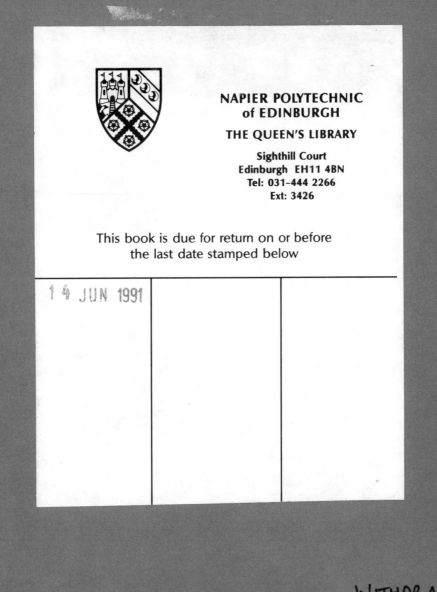

BUSINESS

BUSINESS

Fred Luthans

University of Nebraska

Richard M. Hodgetts

Florida International University

The Dryden Press
Chicago   New York   San Francisco
Philadelphia   Montreal   Toronto
London   Sydney   Tokyo

To the memory of our fathers, Carl H. Luthans and Harold T. Hodgetts, who taught us the fundamentals and spirit of business.

Acquisitions Editor: Mary Fischer
Developmental Editor: Jan Richardson
Project Editor: Paula Dempsey
Design Director: Alan Wendt
Production Manager: Barb Bahnsen
Director of Editing, Design, and Production: Jane Perkins

Text and Cover Designer: Stuart Paterson
Copy Editor: Joanne Fraser
Photo Research: Karen Schenkenfelder
Indexer: Sheila Ary
Compositor: The Clarinda Company
Text Type: 10 point ITC Baskerville

Library of Congress Cataloging-in-Publication Data

Luthans, Fred.
    Business / Fred Luthans, Richard M. Hodgetts.
      p. cm.
    Bibliography: p.
    Includes indexes.
    ISBN 0-03-008949-2
    1. Industrial management—United States.   2. Business enterprises—United States.   I. Hodgetts, Richard M.   II. Title.
HD70.U5L88 1989
    658—dc 19   88-5418
                                                     CIP

Printed in the United States of America
890-039-987654321

Address orders:
The Dryden Press
Orlando, FL 32887

Address editorial correspondence:
The Dryden Press
908 N. Elm Street
Hinsdale, IL 60521

The Dryden Press
Holt, Rinehart and Winston
Saunders College Publishing

About the Cover: Painting by Jerry Rudquist from the collection of Phil Snyder. 84″ × 84″, Acrylic on canvas, 1987.

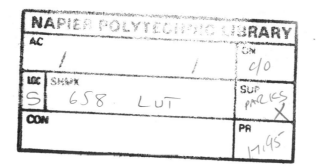
What an exciting time to study business! Consider some major events in recent years.

- The stock market crash of October 1987 sent stock prices reeling and had investors and brokers nervously watching day-to-day stock averages following patterns similar to those after the Crash of 1929.

- The value of the dollar sank to new lows against the German mark and Japanese yen, yet monthly trade deficits reached all-time highs as foreign goods and investments continued to flood into the United States.

- Large firms attempted to become competitive in the global economy by cutting staffs, streamlining structures, and developing intrapreneurial cultures, while small, entrepreneurial businesses continued to hire and to take market share away from the giants.

- Large computer firms introduced new, more powerful microcomputers in an effort to recapture lost market share, but "clones" still offered a more competitive price and high quality.

- The Securities and Exchange Commission investigated stock trading and arrested brokers who had used insider information to make personal fortunes. At the same time, more and more business education programs around the country began introducing business ethics into their curriculums.

These and many other exciting and often alarming events that are happening around us every day signal that the 1990s will not be business as usual. The old standby texts no longer sufficiently cover the dynamically changing world of business.

Business marks the beginning of a new generation in the introductory study of business. The time-tested basic functions of management, marketing, and finance, and their more specialized subfunctions, are given thorough treatment. But unlike previous introduction to business texts, *Business* incorporates themes important to the contemporary business scene.

Change itself is one important focus. The world of business is in a state of flux. Well-known consultant and writer Tom Peters has characterized the modern American business scene as "chaotic" and a "world turned upside down." Yesterday's winners are often today's has-beens, and today's winners may find it impossible to survive in tomorrow's environment. Much of this change comes from technological advancement and the global marketplace. The 1990s will be an era of unparalleled technological and international competitiveness. Only companies and individuals who understand and are able to adapt to such changes will grow or even survive.

A second major focus of the text is on the ethical and social responsibilities of business. Discrimination in employment, pollution of the environment, and insider trading are in violation of the law and cannot be tolerated. Business firms and individuals must operate within the letter and spirit of the law. At the same time, they must fulfill their obligations to stakeholders: quality, safe, and reasonably priced goods and services to customers; good wages/salaries and quality work life for employees; and profits for the owners. These responsibilities to owners, employees, and customers go hand in hand.

Another focus of *Business* is on the important roles of small business, entrepreneurs, and intrapreneurs. Small businesses with fewer than 1,000 employees provide about two-thirds of all new jobs. Every indication is that their influence in revitalizing U.S. business will be great. Entrepreneurs continually commit their talents and fortunes to the creation of new businesses. Well-known examples include Sam Walton of Wal-Mart, Steve Jobs of Apple (and now Next, Inc.), Ben Cohen and Jerry Winfield of Ben & Jerry's Ice Cream, and Debbi Fields of Mrs. Field's Cookies. In recent years, large firms have found it difficult to compete with small business on many fronts. In particular, many small businesses have a more clear understanding of their market and a willingness to work longer and harder to move the company ahead. In an effort to take advantage of the small-business approach and the entrepreneurial spirit, many large businesses today are putting a strong emphasis on creating a climate of intrapreneurship, encouraging managers and staff experts to create and control new, usually risky projects within the existing business. Simply put, an increasing number of large firms are attempting to divide themselves into a host of smaller firms to become more effective and competitive.

The most dominant theme of this text is that the 1990s will not be business as usual. We can expect certain changes, such as the introduction of computers at all levels of the organization and the elimination of smoking on the job, but there will also be changes in fundamental philosophies and strategies. It is becoming increasingly clear that some of the key factors for success during the upcoming decade will be product and service quality, price competitiveness, new product development, state-of-the-art technology, satisfied and productive human resources, an entrepreneurial/intrapreneurial spirit, high ethical standards and socially responsible management, and a clear understanding of the international arena. The overriding purpose of this book is to introduce students to these new developments and explain why and how business can best address them.

Pedagogy

To help convey the new developments as well as the fundamental concepts and principles of business, we have incorporated a number of pedagogical techniques. These features are designed to engage students with the material and help them master the wide array of concepts and vocabulary they encounter.

Learning Objectives Each chapter begins with a series of objectives that cover the key points of the chapter. The objectives are then reviewed in the chapter summary titled "Learning Objectives Revisited."

Your Business IQ Each chapter begins with a short quiz related to the upcoming material. These quizzes will give students a sense of how much they currently know about this material and a brief introductin to some of the topics that will be covered in the chapter. After reading the chapter, they can retake the quiz to ensure that they are now able to correctly answer the questions. Answers to "Your Business IQ" are provided at the end of the chapter.

Checkpoints Designed for active learning, the Checkpoints consist of two review questions at the end of each major section of the chapter so students can continually check their progress. The Checkpoints can also be used to study the chapter material and review important concepts and topics.

Cases There are two cases at the end of each chapter. The first is drawn from actual situations and gives students the opportunity to apply chapter concepts to the real world. The second is a case titled "You Be the Adviser." This latter case has the student assume the role of a consultant in helping a business firm deal with a particular issue or solve a problem by applying ideas presented in the chapter.

Key Terms Every chapter contains a four-way glossary to help identify and define key terms. Each key term is defined in the sentence and margin where it first appears as well as in a glossary at the end of the book. Additionally, the term is listed at the end of the chapter in the Key Terms Reviewed section.

Close-Ups We believe that examples from real companies and recent business events should be interwoven throughout the text rather than inserted arbitrarily in the chapters. Consequently, the student will find hundreds of examples right in the main body of the text. Each chapter also contains two or three more extensive, boxed examples applicable to the discussion at hand—whether about management, marketing, accounting, computers, finance, or law. Each example is referenced in the text so the student will know when to read it. The Close-Up categories we use are Entrepreneurs, Small Business, International, Technology, Computer Technology, Social Responsibility, Ethics, Business Communication, and Competitiveness.

Review Questions and Applied Exercises The Review Questions go beyond basic recall to ask students to apply the chapter to real-world situations. The Applied Exercises give ideas for pursuing concepts in the chapter in business publications and local businesses.

Career Opportunities Each major part of the text ends with a Career Opportunities section. These sections identify careers in the areas discussed in that part of the book. For example, in Part III, which is devoted to managing people and operations, career opportunities in areas such as public relations, production and operations, and personnel are examined. Career Opportunities describes the work responsibilities, identifies the current supply and future demand, and provides salary ranges for these positions.

Supplements

While developing this book, the most common complaint we heard about supplements to accompany introduction to business books is that the pieces are disparate elements only loosely related to the text. Our primary objective in developing the supplements for *Business* was to integrate each item with the text to make them as helpful as possible for you. Each item has been developed with the same care used in developing the text to ensure that it fully supports and enhances the material in the text. Here are just a few examples of this integration:

- First, to save you time, the *Ancillary Resource Guide* provides you with an overview of the entire package. Appropriate *Instructor's Manual* sections, transparencies, videos, and business papers are integrated into outlines of the chapters to show you at a glance the resources that are available for a particular topic.
- All of the written support material for classroom lectures, discussions, and exercises are organized by chapter in a single volume (the *Instructor's Manual*) rather than several.
- The questions in the *Test Bank* have been thoroughly checked by the authors for consistency with the text.
- The supplementary materials for the student—including a computer simulation and career guide—are all in one volume, the *Study Guide*.
- We have developed five professionally produced videos exclusively for this text to help bring to life topics that are typically difficult to convey in the classroom. Each video offered with the book is supported by complete teaching notes that tie the video to the text, highlighting chaper concepts covered in the video and providing discussion questions and class exercises.

These are only examples. Detailed descriptions of each supplement follow.

Ancillary Resource Guide

The *Ancillary Resource Guide* will probably be the place you will want to start as you acquaint yourself with the package. The guide gives you an overview of all of the material we have provided to support the text and then shows how each item can be used in your class. Supplemental items in the *Instructor's Manual,* transparency acetates and masters, videos, and business papers, are integrated into outlines of the chapters to show you at a glance what is available for each topic in the chapter. This guide confirms our commitment to integrate your resource materials and coordinate them with the text.

Instructor's Manual

In writing the *Instructor's Manual,* we have provided a variety of materials that will allow you to choose what is most appropriate for your class and for each topic. Each chapter of the manual includes the following features:

Chapter overview

All key terms in the chapter, with definitions

Detailed lecture outline

Supplemental lecture (Lectures for Chapter 12 through Appendix B were contributed by Richard Randall, Nassau Community College.)

New examples, news items, and "war stories"

Profile of a business leader

Controversial issue for class discussion

Supplemental cases with discussion questions and suggested answers

Discussion topics and in-class exercises

Out-of-class projects

Term paper topics

Guest lecturer suggestions

Annotated supplemental readings

Film and video suggestions

Answers to end-of-chapter questions

Analyses of end-of-chapter cases

Test Bank

An accurate test bank is critical for most professors teaching the introduction to business course. Each question has been reviewed and checked for accuracy and consistency with the text. The *Test Bank* includes approximately 3,000 true/false, multiple choice, and short answer questions, which are organized by chapter learning objective. The key for each question includes the answer, the text page reference, the cognitive type (factual or applied), and the learning goal number. Each chapter also includes two mini-cases with accompanying multiple choice questions. The *Test Bank* was written by Douglas Hibbert, Fayetteville Technical Institute; Jeffrey Mello, Northeastern University; and Philip Weatherford, Embry-Riddle Aeronautical University.

An annual update of the *Test Bank* with 1,000 new test questions will also be provided to adopters of *Business.*

Computerized Test Bank

In addition to the printed version, the *Test Bank* is available in a computerized format for use with IBM-PC and Apple II microcomputers. The computerized test banks contain the same questions appearing in the printed *Test Bank* and allow you to preview and edit the questions, add your own questions, and print multiple versions of test and answer keys.

Study Guide

The *Study Guide* consists of three parts: the study guide proper, a computer simulation game, and a career guide. The study guide section, written by Robert Cox of Salt Lake Community College, will help students master the vocabulary and concepts of the text and apply them to real-world situations. After completing the questions and exercises, students will be prepared for class discussions and examinations. The study guide includes the following sections for each chapter and appendix: learning objectives, chapter summary, key terms matching exercise, true/false questions, completion questions, multiple choice questions, mini-cases, short-answer questions, and answers to all questions. Each part ends with a crossword puzzle of the key concepts in the part.

The computer simulation game, written by Eugene Calvasina of Auburn University–Montgomery, puts students in the manager's seat of a small manufacturing company. The game asks them to make management, operations, marketing, and financial decisions for the company as they progress through the book.

The career guide section, written by Jeffrey Greenhaus of Drexel University introduces students to the basic issues of the career search and career management and provides them with exercises that will help them to actively think about the process. The guide includes sections on occupation choice, the job search, on-the-job issues, and sources of information.

Videos

In talking with intoduction to business professors, we identified a need for assistance in presenting certain topics that are difficult to bring to life in the classroom. In response to this need, we have developed five videos exclusively for *Business: The Great American Dream* (focus on entrepreneurship), *A Plant Tour, A Tour of the Stock Market, Focus on International Business,* and *Close-Up: Wal-Mart Stores, Inc.* These professionally produced tapes, which are 15 to 20 minutes long, can be used either with the appropriate chapter or to introduce or conclude a part of the text. In addition, the text chapters are coordinated with 18 videotape segments from the award-winning "Enterprise" and "60 Minutes" series.

Video Instructor's Manual

The *Video Instructor's Manual,* written by Anthony Lucas of the Community College of Allegheny County and Gayle Marco of Robert Morris College, provides complete teaching notes that integrate each video with a chapter in the text and provide you with suggestions for using the videos. Each chapter includes a synopsis of the video, a list of the chapter concepts covered in the video, teaching objectives, "warm-up" and "recap" discussion questions, and in-class and out-of-class experiential activities.

Transparencies

The transparency package includes 150 full-color acetates of figures not found in the text and over 200 transparency masters of all figures and tables in the text, chapter outlines, and chapter quizzes. Both the acetates and the masters are accompanied by detailed teaching notes that describe the figures and tables and draw out the key points students should note.

Stock Market Game

Developed by Leon Sterdjevich of Montgomery College, the *Stock Market Game* gives students hands-on experience in investing money wisely and provides them with a better understanding of the stock market. The eight- to ten-week game allows students to select and track four stocks on a week-by-week basis and create a profitable portfolio. The workbook includes an overview of stocks and the stock market, information on gathering and analyzing industry and company information, a list of references, and forms for logging in weekly data.

Business Papers

The set of *Business Papers,* prepared by Clyde Neff of South Plains College, contains an assortment of actual business forms and documents— including stock and bond certificates, a small business loan application, a balance sheet, and many others—and teaching notes for each.

Acknowledgments

This book has been developed with the invaluable help of dozens of professors who teach introduction to business. At each stage of development, market surveys, focus groups, and reviewers played a critical role in shaping the book. We would especially like to express our gratitude to the following professors:

Larry Bain
Weatherford College

John Balek
Morton College

John Beem
College of DuPage

Glennis Boyd
Cisco Junior College

Daniel Brady
Highland Community College

Gary Carlson
DeVry Institute of Technology

Helen Davis
Jefferson Community College

Lee Dlabay
Lake Forest College

Carol Ferguson
Rock Valley College

George Hager
College of DuPage

Doug Hibbert
Fayetteville Technical Institute

Garland Holt
Tarrant County Community College

Graham Irwin
Miami University

David Kelmar
Santa Monica College

David Lemak
U.S. Air Force Academy

John Lloyd
Monroe Community College

Paul Londrigan
C. S. Mott Community College

Don Manning
University of Northern Colorado

Jim McAnelly
Waubonsee Community College

Carnella Moore
Glendale Community College

Pat Plocek
Richland College

Richard Randolph
Johnson County Community
College

James Reinemann
College of Lake County

Robert Smoot
Northern Virginia Community
College

Philip Weatherford
Embry-Riddle Aeronautical
University

Charles Woodfill
Franklin University

Larry Zigler
Highland Community College

We believe that an important, but often overlooked, part of the review process is to have the specialized functional areas reviewed. We called on our colleagues at the University of Nebraska in the Departments of Finance (Richard A. DeFusco, Manferd D. Peterson, and Thomas S. Zorn), Economics (Campbell R. McConnell), Marketing (Ronald D. Hampton), Accounting (Thomas E. Balke), and Computers (Krish Muralidhar) to review chapters in their areas of expertise. Gerry Welch, of St. Louis Community College–Meramec, also reviewed the economics appendix. We thank these individuals for the considerable time and effort they gave to us. Interestingly, without exception, they also thanked us for the opportunity to make sure that what was being said in their area of an introductory business text was indeed current and correct.

We would like to acknowledge the dedication, support, and expertise provided to us by the Dryden team. This starts at the top with the leadership of Bill Schoof and our two editors, who have put a lot of heart and hard work into this project, Mary Fischer, Senior Acquisitions Editor, and Jan Richardson, Developmental Editor. We also recognize and would like to thank the help we have received from the rest of the team at various stages. Although there are many who deserve credit, we would like to mention the following: Karen Schenkenfelder in manuscript revisions; Judy Sarwark in the early development stage; Barb Bahnsen, Paula Dempsey, and Alan Wendt in various phases of the production process; Robert Gemin and his marketing staff; and of course, the field sales force who, in the final analysis, represent our book.

Closer to home, we would like to thank the secretarial/word processing support provided by Joyce Anderson, Cathy Jensen, and especially Cheryl Buckridge. Last, but by no means least, we want to thank our families for giving us the time and creating a supportive climate that allowed us to do the best that we could do.

Fred Luthans
Richard M. Hodgetts
September 1988

About the Authors

Fred Luthans and Richard Hodgetts bring a well-rounded combination of teaching, writing, and business experience to this text. Each has been teaching business courses for over 20 years, and each has written several successful textbooks. They coauthored with Kenneth Thompson *Social Issues in Business* and, with Stuart Rosenkrantz, wrote *Real Managers,* which has been acclaimed as the most comprehensive study on how successful and effective managers spend their time. They are actively involved in Wal-Mart's management training program.

Fred Luthans is the George Holmes Distinguished Professor of Business at the University of Nebraska–Lincoln, with a Ph.D. and MBA from the University of Iowa. In 1986 he won the University of Nebraska Distinguished Teaching Award. He has been a visiting scholar at a number of colleges and universities and has lectured in Europe, Japan, Korea, Mexico, the National Republic of China, the People's Republic of China, and Singapore. Besides his extensive training and consulting work with many local and regional businesses, he has worked with a number of national organizations, including Western Electric, Brunswick, Hormel, Blue Cross/Blue Shield, Metromail, U.S. Savings and Loan League, and the F.D.I.C. He has been president of the Academy of Management and is one of the few professors who are fellows of both the Academy of Management and the Decision Sciences Institute. Professor Luthans serves as a consulting editor for the McGraw-Hill Management Series. He is the author of *Organizational Behavior,* fifth edition, coauthor with Robert Kreitner of *Organizational Behavior Modification,* which won the American Society of Personnel Administration Association Award for outstanding contribution to human resource management, and author of several other texts.

Richard M. Hodgetts is a professor of business at Florida International University, with a Ph.D. from the University of Oklahoma and an MBA from Indiana University. He has been named an outstanding teacher of the year twice, at both the University of Nebraska and Florida International University, most recently in 1988. He has lectured in Mexico, Venezuela, Jamaica, Peru, Denmark, Kuwait, and many U.S. colleges and universities. He has worked with Burger King, Exxon International, CIGNA Dental, Eastern Airlines, the government of Kuwait, and the revenue department of Mexico, among many others. Professor Hodgetts is a fellow of the Academy of Management and serves on the review boards of five journals. He is the author of *Modern Human Relations at Work, Management: Theory, Process, and Practice,* coauthor with Donald Kuratko of *Entrepreneurship,* and author of several other texts. He also writes a weekly column on small business and entrepreneurship for the *Ft. Lauderdale News and Sun Sentinel.*

Brief Contents

Contents

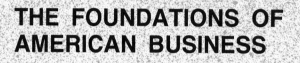

THE FOUNDATIONS OF AMERICAN BUSINESS

The United States has tremendous wealth and, few would argue, offers most of its citizens a good quality of life. A quick tour of most American homes would reveal that the inhabitants have many of the extra conveniences of life: radios, TVs, stereos, VCRs, microwave ovens, personal computers, portable telephones, and cars. How have Americans been able to acquire so much? One cause of this wealth is the U.S. economic system, which encourages creativity, efficiency, and profit. This system has helped initiate and support countless large and small businesses, which provide the goods and services Americans enjoy. Part I examines the foundations of American business. It devotes primary attention to the challenges facing today's businesses and the social responsibilities of free enterprise.

Chapter 1 addresses the nature and challenge of business. In the United States, businesses operate within a system based on three fundamental rights: the right of private property, the right of freedom of choice, and the right to rewards. These rights have helped promote the climate that nurtures success in running businesses. This system allows peo- ple and private firms to decide for themselves what goods and services will be produced. Contemporary businesses face many challenges, including international competition and the need to increase productivity. Chapter 1 identifies some of the ways in which business people are meeting these challenges.

The focus of Chapter 2 is on the social responsibilities of business. Companies want to earn a profit, but they also must know the importance of being good corporate citizens. Businesses have many social obligations, including providing equality in employment, protecting the environment, and producing and selling goods that are safe. Companies are expected to act ethically; if they do not, they must be prepared to pay the price. Chapter 2 describes how business people fulfill their social responsibilities.

When you have finished studying Part I, you should be familiar with the foundations of American business. In particular, you should understand why business people need to balance a concern for profit with a concern for social responsibilities.

Source: Courtesy of Comerica Incorporated.

The Nature and Challenge of Business

LEARNING OBJECTIVES

- Explain the basic rights of the free enterprise system.
- Describe the factors of production.
- Discuss ways of measuring economic well-being.

- Define alternative economic systems.
- Identify the major challenges currently facing American business.
- Relate the benefits of studying business.

Your Business IQ

How much do you already know about the basic nature and challenge of business? Test your business IQ by labeling each statement *true* or *false*. Answers and explanations are at the end of the chapter.

1. America's founders believed that government should leave business alone.
2. The standard of living is now lower in the United States than in many other countries.
3. A socialist government can take over an industry, in which case the business owners lose their entire investment.
4. For a given amount of labor and expense, in recent years American businesses have been able to produce proportionally more goods and services than foreign businesses.
5. Technological developments contribute to long-term unemployment in the United States.

Don't forget to check your answers before reading on.

To meet the challenges of our ever-changing world, business requires the creativity, skills, and energy of many kinds of people.

Looking Back and Ahead

To meet the challenge of having a successful business in a dramatically changing and competitive world, companies must innovate. One example of such an innovative company is Genentech, which after seven years of research, testing, and regulatory review, recently obtained permission from the Food and Drug Administration to sell a new product called Activase. This drug helps prevent heart attacks by dissolving clots. It became the first major gene-spliced drug sold by a biotechnology company, a business that applies techniques and knowledge of biology. Many observers predicted that Activase would not only save lives, but would also bring years of profits for Genentech.[1]

The employees and owners of Genentech and the customers of its products benefit from the company's ability to meet basic business challenges: applying technological developments, coping with government regulation, selling safe products, and, at the same time, making a profit for owners and investors and providing employment to members of society. You, too, are affected by business decisions every day. As a consumer, you have purchased goods and services from business. Probably you have also been an employee of a business. However, this may be your first formal study of the activities and concerns of business.

Now that you have skimmed through the Preface and Table of Contents, you are ready to begin your study. This chapter prepares you by showing you the big picture of business. After defining the nature of business in general, the chapter describes the American economic system: the free enterprise system. Next you will learn about some of the world's other economic systems, the major challenges currently facing American business, and the benefits you can derive from studying business.

What Is Business?

Business An organized, profit-seeking approach to providing people with the goods and services they want.

Profit The difference between revenues and expenses.

The study of business begins with a simple definition of a complex process: **Business** is an organized, profit-seeking approach to providing people with the goods and services they want. The "profit-seeking" part of the definition distinguishes business from nonbusiness activity. **Profit** is the difference between revenues (money received from the sale of products or services) and expenses (the costs of doing business). Business activity plays a vital role in the United States because of its significance in the overall economy and in our daily lives. For example, business provided the textbooks you purchased at the college bookstore, the tapes you bought at the record shop, the car you drove to school, and the pizza you ate last Saturday night.

Even federal, state, and local governments depend on business for goods and services. Business built the publicly owned commuter trains that carry people from the suburbs to the inner cities and the buses that crisscross the streets and avenues of our cities. Business also built the large courthouse that dominates the town square of many small towns. In fact, government agencies spend a large portion of tax revenues in the business arena, purchasing a variety of goods and services. For example, the federal government spends billions of dollars every year purchasing computers from IBM, airplanes from Boeing, and electronic goods from General Electric, to name but a few of the thousands of firms with which it does business.

Checkpoint

1. What is business?
2. How has business contributed to life in the United States?

The Free Enterprise System

More than a half-century ago, President Calvin Coolidge declared, "The business of America is business." This is still true today. In the United States the process of providing people the goods and services they want takes place within the **free enterprise system.** Unlike the other economic systems of communism and socialism, under the free enterprise system businesses are free to decide what to supply and are rewarded on the basis of how well they meet customer needs. Although traditionally this economic system is called capitalism, and it could be said that the American free enterprise system is based on and modified from pure capitalism, we will treat the terms as being interchangeable. A distinguishing feature of capitalism or the free enterprise system is that there is a degree of competition among firms.

Free enterprise system
An economic system under which businesses are free to decide what to supply and are rewarded based on how well they meet customer needs.

The Competitive Environment for American Business

America's founders firmly believed in the doctrine of **laissez-faire,** or government noninterference in the affairs of business. This promotes free competition and is the basis of the free enterprise system. Over the years, however, this laissez-faire doctrine has become less strict. Starting in the late 1800s, it became apparent that big business had to be controlled or it would drive out smaller businesses and exploit consumers. In response, the government outlawed monopolies that restrain trade and began to closely regulate some industries. This trend gained momentum during the 1930s, as the federal government sought to right America's economic ship and steer it through the Depression years.

Laissez-faire The doctrine of government noninterference in the affairs of business.

More recently the trend has reversed, shifting toward deregulation of industry. One of the first major businesses to be deregulated was the telephone industry. The giant American Telephone & Telegraph (AT&T) had its operating divisions spun off into seven regional telephone firms—the so-called Baby Bells. AT&T itself continues to supply long-distance service and telephone equipment but has branched out into computers and information systems. Before deregulation, AT&T's revenues from long-distance service in effect subsidized local service, keeping these rates low. Since the breakup, and the resulting competition in long-distance service, long-distance rates have fallen, but the cost of local service (which is subject to less competition) has increased. In addition, many new makers of telephone equipment have entered the marketplace, offering consumers a greater choice in that area.

At present the Baby Bells, such as US West, are pushing hard for total deregulation of their prices and profits. US West contends that regulation is hampering it in competing against a slew of new, mostly unregulated companies that are chipping away at its business.[2]

As deregulation moves into full swing, despite the push for more deregulation from companies such as US West, there are also cries for a return to more government regulation. Apparently some firms believe that their economic environments are becoming overly competitive and that cutthroat practices are beginning to threaten them. They want the government to play a more active role. In addition, critics of deregulation note that wealthy consumers may have benefited more from deregulation than the less well off. For example, consumers at the lower end of the income spectrum are less likely to do much long-distance telephoning.[3] Customer service may also be affected. Since the airlines were deregulated, passenger complaints have risen sharply. The Transportation Department had 2½ times more complaints in the first six months of 1987 than it had in the same period the year before.[4]

Rights in a Free Enterprise System

The free enterprise system is based on three fundamental rights. These are the right to private property, freedom of choice, and the right to rewards.

Right to private property The right to own, use, buy, sell, or give away property.

Private Property The **right to private property** is the right to own, use, buy, sell, or give away property. For example, if you see a For Sale sign in front of a rundown but formerly beautiful old home, you have a right to make an offer to buy it. If you do buy it, you might decide to make just enough repairs to go into business renting cheap housing to students. Or you might take out a big loan, make major improvements, and ultimately sell the renovated house for a substantial sum. You could even buy the house and then give it away, although this is not a typical business decision.

The right to private property applies in many circumstances. The owner of a printing press can decide whether it would be more profitable to print books or business cards or to sell the operation to someone else. The owner of a small building might want to operate a boutique or to lease the space. Because of the right of private property, the owners of a fast-food restaurant can enforce a dress code on customers, such as "no shirt, no shoes, no service." They own the business. All these options are available to owners under the free enterprise system.

Freedom of choice Businesses are free to hire people, invest money, purchase machinery and equipment, and choose the markets where they wish to operate.

Freedom of Choice The second basic right, **freedom of choice,** means that businesses can hire people, invest money, purchase machinery and equipment, and choose the markets where they wish to operate. Quite simply, a business is free to function in any way it sees fit as long as no laws are broken. This freedom extends to employees and customers. A person working at the college bookstore is free to quit and go to work at a local McDonald's. Or the person can try for a better salary and benefit package at a local Sears outlet and go to work there. As long as it is legal and they have the money, customers can buy whatever they would like. People are free to make whatever career or purchase choices they feel are best.

Right to Rewards The third basic right in the free enterprise system is the **right to rewards.** This is the owner's right to all of the profits, after taxes, that accrue from business activity. The owners of a business may take the profits and use them in any way—put them back into the business or distribute them.

For example, a student group could go into the campus-calendar business. They could round up appropriate campus models, have them photographed, and have the calendars produced at a local printer. The costs involved, such as the photographer's and models' fees and the printing charge, are the expenses. The revenues would come from selling the calendars. If the revenues exceed the expenses, the students have made a profit. After paying the appropriate taxes, they can use the profits to buy photography or printing equipment for future calendars, distribute the profits to the members of the group, or donate the profits to their favorite charity. The owners of a business can even sell the business, pay tax on the gains, and retire on what is left.

The right to profits drives the free enterprise system to continually grow and become more effective. Unfortunately, the profit motive has sometimes been abused; owners have exploited employees or customers. Nevertheless, most business people realize that they can earn the greatest long-term profits when customers and employees are satisfied.

> **Right to rewards** The owner's right to all of the profits, after taxes, that accrue from business activity.

Factors of Production

Besides the three basic rights, free enterprise depends on four factors of production: land, labor, capital, and entrepreneurship. These are the resources on which businesses draw to produce the goods and services they sell. Although other economic systems use some of these factors, notably land and labor, and some free enterprise businesses rely more heavily on one factor than on another, all free enterprise businesses use some combination of the four.

The first three—land, labor, and capital—have been recognized through the years. We have added the fourth—entrepreneurship—because it has now become clear that this is also a vital factor of modern business. Entrepreneurship receives special treatment in Chapter 3; this discussion introduces it along with the other, more traditional factors of production.

Land The term **land** refers to the geographic territory and natural resources used in producing goods and services. Land is literally the foundation of business and includes the site where the enterprise is located. It also includes natural resources for building the facility, heating and cooling it, and supplying the raw materials for making the products or providing the services.

> **Land** The geographic territory and natural resources used in producing goods and services.

Labor Another factor of production has traditionally been called **labor:** the people who produce the goods and services that the business provides. Although the term *labor* has the connotation of operating employees in factories, today this would be expanded to include white-collar workers and even top-level executives, professionals such as accountants

> **Labor** The people who produce the goods and services that the business provides.

or engineers, middle managers, first-line supervisors, and support personnel. All the human resources of the business fall into the category of labor. People, not buildings or capital, run the business.

The labor component represents a significant proportion of the costs involved in operating most businesses. In labor-intensive manufacturing concerns, labor costs may be as much as two-thirds of the budget for operations. At your college, about 90 percent of costs are for administrators, faculty members, and supporting employees.

Capital The money and technology used for operating the enterprise form the factor of production called **capital.** You will learn how businesses obtain and use monetary resources in Part VI. Simply put, businesses need money to buy the necessary land and labor to operate.

Although traditionally capital has been associated primarily with money, we have extended this factor to the concept of the physical resources of a business. In today's businesses the factor of capital includes technology. **Technology** is the application of knowledge to production, physical equipment, and machinery. It has become increasingly visible and important to modern business. For many people, the term *high tech* suggests what modern business is or should be all about.

When firms invest in technology, usually in the form of research and development or advanced equipment, their goods and services are often more useful or attractive. For example, in recent years technology has enabled the television industry to add stereo. More recent developments are enabling TV manufacturers to introduce models that have a very large screen but are less than one foot deep and models that can display multiple channels on one screen. You will learn more about technological advances in the "Technology Close-Up" examples that appear throughout this text.

Capital The money and technology used for operating the enterprise.

Technology The application of knowledge to production, physical equipment, and machinery.

Workers at the *Orlando Sentinel* install a new printing press. See how many factors of production you can identify. A few are the workers (labor), the money spent on and the technology that went into the press (capital), and the ground beneath the press (land).

Source: Photo by Charles Cherney, *Chicago Tribune.* Used with permission.

Entrepreneurship We have added a fourth factor, **entrepreneurship,** to the widely recognized production factors of land, labor, and capital. It is the process of organizing, operating, and assuming the risks associated with a business venture. Entrepreneurship is not new—the founders of American business, including famous business people such as John D. Rockefeller and Cornelius Vanderbilt, were certainly entrepreneurs. It used to be recognized as a factor of production, but only recently has this process resurfaced as the factor that pulls the others together. As one advocate of the importance of entrepreneurship as a factor of production recently noted: "Without this innovative, risk-taking propensity the other factors are basically sterile."[5]

Two important roles are involved in the entrepreneurial process: entrepreneurs and intrapreneurs. The **entrepreneur** is the creator and/or organizer of a venture. A **venture** is a new business or a new or different approach or product/service in an existing business. Typically, the term *entrepreneur* is used for the individual who founds or develops the business enterprise. Three well-known examples are Richard Sears, who started what today is Sears, Roebuck; Edwin Land, who founded the Polaroid Corporation; and An Wang, who built Wang Laboratories into a billion-dollar computer empire. On a smaller scale, but representing the new spirit of entrepreneurial activity that is emerging in modern America, is the success story of Allan Solomon, in "Entrepreneurs Close-Up."

Entrepreneurship The process of organizing, operating, and assuming the risks associated with a business venture.

Entrepreneur The creator and/or organizer of a venture.

Venture A new business or a new or different approach or product/service in an existing business.

ENTREPRENEURS CLOSE-UP

Allan Solomon

Thanks to videocassette players and cable television, more and more people are watching movies at home these days. Some movie theaters are closing as their owners have given up on persuading people to go out more often. Meeting this challenge clearly requires an innovative mind.

Enter Allan Solomon. He bought a theater in Blue Island, Illinois, and turned it into a profitable business by expanding on the way movie theaters have traditionally made most of their money: by selling food. A typical movie theater sells each patron about $2.50 worth of snacks, and only about two-thirds of the price goes to cover the expense of selling them. Solomon has taken this profit-making aspect of the business further by selling an expanded menu. At Solomon's theater, called the Oscar I, patrons can order beer, chicken wings, and pizza, among other items.

Besides food, Solomon draws patrons with comfort. The Oscar I features comfortable leather chairs, soundproof box seats, and butcher-block tables. Waiters and waitresses bring food to the tables. To block out the sound from all that dining, the theater uses an all-around sound system and leaves a foot of space between tables.

Solomon's new approach to showing movies appears to be a hit. Attendance has increased steadily, and the patrons are spending freely. While admission to the movie costs only $1.50, the typical customer spends another $7 on food and refreshments. And the theater keeps costs down by selling only finger food that requires relatively little service and by showing films a few weeks after they are released. The combination of high customer spending and low expenses is making this variation on the dinner theater quite profitable.

It's no wonder, then, that Solomon is planning three more of these innovative movie theaters. All of them will involve rehabilitating old theaters—symbolizing that Solomon's entrepreneurial spirit is bringing new life to a fading business.

Intrapreneuring
Managers and staff experts creating and controlling new, usually risky projects within an existing business.

In recent years, management experts have expanded their understanding of the factor of entrepreneurship to include innovative risk-takers within existing businesses. Gifford Pinchot has coined a term for this role: **intrapreneuring.**[6] The intrapreneuring process consists of managers and staff experts creating and controlling new, usually risky projects within an existing business.

Intrapreneurs do not create new businesses; they move existing ones ahead. For example, on the 25th anniversary of Raychem, a high-tech firm, founder and chairman Paul Cook estimated that the company had developed about 200,000 products.[7] This phenomenal activity was not the work of the entrepreneurial founder, but of in-house intrapreneurs—managers, engineers, and operating employees throughout the firm. At smaller firms, such as Convergent Technologies in Southern California, two- and three-person in-house teams have developed successful intrapreneurial projects.[8] Large, well-known companies such as 3M and Hewlett-Packard also depend on the intrapreneurial approach. IBM recently reorganized to promote such a spirit among its executives.[9]

Success of the Free Enterprise System in America

Standard of living The measure of how well off people of a country are economically.

The economic well-being of Americans suggests that the free enterprise system is succeeding in the United States. The measure of how well off economically the people of a country are is called their **standard of living.** The overall economic activity of a country, measured by the gross national product (GNP), covered in Appendix A, reflects the standard of living. However, a more specific way to measure standard of living is to divide the value of a country's total production by its population. If a nation's businesses produce a great deal compared to the size of its population, then many goods and services will be available to the average citizen, and the standard of living will be high. Conversely, if businesses produce little relative to the size of the population, there will not be as much to go around, and the standard of living will be low.

The American standard of living is high. For example, most American students own a transistor radio; many also have TVs, stereos, and cars. In a recent survey, 13 percent of college students said they owned a personal computer.[10] This wealth is not typical of young people in most other parts of the world. Keep in mind that this standard is the average for all citizens. Some glaring exceptions need attention; pockets of poverty exist in urban and rural areas across the United States. Nevertheless, most Americans enjoy a very high standard of living, which is due in no small part to business.

More consumer goods (televisions, stereos, telephones, VCRs, personal computers, autos, and clothes) are available to consumers in the United States than anywhere else in the world. Figure 1.1 compares the quantities of TVs and telephones owned by the people in selected countries. The difference between the standard of living in the United States and in other countries is even greater if you include popular consumer goods such as houses, automobiles, stereos, VCRs, and personal computers (PCs). For example, VCRs and PCs are still rare in the Soviet Union. As of the mid-1980s, Soviet companies made only 75 VCRs per month. They cost about $1,500 and break down frequently. Foreign-made VCRs sell for as much as $5,000 on the black market. The same situation applies to PCs. They cost over $5,000 in the Soviet Union, compared to

$2,000 or less in the United States, are in limited supply, and require imported floppy disks.[11] Clearly, American consumers enjoy a higher standard of living than those in the Soviet Union and most other countries.

Per Capita Income Statisticians also measure a country's standard of living by determining how much money the average person earns. Such a measurement is called per capita income, or income per person. Figure 1.2 shows examples of per capita income in various countries. Notice that in the United States average income per person is over $14,000, greater than for most countries.

Of course, this is not distributed equally. Some people make a large amount of money, and others make much less. Overall, however, most U.S. families are members of the middle class (earning $25,000 or more). The recent trend toward two-income families, where both the wife and husband work, has helped to increase income per person and to provide even greater purchasing power per family.

Checkpoint

1. What are the factors of production?
2. How do the rights of the free enterprise system affect businesses' control over these factors?

FIGURE 1.1

Modern Communication Technology in Selected Countries

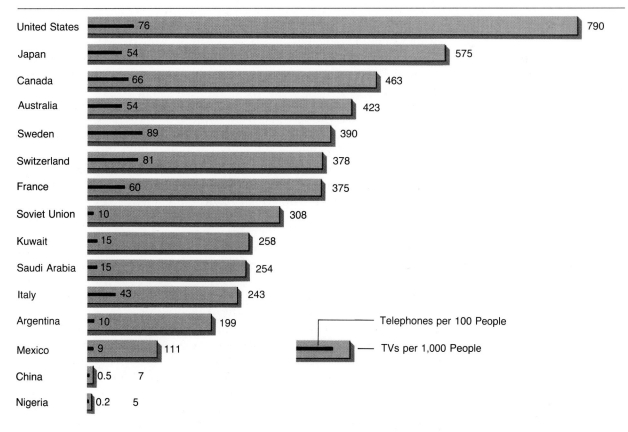

United States 76 790
Japan 54 575
Canada 66 463
Australia 54 423
Sweden 89 390
Switzerland 81 378
France 60 375
Soviet Union 10 308
Kuwait 15 258
Saudi Arabia 15 254
Italy 43 243
Argentina 10 199
Mexico 9 111
China 0.5 7
Nigeria 0.2 5

Telephones per 100 People
TVs per 1,000 People

France	$18,618	West Germany	$9,100
Switzerland	$15,243	Great Britain	$6,916
Kuwait	$14,400	Soviet Union	$6,731
United States	**$14,170**	Italy	$5,314
Canada	$12,800	Argentina	$1,800
Saudi Arabia	$12,615	Mexico	$1,546
Sweden	$10,900	Nigeria	$ 623
Japan	$10,300	China	$ 257
Australia	$10,087		

FIGURE 1.2

Per Capita Income in Selected Countries

Alternative Economic Systems

The free enterprise system under which American businesses operate is only one type of economic system. Most other countries around the world do not operate under this system. Alternative economic systems include communism and socialism. Although no pure form of any of the economic systems currently exists in any country, one of the three types usually predominates, as indicated in Figure 1.3.

Communism

Communism An economic system where the government owns all property and makes all decisions regarding production of goods and services.

At the opposite extreme from free enterprise is **communism,** in which the government (or technically, the people) owns all property and makes all decisions regarding production of goods and services. The Soviet Union, the People's Republic of China, and Cuba are three current examples of countries under a communist system. Under this system, a

FIGURE 1.3

The Basic Economic Systems

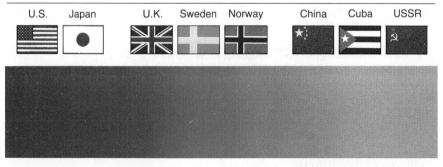

| U.S. | Japan | | U.K. | Sweden | Norway | | China | Cuba | USSR |

Free Enterprise
People are free to determine the goods and services they need.

Socialism
Government owns and controls primary industries, but others are in private hands.

Communism
Property is owned by government, and all decisions regarding goods and services are made by government.

central planning committee decides what will be produced and made available to the people. If the government decides to manufacture radios and few individuals want them, the government pressures the people to buy the radios. Conversely, if the government decides to concentrate on manufacturing defense equipment and to deemphasize consumer goods such as TV sets, most people are forced to go without TV sets even if they want them. The same is true with regard to food and clothing. People are allowed to purchase whatever is available, but if there is no match between the supply of a good and the demand for it, everyone must live with the imbalance.

Under pure communism, profits theoretically are nonexistent, and equality should exist between workers and managers. However, communist countries are finding that profit is a good way to measure performance and that managers strive to do a good job if the government rewards them with a promotion to a better position or with other special benefits. For example, a communist government today may decide to reward managers with a car, a better apartment, or access to stores that sell consumer goods unavailable to the average worker. Although communism is still a major economic system in the world today, it is taking on many characteristics of free enterprise even in traditional strongholds such as the Soviet Union and the People's Republic of China.

Socialism

Another major economic system is **socialism.** Under this system, the government controls primary industries, but most other businesses remain in private hands. If the government does take over these private companies—an act called "nationalizing"—it pays the owners for the business. Usually, however, the price is below fair market value.

Socialism An economic system under which the government controls primary industries, but most other businesses remain in private hands.

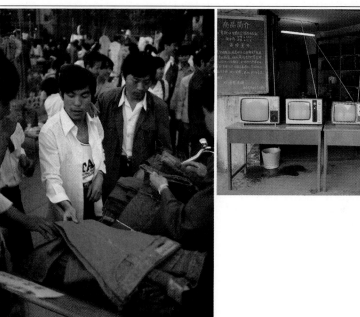

These two businesses show China's move toward a mixed economy. The TV store in Nanning on the right characterizes China's communist economy; the business is licensed and strictly regulated by the government. More recently the government has permitted markets such as the one located in Kunming and shown in the left-hand picture; in such a market, a Chinese entrepreneur can set prices for goods, doesn't need a license, and can keep any profits earned.

Nationalized industries are usually heavy industries such as steel, large-scale manufacturing, banking, and transportation industries such as the airlines and the railroads. To run these operations, the government often employs a large staff. In fact, the governments of socialist countries such as England and the Scandinavian countries often employ a large percentage of the population. Many jobs are given out on the basis of political friendship. If new government officials take charge, many top managers are replaced by individuals more closely aligned with the new party leaders.

As in communism, a major goal of socialism is to enhance the public welfare, and the government often provides many services, including transportation, utilities, housing, education, and medical care, at low or no cost. Consequently, many socialist countries have extremely high tax rates. Anyone making much more than the average worker pays taxes on the additional income at rates that may run as high as 90 percent. This is in contrast to the United States, where under current tax laws hardly anyone pays more than about one-quarter of his or her income in federal taxes and the additional state and local taxes may bring it up to about one-third of one's income.

Mixed economy
Combines characteristics of free enterprise, communist, and/or socialist economies.

Mixed Economies

Over the years, the various economic systems have been merging. Pure forms no longer really exist. Most nations have a mix of government ownership and private enterprise. A **mixed economy** is one that combines characteristics of free enterprise (or capitalism), communism, and/or socialism. Figure 1.4 provides some examples.

Although the United States is known for its free enterprise economy, the government still owns considerable assets. For example, it is the largest landholder in the country. National parks, wilderness lands, government buildings, and military installations are only some of the property the federal government directly owns and controls. State and local governments also have large holdings. On the other hand, the U.S. government owns few businesses that directly provide goods and services. The government fills practically all its needs by purchasing from private business firms. In addition, municipal governments are beginning to turn more public services over to private industry. With shrinking tax dollars, many cities are turning to private business to provide their services more efficiently and at a lower cost. The remaining government-supplied services are also becoming more efficient. The potential for competition from private industry spurs government workers to try harder. As the mayor of Newark observed, "It's amazing what a little competition will do."[12]

In contrast, the communist governments in the Soviet Union and China are directly responsible for providing goods and services. Yet in recent years both countries have softened this position somewhat. The Soviet Union, under Mikhail Gorbachev, has tried to stimulate a deteriorating economy by encouraging plant managers to run more efficient operations and by giving them pay incentives and greater autonomy within their operations. A recent law also allows thousands of Soviet citizens to work for themselves in small family businesses.[13] China, under Deng Xiaoping, now allows small business entrepreneurs to set up their own shops and keep whatever profits they earn. There has been a rush

State and local governments sometimes find it more efficient to turn certain jobs over to private businesses. This move is called *privatization*. One business that has benefited from privatization is Wackenhut, which provides such services as police support, fire protection, and emergency medical services. This parking enforcement officer is a Wackenhut employee.

Source: Courtesy of The Wackenhut Corporation.

in modern-day China to build large capital projects and to buy consumer goods such as washing machines and color television sets.[14] "Pure" communism is a thing of the past.

Socialist countries use a combination of state-owned and privately owned enterprise. In Sweden, for example, the government owns 50 percent of the mining industry but only 2 percent of the chemical industry. This pattern is not uncommon. Many countries that have flirted with government control of industries have found themselves unable to manage some of them and thus have returned them to private hands. Brazil, for example, is in the process of eliminating all unnecessary government holdings. Most of these businesses will be sold back to private industry.[15] And England, long a stronghold of socialism, is undergoing privatization; nearly 40 percent of its state sector has been turned over to private enterprise in the 1980s.[16]

Checkpoint

1. What are the other two basic economic systems besides free enterprise found in the world today?
2. In what ways are the economies of the United States and the Soviet Union mixed economies?

	Airlines	Electric Power	Postal Service	Railroads	Telecommun- ications
United States	P	P	G/P	P	P
Australia	G/P	G	G	G	G
Brazil	P/G	G	G	G	G
England	G/P	G	G	G	G
Canada	P	G	G	G/P	P/G
China	G	G	G	G	G
France	G/P	G	G	G	G
Italy	G	G/P	G	G	G
Japan	P/G	P	G	G/P	G
Soviet Union	G	G	G	G	G
Sweden	P	G/P	G/P	G	G
West Germany	G/P	G/P	G/P	G	G

FIGURE 1.4

Private and Government Control of Enterprises in Selected Countries

P	Privately owned.
P/G	Mostly privately owned, although there is some government ownership.
G/P	Mostly government-owned, although there is some private ownership.
G	Government-owned.

Challenges Facing American Business

U.S. business has provided Americans a high standard of living, but to continue doing so, it must rise to new challenges. Currently, businesses in the United States need to improve productivity, keep up with technology, combat unemployment, fulfill their social responsibility, cope with government regulation, and meet foreign competition.

Productivity

Productivity The amount of output divided by the input.

The term **productivity** is one of the buzzwords of the 1980s. Although it means different things to different people, perhaps the most common measure of productivity is the amount of goods produced (output) divided by the labor or expense required to produce those goods (input). This formula indicates that productivity increases when output is greater or when costs (inputs) are less.

If Company A produces 500 units a day (output) with 10 hours of labor (input), its productivity is: 500 units ÷ 10 hours = 50 units per hour. If Company B produces 600 units with 10 hours of labor, its productivity is 60 units per hour. Clearly, Company B is more productive; every hour, it produces more than Company A. Assuming that the wages and cost of materials are the same for both firms, this means that the more productive firm should be able to sell its product at a lower price than its competitor. Why? Because the cost per unit is less.

This idea applies to many different projects. For example, a student who types term papers with the use of a computer will turn out more completed pages per hour than a student typing with an electric typewriter. This is because the student using a computer can correct errors and make changes more quickly. The student can use the time saved to type additional pages.

The Productivity Challenge In the past, other countries of the world, especially Asian countries such as Japan, have paid their workers much less than U.S. businesses have paid their workers, and thus have had a decided edge in competitive battles for world markets. The wage differential between American and Japanese workers has now almost disappeared, but other problems and other newly developing countries, such as South Korea, provide new challenges. In 1986, the average hourly pay in South Korea was only $1.39 per hour compared to $9.47 in Japan and $13.21 in the United States.[17]

Over the last couple of decades, productivity in the United States has grown more slowly than it has in many other countries. For example, over the past 20 years, the manufacturing output per hour in the United States has grown a little over 50 percent, but Japan's output has leaped ahead about 400 percent, West Germany's about 100 percent, and the United Kingdom's over 80 percent.[18] The 1980s have shown some improvement in U.S. manufacturing productivity. It has risen by an average of 3.8 percent per year over the five-year period of 1982–1986, compared to 1.5 percent in the 1970s.[19] By 1988, many American manufacturers, such as Ford and USX, had made a dramatic revival and could favorably compete for the first time in many years in both Europe and Asia.[20] However, the figures for the nonmanufacturing sector are still pretty bleak. Since 1973 there has been no gain in the average annual nonmanufacturing productivity.[21]

This is especially disheartening in light of the growing dominance of service sector employment in America. From 1950 to July 1987, employment in manufacturing firms dropped from 24 percent to 19 percent, while employment in the service sector dramatically increased from 59 percent to 76 percent of U.S. employment.[22] With 9 out of 10 new jobs in services where productivity problems are the greatest, the challenge is clear.

Although the productivity of both manufacturing and service is most visible and disturbing in relation to foreign competitors, it must be remembered that businesses must also stress productivity to compete domestically. Those firms with the highest productivity rates will grow and prosper.

Meeting the Productivity Challenge How can American businesses meet this productivity challenge? In manufacturing, one way is by using the most up-to-date facilities and equipment. For example, Timken, the giant steel maker, has recently spent $500 million to build an advanced steel mill, and General Motors is putting considerable money into its Saturn project to beat back the Japanese challenge in the market for small cars.[23] Taking care not to grow too fast may also help; for example, see "Small Business Close-Up: Thinking Small."

Another, probably even more important way to improve productivity, especially in the service sector, is to give more attention to new approaches to managing employees. American managers should not necessarily mimic Japanese management techniques, because U.S. workers are different, but they should learn the lesson of giving top priority to human resource management. For example, successful American firms such as Wal-Mart Stores, Inc., and W. L. Gore Company call their employees "associates" to emphasize their importance and to give formal recognition to human resources as a top priority. In reflecting on the key strengths of Procter & Gamble, the head of this successful company, John G. Smale, observed; "I'd say people and then products. Any strong organization, whether it be a business or a university, has to have strong people. And that doesn't just happen."[24] Using up-to-date facilities and equipment is certainly one answer to productivity problems. But, importantly, it is not necessarily the *only* answer. People and the way they are managed are also vital to improving productivity. Chapter 7 will discuss motivating and leading today's employees in greater detail.

Technological Change

Even though the human side of productivity is vital, managers cannot slight the technological side. Technology remains important in helping firms stay up-to-date and effective. Companies use technology in at least two ways:

1. They can invest in the most efficient, state-of-the-art machinery and equipment. For example, auto producers with the most advanced technology use computerized robots to perform much of the work. The result is higher quality and a lower rejection rate.
2. Companies can discover new uses for high-technology equipment. For example, they can use existing equipment to create new goods or services.

Over the last decade, a number of high-tech regions have developed in the United States. In these locations, companies that expend considerable sums for research and development and that hire well-trained employees are creating new technologies and products. These regions are located throughout the country, including the famous Silicon Valley (from Palo Alto to San Jose, California), with firms such as Apple Computer and Silicon Systems; the Research Triangle (Durham, Chapel Hill, and Raleigh, North Carolina), with firms such as Northern Telecom and SCH Corporation; and Route 128/95 (Boston, Massachusetts, and its surrounding area), with firms such as BBN Laboratories and Gen Rad. Recently other high-tech areas have been springing up in such places as Denver, Colorado, and Austin, Texas.

How can business meet the challenge to keep up with technological change? It can ensure that it has state-of-the-art equipment and processes so that it can produce its goods and services as attractively and cheaply as possible and can train its people to use the latest technology.

SMALL BUSINESS   CLOSE-UP

Thinking Small

Small business may be nice, but the real growth and profits are in big business, right? Wrong! Over the last decade, Americans have learned the truth of the cliché "small business is the backbone of the economy." Consider, for example, the growth in new jobs. Years ago, big business used to create most of these. Today, companies with fewer than 100 employees account for over half of all new jobs, and firms with 100–999 employees create another 30 percent. Companies with 1,000 or more employees create less than 20 percent.

What accounts for this dramatic growth of small business? One reason is the entrepreneurial spirit that is sweeping America. Many people want to get into business, small business, for themselves. Another reason is that small businesses often have greater opportunities for intrapreneuring. Managers and staff can pitch in to solve problems and start new, often risky, projects. In contrast, large firms have departmental boundaries that employees seldom cross to work with personnel in other areas. A third reason is that small businesses are often more adept at finding out what the customer wants and can create new products and services. A fourth is that they stay out of big business's way. They know they cannot compete head-to-head, so they pick their markets more carefully. They may charge more, but they often make up the difference in better service.

The lesson here for big business is to think small. If large firms were to adopt the same techniques that small ones use, their performance might improve substantially. Will they do it? A number of large companies already have. Many manufacturing firms are breaking up their large production plants into smaller ones to create more opportunities for intrapreneuring. Steel companies are replacing their huge manufacturing complexes with mini-mills designed to produce innovative specialty steel for selected target markets. In short, big business is beginning to realize the importance of thinking small.

Table 1.1 gives a current evaluation of how various industries are keeping up with technological change.

Unemployment

Another challenge facing American business is to help solve economic ills. One such problem is **unemployment,** the involuntary idleness of people who are actively seeking work. Unfortunately, many people in the United States are without jobs. Some are seeking **blue-collar jobs,** which are jobs in manufacturing or ones that call for employees to work with their hands. Others are seeking **white-collar jobs,** which involve clerical, office, or managerial work. A recently emerging third category of jobs includes the so-called **steel-collar jobs,** which are jobs performed by robots and computers. These have replaced many of the jobs traditionally done by humans.

Unemployment The involuntary idleness of people who are actively seeking work.

Blue-collar jobs Jobs in manufacturing or ones that call for employees to work with their hands.

White-collar jobs Jobs that involve clerical, office, or managerial work.

Steel-collar jobs Jobs performed by robots and computers.

T A B L E   1.1　　　　　**Technological Scorecard**

Industry	The Wall Street Journal Grade	Observations on Technological Status
Airlines (American, United, Delta)	B	The airlines get pretty high marks for advances in the areas of reservations, fares, and scheduling.
Autos (General Motors, Ford, Chrysler)	C	The factories of the future are not turning out as once thought. Robots are not being used as much as expected. There have been a series of embarrassing and costly glitches.
Banking (Bank of America, Citicorp, First Chicago)	C −	Most banks are still paper factories. The technology is available, but has not yet been implemented.
Computers (IBM, Digital Equipment, Apple)	B +	This industry practices what it preaches. Its high-tech members are moving into a world where computers design computers made by robots controlled by still other computers.
Money Management (Dreyfus, Alliance Capital Management)	A −	A technological success story, with desktop computers, telecommunications networks, and other developments helping investment managers make their offices more productive.
Petroleum (Mobil, Royal/Dutch Shell)	A	Even in tough times, this industry has successfully turned to and implemented things such as computer work stations to ride out the storm.
Pharmaceuticals (Hoffman-LaRoche, Merck, Pfizer, Eli Lilly)	B	Although the biomedical breakthroughs rate high, the ability to get these wonders to market rate a weak B.
Publishing (Times Mirror, McGraw-Hill)	B −	On the way up, this industry is doing very well in using technology to revolutionize production and distribution. In other areas it is still lagging.
Telecommunications (AT&T, Western Union, GTE)	C −	Mostly talk rather than action, this industry is still trying to figure out how to sell its impressive technological know-how.

How can business reduce unemployment? One way is to retrain unemployed workers and managers so that they can find jobs in new or emerging industries. For example, Xerox has undertaken an expensive retraining program that, in nine months of intensive, full-time study, prepares outdated employees for new, high-tech careers.[25] Similarly, Rockwell International helped set up a retraining program designed to assist laid-off auto workers in making the transition to high-demand aerospace and defense jobs.[26]

Another proactive approach to reducing unemployment is to remain alert to changing market conditions and to maintain a strong demand for the company's goods and, especially, services. Keeping on top of the changing job market allows business firms to retain employees and even hire more people. To date, these efforts seem to be working. Since 1970, the U.S. economy has produced more than 30 million net new jobs, for an increase of nearly 40 percent. Although some of these new jobs are in relatively low-paying service industries, this increase is still much better than in European countries such as West Germany and England and is even better than in Japan.[27]

Three basic categories of jobs are blue collar, white collar, and steel collar. The Canon employee making a copier in the top photo is a blue-collar worker; her job largely consists of working with her hands. In the center, employees of Cognos Inc. and Hewlett-Packard discuss a new computer development. They are white-collar workers because they do office and managerial work. The bottom photo shows a steel-collar worker: a robot at Caterpillar Inc. that is measuring whether a metal part was machined correctly.

Social Responsibility

Closely related to the unemployment problem is the challenge of meeting social obligations. **Social responsibility** is the obligation of business to the society in which it operates. This responsibility takes a number of different forms. One is providing equal opportunity in employment to everyone, including women and minorities. A second is protecting the environment by conserving energy and not polluting or causing any damage to it. A third is providing customers with safe, high-quality goods and services. A fourth are the ethics that provide the standards of honesty and integrity that govern the conduct of business.

Social responsibility The obligation of business to the society in which it operates.

How can business better meet these social obligations? It can start with several basic approaches:

> Striving to hire the best possible people regardless of race, color, sex, religion, or ethnic origin. Eastman Kodak and Coca-Cola are two companies that have an excellent reputation for initiating proactive programs to ensure equal opportunity in employment.

> Working to provide a safe environment within and outside the organization. The Union Carbide disaster in Bhopal, India, where 2,500 people lost their lives from leaking toxic gases points to problems that can arise when businesses neglect to pay close attention to their environmental responsibilities.

> Providing consumers with information about the way products work and responding to any complaints or inquiries. For example, General Electric has a toll-free number customers can use to inquire about any of its products.

> Adopting a code of ethics and then rewarding specific incidents that reflect the code in actual practice. For example, ITT adopted a 16-page "Code of Corporate Conduct," ranging from antitrust issues to fire prevention, and publicly recognizes incidents that reflect the code.

These are only a few of the ways business has responded to its social obligations. The next chapter will give specific attention to all aspects of social responsibility.

Government Regulation

During the last decade, critics have severely questioned government regulation of business, and in some cases the laws have changed. However, just as individuals have to file income taxes and obey the laws, businesses must file tax returns and other financial reports with governmental agencies and comply with a host of laws that regulate activities inside and outside the firm. The intent of these laws is to ensure that the economic system functions fairly and smoothly. Nevertheless, some would argue that the legal framework is often cumbersome, involves a lot of red tape, and even seems to be antibusiness in some cases.

How can business work more effectively with government? One way is by realizing that an "us against them" attitude is of no value. Business and government must work together as a team. A second way is by fighting unneeded government red tape and regulations through discussions, lobbying, and court cases. Most government agencies are trying to carry out their responsibilities, not give business a hard time.

By interacting honestly with government agencies, business can often work out misunderstandings. When this is impossible, the courts and federal, state, and local lawmakers have often been willing to listen and make fair decisions on matters of concern. Business people should realize that good-faith cooperation and an open exchange of ideas and concerns can resolve many conflicts. Chapter 21 will examine business–government relations in greater detail.

Competitiveness in World Markets

Another challenge facing American business is to become more competitive in the global marketplace. In recent years, Americans have bought more from foreign countries than we have sold to them. Major ways that U.S. companies can compete more effectively are by increasing productivity, keeping abreast of advancing technology, retraining and hiring the unemployed, being socially responsible, and working more harmoniously with government. These goals are not easy, but they are attainable.

For example, companies in the U.S. steel and auto industries, which had some very bleak years throughout the 1980s, are showing some definite signs of a comeback and are competing favorably with the Europeans and Japanese.[28] Some of this comeback can be attributed to the weakening dollar compared to the Japanese yen and European currencies, making imports more expensive and U.S. goods cheaper overseas. But there has also been a major overhaul in these American industries to raise efficiency, slash costs, make better products, and sell them more aggressively.[29] To date, however, even with these changes, U.S. firms are not competitive in many product areas with the newly industrialized countries (NICs) such as South Korea, Taiwan, Hong Kong, Singapore, and Brazil. This inability to compete stems largely from the NICs' lower wages and more favorable trade relations. The U.S. government is trying to help by limiting some of the NICs' trade privileges,[30] but a definite challenge remains for American business to be more competitive in world markets. Chapter 22 discusses in detail all aspects of international business and how business can meet this challenge.

Checkpoint

1. What are two of the major challenges facing American business today?
2. How can businesses meet those challenges?

Why Study Business?

Why study business? What can you gain from such an effort? Studying business pays off in personal and career growth.

Career Choice

Most people spend too little time thinking about what they want to do for a living. They take a job, stay with it for a while, and then move on to something else. In the beginning, this career pattern is neither uncommon nor dangerous. However, over time, these people find that their careers are undirected; they are simply drifting. By the time they finally decide what they want to do, many are well along in age, and the jobs they want are already filled by younger people. As a result, their progress up the ladder is slower than it could have been.

Studying business can help you avoid this pitfall. As you read the chapters in this book, think about careers in the areas of business you study. If some area particularly interests you, investigate it further, starting with the career sections at the end of each part of the book. Perhaps you would like a job in production or sales or accounting. Maybe you would like to go on to law school. All of these are promising career fields—and it is never too early to start thinking about where you want to be in five or ten years. Many successful people have taken such a proactive approach, and many students are already doing it.

Self-Employment One career option open to you is working for yourself. Small business is one of the major areas of opportunity now and in the foreseeable future. To be successfully self-employed, you need to know many different areas: personnel, operations, marketing, accounting, finance, and management. The study of business can help provide this needed base of knowledge. To that end, Chapter 3 examines entrepreneurship and Chapter 4 considers small business. In addition, examples appear throughout the book under the headings "Entrepreneurs Close-Up" and "Small Business Close-Up."

Service to Others With membership in our society goes the obligation to contribute to its betterment. Business can help you fulfill this obligation by teaching you how to identify and solve problems, from working on alternative energy sources to hiring the handicapped to providing quality goods and services. By studying business, you will not only gain insights into how you can help others in a humanitarian sense, but through involvement in the greatly expanding service sector, you also may be able to improve society by providing services such as education, health care, financial and tax planning, travel arrangements, and even eating out.

One of the greatest satisfactions of a career in business can be the opportunities to serve others. Workers at Canon, together with two psychologists, developed a device that enables cerebral palsy victims and others with speech impairments to communicate by typing out messages. This device, called a Canon Communicator, is lightweight and watertight and can type out 150 characters a minute.

Source: Courtesy of Canon U.S.A., Inc.

Relevance

Many fields of study are important to personal enrichment, but they are not always directly relevant to everyday living. Business is. This book applies ideas that you can use in everyday living. A better understanding of the world of business will help you better cope with life in the real world. For example, your knowledge of business may help you make better-informed decisions as a consumer.

Personal Profit and Growth

Business also offers a chance for personal financial gain and psychological growth. On the financial side, successful business people are able to make a good living. On the psychological side, they know they have contributed to society by providing meaningful job opportunities and a better way of life for others.

As you read this book and study for your exams, keep these reasons in mind. Business is an exciting and enriching field to study and practice. As you study business, remain alert to its applications. Keep asking yourself how you can use this information. Also keep in mind a career in business. Millions of Americans have profited from the study of business. You can, too!

Checkpoint

1. What are three reasons for studying business?
2. Why have you chosen to study business?

Closing Comments

This chapter lays the foundation for your study of business. Its purpose is to prepare you for getting involved or, in probably the most famous business manager of our time Lee Iacocca's words, "getting out of your chair and doing something" in the exciting world of business. The chapter provided an understanding of the free enterprise system, the alternative economic systems of communism and socialism, and the current challenges facing American business. This knowledge provides a point of departure and perspective for the rest of the chapters.

Learning Objectives Revisited

1. **Explain the basic rights of the free enterprise system.**
   The basic rights provided by the free enterprise system are the right of private property, which is the right to own, use, sell, or give away property; freedom of choice, which is the right to make business decisions, such as hiring people, investing money, purchasing machinery and equipment, and selecting markets in which to operate; and the right to rewards, which is the owner's right to all of a business's after-tax profits.

2. **Describe the factors of production.**

   The factors of production are land, which consists of the geographic territory and natural resources used in producing goods and services; labor, which is the people who produce the goods and services; capital, which includes the money used for operating the enterprise and the technology used in producing the goods and services; and entrepreneurship, which is the process of organizing, operating, and assuming the risks associated with a business venture. The first three have been traditionally recognized, but entrepreneurship has only recently re-emerged as an important factor of production.

3. **Discuss ways of measuring economic well-being.**

   The measure of economic well-being is the standard of living. Often, this is measured as the value of a country's total production divided by its population. Although there are exceptions, Americans currently enjoy a higher standard of living than the people of most other countries.

4. **Define alternative economic systems.**

   America has a free enterprise or capitalist economic system in which people are basically free to determine what goods and services they want. There are other forms of economic systems found in the world. Communism is an economic system in which the government (the people) owns all of the factors of production and decides what goods and services will be produced. Socialism is an economic system in which the government controls primary industries, but most other businesses remain in private hands. Today most countries have mixed economies, that is, economies that combine characteristics of free enterprise, communism, and/or socialism. For example, the economy of the United States combines free enterprise with a little socialism. The People's Republic of China and the Soviet Union combine communism with a little free enterprise.

5. **Identify the major challenges currently facing American business.**

   Some of the major challenges currently confronting business include increasing productivity, keeping abreast of technological change, helping reduce unemployment, fulfilling social responsibilities, coping with government regulation, and meeting foreign competition.

6. **Relate the benefits of studying business.**

   Some of the benefits of studying business include gaining greater insight into career choices, determining whether self-employment is personally appealing, learning how to contribute to the betterment of society, gaining knowledge of a field that offers relevance to everyday living, and achieving financial gain and psychological growth.

Key Terms Reviewed

Review each of the following terms. For any that you do not know or are unsure of, look up the definitions and see how they were used in the chapter.

business	venture
profit	intrapreneuring
free enterprise system	standard of living
laissez-faire	communism
right to private property	socialism
freedom of choice	mixed economy
right to rewards	productivity
land	unemployment
labor	blue-collar jobs
capital	white-collar jobs
technology	steel-collar jobs
entrepreneurship	social responsibility
entrepreneur	

Review Questions

1. In the United States, why do governments need business?
2. What are the fundamental rights of the free enterprise system? Explain the meaning of each right.
3. George Waterstreet is the accountant for a light manufacturing firm. At the end of last year, George calculated that the company received $2.5 million in revenues for the products it sold. The same year, the company spent $2 million on wages, raw materials, equipment, supplies, and rent for the factory. What is the company's profit? Does the company have a right to this entire sum?
4. What are the four factors of production? Explain how each would be used in starting a restaurant, an assembly plant, and a bookstore.
5. What are the primary differences between the economic system of communism and the economic system of the United States? If Premier Gorbachev begins giving salary increases and bonuses to managers and workers who do an outstanding job, is he changing the Soviet Union's economic system? Why or why not?
6. What is productivity? In general, how can businesses improve productivity?
7. Identify two ways in which companies use technology to stay up-to-date and effective. How can this affect productivity?
8. Nancy Norris is a management consultant. One of her clients has asked her to develop guidelines for how the company can meet its social responsibility. What areas should Nancy's guidelines cover?
9. Another one of Nancy's clients is a shoe manufacturer concerned about foreign competition. Nancy's assignment is to suggest ways to meet the competition. What possible activities might Nancy investigate?
10. How can the study of business help in career planning?

Applied Exercises

1. How does free enterprise work today? How would your answer differ if you were living during your grandparents' generation? (Ask them or someone of that age about it.) What changes have occurred since then?

2. Can business firms successfully set up operations in socialist countries, or do they risk being taken over by the host government? Support your answer.

3. One of the biggest complaints of American manufacturers is that they cannot produce products as cheaply as many Asian manufacturers can. How can an American manufacturer increase its productivity? Define the term *productivity*, and then offer at least four useful recommendations.

4. Choose one of the six challenges facing American business identified in this chapter and do library research on its current status. Does business seem to be meeting, or making any headway, in this area? Support your answer with some facts in a short paper.

Your Business IQ: Answers

1. True. America's founders strictly adhered to the belief that government should not interfere in the affairs of business. However, by the late 1800s, the prevailing belief was that big business must be controlled in order to protect consumers and smaller businesses. To this day, the government regulates business to some extent.

2. False. Only a few nations have a higher income per person, and most people would argue that none has the overall wealth of America or offers the life-style of Americans.

3. False. Under the economic system called socialism, the government can take over an industry, but it generally pays the owners a fair price for the business.

4. False. Producing goods and services more efficiently—improving productivity—is an ongoing challenge facing American businesses. While U.S. businesses are still productive compared to many overseas companies, their productivity growth rates have not been as high as many Asian and Western European countries.

5. True. Technology can create long-term unemployment when it makes people's jobs or skills obsolete. When people are laid off because they work in an industry with slow seasons, they expect to be rehired. But workers who lose their jobs due to technological developments have a hard time finding employment unless they are retrained and acquire new skills.

Case

United Airlines Employees Launch an Airport Battle

Deregulation of the airline industry has led the airlines to compete on major routes with low prices. At Denver's Stapleton Airport, United Airlines employees have found additional ways to go after Continental Airlines, its major competitor in that city.

The offensive started one spring day when a line at the Continental ticket counter at Stapleton grew longer and longer, eventually nearing the United ticket counter. Some grumbling ensued, and soon United's employees began suggesting to the Continental passengers that they move into United's shorter line. Faced with waits of up to an hour, many of the Continental passengers defected.

Inspired by their success, United ticket agents began to spend time wandering into Continental's airport territory, looking for flyers who might be converted to United. Outraged Continental executives demanded that the airport authority put an end to this activity. The airport director did so, because airport leases require that airline employees stick to their own airline's area.

Undaunted, the United employees found new ways to convert flyers. They ride buses looking for Continental passengers. United ticket agents search their computer terminal for names of Continental passengers. When they find one, they page that person to the United ticket counter, where the surprised passenger hears about the advantages of switching to United. "I'm a little surprised that they keep such close tabs on us," exclaimed one such passenger. Industry observers note that the fierce tactics are unprecedented.

Case Questions

1. What evidence in this case indicates that the airlines are operating within a free enterprise economy? What evidence shows limits on the freedom with which these airlines operate?
2. In your opinion, do the activities described in this case demonstrate that deregulation is benefiting passengers? Explain.
3. How would you suggest that Continental respond to United's competition at Stapleton Airport?

You Be the Adviser: Helping Tony

Tony Fascell owns a restaurant that specializes in Italian food and is located in the heart of the business district. Tony does a brisk lunch business, and on weekends his establishment is jam-packed from 6:00 p.m. until 2:00 a.m. In the six months he has been in operation, Tony's business has gone from serving an average of 110 customers a day to over 400. In the process, he has expanded the number of tables from 22 to 45.

Tony started out with $25,000 of his own money and another $75,000 he borrowed from relatives and friends. A local bank gave him an additional line of credit of $100,000. He used these monies to buy equipment, tables, dinnerware, and other necessities to carry the business for the first six months. By this time, Tony felt, the operation should be paying its own way. As it has turned out, business has done even better than he expected. As of last week, Tony had doubled the number of people originally working in the restaurant, and sales are 3½ times his expectations.

Unfortunately, Tony has found that most of the new waiters are unable to provide good enough service and process as many orders as he would like. The same is true for the two new cooks he recently hired. However, Tony is convinced that with more on-the-job experience, they will become as proficient as the regulars.

Yesterday, one of Tony's customers, a manager with a British firm, asked him if he had ever thought of expanding operations. "Your restaurant is distinctive and would do well in Europe," he said. "Have you ever thought about opening another one in, say, London's financial district? I have some partners who would be more than willing to put up the money. Think about it and get back with me, won't you?" Tony promised to do so.

Your Advice

1. What factors of production would Tony be using if he set up a restaurant in London? Which one of these factors would be most important? Why?
2. What types of problems is Tony beginning to have in his current business, and what types of problems will he face if he opens a London restaurant? How can he solve them? Offer some specific advice.
3. What rights of the free enterprise system does Tony have now? Would he also have these in London? If he had a profit in London, would he be as well off as he is in the United States? Why or why not?

The Social Responsibilities of Business

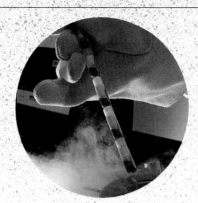

LEARNING OBJECTIVES

- Define the overall nature of social responsibility.
- Describe the social issue of equality in employment.
- Identify the social issue of environmental protection.
- Explain the social issue of consumerism.
- Discuss the nature of business ethics.

Your Business IQ

How much do you already know about the social responsibilities of business? Test your business IQ by labeling each statement *true* or *false*. Answers and explanations are at the end of the chapter.

1. Businesses should exercise responsibility to society, but this inevitably cuts into profits over the long run.
2. The upward mobility of women has been so dramatic in recent years that their participation in professional and managerial ranks almost equals that of men.
3. About half of the air pollution generated in the United States comes from automobiles and other motor vehicles.
4. Customer complaints can help businesses meet their responsibilities to consumers.
5. Employees can and should be fired for blowing the whistle on their employers, reporting their unethical behavior.

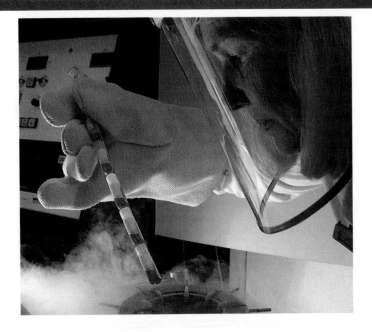

A scientist at Warner-Lambert conducts pharmaceutical research. The company emphasizes treatment of the most widespread chronic diseases, such as cancer, heart disease, and infection. In this way, Warner-Lambert makes its social responsibilities, such as providing opportunities for women and minorities and developing quality products, consistent with its profit objectives.

Source: Courtesy of Warner Lambert Company.

Looking Back and Ahead

Is it irresponsible to sell three-wheeled all-terrain vehicles, recreational vehicles that look like big go-carts with fat tires? Some people say no; these vehicles are simply an exciting form of recreation and they help in certain outdoor jobs. But to others, these products are a hazard. A growing number of state officials claim that the vehicles can flip over and hurt or kill riders. In addition, environmentalists complain that all-terrain vehicles damage the land and its plant life and scare animals. The makers of this product are struggling to contend with threatened regulation or an outright ban, as well as numerous lawsuits.[1] American Honda Corporation stopped producing the three-wheeled vehicles in 1987.

The legal and social environment for the makers of all-terrain vehicles is a particularly challenging one. In the early twentieth century, Henry Ford was on record as putting profit ahead of social responsibility. The business of business was business. What was good for business was good for the country. What Ford and most of the other early industrialists failed to recognize, however, was that what was good for the country—equal opportunity in employment, protection of the environment, and high-quality, safe goods and services—was also good for business. Now businesses realize the importance of social responsibility and are taking an active part in helping solve America's social ills. In fact, Ford's grandson, who was head of Ford Motor Company until his death in 1987, was a major leader in this effort.

Chapter 1 set the stage for a study of business by presenting the overall nature of contemporary business and the challenges facing it. One of the major challenges concerns the responsibilities of business to the society at large.

This chapter focuses on these social responsibilities by first identifying the overall nature of social responsibility and then examining the major issues of equality in employment, environmental concerns, and consumerism, concluding with an assessment of business ethics. This chapter is placed near the beginning of the book to provide an important social framework and perspective for understanding modern business.

The Nature of Business's Social Responsibilities

As you learned in Chapter 1, businesses in a free enterprise system depend on certain resources, or factors of production: land, labor, capital, and entrepreneurship. For example, a construction company might require a plot of land, healthy workers, state-of-the-art equipment, raw materials such as plastic pipes (made from a petroleum product) and wood for doors, and a developer to raise the funds and sell the new construction. But what if the workers are unhealthy because the air they breathe is polluted? What if the supply of petroleum and wood runs out? What if the equipment is unsafe and injures the workers? What if the company loses sales—and hence a supply of capital—because it has a reputation for shoddy work? Businesses depend on society and on the environment. Consequently, many observers believe that business should in turn accept some responsibility for these resources.

Business's obligation to the society in which it operates is called social responsibility. Four areas in particular call for social responsibility on the part of business: equal opportunity in employment, environmental protection, consumerism, and business ethics. Each of these areas will be given detailed attention, but first some of the background of social responsibility is presented.

Past and Present Views of Social Responsibility

The social role of business is certainly not new. During the 19th and early 20th centuries, many business owners and managers took a **paternalistic approach,** which means that the owners/managers took care of their employees similar to the way that parents take care of children. If a worker was sick, the company would bring in a doctor. Likewise, a long-time employee with a large family would receive a bigger salary than a long-time employee with a small family. These paternalistic owners/managers were genuinely concerned for their employees and basically treated them as if they were family members.

Paternalistic approach
Taking care of employees
similar to the way that
parents take care of
children.

Unfortunately, paternalistic managers were in the minority, and even under them, working conditions were often less than ideal. Employees were paid low wages, product quality and safety were often poor, and personal profit was often the only objective of the owner/manager. As a result, early in this century, the public began to pressure the government to regulate some business practices. The government responded by requiring businesses to abide by minimum standards of socially responsible behavior. For example, the government eventually passed child labor laws, minimum-wage legislation, and occupational health and safety acts.

Today these and many other laws regulate business. Among them are laws designed to ensure equal opportunity in employment, prevent unnecessary pollution of the environment, protect consumers, and establish ethical levels of behavior in business practices.

Is legislation necessary to ensure fair and responsible business dealings? The general public obviously thinks so. Most business people agree. While noting that they would never do anything illegal or immoral, they suggest that the laws prevent their competitors from doing these things. But while these laws receive broad support, the general concept of social responsibility has stirred some controversy.

The Case For and Against Social Responsibility

Aside from obeying the laws of the country, does business have any social obligations? Most consumers believe so, arguing that business has to be responsible for the quality and safety of its products. Most Americans also believe that business must keep the environment clean and pay for any damage it does, and that it should give all people, regardless of race, color, creed, or sex, an equal opportunity in employment. Most business people would agree.

Numerous reasons support this view. The most basic is that because business is a vital part of society, it therefore cannot afford to ignore society's problems. By assisting society, business can create a stable environment that is more conducive to its own long-term profit. In addition, business has the managerial, financial, and technical know-how to help solve many of society's problems, so it is obligated to use these abilities to help out. Also, by playing a proactive social role, business can reduce the likelihood that the government will force it to get involved. Governmental guidelines could actually cost business firms more in terms of paperwork and more costly equipment and operating procedures than if the businesses had tackled the social problems on their own.

On the other side of the coin, a few still argue (especially off the record) that social involvement is not business's responsibility. This view contends that devoting company time, money, and talent to social issues will interfere with business's primary responsibility: to make a profit for its owners. Furthermore, since social problems affect the entire nation or the local community, they are the public's responsibility, not private business's. Consequently, elected public officials and government employees should assume the responsibility for society's problems, not business managers. Those who reject social involvement contend that their social obligation begins and ends with running an effective business.

Who is right: those who favor involvement in the social arena or those who oppose it? Most *successful* managers believe that business must not only be socially responsible but also socially active. For example, see "Social Responsibility Close-Up: Leaving South Africa," which describes how U.S. firms are reacting to the situation in South Africa. Enlightened managers view the costs associated with social involvement as wise investments in a better society. The rest of the chapter will take this perspective and examine the various ways that businesses involve themselves in the social arena.

Profits and Social Responsibility

Concern with profits is not inconsistent with fulfilling social responsibility. That is because in addition to business's responsibilities to consumers and employees, companies are also responsible to their investors. Those who invest money in a company expect to receive an acceptable return in exchange for the risks they take. To give the investors a return, the company must be profitable over the long term. Companies can even use social responsibility to directly contribute to profits. For example, a company could reclaim refuse and wastes and remake them into saleable products or they could develop pollution control equipment and sell it to others.

More indirectly, a firm's managers fulfill their responsibility to investors by being honest and avoiding personal gain at the expense of the company. Padding expense accounts or stealing supplies cheats investors of their rightful profits. Besides these relatively small problems, recent scandals in corporate America involving the use of inside stock information to make investments for the personal gain of managers, officers, and directors have led many investors to be wary of unethical conduct on a grander scale. More subtly, recruiting employees from a single ethnic group or of a single sex can also reduce profits by robbing the company of the opportunity to choose the best employee for the job. Also, recent research indicates that when equal-opportunity laws are imposed to erase workplace bias, all workers are spurred to greater efforts.[2] In such cases, managers who fulfill their social responsibility to investors are also fulfilling the broader social responsibility of fair employment practices.

Balancing profits and other responsibilities can be a difficult task. Pollution control, for example, may be costly, and safe products may be more expensive to make than products without safety features. It also may make sense from a marketing standpoint to sell products in South Africa, but threats of consumer boycotts from Americans reflecting ethical consumerism have forced companies such as Coca-Cola and Revlon to rethink such an international strategy. The Council of Economic Priorities has recently issued a book titled *Rating America's Corporate Conscience* to guide consumers on buying from companies that score high on ethical standards. For example, Anheuser-Busch, Avon, and Philip Morris scored high because they have three women among their directors and Coca-Cola, ITT, and Marriott also scored high because each company has four minority officers.

SOCIAL RESPONSIBILITY   CLOSE-UP

Leaving South Africa

In recent years, more and more American businesses have been leaving South Africa. Between 1985 and mid-1987, more than 100 U.S. firms pulled out. Why? Because they are being pressured to do so, and because they believe they have an obligation to oppose apartheid, the South African government's policies of racial segregation and oppression.

Besides their social responsibilities, companies doing business there are getting direct pressure from two directions: political and economic. On the political front, large companies are getting heat from outside activists and, in some cases, their own stockholders to stop doing business with South Africa. Even the board members of many corporations are openly questioning the wisdom of associating with a country whose racial policies are so far out of line with those of America.

On the economic front, the South African economy is weakening. In 1980, American firms in the country earned an average of 31 cents on each dollar invested; by 1983, this return had fallen to 7 cents on the dollar. Additionally, South Africa's unit of currency, the rand, lost half of its value between January and September 1985, and international banks therefore refused to refinance the

country's short-term debt. This meant that South Africa had to come up with $12 billion immediately to repay the international banks. To deal with the crisis, the government was forced to declare a moratorium on repaying the debt, which made the country a less desirable credit risk.

In the meantime, American firms such as General Foods, Pan American World Airways, and PepsiCo have been leaving. Others, some with very large holdings, have been quietly reducing their operations. Even American firms that are not leaving agree that apartheid is unacceptable and changes must be made. For example, General Motors, which operates a plant in Port Elizabeth, has taken a public antiapartheid action. GM is on record as stating that it will give legal aid to any nonwhite employee charged with swimming at whites-only beaches.

The final outcome is yet to be decided, but one thing is clear. Managers of American firms in South Africa feel that they have a social responsibility to speak out or get out—and they are doing either or both in increasing numbers.

Realistically, managers try to strike a balance in meeting their responsibilities to all parties (sometimes called stakeholders): investors, consumers, and employees. In the long run, however, by taking a proactive approach to meeting its social responsibilities, business benefits both itself and society at large (see Figure 2.1).

Checkpoint

1. What are the social responsibilities of business?
2. What are two reasons why businesses should be socially responsible?

Equality in Employment

Perhaps the most obvious and immediate way a company meets its social responsibilities is by being a fair employer. This social role involves offering equal employment opportunity to women and racial minorities. Efforts at equal opportunity should also extend to others who have suffered employment discrimination, such as those with a disability or older workers. These groups receive specific attention in Chapter 8 when we discuss personnel and human resource management.

F I G U R E   2.1

Balancing the Social and Profit Responsibilities of Business

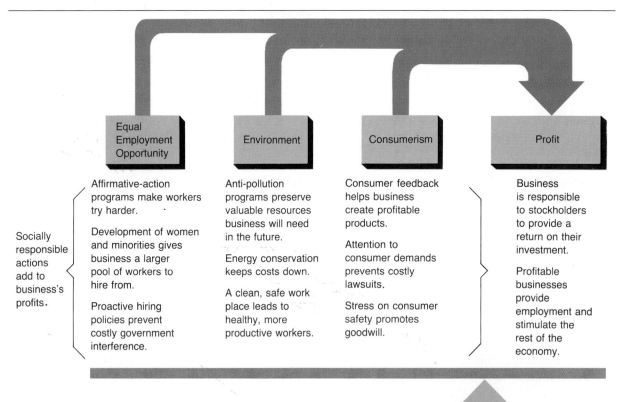

Legislation to Ensure Equality

Congress has passed a number of laws designed to ensure equal employment opportunity. Table 2.1 summarizes the major ones. The landmark legislation is the Civil Rights Act of 1964, which specifically prohibits discrimination based on race, color, sex, or national origin. This law established the **Equal Employment Opportunity Commission (EEOC),** which is charged with overseeing enforcement of the act by investigating complaints and taking appropriate action.

Many firms do more than just comply with this act; they have set up **affirmative-action programs.** These programs are designed to seek out minorities, women, and others who are more likely to have problems finding work, and to hire, train, develop, and promote them. These groups have been discriminated against in the past and still face many problems. In particular, women and minorities have stirred concern in government, private industry, and the public at large.

The Status of Women and Minorities in the Workplace

In spite of laws expressly forbidding discrimination in employment and requiring that all employees receive equal pay for equal work (see Table 2.1), women and minorities still lag far behind white males in these areas. White males tend to earn much higher salaries than do black or Hispanic males. White women do better than black or Hispanic women, but not nearly as well as white men. Women still earn only 60 to 80

Equal Employment Opportunity Commission (EEOC) The commission charged with overseeing enforcement of the Civil Rights Act of 1964 by investigating complaints and taking appropriate action.

Affirmative-action programs Programs designed to seek out minorities, women, the handicapped, and others with problems finding work and to hire, train, develop, and promote them.

Federal Law	Provisions Affecting Business
Davis-Bacon Act, 1931	Requires firms engaged in federal construction projects valued at more than $2,000 to pay the prevailing wage rate.
Walsh-Healey Act, 1936	Requires firms with federal supply contracts in excess of $10,000 to pay a minimum wage and overtime for all hours worked in excess of 40 per week.
Fair Labor Standards Act, 1938	Requires virtually all businesses engaged in interstate commerce to pay the minimum wage and overtime for all hours worked in excess of 40 per week.
Equal Pay Act, 1963	Forbids employers to discriminate on the basis of sex by paying higher wages to one sex than to the other for equal work on jobs requiring equal skill, effort, responsibility, and similar working conditions.
Civil Rights Act of 1964	Prohibits discrimination based on race, color, sex, and national origin.
Age Discrimination in Employment Act, 1967	Originally prohibited discrimination in employment of those 40 to 65 years of age; in 1978, was amended to move the top age from 65 to 70 years; and in 1986, the upper limit was removed.
Vocational Rehabilitation Act, 1973, 1978	Prohibits discrimination against persons with mental or physical handicaps. Employers must make a reasonable effort to accommodate them.

T A B L E 2.1

Major Legislation Affecting Equality in Employment

cents for every dollar earned by men. Women, blacks, and other minorities are also more likely to be unemployed than are white males (see Table 2.2). Overall, black unemployment is 15 percent (2.3 times the rate for whites), the Hispanic rate is 11.2 percent (1.75 times that for whites), and both minorities were worse off in 1985 than five years earlier.[3]

Recent years have witnessed some improvement in the upward mobility of women and, to a lesser degree, minorities (see Figure 2.2). For example, the percentage of white women in managerial, professional, and executive positions has increased. Also, the gap in the median weekly earnings between men and women has been slowly but steadily narrowing since 1979.[4] In that year, women earned only 62.5 percent of men's salaries. In 1986, women's average hourly earnings were 68 percent of men's. Overall, however, women and minorities still have far to go. For example, in 1987, 92.1 percent of directors on boards of major American corporations were white males, and a recent poll found that almost three-fourths of black Americans believe they do not have the same opportunities in employment as do whites.[5]

The Response of Business

To rectify the imbalance, business has taken some steps to ensure equal opportunity in employment. These efforts include:

> Establishing affirmative-action programs designed to target women and minorities with potential.

> Training these people and then moving them up the ranks as quickly as possible.

Mentor An outstanding, experienced manager who provides an identified person with advice and assistance and helps the person achieve career goals.

> Establishing **mentor** programs, whereby an outstanding, experienced manager takes an identified woman or minority member under his or her wing, provides advice and counsel, and helps the person to achieve career goals. Women, in particular, report that mentors have been extremely helpful to them.

Affirmative-action approaches are especially important to business in light of the expectation that minorities and women will account for three-fourths of the growth in the U.S. labor force during the 1990s. This trend means that women and minorities are becoming an increas-

T A B L E   2.2   **Unemployment by Sex, Age, and Race (in Percentages)**

Year	All Civilian Workers	White				Black			
		Male		Female		Male		Female	
		16–19	20+	16–19	20+	16–19	20+	16–19	20+
1974	5.6	13.5	3.5	14.5	5.1	33.1	7.4	37.4	8.8
1977	7.7	17.3	5.4	16.4	6.8	37.5	11.4	41.6	11.7
1978	6.1	13.5	3.7	14.4	5.2	36.7	9.3	40.8	11.2
1980	7.1	16.2	5.3	14.8	5.6	37.5	12.4	39.8	11.9
1982	9.7	21.7	7.8	19.0	7.3	48.9	17.8	47.1	15.4
1984	7.5	16.8	5.7	15.2	5.8	42.7	14.3	42.6	13.5
1986	7.0	16.3	5.3	14.9	5.4	39.3	12.9	39.2	12.5

The Social
Responsibilities of
Business

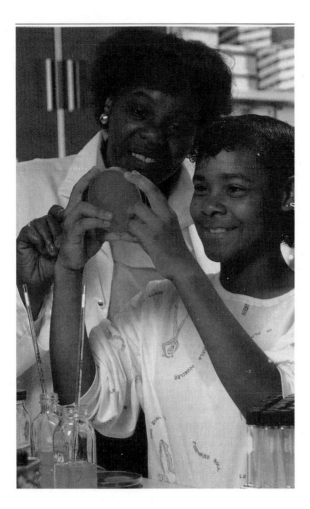

At Pillsbury, willingness to
hire women and minorities is
only the beginning of the company's efforts to provide equal
opportunity. Through Pillsbury's Project Destiny, employees
such as microbiologist Alma
Curry, shown here, act as
mentors to minority junior-
high-school students. The students visit the mentors at work
and learn about the opportunities and requirements of various career paths.

Source: Courtesy of the Pillsbury
Company.

F I G U R E 2.2

**Median Weekly Income
for Whites, Blacks, and
Hispanics**

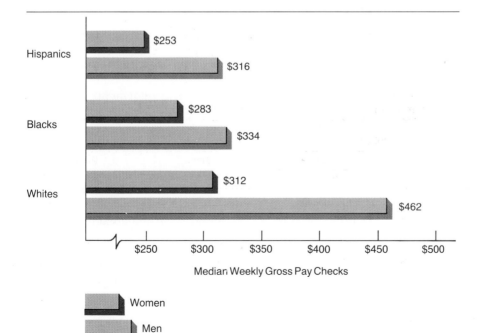

42

ingly important resource for business. Taking an affirmative-action approach, McDonald's cut in half the turnover rate of its minority managers, and General Motors was able to double its proportion of female managers and increase by 50 percent its number of minority managers.[6]

For the past 20 years, the courts have ruled in favor of affirmative-action programs for minorities. In a landmark case in 1987, the Supreme Court ruled that employers may give special preference in hiring and promoting women in order to create a more balanced work force. In this particular case, a man was denied a promotion and the job went to a woman who the man claimed was less qualified. The man charged that he was a victim of reverse discrimination. The court ruled in favor of the woman, even though the justices felt the man might be slightly more qualified (he had scored a little higher on the evaluation). Although this might be interpreted as okaying reverse discrimination, the justices pointed out that their ruling does not mean that unqualified people will be hired or promoted. Instead, they simply stated that sex is now one of several factors that may be taken into account in evaluating qualified applications for a position. Although most companies have been tentative in their use of affirmative-action programs for fear of charges of reverse discrimination, with the Supreme Court ruling, firms now feel that they have legal backing in their efforts to correct the underemployment of women.[7]

Besides using affirmative action, businesses can assist minorities and women in setting up their own small-business ventures. Established firms can provide managerial and/or technical expertise as well as support in the form of orders and subcontracts. Although ventures owned by blacks have received the most publicity, women also are starting their own companies in record numbers. The number of firms owned by women is growing at twice the rate of male-owned business and now represents 27 percent of all businesses in the nation.[8]

Checkpoint

1. What are two laws designed to ensure equal opportunity in employment?
2. How can businesses help ensure equality in employment?

Environmental Concerns

Equality in employment has the greatest impact on workers and their dependents, but all members of society are directly affected by how business is or is not protecting the environment. Environmental issues stem from the biological concept of **ecology,** which is the interrelationship of living things and their environment. Any change, however small, can affect life throughout the environment. Businesses affect the environment in a variety of ways, most of which fall into the categories of energy conservation and pollution control.

Ecology The interrelationship of living things and their environment.

Energy Conservation

Since the Arab oil embargo of the 1970s, the United States has been working hard to conserve energy. Business is certainly one of the largest energy consumers. Thus, conservation measures taken by business can generate tremendous savings of society's natural resources. In addition, by conserving energy, business firms can reduce their costs and eventually benefit individual consumers by keeping prices down.

Companies are taking a number of actions to help meet the challenge of energy conservation. One action is the development of long- and short-range conservation plans. General Motors, DuPont, Exxon, and AT&T, among others, already have such plans in operation. At AT&T, for example, business grew by 50 percent in a recent ten-year period, while its consumption of energy remained the same. Other firms are studying ways of operating machinery more efficiently or replacing it with more up-to-date, energy-efficient equipment. Some organizations have even installed paddle fans in their offices and shut off the air conditioning.

Pollution Control

Besides energy problems, the public is rightfully concerned with pollution of the environment. **Pollution** is any contamination of the air, water, or land in which life exists. For business, there are a number of pollution problems, such as noise and solid-waste, but the two biggest concerns are with air and water pollution.

Pollution Contamination of the air, water, land, or environment in which life exists.

The Ontario Paper Company conserves timber resources by using recycled paper in its production of newsprint. The company conducts research to increase the proportion of recycled paper used. Recent developments have enabled the company's Thorold paper mill to use 50 percent pulp from recycled paper, up from 25 percent—thus reducing expenses, increasing the quality of the product, and saving trees.

Source: Photo by Charles Cherney, *Chicago Tribune.* Used with permission.

Air Pollution Pollution of the air is a major problem. Approximately 200 million tons of pollutants are released into the air each year. Figure 2.3 shows the relative amounts of pollution from various sources. The average person breathes about 35 pounds of air each day, and for those in air-polluted environments, the physical effects can be extremely harmful. Experts estimate that the respiratory ailments and heart disease from breathing polluted air cost the United States approximately $5 billion in medical treatment, lost wages, and reduced productivity. In an effort to address environmental concerns, the federal government has enacted a number of important laws, which are summarized in Table 2.3.

Besides complying with these laws, businesses are taking proactive steps of their own. An increasing number of firms have designated no-smoking areas or banned smoking altogether. For example, the *Pittsburgh Press* bans smoking in its newsroom, and McKesson Corporation and Hewlett-Packard adhere to local bans against smoking in public places.[9] For more examples of limits on smoking, see "Social Responsibility Close-Up: No Smoking." Car manufacturers have redesigned their engines and dramatically cut auto pollution. Utilities and industrial firms have installed special equipment to greatly reduce smokestack pollution. This equipment, which includes filters, after-burners, gas-washing devices, and electrostatic precipitators, is beginning to get results. Although the problem is far from solved, some of the traditional causes of air pollution are being eliminated through legislation and, importantly, the social responsibility actions of business.

TABLE 2.3

Major Environmental Laws

Federal Law	Provisions
Clean Air Act, 1963	Designed to assist local and state government in establishing control programs and coordinating research. Later amendments, among other things, established standards for auto exhaust emissions, set up air-quality regions with acceptable regional pollution levels, required states to meet deadlines for complying with Environmental Protection Agency (EPA) standards, and gave citizens the right to bring suit to require the EPA to carry out approved standards against undiscovered offenders.
Federal Water Pollution Control Act, 1965	Set standards for treatment of municipal water waste before discharge. Later amendments set a national water-quality goal of restoring polluted waters to swimmable, fishable waters.
Noise Control Act, 1972	Required the EPA to establish noise standards for products that are major sources of noise. Also set standards for aircraft noise.
Pesticide Control Act, 1972	Required that all pesticides used in interstate commerce be approved and certified as effective for their stated purpose. An amendment to the act established deadlines for registering, classifying, and licensing pesticides.
Clean Water Act, 1974	Set federal standards for water suppliers serving more than 25 people, having more than 15 service connections, or operating more than 60 days a year. Later amendments required that pollutants be monitored using the best available and economically feasible technology.

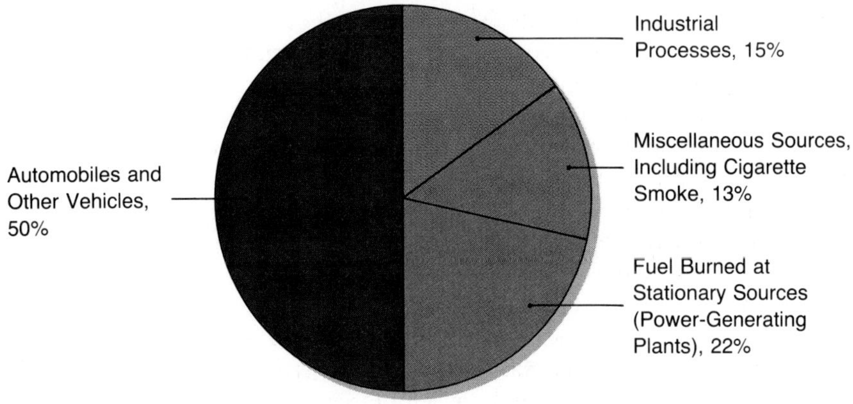

FIGURE 2.3

Sources of Air Pollution

Water Pollution There are many sources of water pollution. Industrial toxic wastes are one of the most common. Other sources are fertilizers, sewage, leakage of underground waste dumps, and acid rain (caused by sulfur emissions from industrial smokestacks) that falls into rivers and lakes.

SOCIAL RESPONSIBILITY   CLOSE-UP

No Smoking

What do the following all have in common: the *Seattle Times,* Group Health Cooperative of Puget Sound (a large health maintenance organization), and the Phoenix headquarters of Greyhound? Answer: They all have banned smoking in their offices. Anyone who wants to light up has to go outside. And these firms are not alone. The Association of Flight Attendants is supporting a recent recommendation by the National Academy of Sciences that will totally ban smoking on airlines, and a number of states have limited smoking at state offices. Northwest Airlines became the first airline to totally ban smoking on its continental domestic flights on April 23, 1988.

No-smoking rules can be traumatic. Smokers at the Group Health Cooperative of Puget Sound threatened to file a labor grievance against management. However, the union's membership included a lot more nonsmokers than smokers, so the employees voted down the proposal to take legal action. In the case of Greyhound, the company tries to soften the blow by offering employees a choice of four free quit-smoking workshops.

Will the future see the abolition of smoking in the workplace? Maybe not, but smokers will increasingly be in the minority, and most companies are firm in their decision to limit smoking to certain areas of the building or to require that smokers go outside to smoke. Many smokers claim that these new rules violate their individual rights in the workplace. However, most organizations feel that it is not a matter of employee rights but of employee health. These firms have concluded that smoking is bad for smokers and nonsmokers. As a result, more and more companies are likely to start kicking the smoking-at-work habit.

Business is taking several actions to control water pollution. The most common actions are to treat waste materials before disposing of them in lakes, streams, or underground dumps, and to recycle the treated water and reuse it in the production process. Many firms are also looking at different ways of handling water discharge, such as alternatives to underground dumps. Other firms, including fertilizer manufacturers, are investigating ways of developing pesticides that, when washed into streams and lakes by the rain, will not pollute the water. For example, Florida Power and Light has a huge grid of cooling canals to prevent their nuclear power plant's warm water discharge from harming the surrounding marine life. The canals have become a breeding ground for endangered crocodiles, and the utility's staff goes out regularly to make sure the nests are protected.[10] Like air pollution, the problems of water pollution are not solved, but businesses are making progress in many areas.

Paying the Bill

How much will it cost to clean up the environment, and who will pay? Business is spending about $50 billion annually to reduce pollution. Experts estimate that during the 1980s, business will have spent approximately $690 billion to create a cleaner environment. A great deal of this expense is borne by "smokestack" industries; they are visible polluters but, unfortunately, currently the least able to pay the costs. Eventually, society will bear much of the cost of environmental protection in the form of higher prices and taxes.

Checkpoint

1. What are the two major types of pollution?
2. How are businesses conserving energy?

Consumerism

Consumerism A movement designed to provide buyers with the information and bargaining power necessary for obtaining high-quality, safe products and services.

Class-action suit A lawsuit in which a group of buyers join together to sue the seller.

Boycott An organized effort to convince people to refrain from buying goods or services from targeted businesses.

The third major social issue facing business is **consumerism,** which is a movement to provide buyers with the information and bargaining power necessary for obtaining high-quality, safe products and services. Consumerism takes many forms, including the following:

Class-action suits, in which a group of buyers join together in a lawsuit against the seller

Boycotts, in which consumers organize to convince people to refrain from buying goods or services from targeted businesses

Individual letters of complaint from dissatisfied customers to the company's management

Consumerism became popular in the 1960s as a result of the work of Ralph Nader and his action groups. Consisting mostly of college students from across the country, "Nader's Raiders" raised the consciousness of the general public about product information and safety and helped mandate safety features (such as seat belts in American automobiles) in consumer products.

Customers have a number of specific gripes, such as with health spas and video clubs that sell long-term memberships and then close, and the problem is not unique to America. For example, a consumer advocate in Mexico claims that because of mismarked labels customers pay for $370,000 worth of tortillas per year that they never see and that many brands of tequila are mostly water. He also found breaded "steak sandwiches" sold at some Mexican soccer stadiums that were really breaded paper. One pet shop sold talkative parrots that fell silent when bought and taken home. It turned out that the proprietor was a ventriloquist.[11] To handle such consumer abuses case by case can be difficult, so consumerism today generally focuses on two major concerns: information and safety. Consumers want information so they can make informed purchase decisions. Consumers also want product safety to avoid injury. Many laws address these two concerns; Table 2.4 summarizes some of the major legislation.

Incomplete Information in Advertising

A common area of consumer complaint is advertising. Many ads give incomplete information or are ambiguous. For example, some companies advertise personal computers at prices hundreds of dollars below those of the competition; however, the ad fails to tell the consumer that the machines are not new, they are reconditioned. Another common practice involves advertising the computer at a low price and, when the customer comes into the store, telling the individual that in order to take advantage of the lower price, it is necessary to buy other equipment and software.

T A B L E   2.4   Major Consumer Laws

Federal Law	Provisions
Wheeler-Lea Act, 1938	Enlarged the Federal Trade Commission's power to prohibit deceptive practices in commerce and false advertising of foods, drugs, and cosmetics.
Fair Packaging and Labeling Act, 1966	Requires that packages and labels identify the article and give the manufacturer's name and location, quantity of contents, and presentation of servings, uses, and/or applications.
Truth-in-Lending Act, 1968	Requires creditors to inform borrowers of the amount of the financing charge and the annual percentage interest rate.
Child Protection and Toy Safety Act, 1969	Forbids the manufacture and interstate distribution of toys and other children's articles that have electrical, mechanical, or other hazards.
Fair Credit Reporting Act, 1970	Requires agencies reporting consumer credit data to follow procedures that ensure the accuracy of their information. If a person is refused credit because of a credit report, the user of the information must inform the consumer of the source of the information.
Consumer Product Safety Act, 1972	Created a Consumer Product Safety Commission to maintain standards for product safety, to require a warning label on potentially dangerous products, and to order recalls of hazardous products.

Still another tactic is **bait and switch,** in which a store advertises a product at a very low price and then tells customers that the product is either out of stock or of low quality and recommends a higher-priced alternative. This is a common practice in many discount retail stores. The store will advertise, say, an RCA video camera at a comparatively low price in mid-December. When the consumer comes in to buy the camera, the sales clerk says the store is out of the RCA and will have to order it, which will take two to three weeks. The consumer wanted it for Christmas, so the salesperson offers to sell a GE model, which the salesperson says has better features anyway. The catch is that the GE model costs substantially more. After the consumer has been baited to come in, the salesperson switches to pushing a similar but more profitable product.

Efforts to Solve the Information Problem

One way business solves information-related consumer problems is to educate employees. A business can make personnel aware of the types of information that buyers need and insist that employees convey this to the customer. Managers must also reward this behavior by attention and specific feedback daily and in performance appraisals.

Companies can also communicate with consumers. They can provide brochures and other written materials that spell out the terms and conditions of the transaction. They also can establish a customer complaint department. Retailers can designate one individual in the store to report all complaints directly to higher management.

When managers know what types of problems customers have, they can work to correct them. Willard Marriott, the founder of the giant hotel chain, was known for reading all customer complaints. As you can guess, he didn't get many to read because employees worked extra hard to see that he didn't receive any complaints from their hotel.

DeSoto, Inc., which manufactures paint for Sears, has applied the principle that good communication is part of satisfying consumers. DeSoto set up a toll-free information number for Sears paint customers. Consumers can call representatives such as the ones pictured here for information, including the best paint for a job and proper painting technique. DeSoto has found that when customers understand how to use the product, they are more likely to be happy with it.

Source: Courtesy of DeSoto, Inc.

Product Safety

For many products, safety is an important issue. Consumers are commonly injured using bicycles, sports-related equipment, and playground climbing apparatus (such as swings, slides, and seesaws). Other injuries involve mechanical equipment (household appliances, tools, and lawn and snow machinery) and products that fail to work as intended, including autos with defective brakes, electrical toys that shock the user, and plastic soft-drink containers with tops that can come loose under pressure and explode in a person's face.

In some cases, problems with product safety result from inadequate engineering or testing. For example, when some American cars first came out with front-wheel drive, a number of problems arose with parts such as the water pump, which would break, causing belts to come off and disable power steering and power brakes.

In other cases, problems stem from failure to anticipate the way the product will be used. For example, some people have been injured when using their household vacuum cleaner to pick up puddles of water. Others have been seriously hurt while using their lawn mower as a hedge trimmer.

Business has taken many steps to solve these problems. Here are some of the major actions:

Product recalls, which are common in the auto industry, designed to repair, replace, or simply check the assembly of various parts to ensure that there is no danger to the user

Warranties or guarantees that cover parts, and often labor, associated with making any necessary changes in the product to ensure its safety

Greater use of in-house checks of product quality and safety engineering to ensure that units are properly designed and built and errors corrected before shipment from the factory

Evaluation of feedback from users

Continued product testing in the research and development laboratory

These are only a few of the steps that business is taking in its effort to meet the challenge of product safety. Although much more needs to be done, most businesses now realize that, with today's safety regulations and litigation-prone customers, they must assume proper responsibility for product safety. Companies that do not are subject to costly lawsuits and the accompanying publicity, which is sure to damage their reputation and future sales. For these reasons, product safety will continue to be a challenge for business.

Checkpoint

1. What are the two major concerns of consumerism?
2. What are three ways that businesses can address these concerns?

Business Ethics

Recognizing and trying to solve the problems involving equality, the environment, and consumerism represent the major part of the social responsibility of business. At the core of social responsibility, though, are the ethics of business. **Business ethics** are standards that govern business behavior.

Business ethics
Standards that govern business behavior.

The honesty and integrity of American business are always under the watchful eye of the public and the media. In recent years, however, this scrutiny does not seem to have prevented what some consider a crisis in ethics. In fact, some critics have begun calling "business ethics" an oxymoron (an expression that combines contradictory words, such as jumbo shrimp). Although most business people are honest, law-abiding citizens, the head of a large accounting firm admits, "We have all been embarrassed by the events that make *The Wall Street Journal* read more like the *Police Gazette*."[12]

Examples of misconduct abound. Prominent businessmen such as Ivan Boesky (a leading Wall Street stock trader), Aldo Gucci (the head of the international fashion empire), and Paul Thayer (former chairman of LTV Corporation) have either served or are facing jail terms for their illegal business activities. Consider the following recent episodes, all hard to believe, but matters of public record.

> A widely admired investment banker making more than a million a year sneaks into Wall Street alleys to sell insider tips on certain companies and later collects a briefcase stuffed with $700,000.

> Officers in a Texas savings and loan association, all with six-figure salaries, loot their company to buy Rolls-Royces and trips to Paris.

> A defense contractor with $11 billion in annual sales bills the federal government $1,118.26 for the plastic cap on a stool leg.[13]

Obviously, these are the rare exceptions; the day-to-day ethical business dealings never make the news. Yet unethical practices do seem to be increasing. To prevent an antibusiness backlash, business people must take proactive steps to ensure ethical behavior.

Communicating Business Ethics

A recent poll of senior executives found that they believed that a code of ethics was the most effective way to encourage ethical business behavior.[14] Sometimes these codes are written down. For example, General Dynamics has a 20-page code of ethics. Figure 2.4 shows the mission

FIGURE 2.4

The Mission Statement of General Motors Corporation

GENERAL MOTORS MISSION

The fundamental purpose of General Motors is to provide products and services of such quality that our customers will receive superior value, our employes and business partners will share in our success, and our stockholders will receive a sustained, superior return on their investment.

GENERAL MOTORS GUIDING PRINCIPLES

- We will establish and maintain a Corporation-wide commitment to excellence in all elements of our product and business activities. This commitment will be central to all that we do.
- We will place top priority on understanding and meeting our customers' needs and expectations.
- General Motors is its people. We recognize that GM's success will depend on our involvement and individual commitment and performance. Each employe will have the opportunity, environment, and incentives to promote maximum participation in meeting our collective goals.
- We recognize that our dealers, suppliers, and all our employes are partners in our business and their success is vital to our own success.
- We recognize that a total dedication to quality leadership in our products, processes, and workplaces is of paramount importance to our success.
- We are committed to sustained growth which will enable us to play a leading role in the worldwide economy.
- We will continue to focus our efforts on transportation products and services, both personal and commercial, but will aggressively seek new opportunities to utilize our resources in business ventures that match our skills and capabilities.
- We will offer a full range of products in the North American market and participate with appropriate products in other markets on a worldwide basis.
- We will maintain strong manufacturing resources at the highest levels of technology and be cost competitive with each manufacturing unit.
- We will operate with clearly articulated centralized policies with decentralized operational responsibilities to keep decisions as close to the operations as possible.
- We will participate in all societies in which we do business as a responsible and ethical citizen, dedicated to continuing social and economic progress.

statement for General Motors Corporation, including a statement of ethics. Often, however, a code of ethics is communicated orally or even through the overall climate or cultural values of the organization. A stated expectation about ethical behavior often implies a broader standard. For example, when top management tells its salespeople, "We do not allow kickbacks," this statement probably covers more than just giving customers money under the table in return for placing orders. It probably also refers to giving customers anything that might be construed as a bribe or attempt at influence, no matter how small its value. The converse applies to employees who do business with outside vendors. In many companies, a purchasing manager who accepts an expensive gift from a supplier at Christmas is subject to reprimand and possible dismissal.

Creating a Climate for Ethical Behavior

How can business create a climate that promotes ethical behavior among its personnel? Communicating a code of ethics is a start but may be too little. Some companies, especially those that have had ethical problems, such as E. F. Hutton and General Dynamics, have turned to experts like the Washington-based Ethics Resource Center to help them put teeth into their codes.[15] For example, General Dynamics has a committee of board members to review the firm's ethics policies, a steering group to oversee policy execution, and a corporate ethics director. They also installed a hot line that allows employees to get instant advice on ethical issues involving their jobs.

One way of strengthening a code of ethics is to make it clear that the company will punish violators and reward ethical acts. A company that fires a manager for giving kickbacks will find that others who are guilty of this behavior will stop and those who are merely thinking about it will

Comerica Incorporated, a banking firm, creates a climate for ethical behavior by actively demonstrating its concern for the community. Here, a bank employee meets with members of a community development organization. Comerica Incorporated provides financial and volunteer support to several community organizations that are rehabilitating housing and commercial areas in their neighborhoods.

Source: Courtesy of Comerica Incorporated.

Whistle blowers
Employees who alert management or public bodies to illegal or unethical practices.

not proceed any further. Likewise, when employees receive attention or even an award for ethical behavior, the message quickly gets out that acting ethically is the way to get ahead.

A second way of encouraging ethical behavior is to reward those who see illegal or unethical practices and call them to the attention of the company or public bodies. These so-called **whistle blowers** can be particularly helpful in stopping the production or sale of defective products and in helping management maintain high standards of ethical behavior throughout the company.

Unfortunately, in some companies, whistle blowers find out that their actions lead to harassment and punishment from those who have been a party to the unethical practices. To prevent such retaliation, the law protects federal employees, and an increasing number of states and cities are also passing laws that prevent private employers from threatening, firing, or discriminating against an employee who reports suspected violations of the law to a public body.

Checkpoint

1. What are two ways that a business can promote ethical behavior among its personnel?
2. What are whistle blowers, and how can they play a role in promoting business ethics?

Closing Comments

This chapter provides the social foundation for the study of modern business. For many outsiders, this is their only view of business. As many of today's headlines attest, the view is not always flattering. Many of today's problems surrounding equality, the environment, consumerism, and business ethics rightfully make news.

But, as this chapter points out, business is responding and making progress. Sometimes these efforts are on business's own initiative, and sometimes they are a response to laws and public pressure. In most cases, being socially responsible makes good business sense. For example, by banning smoking in the workplace, the company can benefit from reduced health costs and even maintenance expenses (burned rugs or painting). Businesses can also avoid costly problems such as the $5 million payment recently made by the Tennessee Valley Authority to settle a sex discrimination suit. An increasing number of business people realize that being socially responsible and ethical pays off. A recent survey of corporate executives found that two-thirds of those questioned believe that it improves their company's competitive position.[16] In any case, the way business responds to the remaining social challenges will determine how business is conducted and may even affect the very survival of business in its present form.

Learning Objectives Revisited

1. **Define the overall nature of social responsibility.**
   Social responsibility is the obligation that business has to the society

in which it operates. These responsibilities include equal opportunity in employment, environmental protection, consumerism, and business ethics.

2. **Describe the social issue of equality in employment.**

   Minorities and women still lag behind white men in terms of employment and earnings. Unemployment is much greater among minorities than whites, and salaries are lower. Women are still paid less and are underrepresented in management ranks but are making some progress. Business's efforts to resolve these problems include affirmative-action programs, training and promotion, the use of mentors, and assisting small-business ventures.

3. **Identify the social issue of environmental protection.**

   In particular, the areas of energy conservation and pollution control are most critical. Business is taking many steps to conserve energy, including developing long- and short-range plans and replacing old equipment with more up-to-date, energy-efficient machinery. In controlling air pollution, business is using special devices on its machinery and equipment and is designing and building products that create less air pollution. Many companies are limiting or banning smoking in the workplace. In controlling water pollution, business is treating waste materials before disposing of them and recycling treated water for reuse in production.

4. **Explain the social issue of consumerism.**

   Consumerism is a movement designed to provide buyers the information and bargaining power vital to obtaining high-quality, safe products and services. In meeting this responsibility, business is providing more information to consumers about the terms of sale and the specifics of the product and building safer products.

5. **Discuss the nature of business ethics.**

   Business ethics are standards that govern business behavior. Some of the ways companies can create a climate for ethical behavior include punishing violators, rewarding those who exemplify ethical behavior, and rewarding those who point out problem areas (whistle blowers).

Key Terms Reviewed

Review each of the following terms. For any that you do not know or are unsure of, look up the definitions and see how they were used in the chapter.

paternalistic approach	consumerism
Equal Employment Opportunity Commission (EEOC)	class-action suit
	boycott
affirmative-action programs	bait and switch
mentor	business ethics
ecology	whistle blowers
pollution	

Review Questions

1. During the nineteenth century, how did business owners and managers view their responsibility to society? Compare this to the dominant view today.

2. What are some arguments against the notion that businesses have a social responsibility? Are these valid arguments? Why or why not?

3. How does the Civil Rights Act of 1964 protect employees against discrimination? What federal laws protect employees from discrimination based on age and handicapped status?

4. Consider the following hypothetical ad, placed in the Help Wanted section of the local newspaper.

> SALESMAN: Looking for a smart, young (age 21–30) man who is eager to get ahead in the financial world. Must have own car. Call 555–5555 and be prepared to send in resume and photo.

What federal laws might the advertiser be violating? Explain.

5. How can the company that placed the ad in Question 4 live up to its social responsibility to ensure equal employment opportunity?

6. How do business efforts at energy conservation benefit society?

7. Is it fair to require everyone to pay to clean up the environment? Why not have businesses pay directly for their share of pollution, so that the biggest polluters pay the most? Explain your answer.

8. What steps have businesses taken to alleviate the safety problems connected with their products?

9. "I'm not worried about ethics," says the owner of a hardware store. "I let the preachers worry about that. I'm a business manager, and my interest is in profits. Being ethical would just cut into my profits." Respond to this statement. Do you agree with the store owner's views? Why or why not?

10. When defense contractors pad their bills to increase their earnings, who benefits? Who loses? What can these companies do to promote ethical behavior among their employees?

Applied Exercises

1. Go to the library and get several recent issues of *Business Week*. Go through each copy and note examples of social actions taken by business firms (or failure to take such actions). Then categorize each story in terms of one of the main categories in this chapter: equality in employment, environmental protection, consumerism, and ethics.

2. At the library, gather information on American businesses in South Africa. Update "Social Responsibility Close-Up: Leaving South Africa," (page 37) by noting some recent developments.

3. Choose a consumer product and explain three ways in which the product could be made safer. Write your answers in the form of a letter. Get the address of the company that makes the products and send your letter to it.

Your Business IQ: Answers

1. False. Businesses *should* exercise social responsibility, but this does not necessarily cut into profits, especially over the long run. For example, fair employment practices enable companies to draw on a wider pool of talent, and satisfying consumer concerns about safety and information can build a base of loyal customers. Furthermore, behaving responsibly can forestall strict government-imposed requirements that may be more costly than responsible behavior initiated by the company.

2. False. Although there has been some improvement, the number of women in professional and managerial positions still falls far short of the number of men. Also, women are underrepresented in management as a percentage of the total number of women in the work force.

3. True. About 50 percent comes from motor vehicles, 22 percent from fuel burned at stationary sources, 15 percent from industrial processes, and the remainder from a variety of sources.

4. True. From customer complaints, business people can learn how to improve products and services and make them safer. They can also find out what kinds of information customers need. For example, a complaint might reveal that a customer is trying to put a product to an unintended, perhaps even dangerous, use.

5. False. Federal law protects federal employees who report misdeeds. A growing number of states and cities have also passed laws that protect whistle blowers. Companies that want to promote ethical behavior will protect and even reward employees who point out illegal or unethical practices.

A Gasoline Leak at the Local Service Station

Times are tough for independent gas stations, like the combination bait-and-tackle shop and service station owned by Harry Hazewinkle located on Highway 151 in Marion, Iowa. These small businesses have been losing customers to convenience stores and gas stations owned by oil companies. Now they are struggling to comply with federal regulations designed to prevent contamination of underground water.

Gasoline leaks from storage tanks have contaminated drinking water—the beginning of what could become a serious public health problem. The Environmental Protection Agency (EPA) has responded by requiring that gas station owners monitor leaks and replace most tanks within ten years. Owners also have to buy insurance policies to cover the cost of cleanup. While this program is expensive, the costs of simply cleaning up leaks as they occur would be even greater. Florida alone already has reported more than 1,000 leaks, each of which will cost $100,000 to $200,000 to clean up.

To Harry Hazewinkle, the EPA program sounds like a good idea, but a potentially impossible one for him to implement. For most of the 27 years Hazewinkle has been in business, he has stored gasoline in two underground steel tanks. He doesn't know whether the tanks are leaking, but he is planning to drill test wells to find out. If gas is seeping into the nearby drinking water, he may have to spend as much as $60,000 to replace his tanks, and he fears that expense could put him out of business.

The insurance requirement could be even a bigger burden. Stations owned by major oil companies can benefit from the parent companies' insurance policies, but Hazewinkle, like other small independent station owners, will have to scramble to find coverage.

Case Questions

1. As the owner of a combination bait-and-tackle shop and service station, what social responsibilities does Harry Hazewinkle have?
2. Who will benefit from the EPA regulations described in the case? Who will lose?
3. Based on the information given in the case and what you have read about the social responsibility of business, do you think the EPA regulations are justified? Why or why not?
4. What steps can Hazewinkle take to fulfill his social responsibilities and also stay in business?

You Be the Adviser: Charlie's Dilemma

For a long time, Charlie Wadkins had wanted to own his own company. Six months ago, the opportunity presented itself. A local manufacturer and golfing buddy of Charlie's told him that he wanted to sell his firm and retire. The terms of sale were attractive, and after having an accountant and lawyer go over the books to verify that everything was in proper order, Charlie closed the deal.

What the financial accounts did not show Charlie is that his golfing friend has two problems in the social arena that are threatening to become major lawsuits. One is a complaint filed by three women who applied for jobs at the firm. They were turned down, and in their complaint to the Equal Employment Opportunity Commission, they have noted that of the 492 people working in the company, only 6 are women. "Quite obviously," reads the complaint, "this firm does not hire women." The personnel department, which provided the court with preliminary employment data, reported that over the past five years, 109 women have applied for work at the firm and 10 of them have been hired. During this same period, 604 men applied and 573 of them were hired. The personnel department's data also show that no woman is in a management position, and, on average, each woman earns about two-thirds of the salary of male workers doing the same job.

The other problem is a formal charge by the union that the company has not done enough to reduce smoke in the plant. According to the union, "in the machine area the environment is dangerous to the health and well-being of the workers, and if nothing is done by the 15th of next month, we intend to file a formal complaint with the Environmental Protection Agency." If Charlie is to resolve this particular problem, he has less than ten days to take the necessary action.

Charlie is determined to resolve both issues. He also wants to examine the company's overall response to its social obligations over the past couple of years. He intends to conduct this evaluation when he is finished with these two pressing issues.

Your Advice

1. Based on the personnel department's data, do the women seem to have a legitimate case? What would you recommend that Charlie do about the situation? Offer some useful recommendations.
2. What should Charlie do about air pollution?
3. How should Charlie go about making an overall evaluation of the firm's social responsiveness over the past five years? Be specific in your recommendations.

Career Opportunities

There are many careers in business that offer challenge, good financial rewards, and interesting work. The "best" careers, however, will depend on a number of factors, and what was an excellent career path five years ago may be a poor one today. During the period 1987–1992, there appear to be five major changes—we will call these "megachanges" for short—that should lead to outstanding career opportunities.

One of these megachanges is government deregulation. Now that the government is moving to the sidelines, the operating ground rules in previously heavily regulated industries are beginning to change and new opportunities are starting to emerge. This is particularly true in the financial and telecommunications industries. Bankers and stockbrokers are now fighting for the same investor markets; and small telecommunications firms are beginning to challenge giants such as AT&T. Some of the careers that are going to be "hot" over the next five years appear to be the following: (1) telecommunication managers, who will help their companies make sense out of the wide array of new high-tech communication equipment coming on the market and ensure that the firm knows what it is buying; (2) bank marketing executives, who will create new products and financial services and formulate strategies that bring them to fruition; and (3) mortgage brokers, who will help home buyers find a bank that will quickly accept and process their home loan.

A second megachange is the movement toward hiring outside consultants in place of full-time staff. Individuals who can help firms get the assistance they need will do quite well. Some of the careers in this area that should blossom in the near future include: (1) employee-leasing executives, who act like personnel managers and provide firms with employees, while assuming all overhead expenses associated with staffing, including severance pay, unemployment benefits, and, to a large degree, health insurance; (2) immigration-law specialists, who help firms deal with the government regulations that are resulting from recent changes in the Immigration Reform and Control Act of 1986; and (3) meeting planners, who help companies take care of out-of-the-office meetings including handling the agendas, transportation, and accommodations.

A third megachange is the increased importance of professional problem solvers who work behind the scenes to help the organization operate more efficiently. These individuals help streamline operations and save money. Examples include: (1) robotics engineers, who design robots for a variety of tasks including manufacturing, quality control, and customer service; (2) logistics managers, who help ensure rapid delivery of inventory and finished products; and (3) security specialists, who help organizations fight employee theft, computer crime, drug use, and organized crime.

A fourth megachange is that of becoming more competitive by developing innovative, customer-appealing strategies. Some of the careers that are emerging as a result of this change include: (1) corporate identity consultants, who help businesses effectively portray themselves to customers and employees; (2) special-events marketers, who help companies become associated with sporting events and, in the process, win customers; and (3) executive recruiters, who help companies recruit the exceptional talent that will give the firm a competitive edge.

A fifth megachange is the emergence of individuals who are helping companies build the bridge to modern technology. These individuals assist the personnel in understanding how new technologies such as computers and office equipment work and how this technology can be used to increase productivity. Some of the specific careers that will be emerging thanks to this megachange include: (1) information center managers, who know how to use computers, evaluate software, and make minor repairs of the equipment; (2) corporate trainers, who can keep the personnel on the cutting edge of technology and management knowledge; and (3) video specialists, who are able to produce in-house videos for use in training, development, and general dissemination of corporate policies.

These trends indicate the types of factors that will influence career opportunities. In each case we have given some examples of the types of careers that will emerge due to the megachange. Others, directly related to functional areas, will be presented at the end of each part of the book. For the moment, keep in mind that business offers many challenging careers, but as the economy continues to grow and change, so will the opportunities available in specific career paths.

PART II

THE SPIRIT AND STRUCTURE OF AMERICAN BUSINESS

America is almost equated with free enterprise. Most Americans acknowledge and are even proud of their association with free enterprise. They value their economic system because it gives them a good life. Most Americans also believe that if they work hard, they can achieve economic well-being. Such thinking has resulted in a widespread entrepreneurial spirit. In large numbers, Americans today want to start their own businesses, become managers, or become intrapreneurs. This spirit underlies what Part II is all about: entrepreneurs and intrapreneurs, small businesses, and how businesses are owned.

Chapter 3 describes entrepreneurs, the creators and/or organizers of a venture, and intrapreneurs, the employees who create and control new, usually risky projects within an existing business. The chapter also discusses an important characteristic of these people: creativity. To show how businesses make the most of creativity, the chapter provides some specific approaches to developing intrapreneurial success. The chapter closes with a look at the current entrepreneurial wave, as evidenced by the trend toward taking public firms private.

Chapter 4 addresses small businesses, the backbone of the American economy. The chapter describes the many challenges that face small-business owners and managers and the skills needed to manage a small business. The chapter also outlines the role of the Small Business Administration in promoting and assisting small enterprises. The last part of the chapter examines franchising, one of the most popular avenues for entering business today.

Chapter 5 examines the various forms of business ownership. The most common is the sole proprietorship. The other forms are the partnership and the corporation. The chapter describes the advantages and disadvantages of owning each of the three types of business. The last part of the chapter examines some interesting corporate trends, including acquisitions, mergers, and divestitures.

When you have finished studying Part II, you should understand the spirit of entrepreneurship and intrapreneurship that has stimulated American businesses to be established and prosper. You should also know the role of small business in the economy and how a franchise works. Finally, you should be able to compare the advantages and disadvantages of the three major forms of business ownership.

Source: Courtesy of RE/MAX International, Inc.

Entrepreneurship and Intrapreneurship

LEARNING OBJECTIVES

- Explain the roles of entrepreneurs and intrapreneurs.
- Examine the creative process.
- Present some creative techniques.
- Relate the work ethic to entrepreneurship.

- Identify some innovative techniques and approaches of successful intrapreneurs.
- Describe some recent entrepreneurial trends represented by business ownership.

Your Business IQ

How much do you already know about entrepreneurship and intrapreneurship? Test your business IQ by labeling each statement *true* or *false*. Answers and explanations are at the end of the chapter.

1. Most new goods and services are not really new; they are more often modifications of current offerings.
2. Creative thinking is an individual process; it does not work in groups.
3. Most of today's rapidly expanding firms were founded by entrepreneurs who had little, if any, previous business experience.
4. The work ethic in America today is almost dead.
5. Successful management is equated with exercising as little control over employees' work as possible.

Mo Siegel, founder of Celestial Seasonings, Inc. The maker of herbal teas prospered, and when the company was 14 years old, Siegel sold it to Kraft.

Looking Back and Ahead

Entrepreneurs put all kinds of experience to work in the businesses they form. For example, Orville Redenbacher, of popcorn fame, has many years of agricultural experience. He earned a bachelor's degree in agriculture from Purdue University, and gained experience the hard way by supporting himself with jobs such as delousing chickens and scrubbing hoghouses. During the 1930s he developed corn hybrids, and during the 1940s he managed a farm that raised various types of popcorn seed. A decade later, Redenbacher started his own seed plant, and in the 1960s he developed Gourmet Popping Corn. Today, thanks to an appealing product and Redenbacher's hard work, practical experience, and creative selling, his Gourmet Popping Corn is a big seller nationwide and he is a well-known entrepreneur.[1]

The "spirit" of American business is entrepreneurship and the more recently recognized intrapreneurship. Entrepreneurship has been part of the business scene since commercial ventures predating the Industrial Revolution, but it is only now getting its just recognition. As pointed out in Chapter 1, *intrapreneur* is a new term coined by author Gifford Pinchot[2] to recognize existing employees, not necessarily the business's creators, who are the "maintainers," the "expanders," and the "changers." As one recent publication devoted to intrapreneurship put it:

> The intrapreneur is an employee with an idea and an itch to try it out . . . a self-selected doer with a vision. . . . He [or she] is a thinker . . . a networker . . . a facilitator . . . a craftsman, and an unbridled believer in the power of a few inspired people to "imagineer" their company into new areas of growth and profit.[3]

Intrapreneurs work in the boardrooms and the workshops of companies across America.

In discussing entre- and intrapreneurship, this chapter builds on the overall foundation laid in Part I, the introduction to modern business. The chapter starts by defining the nature of entre- and intrapreneurship. Next, it examines the creative process, so vital to entre/intrapreneurship, and presents some creative techniques. The next section analyzes the other important dimensions of entre/intrapreneurship: hard work and innovative approaches to doing business. Finally, the last section examines entrepreneurial trends in business ownership.

The Nature of Entre- and Intrapreneurship

Chapter 1 defined entrepreneurship as the process of organizing, operating, and assuming the risks associated with a business venture. The risk-taking part has recently been termed *entrepreneurial terror*. In other words, it takes courage to be an entrepreneur. One Florida-based entrepreneur believes that "the ability to handle terror, to live with it, is the single most important—and, yes, necessary—ingredient of entrepreneurial success."[4]

From the French word *entreprendre*, to undertake, an entrepreneur is the creator and/or organizer of a venture. Chapter 1 also pointed out that some business people play an entrepreneurial role in existing businesses. These intrapreneurs may differ from the traditional entrepreneur. The intrapreneur is not just an originator and creator, but also a maintainer and changer. Following the definition in Chapter 1, the **intrapreneur** is a manager or staff expert who creates and controls new, usually risky projects within an existing business.

Successful enterprises require both entrepreneurs and intrapreneurs. An entrepreneurial type, such as one of Apple's founders, Steven Jobs, starts the enterprise and comes up with original ideas, products, and services, as well as creative or unique ways of doing things. Intrapreneurial types then keep the enterprise growing and make it more profitable. For example, Alfred P. Sloan did not found General Motors, but through innovative organization design and reward policies, he was able to shape the giant automaker into a growing and prosperous concern.

Some start off as entrepreneurs, by founding a company, and then use intrapreneurship to develop it. Jobs was not able to make this transition from creative founder to developer at Apple Computer. However, some are able to do it. For example, in rural Italy, Sergio Rossi recently took the risk of starting his own leather goods operation. He could not afford a big factory, so he uses his home. In the garage, three high-paid workers use ultramodern machines to produce 100 top-quality leather bags daily, many of which are exported to New York for sale in Alexander's department stores.[5] Starting the operation was entrepreneurial, but using his home, paying his workers high wages, using technologically advanced equipment, and selling his product in foreign markets was intrapreneurial.

Intrapreneur Manager or staff expert who creates and controls new, usually risky projects within an existing business.

Who Are the Intrapreneurs?

The people who maintain and change organizations for profit and growth are the largely unknown intrapreneurs. Examples of intrapreneurs include those responsible for innovations such as the Pontiac Fiero sports car and Texas Instruments' Speak & Spell. Other less known but equally important intrapreneurs do not necessarily develop new products. They develop new approaches to human resource management, such as in Publix, a Florida-based retailer, where someone was responsible for across-the-board employee ownership long before it was popular. They also develop new perspectives and new ways of doing business, such as at Sunset Scavengers, a San Francisco–based garbage company where the boss, Len Stephanelli, says he "loves garbage," requires that employees own their trucks, and stresses customer service.[6]

Where Do Entre- and Intrapreneurs Come From?

In recent years, many employees have been realizing that the experience they are gaining in everyday operations can help them become entrepreneurial and intrapreneurial. For example, one research effort found that three-quarters of the 161 rapidly expanding firms studied had been started by people who had previously worked for big industrial companies.[7] From their former large employers, these entrepreneurs learned how to organize operations, order inventory, sell products, and finance and manage the business. This experience proved to be invaluable in their entrepreneurial activities.

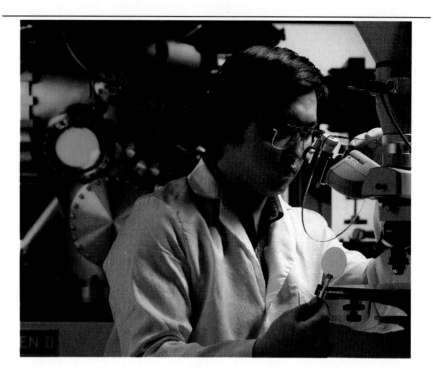

Yi-Ching Pao is an intrapreneur at Varian Associates,
Inc., an international electronics company. Pao developed
innovative procedures for
making microwave devices.
The new procedures allow the
company to increase production dramatically.

Source: Courtesy of Varian Associates, Inc.

The same is true of intrapreneurs. People with valuable job experience in an organizational and supervisory climate that is open to change
and innovation can make valuable, creative changes in existing processes,
products, or services. Their intrapreneurial activities can help their present company grow and profit.

Many entrepreneurs and intrapreneurs also come from the ranks of
minorities. In the past, minority entrepreneurs largely were concentrated in mom-and-pop businesses such as groceries, barber shops, and
cleaners. Today, there is evidence that they are increasingly moving into
fields such as electronics, health care, advertising, real estate development, insurance, and computer software. For example, the percentage
of Hispanic-owned U.S. computer-related businesses more than doubled
in the 1980s.[8] Today's minority entrepreneurs are better educated than
their predecessors, and many are gaining valuable experience in large
companies before starting their own.

Checkpoint

1. What are entrepreneurs and intrapreneurs?
2. What kind of background do these people have?

Creativity for Entre- and Intrapreneurship

Perhaps the dominant characteristic of entrepreneurs and intrapreneurs
is creativity. Creativity refers to inventiveness and originality, as the following creative enterprises show.[9]

Ho, Ho, Ho. Thoughtware, Inc., of Coconut Grove, Florida, offers Christmas cheer through the personal computer. Its $9.95 floppy disk, available at many retail outlets, plays a Christmas carol and prints out a Christmas card. The card can be specially designed for business customers or personal friends, and the diskettes are playable on Apple, Commodore, and IBM personal computers.

It's for the Dogs. The Doggery Animal Center in Los Angeles has taken the fitness craze to heart. It offers dogs a lap pool, sauna, and jogging track, as well as grooming. The therapeutic regimen is particularly useful for injured, arthritic, or postoperative dogs.

One-Stop Shopping. The Executive Express Service of Middletown, Connecticut, a women's department store, offers customers a $50 consultation with its fashion consultant. The consultant evaluates the client's size, hair, coloring, and life-style and keeps a record of her size and colors. The store then encourages the client to do all of her shopping there, since it knows the best clothes for her to wear.

Dishwater Power. Hart Industries of Laguna Hills, California, offers a $350 machine that cleans dishes with a multidirectional spray that is less forceful than that of the typical dishwasher. All the user needs is a teaspoonful of liquid detergent, a water faucet, the company's Ecotech dishwasher, and three minutes of time. This machine is very economical.

Uncanny Veggies. The DNA Plant Technology Corporation is breeding a race of super vegetables that have enhanced taste, appearance, and freshness. Using a variety of tissue-culturing methods, the firm is able to regenerate plants and to elicit their most desirable traits. The company is now working on a number of different products, including a meatier tomato.

Unfortunately, such creative, innovative products are not common in American firms. Almost two-thirds of recently surveyed executives said they felt constrained from developing such products for fear of liability suits and because of their companies' focus on short-term results.[10] Obviously, these types of barriers must be eliminated in order for entrepreneurs and intrapreneurs to use their creative talents.

Types of Creativity

Two types of creativity apply especially to entrepreneurs and intrapreneurs: new-new and new-old. "New-new" creativity applies to inventing goods and services that have never been offered before. One example of this is the Polaroid camera, which revolutionized the industry by helping create a market for instant pictures. This camera did not merely improve upon an existing model, it was an original idea.

"New-old" creativity refers to goods and services that are modifications of past offerings. For example, before McDonald's, there were other fast-food chains such as White Castle and Horn and Hardart. However, under the direction of entrepreneur Ray Kroc, McDonald's revolutionized the fast-food business by offering fast, high-quality, inexpensive food at easy-to-reach locations all across the country. Another example is Holiday Inns. When entrepreneur Kemmons Wilson built the first Holiday Inn in Memphis in 1952, motels already existed in America. However, Wilson offered additional services such as free cribs for babies, free

TVs in every room, telephones in every room, a swimming pool in every motel, and no charge for children who shared a room with their parents. Holiday Inns soon became the largest motel chain in America. A more recent example is the work in the computer field of William Gates, which is described in "Entrepreneurs Close-Up." Even whole companies develop a climate for "new-old" creativity. For example, companies such as Citicorp, Gannett, and 3M have been rated to have the best reputation for creativity and innovation, and Amax, Bethlehem Steel, and Bank of America the worst.[11]

ENTREPRENEURS   CLOSE-UP

William H. Gates III

Through a combination of luck and negotiating skill, William H. Gates III has been able to create a near-monopoly position for operating systems, the instructions that tell personal computers what to do. His business, Washington state–based Microsoft Corporation, sells software (computer programs) designed to set standards for the personal computer industry.

Gates was lucky at the beginning. In 1980, IBM asked Microsoft to develop the operating system for its new personal computer. Gates doubted that his company could handle such a big job and turned IBM down. By the time a competitor had also turned down the assignment, Gates had located a programmer who had already developed a rough program. Gates bought the rights to it, refined it, and sold it. It became MS-DOS, the operating system of IBM's standard-setting personal computer. Today, Microsoft is developing the operating system for IBM's latest generation of personal computers as well.

Microsoft also provides the software for IBM's biggest competition in the personal computer business, Apple Computer Inc. Microsoft licenses to Apple the language that runs on the popular Apple II. When Apple decided to bring out a language called Mac-Basic for its Macintosh, Gates threatened to cut off Apple's license for the Apple II software if it didn't sign over the rights to Mac-Basic. Apple's president saw no alternative and gave in, losing the program plus several key engineers who resigned in disgust.

Today Microsoft provides most of the computer languages that professional programmers use on IBM and Apple computers. Since most other personal computers are compatible with IBM, this covers essentially the whole market. In addition, the company has products or partnerships to make products that set the standards for devices that plug into personal computers or enable communication among them. The more links with computer makers that Gates creates, the harder it is for the companies to break away. Says one industry expert, "There's no way IBM can get off Microsoft's bus now, because Microsoft has gotten too deep into IBM's own strategy."

The Wall Street Journal has called Gates "the industry's most influential individual." Nevertheless, some observers question whether his company can maintain its near-monopoly position much longer. The company may not be able to continue growing fast enough to keep up with the many projects it is taking on.

More business successes result from new-old creativity, which is more closely associated with intrapreneurs, than from new-new creativity, which is more closely associated with entrepreneurs. For example, the original ideas for a microwave oven lay around Raytheon, a U.S. defense equipment company, for more than 20 years before Japanese competitors developed the idea and obtained the largest share of the market.[12]

Researchers and practitioners generally agree that entre- and intrapreneurs do not necessarily learn how to be creative; it is more like a talent. However, understanding the creative process and learning some creative techniques can help develop entre- and intrapreneurship.

The Creative Process

The **creative process** is a way of generating unique or novel ideas, many of which can be used in a business. As illustrated in Figure 3.1, this process has four steps: preparation, incubation, illumination, and verification. A closer look at each step shows what is involved in generating a creative idea to start a new business or to make an existing one grow and become more profitable.

Creative process Generating new or unique ideas, involving four steps: preparation, incubation, illumination, and verfication.

Preparation The first stage of the creative process is **preparation.** This step involves gathering information on the problem or issue under analysis. For example, consider Ray Kroc, the McDonald's entrepreneur who many years ago made a deal with the person who invented a machine to make thick frozen milkshakes (the kind sold at McDonald's). Originally, when employees put this frozen milkshake into a regular blender, it burned out the machine. The blender was not built to mix a thick, frozen drink; it was designed to mix regular malts and other light drinks. When Kroc, then a salesperson for a paper cup company, saw the new machine, which could mix six milkshakes at a time, he began to think about how restaurants and other food establishments could use the machine.

Preparation Stage of the creative process that involves gathering information on the problem or issue under analysis.

Incubation The second stage, **incubation,** involves sitting back and letting the subconscious mind work on the problem. Often the brain rearranges information in a logical, straightforward way that makes the solution easier to understand.

Incubation Stage of the creative process that involves sitting back and letting the subconscious mind work on the problem.

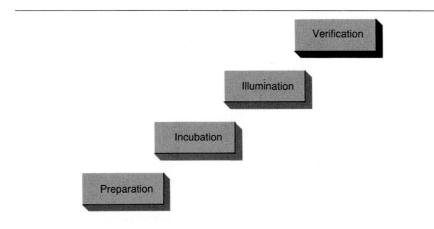

FIGURE 3.1

The Four Steps of the Creative Process

The more information collected in the preparation stage, the more likely the incubation period will provide an answer or a general direction to take in resolving the matter. If no ideas surface after a period of time (the length depending on the problem), the creative process returns to the preparation stage. In the case of Ray Kroc's frozen-milkshake problem, he allowed time to mull over the problem and think about solutions. His experience in calling on retail food establishments helped him decide who would be the best targets for this machine.

Illumination   Stage of the creative process during which the answer to the problem or issue becomes apparent.

Illumination   In the third step of the creative process, **illumination,** the answer to the problem or issue becomes apparent. In the case of the milkshake, Kroc realized that frozen milkshakes were going to become a major food offering in fast-food units. So he made a deal with the inventor to let him sell these multimixers nationwide.

Verification   Stage of the creative process that involves testing the solution and, if necessary, modifying it.

Verification   The final step, **verification,** involves testing the solution and, if necessary, modifying it. As Kroc traveled his route selling paper cups to retail food establishments, he would bring one of the multimixers with him. He would demonstrate how the machine worked and then take the order. Today, fast-food franchises use this type of machine to mix their "frosties" and thick milkshakes. Kroc's entrepreneurial creativity led to the development of a new technique and resulting product, helping spur the growth of fast-food franchises in America.

Notice that the example used the term *entrepreneur* instead of *intrapreneur*. Ray Kroc is usually considered to be an entrepreneur because he popularized the fast-food industry with McDonald's. This came about because the McDonald brothers placed a large order for multimixers. Kroc was pleasantly surprised and decided to look in on their operation and see how it worked. When he did, Kroc became convinced that the McDonald's approach to fast food was brilliant. He talked them into letting him franchise the operation nationally — and the rest is history.

Dave Packard *(left)* and Bill Hewlett at work on their first product—an audio oscillator, a device that Walt Disney Studios used in developing the soundtrack for *Fantasia*. The two men founded Hewlett-Packard in 1939 in a garage behind the Packards' home in Palo Alto, California. Today, Hewlett-Packard is one of the 100 largest industrial corporations in America, and creative ideas continue to be an important source of its growth.

Source: Courtesy of Hewlett-Packard Company.

Individual Techniques for Creativity

One useful approach to developing creative thinking is to use mental exercises that force the individual to look at problems differently. The following guidelines can be used for thinking more creatively:

Look at the space around the problem rather than just the problem. For example, if an employee is showing up late for work and not producing up to expectations, look at the environment in which the person works. Is this person's desk tucked away in the corner? Does the individual have trouble breaking into the office's social circle? Is the person being assigned boring work? Rather than assuming that the employee is at fault, look for conditions in the environment that may be adding to the problem and work to change these.

Visualize the opposite of the situation. Instead of focusing on the fact that absenteeism is at an all-time high, assume that it is nonexistent. Write down why there is no absenteeism. What is causing people to come to work every day? Now ask yourself how it is possible to change current conditions so that they look like those that exist in a situation without absenteeism. Start working in that direction.

Reverse the physical characteristics of every object in the problem. For example, suppose a warehouse is filled with material, and there is no way of squeezing any more units onto the floor. How can more units be stored? One way is by making the units smaller or retractable. Another is by using the space between the units and the ceiling above. Can shelves or racks be installed to hold more goods? Can some units be suspended from the ceiling? Is it possible to convert the roof to a storage area by installing inexpensive plastic bins?[13]

These exercises are not difficult, but they do require practice and a desire to break out of some old ways of thinking and to look at problems in new and different ways. Many intrapreneurs are doing just this as they develop new goods, services, and procedures that the business they own or work for will use to gain a competitive edge. For examples, see "Technology Close-Up: New Ideas That Work."

TECHNOLOGY CLOSE-UP

New Ideas That Work

Creativity and ingenuity can be extremely useful in developing new goods and services. Entrepreneurs and intrapreneurs thrive on new, creative ideas and must have them to start new businesses or expand existing ones. Creative, innovative products and services are what separate successful entrepreneurs and intrapreneurs from their more mundane counterparts.

For example, until recently, gamblers in Las Vegas used to feed coins into slot machines one at a time. Now casinos offer machines that take debit cards. The gambler buys a card with a dollar amount magnetically encoded on its plastic strip. When the person bets, the machine deducts the amount from the total on the strip. When the gambler wins, the coins drop out of the machine as they always do. These new plastic cards make slots more profitable, because on small bets, the profit (5.5 percent) is often eaten up by the cost of labor for providing change to the customers, collecting the money from the machine, and so on. Also, since the card makes gambling easier, management finds that people stay at the machines longer.

Another idea applies to automobile tires. The biggest problem many people have with their tires is that they fail to maintain proper pressure and end up getting flats. Michelin has developed a system that keeps tabs on the pressure and temperature of tires, including the spare. Miniature radio transmitter-receivers on the wheel mounts monitor tiny sensors inside each tire and relay the data to a read-out on the dashboard. Because 90 percent of all tires are improperly inflated, this new approach is likely to earn the firm large profits and save customers headaches.

A prevalent oral hygiene problem for adults is plaque buildup, which can cause gum disease and often results in tooth loss. Oral Research Laboratories of New York has formulated a product called Plax. It is a mouthwash designed to loosen and detach plaque before brushing. The firm hopes that by selling Plax for $2.79 to $3.59 per 16-ounce bottle, it will cash in on a lucrative market.

Group Techniques for Creativity

At the opposite extreme of highly individualized creative techniques for creativity are group techniques for creativity. The intrapreneur brings together those who are actively involved in the operations to offer new ideas or solutions. Companies that have lost out to Japanese companies in recent years are trying such group approaches to regain ground. For example, Eastman Kodak set up what they call small entrepreneurial business units. They also use informal group techniques, such as the monthly pizza lunches held by the bio-products division, where employees are encouraged to come up with new ideas in a relaxed atmosphere.[14] Besides such company-specific approaches, there are a number of formal group techniques available,[15] but the most popular is brainstorming.

Brainstorming A creative technique for groups in which participants generate as many ideas as possible for solving a problem without considering at first the merits of each idea.

The Brainstorming Technique Brainstorming is a creative technique for groups in which the leader presents the problem and encourages participants to generate as many ideas as possible for solving it (see Figure 3.2). Brainstorming has four important rules:

1. Anyone can put forth any idea that seems useful to the problem under discussion.
2. Everyone is encouraged to come up with as many ideas as possible.
3. Participants may improve on someone else's idea or combine it with another idea.
4. Criticism and evaluation of ideas are forbidden.

FIGURE 3.2

The Brainstorming Process

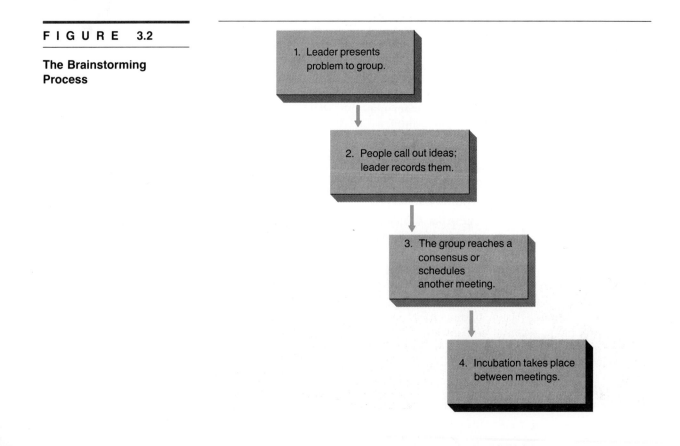

1. Leader presents problem to group.
2. People call out ideas; leader records them.
3. The group reaches a consensus or schedules another meeting.
4. Incubation takes place between meetings.

Brainstorming sessions generally follow a set procedure. The leader, who may be an intrapreneur, begins by presenting the problem to the group. If the participants need some specific technical or descriptive information, they receive it at this time. For example, if the problem involves a small product, such as a hand-held calculator, samples would be available for everyone. Then the brainstorming begins. As people call out their ideas, the leader records them. By the end of the session, which usually lasts about an hour on most small-business problems, the group reaches a consensus about how to handle the problem, or another meeting is scheduled to continue the process.

If the latter happens, the information generated at the first meeting serves as the preparation step in the creative process. During the period between meetings, incubation takes place. By the next meeting, or perhaps during it, illumination may occur. Then the final recommendations can be modified and tested in the verification stage.

How to Make Brainstorming Effective A number of guidelines help make the brainstorming process most effective. One is to choose the participants carefully. For example, if the problem involves advertising, the group should include people with experience in this area. If the problem is more broadly based, such as how to generate additional sales for a product, people from sales, advertising, production, design, and consumer research would all be useful participants in the group.

Another important guideline is to get a balance of personalities: some vocal and uninhibited, others quiet and insightful. Otherwise, there is too much talking or too little, and the final outcome suffers. In a balanced group, the leader must make sure that the quiet participants get a chance to talk.

Still another guideline is to keep the size of the group manageable. Six to nine is a good number of participants. Using a smaller group may limit the number of ideas, and a larger group is hard to control and may not have a friendly, intimate atmosphere.

Brainstorming is a useful technique for viewing a problem from many angles. The initial result is often pages of ideas.

Finally, it is important to appoint as the group recorder someone who takes fast, complete notes. This ensures that no ideas are left out. Sometimes it pays to also use a tape recorder to make a backup of everything that takes place.

Checkpoint

1. What are the steps in the creative process?
2. How can intrapreneurs use brainstorming to generate creative ideas?

Hard Work as a Dimension of Entre- and Intrapreneurship

Besides creativity, the other important characteristic of entrepreneurs and intrapreneurs is their capacity for hard work. Entre/intrapreneurs have a strong work ethic. Many people claim that the work ethic in America is dead. "You can't get good help anymore," they say. "No one works hard the way people used to in my day." Yet recent research indicates that not only is the work ethic in America still alive, it is actually thriving.

The Protestant Work Ethic

Protestant work ethic A belief that people should work hard and save their money.

A hundred years ago, Americans with European roots were said to possess the **Protestant work ethic,** which holds that people should work hard and save their money. This work ethic had both religious and economic significance. Many Protestants, particularly a branch called Calvinists, believed that God would give people a sign if they were to be saved. This sign came in the form of success and material wealth. Those who did well in this life were destined for salvation, and their wealth was an early indication that they were being favorably viewed. Those who believed this were spurred on to work very hard so that they could prosper and see that they were assured of salvation. Additionally, they saved their money in the bank or invested it in entrepreneurial activities. In either case, their savings would grow, as would their belief that they were predestined for salvation.

In the process, the Protestant work ethic helped the early American economy because it encouraged hard work, savings, and entrepreneurial activities. Savings were reinvested in the economy, allowing businesses to expand and hire more people, and entrepreneurial activities led to new businesses and expansion of existing ones. In turn, new employees had money to spend on goods and services, so business created more customers in the process. At the same time, new employees who believed in the Protestant work ethic would save their earnings and strike out on their own in entrepreneurial activities. Simply stated, the work ethic helped the American economy grow because it fostered the ambition to work hard, save, and start new ventures, the very elements needed for economic growth in a free enterprise system.

The Modern Work Ethic

Today, adherence to the work ethic persists, although it usually lacks the religious undertones of previous centuries. People work hard for various nonreligious reasons, including:

Pride in the job

Personal desire to do the best job possible

Belief that hard work is honorable

Desire for advancement and promotion

Chance to earn more money

In terms of getting ahead and making money, the retiring head of Westinghouse Corporation, when asked in an interview, "Let's say you were a new college graduate, what would you do?" responded, "I think I'd try to spend 10 years with the best company I could find, that I could learn the most from—not necessarily the biggest—and then I would become an entrepreneur." When asked why he would do it this way, he declared, "For the average individual who has the drive, the education and the willingness to gamble, you probably have a greater chance at success earlier (by being an entrepreneur) than by going through the corporate system."[16]

A survey found that the work ethic is still very much alive.[17] Regardless of pay, a majority of resondents indicated they had the old-fashioned work ethic. A recent survey comparing job attitudes in the 1970s with those in the 1980s found "important and meaningful work" still more than twice as important as any other job characteristic.[18] As expected, this work ethic was even more common among entrepreneurial types.

Entre/intrapreneurs like to attain goals and to feel that what they are doing is important and meaningful. A couple of examples of these characteristics are found in the intrapreneurs responsible for the Post-It notepads and the anti-ulcer drug Tagamet. Even 3M, a company known for fostering innovation, almost managed to stifle the breakthrough Post-It notepad. The intrapreneur on the project only got the product accepted after persistence, belief in what he was doing, and much hard work. The same was true of Tagamet, the world's first drug to achieve sales of over $1 billion. It was turned down by Britian's largest chemical firm and was only accepted by the American firm Smith-Kline because of the persistence and hard work of the intrapreneur.[19] Like creativity, the capacity for hard work cannot be taught, but it seems to be a necessary requirement for entre/intrapreneurship.

Checkpoint

1. What is the Protestant work ethic?
2. Why do so many people value hard work today?

Innovative Approaches to Intrapreneurial Success

Besides creativity and hard work, intrapreneurs can ensure success by getting a new or modified idea to work and be carried out. Study of innovative companies has uncovered some clear guidelines for managing this process. In their "search for excellence," Peters and Waterman found eight common approaches that characterized the firms they admired.[20] Peters has subsequently stated that "excellence" has become an overused term and the well-run companies today are even more intrapreneurial—they believe in constant improvement and constant change.[21] The eight approaches can be used as guidelines and a framework for intrapreneurial success.

Bias for Action

Successful intrapreneurs avoid long, complicated delays. If an idea does not work out as intended, intrapreneurs analyze the situation, learn a lesson from the failure, and implement a new course of action. If intrapreneurs have an idea for a new product or service, management should encourage them to explain it orally or to write it down in comprehensible, short reports. Procter and Gamble has a one-page memo rule: If you can't say it in one page, you don't say it.

The active company's focus is on determining what has to be done and then doing it. Peters and Waterman summarize this bias for action with the slogan: "Ready, fire, aim." What this unique slogan says is that you have to be ready; successful intrapreneurs prepare and gather information, they don't fly by the seat of their pants. But, importantly, they also "fire"; they try things now. Then they "aim"; they verify, they learn, and they perfect.

Closeness to the Customer

Successful intrapreneurs also keep in close touch with their customers. They treat customers as human beings and listen to them. They find out what customers want and what bothers them. The 3M Company estimates that half of its current products are the result of customer complaints. In a manufacturing firm, successful intrapreneurs examine how product modifications can permit the company to tailor-make the good to the customer's specific needs; in an advertising firm, intrapreneurs find out how their clients view their goods and services and what image they would like to convey. Additionally, successful intrapreneurs get out from behind clean desks and closed doors and into the field to talk directly with customers and get firsthand feedback. For example, Al Boyajian, who owns and runs the popular Sears Restaurant in San Francisco, is constantly in touch with his customers. Although his breakfast and lunch restaurant averages 800 to 900 checks a day and the wait is up to 45 minutes to be seated, he still personally interacts with customers, asks for their suggestions, and believes that "my customers should be treated like guests in my own home."[22]

Peters recommends that managers in general, and we would say intrapreneurs in particular, should spend up to three-fourths of their time "managing by walking around" (MBWA). In other words, they should put a priority on going out and talking to customers and people they work with. When successful intrapreneurs are asked how can they afford to spend so much of their time in MBWA, they shoot back: "How can *you* afford to spend so much of your time on paperwork and attending meetings?" Sam Walton, one of the most successful entrepreneurs of all time with his chain of Wal-Mart stores, makes a point of visiting all of the more than one thousand stores and talking to customers and employees firsthand. He appears at a store unannounced and asks how things are going and how things can be improved.

Autonomy

One source of personal development and creative thinking is autonomy. Peters and Waterman found that excellent firms give their personnel the freedom they need to think independently, make decisions, and, in essence, act like intrapreneurs. In companies with a series of products, each division or group is encouraged to act like a small firm within the overall structure. For example, Chevrolet acts like a separate company within General Motors. Even in large organizations such as GM, this creates the feeling of entrepreneurship and the resulting dynamism, energy, and new ideas that are often generated in small enterprises, where intrapreneurs have wide latitude in making decisions.

Productivity through People

Successful intrapreneurs encourage their workers to contribute to productivity. These managers know that maximum productivity does not result from relying exclusively on technology and machines; subordinates also have important contributions to make. One way to inspire people-generated ideas and effort is with increased autonomy. Some intrapreneurs put their people into autonomous work groups and let them operate any way they want as long as the job gets done. This "free" environment often results in creative, productive ideas that help the firm stay ahead of the competition. North American Tool and Die, Data Design, Fel-Pro, and JBM Electronics are just a few of the excellent companies known for placing top priority on their people and creating an open, positive climate of work.[23] Part III will give more detailed attention to this human side of enterprise.

Emphasis on Key Business Values

Another way to encourage innovation is to emphasize key business values. Every successful intrapreneur has one or two business values that are the keys to success. In some firms, such as Dana Corporation, the focus is on reducing costs and improving productivity. Intrapreneurs in this company direct all their efforts toward these two aims. Other firms, such as 3M Corporation, emphasize new-product development. Others, such as Deluxe Check Printers, Inc., value superior service. At this successful firm (they have about 50 percent of the check printing market, making them three to four times larger than their nearest competitor), they do things such as closely monitor the average "ring time"—the number of times the phone rings before it is answered. This simple but generally ignored measure is highly correlated to customer satisfaction

AT&T's Bell Labs is known for inspiring intrapreneurship by bringing together talented scientists. Physicists Hans Peter Graf *(seated)* and Paul de Vegvar are part of a research team developing a type of computer chip called a neural network. These chips are designed to mimic the functioning of the human brain and could bring about radical change in the way computers operate.

Source: Courtesy of AT&T.

with service.[24] These business values become focal points for the effort of the intrapreneurs in these firms. The result is that intrapreneurs move in the same general direction, driven by the same values, and eventually achieve and maintain their lofty goals of growth, profit, and personal achievement.

Sticking to the Knitting

Successful intrapreneurs find out what they do best and specialize in it. In other words, they stick to their knitting. If they are good at new-product development, they enter markets where new products tend to capture large market share and redesigned or revamped products find it hard to compete. If they excel at personal service, they choose markets where price is less important than service. If they are a low-cost producer, they pick markets where people buy based almost exclusively on price. If they merge or acquire another firm, they choose one that is in a business they understand. Successful intrapreneurs emphasize doing what they know best but, importantly, in a new and creative way.

Simple, Lean Organization Structure

Successful intrapreneurs depend on simple structure. For example, at Hewlett-Packard, product development intrapreneurs face no bureaucratic obstacles. In this no-nonsense system, everyone knows to whom they report and who reports to them. In few instances, if any, do intrapreneurs have two or more bosses. If a department or division contains a large number of people, the company breaks it into smaller groups — sometimes even moving people to other geographic locales — so as to reduce the inefficiency that often accompanies large size. Intrapreneurs also minimize the number of support staff.

Many major firms today are trying to make their organizations into a series of small firms all operating under one roof. This gives them the

Levi Strauss sticks to its knitting by building its product line around the product the company is known for: high-quality blue jeans. This ad explains that Levi's 501 jeans used to be cut only for men but now are available in women's sizes. It is a new variation of a product the company is thoroughly familiar with.

Source: Courtesy of Levi Strauss & Company.

benefits of being small while remaining quite large overall. Organization structures receive more detailed attention in Chapter 6.

Simultaneous Loose-Tight Controls

Successful intrapreneurs apply some controls tightly, leaving others flexible and loose. For example, some intrapreneurs use stringent profit and other financial controls. If a product is unprofitable or fails to achieve anticipated sales, the company drops it. These same intrapreneurs may then apply many other controls loosely. For example, in day-to-day operations, some intrapreneurs may allow their employees a great deal of leeway in the routine aspects of their jobs. Successful intrapreneurs know when to use tight controls and when to loosen the reins.

Innovative Approaches in Perspective

These guidelines for intrapreneurship are not guarantees for success;[25] they are important lessons from which intrapreneurs can learn how things are done in the "excellent" firms in America. The ideas are innovative and in some ways contradict traditional notions about effective management. By the same token, intrapreneurs can also draw on the management concepts in Part III.

Checkpoint

1. What are three ways intrapreneurs can ensure that their ideas will be successfully implemented?
2. What does the slogan "Ready, Fire, Aim" mean?

The Entrepreneurial Wave

Paralleling the growing interest in promoting successful innovation and intrapreneurship is a surge of interest and actual activity in entrepreneurship. This trend has taken a number of different forms. The most obvious is that the number of new ventures is dramatically increasing. In 1950, Americans started just 90,000 companies, but in 1985, 1.4 million new ventures were launched.[26] An increasingly proportionate number of these new ventures are started by women. A recent estimate is that there are 3.5 million women entrepreneurs.[27] This wave of female entrepreneurship is attributed to two major factors: the large movement of women into the labor force and advancements in computer technology that make home-based businesses more feasible.[28] Although new ventures started by women and men are most closely associated with entrepreneurship, the entrepreneurial wave is also represented, at least indirectly, by the increasing number of privately held enterprises.

Although Chapter 5 will discuss in detail the various types of business ownership, an example of the entrepreneurial wave occurring in America is privately held enterprises (companies that do not offer ownership to the general public through the sale of stock). The unwillingness of the owners of privately held companies to share ownership with the general public suggests that they place great value on their role as owners and entrepreneurs. Few privately held firms are well known, although their number has increased dramatically over the last decade.

Other ownership patterns illustrate the importance of entrepreneurship. For example, many of the extremely large companies are privately held, including Bechtel (construction), M&M Mars (candy), Milliken (textiles), and Dubuque Packing (meat packing). In addition, a few major firms have gone from public to private in recent years, including Levi Strauss (jeans), Uniroyal (tires), R. H. Macy (retail), and the Jack Eckerd Corporation (drugstores).[29]

However, the not so well-known fast-growing privately held enterprises provide the best examples of an entrepreneurial influence in the economy. Here are some examples.

The Staubach Co. (Dallas, Texas) Founded by the former Dallas quarterback Roger Staubach, the firm leases and brokers commercial real estate. The business started in 1977 as a partnership, then Staubach bought out his partner in 1982. In 1983, revenues were $1.05 million; three years later, they stood at $5.4 million.

Akal Security, Inc. (Santa Cruz, New Mexico) Founded in 1980 by four American converts to Sikhdharma, an offshoot of Hinduism, the owners dress in traditional Sikh clothing. One of the partners started out as head of security for a small college and then brought his partners into the business. Their first job was an all-night guard patrol service for the shopkeepers in Espanola, New Mexico, near an active Sikh community. Since then, they have expanded into guarding gold mines and providing security at rock concerts and movie productions. At the end of their fourth year of operations, they were grossing almot $2 million annually.

Shader's China Doll Inc. (Wilmington, Delaware) In 1976, Ken Shader found his job a lot less interesting than his hobby, making poreclain dolls for his little daughter. Together with his wife, he began making dolls for specialty stores. In 1979, Bloomingdale's began buying his dolls, and F. A. O. Schwartz, the giant toy store, soon followed. By 1985, Shader had 120 employees, a 13,000-square-foot factory, and annual revenues of $4.1 million.[30]

What is interesting about most of these firms is that they were founded within the last ten years or so. The emergence of these new entrepreneurial driven private businesses in recent years has been phenomenal.

Checkpoint

1. What evidence indicates that the United States has seen a surge of entrepreneurial activity?
2. What are some examples of privately held businesses?

Closing Comments

With so many new businesses starting up each year in the United States and with existing ones struggling to remain competitive, survive, profit, and grow, the entrepreneurial spirit is alive and well. Some entre- and intrapreneurs are not satisfied to just "build a better mousetrap." In fact, Ken Gidrey of Bell Gardens, California, had the idea to trap ants instead of mice. At last count, he was making $3,000 a week selling live ants to a wholesaler dealing in ant farms.[31] Entrepreneurs like Gidrey are needed to start new ventures, and intrapreneurs are needed to make existing companies grow and prosper.

This topic has not traditionally been included in the introductory study of business. Although entrepreneurship played a vital role in the founding of the American business system, it has only recently been recognized as a vital part of modern business. Intrapreneurship has emerged even more recently. It recognizes that the entrepreneurial spirit of discovery, innovation, and change is important in all employees—managers, staff specialists, and operating employees.

Learning Objectives Revisited

1. **Explain the roles of entrepreneurs and intrapreneurs.**
   An entrepreneur is the organizer or manager of a venture. An intrapreneur is a manager or staff expert who creates and controls new, usually risky projects within an existing business. Successful enterprises need both, because organizations need bold, creative people to start ventures and to maintain and change them.

2. **Examine the creative process.**
   The creative process involves a series of steps: preparation, collecting information on the problem; incubation, letting the mind work on the problem; illumination, when the solution to the problem becomes apparent; and verification, testing and possibly modifying the solution.

3. **Present some creative techniques.**
   Some of the ways to trigger creative thinking include: looking at the space around the problem rather than just the problem, visualizing the opposite of the situation, and reversing the physical characteristics of every object in the problem. A popular group technique is called brainstorming, which is a creative thinking process in which the participants generate as many ideas as possible for solving a problem. Participants can put forth any ideas they think are useful, are encouraged to come up with as many of these ideas as possible, and can improve on other people's ideas if they want, but are forbidden to criticize and evaluate.

4. **Relate the work ethic to entrepreneurship.**
   The work ethic places high value on working hard and saving money. This ethic has helped move the U.S. economy forward, because by saving their money and investing in entrepreneurial activities, people helped generate sources of capital for business expansion and growth; and by working hard, they helped businesses operate efficiently. People today still adhere to the work ethic.

5. **Identify some innovative techniques and approaches of successful intrapreneurs.**

   Some innovative techniques and approaches drawn from Peters and Waterman's analysis of "excellent" firms include the following: Have a bias for action. Stay close to the customer. Use autonomy. Achieve productivity through people. Emphasize key business values. Stick to the knitting. Have a simple, lean organizational structure. Use simultaneous loose/tight controls.

6. **Explain some recent entrepreneurial trends in business ownership.**

   One entrepreneurial trend is the growth of new ventures. A second is the increasing number of women entrepreneurs. A third is that some of America's fastest-growing companies are privately held. Most of these fast-growing, privately held firms have been founded within the last ten years, indicating that entrepreneurial activities have emerged on all levels of business.

Key Terms Reviewed

Review each of the following terms. For any that you do not know or are unsure of, look up the definitions and see how they were used in the chapter.

intrapreneur

creative process

preparation

incubation

illumination

verification

brainstorming

Protestant work ethic

Review Questions

1. How are entrepreneurs and intrapreneurs different? How are they the same?

2. Pete Dunlop's supervisor has asked him to come up with suggestions for modifying the company's billing procedure. Pete has been thinking all afternoon about the request without coming up with a single idea. He is discouraged and almost ready to give up on fulfilling his supervisor's request. Does Pete's situation sound hopeless? Use what you know about the creative process to come up with some guidelines to help Pete with his problem.

3. You work for an advertising agency that has obtained a new account from a company that sells athletic shoes. The new client wants your agency to come up with a new, creative advertising campaign that will help it capture a large share of the market for athletic shoes. How can you use brainstorming to accomplish this objective? Whom would you include in the brainstorming session(s)?

4. You are leading a brainstorming session to consider possible markets for an electric dish dryer. "Well, working women would really be the key market," says one participant. "I think housewives would be more receptive," says another. A third participant objects: "Hey, what about men? You're wrong to exclude them, because they do dishes, too." As the group leader, what should you say at this point?

5. Is the work ethic dead? Explain.

6. How can intrapreneurs stay close to their customers?

7. In explaining how her business has prospered, owner Kate Kesler says, "I stick to the knitting." What does this expression mean? How do business people stick to the knitting?

8. What does the recent growth in privately held enterprises indicate about the role of entrepreneurship in U.S. business today?

Applied Exercises

1. Get the latest issue of *Business Week* and read the "Developments to Watch" section. How many of these new developments would you categorize as "new-new," and how many would be "new-old"? Defend your reasoning.

2. In the November 5, 1984, issue of *Business Week,* an article titled "Who's Excellent Now?" (pp. 76–88) reported that some of the companies (such as Johnson & Johnson, Dana, and 3M) that were considered excellent companies in the early 1980s have experienced some problems. Take one of these three companies and using library resources see if you can analyze what happened and where this company stands today.

3. *Inc.* magazine publishes an annual list of the fastest-growing firms in America. Determine from this or other sources which companies are privately held. Compare the latest list with that of three years ago. What conclusions can you draw from this?

Your Business IQ: Answers

1. True. Few offerings are unique; most are developments or modifications of some existing good or service.

2. False. While creative thinking often takes place at the individual level, groups can use it through such techniques as brainstorming.

3. False. Most (one study found seventy-five percent) of today's rapidly expanding firms were founded by entrepreneurs who came from big firms. Their experience proved invaluable in getting the firm started and making it successful.

4. False. If anything, it is more alive than ever. Millions of Americans in large and small firms are willing to work hard in an effort to get ahead.

5. False. The most successful approach is to combine loose and tight controls. For example, a manager might set tight controls for profit and other financial goals, while controlling subordinates' day-to-day activities loosely.

Case

Calibrake's Entrepreneurial Approach

Several years ago, Steven Frisbie and Russell Swan started their own business: rebuilding automotive parts, specifically brake calipers and master cylinders. This market is already glutted with firms providing these products, but Frisbie and Swan have been able to find a profitable niche between the big firms and the small firms.

Big firms can rebuild auto parts much more cheaply than small ones can. However, these products contain a lot of heavy cast iron so the cost of shipping is high. When big firms pass these costs on to the customer, their price advantage shrinks dramatically. The time required to ship the product means that large firms also have difficulty providing rapid service.

Small firms can provide quick service. However, because the machinery and equipment in this industry are so expensive, their cost of rebuilding auto parts is high. Small firms can be competitive in the local market, when service is a key factor, but they lose the race when costs enter in. Also, small companies have difficulty filling big orders, since their plant facilities are limited.

Frisbie and Swan's company, Calibrake, Inc., has the best of both worlds. Their plant is big enough to handle large orders and to keep their production costs down. At the same time, they think like a small business in that they avoid competing head-to-head with the large firms. They know that the farther they ship from their factory in Kansas City, Missouri, the higher their costs and the lower their competitiveness. For this reason, they remain local and have tried to dominate the market in Kansas City and the adjoining area.

How well have they done? In 1980, they had sales of $181,000. Five years later, their revenues exceeded $1.7 million and they were number 466 on the list of the fastest-growing private firms in America. Their sales growth during this period was 495 percent.

They attribute their success to three simple rules:

1. **Argue the facts.** If the partners disagree about whether to buy a major piece of equipment, they gather as many facts as possible before making the decision.
2. **Keep egos out of the decision.** They do not allow themselves to get carried away with their own self-importance.
3. **After reaching a decision, speak with one voice.** The partners act in unison on business matters.

Case Questions

1. Do these entrepreneurs adhere to the work ethic? Explain, being sure to incorporate a discussion of this ethic into your answer.
2. Do the owners use the entrepreneurial characteristic of creative thinking in any of their business decisions? Explain.
3. Which of the innovative approaches drawn from Peters and Waterman's "excellent" firms do the entrepreneurs in this case follow? Identify and describe at least three of them.

You Be the Adviser: Reducing Turnover

Management turnover at the Jefferson Company has been unusually high this year. The firm, which has over 15,000 employees in a 12-state area, typically has to replace 5 percent of its workers and 3 percent of its managers every year. However, this year it lost 14 percent of its management staff, including seven senior-level managers.

Jefferson was founded 19 years ago and has witnessed dramatic growth over the last 7 years. During these latter years, the number of employees quadrupled, and management moved from an informal structure to a highly complex, bureaucratic design. To maintain efficiency, top management introduced a series of control measures that ensure everyone is following the rules and abiding by company policy. The president of Jefferson likes to say, "Around here, we are all one big team, and like any successful team, we all have to be moving in the same direction at the same time."

The heavy turnover in the management ranks has not escaped the attention of the board of directors. The chairman of the board has asked the head of the personnel department to put together a brief report indicating why the firm is losing senior-level people. In doing so, the personnel manager contacted the seven executives who had left to find out what they were doing and why they had left. Here is what he discovered:

Five of them left to start their own company.

The other two are partners in new ventures that are just getting off the ground.

Four of them said that they wanted the opportunity for more freedom and decision-making authority.

The other three said they wanted to use what they had learned in the business to run an operation of their own.

All said that they wanted the chance to make more money than they could earn at Jefferson.

Your Advice

1. Using the innovative approaches drawn from Peters and Waterman's study of "excellent" firms, in what areas does Jefferson need to make changes?
2. What advice would you give to the chairman of the board about how to change each of the areas you have identified in Question 1?
3. How can your advice help the company recruit and maintain people with intrapreneurial tendencies?

Small Business and Franchising

LEARNING OBJECTIVES

- Define small business and its impact.
- Identify the types of small businesses.
- Analyze some of the major advantages and disadvantages of owning a small business.

- Discuss how to start a small business and effectively operate it.
- Describe how the franchise form of business works.
- Relate the major advantages and disadvantages of franchises.

Your Business IQ

How much do you already know about small businesses and franchises? Test your business IQ by labeling each statement *true* or *false*. Answers and explanations are at the end of the chapter.

1. Approximately two-thirds of all businesses in the United States fit the Small Business Administration's definition of a small business.
2. About 2 out of 10 new businesses fail each year.
3. Most small-business owners work more than 70 hours a week.
4. To grow and expand, most small-business owners get funding from venture capitalists and the Small Business Administration.
5. One of the biggest complaints against franchisors is that they often refuse to sell franchises to minority entrepreneurs.

Like this Cincinnati grocer, many small-business owners are retailers.

Source: © 1988 Paul Poplis: CLICK/ Chicago.

Looking Back and Ahead

About 30 years ago, two sets of brothers each borrowed a few hundred dollars and opened the same type of small business. The Monaghan brothers opened pizza shops in Ypsilanti, Michigan, and the Carney brothers opened pizzerias in Wichita, Kansas. The rest is history. Tom Monaghan (who bought out his brother's share for a used Volkswagen) founded Domino's Pizza, which at last count had close to 4,000 stores and was growing so rapidly that the company expects to soon have 5,000 stores. Frank and Dan Carney founded Pizza Hut, now the largest pizza restaurant chain in the world. At last count, the company had over 4,000 stores in 17 countries. Tom Monaghan and Frank Carney fit the classic entrepreneurial profile that was discussed in the last chapter.

This chapter looks at the kinds of organizations that these men started (small businesses) and have built (franchises). The chapter begins by describing the nature and impact of small business, then discusses the common types and the major advantages and disadvantages of owning a small business. The next part of the chapter describes some of the details of a small-business plan and identifies the critical aspects of effectively managing a small business. The last part of the chapter covers a special way to own a small business — through franchising.

Nature of Small Business

Small business
Independently owned and operated business that is not dominant in its field of operation and meets certain standards of size in terms of employees or annual receipts.

According to the Small Business Administration (SBA), a **small business** is one that "is independently owned and operated, [is] not dominant in its field of operation, and meets certain standards of size in terms of employees or annual receipts." The standards vary with the industry in question. Using this definition, approximately 97 percent of all nonfarm businesses in the United States are small businesses. Over the last few years, about two-thirds of all new jobs in the United States have been created in firms with fewer than 1,000 employees.

The Backbone of the American Economy

Small businesses are the backbone of the American economy. They not only provide millions of people with jobs, they also help big businesses remain profitable by filling small or specialized orders. Large firms cannot fill such orders profitably because the special equipment and personnel needed are not economical for a company that serves a broad market. Small businesses, in contrast, have lower overhead and can handle all sorts of specialized, piecemeal jobs at a profit. Estimates indicate that for every large manufacturing firm in this country, there are 600 small ones, many of which supply the large firm with services, parts, and materials vital to their production process.

Taking up the Slack

In some markets, small firms have secured themselves a niche by catering to the needs of customers who can't get what they want from larger firms. Banking is a good example. In particular, minority bankers (blacks, Hispanics, and Chinese-Americans) have provided services, financed ventures, and reached out to customers in areas the larger banks have ignored or avoided.

Small business also offers career prospects to people who have traditionally had limited opportunities in major corporations. The SBA reports that approximately 4.4 percent of all businesses in this country are owned and operated by minorities and take in over $30 billion a year in receipts. In addition, an estimated 3.5 million women own small businesses. This represents 27 percent of all U.S. businesses.[1] Minorities and women who have been stifled by the lack of opportunities in large organizations often have found successful careers in small businesses.

Common Types of Small Businesses

Small businesses most often operate in one of three broad nonfarming areas: light manufacturing and construction, merchandising (retailers or wholesalers), and service industries.

Light Manufacturing and Construction Many types of small firms do light manufacturing — machine shops, bakeries, ice cream plants or dairies, and furniture makers — and construction of buildings (residential and commercial) and other projects. They take raw materials and convert them into finished products. For example, machine shops turn iron and steel into special parts used by big auto or appliance factories, bakeries turn flour into bread, dairies turn milk and cream into ice cream and specialty items, furniture shops turn wood and cloth into furniture, and construction firms turn lumber, bricks, and mortar into buildings.

As a whole, a small number of manufacturers account for a large percentage of total employment; only 3 percent of the firms account for almost three-fourths of all manufacturing employment. Thus, there are many very small manufacturing firms that employ fewer than ten people.[2] To learn about one such business based in Iowa, see "Small Business Close-Up: Homegrown Snacks."

Merchandising Merchandisers are of two kinds: retailers, which sell products to the final customer, and wholesalers, which buy goods to sell to retailers. Retailers are more common than wholesalers. Typical retailers include auto dealers, department stores, discount stores, clothing stores, drugstores, supermarkets, and service stations. Although some department stores, such as Macy's in New York, Dillards in Little Rock, or Dayton's in Minneapolis, are large, most of the retail establishments in the United States have fewer than four employees. Wholesalers, on the other hand, are slightly larger, averaging between four and ten employees. In recent years, wholesalers have grown more slowly than retailers, but they still manage to generate over $750 billion annually.

Services The modern economy includes many small service firms. Although large financial and insurance firms covered in Part VI are service industries, some examples of small service firms are restaurants, dry cleaners, auto repair shops, and accounting services. Most of these small service companies are labor-intensive, which means that a large part of their costs goes for employee-related expenses. Restaurants are a good example. A waiter can serve only a limited number of tables. As the size of a restaurant increases, the restaurant manager eventually has to hire more waiters.

As the economy has grown in recent years, service has proved to be one of the fastest-growing sectors. Of the 12.6 million new jobs created since the 1982 recession, about 85 percent have been in the service sector.[3] This portion of the economy also promises a good chance for success for the small business. As Chapter 1 pointed out, the productivity record in the service industry is poor, and unlike in the manufacturing sector new technologies and human resource management techniques are untapped. There is considerable potential for improvement in the service sector.

One important area for growth among service businesses has been that of convenience services. The growth in the number of single-parent households and especially the growth in the number of two-earner households has created a pool of people for whom time for household chores is scarce and who are willing and able to spend money to make their lives easier. The result has been a boom in services geared toward providing convenience. For example, Austin, Texas–based EatOutIn will deliver a meal from a local restaurant; The Busy Body's Helper will water your plants in New York; and Personalized Services will walk your

SMALL BUSINESS   CLOSE-UP

Homegrown Snacks

When Alan Schillerberg wanted to start a small business, he drew on his background in selling seeds and exporting corn and soybeans. Through his export business, Schillerberg learned that people overseas enjoy snack foods made from soybeans, a major crop in Schillerberg's home state of Iowa.

So Schillerberg started a snack-food business with a $50,000 investment. One year later, he was selling about 1,000 pounds of flavored Iowa Nuts to stores in northwestern and central Iowa. The entire payroll of the company consists of Schillerberg, a sales and production manager, and an office manager. The company buys fresh soybeans, sends them to a food-processing company to be steam-cooked into a nutlike product, and them has them shipped to a company called Consolidated Popcorn, Inc., which adds the flavorings and packages the snacks. The product comes in 5-ounce resealable cans in four flavors: sour cream and onion, cheddar and bacon, nacho cheese, and barbeque.

Smaller packages are planned for vending machine sales. In addition, the company has developed a chopped-soybean topping for ice cream, to be prepared in butterscotch and caramel flavors.

According to Schillerberg, the biggest obstacle for Iowa Nuts, Inc., is obtaining financing to expand the company. With another $90,000, they could expand statewide and hire part-time distributors. The next step would be to establish a midwestern sales territory, which might require a $1 million investment in a factory. Eventually Schillerberg hopes to expand nationwide and into Canada. He notes that people outside the company's current marketing area ask where they can buy Iowa Nuts, "and the response is they can't." In the meantime, the company has asked county organizations of the Iowa Soybean Association to sell Iowa Nuts at county fairs.

dog or run your errands in Chicago.[4] Other businesses do household
chores, manicure your lawn, baby-sit, or shine your shoes in your home.
Many of the providers of these services are small businesses.

Advantages of Owning a Small Business

Many business people would rather own a small business than head up a
division of a larger company. Both positions offer many responsibilities
and rewards, but the owner of a small business has the additional benefit
of independence. The small-business owner can run the operation the
way he or she thinks is best. Closely tied to this freedom is the challenge
of pitting one's skills and abilities against those of competitors and the
possible satisfaction of success. When the business succeeds, the owner
often is able to make more money than would be possible working for
someone else. Along with this reward is the intangible satisfaction of
providing a community service by supplying needed goods and services.
In fact, in a recent survey, small-business owners ranked pride in offering a product or service as their most important source of satisfaction.[5]

Disadvantages of Owning a Small Business

Owning a small business is not for everyone. For some people, independence and challenge sound more threatening than inviting. These fears
have some justification. Business owners risk losing their money and perhaps having to declare bankruptcy. In 1986, 61,000 U.S. businesses
failed, which was a 6.9 percent increase from the year before.[6] The
great majority of these were in the industries of service, retail trade, construction, light manufacturing, and wholesale trade; the strongholds of
small business.

One source of this risk of failure is that small-business owners are often unable to raise large sums of money for expansion. In most cases,
small firms have to rely on internal profits as their main source of funds.
Running a small business also places stringent demands on the owner's
time and ability to make decisions that will keep the business competitive
and ensure that it has the financial resources to continue operating.
Small-business owners also are often dismayed when they find that the
government requires them to comply with a myriad of regulations and a
frustrating amount of red tape. For example, a recent nationwide survey
found that small businesses spend about as much time complying with
government information requirements as do large businesses.[7]

Checkpoint

1. What are three common types of nonfarm small businesses?
2. Name one advantage and one disadvantage of owning and running
   your own small business.

Starting a Small Business

A person who wants to start a small business needs to do three things
before obtaining the needed funds and finding a location and facility:

assess his or her abilities and interests, look for a viable opportunity, and draw up a business plan.

Personal Assessment

To reduce the likelihood of failure, prospective business owners should start by assessing their strengths and weaknesses. Some small-business owners try out a number of different business opportunities before settling on the one they like best. An honest personal appraisal can help eliminate the time-consuming and potentially costly (in terms of both money and pride) experiments.

A candid personal assessment helps a potential owner decide whether he or she is able to run a business. For example, the average small-business owner works 70 to 80 hours per week. A person thinking of going into business has to ask, am I *willing* to work long hours? Even if the answer is yes, a follow-up question is, am I *able* to work long hours? Good physical and mental health and a full-time commitment are mandatory to success.

For example, it would be difficult, though not impossible, for a full-time student to go into most businesses, simply because of the amount of time and physical and mental energy required. The same is true of some successful athletes. They try to run a business as a sideline, rather than devoting their full efforts to it. As Gil Brandt, director of player personnel for the Dallas Cowboys recently stated, athletes "don't realize that you have to be [with the business] 18 hours a day."[8] Therefore, before embarking on a small-business venture, the potential owner should undertake some form of self-assessment, such as completing the questionnaire in Figure 4.1.

Opportunity Identification

Businesses don't prosper just because their owners are hard workers; they have to meet a need. Therefore, the next step before starting a small business is to identify an opportunity to meet a need.

One way to do this is to spend several years working in a field that interests you. While you are working, keep your eyes open. What products and services are companies already providing? Who is buying them? Are the customers satisfied? Are the existing companies meeting the full demand for these products and services? Do customers want something that existing companies aren't providing? The answers to questions such as these may suggest an opportunity for a new business. You might also find the answers to these questions by doing research in the library and by interviewing people who might be a potential market for the product or service you are interested in providing. For example, the National Federation of Export Associations provides evidence that small businesses are not taking advantage of overseas markets for their goods and services.[9]

You might also choose a field based on your particular knowledge, interests, skills, or personal contacts. The admonition to "stick to the knitting," described in Chapter 3, applies equally well when entering into a new small-business venture. Build on your strengths.

Check the statement that best describes you.

1. Are you a self-starter?
   ☐ I can get going without any help from other people.
   ☐ Once someone helps me get started, I can maintain the momentum.
   ☐ I take things nice and easy and do not get started until the last minute.

2. Can you assume responsibility?
   ☐ I can take charge and see things through to completion.
   ☐ I can take the reins if it is necessary, but I prefer to let someone else handle the responsibility.
   ☐ I prefer to let others handle responsibility.

3. Can you lead people?
   ☐ I can get most people to follow me once I get something started.
   ☐ If someone can help me understand what needs to be done, I can usually take it from there.
   ☐ I prefer to let other people lead and go along if I like it.

4. How good an organizer are you?
   ☐ I am orderly and work from a predetermined plan or design.
   ☐ I can usually get things organized, but if the situation gets too confusing, I give up.
   ☐ Most situations change so rapidly that I find it is a waste of time to organize anything, and I never do.

5. Can you make decisions?
   ☐ Yes, and they usually turn out well.
   ☐ If I have to, but I like plenty of time to think things through.
   ☐ I prefer to let others make decisions and then react to them.

6. How well can you get along with others?
   ☐ Very well. I like people and they like me.
   ☐ I'm as good as the next person and can usually get through just about any situation.
   ☐ I'm a little nervous around people and sometimes find it hard to work with them.

7. How hard a worker are you?
   ☐ I have tremendous drive and stamina and can keep going for a long time.
   ☐ I can work hard for a while, but then I taper off.
   ☐ I do not care to work hard and seldom do.

8. Can people rely on your word?
   ☐ Absolutely. I always stick by what I say.
   ☐ I usually stand by my word, but sometimes it is necessary to change my mind.
   ☐ I often break my word, but that's because things have changed so much that I just don't feel I should go through with my promise.

9. How good are you about seeing things through to completion?
   ☐ Once I set my mind to it, I can see anything through to the end.
   ☐ I usually stick with a task until it is completed.
   ☐ I try hard, but if the situation gets too complicated, I usually bail out.

10. How good is your health?
   ☐ Excellent.
   ☐ Good.
   ☐ All right, but it has been better.

Although there are no right or wrong answers, the first response can be considered the best, the second the neutral, and the last the worst in terms of going into business for oneself. To score yourself, give 3 points for each first response box checked, 2 points for each middle response box checked, and 1 point for the bottom response box checked. As a guideline, if you scored 25–30 points, you may be a very good candidate for going into business for yourself. If you scored 20–24 points, you may not be suited for self-employment. If you scored below 20 points, self-employment is probably not for you.

FIGURE 4.1

**Going into Business:
A Self-Assessment
(Representative
Questions)**

The Business Plan

Prospective small-business people today usually draw up a business plan. In fact, most banks consider lending only to a small business that has such a formal plan. This plan usually covers marketing, operations, and finance. The finance part of the plan is most relevant to lenders because it explains how the owner will keep the business afloat. The statistics are frightening: Most small businesses close their doors within five years of their founding. Although overall poor management is the primary underlying reason for most small-business failures, the last straw is often a lack of money for continuing the operation. The business plan should address the major financial considerations of obtaining funds needed to get started and then having the money to keep the operation going.

Checkpoint

1. What three activities are required before starting a small business?
2. What information should go into a business plan?

Operating a Small Business

Operating a small business is in many ways similar to running a large firm, but it takes place on a smaller scale. The smaller size means that managing a small business is unique in some ways. In general, small-business owners must be concerned with three major areas: management, marketing, and finance.

Management

Small-business owners need to pay particular attention to two areas of management: staffing and operations. Staffing a small business is especially critical because the company has only a few employees, each with a great deal of responsibility. If only one employee leaves, day-to-day operations could change drastically, and the remaining employees must share the work until the company finds a replacement. Another dimension of staffing in small businesses is the development of managerial succession. Who will replace the manager or owner when he or she dies, retires, or quits? In many small firms, managers never answer this question; when the head person leaves, chaos results and the small business may even fail.

The operations function, which is covered in Chapter 10, addresses several questions: What types of machinery and equipment does the enterprise need? What is the best layout for the facilities? How much inventory and what types of storage facilities will the business require? The answers to these types of questions will influence the small company's ability to produce its goods efficiently and to store them at minimum cost. For example, small firms such as Lifeline Systems of Watertown, Massachusetts, and Fireplace Manufacturers of Santa Ana, California, have recently converted to modern but simple production and inventory systems that have had a dramatic impact on their efficiency and profits.[10] The effective small-business owner is as interested in maintaining high productivity and low cost as is the president of a large corporation. Part III discusses management in greater detail.

Marketing

A vital area of running a small business is marketing (covered in Part IV). The hard fact is that inadequate sales will force small businesses to cease operations. Well-planned marketing activities can minimize these problems. Particularly important dimensions of marketing in small business are personal selling and advertising. For a retail establishment, location is also a primary concern in the marketing effort. A well-placed business helps attract customers and increase sales. For example, a men's or women's apparel shop or other specialty stores could benefit from locating near a large department store, because this location would help generate customer traffic. Restaurants, barber shops, candy stores, and jewelry stores often prosper near movie theaters. Women's clothing and shoe stores are grouped together. Furniture stores often do better if they are located near each other, because most people comparison shop for furniture. Two furniture stores located down the block from each other will generate more total sales than if they are located across town from each other. In most cities, you will find a Burger King and a McDonald's near to one another for the same reason.

Babs Eyerly Pruden operates the Inn at Turkey Hill in Bloomsburg, Pennsylvania. She advertises her inn and restaurant in the Bell of Pennsylvania Yellow Pages. The Yellow Pages sales agent helps her develop ads that project the image she wants for the inn.

Source: Courtesy of Bell Atlantic Corporation.

Financing

Like managing and marketing, financing is important to the success of a small business. The general topic of financing receives more detailed coverage in Part VI. Managers of small businesses need to pay particular attention to two areas: credit and expansion capital.

Credit Most businesses are givers and receivers of credit. Few businesses, large or small, pay cash for the things they buy. Most use credit and then pay the bills at the end of the month. However, the company may be short of cash when bills come due, in part because it extends credit to its own customers.

Business managers usually resolve this problem by securing a "line of credit" from a bank. This is a bank's agreement to let the business borrow funds as needed up to a specified limit. An example of this type of credit would be a wholesaler whose biggest sales season is September 15 through November 1. Most of these sales are on credit to retailers who pay for them within 90 days, so between December 15 and February 1 the wholesaler will be getting a large inflow of cash payments. However, before this period, the wholesaler will need money to stay afloat. After all, this wholesaler spent a lot of money to acquire the inventory that it has sold but not received payment for. A line of credit from the bank that the company repays by February 15 will tide the wholesaler over.

The big question is whether the small business will be able to secure such a line of credit from a bank. This depends on the owner's ability to show the financial institution that the business is a good risk. The owner does this by demonstrating to the bank that the company has a good record of paying off debts in a timely fashion and that the sales forecast is accurate. A company that can show this, along with the owner's personal guarantee backed by personal assets, seldom has trouble obtaining credit.

Venture capitalist An investor who specializes in small firms that offer potential for rapid growth and high returns.

Expansion Capital Besides credit for daily operations, a small business needs funds for expansion. For such funding, most small businesses reinvest profits from the business or rely on the owner's personal funds. However, a company that can generate outside sources of capital can more easily accomplish expansion plans. Small businesses have various sources of expansion capital. One source of funding is a **venture capitalist,** an investor who specializes in small firms that offer potential for rapid growth and high returns. In some cases, state and local governments also provide funding.

Checkpoint

1. Why is location so important to small businesses?
2. What are two ways in which small-business owners obtain financing?

The Small Business Administration

Small Business Administration (SBA) The principal government agency concerned with the economic welfare of small U.S. firms.

The principal government agency concerned with the economic welfare of small firms in the United States is the **Small Business Administration (SBA).** Congress created the SBA in 1953 with the Small Business Act.

Since then, the SBA has played an important role in American small business. In recent years, however, it has been the target of budget-cutting efforts, and its future is uncertain.

The Small Business Administration provides services in several areas. It helps small businesses receive a share of government contracts, in accordance with federal regulations requiring the government to make some of its purchases from small businesses. The agency also has available limited financing assistance and information on business management.

Financing Assistance

The SBA offers several programs to help businesses obtain financing. It guarantees repayment of loans of up $500,000 that private lenders make to businesses that have been unable to obtain a loan from at least two banks. The guarantee makes lenders more willing to take the risk of extending a loan to a small business. For businesses that have been unable to obtain a guaranteed loan, the SBA also loans up to $150,000 directly. These loans are not easy to obtain; the borrower must fill out a detailed credit application, and funding has always fallen short of the demand for loans.

The SBA also offers loans to special groups. Groups qualifying for such loans include disadvantaged or handicapped business people, business people involved in conservation endeavors, and development companies helping small businesses in rural or urban areas. Loans are also available to assist small businesses in moving into international markets.

The SBA licenses **small business investment companies (SBICs)** to provide venture capital to small businesses. The SBIC borrows from the government on attractive terms and then invests the money in small businesses. It may be willing to consider less glamorous enterprises than a private venture capitalist would. A type of SBIC called a **minority enterprise small business investment company (MESBIC)** provides financing to small businesses whose owners are economically or socially disadvantaged.

Information and Advice

Besides money, the Small Business Administration provides small enterprises with information and advice. Management assistance officers provide individual assistance and counseling to small-business owners. The SBA sponsors publications, both free and for sale, that discuss management, marketing, finance, and other technical aspects of small-business ownership.

The SBA sponsors and administers special programs that provide free counseling to small businesses. Two of these programs are the Service Corps of Retired Executives (SCORE) and the Active Corps of Executives (ACE). These two groups consist of experienced volunteers who want to help small businesses. Today, 400 SCORE and ACE chapters are in operation, staffed by 2,000 volunteers, in all 50 states, Puerto Rico, Guam, and the Virgin Islands.

Another education program is the Small Business Institute (SBI). In cooperation with colleges and universities, SBI conducts programs in which student teams assigned to small businesses provide free management counseling and work alongside the owner in identifying solutions

Small business investment company (SBIC) A company licensed by the SBA for the purpose of providing venture capital to small businesses.

Minority enterprise small business investment company (MESBIC) An SBIC that provides capital and equity financing to small businesses whose owners are economically or socially disadvantaged.

to operational problems. Today over 400 universities have SBIs. Besides helping the small businesses involved, they provide valuable learning and hands-on experience for business students.

Small Business Development Centers (SBDCs) are still another program funded by the SBA that provide a full range of services to assist small businesses by drawing together local, state, and federal resources. With public and private educational institutions and business associations, the SBDCs sponsor courses in small-business management. They also run conferences and workshops on topics such as business forecasting, sources of financing, types of business organizations, and choosing a site location.

Checkpoint

1. What are two kinds of services the Small Business Administration (SBA) offers?
2. Suppose that you owned a small business and were struggling to make ends meet. What help could you expect from the Small Business Administration?

Franchise A system of distribution in which a producer or supplier arranges for a dealer to handle a product or service under mutually agreed-upon conditions.

Franchisor The supplier in a franchise system.

Franchisee The dealer in a franchise system.

Franchising

In recent years, many would-be entrepreneurs have been attracted to a special form of small business, the **franchise.** Under a franchise arrangement, a producer or supplier arranges for dealers to handle a product or service under mutually agreed-upon conditions. The supplier is known as the **franchisor;** the dealers are known as the **franchisees.**

Franchises are one of the most popular ways of getting into a small business. "Entrepreneurs Close-Up" gives an example of how a father-son combination used the franchise route to get into business for themselves. This arrangement appeals to many people wanting to get into

FIGURE 4.2

Sales and Growth of Franchising

Sales (in billions)		Number of Establishments	
1970	$120		396,000
1979	287		452,000
1982	376		439,000
1983	423		442,000
1984	492		444,000
1985	530		454,000
1986	576		478,000
1987[a]	625		500,000

business because it avoids the risk of starting a business from the ground up and the expense of buying an ongoing firm. As one spokesperson puts it, "Franchising is one of the few ways to combine a spirit of enterpreneurship with the lessons of a proven system."[11] Consequently, franchises are one of the fastest growing and most important modern forms of business. Figure 4.2 graphs the tremendous growth in the number and sales of franchises over the past several years. At present, franchising accounts for one-third of retail sales and over 7 million workers — 6.3 percent of the U.S. work force — are employed by franchised businesses.[12]

Franchises meet many different customer demands. Some of the best-known franchises are in the fast-food industry, including McDonald's, Burger King, Wendy's, and Kentucky Fried Chicken. A total of 188,871 employees work in California's fast-food restaurants alone.[13] One success story in the fast-food area is Mehdi Mohannadi, an Iranian citizen who had never had a submarine sandwich when he bought his first franchise of Subway Sandwich & Salads in Columbia, South Carolina. Thanks to the guidance and assistance given to him by the franchisor, within five years he had two franchises and combined annual gross revenues of $360,000.[14]

Besides fast food, franchises are popular in other service industries. For example, Ramada Inn Motels, Maids International, Dollar Rent a Car, One Hour Martinizing Drycleaner, and Suddenly Slender and Designer Body weight-loss centers are all franchises.

ENTREPRENEURS   CLOSE-UP

Bruce and Barry Donahue

A father-and-son franchise provided an attractive opportunity for Barry Donahue and his father, Bruce, to launch a business. They decided to team up when each was at a crossroads in his career: Barry Donahue had grown tired of his job, and Bruce had sold a previous business.

Barry researched franchise opportunities for almost a year and then found one that looked interesting: a chain of pet stores called Docktor Pet Centers. The pet stores appealed to Barry because he loves animals and because a Docktor Pet Center requires a relatively small investment for a franchise ($50,000 to $80,000, including a $15,000 franchising fee).

Barry and Bruce pooled their funds to make their investment of less than $80,000 in a Niles, Illinois, store. "It didn't break us,"

reports the younger Donahue. "There was no problem for us to get our money together. I think the only thing we worried about was how we were going to work together as a family. So far, so good."

Depending on a store's location, a Docktor Pet Center brings in more than $500,000 a year. Sales for the Donahues' store are boosted by its location in a shopping mall. Visitors to the mall are attracted to the pets in the store windows. In effect, the animals are their own advertising.

Although the Docktor Pet Center chain had been struggling during the 1970s, its performance in more recent years bodes well for the Donahues. The company has grown steadily over the past 15 years.

Companies that service other businesses also frequently use franchises. These organizations include collection agencies, employment services, printing and copying services such as Postal Instant Press, and tax preparation companies such as H&R Block. One success story in service franchising is Timothy Wagner, who quit his $60,000-a-year job as head of operations for Sheffield Hotels in Alaska, and for $50,000 became an Anchorage franchisee for Mail Boxes Etc. USA. The franchise sells stamps and office supplies and rents mailbox space. Within a year, he was grossing $250,000 and began selling franchises of his own. For every franchise he sells, Wagner gets 40 percent of the franchise fee and 5 percent of the royalties paid by the new store.[15]

The Franchise Agreement

While the products of franchises vary widely, the basic business arrangements have much in common. These arrangements are contained in a franchise agreement, which is a contract between the supplier and dealer that spells out what each party will do. Typically the dealer (franchisee) agrees to:

Pay a franchise fee for the right to run the operation

Pay a percentage of the gross revenues to the supplier (franchisor)

Follow the operating procedures that have been set forth by the franchisor

The buyer of a fast-food franchise might be required to pay as much as $750,000 to $1,300,000 for a Wendy's or $350,000 for a McDonald's, and as little as $9,750 for a Coustic-Glo firm, which specializes in cleaning ceilings. Since the buyer must lay out the facilities in a manner specified by the franchisor, all franchisees often have the same external and internal decor, table arrangements, menu, and preparation techniques. The result is that a customer in Dallas and one in Detroit will be eating the same food in the same basic environment. The customer will always know what to expect from the business, regardless of location.

The franchisor, in turn, usually promises to do the following things:

Allow the franchisee the right to use the company's name, logo, and symbols (such as the golden arches in the case of McDonald's)

Provide advertising and marketing support at both the local and national levels

Provide professional, standardized training so the franchisee learns how to run the unit correctly

Provide the franchisee with merchandise (food and equipment) at wholesale prices

Assist the franchisee in getting financial assistance, such as a line of credit with a local bank

Provide ongoing help for the duration of the contract

If you want to enter into a franchise agreement, begin by learning what franchises are available. Excellent sources of information are the *Franchise Annual Handbook and Directory* and the *International Franchise Association Membership Directory*. When you have identified a local franchise that looks promising, investigate it by talking to some of the current franchise owners.

When you receive a contract, have a lawyer look it over and comment on the advantages and disadvantages of the agreement. Also have an accountant or banker examine the initial investment, the likely annual revenues, the potential return on investment, and the overall financial risks. In entering the world of franchising, as with other small-business ventures, you must look before you leap.

Advantages of Franchising

Franchising offers a number of important advantages. One is that the franchisor provides you with management and operational training, showing you how to organize and operate the unit. Since the franchisor knows the best ways to produce the product or service, keep records, control inventory, and manage cash, you quickly learn what to do and what not to do. This greatly increases your chances of making the venture a success. However, there is also room for innovative approaches. For example, the head of Domino's Pizza's Washington, D.C.–area franchise requires his 11 store managers to run a 10-kilometer race before weekly sales meetings and go on group vacation-business trips every three months, and awards free family vacations to top-performing managers. This innovative approach is paying off. His franchise has the chain's highest sales volume per store.[16]

A second advantage is that the good or service has already been tested in the marketplace, has proved to be in demand, and has instant name recognition. You need not worry about whether anyone will buy the hamburgers or auto parts. The franchisor has already identified and demonstrated the market demand and has the name before the public.

Real estate brokers who join the RE/MAX franchise benefit from RE/MAX's promotional activities. For example, the RE/MAX balloon builds name recognition among potential buyers and sellers. Some of these people may look for a RE/MAX agent when they want to buy or sell real estate. Part of the cost of joining a franchise goes to cover benefits such as this.

Source: Courtesy of RE/MAX International, Inc.

In addition, the franchisor often helps with advertising and promotion. For example, the franchisors pay for the TV ads for national franchises such as Holiday Inn, Kentucky Fried Chicken, and Burger King. However, the franchisee pays for these benefits with the original franchise fee and may pay a percentage of sales to the franchisor for such services.

Finally, in many cases, the franchisor helps secure financial assistance. For example, a bank might refuse to lend money to Carl and Jennifer Smith, who want to open "Smith's Muffler Shop." The bank would more likely make a loan if the Smiths had a Midas Muffler franchise. Also, the SBA and about 1,000 private lenders participate in a program that provides loans, and franchisors themselves will often provide necessary start-up capital.

Disadvantages of Franchising

As does any other area of business, franchising has some disadvantages. The hard facts are that the average franchise owner nets a modest $21,000 per year, can work 12-hour days, seven days a week, and may still see the business fail.[17] One of the first drawbacks is that the larger and better known the franchise, the greater the initial fee and the percentage of revenues that must be paid to the franchisor. To avoid this, many people invest in small, unknown franchises with the hope that they will become well established. Unfortunately, many of them do not make it, and the franchisees lose their investment.

A second drawback is that the franchisor usually maintains strong control over the way the operation is run. Local conditions may call for a modification, but if the business is not operated according to the book, the franchisor can terminate the arrangement. This is why those with a strong entrepreneurial orientation or those who managed in large corporations may have trouble as franchisees. Instead of hands-on operation of their franchises, as the head of franchise sales at Window Works, Inc., recently noted, "The number-one problem is they [former corporate managers] like to sit behind the desk and give out orders."[18]

Another drawback arises because the franchisee usually agrees to buy all equipment, materials, and supplies from the franchisor. This gives the franchisor a ready, profitable market for its goods. The franchisor may promise to sell all equipment, materials, and supplies at wholesale, implying low prices, but the franchisee might be able to find a local source of these goods at much lower prices. Furthermore, some franchisors might not deliver on their promises. For example, management training may be scheduled for one week a year, but the franchisor may only pay for the initial training.

Finally, some franchisees have found that their agreement allows the franchisor to buy them out at the end of their original contract, say, after 5 or 10 years, at a price stipulated by the contract. If the franchise has done well, the unit may be worth a lot more money, with even greater future potential. However, if the product or service does not sell, franchisees lose their investment, while the franchisor goes right on selling to other franchisees.

Trends and Outlook

Despite its drawbacks, franchising is proving to be extremely attractive to small enterprises that want to expand (by becoming franchisors) and to individual enterpreneurs who are looking for a chance to operate their own businesses (by becoming franchisees). Franchising enables enterprises to move out of their local area and into regional and national markets. For example, the owners of a popular local sandwich shop may feel their sandwiches are so good and unique that they could become a franchisor. They could sell their name, recipes, and style of service to franchisees in surrounding cities or in other parts of the city. The opportunities are so good that franchisees of some chains are buying units in several locations, and some franchisors are beginning to buy back units or build company-owned units.

The Department of Commerce predicts that restaurants will continue to be the most popular sector of franchising. These restaurants are likely to move toward more diversified menus, including salad bars, fish, and poultry, as personal health concerns influence the consumption of such items. There is also a shift toward ethnic foods, allowing franchises to more effectively win a market share in a local area. Business and personal service franchises are also expected to continue to increase significantly. For example, business people can seek advice on how to organize their time from Priority Management Systems franchises. Consumers in a growing number of cities can get a haircut at Hair Performers, buy hearing aids at Miracle-Ear, and do their laundry at Duds 'N Suds.[19]

International Markets As illustrated in Figure 4.3, U.S. franchisors are moving into overseas markets. Large franchisors (those with 1,000 or

F I G U R E 4.3

International Franchising

Franchising companies: 305
Number of franchising outlets: 26,598

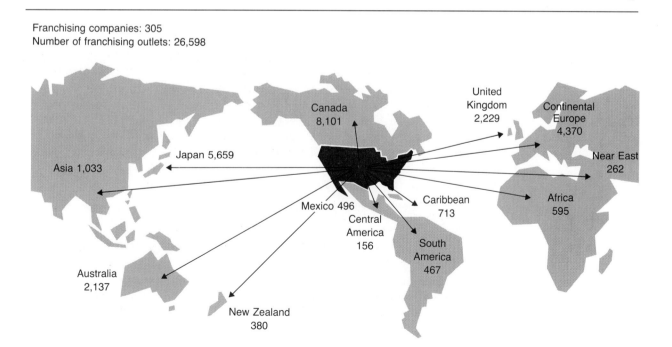

more units each) dominate this market. About 50 companies account for the majority of international franchise establishments.

Because the young people in many foreign countries like to try new products and concepts, overseas franchises often gain quick acceptance. Once again, fast-food outlets are a good example. McDonald's has made the hamburger an international food. Kentucky Fried Chicken recently opened mainland China's first fast-food restaurant, a huge facility with 500 seats and employing 150 workers. It may take time for Chinese customers to get used to "haodao yun shouzhi," translated as "so good you suck your fingers" from the franchise's slogan of "it's finger-lickin' good." A two-piece chicken meal and drink cost the equivalent of about two days' wages for employees at the restaurant. Yet the outlet is doing great business, serving 2,000 to 3,000 customers a day (including many foreign tourists).[20] Other popular international franchisors include those selling automotive products and services.

Minority Franchises Minorities are finding franchising to be an excellent route for getting into business. Many of the start-up hassles and barriers are eliminated and the probabilities of success are greatly enhanced by the franchise arrangements discussed. The Department of Commerce

Overseas markets are providing attractive opportunities for many franchisors. Häagen-Dazs outlets in Japan are setting sales records at the same time intense competition has caused U.S. sales to decline.

Source: Courtesy of The Pillsbury Company.

recently reported a 13 percent increase in minority ownership of franchises. Some of the major increases have occurred in automotive products and services, restaurants, business services, and retailing.

CHAPTER 4

105

Small Business and
Franchising

Checkpoint

1. How does a franchise work?
2. Name two advantages and two disadvantages of the franchise form of small business.

Closing Comments

The Monaghan and Carney brothers of pizza fame show that owning a small business and franchising can be a satisfying route to business success. While not all business owners will match the record of these entrepreneurs, they can enjoy the thrills of starting and nurturing one's own business.

As you learned in this chapter, small-business ownership offers many advantages but is not for everyone. Those who conclude that they are suited for this role should look for an opportunity and prepare a business plan. In operating a small business, the owner should focus especially on management, marketing, and finance. A possible source of assistance is the Small Business Administration, and a business arrangement that might simplify the owner's role is the franchise. John Naisbitt, author of *Megatrends,* estimates that within 20 years franchising will generate $1 trillion in sales, or half of all sales.[21]

Learning Objectives Revisited

1. **Define small business and its impact.**

   A small business is independently owned and operated, is not dominant in its field of operation, and meets certain standards of size in terms of employees or annual receipts. Small businesses account for about 97 percent of all nonfarm businesses and about two-thirds of all new jobs.

2. **Identify the types of small businesses.**

   Some of the most common types of small businesses can be found in three main areas: light manufacturing and construction, merchandising, and service enterprises.

3. **Analyze some of the major advantages and disadvantages of owning a small business.**

   Some of the major advantages of owning a small business include independence, a chance to make a good living, the challenge involved, and the opportunity to provide a community service. The disadvantages of owning a small business include the risk of losing money, great time demands, difficulty raising large sums of money for expansion, and the need to comply with government regulations and red tape.

4. **Discuss how to start a small business and effectively operate it.**
   The small business should start with a plan, which usually covers marketing, operations, and finance. The financial portion is especially important to lenders. Effectively operating the small business involves three functions: management, marketing, and finance. Management focuses on staffing and production. Marketing addresses personal selling, advertising, and location. Finance considers credit and expansion capital.

5. **Describe how the franchise form of business works.**
   A franchise is a system of distribution in which a producer or supplier arranges for a dealer to handle a product or service under mutually agreed-upon conditions. The dealer, known as the franchisee, pays a fee and a percentage of the revenues to the supplier and operates the unit in a specified manner. The supplier, known as the franchisor, allows the franchisee to use the company's name and reputation; provides professional, standardized training in running the unit; provides merchandise at wholesale prices; and assists the franchisee in getting financial assistance.

6. **Relate the major advantages and disadvantages of franchises.**
   Some of the major advantages of franchising are that the franchisor provides management and operational training to the franchisee; the good or service has already been tested in the marketplace; the franchisor often helps with the advertising and promotion; and, in many cases, the franchisor helps the franchisee secure financial assistance. Some of the major disadvantages are that the franchisee must pay a high initial fee and percentage of revenues; the franchisor usually maintains strong control over the way the franchisee runs the operation; the franchisee usually has to buy all operating equipment, materials, and supplies from the franchisor; some franchisors do not deliver on their promises; and, in some cases, the franchisor has the right to buy out the unit at the end of the original contract.

Key Terms Reviewed

Review each of the following terms. For any that you do not know or are unsure of, look up the definitions and see how they were used in the chapter.

small business

venture capitalist

Small Business Administration (SBA)

small business investment company (SBIC)

minority enterprise small business investment company (MESBIC)

franchise

franchisor

franchisee

Review Questions

1. In what ways are small businesses important to the economy of the United States today?

2. Anita Summers is considering whether to go into business for herself. Anita is punctual and meticulous and works best when she has clear instructions. She doesn't like surprises and avoids risks. She is willing to work long hours. Based on this information, do you think Anita is a good candidate to be a small-business owner? Support your answer with principles described in the text.

3. Peter Dreyfuss likes dogs and thinks he has the characteristics of a good business owner. Therefore, he has decided to start up a business to provide dog-sitting services. What else should Peter consider before he arrives at such a decision?

4. What aspects of marketing are especially important to the owner of a small business? Why?

5. How do small-business owners obtain financing?

6. What is the Small Business Administration (SBA)? In what ways has this organization helped small businesses? If you were starting a small business, would you count on this organization for financing help? Why or why not?

7. Under a typical franchise arrangement, what are the responsibilities of a franchisee and a franchisor?

8. Lisa Crawford wants the independence of being in business for herself. What advantages and disadvantages of franchising should she consider?

9. If Lisa goes ahead with the franchise, what steps should she take to get started?

Applied Exercises

1. Interview a small-business manager or owner who has started a small business within the last year. Interview a small-business manager or owner who has been in business for more than five years. Ask them what they see as the advantages and disadvantages of small business. Compare and contrast the answers and report your findings to the rest of the class.

2. Go to the local Small Business Administration office or your library and get an SBA pamphlet that describes how to make a personal assessment of one's abilities, drive, and other characteristics before going into small business. Fill out the form and compare your answers with those of others in the class. (If you get the form from the library, make a copy to write on.)

3. Visit a local banker who makes small-business loans. Ask the banker to describe what a small-business plan should look like and why such a plan is important when seeking a loan. Based on your interview, write a brief paper describing what every small-business owner should know about putting together a business plan.

4. Visit two different types of relatively new small businesses, such as a florist, a jewelry store, and a furniture store. Ask the manager or owner of each how he or she went about choosing a site. Note what factors each person considered important. Compare and contrast the reasons. Were any mentioned by both owners? What conclusions can you draw regarding how these managers or owners went about choosing a location for their business?

Your Business IQ: Answers

1. False. About 97 percent of all businesses in the United States fit the Small Business Administration's definition of a small business.
2. False. Depending on the state of the economy, usually more than half of all new small businesses fail each year.
3. True. Although this depends on the person and the business, most small-business owners work 70 to 80 hours a week and more. Many of them would make more money per hour if they worked for someone else, but owning one's business can have many nonfinancial rewards.
4. False. Most small-business owners get money by putting profits back into the business and using their personal funds. Venture capitalists back only a few select firms, and the Small Business Administration has strict requirements and little or no money to lend in recent years.
5. False. Franchisors readily sell outlets to minority members. Many minority entrepreneurs already own franchises, and their number is growing.

Freedom Tire Adds a New Dimension to the Tire Business

Auto-related services have been franchised for years. But the Brookfield, Wisconsin–based Freedom Tire Company has taken the business into a new dimension: service plus convenience. They will not only sell you tires, but they will put them on the car wherever you prefer — at home, at your workplace, at the golf course. Freedom Tire's founder, Monte B. Tobin, observes that the average customer "is doing something he doesn't like to do anyway: spending $200 to $300 on tires. And most tire stores aren't the nicest places to spend two to three hours. Customers often leave unhappy." In contrast, a Freedom Tire customer simply telephones for an appointment; a day or two later the tire team arrives to replace and balance the tires.

Consumer convenience is only one reason that Freedom Tire delivers its product. Another reason is low overhead costs, which keep down the cost of a franchise. A Freedom Tire franchise costs $144,500 — not cheap but, according to Tobin, considerably less than it would cost to operate out of a retail store. Because of the lower overhead, Freedom Tire charges less for its tires than a garage or tire store would, even though the price includes the extra service.

So far Freedom Tire has one franchise outlet, but the company hopes to expand. Some observers question whether the business can succeed for long. One of Tobin's competitors asks, "Have you ever had to change a spare tire in a rainstorm? Well, imagine doing that all day. And imagine not just bolting on the spare but removing all four tires from their rims and putting on new ones."

Also, auto-service franchises are fairly easy to copy, so Freedom Tire may eventually face tough competition. For that reason, the company is budgeting $30,000 out of its franchise fee for advertising. Says Tobin, "A brand name is the greatest barrier to entry."

Case Questions

1. Freedom Tire charges less for its tires than a retail store would. Do you think the business's pricing policy is wise? Why or why not?
2. What kind of problems is Tobin's competitor predicting when he describes how irksome it is to change tires in bad weather? How might the company address this problem?
3. If you knew someone who wanted to become a small-business owner, would you recommend buying a Freedom Tire franchise? Why or why not?

You Be the Adviser: A Lack of Funds

When Delores Reyes opened her office supply store, she was sure she would be successful. After ten years as an office manager with a large insurance firm, she knew what types of supplies businesses need. In fact, whenever she had ordered supplies for her employer, Delores had personally gone to the store and talked to the manager. Since the insurance company was the store's biggest account, the owner had gone out of his way to give Delores the best prices and fastest delivery. About three months ago, the supply store had been late in delivering a crucial order, and the insurance firm had to delay an important customer mailing by ten days. Top management decided that it would no longer do business with the store. Delores's boss asked her to find another supplier who would be reliable.

After thinking the matter over, Delores approached her boss with the idea of opening her own store and bidding on the company's business. "You don't have to bid on our business," he told her. "If you want to go into this business, I'll give you a two-year contract for all of our office supplies." With this amount of business guaranteed, Delores was able to get her operation up and going within 30 days. Unfortunately, a problem has now developed.

The insurance company does about $10,000 a month of business with Delores. Her walk-in business, much of it from other insurance companies she knows from her years in that field, adds another $12,000 monthly. This is much more than Delores thought it would be, but because of payment delays, she is running out of operating money. The insurance companies pay within 90 days of delivery, which means that Delores has approximately $12,000 in bills outstanding at any time. She also needs expansion capital so she can carry more supplies and negotiate a lease arrangement for the vacant store next to hers. If she can get this store, she will be able to double her current floor space.

Delores cannot continue for more than two weeks unless she gets additional capital. She estimates that she will need about $5,000 for day-to-day working cash, $25,000 for additional inventory, and $20,000 to renovate the store next door.

Your Advice

1. Where can Delores go to get this expansion capital? Identify at least two sources and relate which one you favor and why.
2. How important would a business plan be to Delores's efforts? Support your answer.
3. What areas of the business should Delores emphasize? Identify and describe what she should do to make her business a success.

C H A P T E R 5

Forms of Business Ownership

![black bar]

LEARNING OBJECTIVES

- Describe the nature of sole proprietorships.
- Describe the nature of partnerships.
- Explain how a corporation is structured.

- Analyze the advantages and disadvantages of corporations.
- Discuss acquisitions, mergers, and divestitures.

Your Business IQ

How much do you already know about forms of business ownership? Test your business IQ by labeling each statement *true* or *false*. Answers and explanations are at the end of the chapter.

1. Most businesses operating in the United States are corporations.
2. To set up a one-person business, the owner must fill out a considerable number of special forms with the federal, state, and local governments.
3. When partners go into business, they may divide the financial responsibility among themselves however they see fit. Some partners may have more responsibility than others.
4. To form a corporation, the owners must obtain the permission of the state in which they incorporate.
5. Corporations have limited liability, so angry stockholders may not sue their officers.

Herman J. Russell, who has been a sole proprietor, partner, and corporation owner.

Source: Courtesy of H. J. Russell & Company.

Looking Back and Ahead

When he was still a student in high school, Herman J. Russell bought a neighborhood lot for $250 and got some friends to help him build a duplex on it. A year later, he sold the building for $12,500. He paid his way through college by working on weekends as a plasterer. Upon graduating, Russell hired an assistant and started his own plastering business. At first, he built on small parcels of land, then entered into ventures with larger companies, and eventually bought other firms. Today, H. J. Russell & Company is one of the largest black-owned enterprises in the United States and has built a legacy of thousands of apartments and dozens of office buildings in Atlanta.[1]

As Russell's business grew, he used several forms of business ownership, each of which offered different benefits. When he was starting out alone, Russell took advantage of the flexibility of the sole proprietorship. As the company grew, the more formal corporate form of ownership was more suitable and enabled Russell to hire managers with special skills. In addition, joint ventures — a special form of partnership between two companies — enabled Russell to learn new areas of business by working with a company that had the experience he needed.

Building on the skills of entrepreneurship and small-business ownership discussed in the preceding two chapters, Russell also knew how to select ownership forms that combine the right mix of autonomy and shared knowledge. This chapter helps you learn how to make similar choices. It explains the basic elements of each ownership form — sole proprietorship, partnership, and corporation — and identifies some of their advantages and disadvantages.

The Sole Proprietorship

An entrepreneur often strikes out alone, for example, starting a construction firm to build homes or setting aside space in the garage to make a product. Sometimes the business grows to a point where the owner wants to share ownership, but often the entrepreneur enjoys and profits from going it alone. A business owned by one individual is called a **sole proprietorship.**

This is the most common form of business ownership in the United States, and because of the entrepreneurial spirit sweeping America, the number of sole proprietorships is still growing. One research report estimates that in 1985 alone, about 300,000 individuals became sole proprietors.[2] Figure 5.1 shows the proportion of proprietorships relative to partnerships and corporations in terms of number, sales, and profits.

Advantages of the Sole Proprietorship

The sole proprietorship is a popular form of ownership for good reason: It offers many benefits. The major ones are the ease of starting and dissolving the company, the retention of all profits, and the control over operations and information.

Ease of Formation Setting up a sole proprietorship is relatively simple. Except when the owner needs a license, such as for a liquor store or a barbershop, he or she need not obtain government permission. Further-

---

Sole proprietorship   A business owned by one individual.

According to a January 1988 article in *Inc.* magazine, the most frequently started businesses include eating and drinking establishments, automotive repair shops, and residential construction businesses. However, the businesses most likely to survive include veterinary services, funeral services, hotels and motels, and barbershops. Shown here is a barbershop in Wilmington, Ohio. Because a barbershop can start out very small, this type of business lends itself to a sole proprietorship form of ownership.

Source: © 1985 Jim Pickerell: CLICK/Chicago.

more, other than some paperwork pertaining to sales tax, the government does not require the owner to fill out special forms. And in many areas, businesses selling services don't even have to contend with sales tax. In sum, getting started merely entails laying out a plan of action and beginning operations. For example, a student who wants to earn extra money doing word processing simply needs to advertise in the student newspaper; as soon as a customer submits a paper, the student is in business.

Retention of All Profits After paying taxes, the owner keeps all profits. The owner of the word-processing business does not have to share the money with anyone. An owner who can figure out how to increase profits by working harder or being more efficient can enjoy the entire benefit of the extra effort or insight. Additionally, the federal government taxes all business revenues under this form of ownership at the same rate as individuals pay. Depending on how much the business makes, this rate can be lower than that for corporations.

Direct Control The sole proprietor controls operations directly. The owner does not have to hold meetings, consult with or get approvals from partners or stockholders, or secure compromises from business associates. This allows the owner to respond quickly to changes in the marketplace and to take advantage of developments. For example, the owner of the word-processing business could decide to specialize in statistical typing. No co-owners would protest that this would be dull or overly difficult.

Ease of Dissolution The sole proprietor can cease operations quickly and easily. Someone who has had enough of the business merely has to pay any outstanding bills, such as rent, utilities, salaries, and loans, and meet any contractual obligations, such as lease arrangements. Aside from these limitations, virtually nothing can stop the proprietor from going out of business. At the end of the school year, the student with the word-processing business could stop working and go home for the summer.

Secrecy Since the owner is seldom burdened with government forms or reports and is not required to divulge operating information to stockholders or partners, operations can remain relatively secret. They are

FIGURE   5.1

Sole Proprietorships, Partnerships, and Corporations in the United States

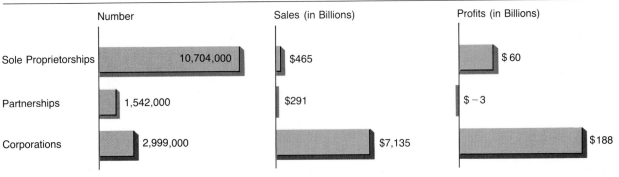

	Number	Sales (in Billions)	Profits (in Billions)
Sole Proprietorships	10,704,000	$465	$ 60
Partnerships	1,542,000	$291	$ –3
Corporations	2,999,000	$7,135	$188

nobody's business but the owner's. The owner can personally formulate strategy and then implement it without telling anyone what he or she is up to. This can be important, considering how closely competitors try to keep tabs on one another.

Disadvantages of the Sole Proprietorship

Even though business owners enjoy the freedom of running a sole proprietorship, this form of ownership does have some distinct disadvantages. Some of the major ones are unlimited liability, difficulty in borrowing money, limited expertise, long hours, limited opportunities for subordinates, and the fact that the life of the business is tied to the owner's involvement.

Unlimited liability Total responsibility for all debts of a company.

Unlimited Liability The owner of a sole proprietorship is subject to **unlimited liability,** which means that the owner has total responsibility for all debts of the company. This liability extends to the owner personally as well as to the business. Under the sole proprietorship, the business and personal property are legally considered to be the same. If the proprietorship cannot pay its debts, the creditors can force the owner to sell his or her car, home, and other personal assets to meet the business's outstanding bills.

Often, a proprietor who goes bankrupt (commonly called going "belly up") loses everything he or she owns. For example, if the student with the word-processing business had borrowed to buy a computer and found that the business's income did not cover the monthly bank payments, the bank could force the student to sell off personal assets such as a car or stereo system to cover the debt of the word-processing business.

Difficulty in Borrowing Money A sole proprietorship has more limited ability to borrow money than do other kinds of businesses. This is because the owner is the only person who stands behind the loan; banks are reluctant to extend large sums of money unless the individual has substantial assets to back up the loan. Thus, the proprietor's ability to borrow money is limited not only by the past and potential profitability of the firm, but also by his or her personal wealth. In the case of the word-processing business, a bank would probably require that a big down payment be made on the computer if it felt that the student would have difficulty generating a great deal of monthly income or if the student owned little of value.

Limited Management Expertise A sole proprietor must excel at many things: planning for the goods and services, supervising operations, promoting and selling the product or service, hiring competent personnel, keeping books and financing operations, and so forth. But it is difficult to excel at any one of these functions, let alone at all of them. The owner's limitations inhibit the ability of most proprietorships to expand and grow. For example, the student's word-processing business would have difficulty competing with larger companies that have experts in selling, financing, and word-processing technology.

Long Hours Since sole proprietors are totally responsible for day-to-day operations, most of them have to put in considerable amounts of time in order to succeed. If the sole proprietor takes a vacation, no other owners are around to keep an eye on the business. Hired employees seldom share the owner's intense commitment to the business's success.

Nevertheless, the owner can sometimes reduce the time commitment by delegating authority to well-trained, trusted subordinates and by effectively managing his or her time. For example, the student in the word-processing business can work "smarter" (say, by setting up control reports and procedures) rather than "harder" (personally checking all manuscripts for errors).

Lack of Opportunities for Subordinates Because they tend to be small, sole proprietorships sometimes offer only limited opportunities to those who work for proprietors. As a result, owners may have a difficult time attracting and keeping talented people. Proprietorships sometimes cannot afford to pay high salaries or offer the benefits, such as a pension plan for retirement, that a larger company can, and they usually do not turn over as much decision making to others. Thus, talented subordinates may move on to other organizations that offer greater opportunities. They may even try to set up a competing business of their own that duplicates what they have learned from their employer. It may be hard for the student owner of the word-processing business to get good help. As soon as a good employee learns the ropes, that person might quit and start his or her own business.

Noncontinuous Business Life The business's life ends with the end of the proprietor's involvement. If the owner dies, the business usually does, too. If the owner becomes ill and is hospitalized for an extended period of time, the business may have to close its doors. Regrettably, many proprietorships depend exclusively on their owners, and the business cannot be passed on after death. Heirs and subordinates cannot replicate the insight, judgment, and business skills of the disabled or deceased owner. To offset some of the problems that could accompany such a development, many banks or creditors require a proprietor to carry a life insurance policy that will cover financial obligations outstanding after the person's death.

In deciding whether to use a proprietorship, the owner must balance the advantages against the disadvantages in each particular situation. If the disadvantages outweigh the advantages, or if other circumstances such as size come into play, then another form of ownership such as a partnership or corporation would be preferable.

Checkpoint

1. What is a sole proprietorship?
2. What are two major advantages and two major disadvantages of this form of ownership?

The Partnership

Rather than go it alone, many entrepreneurs team up with one or more partners. According to the Uniform Partnership Act, in effect in most states, a **partnership** is an association of two or more persons to carry on as co-owners of a business for profit. As Figure 5.1 shows, almost a million and a half partnerships are operating in the United States, with total business receipts of more than $262 billion. Most partnerships have two partners, although the law permits more. Each of these partnerships started with an agreement between the partners.

Partnership An association of two or more persons to carry on as co-owners of a business for profit.

The Partnership Agreement

The agreement to form a partnership may be informal, but the partners usually sign a formal written agreement to avoid future misunderstandings. This partnership agreement is a contract that sets forth the specific terms for operating the business. Some of the most common provisions of such a contract include:

Date of the agreement

Name of the partnership

Partnership's business and principal place of operation

Names of the partners, amount of their investment, and the way profits and losses will be distributed

Duties of each partner

Provisions for paying salaries and withdrawing capital from the firm

What to do if a partner withdraws or dies

Length of time the agreement will be in force

Types of Partners

The partners need not necessarily share the same involvement in the business and the same liability for the company's debts. Based on differences in sharing involvement and liability, partnerships fall into different categories, the most basic of which are general and limited partnerships.

General partner A partner who is active in the operation of a business and has unlimited liability.

General Partners A **general partner** is active in the operation of the business and has unlimited liability. Every partnership must have at least one general partner. General partners have the authority to enter into contracts on behalf of all the partners. A group of students who form a partnership to paint houses during the summer would usually opt to be general partners. Everyone agrees to be responsible for the debts of the business and to make joint decisions.

Limited partner A partner whose liability is limited to his or her investment in the business.

Limited Partners A **limited partner** is a partner whose liability is limited to his or her investment in the business. The partnership agreement usually specifies that the limited partners are not active in the business operation. If the parents of one of the students were to put up $500 to help them get started in the painting business, the parents would most likely be specified as limited partners. They would not participate in the business's day-to-day operations and could lose no more than their $500 investment. Big real estate deals and many other popular investment partnerships consist of numerous limited partners and only one or a few general partners.

Special Kinds of Partners   Depending on their role in the partnership, general and limited partners fall into special categories, including:

> **Silent partner** — A partner who is known as an owner in the business but who plays no active role in running the operation
>
> **Secret partner** — A partner who is not known as a partner to the general public but plays an active role in running the company
>
> **Dormant partner** — A partner who is not known as a partner to the general public and plays no active role in the company
>
> **Nominal partner** — A partner who lends his or her name to the partnership but plays no role in the operation

Secret partners are usually general partners; the others are usually limited partners. In the students' painting business, the parents who put up some of the money could be any of these, but typically would be dormant partners. A highly visible, respected member of the community, such as a football coach in a college town, often may be a nominal partner in a business such as a restaurant or sporting goods store.

Sometimes, partners with a limited role come to regret their lack of involvement. For example, Mary Garvey, a silent partner in Grocery Ex-

Silent partner   A partner known to be an owner in the business but who plays no active role in running the operation.

Secret partner   A partner who is not known as a partner to the general public but who plays an active role in running the business.

Dormant partner   A partner who is not known as a partner to the general public and plays no active role in the company.

Nominal partner   A partner who lends his or her name to the partnership but plays no role in the operation.

The limited partnership is a popular arrangement for risky ventures such as oil and gas exploration. This rig, owned by Union Exploration Partners (UXP), is the site of a natural gas discovery. Individuals who invest in UXP contribute funds to the company in exchange for being made limited partners.

Source: Photo courtesy of UNOCAL. © 1986 Bob Thomason.

press, was dismayed by the performance of the San Francisco phone-order grocer. The Internal Revenue Service was about to padlock the warehouse for overdue payroll taxes, and Garvey discovered that the store was losing customers because it was constantly out of stock and delivery service wasn't always reliable. Garvey wrested control of the business from her partners, improved services, restocked the shelves, and turned Grocery Express into a prospering enterprise.[3] In so doing, she abandoned her status as a silent partner but turned the business into a success.

Advantages of the Partnership

Like proprietorships, partnerships offer advantages and disadvantages. Some of the more important benefits are ease of formation, expanded financial capacity, the opportunity to draw on complementary skills, the potential for profits, and lower taxes.

Ease of Formation Forming a partnership is relatively easy. The legal requirements are typically limited to registering the name of the business and securing whatever licenses are needed. If the partners want a formal agreement, they have to pay an attorney's fee, which is relatively small. In the case of the house-painting partnership, start-up costs might involve getting a license and, if a formal arrangement is felt to be needed, arranging for an attorney to draw up the agreement. In total, only about $100 is needed to get started in most locations.

Expanded Financial Capacity A partnership expands the financial capacity of a business. In contrast to the sole proprietorship, which relies exclusively on the financial resources of one person, the partnership can draw on the funds of two or more owners. This usually makes the business a much better risk, meaning that lenders are more likely to grant a line of credit (a specified amount of funds that the partnership can draw from a bank) or make a loan. Additionally, suppliers and other creditors are usually more willing to extend credit because the general partners are personally responsible for the debts. Two or more partners in the house-painting business would be more likely to have the needed money themselves, to receive a loan for needed equipment, and to get credit from a paint store than would a single student starting this business.

Complementary Business Skills Since the partnership has two or more owners, the business can draw on complementary business skills. For instance, one partner may be effective at selling, while another is a whiz in financial matters. A third may know a great deal about the technical aspects of the operation. Collectively, the partners can make better decisions than the average sole proprietor. In the painting partnership, one partner might be good at soliciting new jobs. Another might be good at keeping the books and getting the best deals on supplies. Still another might be a good on-site supervisor, assuring quality and keeping everybody motivated and working hard. These complementary skills also have a beneficial side effect. By sharing and dividing up the work, the partners can reduce the number of hours each has to work.

Profit Potential Although many large partnerships such as real estate ventures are set up so that the limited partners can show losses for tax purposes in the early years, there is nevertheless great potential for profit in the partnership form of ownership. The expertise and resources of the partners often allow the partnership to develop and cater to a market that is beyond the capabilities of a sole proprietor but is too small to attract the competitive attention of a large corporation. In contrast to a sole proprietorship, the painting partnership could cover a larger area and do more work. It might also receive quantity discounts on painting supplies.

Lower Taxes Partners, like sole proprietors, are taxed as individuals. Depending on the amount of profits the partnership generates, a partner's tax liability could be lower than if the business paid corporate rates and he or she paid taxes on income from the corporation. Thus, the painting partners may pay less tax than if they had incorporated.

Disadvantages of the Partnership

Business people considering a partnership need to be aware of the drawbacks of this form of ownership. Some of the major disadvantages are unlimited liability, the potential for conflicts among the partners, lack of continuity, lack of flexibility, and a complex procedure for dissolution.

Unlimited Liability General partners face unlimited liability for the partnership's debts. If the partnership's obligations exceed its income and ability to borrow, the general partners must make up the difference from their personal assets.

In a general partnership, where all owners are general partners and therefore have unlimited liability, the agreement usually states that partners will share profits and losses according to the percentage of their contribution. For example, a partner who puts up half of the initial capital and does half the work receives half of the profits and must pay half of the losses. On the other hand, a partner who puts up only one-fifth of the capital and does little of the work will get one-fifth of the profits and must pay one-fifth of the losses.

If any of the partners are unable to pay their share, the other general partners are personally liable. The same is true of lawsuits; each general partner is liable for the actions of all the partners. Thus, relatively wealthy partners could find their liability expanded to include the operating debts of their less well-off partners. If the painting partnership owed $800 at the end of the summer and one of the partners was unable to pay, the other partners would have to come up with the whole amount. Although the paying partner or partners can sue the delinquent partner, they may not get anything.

Interpersonal Conflicts Sometimes conflicts arise among the partners. While partners often initially agree on which areas of operation each will handle, this agreement often breaks down. A partner begins making decisions that one of the others is supposed to handle, or the partners begin challenging each other's judgment. This squabbling and interpersonal conflict can seriously cut into business efficiency and, in some cases, can set the business back financially. For example, if one of the partners had agreed to paint full-time but now wants to start soliciting business for the partnership or keeping the books instead, the consequences could be arguments, hard feelings, and inefficient operations.

Lack of Continuity If one of the partners dies, becomes disabled, moves out of town, goes to jail, or simply wants to withdraw from the partnership, the existing partnership terminates. When there are only two partners, this is seldom a major problem. The remaining owner may choose to operate the enterprise as a sole proprietorship. However, when several partners are involved, one partner's withdrawal may spell trouble for the entire operation. For example, if the wealthiest member withdraws out of dissatisfaction at having been obligated to pay more than her share of last year's losses, the business may be unable to continue under any circumstance.

Lack of Flexibility Closely related to the continuity problem is the inflexibility of adding new partners. This may happen when some, but not all, of the existing partners want to bring in another partner. The agreement usually spells out that everyone must concur with such a decision, but as the number of partners increases, unanimous agreement usually becomes extremely difficult to achieve. Thus, flexibility suffers. In the painting partnership, one partner might welcome the enthusiasm of a prospective new partner, while the other partners might doubt the prospect's reliability.

Complex Dissolution Dissolving a partnership is more complex than ending a sole proprietorship. The agreement usually spells out the method of dividing up and dissolving the business. In the case of a two-person partnership, this seldom presents a major problem. However, if there

These color tubes for televisions are the product of a joint venture between Westinghouse and Toshiba. The plant is located in Elmira, New York. While Japanese companies such as Toshiba use joint ventures to enter the U.S. market, U.S. companies use joint ventures with foreign companies as a way to grow internationally.

Source: Courtesy of Westinghouse Electric Corporation.

are a number of partners, even a written partnership agreement may fail to prevent disagreements about how much the enterprise is worth and who gets what. The problem is worse when some of the partners feel, rightly or wrongly, that they contributed relatively more to the business. Another problem arises if only some of the partners want to dissolve the current partnership and start a new one. This entails buying out some of the present partners at a mutually agreed-upon price. In the painting partnership, the wealthy partner who bailed out the business during a bad year might object to a final distribution that does not favor her.

Business people considering a partnership must weigh its pros and cons in a given business situation to determine whether this is the best form of ownership. The ideal form of ownership may turn out to be a variation of a partnership, such as a joint venture.

Joint Ventures

Particularly important in today's entrepreneurial climate is a special form of ownership called a **joint venture.** In this form of ownership, described in Chapter 1 as a venture, two or more investors or firms share the control and property rights of an enterprise. When viewed as a partnership, it is usually temporary and has the purpose of carrying out a single business project. When the project is completed, the participants dissolve the joint venture. During the life of this form of business ownership, each partner is a general partner.

Joint ventures have become popular in real estate developments. A group of investors pool their funds to build or purchase houses or apartments. Once they are sold, the partnership arrangement comes to an end.

Although joint ventures viewed as partnerships usually involve individual investors, joint ventures can also involve separate businesses serving in a more long-term relationship. For example, high-tech firms use them to combine their talents to develop, manufacture, and market such products as drugs, chemicals, and computer hardware. Automakers from the United States and Japan (for example, GM and Toyota) have used joint ventures to attempt to gain market share by combining their manufacturing and marketing efforts.

> **Joint venture** A type of joint ownership that, when viewed as a partnership, is usually temporary and is created for the purpose of carrying out a single business project.

Checkpoint

1. Define three types of partners.
2. What are two advantages and two disadvantages of partnerships?

The Corporation

Some business owners seek a form of ownership that is more durable than a sole proprietorship or partnership, which have no legal existence apart from their owners. They might prefer a business that constitutes a separate artificial entity in the eyes of the law. These owners would want to form a **corporation,** a body established by law and existing distinct

> **Corporation** A body established by law and existing distinct from the individuals who invest in and control it.

from the individuals who invest in and control it. The corporation may take one of a variety of forms, described in Table 5.1.

The corporate form is particularly important in the study of modern business because so many of the country's largest and most powerful firms are incorporated. In fact, while corporations constitute just over 20 percent of all business firms, they account for more than 90 percent of all sales and 80 percent of all profits. Corporations also account for more than 70 percent of all wages paid to workers in the United States. Many corporations have payrolls of over 100,000 employees. No wonder that in most people's minds, American business—especially big business—and corporations are one and the same.

Table 5.2 reports the sales and profits of the ten largest industrial corporations in the United States. These corporations, of course, are much larger than any sole proprietorships or partnerships. However, despite the visibility and power of these large corporations, some of which generate more revenues than the economies of many countries around the world, most corporations are relatively small. In fact, three-fourths of U.S. corporations generate less than $500,000 in annual sales.[4]

T A B L E   5.1   **Types of Corporations**

Type	Definition	Example
Public corporation	A business that operates for the purpose of making a profit for the shareholders and has its stock traded in the open market.	General Electric
Private corporation	A profit-making enterprise whose stock is held by a small group of owners and is unavailable for purchase by the general public.	Levi Strauss
Municipal corporation	A city or township that carries on its governmental functions under a charter granted by the state.	City of Chicago
Government-owned corporation	A federal, state, or local business that is controlled by the government and functions for the welfare of the public.	Tennessee Valley Authority
Quasipublic corporation	A business that is partly owned by the government and partly owned by private investors; can also be a private venture that is subsidized by the government because its operation is important to society.	Comsat (Communication Satellite Corporation)
Nonprofit corporation	An enterprise that is incorporated in order to limit liability and whose purpose is for social service rather than profit.	Stanford University
Single-person corporation	A corporation owned by one individual, usually with the purpose of escaping high personal income taxes.	Authors, consultants, athletes, movie stars
S corporation	A corporation that elects to be taxed as a partnership, while maintaining the benefits of incorporation such as limited liability. Used to be called a "subchapter S" corporation.	A small number of investors (fewer than 35 under current law) who get together for a real estate project or to buy a small business

Corporations are the biggest employers. The 24,000 employees of publisher Knight-Ridder, including the ones shown here, include white- and blue-collar workers with jobs around the nation. In fact, Knight-Ridder journalists even have assignments overseas.

Source: Courtesy of Knight-Ridder, Incorporated.

Forming a Corporation

To incorporate, the owners must obtain the permission of the state in which they want to incorporate. Most firms incorporate in the state where they intend to do business. However, large corporations, or those that intend to do business nationwide, typically compare the benefits different states offer. Many prefer Delaware because of its lenient tax structure. An incorporated business is called a **domestic corporation** in

Domestic corporation A business operating in the state where it is incorporated.

T A B L E 5.2 **The Ten Largest Industrial Corporations in the United States**

Company	Sales (in Thousands)	Profit (in Thousands)
General Motors	$101,781,900	$3,550,900
Exxon	76,416,000	4,840,000
Ford Motor	71,643,400	4,625,200
International Business Machines	54,217,000	5,258,000
Mobil	51,223,000	1,258,000
General Electric	39,315,000	2,915,000
Texaco	34,372,000	(4,407,000)[a]
American Telephone & Telegraph	33,598,000	2,044,000
E. I. du Pont	30,468,000	1,786,000
Chrysler	26,257,700	1,289,700

[a]Loss.

the state where it is incorporated, and a **foreign corporation** in all other states. Not to be confused with a foreign corporation, an **alien corporation** is incorporated in one country but operating in another. Most large corporations are all three—domestic in the state where they incorporate, and because they have facilities in other states and countries, they are also foreign and alien corporations.

The first step in forming a corporation is to submit articles of incorporation to the appropriate state official, usually the secretary of state. These articles are documents that describe such things as:

Name of the corporation

Purposes for which the business is being organized

Number and types of stock that the corporation will have the authority to issue

Rights and privileges of the stockholders

Address of the office of the corporation

How long the company will remain in existence

Names and addresses of the initial board of directors

When the filing is complete and the state gives its approval, the secretary of that state will issue the company a corporate charter. This charter is a contract between the corporation and the state and recognizes the formation of the company in the eyes of the state. Any major changes in the way the company does business will require a change in this charter.

Corporate Structure

According to the corporate charter, the stockholders own the corporation and have the right to elect a board of directors to oversee the company's activities. The board chooses officers; the officers, in turn, hire the personnel to run the organization. Figure 5.2 illustrates this process.

Stockholders The corporation's **stockholders** are individuals who have purchased shares of stock in the corporation. The stockholders who own shares in the company and elect the board of directors are called common stockholders. (Preferred stockholders are a special case, and their rights are described in Chapter 18.) Each stockholder receives a stock certificate that indicates the number of shares purchased. Figure 5.3 is an example of such a certificate. Each share entitles the stockholder to one vote.

The number of shareholders of a corporation varies greatly. Small privately owned corporations often issue relatively few shares of stock, perhaps 1,000. The owners of these shares are typically the president of the firm and perhaps immediate family members or those who helped start the company. On the other hand, large public corporations, such as General Motors or IBM, issue millions of shares. The average stockholder generally holds only a few shares, perhaps 100 to 200.

Stockholders typically have the following rights:

To sell their stock whenever they want

To buy newly issued stock before it is made available to the general public

Foreign corporation A business that has been incorporated in another state.

Alien corporation A business incorporated in one country but operating in another.

Stockholders Individuals who have purchased shares of stock in a corporation.

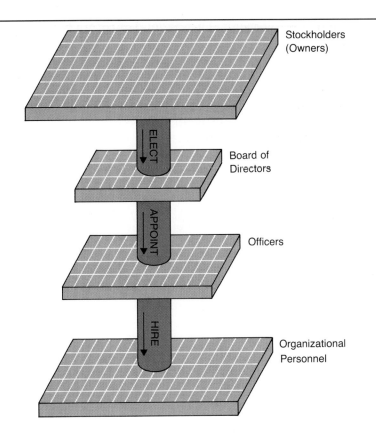

FIGURE 5.2

The Corporate Structure

FIGURE 5.3

Sample Stock Certificate

Source: Reproduced with permission of NCR Corporation.

To inspect the company's records if good cause can be shown for requesting such action

To vote on proposed amendments to the corporate charter

To vote on the certified accounting firm that will audit the company's books

To vote on the retirement or pension plans the company will offer its employees

To elect the board of directors

Proxy A written authorization that allows a specified person to cast a stockholder's vote.

Common stockholders are entitled to cast their votes to elect whichever board member(s) they want. If a common stockholder does not attend the annual meeting, which is usually the case, that person may cast votes by **proxy.** This is a written authorization that allows a specified person to cast a stockholder's vote. Often, the corporation will ask its stockholders to give their proxy to management to vote for its own proposed slate of directors. Figure 5.4 shows such a proxy card.

Board of directors The top governing body of a corporation.

Board of Directors The **board of directors** is the top governing body of the corporation. Its duties include:

Appointing and reviewing the performance of the officers

Helping formulate long-range strategies

Approving top management plans

Setting major policies within which all operations are carried out

Declaring dividends from earnings to be paid to the stockholders

Inside directors Directors who are employees of the firm.

Outside directors Directors who come from outside the company.

Large boards usually consist of a combination of inside and outside directors. **Inside directors** are directors who are employees of the firm. These people are often members of top management, such as the president, the executive vice president, and the controller. **Outside directors** are directors who come from outside the company. They are generally experienced executives with proven leadership ability or specific talents. For example, a corporation that needs help in raising funds might benefit from having a banker or financial analyst on the board.[5] The outside directors are usually from firms in other industries, so that their interests will not conflict with the corporation's.

FIGURE 5.4

Sample Proxy Card

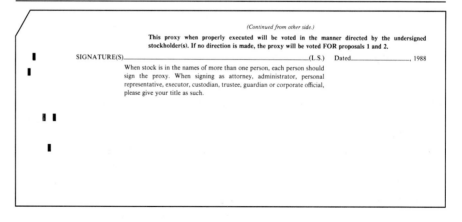

(Continued from other side.)

This proxy when properly executed will be voted in the manner directed by the undersigned stockholder(s). If no direction is made, the proxy will be voted FOR proposals 1 and 2.

SIGNATURE(S)_____(L.S.) Dated_____, 1988

When stock is in the names of more than one person, each person should sign the proxy. When signing as attorney, administrator, personal representative, executor, custodian, trustee, guardian or corporate official, please give your title as such.

Source: Courtesy of Freedom Federal Savings Bank.

Boards under Attack In recent years, board members of public corporations have increasingly come under attack from irate stockholders. In fact, it is estimated that the number of shareholder rights suits filed has quadrupled over the past decade.[6] Stockholders have brought negligence lawsuits against boards that have not kept up with the competition by merging with other firms, buying other enterprises, or increasing market share or profits. For example, when the Penn Central Railroad collapsed a number of years ago, the stockholders sued the directors for negligence in their duties.

As a result of these developments, some board members now refuse to serve unless the corporation insures them against any claims arising from such lawsuits. For example, Lear Petroleum Corp. in Dallas recently lost its liability insurance and some of its directors resigned. To help solve the problem, the shareholders of this company approved a change in the corporate charter to shield board members from personal monetary liability in certain cases. A recent study found that 20 percent of the corporations surveyed had been turned down by a prospective director, and according to the study, the problem of getting qualified people to serve on boards seems to be getting worse.[7]

Officers of the Corporation Besides stockholders and directors, the third major group in the corporate structure consists of **corporate officers.** They are legally empowered to represent the corporation and to bind it to contracts. The board of directors designates officers through election or appointment. Typical officers include the chairperson of the board, the president, the executive vice president, the corporate secretary, and the treasurer.

Officers have several responsibilities. They help the board formulate plans, implement strategy, and manage day-to-day operations of the business. The also report to the board and keep it apprised of what is going on in the firm. They usually do this through monthly or quarterly meetings, in which they report on operating activities and results. The officers are answerable to the board, which gives the board overall control of operations and enables it to fulfill its responsibilities to the stockholders.

Advantages of the Corporation

Business people incorporate because this form of ownership offers a number of important advantages. The major ones are limited liability, simple transfer of ownership, continuous existence, ease of raising capital, and professional management.

Limited Liability The owners of a corporation limit their liability to the money they have invested in the purchase of shares of stock. If an investor buys 100 shares of stock in, say, Chrysler Corporation, and this firm declares bankruptcy (which it almost did a number of years ago), the most the stockholder would lose would be the price of the 100 shares. Suppliers and bankers could sue the corporation for their unpaid bills and uncollected debts, but they could not get a legal judgment against the stockholders, officers, or managers of the corporation. This gives considerable protection to and greatly reduces the risks of those who incorporate.

Corporate officers
Individuals legally empowered to represent the corporation and to bind it to contracts.

The board of directors of SmithKline Beckman Corporation. These people, shown in the 1986 annual report, have ultimate responsibility for the company's policy and performance, although others may oversee day-to-day activities. Typically, directors are executives of the company, consultants, attorneys, and present or retired executives of other companies. Together, they offer expertise in a variety of areas of business.

Source: Courtesy of SmithKline Beckman Corporation, Philadelphia, PA.

Nevertheless, if a corporation is small and the owner wants to borrow a large sum of money for expansion, the bank is likely to ask the individual to sign the loan both as the corporation president *and* as a private individual. In this case, if the corporation goes bankrupt, the bank would bring action against the president as a private individual and force him or her to sell off personal assets in order to meet the outstanding debts of the business. But except for this case of borrowing as an individual, the bank's only recourse is against the corporation as a legal entity that can both sue and be sued.

Simple Transfer of Ownership If stockholders want to sell their shares of ownership in the corporation, they can do so relatively easily. For major corporations, where the stock is traded on regulated stock exchanges such as the New York Stock Exchange or the American Stock Exchange, the stockholder merely needs to contact a stockbroker at a bank or brokerage house, such as Merrill Lynch or Dean Witter, and have the stock sold. The broker will sell the stock quickly and issue the seller a check for the amount that the stock was trading for at that moment, minus a commission. If the corporation is a small one that is not listed on a stock exchange, or if it is a privately held corporation, the stockholder may have to seek out a buyer for the stock. Having found such a person, the shareholder is then free to transfer the shares of ownership to the buyer at the agreed-upon price.

Continuity of Existence Although the articles of incorporation specify the life of corporations, practically speaking, they can exist for an indefinite period of time. The founders of the company can die, the officers can leave, or the stockholders can pass their shares to their heirs or sell them to outsiders; none of this affects the corporation's life. In fact, many of the major corporations in America have existed for decades. For example, Standard Oil of Indiana was founded in 1889, General Electric in 1892, IBM in 1911, and General Motors in 1916.

Employees of the original Helvetia Milk Condensing Company plant in Highland, Illinois. The company, founded in 1885, later became Pet Incorporated, now headquartered in St. Louis, Missouri. Today with over 7,000 employees, the company manufactures and markets dozens of well-known consumer food products throughout the United States and internationally. Among the more popular brands marketed by Pet are Old El Paso Mexican foods, Progresso Italian foods, Underwood meat spreads, Pet-Ritz pie shells, Downyflake frozen waffles, Ac'cent flavor enhancer, and, of course, Pet Evaporated Milk.

Source: Courtesy of Pet Incorporated © 1985.

Ease of Raising Capital Corporations have a relatively easier time raising capital than do sole proprietorships or partnerships. The reason is that corporations generally have more assets and greater profits than most proprietorships and partnerships. Size alone makes corporations more attractive investment prospects. Large, successful corporations, such as General Electric or IBM, can raise millions of dollars in short-term loans by simply going to the large banks and asking for money. Such corporations are able to raise long-term funds through the sale of bonds (long-term loans, which receive detailed attention in Chapter 18) or additional stock. This is attractive to potential investors because they know that there is a ready market for corporate bonds and stocks, so they are not tying up their funds forever. Thus, if General Motors decided to build a highly modernized auto plant, it could readily raise the necessary funds by selling bonds or by issuing and selling more stock.

Professional Management Corporations have the advantage of professional management. While sole proprietorships and partnerships are generally managed by the self-employed manager or one of a few general partners, the owners of corporations, especially large ones, are not necessarily the managers. The owners purchase stock and elect the board of directors, which in turn brings in professional managers to run the operation. Although corporate managers generally own shares of stock in the company, they generally do not represent a significant percentage of the ownership.

The top managers (the corporate officers) hire specialists to handle areas such as advertising, accounting, engineering, and legal duties. They also employ skilled functional managers to handle the areas of production, marketing, personnel, and finance. These professional managers and specialists bring a degree of skill and knowledge that the average proprietor or general partner simply cannot match. This allows the corporation to operate efficiently and take advantage of market opportunities. The result can be dynamic growth and high profits.

Disadvantages of the Corporation

Along with these benefits of corporate ownership come some disadvantages. The primary ones are taxation, costs of formation, and government restrictions.

The Tax Burden Although the latest tax laws have offered some relief, the owners of corporations still can have a relatively heavy tax burden. Corporations may be subject to higher tax rates than sole proprietorships or partnerships, which are taxed at individual rates. Additionally, any dividends the stockholders receive come from after-tax earnings of the corporation, and these dividends are *again* eligible for taxation on the individual stockholder's income tax return. Sole proprietors and partnerships can avoid this double taxation.

Some states provide tax relief to businesses that take the form of **S corporations.** These are small corporations (fewer than 35 stockholders) that are taxed as partnerships but maintain the rights and liabilities of the corporate form of ownership. S corporations were formerly called subchapter S corporations.

S corporation A corporation that has fewer than 35 stockholders and is taxed as a partnership but maintains the rights and liabilities of a corporation.

Cost and Trouble of Formation Forming a corporation can be expensive. Corporations encounter a number of different types of organizing fees, such as expenses associated with securing the original charter, fees that must be paid to do business in states where the business is not incorporated, and legal expenses associated with the start-up activities. Besides these monetary costs, the original owners must expend time and trouble to go through all the procedures required for incorporation. The previously discussed student-run businesses of word processing and house painting would not be good candidates to form corporations, because the expense and effort required may outweigh the potential benefits.

Government Restrictions The government regulates public corporations more closely than sole proprietorships or partnerships. For example, they must file reports related to any sale of stocks or bonds, and these sales are monitored by governmental agencies. All corporations must comply with certain laws if they decide to merge or consolidate their holdings with those of another firm. Corporations must also file financial reports with the government and, in the case of regulated industries such as utilities, must submit them periodically. Thus, not only is starting a corporation relatively difficult, but the business must follow many procedures and regulations once it gets going.

When starting a new business or evaluating an existing one, entrepreneurs, managers, and investors must weigh the advantages and disadvantages of each form of ownership in order to determine which is best for them. Table 5.3 summarizes the advantages and disadvantages of the three major forms: sole proprietorships, partnerships, and corporations.

T A B L E   5.3   Advantages and Disadvantages of Sole Proprietorships, Partnerships, and Corporations

	Advantages	Disadvantages
Sole proprietorships	1. Ease of formation	1. Unlimited liability
	2. Retention of all profits	2. Difficulty of raising capital
	3. Direct control	3. Limited management expertise
	4. Ease of dissolution	4. Lack of employee opportunities
	5. Secrecy	5. Lack of continuity
Partnerships	1. Ease of formation	1. Unlimited liability
	2. Expanded financial capacity	2. Interpersonal conflicts
	3. Complementary business skills	3. Lack of continuity
	4. Profit potential	4. Difficulty of dissolution
Corporations	1. Limited liability	1. Heavy taxation
	2. Simple transfer of ownership	2. Cost of formation
	3. Continuity of existence	3. Government restrictions
	4. Ease of raising capital	
	5. Professional management	

Checkpoint

1. What is a corporation?
2. What are two advantages and two disadvantages of the corporate form of ownership?

Corporate Trends: Acquisitions, Mergers, and Divestitures

Business ownership is constantly changing. Fast-growing sole proprietorships and partnerships often incorporate. Businesses of all kinds enter into joint ventures with one another. Among corporations, major changes that have been important in recent years include acquisitions, mergers, and divestitures.

Acquisitions

When one company buys another and takes over its operations and property, this is called an **acquisition.** Large corporations such as General Electric and Chrysler are acquiring other businesses in their industry to reduce competition and increase profitability. For example, in the past six years GE has bought 338 businesses. The company is doing this to spread its risk, take advantage of the dynamic growth of the acquired firms, and diversify into other products and services. To get the NBC television network, which RCA owned, GE bought RCA. Likewise, Chrysler (the third-largest U.S. automaker) recently acquired American Motors Corp. in a deal valued at $757 million.

Sometimes these takeovers are friendly, but not always. Chrysler's takeover of American Motors was friendly because Chrysler was profitable and American Motors was deeply in debt; American Motors officers and employees welcomed the more secure company. In other cases, however, the board of directors and management of the firm being acquired is unwilling or reluctant to be swallowed up by another firm or by so-called corporate raiders. For example, one well-known corporate raider, Carl Icahn, has taken over companies such as ACF and TWA against the wishes of existing officers and management by purchasing enough stock to control the ownership and make the decisions. In these unfriendly or hostile takeovers, the acquiring company may dismiss the management team of the acquired firm, lay off workers, and diminish the identity and pride of the acquired firm. When Icahn took over TWA, he replaced the flight attendants who had walked off the job and paid the replacements an average salary of $12,000, compared to $35,000 for the strikers. He also slashed costs by $400 million and swallowed up Ozark Air Lines to bolster TWA's routes. This resulted in a dramatic turnaround and doubled Icahn's investment. Icahn's recent statement that "If I hadn't come along, the airline would have unquestionably gone bankrupt by now," is probably true.[8]

Acquisition The purchase of one company by another, in which the purchasing company takes over the acquired company's operations and property.

134

Mergers

Merger The joining together of two companies to form a new company.

A **merger** is the joining together of two companies to form a new company. Some of the nation's largest corporations have been formed through mergers. For example, General Motors merged with Chevrolet and with Cadillac in creating its modern automotive empire.

A number of mergers have taken place in recent years. The airline industry in particular has experienced a number of mergers in the aftermath of deregulation. Other industries that have witnessed many mergers include insurance, publishing, and retailing. For example, INA and Connecticut General merged to form CIGNA Insurance.

Divestitures

Divestiture The selling off of a business holding.

While many companies have been getting bigger by merging, some large corporations have recently been getting smaller by divesting. A **divestiture** involves selling off a business holding. This process has had a dramatic effect on forms of business ownership. Some companies such as Beatrice Foods, which started off by making many acquisitions, have in recent years found divesting to be the appropriate strategy.

Some divestitures have resulted from court orders for antitrust reasons (preventing monopolies and restraining free trade). For example, as was noted in Chapter 1, one of the biggest divestitures in American business history occurred when the courts forced American Telephone &

SOCIAL RESPONSIBILITY   CLOSE-UP

Looking After the Employees

When a company decides to sell one of its operations or to stop providing some good or service, one of the first questions it has to answer is: What will management do for those who will lose their jobs? Large corporations especially have been giving a great deal of attention to the company's social responsibility to its employees after an acquisition or merger. Some of the most common benefits being offered include the following.

Early-retirement privileges. Under this arrangement, the company gives employees extra time toward their retirement pay. For example, a person who has 20 years on the job will be offered another 5 years for taking early retirement. If the organization applied toward retirement 2 percent of the employee's annual salary for every year worked, the person with only 20 years' employment

would be able to retire at 50 percent of regular pay. Other companies are sweetening the pie by offering 5 additional years' worth of benefits to those who agree to retire within 12 months. This would raise the retirement pay of the person in the example to 60 percent of regular pay.

Free lifetime health benefits. People who retire with this benefit will get to keep their health insurance coverage.

Preretirement counseling and guidance. This benefit shows the affected people the work and leisure options available and helps them develop a financial plan for the future. As a result of these types of programs, many firms are finding that employees are more optimistic about leaving the company if this becomes necessary after an acquisition or merger, and begin to look forward to what the future will bring.

Telegraph Company (AT&T) to release control of its 22 operating companies. These were formed into seven independent regional firms, the "Baby Bells," that now handle local phone service.

Besides court action, divestitures result from a firm's decision that it cannot profitably operate one of its holdings. The company therefore decides to sell it. In recent years, Gulf & Western spun off 65 diverse subsidiaries worth more than $4 billion, Coca-Cola sold its Taylor Wine division to Seagrams, and ITT sold off more than 100 businesses in an effort to drop its marginally profitable lines and focus more attention on its high-profit products. Even while acquiring other businesses, GE shed 232 businesses worth $5.9 billion and closed 73 plants and offices in the first part of the 1980s.[9]

In the process of carrying out these divestitures, many firms are finding that the buyer often wants their products but does not intend to hire all of the current personnel. In these cases, the company selling the operation often provides its personnel with an early-retirement program or a severance package. For some examples of these programs, see "Social Responsibility Close-Up: Looking After the Employees."

Checkpoint

1. What is an acquisition? A divestiture?
2. What are two reasons a company might acquire or merge with another company? Why would a company want to get rid of one of its holdings?

Closing Comments

One of the most basic decisions in the field of business involves how the business is to be owned. The choices are for the organization to be a sole proprietorship or some form of partnership or corporation. Because each of these forms has distinct advantages and disadvantages, skilled business owners have to weigh the alternatives and often use more than one form of ownership during the course of their business career.

Learning Objectives Revisited

1. **Describe the nature of sole proprietorships.**
   A sole proprietorship is a business owned by one person. Some of the major advantages of this business form are ease of formation, retention of all profits, direct control, ease of dissolution, and secrecy. Some of the major disadvantages are unlimited liability, difficulty in borrowing money, limited management expertise, long hours, lack of employee opportunities, and lack of continuity.
2. **Describe the nature of partnerships.**
   A partnership is an association of two or more persons to carry on as co-owners of a business for profit. Some types of partners are the

general partner, who is active in the business and has unlimited liability; the limited partner, whose liability is limited to his or her investment in the business; the silent partner, who is known as an owner but who plays no active role in running the operation; the secret partner, who is not known as a partner to the general public but is active in running the business; the dormant partner, who is not known to the general public as a partner and plays no active role in the company; and the nominal partner, who lends his or her name to the partnership but plays no role in the operation. The advantages of the partnership include ease of formation, expanded financial capacity, complementary business skills, and profit potential. The disadvantages include unlimited liability, interpersonal conflicts, lack of continuity, lack of flexibility, and complex dissolution.

3. **Explain how a corporation is structured.**

A corporation is a body established by law and exists distinct from those who invest in and control it. Its owners are the common stockholders. Common stockholders elect the board of directors; sell their stock whenever they want; purchase additional shares of newly issued stock before the corporation offers it to the general public; inspect the company's records if they can show good cause; and vote on amendments to the corporate charter, on the accounting firm that will audit the company's books, and on the retirement plans the corporation will offer the employees. The board of directors appoints and reviews the performance of the officers; helps develop and approves long-range strategy, management plans, and major policies; and declares dividends. The officers are legally empowered to represent the corporation and to bind it to contracts. They also help formulate plans, implement strategy, and manage day-to-day operations.

4. **Analyze the advantages and disadvantages of corporations.**

The major advantages of the corporate form of ownership include limited liability, ease of transfer of ownership, continuity of existence, ease of raising capital, and professional management. The major disadvantages include heavy taxation, cost and trouble of formation, and government restrictions.

5. **Discuss acquisitions, mergers, and divestitures.**

In an acquisition, one company takes over the property and operation of another, whereas in a merger, the companies join together to form a new company. Sometimes acquisitions are friendly (the officers and employees welcome the buyer), but sometimes the officers and employees are leery of what will happen to them and they resist the takeover. A divestiture is the selling off of a business holding. By enlarging or shrinking an enterprise, the corporation attempts to make the enterprise more competitive and profitable.

Key Terms Reviewed

Review each of the following terms. For any that you do not know or are unsure of, look up the definitions and see how they were used in the chapter.

sole proprietorship	foreign corporation
unlimited liability	alien corporation
partnership	stockholders
general partner	proxy
limited partner	board of directors
silent partner	inside directors
secret partner	outside directors
dormant partner	corporate officers
nominal partner	S corporation
joint venture	acquisition
corporation	merger
domestic corporation	divestiture

Review Questions

1. What are the major advantages of a sole proprietorship? What are the major disadvantages of this form of business ownership?
2. Three neighborhood friends want to form a partnership to sell neck and shoulder massages to weary executives. What steps should they take to form the partnership? What should they specify in their partnership agreement?
3. Sandra Longstreet invests $10,000 as a limited partner in a partnership set up to construct and lease an office building. A total of 100 partners participate. Unfortunately, so many other buildings are being constructed in the area that the competition overwhelms Sandra's partnership, and it goes bankrupt, owing $1.5 million. Sandra has $20,000 in the bank. How much of this will she have to spend toward the debts of the partnership?
4. Identify each of the following types of corporations.
   a. Tandy's stock trades on the New York Stock Exchange; anyone who has enough money can buy shares.
   b. ABC Real Estate Group, Inc., consists of 20 investors who have formed a company to develop a parcel of real estate; they have elected to be taxed as a partnership.
   c. The City of Seattle has a state charter to carry on its governmental functions.
   d. ComSonics, of Harrisonburg, Virginia, is a cable TV contractor owned by its founder and employees.
5. What rights do common stockholders have?
6. What is a proxy? Why do you think stockholders often vote by proxy?

7. Why do corporations include outside directors on the board of directors?
8. The neighborhood friends' massage business is prospering (see Question 2), and they are thinking of incorporating. What are some reasons they might want to do this? What are some potential pitfalls?
9. What is the difference between a merger and an acquisition?
10. Why do successful corporations such as General Electric divest themselves of business holdings?

Applied Exercises

1. Go to the library and get data to update Figure 5.1. What do these data reveal about the three business ownership forms? Are these data basically the same as those in Figure 5.1, or have they changed?
2. Interview a local small-business owner. Find out what type of ownership he or she has for this business. Ask the owner to identify the reasons why he or she chose this form and the degree of his or her satisfaction with it. Write up your findings in a two-page report.
3. Find three people who own stock in a large corporation. Use relatives and friends if you wish. Without having them do any homework, ask them details about the company they partly own (for example, where is it headquartered, what are the major products or services, who are the officers, and so forth). What kind of responses do you get to your questions? Why do you think you get these answers? What implications do these answers have for business ownership?

Your Business IQ: Answers

1. False. There are many more sole proprietorships (one-owner businesses) in the United States than there are corporations. Corporations do, however, have the large majority of sales and profits.
2. False. In general, to set up a one-person business (called a sole proprietorship), a person goes into business merely by trying to make a profit. However, some types of businesses, such as a liquor store, real estate brokerage, or medical care facility, do require the owner to get a license first, which requires some paperwork.
3. True. Usually, they sign a formal agreement that allocates the responsibility. In most cases, partners who accept more responsibility are allocated a greater share of the profits.
4. True. The first step in forming a corporation is to request permission from the state by filing articles of incorporation.
5. False. Corporations do have limited liability; this means the owners are not personally liable for actions of the corporation. However, if stockholders believe that the officers carried out their duties negligently or improperly, they can sue the officers for any losses that resulted. This would be holding the officers liable for their own actions.

Amsterdam Landscaping's Independent Proprietor

You'd be hard-pressed to find a more independent-minded business owner than Robert Mulder, owner of Amsterdam Landscaping of Raleigh, North Carolina. The business, a sole proprietorship, brings in all of $50,000 a year. After expenses, including wages for the three part-time employees and the cost of running a 1976 Ford pickup truck, that leaves Mulder something less than $16,000.

While many business owners would be eager to make their business grow and bring in more money, Mulder is happy with things just the way they are. He opened his business for two reasons: he likes working with plants and shrubs and he prefers being his own boss. He believes he has achieved those objectives by setting up a business in which he is able to do what he likes doing every day and has the freedom to come and go as he pleases. He has enough work to keep him busy and, in fact, has turned away many prospective customers. He limits his business's growth in favor of spending time with his family.

Not long ago, Mulder had an opportunity to expand his business. He was offered a large commercial landscaping contract with a builder who was constructing houses that would sell for $150,000 to $200,000. If Mulder were to take the account, similar contracts would likely follow, and Amsterdam Landscaping would begin growing rapidly. Taking the account would mean Mulder would have to borrow about $30,000, hire more employees, and manage the landscaping projects instead of doing them himself. Mulder turned down the offer.

While Mulder's company is small, he considers it to be important. He notes that in a recent year, he pumped almost $23,000 into the local economy. Multiplying that amount by the thousands of other small businesses in the Raleigh area, Mulder estimates that their contribution plays a significant role in building a stable and healthy local economy.

Case Questions

1. Mulder says that many of his friends and customers think he lacks ambition. Do you think Mulder is ambitious? Why or why not? Is Amsterdam Landscaping a successful business? Why or why not?
2. Should Mulder have taken the major commercial account that would have enabled him to expand his business? Give your reasons. If he had taken the account, would he have been better off with another form of business ownership? If so, which form?
3. Could Mulder make his business more successful with another form of ownership? Explain.

You Be the Adviser: Sara's Decision

Sara Holmes owns a successful porcelain shop in a major metropolitan area. Sara's store is located in a large shopping mall in midtown. Although she pays a substantial monthly rent, Sara's store is so well situated that she has three times the walk-in traffic of her nearest competitor. Additionally, while porcelain carries a high markup, Sara's prices are 20 percent lower than those of the competition. In the three years she has been located in the shopping mall, Sara's sales have increased 47 percent annually.

Despite her high sales volume, Sara must carry a large inventory. That is because most of the porcelain is imported from Europe and delivery time runs six to seven weeks. As a result, Sara must reinvest much of her profits in inventory.

Last month, Sara learned that a store farther down the mall was going out of business. She would like to move into this new location because it is twice the size of her current shop. However, to do so, she would have to double the size of her inventory, and she does not have the necessary funds. Her banker has offered to give her a line of credit equal to 20 percent of the value of her inventory, but Sara believes there may be an easier way to finance the move.

She has two ideas. One is to take in two new partners who would each put up a sum of money equal to her current investment in inventory. For this investment, each would receive 25 percent ownership in the partnership. Sara knows two people who are willing to do this. The second idea is to form a corporation and sell these two people a total of 50 percent of the stock for the same amount of money as they would have invested in the partnership. Both of these ideas sound good to Sara, but she cannot decide which course of action to take.

Your Advice

1. What are the benefits to Sara of forming a partnership? What are the drawbacks to this arangement?
2. What are the benefits to Sara of forming a corporation? What are the drawbacks to this arrangement?
3. What would you recommend that Sara do? Why? Be complete in your answer.

Career Opportunities

Many of the most exciting opportunities in today's business world are for entrepreneurs and in franchising. Rarely do these people get started by reading the want ads; after all, few ads read, "Would-be entrepreneur needed to start company to sell a new product." But for those who can generate an idea and motivate themselves to carry it out, owning or consulting at small enterprises offers a host of possibilities.

Small-Business Owners

During the last few years, small businesses have provided two out of every three new jobs. Small businesses operate in virtually every sector of the economy. Even industries dominated by large corporations include many small enterprises that supply and support the giants by providing them with goods and services.

The specific tasks of small-business owners depend on the particular goods and services their business provides, such as helping produce the goods, selling directly to customers, and working with banks to obtain lines of credit and other financial assistance. Most small-business people spend 70 or more hours a week in their firm, often working Monday through Saturday.

Earnings vary widely. In many cases, owners make less than they could if they worked a 40-hour week for a large company. However, they feel that the opportunity to do things their own way more than outweighs the higher salary available in a large bureaucracy. Most small-business owners earn between $20,000 and $40,000 annually, but they can earn considerably more.

The long-run outlook for small business in general is promising. In particular, with the demand for services continuing to increase, small businesses providing services should grow steadily during the next decade. A couple of examples might be a type of "kids only" shop or a temporary help business.

Small-Business Consultants

Most small businesses were founded by entrepreneurs, who, as Chapter 3 pointed out, are not necessarily effective managers. Entrepreneurs know how to generate new ideas, and sometimes they can turn creative ideas into successful product lines or services. However, they often know little about the managerial or financial side of enterprise. As the operation grows and hires more people, the entrepreneur needs to develop a long-range plan and to coordinate this plan with a carefully designed budget. He or she also needs to know how to identify problem areas and to formulate steps for resolving bottlenecks. This is where the small-business consultant can be of value.

Preparation for this career includes education and experience. Consultants have often had a great deal of practical business experience. In some cases, they have been associated with professional consulting groups and have broken away to start their own business. In other cases, they have been executives in large organizations or have run their own business. While there are no specific educational requirements for becoming a small-business consultant, it helps to have a solid understanding of business fundamentals, including economics, management, marketing, accounting, computers, finance, and law.

The best place to start is often with a consulting firm or an accounting firm that has a management services division. These firms typically hire business graduates and pay around $20,000 to start. However, those who break away and do independent consulting can make considerably more. Consultants often earn large salaries by bringing on associates so that they can handle ever-larger consulting contracts.

The outlook for small-business consulting through the mid-1990s is expected to be very good. This is because so many businesses start up every year, and most of them will need expert help.

Franchisees

Franchisees are business people who have purchased a franchise in exchange for a fee and a royalty payment on sales. Franchises provide a variety of goods and services, from fast foods to auto parts to lodgings. There are over 320,000 franchisees in the United States, and this number is likely to increase by about 5 percent per year.

The franchisees' work is challenging. Although many franchisors train their franchisees and help them get the operation off the ground, a great deal of work remains to be done. Many franchisees work 10 to 12 hours a day, seven days a week, for at least the first year or two. The challenges and demands of the business are similar to those faced by owner-managers. Franchisees must be able to work well with others and to set goals and accomplish them. They also must know how to communicate effectively and to control operations.

Annual income depends on the success of the franchise. National franchises tend to be more profitable than regional or local ones. In most cases, franchisees earn between $10,000 and $40,000 after expenses, although well-established, well-located franchisees can make $75,000 or more.

MANAGING PEOPLE AND OPERATIONS

A critical challenge facing American business today is to maintain competitiveness. More effective management of people and operations is a key to meeting this challenge. The overriding objective of Part III is to study the ways in which business managers can most effectively get this important job done.

Chapter 6 starts with a broad view; it examines the management processes of planning, organizing, and controlling.

Chapter 7 addresses the human side of organizations, with particular attention to motivating and leading. Over the years, managers have taken different approaches to motivating employees. It is generally recognized today that money is not the only way to motivate people.

Chapter 8 focuses on a specific function of the modern business firm: personnel and human resource management. This function involves planning personnel needs; staffing the organization; and training, developing, maintaining, and appraising an organization's personnel. Modern companies anticipate personnel shortages ahead of time and develop strategies for handling these staffing needs.

Chapter 9 examines union-management relations. If a majority of employees vote to have a union represent them, then the union has the legal authority to collectively bargain with the employer over wages, hours, and conditions of employment. In these cases, managers need to understand ways to work constructively with the union.

Chapter 10 addresses production and operations management. The production or operations system for most goods and services involves input, a transformation process, and output. To use the operations system effectively, the production manager must oversee production planning, production scheduling, plant location, and plant layout.

When you have finished studying Part III, you should understand how effective managers go about managing their people and their operations.

Source: Courtesy of AAR Corporation.

Management and Organization

LEARNING OBJECTIVES

- Explain what skills are involved in the management process.
- Present the dimensions of the management function of planning.
- Describe the principles of the management function of organizing.

- Analyze how an informal organization works.
- Discuss the various aspects of the management function of controlling.
- Identify characteristics of organizational culture and ways to change it.

Your Business IQ

How much do you already know about management and organization? Test your business IQ by labeling each statement *true* or *false*. Answers and explanations are at the end of the chapter.

1. All kinds of managers need the same basic categories of skills.
2. Once managers have short-range objectives in place, they are ready to establish long-range objectives.
3. Managers should delegate responsibility to subordinates, but not authority; to do so would undermine their power.
4. Some successful retail executives believe that their store managers will do a better job if they have no formal office set aside in the outlet.
5. Regrettably, the only way to change an organization's culture is to fire long-time personnel and replace them.

Managers need to be able to work together to plan, organize, and control the activities of the organization. Here, top-level managers of Tasty Baking Company review the company's plans.

Source: Courtesy of Tasty Baking Company.

Looking Back and Ahead

Recently, Philip L. Smith applied the principles of management and organization. As chairman of General Foods, Smith led a reorganization effort to make the firm more profitable. First, he directed his staff to gather details on the organizational structure of several food companies and from this information developed a plan for reorganizing General Foods. He put into place a new organization structure that split General Foods into three independent divisions: General Foods USA; a coffee and international division; and Oscar Mayer Foods. This reorganization involved laying off nearly half the employees at corporate headquarters. Besides reducing payroll costs, the changes should help the company's profits by giving managers greater control. Instead of going through eight levels of management to get approval, product managers can now make many decisions themselves. They can move faster and feel a greater sense of responsibility. Smith, in turn, is freed up from day-to-day operations and can concentrate on more conceptual matters such as corporate strategy.[1]

Building on the foundations of modern business, which were described in Parts I and II, this chapter begins a discussion of managing people and operations. After first identifying some important managerial skills, this chapter describes the management process in terms of the functions of planning, organizing, and controlling. Directing, the fourth major function of management, receives separate, more detailed treatment in Chapter 7.

The Overall Management Process

Management The process of setting objectives and coordinating employees' efforts to attain them.

Management is the cornerstone of all business organizations. Like business, the term *management* has many dimensions and definitions. A simple yet comprehensive definition is that **management** is the process of setting objectives and coordinating employees' efforts to attain them. When managers do this well, the company prospers. Usually this means the company is growing and its profits and share of customers are increasing.

Managerial Skills

Every manager—whether the supervisor on a construction crew, the executive of a large high-tech firm, the accounting manager of a nonprofit organization—needs the same kinds of skills. Each manager must have technical skills, human relations skills, and conceptual skills.[2] What makes management jobs different is the way these skills are emphasized and combined.

Technical Skills Managers must be able to use the techniques and knowledge of a particular functional area or type of business; these are called technical skills. In the case of the construction supervisor, these skills might include understanding how to use and maintain the heavy equipment, fill out time sheets, and read blueprints. For the head of the high-tech firm, technical skills would include a basic understanding of the company's manufacturing processes, the ability to evaluate budget proposals, and insights into market trends and new product needs. For the accounting manager, these skills would include knowledge of accepted accounting practices and the administrative procedures of the company. In other words, technical skills are associated with the areas of production, accounting, information systems, marketing, and finance.

Human Relations Skills Managers also have to be able to understand, motivate, and lead people. In fact, one management expert has recently noted that, "the major difference between nonmanagers and managers is the shift from reliance on technical skills to focus on human skills."[3] Managers use these human skills when they motivate their subordinates to do their best, when they effectively coordinate efforts of the work group, and when they recognize and reward employee performance. These human relations skills are operationalized by managers at all levels by motivating and leading their human resources.

Conceptual Skills Finally, managers must be able to interpret information, provide policy guidelines, and see the relationship of the parts to the whole. For top executives, this may mean defining what business their company is really in. (For example, is Union Pacific in railroading or transportation, are Hollywood studios in film making or entertainment?) Or it may mean seeing an immediate difficulty such as a fall in profits as a symptom of a larger problem such as a failure to keep up with a change in customer tastes and demand. Lower-level managers also must be able to understand how the parts relate to the whole. Often, this involves seeing how one's department fits into the big picture of the entire company. These conceptual skills are operationalized by managers at all levels by the functions of planning, organizing, directing, and controlling.

A supervisor at AAR Corporation checks repairs of aircraft accessories. Like other lower-level managers, this supervisor needs strong technical skills, including understanding how the accessories work and how to fix them, knowing how to prepare a budget, or making sales calls.

Source: Courtesy of AAR Corporation.

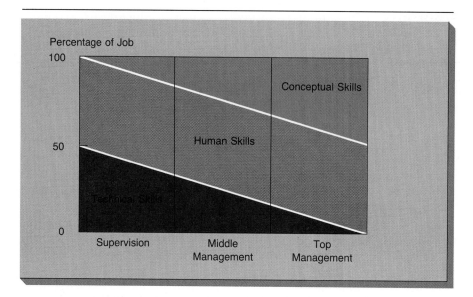

Levels of Management

The relative importance of these three managerial skills varies at different levels of the organization, because the perspective and day-to-day activities of management jobs change. In general, technical skills are relatively more important at the lowest levels of management. Lower-level supervisors, depending on the job, need to know how to run the equipment, set up the accounts, program the computers, and provide answers to technical questions. However, a large part of the supervisor's job is still concerned with human relations and conceptual skills. For middle managers (e.g., department heads, office managers, and product managers), the three skills are about evenly divided. For top-level managers, the conceptual skills dominate, the human skills are still important, but the technical skills have a decreased importance. Figure 6.1 shows this relative proportion of the managerial skills by organizational level.

Traditionally, American managers at all levels have stressed and been very good at the technical skills. However, recent successful company experience and comprehensive research shows that effective management is more than just a series of routine activities and technical know-how.[4] It is a complex process in which the effective manager uses the conceptual and human skills as well. This chapter focuses primarily on the conceptual managerial skills expressed through the functions of planning, organizing, and controlling. Chapter 7 discusses the human relations skills expressed through the directing function of motivating and leading. Figure 6.2 illustrates these functions in the management process. Other chapters of the book, such as Chapter 10 on production, Part IV on marketing, Part V on accounting and computers, and Part VI on finance are more related to the technical skills.

Checkpoint

1. What skills must managers have?
2. If you were a lower-level supervisor, how would your job differ from that of a top-level manager? Identify two differences.

Planning

Many years ago, Dick Gelb, the CEO for Bristol-Myers, overcame tremendous odds (about 1,000 to 1) and caught a 13-foot blue marlin. Now he is attempting to overcome similar odds by leading his company in the development of a blockbuster drug that could serve as a cure for cancer.[5] However, instead of relying on luck, Gelb is employing a systematic planning approach to accomplish his company's objective.

The modern management process starts with **planning,** which involves setting objectives and formulating the steps to attain them. The planning process incorporates five specific steps. As shown in Figure 6.3, planning starts when the manager becomes aware of an opportunity and ends with budgeting the overall plan.

Planning Setting objectives and formulating the steps to attain them.

Awareness of an Opportunity

The first step in the planning process, becoming aware of an opportunity, requires that the company's managers remain alert to changes in the marketplace. As customers' needs change or the competition offers new goods and services, management must look for ways to exploit these developments. For example, when people, especially young adults, became interested in physical fitness, aerobics classes became popular and makers of athletic shoes became aware of an opportunity. They designed shoes that would support and protect the heels and ankles of aerobic dancers and also looked stylish. Before long, Reebok, Avia, and other aerobics shoes were popular among those who participated in this activity, as well as those who wished to look like they participated. When research more recently showed walking to be the most popular form of exercise for Americans, the makers of athletic shoes again saw an opportunity and introduced or expanded lines of shoes designed for walkers.

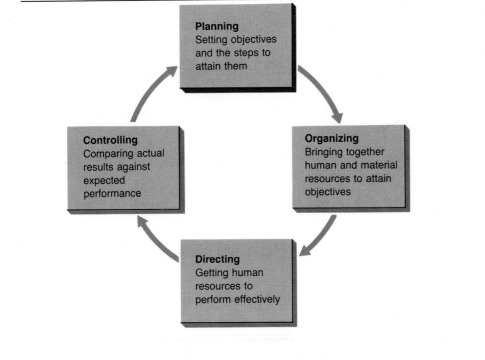

FIGURE 6.2

The Functions in the Management Process

FIGURE 6.3

The Planning Process

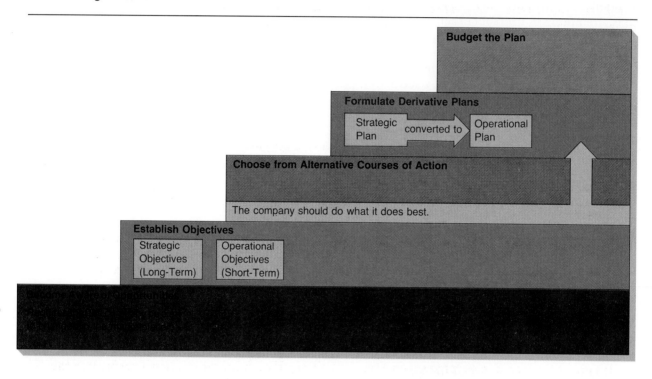

In both cases, when one company introduced a product, competitors quickly followed with their own versions.

Establishment of Objectives

In light of the opportunities they see, managers set objectives. These may take two basic forms: strategic and operational.

Strategic objectives Long-range objectives that help an organization compare itself with the competition.

Strategic Objectives An organization's **strategic objectives** are long-range objectives that help it compare itself with the competition. Increased profits, growth, and market share are typical strategic objectives. Another long-range objective is improving the organization's reputation in the industry and the business community at large. Achievement of strategic objectives requires the efforts of more than one department. For example, profits are greater when the production department keeps costs low and salespeople keep the orders coming in. A good reputation depends on a variety of accomplishments, including financial soundness and a quality product. Management also uses strategic objectives in developing a long-range plan, called a **strategic plan.**

Strategic plan A long-range plan.

Operational objectives Short-range objectives that help management control its internal resources and implement the strategic plan.

Operational Objectives A company's **operational objectives** are short-range objectives that help management control its internal resources and implement the strategic plan. For example, to increase profits (a strategic objective), managers want high productivity, low costs, and low employee turnover (operational objectives). The companies described in "Competitiveness Close-Up: The Internal Customer" set operational objectives to attain their strategic objectives. The operational objectives are the basis for a firm's short-range plan, called its **operational plan,** or sometimes its tactical plan. To ensure that the company is meeting its objectives and carrying out its plan, management will often evaluate progress each month or quarter.

Operational plan A short-range plan.

COMPETITIVENESS   CLOSE-UP

The Internal Customer

For many businesses today, the competitive edge is gained through customer satisfaction and service. Satisfied customers become repeat buyers and help businesses satisfy their long-term objectives for profits, growth, and reputation in the community.

At some businesses, managers have recognized an opportunity to extend this emphasis on the customer even further. They have determined that companies achieve good customer service through a chain extending from the customer back to employees who have no customer contact at all. An employee in the accounting department may never see a customer, but an accounting error in billing can frustrate a customer. Employees without customer contact can therefore contribute to customer satisfaction by satisfying whoever is at the next link in the chain. Managers who have recognized this interdependency have tried assigning customer service goals to all employees. Even employees who have no direct contact with the company's customers try to service internal "customers" — the departments or other employees to whom they provide services.

At Bell Canada, there was a 10 percent error rate in assigning and scheduling telephone installers. While these schedulers had no customer contact, their errors were causing a lot of dissatisfaction when installers didn't show up for appointments. To achieve the objective of better service, the managers of the assignment group met with managers

responsible for installations and service orders. Together they looked for ways to reduce the errors, considering their interdependent roles. With their new cooperation, the error rate fell to 1 percent.

At IBM, people in different departments set "contracts" with each other. For example, managers of the accounting department found that when their data processors entered data from various departments into the company's accounting system, they were making coding errors. The miscoding meant that errors appeared in the reports managers in various departments received from accounting. To remedy this, the accounting department first negotiated objectives that spelled out acceptable levels of accuracy for information to and from their department. Then they identified and developed ways to fulfill their commitment to attaining these objectives. Finally, they established a system to provide the internal customers with feedback identifying and correcting errors. This objective setting and follow-up have reduced the miscoding rates at IBM to one-fifth of the previous level.

Setting operational objectives such as reducing error rates helped these companies attain their broader strategic objectives of customer satisfaction and service.

Choice of Alternative Courses of Action

After setting objectives, managers must choose the courses of action that will achieve the objectives. In doing so, they follow the first rule of strategy: Lead from strength. This means the company should do what it can do best. If the company is a large manufacturer with low cost per unit, it will seek markets where price is important in selling the product. If the firm is small but provides excellent service, it will seek markets where customers are willing to pay more because the company caters to their needs.

Some industries use both of these approaches profitably. For example, in the airline industry, a low-price strategy will attract many vacationers who find it cheaper to fly than to drive or take a bus. The airfare wars that resulted from deregulation have clearly illustrated this. Other passengers fly first class because they want the comfort and convenience. This group includes business people who need to work during the trip. Even though it costs quite a bit more to fly first class, the extra comfort and convenience may be worth the price.

Formulation of Derivative Plans

Derivative plan The plan for a series of actions that convert the strategic plan into an operational plan.

The chosen courses of action become part of the organization's derivative plan. A **derivative plan** outlines a series of actions that convert the strategic plan into an operational plan. The example in Figure 6.4 focuses on the objectives that are part of these plans. Notice how the strategic objectives of profit, sales, and market share are broken down into operational objectives. The derivative plan helps convert the strategies

FIGURE 6.4

Hierarchy of Objectives for Derivative Plans

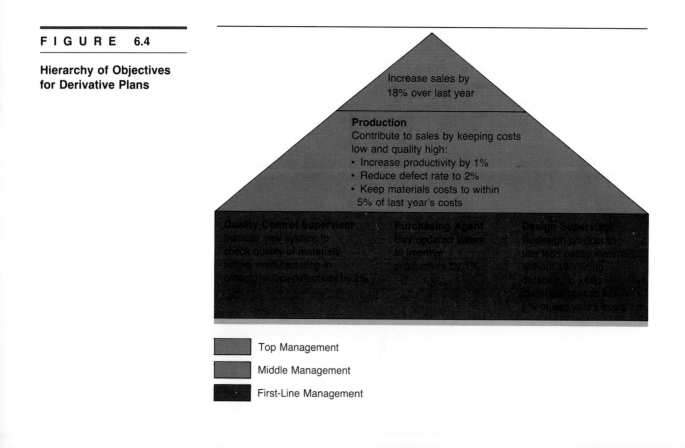

Increase sales by 18% over last year

Production
Contribute to sales by keeping costs low and quality high:
• Increase productivity by 1%
• Reduce defect rate to 2%
• Keep materials costs to within 5% of last year's costs

Quality Control Supervisor
Institute new system to check quality of materials before manufacturing in order to reduce defect rate by 2%

Purchasing Agent
Buy updated lathes to improve productivity by 1%

Design Supervisor
Redesign product to use less costly materials without sacrificing durability to keep materials cost to within 5% of last year's costs

■ Top Management
■ Middle Management
■ First-Line Management

into more and more specifics going from top to intermediate to lower
levels of management.

Budgeting of the Plan

The last step in the planning process is budgeting the plan. A budget is
a statement of expected results expressed numerically. (For more detail,
see Chapter 15.) Examples include the sales budget, the production
budget, the purchasing budget, the maintenance budget, the advertising
budget, and the personnel budget. The budget indicates the goals in
each area and may list the amounts the company plans to spend to
achieve the goals. For example, most companies spend money on salespeople and advertising in order to meet sales goals. They don't spend
the money arbitrarily; they follow a budget. The budget may also contain nonfinancial information on resources such as people, equipment,
or materials that are needed to attain the objectives.

Management by Objectives

One way to plan formally is to use a technique outlined a number of
years ago by management consultant Peter Drucker. This technique,
called **management by objectives (MBO),** is a system in which managers
and subordinates set objectives jointly and use these objectives as the basis for operating the business and evaluating performance. Although not
always labeled as such, MBO helps planning in many organizations today, from the biggest corporations to the local department store.

**Management by objectives
(MBO)** The system in
which managers and
subordinates jointly set
objectives to use as the
basis for operating the
business and evaluating
performance.

The generally recognized steps of MBO are to (1) identify the overall
goals, (2) sketch out the responsibilities of each subordinate, (3) have
subordinates identify the goals they want to pursue, (4) have the manager identify the goals he or she wants the subordinate to pursue, (5)
mutually set the goals, (6) periodically appraise progress, (7) evaluate
overall results, and then start the cycle over again.

The MBO process has received its share of criticism over the years.
When applied, problems can enter at each step. For example, top management may not communicate the purpose of the system, and subordinates may feel pressured to go through a "paperwork exercise" and
"keep score" of how many objectives they did or did not attain. If carefully implemented, these problems can be overcome, and MBO can be
an effective way of linking the overall goals of the enterprise to those of
the various departments and units.

For proper implementation, the manager must consider the overall
company goals when setting departmental goals. Then, the manager
links departmental objectives to employee objectives when planning subordinates' responsibilities and discussing their objectives with them. The
link to overall goals provides a basis for managers and subordinates to
determine objectives jointly and get everyone moving in the same direction.

MBO also stimulates communication between managers and subordinates. It encourages frequent follow-up to discuss performance and to
offer assistance. Employees usually appreciate knowing exactly what is
expected of them, stated in the form of goals they helped set. The evaluation, which occurs at the end of a predetermined period, usually one
year, also lets employees know what to expect.

156

1. What are the major steps in the planning process?
2. What are two reasons managers use management by objectives?

Organizing

Organizing Efficiently bringing together human and material resources to attain objectives.

Whereas the management process in general can be thought of as the cornerstone of business, organizing could be called the skeletal framework of business. The management function of **organizing** involves efficiently bringing together human and material resources to attain objectives.

The Impact of Organizing on Performance

Organizing can greatly affect performance for two reasons. First, work proceeds more smoothly at a well-organized company. If employees must cut through a mass of red tape or forward all decisions up the line for a final OK, they may waste time and effort and grow frustrated in the process. To avoid this, managers must develop an organization that facilitates decision making, communication, and work performance. The importance of an effective organization structure was brought out by the intensive investigation following the explosion of the space shuttle *Challenger*. The investigation concluded that management failure in general and an ambiguous system of authority in particular led to the disaster. Although there were technical problems such as with the O rings, the organization structure did not allow the essential communication to reach critical decision makers before and during the launch process.[6]

Organizing is also important because it enables managers to meet the challenges of the external environment, so that they can keep up with competitors. This often requires flexibility and change. Some innovative managers have responded by greatly reducing or eliminating levels of bureaucratic structure and accompanying rules and regulations. For example, Marcus Sieff, the former chairman of the British retail chain of Marks & Spence, took a year off to search through, evaluate, and then eliminate 80 percent of the company's paperwork. At the end of the year, Sieff piled up five tons of useless paper and hosted a companywide bonfire.[7] This extreme approach to streamlining the organization helped make this company one of the most respected in the retail industry. Other firms, however, have found that as they grow and need more consistency, they need to tighten up operations and create formal rules and procedures for paperwork.

Determining the Organization's Structure

The process of determining the best structure for an organization follows the steps shown in Figure 6.5. These steps involve formulating goals and objectives, developing coordination, delegating authority, shaping the structure, and dividing the overall structure into departments.

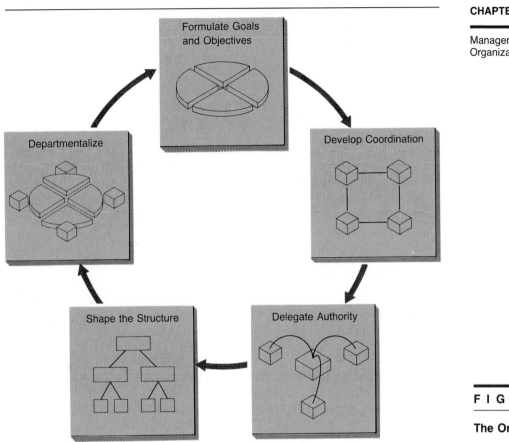

Formulation of Goals The first step in creating the organization structure
is similar to the planning process in its emphasis on goals. The goals of
the company need not be set forth in an elaborate policy manual, but
they should be in writing. For example, Dana Corporation, an Ohio firm
that manufactures axles, has no overall policy manuals but instead has a
one-page policy sheet.[8]

Goals should be specific. This helps management break them down
and assign them to existing organization units or create new ones. Examples of goals that would start the organizing process are:

> Attain a 15 percent growth in productive capacity.
>
> Expand sales regions to cover the Pacific coast states.
>
> Develop two new product lines.
>
> Establish branch offices in Paris and Rome.

Development of Coordination For separate divisions to attain overall company objectives, their work must be coordinated. **Coordination** is systematic, unified group effort in the pursuit of common objectives. When
coordination exists, everyone works in harmony. Coordination depends
on two things:

1. Well-defined tasks and objectives. When people know and agree
   about what they are supposed to be doing and when they should do
   it, coordination increases.

Coordination A
systematic, unified group
effort in the pursuit of
common objectives.

2. Willingness of managers to cooperate. The desire for teamwork is necessary for coordination.

Coordination is particularly important when more than one unit or department is involved. For example, Hallmark's biggest selling season for Christmas cards is November and early December. Thus, the production department must have enough cards made and distributed before November. Since Hallmark sells to retailers, the retailers need to receive the cards a few weeks in advance, in order to properly price and display them on the sales floor. Hallmark's wholesalers who sell to retailers need even greater lead time. It may be necessary to have the cards in the wholesalers' hands by October 15. Thus, the marketing and production departments at Hallmark must coordinate their efforts so that the Christmas cards arrive in the marketplace at the right time.

Authority The right to command.

Delegation The distribution of work and authority to subordinates.

Centralization Upper management levels make most of the important decisions.

Decentralization Delegation of many important decisions to lower management levels.

Delegation of Authority After developing coordination, managers next decide how they will delegate authority. **Authority** is the right to command. All managers have authority, but unless they intend to do everything themselves, they must also delegate. **Delegation** is the distribution of work and authority to subordinates.

How much should the manager delegate? This depends on the nature of the business or the particular task. Some firms, such as ITT, Polaroid, and Marshall Field's (the large Chicago department store), employ strong **centralization,** which means that the upper levels of management make most of the important decisions. Other firms, such as Sears, Exxon, Mobil, Dean Witter, and DuPont, use strong **decentralization,** which means delegating many important decisions to the lower levels of management. Some companies switch back and forth from centralization to decentralization, depending on the situation they are facing. For example, to become more flexible and respond faster to changing market needs, the head of IBM recently announced a switch to a highly decentralized organization in order to give more decision-making authority to division managers.[9] The manager's job is to determine the right amount of work and authority to delegate to each subordinate.

In highly decentralized firms, managers delegate important work, freeing themselves for other tasks. One example of extreme delegation occurs at the Ford Motor plant in Edison, New Jersey, which allows its assembly-line workers to use the Japanese-derived "stop button" to halt the entire line in order to correct a quality defect. This gives the lowest-level worker a feeling of control over the whole operation.[10] An example in the service industry would be the general manager of a Marriott hotel who tells all employees (from desk clerks and bellhops to department managers) they have the right to make on-the-spot decisions (concerning refunds or any customer request). For example, when a customer complained that he was told that the hotel had free strollers (which they never have had), the desk clerk made a decision to rent a stroller for the customer's use at the hotel's expense. Obviously, such a policy of delegation to front-line employees can have a tremendous positive impact on customer satisfaction.

When delegating, managers must keep in mind two important principles of organizing. Both principles consider responsibility, the obligation to meet the demands of the job. The first is the principle of equal authority and responsibility, which holds that if people are given responsibility, they must have the authority to carry it out. The manager should not delegate one without the other. The second is the principle of absoluteness of responsibility, which holds that while authority can be delegated, the manager still has responsibility. While managers may realistically pass on some responsibility, according to this principle, they cannot try to use delegation as a way to shirk their duties.

The extent to which managers delegate authority and the way they treat responsibility varies among cultures as well as among organizations. For example, no American executives of the Union Carbide Corporation resigned after the poison gas leak in Bhopal, India, several years ago, and no executives of Morton Thiokol resigned over the company's involvement in the loss of the space shuttle *Challenger*. In contrast, when Toshiba was accused of allowing a subsidiary to sell militarily sensitive technology to the Soviet Union, the Japanese company's two top executives resigned.[11] In contrast to the executives at Union Carbide and Morton Thiokol, the executives at Toshiba assumed ultimate responsibility for their company's problems.

Shaping the Structure Most important to developing an appropriate structure is to allow the enterprise to function in a way that is most effective for its particular situation. To achieve this, businesses often adhere to a number of basic organizing principles:

The principle of flexibility. An organization must be able to adjust to changing conditions. For example, 3M Company uses a "biological organization." To preserve the flexibility of smallness within a large organization, 3M creates a new division for any product that sells well enough.[12] This principle has also contributed to the highly successful Worthington and Nucor steel companies (in a depressed industry) who use minimills for flexibility in making specialty products.[13]

The principle of minimum levels. A firm should have as few levels in the hierarchy as possible. For example, Dana Corporation successfully went from eleven levels to five, even while growing rapidly.[14]

The principle of span of control. The **span of control** refers to the number of subordinates directly reporting to a supervisor. The principle holds that supervisors should have only as many subordinates as they can manage efficiently. While classic management theorists have recommended that the span be kept small, many successful firms such as Sears have deliberately increased the span in order to give subordinates more autonomy. Thus the length of the span may vary widely, depending on the manager and the situation.

The principles of minimum levels and span of control help determine the "shape" of the structure. For example, if managers can effectively handle only two subordinates, the structure needs a different shape than if all of the managers have ten subordinates. Figure 6.6 illustrates this concept. Notice that a **tall structure** is one with many levels and short spans, and a **flat structure** is one with few levels and wide spans.

Departmentalizing the Structure Taking into account a given level, managers structure the organization on the basis of some common characteristics. This process is called **departmentalization.** The most popular forms

Span of control The number of subordinates directly reporting to a supervisor.

Tall structure Structure with many levels and short spans of control.

Flat structure Structure with few levels and wide spans of control.

Departmentalization The structure of a given level of an organization on the basis of some common characteristics.

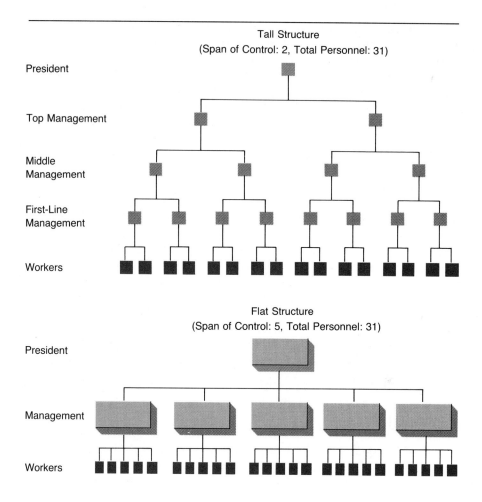

Tall Structure
(Span of Control: 2, Total Personnel: 31)

Flat Structure
(Span of Control: 5, Total Personnel: 31)

of departmentalization are by function, product, geographic area, and customer.

Managers use **functional departmentalization** when they structure an organizational level on the basis of major activities. For example, in a manufacturing firm, the primary activities are personnel, production, marketing, and finance. The heads of these four activities would be located far up the hierarchy, in most cases reporting directly to the general manager at the plant level or the president at corporate level. In an insurance company such as State Farm, departmentalized functions reporting to the president include actuarial, personnel, public relations, claims, underwriting, law, and data processing.[15]

Structuring a level of the organization on the basis of product lines is **product departmentalization.** Many communications firms are organized this way, with major departments or divisions for TV production, movie production, music publishing, TV stations, and radio stations. General Motors has divisions for its automotive lines, such as Chevrolet and Cadillac, and for its nonautomotive lines, such as General Motors Acceptance Corporation, which finances auto loans. Other large multiproduct firms such as Procter & Gamble are also organized by product. Large companies such as IBM have moved to product departmentalization in order to create larger numbers of smaller entrepreneurial units. The

Functional departmentalization The structure of a level of an organization on the basis of major activities.

Product departmentalization The structure of a level of an organization on the basis of product lines.

five new departments consist of separate, relatively autonomous units for IBM's large, mid-range, and small computers and for its communications and semi-conductor products.[16]

Structuring a level of the organization along territorial lines is **geographic departmentalization.** For example, Dallas-based Southland Corporation has about 7,000 7-Eleven stores grouped into five regions: eastern, central, western, southwestern, and southeastern. Each region is then divided into territories.[17]

The final form, **customer departmentalization,** structures a level of the organization on the basis of customer needs. For example, many banks have departments such as corporate banking, community banking, international banking, real estate lending, and portfolio and investment banking. Each department addresses the needs of a particular group of customers.

Depending on the industry and the nature of the good or service, any one of the departmental arrangements can work well. In fact, most large companies use combinations of them. For example, in a company that uses product departmentalization, the division handling a particular product is typically responsible for producing, marketing, and financing the product line. Within the product division, the organization is based on functional departments. Figure 6.7 illustrates this arrangement. For another example of departmentalization as well as other organizing principles discussed so far, see "Small Business Close-Up: Catering to the Customer."

Types of Organization Structures

When an enterprise adheres to the principles of effective organizing, an overall structure for the organization begins to take shape. While it can take many forms, the structure usually fits one of four basic designs: line, line and staff, functional, or matrix and project. Each type gives management a framework for coordinating overall organizational activity. In practice, most managers prefer to combine types of organizations.

Line Organization Structures A **line organization structure** is one in which authority flows directly from the top of the organization to the bottom. This structure adheres to the organizing principle known as **unity of command,** which holds that every person should have only one

Geographic departmentalization The structure of a level of an organization along territorial lines.

Customer departmentalization The structure of a level of an organization on the basis of customer needs.

Line organization structure Authority flows directly from the top of the organization to the bottom.

Unity of command Every person should have only one boss.

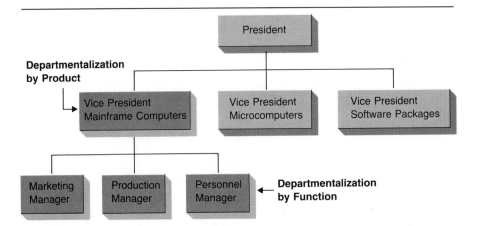

FIGURE 6.7

Departmentalization by Product and Function (Portion of Organizational Chart)

boss. Moving from the top of the hierarchy to the bottom, there is a scalar chain of command, meaning that every subordinate is a superior to another subordinate, on down to the lowest member of the enterprise. Every manager has direct control over his or her subordinates. Additionally, department or unit managers have authority over their own operations; they do not share control with other managers.

The line structure offers the advantage of being easy to understand and put into action. Authority and responsibility are clearly spelled out. Everyone has a single boss, so no one is left wondering who gives orders or whom to see with problems or questions. This means that decisions can often be made quickly and efficiently.

Most of the disadvantages of line organizations stem from the heavy responsibilities of the managers. Managers have to be good at handling many different situations, because all problems or decisions come directly to them. Being responsible for every aspect of their unit's operations may also mean that managers are swamped with work. When managers retire or are transferred, it often takes a great deal of time to

SMALL BUSINESS CLOSE-UP

Catering to the Customer

The banking industry is undergoing a wave of mergers and acquisitions. Big banks are buying out profitable and/or well-established small banks or merging with other large banks in an effort to create regional banking systems. However, this does not mean that small banks are doomed; far from it. Some small financial institutions are doing just fine because they have organized to service various customer needs.

The Stillwater National Bank of Stillwater, Oklahoma, is such an institution. Over the last 15 years the organization has dramatically changed the way it does business. Today authority is much more decentralized, and the personnel are expected to assume the responsibility of their positions. Central management no longer decides everything from lending $5,000 to purchasing toilet tissue.

Stillwater National looks carefully at the financial needs of its customers and organizes to meet these needs. For example, while most banks stay away from home mortgages, Stillwater National packages and resells them to investors all over the country. It also found that most of the banks in town were not ac-

tively soliciting the accounts of students at the local university, Oklahoma State. The bank began blitzing the students, offering free pizzas and movie tickets in exchange for opening new accounts. Before long, 70 to 80 students a day were coming into the bank to open accounts. The bank has become an active lender to small businesses and has hosted bank seminars on how to structure deals. The Small Business Administration has designated Stillwater National as one of approximately 100 "preferred" lenders in the country.

By creating specialized departments to accommodate these various types of customers, the bank has been able to improve its performance. For example, relative to its size, Stillwater's earnings top those of the average U.S. bank. It has a lower percentage of bad loans and lower overhead than its competitors. Overall, the bank has shown how an effective organization structure can enhance the bottom line.

train replacements and give them the experience necessary to meet the challenges they face each day. In addition, each department or unit is primarily concerned with its own goals and work assignments. Employees pay little attention to what is going on in other areas. When interdepartmental coordination is required, employees often have trouble working with outside groups.

Line-and-Staff Organization Structures When companies are relatively small, the line organization can often handle management's needs. As firms get larger, however, they need staff specialists in areas such as personnel management and law. As the enterprise adds these types of specialists, a line-and-staff organization emerges. A **line-and-staff organization structure** is one in which specialists help those directly responsible for attaining organization objectives.

A simple distinction between line and staff positions in an organization is that those holding a line position give orders and make decisions in their area of responsibility, while those in a staff position give advice and assist the line manager. Although it doesn't always happen in actual practice (except in the military), staff personnel are technically not supposed to give direct orders or make final decisions. Figure 6.8 illustrates what the line-and-staff structure looks like in a manufacturing firm.

Line-and-staff organizations are common in large companies. Several advantages underlie this popularity:

> Skilled professionals are available to provide advice and assistance in areas where the average manager is not particularly knowledgeable.

Line-and-staff organization structure Specialists help those directly responsible for attaining organization objectives.

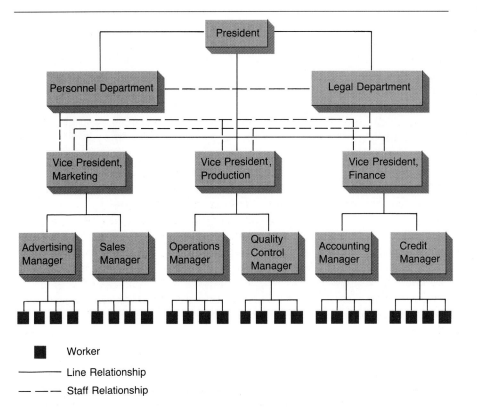

F I G U R E   6.8

Line-and-Staff Organization of a Manufacturing Firm

■ Worker

——— Line Relationship

— — — Staff Relationship

Line managers are free to devote their time and energy to producing goods and services. They do not have to be concerned about handling highly specialized matters.

While the structure is more sophisticated than a line organization, it still follows the principle of unity of command, ensuring a clear line of reporting relationships throughout the structure.

Despite these advantages, the line-and-staff organization may encounter additional tensions and costs. Although technically line managers do not have to accept staff input, they still may resent getting advice from staff people. Staff specialists may come on strong by telling experienced line managers what they are doing wrong and how they should be doing the job. If the staff people give wrong advice, it is the line managers who must bear the ultimate responsibility for the decision, since they are held accountable for results.

Line-staff conflicts can be overcome if staff would sell rather than tell their ideas to line managers. Furthermore, the use of staff specialists can greatly increase the administrative expenses of running the organization. Many large companies in recent years have been cutting back on their

FIGURE   6.9

Line versus Functional Organizations

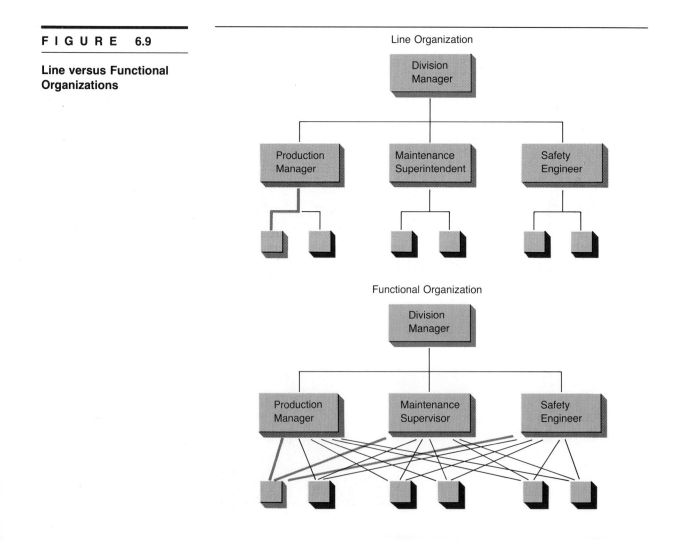

staff positions to reduce expenses. For example, in 1986, ITT cut its headquarters staff from 850 to 350.[18]

Functional Organization Structures In a functional organization structure, specialists are placed in line positions and have the authority to give orders in their areas of expertise. Figure 6.9 illustrates this arrangement. Some managers dislike a functional design because it violates unity of command and so may lead to confusion. For example, in Figure 6.9 each of the workers receives orders from several different managers, each of whom is an expert in his or her area. Conflicting orders may lead to frustration and confusion. Nevertheless, some managers feel that the benefits of this arrangement more than offset its shortcomings.

Project and Matrix Structures The line, line-and-staff, and functional structures are the traditional types used in most businesses. Recently, however, certain industries have become interested in two newer types: project and matrix structures. A **project organization structure** is formed for the purpose of attaining a particular objective and is then disbanded. A **matrix organization structure** combines elements of a line organization with elements of a project organization. These structures were first adopted by, among others, the aerospace industry (Figure 6.10). Now some large construction firms, such as Bechtel; banks, such as Citibank; and professional service businesses, such as certain accounting and consulting firms, use these forms as well.

Project organization structure A structure formed for the purpose of attaining a particular objective and then disbanded.

Matrix organization structure Combines elements of a line organization with elements of a project organization.

The Aerospace Corporation, which provides the federal government with architect and engineering services for military space programs, is functionally departmentalized into four groups: programs, engineering, development, and administration. Since its inception, the Company has accomplished its mission by using the matrix form of organizational structure. Technical working groups, such as the one shown here, provide diverse skills in a broad range of technical areas. In this group, engineers are discussing the structural mechanics of a launch vehicle.

Source: Courtesy of The Aerospace Corporation.

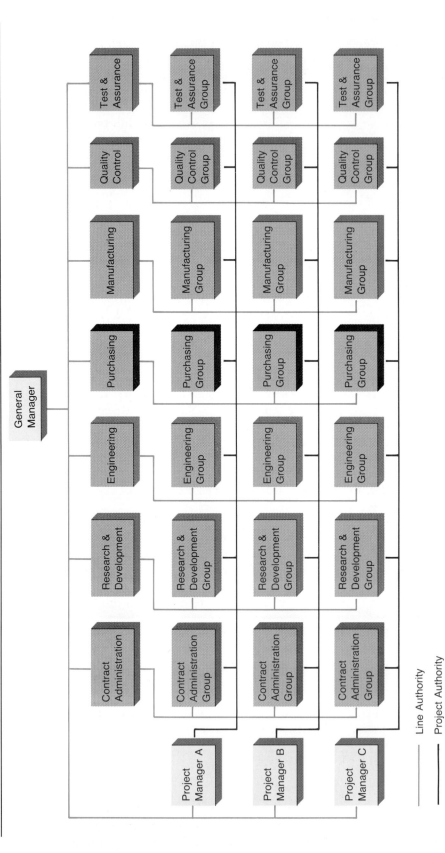

Informal Organizations

Through the organizing function described so far, management designs the **formal organization structure,** the explicitly established lines of authority and responsibility. But not all work takes place along formal lines. Often, employees find that using informal channels enables them to avoid red tape, cut across departmental boundaries, and get things done much faster and more efficiently. Research has found that successful managers, those experiencing relatively fast promotions, engage in significantly more of these informal network activities than do their less successful counterparts.[19]

The **informal organization structure** consists of the paths of communication and work created by the personnel themselves, on the basis of friendship and common interests. People who work with each other informally do so because they like each other or because it brings them certain benefits, such as mutual assistance or information. This informal organization exists within the formal organization structure. Rather than boxes on a formal organization chart, the informal organization involves people talking and interacting with each other. The communication part of this network is often called the company's "grapevine." Employees using the grapevine are following lines of communication they established themselves rather than the formal chain of command.

Formal organization structure The explicitly established lines of authority and responsibility designed by management.

Informal organization structure The structure created by the personnel on the basis of friendship and common interests.

Advantages of the Informal Organization The informal organization provides the company with a number of important advantages. It contributes to efficiency by providing a means of cutting across departmental lines and expediting things that need to get done. It lightens work loads for both managers and subordinates by allowing them to cut through some of the tedious, formally prescribed rules and procedures that often take considerable time and effort. Still another advantage is that it provides personal satisfaction in the form of social interaction and friendship with others.

The grapevine can serve as a safety valve for employee emotions, allowing them to blow off steam without going through formal channels and, perhaps, endangering their jobs with the firm. Finally, the informal organization provides the manager with feedback on what is going on in the department or unit. By tapping into the grapevine, the manager can learn a great deal about worker concerns, interests, and attitudes. It therefore provides a means of upward communication that is lacking in the formal structure.

As a result of these advantages, some companies have deliberately tried to use the informal organization. For example, W. L. Gore & Associates of Newark, Delaware, the successful company that makes Gore-tex, a fabric popular in sports and military clothing, has an organization where everyone deals *directly* with everyone else. There are no formal job titles, no bosses, and no formal lines of authority.[20]

Disadvantages of the Informal Organization The informal organization can cause problems because its goals are not always consistent with those of the formal organization. For example, while the informal organization may want workers to resist new work quotas, the company may need the work quotas to accomplish its objectives. Likewise, the informal organization sometimes resists changes such as new work designs because they alter the way the work is done and break up the current pattern of social interaction among the existing work groups. The informal organization often demands conformity to informal norms of behavior. Those who do not comply may be subjected to harassment or find themselves ostracized. In addition, the informal organization sometimes promotes false or malicious rumors.

Despite these problems, managers must recognize and learn how to live with and use the informal organization. There is some evidence that college students do not recognize it. A recent survey of undergraduates found that "knowing the ropes, being a team player and other important workplace concepts are not part of students' consciousness."[21] They need to know about the informal, as well as the formal, aspects of the job. Fortunately, the informal organization usually has more advantages than drawbacks. Effective managers accept the fact of informal organization and focus on learning to influence it and getting it to work for instead of against them.

Checkpoint

1. What steps do managers follow when they organize?
2. Why do employees create informal organizations?

Directing

Directing Getting human resources to work effectively and efficiently.

The management process is concerned with getting the job done through people. Managers have responsibility for the performance of subordinates. The manager has to see to it that subordinates do their part in helping to achieve the organization's objectives. Managers do this through the function of **directing,** or getting employees to work effectively and efficiently.

Directing today's employees is complex. It involves the two major human relations dimensions, motivating and leading. Because of the complexity of the subject, we investigate motivation and leadership in depth in Chapter 7. For now it can simply be said that along with planning, organizing, and controlling, directing is usually considered to be one of the major functions of management. However, since it draws mainly on the important human relations skills of the manager, it is given separate, detailed attention in this text.

Controlling

Controlling Comparing actual results against expected performance.

What do Swift, International Playtex, and J. P. Stevens have in common? They are examples of companies who had problems stemming from their control system. Swift had an oversupply of canned turkey, Playtex was stuck with 2 million pairs of pantyhose in outdated packaging, and J. P. Stevens had overproduced a large amount of kitchen towels.[22] These problems would not have happened if management had been effectively controlling the operation.

Controlling is the process of comparing actual results against expected performance. Effective control systems are designed to prevent problems such as those of Swift, Playtex, and J. P. Stevens or to catch them early enough so that management can take corrective action.

Controlling, like planning and organizing, begins with setting objectives or standards for performance. Without them, employees will cast about aimlessly, trying to guess what they should be trying to achieve, and any evaluation managers try to make will be arbitrary. Using the initial performance standards, the manager compares the actual performance with the standard. Are salespeople meeting quotas? Are inventories at the target level? Have complaints about customer service dropped to meet goals? If actual performance meets or exceeds the standards, the manager may want to recognize and reward those who are responsible.

If performance falls short of the standards, the manager is responsible for finding ways to correct the problem and to ensure that it does not happen again. This is called *feedback control*. In addition, effective managers monitor on the "front end"; for example, they carefully watch inventories and do preventative maintenance so that they can correct problems before they become serious. This is a proactive approach to control and is sometimes called *feedforward control*.

Requirements of Effective Control Systems

To be effective, a control system must be useful, timely, economical, and action-oriented. To meet the first requirement, the system must provide the manager with information that is useful and understandable. If managers receive volumes of computer printouts filled with columns of statistics, they aren't likely to know what to do with the information, have time to get through it, or be able to understand it. For example, a

Technicians use a computerized control system at Methodist Hospital of Indiana. The system automatically monitors the vital signs of 80 patients and displays information on video screens at a single location. If a patient's heartbeat becomes irregular, an alarm alerts a technician to summon a cardiac team. This is an effective control system because it provides timely, relevant information, is action-oriented, and frees nurses to spend time with patients.

Source: Courtesy of Hewlett-Packard Company.

manager in a metal-fabricating company received no less than 600 pages of computer print-out describing his operation each day. He said it would take him three full days to simplify one day's information into understandable, usable form. The manager's solution was to stack the print-outs in an empty storage room and subcontract with a trash-removal firm to remove them, untouched, once a month.[23]

The information must also be timely. Daily reports are better than weekly reports, weekly reports are better than monthly ones, and monthly reports are better than quarterly ones. Semiannual and annual reports are necessary for legal purposes and long-range, strategic planning but do little for day-to-day managerial control.

The system must be economical. The benefits it provides should exceed the costs of using it. It makes no sense to install a $5,000 control system that saves the company $50 a year.

The system must lead to corrective action by helping managers identify where the problem areas are and who is responsible for them. Managers can use this information to decide how to correct the problem. This action requirement makes the control system a reality in today's effective organizations.

Useful Control Techniques

In controlling operations, many managers rely heavily on two simple techniques: management by walking around and management by exception.

Management by walking around (MBWA) The management practice of visiting the workplace to find out what is going on.

Management by Walking Around (MBWA) To practice **management by walking around (MBWA),** managers visit the workplace and find out what is going on with employees and customers. Often they learn more by directly talking to people out on the floor and in the field than they do by studying quality-control reports and other types of formal feedback. For example, top managers of Campbell Soup Company do their own grocery shopping and regularly visit household kitchens to see how meals are prepared.[24] Many retail stores deliberately do not construct an office for the store managers, so they are forced to get out in the store and practice MBWA.

First-hand information allows managers using MBWA to assess more accurately what is happening and why it is happening. Many times, employees and customers know what is going wrong and how it can be corrected. By actively listening to them, the manager is able to identify problems and formulate corrective actions.

Exception principle Management should concern itself only with significant deviations or exceptions.

Management by Exception A second control technique is the **exception principle,** which holds that management should concern itself only with significant deviations or exceptions. For example, if the company projects sales of 8,000 units for the month and sells 7,991, the forecast was accurate, and no corrective action is needed. Minor problems do not warrant attention.

On the other hand, major discrepancies do require action. If sales were only 4,300 units, then the manager would want to follow up and find out what had gone wrong. The product may be falling short of customer expectations; the price may be too high; the competition may have increased dramatically; the sales force may not be selling the product properly; the advertising or promotion campaign may have been poorly implemented; or perhaps the standard was set unrealistically high. Whatever the reason, the exception principle calls for an evaluation and correction of the situation.

Checkpoint

1. What are the four basic requirements of an effective control system?
2. Describe two ways by which managers can effectively control operations.

Organizational Culture

Managers perform the planning, organizing, directing, and controlling functions within the context of the organization's culture. This culture is all-encompassing. An expert on organizational culture notes:

> The organization itself has an invisible quality — a certain style, a character, a way of doing things — that may be more powerful than the dictates of any one person or any formal system. To understand the soul of the organization requires that we travel below the charts, rule books, machines, and building into the underground world of corporate culture.[25]

More precisely, **organizational culture** consists of the organization's norms, beliefs, attitudes, and values. This culture was initially shaped by the beliefs and values of the entrepreneur who founded the company and is maintained by the managers who follow. In successful companies, these managers shape and encourage the "right" values.

Organizational culture
An organization's norms, beliefs, attitudes, and values.

Cultural Values

What values are the right ones? Research shows that successful firms share three common cultural characteristics:

1. They stand for something; that is, they have a clear and explicit philosophy of how they should conduct their business.
2. They pay a lot of attention to shaping and encouraging values that conform to the environment in which they operate.
3. These values are known to and shared by the organization's personnel.[26]

Federal Express is often cited as a good example of a company with the right cultural values for success. The dominant values of the culture of this company are customer service and loyalty to the company. Federal Express shapes and encourages these values by *doing* customer service (not just having a slogan) through personalized follow-up and assistance. Management promotes employee loyalty with an up-the-ranks complaint system and by rewarding employee performance. An interesting contrast, and a growing competitor for Federal Express overnight mail, is United Parcel Service. UPS's culture has values of efficiency. The differing cultures of Federal Express and UPS are symbolized by such contrasts as the lively orange and purple colors of Federal Express versus the dull brown trucks and uniforms of UPS, and the easy-going velvet-glove management of Federal Express versus the stopwatch, highly engineered UPS style.[27] Importantly, even though they have vastly different cultures, both companies are successful.

Types of Organizational Cultures

One of the easiest ways to describe an organization's culture is in terms of risk and feedback. The decisions managers make can involve high or low risk to the company and the manager's career. Feedback on whether the decisions worked can be fast or slow. Combining these characteristics results in the following four categories of organizational culture:[28]

> The *tough-guy macho culture* is common in organizations such as those in the construction industry, where people have to make high-risk decisions and thrive on fast feedback. Those who do well in this environment are often young and stress speed over endurance. They tend to be individualistic and enjoy winning.

> The *work hard/play hard culture* is characterized by low risk and fast feedback. Many sales organizations such as insurance agencies or car dealerships fall into this category. Successful people in this organizational culture tend to be team players who are also high achievers.

> The *bet-your-company culture* offers high risk and slow feedback. Firms that have to wait a long time before knowing the outcome of their decisions fall into this category. Examples are oil-well explorers and manufacturers who design and produce expensive, tailor-made equipment. In this culture, successful people tend to be technically competent and able to withstand long-term ambiguity.

> The *process culture* is characterized by low risk and slow feedback. Bureaucratic organizations such as accounting offices or routine manufacturing fall into this category. Successful people in this culture tend to be cautious and to follow the rules meticulously.

How Organizational Culture Develops

Despite their differences, the types of cultures develop and change through similar processes. The process of cultural development is complex. Creation of a culture is based on three important elements: heroes, rites and rituals, and communications networks.

A hero is a role model who embodies the organizational culture — someone employees look up to and admire. The public sees such heroes as representatives of the company. Well-known heroes in today's business world include Lee Iacocca at Chrysler, Sam Walton at Wal-Mart, Victor Kiam at Remington Products, and Mary Kay Ash at Mary Kay Cosmetics.

Rites and rituals reinforce desired behavior. Examples are an employee-of-the-month award and an awards dinner at which the company's leading salespeople are honored. Some organizations have even created their own reward rituals. When an employee of the Intel Corporation does a good job, he or she gets a handful of M&Ms as a sign of recognition. The ceremony began years ago, and everyone now keeps a supply of this candy available.

Communications networks are used to keep alive the stories of heroes and to ensure that employees adhere to the corporation's culture. For example, stories about Sam Walton bringing donuts to dockworkers and having a can of tuna fish and crackers for lunch with employees in their lounge are well known throughout the more than 1,200 Wal-Mart stores. The important roles in communications networks are storytellers and organizational priests.

A storyteller is a person who has been around for a long time and who tells stories of the "good old days" to reinforce the organizational culture. While these stories vary from one storyteller to another, the basic themes are usually that hard work will get you ahead and the firm really cares about its people.

An organizational priest helps guard the group's values, keeps everyone together, and offers recommendations for action. These people have usually been around the company for a long time and are familiar with its history. They use this experience to guide other employees. If a new manager has a proposed plan of action, the boss may say, "Check your idea out with Harry." Harry, the organizational priest, will either give the idea his blessing or tell the manager that it will not fly because top management always turns down such ideas. If the priest approves the idea, the manager then proceeds; otherwise the manager drops it.

Changing an Organization's Culture

Sometimes a corporate culture must change. This need for change often arises when the environment changes quickly. For example, Apple Computer was initially able to dominate the personal computer market with a culture stressing innovation. When IBM entered the market, followed by

At Mary Kay Cosmetics' annual sales seminar, the company combines training with inspirational programs and awards ranging from jewelry to automobiles. Here, the founder and Chairman Emeritus of this successful company Mary Kay Ash crowns Director Sandie DeVlieger Queen of Personal Sales during Seminar '87 in Dallas, Texas. Ash's visibility as a role model who succeeded at selling cosmetics, combined with the ceremony of the sales seminar, creates an environment in which the company's representatives believe in their own capacity for achievement.

Source: Courtesy of Mary Kay Cosmetics, Incorporated.

a host of other competitors, Apple tried to compete by selling costlier machines to the business market. The strategy failed. Apple found that in a more competitive environment, it needed a new culture that emphasized marketing. With a changeover in top management, Apple has since shown signs of moving toward a marketing-oriented culture.

Culture also must change when a firm starts growing. The culture that worked when a company was small seldom remains the best one. A small company's strong focus on individuality must give way to a concern for the management functions. To remain successful, fast-growing companies, such as Wang Laboratories and Wal-Mart Stores, Inc., which had or still have a culture shaped by the founders, have had to change, but not too much or too fast.

Changing an organization's culture usually takes a long time, but managers can guide the process. Experts recommend guidelines such as the following:

Put a hero in charge of the process.

Use rituals such as meetings to let people talk about their concerns and to win support for the new values.

If necessary, bring in outside consultants to help out.

Ensure that no one is fired as a result of the change. This helps generate further support for the new culture.

Checkpoint

1. What are the types of organizational culture?
2. Under what circumstances does an organization's culture need to change?

Closing Comments

This chapter identified the technical, conceptual, and human skills needed for effective modern management. The heart of the chapter described the management functions of planning, organizing, and controlling. Following the steps of the processes outlined in this chapter can simplify management and improve performance. The challenge for managers of today's organizations is to understand and prioritize managerial problems and to apply some of the emerging, proven approaches to planning, organizing, and controlling in a way appropriate to the organization's culture.

Learning Objectives Revisited

1. **Explain what skills are involved in the management process.**
   Management is the process of setting objectives and coordinating employees' efforts in attaining them. It consists of planning, organizing, directing, and controlling. While all managers use technical, hu-

man relations, and conceptual skills, the nature of the job changes by level in the company hierarchy. Technical skills are relatively more important at the lowest level of management, but the conceptual and human relations skills are also important. At middle management levels, the three managerial skills are about equally weighted. At top management levels, the conceptual and, secondarily, the human relations skills take on relatively more importance, while the technical become relatively less important.

2. **Present the dimensions of the management function of planning.**
   The planning function of management involves setting objectives and formulating the steps to follow in attaining them. This involves being aware of an opportunity, establishing objectives, choosing alternative courses of action, formulating the derivative plan, and budgeting the plan. Many firms today conduct their formal planning with the management by objectives (MBO) approach.

3. **Describe the principles of the management function of organizing.**
   Organizing involves efficiently bringing together human and material resources to attain objectives. The steps involved are formulating organizational goals and objectives; coordinating work; delegating authority; shaping a tall or flat structure; and departmentalizing the structure along functional, product, geographic, or customer lines. The resulting structure may be a line organization, a line-and-staff organization, a functional organization, a project organization, or a matrix organization, which combines elements of line and project organizations.

4. **Analyze how an informal organization works.**
   Unlike the formal organization, which is designed by management, the informal organization is created by personnel on the basis of friendship and common interests. It consists of people interacting and communicating with one another outside of the formal organization structure. Research indicates that successful managers use the informal network.

5. **Discuss the various aspects of the management function of controlling.**
   Controlling involves establishing initial performance standards, measuring actual performance, determining whether the performance was adequate, and taking corrective action if performance has been inadequate.

6. **Identify characteristics of organizational culture and ways to change it.**
   Modern management functions within the context of the organization's culture. This culture contains the organization's norms, beliefs, attitudes, and values. The four types of culture are tough-guy macho (high risk and fast feedback), work hard/play hard (low risk and fast feedback), bet-your-company (high risk and slow feedback), and process (low risk and slow feedback). Managers can change an organization's culture in a number of ways, including putting a hero in charge of the process; using rituals such as meetings to let people talk about their concerns and to win support for the new values; bringing in outside consultants to help if needed; and ensuring that no one is fired as a result of the change.

Key Terms Reviewed

Review each of the following terms. For any that you do not know or are unsure of, look up the definitions and see how they were used in the chapter.

management

planning

strategic objectives

strategic plan

operational objectives

operational plan

derivative plan

management by objectives (MBO)

organizing

coordination

authority

delegation

centralization

decentralization

span of control

tall structure

flat structure

departmentalization

functional departmental- ization

product departmental- ization

geographic departmental- ization

customer departmental- ization

line organization structure

unity of command

line-and-staff organization structure

project organization struc- ture

matrix organization struc- ture

formal organization struc- ture

informal organization struc- ture

directing

controlling

management by walking around (MBWA)

exception principle

organizational culture

Review Questions

1. What is management? What skills does managing require?
2. Why is planning important?
3. Why is organizing important?
4. Christina King works in the payroll department of a corporation with six divisions. Two weeks ago, Christina's boss said, "You've been doing a great job, and I think you're ready to take on something else. From now on, each Friday I want you to follow up with each division to make sure they get their time sheets in by 2 o'clock." When Friday came, Christina found that she had a difficult time persuading two division administrators to turn in the time sheets by

the deadline. When she talked to her boss, he said, "It's up to you to take care of that now." Does Christina have authority? Does she have responsibility? Why or why not? Has Christina's boss followed the principles of delegating? Explain.

5. How do managers decide on a shape for the organization's structure?

6. What is unity of command? Which organization structures adhere to this principle? Which do not?

7. How does a matrix organization work? Would it be a suitable arrangement for a store with ten employees? Why or why not?

8. How are informal organizations created? How can lower-level operating employees benefit from them? How can upper-level managers benefit from them?

9. Pete Maahs is the president of Wonderful Home Improvement Company. He has hired a consultant to develop a control system for his business. Pete has always thought that consultants only give answers and don't ask questions, so he was surprised when his consultant asked him what criteria the control system should meet. Pete said he'd think it over and give the consultant some specifications the next day. What requirements should Pete ask for?

10. What is the exception principle? How can managers use this principle to control operations?

11. When do managers need to consider changing the organization's culture? How can they bring about positive change?

Applied Exercises

1. From the most recent January edition of *Fortune* magazine, get the names of the latest group of America's ten most admired corporations. How does this most recent list differ from one five or six years ago? What conclusions can you draw as a result? Explain.

2. Two major U.S. companies are Ford Motor Company and General Electric. At the library, review what these companies do. Then, if possible, draw the organization chart of each and identify what form of departmentalization each uses. (Hint: Try to get a recent annual report.)

3. Wecleen Janitorial Service is a successful business providing cleaning services to the major office buildings downtown. Next week, Wecleen's managers will be meeting to develop company strategy for the next five years. As a member of the management team, you have been asked to prepare a preliminary plan. Following the process in Figure 6.3, briefly outline such a hypothetical plan.

4. Look through recent issues of business periodicals such as *The Wall Street Journal*, *Business Week*, *Fortune*, *Nation's Business*, and *Forbes*, and identify at least one firm that is best described as tough-guy macho. Defend your answer. Then find at least one firm for each of the three other kinds of cultures, noting your reasons for each choice.

Your Business IQ: Answers

1. True. Managers at all levels and all types of organizations need some combination of technical, human relations, and conceptual skills. However, the degree to which individual managers draw on each type of skill may vary.

2. False. First the manager sets long-range, or strategic, objectives. The manager then establishes short-range, or operational, objectives to meet the strategic objectives.

3. False. A classic principle of management is that subordinates who are given responsibility should also receive the authority to carry out their responsibility. The idea here is that subordinates must have some authority if they are to be effective. However, the delegator may be held ultimately responsible for the acts of his or her subordinates.

4. True. Some successful retailing businesses deliberately set up stores without an office for the store manager. This is so the manager will manage daily operations by spending time out on the floor directly observing what is happening and talking with employees and customers.

5. False. This actually may be one of the worst things to do. Firing long-time personnel may simply cause the remaining employees to oppose changes. Generally, the organization's managers should attempt to change the culture in other, less threatening ways.

Apollo and Sun Try Different Cultures

Two computer firms with quite different corporate cultures and approaches to management and organization are trying to beat each other in the same marketplace. Both sell products called work stations, powerful personal computers that engineers, scientists, printers, and money managers use for tasks such as designing products and planning investments. One company is Apollo Computer Inc. of Chelmsford, Massachusetts, a traditionally managed company with corporate values and beliefs that its managers have learned from experience. The other company is Sun Microsystems Inc. of Mountain View, California, an uninhibited group that seems to violate many of the traditional management approaches and cultural values.

Apollo, which basically invented the work station, has built on a reputation for quality and engineering expertise. Apollo's original systems were custom-designed, relatively expensive, and highly regarded. In contrast, Sun was the product of two Stanford business school graduate students who joined forces with two local computer experts. Sun competed by building a less expensive machine that used a standard operating system, so that it could communicate with other computers.

Apollo ran into problems when its main customers experienced a slump in business and stopped ordering. At the same time, customers encountered quality problems with Apollo's machines and began to be enticed by Sun's lower prices and standardized designs. Apollo redesigned its system to run on standard software, but has had to rebuild its profits and share of the market. The company's chairman says that the experience has made them more competitive and mature.

In the meantime, Sun employees are having fun. Every Friday is dress-down day, with most employees wearing jeans and sport shirts. An April Fool's Day tradition stipulates that engineers must torment their bosses. One year, the engineers disassembled their boss's Ferrari and reassembled it inside his office. The next year, they disassembled his office and reassembled it on a platform in the middle of the company's decorative pond. The third year, they placed the Ferrari on the platform in the pond. The boss worries that the next step is to bring the pond into his office.

Frivolity aside, Sun is growing faster than Apollo. Sun's management credits their dynamic growth to open discussion and debate. Yet Apollo's managers dispute whether their more formalized structure is hurting them. "There's a lot to be said for being professional," observes Roland Pampel, the company's senior vice president. Observers have wondered whether Sun can continue to keep up their current pace if the industry takes another downturn.

Case Questions

1. Which of the types of corporate culture characterizes Apollo? Which characterizes Sun?
2. Have the managers of both companies chosen the most appropriate approaches to the management functions of planning, organizing, and controlling? Explain and, where appropriate, recommend changes.
3. Why might Sun's management approach and cultural values hurt the company if the industry experiences a decline? What can Sun's managers do about that?

You Be the Adviser:
An Expansion Proposal

The Merkoff Corporation was founded over 80 years ago when a group of wildcatters pooled their funds and drilled for oil in Oklahoma. Their first well was one of the biggest in the region, and the Merkoff brothers not only became rich but took their early profits and used them to buy out the rest of the group. Since then, the Merkoffs have been in the business of oil exploration and drilling.

Over the last three years, the family members who now run the company have been thinking about expanding its scope of operations. They would like to do more than just discover oil and sell it to the large refiners. They would like to buy some refineries and a large number of service stations and move the oil from the ground right through to the final user. While it will cost approximately $1 billion to implement this plan, the chief financial officer for the corporation has reported that the necessary financing can be arranged. It is now up to the board of directors to decide whether or not to go ahead.

Management believes that a number of steps are necessary before it approves the plan. Most important is to anticipate how this change will affect the current organization. "We're going to be getting into new areas, and this will mean having to hire plenty of personnel, while still hanging on to the ones we have now," the chairman of the board reminded the other members. "Also, it will mean a major revision in our strategic plan and the need to control operations in a lot more than the five states where we now operate. Before we do anything, I think we need to discuss the impact of the change." The other board members agreed.

Your Advice

1. If you were a member of the board, how would you describe the company's current organization structure? How would you describe the organization's culture? How will this culture change if it expands into the proposed new areas? Explain.
2. What types of objectives would you expect the Merkoff Corporation to be pursuing in its strategic and operational plans? How would these objectives change if it expanded into the proposed new areas? Explain.
3. Would management by objectives be of any value to this firm if it decided to pursue its acquisition plans? What would be the steps they would follow to implement MBO?
4. Could the control mechanisms of MBWA and/or management by exception be used by Merkoff's managers in this business? How?

Human Relations: Motivating and Leading

LEARNING OBJECTIVES

- Describe how the major management approaches have changed over the years.
- Discuss approaches to understanding motivation.
- Present some techniques for motivating employees by improving the work environment.

- Describe the techniques managers use to motivate individual employees.
- Identify some basic leadership styles.
- Explain how leaders can choose an effective style.

Your Business IQ

How much do you already know about human relations in general and motivation and leadership in particular? Test your business IQ by labeling each statement *true* or *false*. Answers and explanations are at the end of the chapter.

1. The modern view of employees is to consider them resources of the company.
2. Flexible work schedules are mainly concerned with how hard employees work; they can work at their own pace as long as they get all of their work done by the end of the day.
3. Encouraging employees to "do the best you can" will result in better performance than will setting specific and difficult goals for them.
4. The most effective organizations report that they have been able to virtually eliminate stress among their personnel.
5. Research shows that effective managers are almost always described by their subordinates as friendly, kind, and concerned, while ineffective managers are the opposite.

Mike Ditka coaching the Chicago Bears.

Source: UPI/Bettmann Newsphotos.

Looking Back and Ahead

To motivate their employees and inspire loyalty, White Castle System, Inc., the nation's oldest fast-food chain, offers compensation and benefits that are generous for the industry. For example, the company provides all employees with profit sharing, an annual bonus, a pension, and life and health insurance. In addition, the company has a policy of promoting only from within. Employees who stick with White Castle for 25 years get the royal treatment: a limousine ride to a country club banquet at which the employee is presented with an engraved gold watch in recognition of his or her service. White Castle's president also tries to show his concern for everyone by visiting each store every year. This approach seems to work; White Castle reports a rate of turnover (the proportion of employees leaving the company) that is much lower than the industry average, and the stores have generated an impressive level of sales and profits over the years.[1]

Most management research and effective practicing managers say that employees are a business's most important asset. They are the key to every successful enterprise. Support for this idea comes from Sam Walton, who is worth several billion dollars and is the founder and head of the successful Wal-Mart chain of stores. Describing the basis for his success in business, Walton said, "It can be summarized in one word — people."

The human aspects of management received only brief mention in the previous chapter's look at the functions of planning, organizing, and controlling. This chapter focuses on the directing function of management. It describes how managers motivate and lead their employees to achieve organizational and individual goals.

The Emergence of Modern Human Relations

Human relations A management approach that brings employees and the organization together to achieve the objectives of both.

The directing function is concerned with managing the human side of an enterprise and can be called **human relations.** This management approach brings employees and the organization together in a way that achieves the objectives of both. For example, if employees find that by working hard they can meet their own objectives of earning more or feeling proud of their work, they will put forth extra effort. This effort helps the organization meet its objectives for productivity and profits. This chapter describes ways managers can reap such benefits from human relations.

Modern human relations results from an evolution of management styles. That process began before the turn of the century with the scientific management movement.

Scientific Management

Scientific management An approach started around 1900 that used engineering techniques such as time-and-motion analysis to increase plant efficiency by establishing the one best method for each task.

About 100 years ago, America was in the throes of the Industrial Revolution. Huge factories, each employing hundreds or thousands of workers, were springing up across the country, and managers primarily focused on how to get workers and machines to operate as efficiently as possible. Around the beginning of the century, companies began using **scientific management,** which was an approach that used engineering techniques such as time and motion analysis to increase plant efficiency. Pioneering scientific managers helped solve such problems as laying out the plant efficiently, determining the best machine speed, and figuring out how employees could work most productively and quickly. Some of the basic beliefs of the scientific managers during this time period are summarized in the first column of Figure 7.1.

The founding father of scientific management was Frederick W. Taylor, who analyzed tasks and conducted time-and-motion studies to determine the one "best way" to perform a job. To do this, scientific managers such as Taylor divided jobs into elementary movements, then discarded the nonessential ones. They determined the most efficient way of performing each essential movement; and then they prepared written instructions for how to perform a job, down to the minute details. Workers were to follow these instructions without deviation.

For example, through scientific analysis, Taylor was able to almost quadruple the output of pig-iron handlers (those who loaded slabs of iron weighing about 92 pounds that were shaped somewhat like a pig) and shovelers at steel plants. Scientific managers also planned the sequence of machines used and the route the materials followed. Under this approach, the company's managers were responsible for seeing that the work was carried out in accordance with the scientific managers' instructions.[2]

Although these efforts enabled companies to improve their efficiency and productivity, other problems arose. Managers and workers resisted the loss of autonomy in deciding how they did their jobs. Although so-

F I G U R E   7.1

Management Approaches through the Years

	Elements of Scientific Management	Elements of Early Behavioral Management	Elements of Human Resources Management
Treatment of Employees	Supervise and control workers closely. Treat them as a factor of production.	Make employees feel that they are important. Give them fringe benefits and good working conditions.	Try to tap each employee's full potential by giving increased responsibility and challenging work.
Employee Relationship to Work	Reduce all work into simple repetitive processes. Use scientific method.	Give employees some self-direction and self-control over their work.	Encourage subordinates to participate in decision making.
Employee Role in a Firm	Make sure employees follow the rules. There is no room for flexibility or initiative.	Keep subordinates informed about what is going on. Make them feel like they are insiders.	Keep in mind that employees are the enterprise's most important asset.
Motivation of Employees	Money motivates.	Money and a friendly work environment are the two most important motivators.	Interesting and challenging work and good wages motivate most people.
		Labor unions and personnel departments gain strength.	World competition and recognition that human resources are recognized as the key to increased productivity.
	Frederick W. Taylor applies scientific management in steel plants successfully.	Hawthorne studies provide new insights into human behavior.	Human relations provides good wages and working conditions.

Industrial Revolution	1880	1890	1900	1910	1920	1930	1940	1950	1960	1970	1980	Present

phisticated wage incentives were used, advocates of scientific management generally regarded the worker more as a machine to be manipulated than as a thinking, feeling person.

Early Behavioral Management

Beginning in the late 1920s and early 1930s, the approach to managing people began to change. The labor union movement was gaining momentum, forcing companies to consider the interests of workers. As a result, companies began to form personnel departments. Management experts were also learning more about workers. They looked beyond the job itself to the person holding the job.

The Hawthorne Studies One famous examination of the dynamics of human behavior at work was a series of pioneering studies conducted between 1924 and 1932 at the Hawthorne works of the Western Electric Company. The **Hawthorne studies** provided important insights into worker motivation and behavior. The initial phase of the studies was intended to determine whether the level of illumination affected worker productivity. In the experiment, the researchers increased the illumination level for workers who were doing simple assembly tasks. As expected, productivity increased. Then the researchers *decreased* the level of light. To their bafflement, the performance increased again. The researchers decreased the illumination again until it was comparable to that of moonlight, and still the workers' productivity improved.

Clearly, something besides the level of light was influencing performance. As further studies showed, this "additional influence" was the human element. The workers put forth extra effort in part because they saw the research as a sign of management's interest in them.[3] In another phase of the Hawthorne studies, the informal work group was shown to have considerable influence on individual workers. The Hawthorne workers needed to be accepted by their work group, to be able to talk to their boss, and to feel that the company in general and managers in particular cared about them. The researchers concluded that workers are more complicated than just another factor of production and that aspects of the work setting other than the job itself influence worker behavior.

A More Humanistic Approach As a result of the Hawthorne studies and a growing body of other research, management began to adopt a more humanistic approach. Companies still valued scientific management's emphasis on efficiency, but came to appreciate an additional element of management: the way in which managers attempt to motivate and lead their employees. For example, Cleveland-based Lincoln Electric, the world's largest manufacturer of welding machines and electrodes, was one of the first firms to implement a lifetime employment policy, promotion from within, performance appraisals, pay-for-performance incentive systems, an employee stock ownership plan (employees currently own about half of the company's stock), pensions and extensive fringe benefits (a company cafeteria serves meals at about 60 percent of usual costs), and employee participation in decision making. The second column in

Hawthorne studies
Pioneering research studies on worker behavior and motivation.

Figure 7.1 summarizes this early behavioral management approach.

Just as scientific management led to some dramatic increases in productivity and profits, so did the early behavioral management approach. For instance, at Lincoln Electric, profits and productivity grew rapidly. Between 1934 and 1941, productivity per employee at this innovative company more than doubled.[4]

Human Resource Management

Beginning in the 1970s, a newer approach to managing employees developed. Today's effective managers regard their employees as important resources — "human resources" — having a great deal of untapped potential. Under human resource management, the manager's job is to create an environment in which employees can unleash their considerable potential and use it for the good of both the organization and themselves. Instead of trying to structure jobs rigidly and monitor employees' behavior closely (as under scientific management) or trying to make employees feel that they are all part of one big, happy family (early behavioral management), the human resource approach recognizes the importance of people to organizational performance and seeks to provide them with the opportunity to develop their full potential. Unfortunately, a recent comprehensive study found that not enough American companies recognize this human resource approach and this is cited as a major reason for our productivity problems.[5]

The human resource approach takes many forms, ranging from recruiting, selecting, training, and developing personnel to motivating and leading them. For example, the Sherwin-Williams Paint Company instituted a human resource approach in its Richmond, Kentucky, plant. It hires only those who would enjoy working on challenging and important tasks, then it groups the employees into teams. These teams have complete autonomy to determine where members work, what work they do, and how to train a newcomer. The teams are also responsible for the results, and pay is based on performance.

Like scientific management and the early behavioral approaches, the human resource approach has had considerable success. At the Richmond Sherwin-Williams plant, absenteeism is much lower than at the company's other plants, and productivity is greater.[6]

The human resource approach to management is the basis for modern human relations techniques. Modern human relations takes many different forms, but the focus is on two major areas: motivation and leadership.

Checkpoint

1. What approaches to management have led to the development of modern human relations?
2. What have managers learned from each of these management approaches?

Understanding Motivation

To manage human relations effectively, the organization must motivate its employees. **Motivation** is a complex psychological process in which needs or wants lead to drives (behavior intended to satisfy a need) aimed at goals or incentives. Attaining the goals or incentives reduces the intensity of the drives and fulfills the needs. As shown in Figure 7.2, the needs are really the mainspring of the motivation. For example, if you have a need for achievement, your behavior aimed at satisfying that need (that is, your drive) may be to study hard. Your goal might be straight A's. If you get straight A's, your drive will be less intense and your need satisfied. Consequently, after final exams, your need for rest might seem more important than your need for achievement.

To know what motivates people, you must look at the world the way they do. One representative survey asked managers to rank the rewards that workers desired from their jobs and then asked the workers to rank the things that motivated them. It was found that the three factors the supervisors rated lowest were rated highest by the workers. This finding shows that many managers really do not know what motivates their employees. Furthermore, a recent large survey found fewer than half of American workers think their bosses properly motivate them.[7]

Needs and Motivation

Employees may be motivated by challenging work, good wages and salaries, or fringe benefits (a company car, free life insurance, or low-cost health insurance). Each employee will seek to satisfy personal needs. A person with a strong need for job security may gravitate into a government bureaucracy, where lifetime employment is common. An individual with a high need for achievement may seek a job in sales, where progress is largely up to the individual and security is less important. The influence of motivational needs helps explain employee behavior.

Primary and Secondary Needs People have two major types of needs, primary and secondary. **Primary needs** are physiological; they include the needs for food, water, sex, sleep, clothing, and shelter. Students who work part-time at the library to cover living expenses do so to fulfill some of these primary needs. **Secondary needs** are psychological; they include the needs for friendship, recognition, control or power, and achievement. Students who join a fraternity, sorority, or social club do so to fulfill some of these secondary needs.

The two kinds of needs have different sources. Primary needs are innate, meaning that people are born with them. Secondary needs are learned, meaning that people acquire these needs from parents, friends, and society as they mature.

FIGURE 7.2

The Process of Motivation

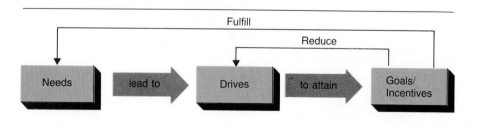

Maslow's Hierarchy of Needs The best-known explanation of motivation based on needs is that of the famous humanistic psychologist Abraham Maslow. He described a five-step hierarchy of needs people strive to attain:

Physiological needs—the primary needs for survival: food, water, clothing, shelter, sex, and sleep

Safety needs—the need to protect yourself from physical and financial risks

Social needs—the needs for friendship, affection, and acceptance

Esteem needs—the need to be recognized and to have status and power

Self-actualization needs—the need to reach your potential, to be the best you can be

Figure 7.3 summarizes and gives examples of Maslow's hierarchy of human needs.

Once a person fulfills a particular level of need, it no longer serves to motivate. The next level of need then serves to motivate the individual. For example, suppose Mary Smith has just been laid off and has no money saved up. Her primary concern is how to buy groceries and pay the rent; she is motivated by physiological needs. Then Mary starts receiving unemployment compensation, so she knows she can satisfy her basic physiological needs. Now she is interested in a job that will offer her safe working conditions, health insurance, and job security; these are safety needs.

FIGURE 7.3

Maslow's Hierarchy of Needs

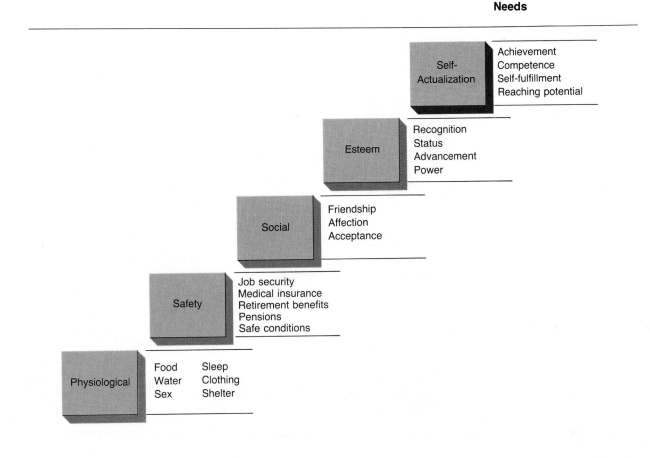

If Mary finds such a job, she will probably start devoting more energy to fulfilling social and esteem needs — spending more time with family, friends, and co-workers, and seeking a promotion and recognition at work. If she doesn't feel like part of the group at work, she might start looking for another job. Finally, Mary hopes that someday she will be free to devote more energy to attaining her full potential. This motivation to achieve self-actualization may lead to accomplishments in areas as diverse as career advancement, body building, child rearing, and charity work.

Maslow's approach to motivation is useful in helping identify the types of needs people have and the role of the manager and the organization in motivating employees. Maslow's theory points out that the sources of motivation are diverse. It explains why some workers may be unmotivated in an organization that pays good wages, offers fringe benefits, and has excellent working conditions. The company is taking care of the lower-level needs, but not the higher-level needs for esteem and self-actualization.

In order to fulfill their need to realize their potential, some employees may feel forced to leave a company and become entrepreneurs. However, as Chapter 3 pointed out, companies can appeal to their employees' need for self-actualization, and reap benefits from their increased motivation, by encouraging and creating a climate of intrapreneurship. Employees are thus able to fulfill their need for self-actualization on the job through intrapreneuring, and both the individuals and the company benefit.

Two-Factor Theory of Work Motivation

Motivator factors Job characteristics that make people feel exceptionally good about their jobs, including challenge, recognition, and responsibility.

Although Maslow provides a beginning for understanding work motivation, Frederick Herzberg has developed an even more relevant theory: the two-factor theory of work motivation. Whereas Maslow never tested his theory in the workplace, Herzberg based his theory on industrial research. Herzberg and his research associates asked two basic questions of employees: What makes you feel exceptionally good about your job? What makes you feel exceptionally bad about your job? Figure 7.4 illustrates the specific factors that workers mentioned.

Herzberg termed as **motivator factors** those job characteristics that make people feel exceptionally good about their jobs. These include the

FIGURE 7.4

Herzberg's Two-Factor Theory

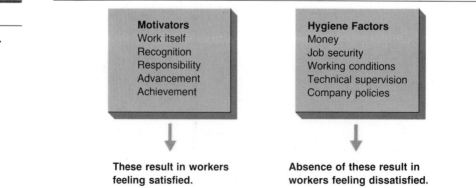

Motivators	**Hygiene Factors**
Work itself	Money
Recognition	Job security
Responsibility	Working conditions
Advancement	Technical supervision
Achievement	Company policies

These result in workers feeling satisfied.

Absence of these result in workers feeling dissatisfied.

challenge of the work, recognition for doing a good job, the responsibility associated with the work, prospects for advancement, and a sense of achievement. According to Herzberg, these factors lead to job satisfaction and motivate employees.

He called **hygiene factors** those job characteristics that do not directly motivate workers but that cause dissatisfaction when they are absent. These factors include money, job security, working conditions, technical supervision, and company policies. By giving people competitive salaries, good working conditions, and job security, managers can prevent dissatisfaction. However, to create satisfaction, managers also must provide motivator factors. Surveys indicate that today's workers want such satisfaction more than the hygiene factors.[8]

For example, at a branch office of AT&T, the computer operators were well paid and had good fringe benefits and working conditions, but they were not satisfied with their jobs. Absenteeism was high, and quality of work was low. The operators simply did their assigned pile of work every day and then passed it on, whether it was correct or not. If they didn't feel like working they stayed home, because someone would cover for them. To motivate the employees, AT&T tried assigning each computer operator a specific area of responsibility, such as payroll or billing. In other words, the operators received the motivator factors of responsibility, recognition, and opportunity for growth and achievement. As a result, the operators became more satisfied with their jobs. Absenteeism and the quality of work improved dramatically.

Hygiene factors Job characteristics that do not motivate people but that cause dissatisfaction when absent, including money, working conditions, and job security.

Checkpoint

1. How do Maslow's hierarchy and Herzberg's two-factor theory explain motivation?
2. How can companies use these theories to motivate their employees?

Techniques for Motivating Employees

Maslow's and Herzberg's models provide some understanding of what motivates employees. For example, both models demonstrate that money is important to one's physiological needs (Maslow's first level) and to prevent dissatisfaction (Herzberg's hygiene factors). However, these models also point out that an employer can also expect that if money satisfies workers' physiological needs, they next should try to meet the workers' safety needs by providing safe working conditions and insurance and retirement benefits. But as Herzberg's model shows, money, fringe benefits, and safe conditions may only prevent dissatisfaction; these factors may not motivate employees. Workers also look for the motivator factors (recognition and responsibility) that help them meet their higher-level needs (esteem and self-actualization).

Employers' efforts to motivate employees typically fall into two categories. Businesses try to improve the work environment so that it will facilitate motivation. They also focus on ways to motivate individual employees.

A vice president at Valley National Bancorp takes time to go over work with an employee. Most employees tend to be motivated with jobs that provide responsibility and challenge as well as compensation and security. Training employees also provides them with opportunities for achievement and advancement, two more motivators in Herzberg's model.

Source: Courtesy of Valley National Bank.

Improving the Work Environment

One of the most important concerns affecting employee motivation is the dramatically changing technological environment of work. Increasingly sophisticated technology has simplified many jobs and made others obsolete. For example, steel-collar jobs performed by robots and computers are replacing many factory workers' jobs and making other workers feel that they are merely part of the machine. Many workers feel that their work is no longer meaningful; it is simply a way to earn a living. The company in general and their supervisors in particular do not seem to care about them or their ideas on how to improve productivity. To overcome these feelings of being left out and at the same time make the job more interesting and rewarding, many firms are developing quality of work life programs.

Quality of work life (QWL) refers to efforts to improve the job environment and make work life more enjoyable and meaningful. Such efforts may extend beyond the job site and include providing day care centers and recreational activities. The idea is to create a total supportive, quality environment for the employees. Some of the most widely recognized specific techniques associated with QWL at the workplace are job enrichment, quality-control circles, flexible work schedules, and job sharing.

Quality of work life (QWL) Efforts to improve the job environment and make work life more enjoyable and meaningful.

Job Enrichment Management can use the Herzberg two-factor theory to improve employee performance by adding motivators to the job design.

This approach has been termed **job enrichment.** Managers can add motivators in a variety of ways:

Varying the work so that employees are able to use more of their skills and abilities

Giving employees a chance to complete a whole or identifiable piece of work, as opposed to doing just one small task in a large project

Making workers aware of how important their jobs are

Giving employees more autonomy, freedom, and responsibility to do the job their own way

Providing employees with immediate feedback so they know how they are doing

Many employers have tried job enrichment approaches. Sherwin-Williams, mentioned earlier, has combined a well-designed work layout with the use of autonomous work groups that set their own pace. When the company instituted this arrangement, the cost per gallon of paint declined, productivity rose, product quality hit an all-time high, and work time lost through accidents was virtually eliminated.[9] In another case, a major insurance company gave its workers greater control over their work and used their ideas to redesign the jobs. Work output rose significantly.[10] Examples such as these show that job enrichment can make the job more interesting and challenging for the employee, while simultaneously increasing productivity and lowering costs.

Job enrichment A technique for motivating employees by adding motivator factors to their jobs.

Quality-Control Circles Companies also challenge employees and give recognition through the institution of quality-control circles. A **quality-control circle** consists of a group of workers who meet regularly to discuss the way they do their jobs and to recommend changes. Quality-control (QC) circles have been popular in Japan. For example, Toyota has had QC circles for over 20 years and now has several hundred circles involving thousands of its employees. The circles have also gained wide use in the United States at firms such as General Foods, Weyerhaeuser, Heinz, Nabisco, Honeywell, and Lockheed.

Quality-control circle
A group of workers who meet regularly to discuss the way they do their jobs and to recommend changes.

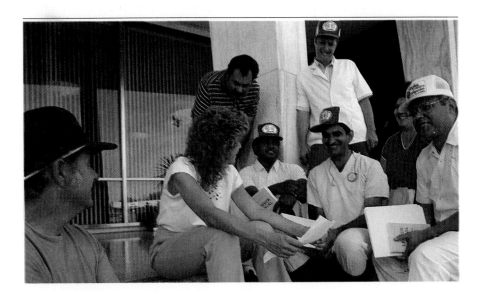

A quality-control circle at Campbell Soup Company. The company has established almost 500 of these employee groups worldwide. The production and office employees discuss ways to improve quality and keep costs down. Their input helps managers keep pace with developments in a company that is rapidly becoming more complex.

Source: Courtesy of Campbell Soup Company.

Quality-control circles typically consist of five to ten employees and a group leader. Membership is voluntary. The objective of each group is to study problems of production or service that fall within their scope of work, such as how to assemble more TVs per hour or reduce the number of defects per TV set. Quality-control circle participants are trained in how to identify areas that warrant consideration and how to work harmoniously with others in a group setting. The group usually meets for one or two hours a week to discuss projects it wants to undertake and changes it wants to make as a result of its investigations of current work procedures.

After the QC group has completed its study of a problem, it suggests what should be done to improve quality and productivity. In one case, a quality-control circle began by counting the number of defects at each of the stages of the production process covered by members of the group. The circle members then identified what was causing each of these defects (incorrect engineering specifications, a part produced improperly by one of the subcontractors, a defective processing machine, and so on) and suggested ways of correcting each problem. The group then reported its findings to management for action.

Besides the quality-control circles that identify and attempt to solve specific problems in manufacturing operations, similar groups meet to discuss other types of issues:

At Olga, a maker of women's undergarments, managers hold regular "Creative Meetings" with employees to ask how they would run the company if they were the president.

At Electro Scientific Industries, managers have what are called "Doing Well/In the Way" meetings with employees to learn what is going well and what is interfering with work.

At Preston Trucking Company, the drivers meet in groups of 20 every few weeks to discuss ways of doing their jobs better.

At Kollmorgen Corporation, managers have monthly "People Meetings" at which employees discuss what issues and problems are facing the company and how to solve them.[11]

Flexible work schedule
A schedule that allows workers to set their own work hours, within limitations established by the organization.

Flextime Another name for a flexible work schedule.

Core hours Those times when everyone must be on the job under a flexible work schedule.

Flexible Work Schedules Companies also improve the work environment through the use of **flexible work schedules,** which allow workers to set their own work hours, within limitations established by the organization. Sometimes this arrangement is called **flextime.** The firm establishes **core hours,** which are the times when everyone must be on the job, say, from 10:00 a.m. to 3:00 p.m. (see Figure 7.5). In addition to these five core hours, everyone must put in an additional three hours, but these specific

FIGURE 7.5

A Flexible Work Schedule

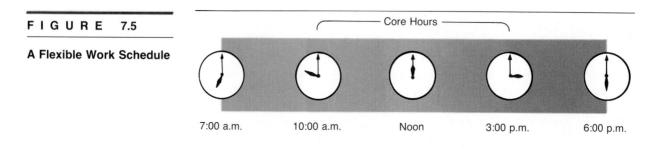

Core Hours

| 7:00 a.m. | 10:00 a.m. | Noon | 3:00 p.m. | 6:00 p.m. |

times are flexible. The flexibility of the work schedule allows people to adjust their work life to their personal life. For example, if a working mother has to drop the children at school at 8:30 a.m., she can start work at 9:00 a.m. and work until 5:00 p.m. (If a friend or her husband also has flexible hours, that person could agree to work early hours and pick up the kids after school.) Likewise, a person who wants to pursue a hobby or exercise after work can schedule the work day to start at 7:00 a.m. and work until 3:00 p.m. For example, at Hewlett-Packard, employees can start work at 6:00 a.m., 7:00 a.m., or 8:00 a.m.

In addition to flexible work hours, some firms are also experimenting with flexible work weeks and even "flexyears." For example, in the summer months at Baxter Travenol, the large producer of medical-care products, employees who work an extra hour Monday through Thursday can have Friday afternoon off. Some companies use such compressed work weeks year-round. At Quad/Graphics, employees can work three 12-hour days and then have long weekends. At Firestone and Goodyear, employees who work two 12-hour shifts on weekends are paid for 36 hours and can have the rest of the week off. The German department store Beck-Feldmeier KG uses the concept of flexible years, by allowing employees to contract to work a certain number of hours during the year.[12]

Many firms have reaped benefits from flextime. For example, the State Street Bank of Boston was able to reduce its overtime cost and employee turnover. The Metropolitan Life Insurance Company reduced tardiness and improved employee morale. At Control Data, a three-year study revealed that flextime had increased morale and productivity. The U.S. Geological Survey introduced flextime and after a year found that use of sick leave had dropped and the turnover rate was the lowest it had been in five years.[13] At Quad/Graphics, productivity increased 20 percent when the company moved to its flextime work weeks.[14] Because of this type of success, the use of flextime appears to be dramatically increasing. A recent study found one-third of the businesses surveyed were using it, which was double the percentage of ten years earlier.[15]

Job Sharing Another way companies can enable employees to combine career and personal objectives is through job sharing. **Job sharing** consists of employing two or more part-time workers to fulfill the requirements of a single full-time position. Under this arrangement, a student can work part-time while attending school, or a parent can have more time to be with the children. This enables the employee to earn some income and keep abreast of job developments while still meeting other obligations. The employer, in turn, benefits from not losing a valued employee who otherwise could not put in the hours required for a full-time position.

Job sharing Employing two or more part-time workers to fulfill the requirements of a single full-time position.

Motivating Individual Employees

Besides modifying the work environment to motivate employees, another approach is to focus on the individual worker. The work motivation theories state that both the individual employee and the context or environment in which the employee works are important to motivation. Although it is relatively easier to change and manage the environment, in the final analysis it is the individual worker who must feel motivated to perform. Fortunately, some effective techniques to motivate on the level of the individual have recently emerged. These include goal setting, stress management, and retraining.

Goal Setting Employees want to know what their employer expects of them and to feel part of a team effort. Businesses can motivate employees to improve their performance by setting goals. Applied to work motivation, **goal setting** is the process of establishing specific objectives for an individual to pursue. Chapter 6 described a comprehensive goal-setting approach used for management planning and appraising employees — management by objectives (MBO).

Research has uncovered some important guidelines for effective goal setting:

> Specific goals lead to more effective task performance than those that are vague or simply encourage employees to "do the best you can."[16]

> Goals that are difficult but attainable lead to higher performance than do easy goals, as long as the employee accepts these goals.[17]

> Employees tend to work harder in pursuing goals that they have helped set than those that have been assigned to them.[18]

> Frequent feedback on how well an employee is doing typically generates higher performance from that employee.[19]

Simply put, goal setting works; it leads to better performance. One manager who experienced this is the successful general agent of an office of Mutual of Omaha who each quarter determined sales goals together with his agents *and* their spouses. Most sales managers find it effective to set goals for their sales force. However, this manager got even better performance because he allowed his sales agents to participate in the goal-setting process. By involving spouses, he obtained for his salespeople their families' support for their selling after hours and on weekends.

Goal setting The process of establishing specific objectives for an individual to pursue.

T A B L E   7.1

Type A and Type B Personality Profiles

Type A	Type B
Is always moving	Is not concerned about time
Walks rapidly	Is patient
Eats rapidly	Doesn't brag
Talks rapidly	Plays for fun, not to win
Is impatient	Relaxes without guilt
Does two things at once	Has no pressing deadlines
Can't cope with leisure time	Is mild-mannered
Is obsessed with numbers	Is never in a hurry
Measures success by quantity	
Is aggressive	
Is competitive	
Constantly feels under time pressure	

Stress Management Businesses can also motivate employees to do their best by showing them how to manage stress. **Stress** is the body's response to an action or situation that places demands on a person.[20] We all must meet demands, and we even choose many of those demands. Taking an exam causes stress, and so does meeting a deadline at work or getting married. If you've ever started writing a term paper at the last minute, you know that the stress response can spur you on to great efforts (and long hours). Life would be dull if you were never subject to any stress.

However, intense or continuous stress can be harmful. People under stress can become tense, anxious, and mentally and physically exhausted. Health problems such as ulcers or heart disease can also develop. To prevent these problems, people need to avoid excess stress or to cope with it by adopting healthy behavior such as exercising and learning to be assertive.

Some jobs put so much pressure on employees that they suffer **burnout,** which is mental and/or physical exhaustion caused by excess stress. Typically, these jobs are demanding and offer employees few opportunities for feeling recognized or rewarded. People at risk for burnout include air traffic controllers, medical personnel, teachers, and stockbrokers.

Researchers have tried to determine whether some characteristics make people especially susceptible to stress and burnout. Some evidence suggests that a certain type of personality is at risk. This personality, described in the left column of Table 7.1, is called a **Type A personality.** It includes a drive to get more and more done in less and less time. At first it was reported that Type A people wear themselves down and are even more likely to have heart attacks or other serious health problems than those with a so-called "Type B personality." Now the research is less clear.[21] People who hold frustration in and keep their problems to themselves may be more susceptible to serious problems than Type A personalities.

Many companies are beginning to help their personnel eliminate or cope with excess stress. For example, Johnson and Johnson and IBM have instituted comprehensive programs of health checkups, exercise, and "lifestyle" classes for stress management.[22] In addition to encouraging employees to watch their diet and give up smoking, some business firms are providing on-site facilities for exercising. These programs — sometimes called wellness programs — are keeping personnel healthier, happier, and more productive. As a result of its wellness programs, New York Telephone estimates it saves at least $2.7 million on its health costs annually, and Lockheed estimates $1 million in savings on its life insurance premiums.[23] These companies are also showing the workers that they actively promote the well-being of their employees.

Retraining A particularly stressful situation is job insecurity caused by the threat of layoffs or new technological developments. When workers are worried about losing their jobs, they may not think it is worthwhile to do their best. They will not come forth with new ideas for fear it may eliminate their job or the jobs of their friends. Some workers may even turn to drugs or alcohol to dull their fears.

Companies can help workers cope with this problem more productively. Some companies have followed the lead of many Japanese compa-

Stress The body's response to an action or situation that places demands on a person.

Burnout Mental and/or physical exhaustion caused by excess stress.

Type A personality A personality characterized by a drive to get more and more done in less and less time.

nies by having a lifetime employment policy. For example, at Worthington Steel, once employees pass a rigid probationary period (they are voted on by their co-workers), they are guaranteed a job for life.

Another approach, which can be used alone or in conjunction with lifetime employment, is to provide workers with retraining in skills the employer is more likely to need after cutbacks or technological changes. The federal government even has programs that will help employers pay for the retraining costs. The state of Illinois has proposed an innovative program whereby employers in a city would contribute to a fund used for retraining that is matched by worker contributions. A survey indicated that 40 percent of employers favor the idea, and 25 percent of workers said they should chip in.[24] If employees see hope for their future and have a sense that management values them, they are more likely to respond to such programs and be motivated to perform. To learn how one company has successfully used retraining, see "Social Responsibility Close-Up: Hallmark Cuts Costs without Cutting Staff."

Checkpoint

1. What techniques are available to motivate today's employees?
2. How do improvements in the quality of work life enhance employees' performance?

SOCIAL RESPONSIBILITY   CLOSE-UP

Hallmark Cuts Costs without Cutting Staff

Many companies attempt to lower their costs by laying off employees, but Hallmark has found a different approach. The Kansas City–based maker of greeting cards has improved efficiency while keeping employees on the payroll.

Printing is a major part of Hallmark's operations. The company's four printing plants produce millions of greeting cards each day, plus wrapping paper and party goods. But the printing industry has undergone major technological advances that mean companies can produce more with fewer workers.

In response to these changes, Hallmark has instituted a continuous retraining process. As a result, employees have learned a variety of skills. For example, Ray Smith, a cutting machine operator, also can work as a custom-card imprinter, a painter, or an assembler of

modular offices. At headquarters, factory personnel may work in the kitchen of the company cafeteria for a while, but they still earn factory wages. The company has also taught factory personnel shorthand and typing, enabling them to fill clerical positions as they become available.

In addition, Hallmark has improved productivity in the creative area by establishing a team approach. An artist, writer, and marketing expert work together to develop a broad category of cards, say, the entire Thanksgiving line. With this approach, the company's artists are producing more designs than when each employee worked individually. The team members can spot problems before someone has spent a lot of time trying to develop an idea.

Leadership Styles

Along with motivation, modern human relations involves leadership. A comprehensive definition of **leadership** is that it is the process of influencing people to direct their efforts toward the achievement of particular objectives. Although there are many different views and it is hard to pin down, both researchers and practitioners would agree that effective leadership is a major contributor to successful organizations.

Every manager has a style of leadership or a particular way of using power to lead. These leadership styles fall into three broad categories: autocratic, democratic, and laissez-faire. In an autocratic style, the leader exercises the greatest amount of authority, leaving little freedom to the workers. A democratic leader shares authority with the workers. Laissez-faire leadership leaves a great deal of freedom to the workers, with the manager merely establishing some broad limits. (The term *laissez-faire* is a French expression that roughly translates as "leave it alone.") These leadership styles are not absolutes; they fall along a continuum, as illustrated in Figure 7.6.

In evaluating how managers lead, researchers have developed several theories. These theories describe the assumptions that underlie a manager's choice of leadership style. They are known as Theories X, Y, and Z.

Leadership The process of influencing people to direct their efforts toward the achievement of particular objectives.

Theories X and Y

The pioneering human relations theorist Douglas McGregor recognized that leadership style is heavily influenced by leaders' assumptions about their subordinates. A manager who thinks employees are lazy and will cut corners whenever possible will adopt a much different leadership style than will a manager who believes employees generally work hard and are reliable. McGregor called these assumptions Theory X and Theory Y.

Theory X assumes people are basically lazy and have to be threatened before they will work. Some of the specific assumptions of this theory include:

People dislike work and will avoid it when possible.

Theory X The assumption that people are basically lazy and have to be coerced or threatened before they will work.

FIGURE 7.6

Leadership Styles

Autocratic			Democratic			Laissez-faire
Leader exercises considerable authority.						Subordinates have considerable freedom
Leader makes all decisions with no input.	Leader makes all decisions and tries to convince subordinates.	Leader asks for input from subordinates but makes decisions.	Leader makes decisions but will change on basis of subordinate input.	Leader gets participative input and makes decisions based on this input.	Leader spells out limits in which subordinate group makes decisions.	Leader allows full freedom and makes a decision on democratic or consensus basis.

Employees have little ambition, shun responsibility, and like to be directed.

Employees want security above all else and actually like to be told what to do.

To get employees to attain organizational objectives, the leader must keep a close watch over them and use threats of punishment.[25]

Based on these assumptions, a manager who adopts Theory X is likely to use a relatively autocratic management style.

Theory Y assumes people are creative and responsible and will work hard under the proper conditions. Some of the specific assumptions of this theory include:

> **Theory Y** The assumption that people are creative and responsible and will work hard under the proper conditions.

Work is as natural as play.

If people are committed to objectives, they will exercise self-direction and self-control.

Commitment to objectives depends on the rewards associated with achieving the objectives.

Under proper conditions, people will seek responsibility.

People are highly creative.

In industrial life, the intellectual potential of the average employee is only partially tapped.[26]

A Theory Y manager is likely to choose a democratic or laissez-faire leadership style. Most successful leaders make Theory Y assumptions about people. They feel most subordinates will work hard if given the proper environment.

Theory Z

A third, more recent, theory of how managers should lead is Theory Z, proposed by UCLA professor William G. Ouchi.[27] This is sometimes referred to as a Japanese approach, because it is based on a style of management found in typical Japanese companies. According to **Theory Z,** the key is to create a culture or climate that lends itself to openness, trust, and employee involvement. Managers who adhere to Theory Z try to make workers feel like family, involving them in decision making and seldom if ever laying off anyone. In addition, Theory Z companies provide employees with broad experience and cross-training to avoid boredom and broaden career paths. They may also use the quality of work life techniques discussed earlier.

> **Theory Z** The assumption that the key to productivity is to create a climate or culture of openness and trust that leads to increased employee involvement.

Choosing a Leadership Style

Choosing a style of leadership is a complicated process. Some leaders seem able to lead naturally. Others turn to experts for help. For example, some seek guidance from computerized training, such as the program described in "Computer Technology Close-Up: Improving Leadership Style."

Research and experience concerning leadership styles have led to the conclusion that the best leadership style must consider the nature of the subordinates, the leaders themselves, and the situation. Some subordinates, such as factory workers, perform best when they are closely monitored; others, for example, scientists in a research laboratory, do well when they have free rein. Some leaders operate more effectively when they exercise close control; others do better when they delegate a great deal of authority and let the subordinates set their own pace. Some situations require managers to monitor personnel with care because any mistake can be very costly (making heart pacemakers), while other situations allow for more general control because the work is basically simple and mistakes matter less (making shipping containers).

Because of these variables, modern managers often find they get the best results when they don't settle for one leadership style. Instead, they practice **contingency leadership,** which calls for using the style that will be the most effective in a specific situation. Specifically, research indicates that an autocratic style is most effective in two situations:

1. A very favorable leadership situation, which includes a structured task, a great deal of formal power and authority, and respect and loyalty from subordinates. An example of such a very favorable situation would be that facing an airline pilot.
2. A very unfavorable leadership situation, which includes an unstructured task, no formal power or authority, and a reluctant, "volunteered" group of subordinates. An example of a leader in such a situation is the chairperson of the annual company picnic.

Contingency leadership
The leadership technique of using the style that will be most effective in a specific situation.

COMPUTER TECHNOLOGY   CLOSE-UP

Improving Leadership Style

In recent years, some computer software firms have come up with ways to help managers improve their leadership style with self-paced computer programs. These programs give the individual immediate feedback. The idea is quite simple. For a fee, the manager receives a set of diskettes accompanied by an instruction manual. The computer program leads the user through the lessons, displaying questions on the screen. The user types in responses, which the computer analyzes. The computer informs the user how he or she ranks in comparison to other users throughout the country.

Typically, this feedback is in the form of bar charts and graphs that illustrate the manager's answers and what they mean in terms of leadership style and decision making. For example, those using the program are asked to decide how they would handle certain situations. These answers are used to provide a visual presentation of the manager's leadership style. The individual can see what primary leadership approach he or she used, and compare it to those available. In another instance, users learn about their style of conducting meetings, including how much attention they give to preparation, participation, implementation, and control. The software helps the participant identify leadership weaknesses and develop a plan of action for overcoming them.

Some of the biggest advantages of these computer programs is that they allow managers to work at their own pace. The manager does not have to break away from the job to attend a seminar downtown or in another city. Another advantage is that the manager can reuse the program or pass it along to others in the firm who would like to learn more about their leadership styles and ways to improve them. Computers are helping managers do more than just control inventory and finances; they are helping them learn how to manage people more effectively.

In contrast, a human-oriented style is most effective between these extremes, in moderately favorable or moderately unfavorable situations, which make up most modern jobs.[28] Thus, except in the few situations that are very favorable or very unfavorable, most managers would be better off using Theory Y or Theory Z styles.

Despite the general preference for a Theory Y or Z approach, a Theory X style may be more appropriate when economic or competitive times are tough. For example, the former head of E. F. Hutton did not make a change in leadership style, and this eventually led to the downfall of his company. His style was to take risks and make quick decisions. He considered traditional techniques such as budgets and organization charts a waste of time. During the boom of the 1970s this style worked. He assembled the best sales force on Wall Street, and Hutton's profits were the envy of the industry. But when the securities industry entered a new competitive era in the 1980s, a new style of leadership was needed. Tighter controls and a more forceful, Theory X type of leadership was needed. He either couldn't or wouldn't make the transition to a new style of leadership, and as a result Hutton succumbed to a takeover by Shearson Lehman, and 5,000 Hutton employees lost their jobs.[29] In other words, managers have to be somewhat flexible and change their styles with the conditions they face.

Whatever style they choose, managers must avoid being inconsistent or vacillating between styles *within* a given situation. It is probably better to use a consistent Theory X style of leadership (because the subordinates at least know what to expect) than an inconsistent or wishy-washy Theory Y or Z style of leadership. The key is to be flexible in choosing the style to fit the situation and consistent within the identified situation. Unfortunately, there is some evidence that leaders are not differing their styles to fit the situation. A recent study of 163 Army generals and 120 corporate chief executive officers found they use remarkably similar styles.[30] Although the situations may have similarities, there are undoubtedly enough differences that different styles would be more effective.

When these medical professionals perform surgery — and when Merck & Company employees prepare special cleansers for the surgical instruments — the cost of making a mistake can be enormous. In situations such as these, the need for close control may make the autocratic style of leadership most appropriate.

Source: © Mark Joseph/Chicago.

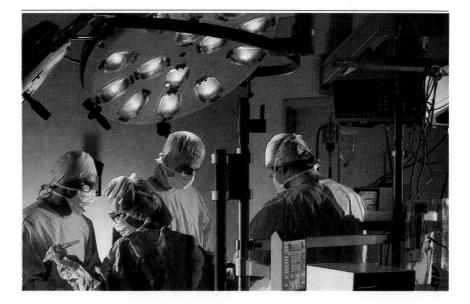

Checkpoint

1. What are some basic leadership styles?
2. When would you use a Theory X style? When would you use a Theory Y style?

Closing Comments

This chaper discussed what Sam Walton, the richest person in America and the head of Wal-Mart, identified as the major single reason for his business success: people. Modern human relations takes many forms but mainly focuses on motivation and leadership. Motivation stems from formal reward systems, such as wages and promotions, and also from interesting and challenging work. Effective leadership balances a concern for getting the job done with a concern for the worker. From Exxon and Texaco to Bank of America and Chase Manhattan to Digital Equipment and Hewlett-Packard, most major corporations in America spend millions of dollars annually training their managers to motivate and lead their employees more effectively.

Learning Objectives Revisited

1. **Describe how the major management approaches have changed over the years.**

   Beginning at the turn of the century, the scientific management era focused on achieving increased efficiency through the application of scientific procedures in the workplace. Workers were treated as if they were merely factors of production. During the early behavioral management era, which began about 1920, management came to realize that treating workers as thinking, feeling human beings both motivated them and improved productivity. Finally, the human resource management era emerged around 1970. Management has realized the importance of employees to organizational performance and has begun providing them with the opportunity to use their full potential and ability.

2. **Discuss approaches to understanding motivation.**

   Maslow's hierarchy of needs explains that people are motivated, in turn, by physiological, safety, social, esteem, and self-actualization needs. The two-factor theory proposed by Herzberg holds that work motivation and resulting employee satisfaction has two dimensions: hygiene factors and motivator factors. Hygiene factors such as money and working conditions can help prevent employee dissatisfaction, but only the motivator factors — responsibility, recognition, and opportunities for achievement — motivate employees directly and lead to satisfaction. To improve performance and satisfaction, managers need to offer motivator factors as well as hygiene factors.

3. **Present some techniques for motivating employees by improving the work environment.**

   Quality of work life (QWL) programs are used to manage the technological and social environment of the workplace. Some QWL techniques are job enrichment, quality-control circles, flexible work schedules, and job sharing. Job enrichment redesigns jobs, building in psychological motivators such as increased responsibility. A quality-control circle is a group of workers who meet regularly to discuss and recommend changes in the way their jobs are being done. With flexible work schedules, also called flextime, workers may set their own work hours as long as everyone is on the job during specific core hours. Job sharing means employing two or more part-time workers for one full-time position.

4. **Describe the techniques managers use to motivate individual employees.**

Techniques to motivate today's employees include goal setting, stress management, and retraining. Goal setting is the process of helping employees to set clear, specific, and difficult but attainable performance goals, and providing them with feedback on progress. Stress management techniques help employees find constructive ways to respond to the demands placed on them. Job retraining equips employees with the skills the employer is more likely to need after cutbacks or technological changes.

5. **Identify some basic leadership styles.**

Broadly stated, a leader's style can range from autocratic to democratic to laissez-faire. Some theories describe the assumptions underlying the way a manager leads. Theory X managers assume workers are basically lazy and have to be threatened. Theory Y managers assume people are creative and responsible and will work hard under the proper conditions. Theory Z managers assume that creating an open, trusting climate or culture will lead to increased employee involvement and improved performance.

6. **Explain how leaders can choose an effective style.**

The best leadership style depends on the nature of the subordinates, the leaders themselves, and the situation. Contingency leadership calls for using the style that will be most effective in a specific situation. An autocratic style is most effective in very favorable or very unfavorable leadership situations. In most situations, however, a human-oriented style is most effective.

Key Terms Reviewed

Review each of the following terms. For any that you do not know or are unsure of, look up the definitions and see how they were used in the chapter.

human relations	flextime
scientific management	core hours
Hawthorne studies	job sharing
motivation	goal setting
primary needs	stress
secondary needs	burnout
motivator factors	Type A personality
hygiene factors	leadership
quality of work life (QWL)	Theory X
job enrichment	Theory Y
quality-control circle	Theory Z
flexible work schedule	contingency leadership

Review Questions

1. Frederick W. Taylor wanted managers to use the scientific method. Did this happen? Explain.
2. What lessons can managers learn from the Hawthorne studies?
3. What beliefs about workers and motivation underlie the human resource approach to management?
4. Give an example of how a company can enable an employee to meet each of the types of needs in Maslow's hierarchy. Give one example for each type of need.
5. Bob Crunch, president of a manufacturing company, called the personnel director into his office. "You're the expert on employees," said Bob, "so please explain to me why our turnover is so high and our quality is so low, when our salaries are above industry average and we have one of the safest, cleanest plants in the country. Our people just don't seem motivated." Based on your reading of the two-factor theory of motivation, offer a possible explanation for the high turnover and low quality at this company.
6. Why are employers concerned about the quality of work life? What techniques do they use to improve the quality of work life?
7. How can employers and employees benefit from flextime?
8. Every year, Martha Moore gives each member of her staff a list of goals for the year. At the end of the year, Martha sits down with each worker to discuss the achievements for the year. To Martha's dismay, she finds that staff members often fall short of the goals, even though she makes them easier every year. What principles of goal setting has Martha failed to take into account? How could she better use goal setting to motivate her staff?
9. Is all stress harmful? Write a short description of totally stress-free living.
10. The sales manager for Wonder Washers prefers to let his salespeople use whatever style works for them. He helps them set sales goals, and then he leaves them alone unless they ask for assistance. The salespeople send in weekly sales reports but set their own hours and decide which customers in their territory to call on. What is the sales manager's leadership style?
11. In general, what kind of leadership style would a Theory X manager adopt? A Theory Y manager?
12. How do Theory Z managers motivate and lead their employees?
13. Which leadership approach is usually more suitable — Theory X or Theory Y? Explain.
14. Pat Petro tries to use contingency leadership. Every morning when she plans her day, Pat decides what management style will be most appropriate for achieving the day's goals. What is wrong with this approach to leadership?

Applied Exercises

1. How would you enrich a computer operator's job? Would you expect this approach to motivate the operator? Have you ever held a job that needed enrichment? Explain.
2. At the library, get a list of the compensation paid to the top 20 executives in the most recent year. (*Business Week* contains this informa-

tion once a year.) Based on this information, how much of a motivator is money? Defend your answer.

3. At the library, investigate current information on managing stress. Prepare a list of five stress management techniques. Your instructor may compile a master list of everyone's suggestions.

4. Construct in detail a situation where a Theory X style of leadership would be most effective. Do the same for a Theory Y situation.

Your Business IQ: Answers

1. True. Beginning in the 1970s, effective managers began to regard their employees as human resources. They try to create an environment in which employees can live up to their potential to be productive and creative.

2. False. Flexible work schedules allow people to determine the time when they will start and finish work during the day rather than the amount or pace of work during the day.

3. False. On the contrary, considerable research shows that setting specific and difficult work goals will lead to better performance than merely encouraging employees to "do the best you can."

4. False. Organizations have not been able to completely eliminate stress. They often are able to help their employees better cope with stress and in some cases eliminate it. However, effective organizations do not necessarily want to eliminate all stress.

5. False. Some effective managers are described by their subordinates as friendly, kind, and concerned people, but other effective managers are regarded as hard-nosed, demanding, and work-centered bosses. The most effective leadership style depends on the situation and the type of people being led.

Creel Morrell Copes with Growth

Business was booming at Creel Morrell, Inc., a Houston-based graphic design firm, but the company and Wes Creel, its chief executive, were in trouble. Orders were coming in faster than the employees could handle them, work was being completed at the last minute, and turnover was high. Wes Creel was overweight, exhausted, and in poor health. His wife and business partner Nancy couldn't remember the last time she had seen him in a good mood. His two daughters rarely saw him at all.

Creel Morrell's reputation brought in many orders. And the company's practice was to take on any work that was offered, whether the job was large or small. The company hired more and more people to do the work, but there was less and less time to train them. An artist working on one last-minute job might be pulled off it at a moment's notice to work on an even bigger rush. In addition, Wes and Nancy Creel had a habit of showing up unannounced to discuss ideas, further distracting employees from their day-to-day work.

A common complaint among staff members was Wes Creel's involvement in the details. Employees felt that he was the only person who knew what was going on, and that they didn't have a clear sense of direction. At the same time, Wes was frustrated with trying to juggle long-range planning and traveling to meet clients, while at the same time authorizing $100 checks and deciding what kind of soft drinks to put in the company vending machine.

The company's designers were frustrated, too. They joked about putting a mobile home on the roof so that they could get some rest. They were exasperated at being pulled from more complex projects to prepare business cards and order supplies.

Case Questions

1. What evidence can you cite to demonstrate that Wes Creel and his employees are experiencing burnout? What are some of their sources of stress?
2. What is Wes Creel's leadership style? Based on the information given, is it an appropriate style? Explain.
3. Eventually, Wes Creel hired a business consultant, who helped the company organize to reduce the sources of stress. What are some basic steps the company might take to operate more smoothly and reduce turnover? (You have less information than the consultant did, but you have some clues.)

You Be the Adviser: Helping Howard

As the Lorek Company expanded, it began filling many of its new supervisory positions with people from inside the firm. That is how Howard Iznek got his promotion. Howard has been with the firm for three years and has continually been evaluated as one of the highest performers in his department. Based on this performance, the company decided to promote him into the management ranks.

Howard is in charge of nine assemblers, each of whom puts together a hand-held calculator. The workers are expected to assemble 15 calculators an hour. Before Howard took over the unit, the average worker was assembling 13.5 calculators per hour. Management asked Howard to get the number up to 15, but it appears that just the reverse has occurred. Since Howard took command, the average worker's output has fallen to 11.7 an hour.

Howard is not the only new supervisor having productivity problems. As a result, management decided to investigate why. To date, the company has interviewed the supervisors and the workers and put together a general picture of Howard's leadership approach. It also gave Howard and the workers a questionnaire to fill out. Howard's questionnaire asked him to describe his leadership style; the workers' questionnaire asked each of them to describe Howard's leadership style. In both cases, the answers were the same: Howard has an autocratic style.

Your Advice

1. If you were advising Howard on how he could improve worker output, what would you tell him about motivation and leadership?
2. What type of motivation techniques and leadership style would you recommend that Howard use? Why?
3. How would you suggest that Howard change to or maintain the recommended leadership style? Be as specific as you can.

Personnel and Human Resource Management

LEARNING OBJECTIVES

- Describe human resource management.
- Explain the processes of human resource planning and staffing.
- Discuss employee training and development.

- Define and analyze the techniques for performance appraisal.
- Present the ways compensation and benefits maintain employees.
- Identify the important issues surrounding employee rights.

Your Business IQ

How much do you already know about personnel and human resource management? Test your business IQ by labeling each statement *true* or *false*. Answers and explanations are at the end of the chapter.

1. Some companies recruit new employees by paying current employees for recommendations.
2. An employment test that is consistent (the test-taker gets the same score time after time) may still be an inappropriate tool for screening employees.
3. Because of the great expense involved, few firms today make background and reference checks of job applicants.
4. The most widely used form of training is informal instruction at the job site.
5. Federal law requires employers to pay equally for jobs of comparable worth.

Coldwell Banker develops its employees' skills through a variety of techniques. In this training session, managers of residential brokerage offices use computer simulations to practice solving typical problems they might encounter in the course of their duties.

Source: The Sears, Roebuck and Co. 1986 Annual Report. Photographer, Jay Silverman, Hollywood, CA.

Looking Back and Ahead

Successful businesses don't take chances on having unknowledgeable personnel. Take, for example, L. L. Bean, a mail-order company specializing in camping and hunting equipment, which calls itself "the store that knows the outdoors." As the company has grown from a handful of employees to thousands, this expertise has begun to require special training. Moving beyond mere lectures, L. L. Bean has its employees actually put its merchandise to use by participating in activities such as backpacking, kayaking, and snowshoeing. For example, on one recent October outing, ten employees hiked the Appalachian Trail to become familiar with backpacking apparel and equipment.[1]

For motivating and leading to bring results, employees must also be qualified and well trained. This chapter moves beyond the general issues of motivation and leadership, discussed in the last chapter, to the more specialized personnel or human resource management function of businesses. This function is as important as the widely recognized business functions of operations (production), marketing, and finance.

After discussing the overall nature of human resource management, this chapter examines the specific activities involved: human resource planning, staffing, training and developing, appraising performance, maintaining staff with compensation and benefits, and managing careers and outplacements. The last section of the chapter explores the recently emerging issues surrounding employee rights.

Another, often major, responsibility of human resource management is union-management relations. This subject is so important that it will receive separate attention in Chapter 9.

The Nature of Human Resource Management

Human resource management The process of planning personnel needs; staffing the organization; and training, developing, appraising, and maintaining an organization's personnel.

Human resource management is the process of planning personnel needs, staffing the organization, and training, developing, appraising, and maintaining an organization's personnel. The terms *personnel management* and *human resource management* refer to the same basic organizational function. The newer of these terms, *human resource management,* recognizes that employees are not merely an expense but a resource of the firm, just as capital and equipment are resources.

Human resource management takes place on two levels. On one level, *all* managers, whether in the production, marketing, finance, or personnel departments, are human resource managers as long as they manage others. These managers provide their staff with assistance, counseling, guidance, and training, no matter what their technical specialty. The last chapter examined this responsibility. It is an important responsibility for overall effective management but one that managers often neglect. Many managers get so caught up in their technical specialties that they forget they have a human resource role as well.

Personnel managers Managers responsible for staffing the organization and training, developing, appraising, and maintaining its employees.

Human resource management is also a specialized area of the organization. Specialized managers, called **personnel managers,** are responsible for staffing the organization and training, developing, appraising, and maintaining its employees. Figure 8.1 illustrates the responsibilities typically associated with modern human resource management. This chapter focuses on the organizational level of human resource management, beginning with its historical background and present status.

213

CHAPTER 8

Personnel and
Human
Resource
Management

Historical Background

Over the last 60 years, the personnel or human resource department has evolved greatly. At the beginning of the century, although there were a few companies such as NCR and Ford that had departments handling personnel matters, foremen and supervisors largely took care of hiring, firing, and paying their own employees. The Great Depression in the 1930s brought legalization and power to trade unions through labor laws. To handle this more complex situation, companies created personnel departments. Personnel managers became responsible for hiring, firing, wage and salary administration, handling discipline problems, and administering benefit plans. They also handled employee relations and the negotiation and administration of union contracts.

The Current Status of Human Resource Management

Today, personnel managers carry ever-greater responsibilities. The human resource function is now being recognized as making a valuable contribution to the goals of businesses. In particular, many large firms rely heavily on their human resource departments to help plan for human resource needs and to advise top management in such areas as acquisitions and mergers. As one human resource manager recently commented, "We used to be an insecure bunch, but today we're being invited to a lot more parties."[2] This manager was referring to the fact that top management is coming to rely more and more on its human resource managers for help in making critical decisions.

At General Electric, Ford, General Motors, IBM, Mobil, Chase Manhattan, and many other large corporations, the head of the human resource (or personnel) department reports directly to the chief executive officer. From this vantage point, the personnel manager helps influence the overall direction of the company.

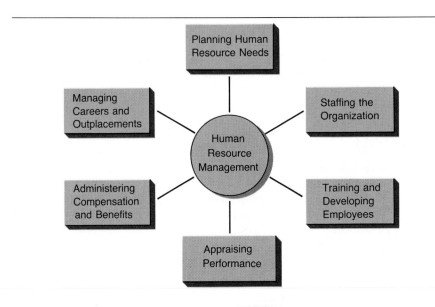

214

Checkpoint

1. What activities are involved in human resource management?
2. How has the management of human resources changed since the 1930s?

Human Resource Planning

The many activities included in the human resource function start with **human resource planning** (HRP), the process of forecasting personnel needs and developing the necessary strategies for meeting those needs. This information helps managers in several ways:

> Managers can anticipate personnel shortages or vacancies and act to create or fill jobs before problems arise.
>
> Managers can anticipate the types of training and development the personnel will need.
>
> Managers can identify the particular skills and abilities of the present employees to help develop effective career paths for them.
>
> Managers can evaluate the effect of human resource decisions and make any necessary changes.

Forecasting Human Resource Needs

Effective HRP starts with a forecast. The human resource forecast estimates the number and types of employees the organization will need over the next one to two years. The forecast also predicts the supply of employees to fill these needs. In predicting supply, the human resource manager considers internal sources, or employees who could be promoted or shifted into the vacant positions, as well as external sources: people currently in school, working for another company, or actively seeking employment.

For the owner of a small company, a forecast may be the only information needed to plan for human resource needs. The owner usually has a good idea of what kind of person would fill the needs of a new position. But in a larger, more complex organization, the human resource manager cannot possibly keep track of all the requirements for employees doing many different kinds of work. In these cases, HRP has a second step, job analysis.

Job Analysis

Job analysis is a comprehensive step in HRP that involves creating job descriptions and job specifications. First, an analysis is made of the jobs in the organization, with particular attention given to the tasks and skills involved in performing them. This list of the specific duties of a particular job is called a job description. The human resource manager next lists the qualifications for each of these duties—the education, abilities, and experience required of the person who fills the position. This list of qualifications is called the job specification. Often, a job description and

Human resource planning The process of forecasting personnel needs and developing the necessary strategies for meeting those needs.

215

CHAPTER 8

Personnel and
Human
Resource
Management

a job specification appear together on a single form and are referred to jointly as a job description.

Checkpoint

1. What activities are involved in human resource planning?
2. What is involved in job analysis?

Staffing the Organization

A major function of human resource managers is making sure that the company has the staff it needs. This staffing function involves more than simply hiring personnel. Staffing has several phases: recruiting, screening, testing, interviewing, conducting background checks, overseeing physical examinations, making employment decisions, and administering orientation and placement. Figure 8.2 illustrates this process.

Recruiting

The recruiting process involves locating and attracting qualified job applicants. Managers can find candidates both inside and outside the company.

Hiring from Within Most organizations prefer to recruit existing employees and promote them when possible. This policy helps motivate present

F I G U R E   8.2

The Staffing Process

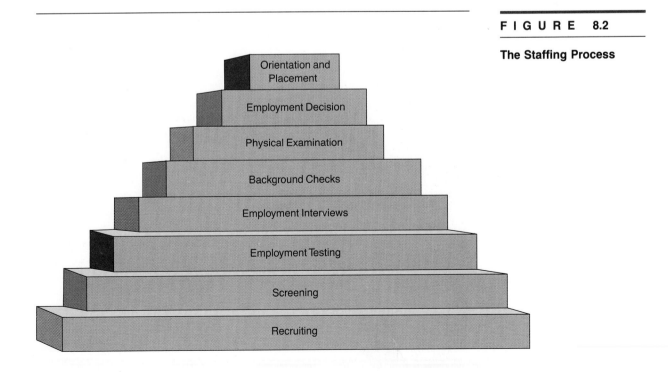

216

employees because they realize that if they do a good job, the organization will reward them with a promotion. Promoting from within also eliminates the cost of placing employment ads in newspapers and trade journals, sending recruiters out to interview, and paying private employment agencies and executive search firms.

Outside Sources A firm that recruits on the outside has many potential sources of employees. Some of the most common sources include private and public employment agencies and educational institutions. An often overlooked source of leads is present employees. Some companies even pay employees for their recommendations. For example, Baxter Travenol pays $350 to $500 to employees if a person they recommend is eventually hired.[3]

This recruiting advertisement appeared in several publications and employment directories published for prospective college graduates. College recruitment is popular among high-tech firms such as Perkin-Elmer. Among this company's products are analytical instruments and sophisticated optical systems; to develop and manufacture such products, the company hires graduates with degrees in engineering, computer science, and the natural sciences.

Source: Courtesy of The Perkin-Elmer Corporation.

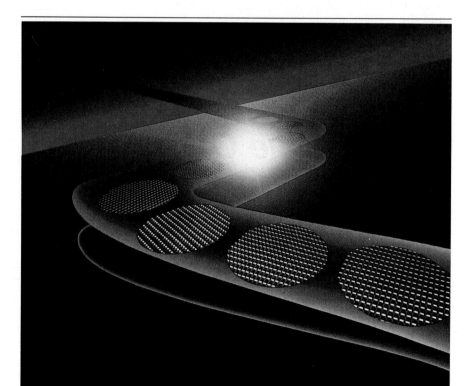

Next Assignment: The Future

And what a future it will be at Perkin-Elmer. Filled with challenging projects, opportunities for career advancement, and the satisfaction of being on the leading edge of technology in analytical instruments, semiconductor processing equipment, electro-optical systems, and surface science systems.

Perkin-Elmer is on the vanguard of technological advancement for this decade... this century...and beyond.

An Equal Opportunity Employer

PERKIN-ELMER

217

CHAPTER 8

Personnel and
Human
Resource
Management

Most organizations find that certain sources of recruits are more likely than others to provide them with qualified applicants for their particular needs. For example, insurance and high-tech firms have found university and college recruitment to be extremely effective. Most personnel managers, however, seem to prefer using newspaper ads and private employment agencies. The Bureau of National Affairs reports that community agencies and referrals are the best sources for locating minority and handicapped workers, and advertising is the best way to attract female applicants.[4] To recruit married candidates from out of the area, an attractive approach is often to help their spouses find work. For more details on this technique, see "Social Responsibility Close-Up: Relocating the Spouse."

Legal Climate Throughout the recruiting process and the employment steps that follow, the organization must take care to adhere to the letter and the spirit of legislation designed to regulate hiring practices. Firms have to avoid possible charges of discrimination on the basis of race, color, sex, or national origin. Table 8.1 summarizes some of the most important statutes pertaining to the employment process.

SOCIAL RESPONSIBILITY CLOSE-UP

Relocating the Spouse

The executive vice president of a large bank recently remarked, "We've found that talented people are frequently married to other talented people." This executive was discussing one of the major hurdles of attracting a top job applicant from another part of the country: These individuals will not accept a job offer unless their spouse also finds a good job.

Some firms have not yet learned this lesson. In one case, a woman who was receiving her MBA from a midwestern university asked a recruiter from a Chicago firm about job prospects for her fiancé. The recruiter handed her the Yellow Pages. Another brushed aside her question by saying, "Oh, he'll have no trouble. This is a big city." One firm, however, asked for the man's resume and gave the woman names of people in personnel departments in the Chicago area. The woman wound up accepting this company's job offer. The firm understood her desire to be in the same location as her husband-to-be.

More and more business firms are realizing that when they try to hire someone from another geographic area, they can sweeten the offer by providing relocation services. Few couples these days are going to jeopardize their marriage in exchange for a better job opportunity. As a result, firms are now beginning to provide resume advice, employment leads, and financial assistance to spouses, who often have to remain behind to sell the house and close up things on the other end. For example, IBM reimburses spouses up to $500 for expenses related to their own job search, and GM often spends twice this amount per spouse. Other firms provide airplane tickets so that the spouses can spend time together until one sells the house and joins the other. Businesses are finding that hiring a manager from out of town is becoming a two-part challenge.

**T A B L E   8.1   Important Laws
Regulating Hiring**

Law	What It Requires
Title VII of the Civil Rights Act of 1964 (as amended by the Equal Employment Opportunity Act of 1972)	Prohibits discrimination in employment on the basis of race, color, religion, sex, or national origin. Includes discrimination in hiring, firing, wages, benefits, classifying, referring, assigning, promoting, training, or apprenticeships.
Age Discrimination in Employment Act of 1968 (as amended)	Prohibits discrimination in employment against any person 40 years of age or over in hiring, firing, compensating, or any other conditions of employment.
Executive Order 11246 (1965)	Prohibits employment discrimination based on sex, race, color, religion, or national origin by federal contractors or subcontractors and on federally assisted construction contracts.
Equal Pay Act of 1963	Requires equal pay for men and women who work in the same establishment and whose jobs require equal skill, effort, and responsibility.
Rehabilitation Act of 1973	Requires employers to take affirmative action to employ and promote qualified handicapped individuals.
Pregnancy Discrimination Act (1978)	Requires business to treat pregnant women and new mothers the same as other employees for all employment-related purposes, including receipt of benefits under fringe benefits programs.
Vietnam Era Veterans Readjustment Assistance Act of 1974	Requires government contractors and subcontractors to take affirmative action to employ disabled veterans.

After a number of court cases where firms were tried and convicted of discriminatory hiring practices, many firms shied away and even dropped some of their procedures for systematically recruiting and selecting new employees. However, this reaction was not really justified or warranted. The courts and the general public never intended for companies to drop all recruitment and selection procedures, only those that discriminate on the basis of race, color, sex, age, or national origin. More recent prohibitions extend to discrimination against Vietnam-era veterans, women who are pregnant or new mothers, and the handicapped. The intent of these laws is to secure equal employment opportunities for everyone.

Screening

After recruitment, the human resource staff begins the selection process. This starts with screening, or eliminating applicants who are unlikely to succeed on the job. Screening takes place in a number of ways. One is to have job seekers fill out an application form. The recruiter compares the information from the application with the minimum training and experience specified in the job description for the position. For example, a life

219

CHAPTER 8

Personnel and
Human
Resource
Management

insurance company usually hires salespeople with a college degree. Applicants without a degree would therefore be screened out.

Another source of information for screening is resumes. Job seekers often prefer resumes over application forms because they have more control over the format; they can arrange the information in the most flattering way. However, human resource managers are often inundated with resumes and may feel that they all look alike after a while. Some job seekers have responded to this by looking for ways to make their resumes stand out, such as enclosing a short videotape of themselves being interviewed (see Technology Close-Up: Video Resumes).

Employment Testing

For the applicants who pass the initial screening, the next step in the selection process is often some form of employment testing. Whereas the screening determines whether applicants have the necessary background to do the job, the testing helps determine whether they can really meet the demands of the job.

TECHNOLOGY   CLOSE-UP

Video Resumes

Afraid that the traditional resume will only get lost in the paper shuffle of employers, some job hunters are taking a new approach. They are going on camera. These people are taping interviews about themselves and sending them out as "video resumes." For up to $300, job-search firms help the job hunters put themselves and their credentials on tape. The videos usually show the applicants from the waist up talking about themselves, their job experiences, and the kinds of positions they are looking for. Sometimes the tape shows the applicant answering questions posed by an off-screen narrator. Most videotapes run 3 to 5 minutes, but they can be as long as 20 minutes.

The companies that prepare the videotaped resumes usually coach the interviewees and practice the sessions. They also provide tips such as how to dress and relax. One checklist notes: "To avoid dry cotton-mouth, a bit of Vaseline can be applied to the inner upper and bottom lip."

Many job hunters like the video resumes because they present them in a flattering light, discussing the questions they want to answer. They also demonstrate how well the candidate can make presentations. Dancers and actors use them because they allow for a visual display of talent. A recruiter of salespeople found video resumes helpful in determining whether candidates had the right appearance, language skills, and presentation abilities. However, personnel managers and recruiters are less than uniformly enthusiastic about video resumes. They doubt the value of an interview in which someone else is asking the questions, and they resist taking the time to view them. Quality is also a problem. Some videos are no better than home movies, while others are so polished and acted out as to be unbelievable.

Job seekers rushing to the nearest video camera should first listen to James Schmidt, director of human resources for Apple Computer, Inc. When he recently received a video resume with a paper one, he sent back the taped version. "We get 9,000 resumes a month," Schmidt explained. "We don't have time to watch videos."

220

Types of Tests For jobs that depend on specific, measurable skills, the staff of the human resource department tries to assess whether applicants possess those skills. For example, does the applicant for the job of computer programmer have knowledge of the relevant computer languages? Can the machinist applicants operate a lathe properly? Can the proofreading applicants spell accurately? The tests that answer these questions are skill tests. For other jobs, skill in performing specific tasks is less important than the applicant's potential and personality. Aptitude and personality tests try to measure characteristics such as interests, attitudes, and feelings. Companies often use such tests for sales and managerial positions, where the skills of interacting with and leading people are important to job success, but evidence suggests that a growing number of firms are using them for entry-level, blue-collar jobs as well.[5] Most U.S. firms give about an hour-long test for entry-level, blue-collar workers, and candidates for top-management jobs take personality tests requiring a day or less. Toyota Motor Corp., by contrast, put applicants for entry-level, shop-floor jobs at its Georgetown, Kentucky, plant through 14 hours of testing.[6]

Validity and Reliability No matter what the purpose of an employment test, it must be both valid and reliable. A **valid** test measures what it is intended to measure. For example, if an applicant for the job of executive secretary is given a typing test for speed and accuracy, this would validly demonstrate typing skills. The test measures what the company wants it to measure. If the applicant takes a personality test and is turned down for the job because the results show characteristics that the firm considers inappropriate for a good secretary, the test is not valid unless the company can prove that these personality characteristics are required for the position and that the test really measures them.

For a test to be **reliable,** its results must be consistent and accurate. For a test of dexterity to be reliable, an applicant for an assembler's job who scores poorly should score poorly again if he or she repeated the test. A test must be reliable in order to be valid. However, a test may be reliable but not valid. In that case, the test is consistently and accurately measuring the wrong thing.

Most employment tests are reliable, and the ones used to determine specific skills, such as typing or hand-eye coordination, are also valid. The challenge facing human resource management is to develop and use valid and reliable tests for assessing leadership, personality, and certain complex abilities such as selling. Valid tests in these areas are needed not only to counter charges of discrimination in court, but more importantly to enable effective selection—getting the best person to fill the job.

Employment Interviews

After the initial screening and testing, the next step in the selection process is usually to interview the remaining applicants. The employment interview enables the interviewer to size up the applicant in person.

The interview may be structured or semistructured. A **structured interview** is one in which the interviewer follows a prepared format that consists of a series of direct questions. These questions specifically re-

Valid Tests that measure what they are intended to measure.

Reliable Tests that give consistent and accurate results.

Structured interview An interview that follows a prepared format that consists of a series of direct questions.

221

CHAPTER 8

Personnel and
Human
Resource
Management

quest desired information, for example, "Why did you leave your last job?" or "How did you find out about this current opening?"

In contrast, a **semistructured interview** is one in which the interviewer uses prepared questions to direct the interview but allows the interviewee to develop ideas that seem important. This interviewing style uses indirect questions such as "What do you expect of the company?" or "What can you contribute to the company?" to try to find out whether the individual seems interested in the job, has the right temperament to fit in with the existing personnel, and meets the job requirements. Most human resource managers prefer the semistructured interview, because the environment is more relaxed and allows the interviewer to obtain information beyond the application blank and test.

Regardless of the method, however, the interviewer must avoid questions that are considered discriminatory. For example, even if the company needs to know the applicant's marital status for insurance purposes, the interviewer must wait until after the individual is hired to obtain this information. Table 8.2 shows guidelines as to which questions are considered fair to ask and which are considered unfair.

Semistructured interview An interview that consists of prepared questions to direct the interview but that allows the interviewee to develop ideas that seem important.

Background and Reference Checks

After the initial screening, tests, and interviews, the human resource staff conducts background and reference checks of candidates still under consideration. Because of the employee's rights of privacy (discussed more fully in a later section), an increasing number of employers are unwilling to answer questions related to a former employee's education, overall character, safety record, union activity, or family background.[7]

T A B L E 8.2	Pre-employment Inquiries: Guidelines for Fairness	
Topic	**Fair Inquiry**	**Unfair Inquiry**
Age	Are you the minimum legal age?	How old are you? (Any inquiry that implies a preference for candidates under 40 years of age.)
Citizenship	Are you prevented from being lawfully employed in this country because of a lack of a visa or because of your immigration status? Are you a citizen?	Are you a naturalized citizen? What country did your parents come from?
Family	Will you have any problems meeting our work schedules? We start at 7 a.m. every work day, you know.	Does your spouse work? How much does he (or she) make? How many children do you have? What types of arrangements have you made for taking care of your children while you are at work?
Handicaps	Do you have any handicaps that would prevent you from doing this job?	Do you have any handicaps?
Marital Status	None.	Are you single, married, or divorced?
Military Record	What type of work experience did you gain in the military?	What type of military discharge did you receive? Can I see your records?
Name	Have you ever worked for this company before under a different name?	Your name is Polish (or any other ethnic reference) isn't it? Do you use Miss, Mrs., or Ms.?
Religion	None.	To what church do you belong? Are there any specific religious holidays that you observe?

Nevertheless, the personnel staff usually should still verify the basic information on the application blank. If an applicant has lied about anything, most firms will automatically drop the individual from further consideration.

Physical Examination

Many enterprises require job applicants to take a physical examination. One reason is that the firm wants to ensure that the individual is physically able to perform the job. An incoming top executive who is found to have a serious heart ailment may not be able to stand up to the pressures of the job. A loading-dock laborer with a slipped disk may not be able to carry anything weighing more than 10 pounds.

A special case in recent years has been AIDS victims. If co-workers find out that a new employee has this dreaded disease, they may raise a storm of protest. A recent poll of full-time working people found that 66 percent of them would be concerned about using the same restroom on the job as a person with AIDS, 40 percent would be bothered about eating in the same cafeteria, and 37 percent said they would not share tools or equipment.[8] Besides the obvious problem of getting along with co-workers, the afflicted person will also cost the company a great deal of money in disability payments and/or insurance premiums. However, the legal decisions so far have generally protected the rights of people with AIDS to keep working. Business will have to help contribute to the effort to better educate people how AIDS is transmitted and help in the fight against this growing problem.

Employment Decision

The final step in the employment process is the actual decision to hire. This final decision is usually made by the manager in the department where the individual will work. Staff in the human resource department usually take care of the preliminary steps and then recommend a candidate. The supervisor for whom the applicant will work reviews this recommendation, may conduct another interview with the candidate, and then decides to either hire the candidate or ask for another recommendation.

All newly employed people become part of the in-house pool of talent that serves as a source for future internal recruiting. Today, more and more companies are keeping track of this pool of talent by maintaining records of employees in specially designed computer programs. For example, a company's records could contain evaluations of all workers. When vacancies occur, managers can scan the evaluations to identify the ones that indicate supervisory potential or the best performance. The records can also contain special credentials, such as ability to speak French or experience with personal computers. When the company needs a person with such credentials, the computer can search the files and retrieve the appropriate records.

Orientation and Placement

Staffing the modern organization continues beyond selecting employees and includes orienting them and placing them in their new jobs. Orientation is the process of introducing a new employee to the job and creat-

223

CHAPTER 8

Personnel and
Human
Resource
Management

ing a basis for the employee to cooperate with the work unit as part of a team. A good orientation offers a number of important advantages. One is that well-oriented workers tend to get off on the right foot. They learn the "ropes to skip and the ropes to know"[9] in order to get along and be productive. Also, the orientation helps reduce anxiety associated with a new job and frees supervisors and co-workers from having to take time to answer questions or explain why things are being done in a particular manner.

Orientation Techniques In small companies, orientation often takes place informally. The new employee's boss or someone from the human resource department takes the employee around the facilities and introduces him or her to everyone. Then the direct supervisor fills in the newcomer on company procedures. In larger companies, the orientation process is often much more formal. A new employee receives a briefing and usually a booklet from the human resource department regarding company policies, rules, benefits, services, and other information.

Traditionally, companies presented such orientations in glowing terms, saying that this is the greatest job in the greatest company in the world. Now, research findings have led many companies to adopt what are called **realistic job previews**, which attempt to tell the full story about the job instead of creating false expectations. Considerable evidence suggests that realistic orientations significantly reduce turnover.[10]

Realistic job previews Orientations that attempt to tell the full story about the job instead of creating false expectations.

Placement Decision After the company has oriented the new employee, it places that person into the new job. This first assignment, and who the new employee works with and for, can affect this person's career and long-run contribution to the organization. This step will be crucial to the new employee in learning the proper values of the company. For example, is customer service just a slogan or a reality? Are people who take a risk and try something new rewarded? Human resource management often slights placement, but increasing evidence shows that this activity is as important as the preceding steps in the staffing process.

Checkpoint

1. What are the steps in staffing an organization?
2. Describe two ways managers can ensure they follow fair employment practices during the staffing process.

Training and Developing

To treat the company's employees as resources, managers cannot simply hire the necessary staff and call their job finished. Rather, managers need to help employees fulfill their potential by learning new skills and developing their abilities. Managers accomplish this through training and development.

Training is the process of teaching employees the procedures and techniques to do their job efficiently. A great deal of training takes place at the lower and intermediate levels of organizations. Examples include teaching employees to fill out a new cost-control report, run a simple program on the computer, process a customer order, or operate a machine or specialized piece of equipment.

A broader approach than training, development is the process of helping people gain the necessary skills and experiences they need to become or remain successful in their jobs. Whereas training is aimed more at lower-level operating employees, development takes place at the middle and upper levels of the organization. Examples include programs designed to help managers manage their time more effectively, build teamwork among their subordinates, and cope with stress.

Types of Employee Training and Development Programs

Human resource managers have a variety of choices in selecting training and development programs. The most common training approach is **on-the-job training,** which is informal instruction conducted at the job site. In the actual job environment, the trainee mainly learns by doing the job, with help provided by an experienced partner. Another traditional training approach used with operating employees is **apprentice training,** an approach that is similar to but more formal than on-the-job training. The employee learns a job by spending a relatively long time working directly with a more experienced employee, who teaches procedures, rules, and techniques.

A newer, less traditional approach to training is called mentoring. Specifically, a **mentor** is an experienced employee who coaches and counsels a less experienced employee in the latter's training and development. Mentors take the person "under their wing" or act as sponsors. A new salesperson may start out by teaming up with a mentor to make calls on

On-the-job training
Informal instruction conducted at the job site.

Apprentice training
Training a new employee by assigning a more experienced employee to teach procedures, rules, and techniques over a relatively long period.

Mentor An experienced employee who coaches and counsels a less experienced employee in the latter's training and development.

Often companies provide training by sponsoring employee attendance at professionally conducted seminars. The speaker shown here is one of 55 presenters on the staff of Padgett-Thompson Management Industries, which develops and conducts seminars on a variety of business topics. The programs emphasize skills and techniques that participants can immediately apply on the job.

Source: Courtesy of H&R Block, Inc.

225

CHAPTER 8

Personnel and
Human
Resource
Management

customers and prospects. During the calls, the new employee watches how the experienced mentor handles questions and closes sales; after a while, the mentor may have the new employee do more of the talking. The mentor will also provide guidance on how to get along with important managers and customers, and can transmit the cultural values of the organization. One study of a large group of successful executives found that over 60 percent had received help from a mentor.[11] Women and members of other groups that have traditionally experienced discrimination have successfully used mentors to get ahead in organizations.

To provide broader experience, companies may use **job rotation,** which involves moving an employee from one job to another. Although the approach is commonly used with operating employees to reduce boredom, it is becoming an increasingly popular approach to management development. This is especially true when the person not only moves from one routine job to another, as in traditional job rotation, but also learns new jobs requiring different skills or perspectives. This expanded version of job rotation is called **cross training** and in management ranks might involve moving an engineering manager into a short assignment in customer service and then on to a stint in sales. This provides managers with a broad understanding of how the overall business functions.

Job rotation Development of broad experience by moving an employee from one job to another.

Most companies also provide or encourage participation in off-the-job programs, formal training and development that takes place away from the job site. Such a program may be conducted by company trainers at a local motel or at corporate headquarters located in another city. Other programs are presented by professional training organizations such as the American Management Association or the American Society for Training and Development (ASTD), or by local colleges and universities that sponsor one-day training workshops and longer comprehensive programs. Examples might be a stress management workshop sponsored by ASTD held at a local hotel or a short course on personal computers given at the local college. One estimate is that there are 100,000 such programs offered annually and that corporations send 8 million of their people for such outside training at a cost of $4 billion.[12] In other words, training and development is big business.

Cross training An expanded version of job rotation, in which the employee learns different skills or perspectives.

These training and development techniques are helping businesses abroad as well as those in the United States. For some examples, see "International Close-Up: Human Resource Development Abroad."

Checkpoint

1. What are two ways companies train employees and two ways they develop employees?
2. How do managers decide on the kinds of training the company should offer?

Performance Appraisal

Once employees are in place and learning new skills, managers need to keep track of how the employees are doing. Human resource managers take responsibility for this activity by making sure the company has an effective means of performance appraisal. Performance appraisal is the systematic observation and evaluation of worker behavior. Managers use these evaluations to make decisions about promotion and compensation, as well as to uncover needs for training and development and to identify employees who have potential for advancement.

Types of Appraisals

Supervisory appraisal A performance appraisal in which the immediate supervisor evaluates the performance of a subordinate.

Performance appraisals take many forms. The most common is an evaluation by the supervisor. A **supervisory appraisal** is when the immediate superior evaluates the performance of a subordinate. Sometimes the human resource department supplements the supervisory appraisal with other forms of performance appraisal, such as peer ratings, subordinate

---

INTERNATIONAL **CLOSE-UP**

Human Resource Development Abroad

Many American businesses spend thousands (even millions) of dollars to train and develop their personnel. They also invest heavily in training in their overseas branches and subsidiaries. In fact, American firms typically spend more on training and development in other countries than do businesses based in those countries.

Consider the case of Taiwan, one of the most competitive business environments in the Far East. Recent research shows that American multinational firms in Taiwan spent more than Taiwanese firms in virtually every phase of training and development:

Annual Expenditures per Person for Training and Development

	Taiwanese Firms (22 firms)	American Multinationals (30 firms)
Unskilled and semi-skilled workers	$ 97	$125
Skilled workers	306	383
Administrative, professional, and managerial staff	148	176

Among high-tech firms, the expenditures per employee were even higher than these averages. This has led one high-ranking Taiwanese official to note, "Unless we start following the lead of the American multinationals and investing more money in the training and development of our people, we are going to find that our guests are able to produce and sell goods at much lower prices than our national firms. American companies have learned something that we here in the Far East must recognize — technology is important, but human resources are an organization's most important asset." The Japanese, of course, already know this. A National Bureau of Economic Research study concludes that Japanese workers stay in a job longer than U.S. workers, not because of cultural reasons, but because they are trained more.

ratings, and self-rating. A **peer rating** is one in which the workers all rate each other. The company sometimes uses this approach when it wants to give an award to the best worker in each unit and is interested in the workers' opinions about who should get the award. A **subordinate rating** is one in which the workers evaluate their superior. This reverse appraisal is particularly useful when the organization wants feedback on how the workers view their boss's leadership style. A **self-rating** is one in which the employees evaluate themselves. This rating is useful when management wants to compare how people see themselves against how their bosses see them. The evaluations indicate areas where disagreements exist. As might be expected, most employees rate themselves higher than their supervisors do.[13]

Personnel and
Human
Resource
Management

Rating Errors

In conducting performance appraisals, managers must be careful to avoid making rating errors. One common error is the **halo effect,** which is the tendency to allow an overall positive evaluation of the person to influence the specific characteristics being rated. For example, the supervisor likes Bob because he is so friendly and cooperative. The halo effect leads Bob's supervisor to automatically rate him high on all evaluation factors, including work quality and quantity as well as his ability to get along with the other members of the unit.

Another rating problem is the **severity error,** which occurs when a manager rates all of the subordinates lower than they deserve. For example, a supervisor may believe that no one ever deserves an outstanding rating in her department and therefore gives mostly average and poor ratings. This severity error may be punishing relatively good subordinates.

The opposite kind of error is the **leniency error,** which occurs when a manager rates most employees as above average or excellent. If a supervisor rates 75 percent of the employees as outstanding and the rest as good, the supervisor is probably making leniency errors. Just as the severity error punishes good employees, so does the leniency error. The supervisor who is too lenient penalizes the best performers by preventing them from building performance records that are clearly superior to those of the average performers.

Peer rating A performance appraisal in which the workers all rate each other.

Subordinate rating A performance appraisal in which the workers evaluate their superior.

Self-rating A performance appraisal in which the employees evaluate themselves.

Halo effect The tendency to allow an overall positive evaluation of a person to influence the specific characteristics being rated.

Severity error A rating error in which a manager rates all of the subordinates lower than they deserve.

Leniency error A rating error in which a manager rates most employees above average or excellent.

Checkpoint

1. What are two ways of appraising an employee's performance?
2. What are two ways in which supervisors can make errors in appraising performance?

Maintaining Human Resources: Compensation and Benefits

Human resource managers know that to retain their good employees, they must reward them fairly for their time and effort. The formal reward system takes the form of compensation and benefits. Supervisors use informal rewards such as increased responsibility and other techniques discussed in Chapter 7, and they often also make decisions concerning what to pay individual employees. The human resource department, on the other hand, is responsible for managing the overall package of compensation and benefits that the company offers.

Compensation Management

Compensation serves as both a payment to employees for their past efforts and an incentive for future performance. The payment for past efforts may take the form of wages (payment per hour worked) or salaries (payment at a flat monthly or annual rate). Incentive pay is usually tied to performance.

To assemble a compensation package, human resource managers weigh wage and salary levels for the industry and geographic area against the firm's ability to pay. Most companies pay about what the competition is paying. If they pay less, they may have trouble attracting and keeping good workers. If they pay more, they may have a hard time keeping the prices they must charge for their goods or services competitive. If management determines that it is overpaying an individual or type of job, the company can freeze the pay at that level until the market catches up. If the company is underpaying, it can increase the compensation until it eliminates the difference. There are a number of important current issues related to this compensation process.

Equal Pay for Equal Worth The Equal Pay Act of 1963 and the Civil Rights Act of 1964 require employers to pay employees equally for doing the same job (see Table 8.1). Therefore, under the law, a female accounting clerk must be paid the same as a male accounting clerk with similar experience in the same office. Likewise, a black or Hispanic welder with two years' experience must receive the same pay as a white welder with two years' experience.

The City of Colorado Springs was the first city in the United States to adopt a policy of comparable worth. City officials analyzed the responsibilities, skills, and difficulties of various jobs and assigned points to each job to represent its worth. For example, the officials determined that a senior accounting clerk and an on-site carpentry foreman were doing jobs of comparable worth. The city then accelerated salary increases for the lower-paying, female-dominated positions until the lower salaries were at least 80 percent of those paid for the male-dominated jobs.

Sources: © 1986 John Lawlor/The Stock Market. © 1984 Craig Hammell/The Stock Market.

Comparable Worth A controversial issue facing compensation management is whether employers should pay equally for different jobs that have comparable worth to the company. Some people argue that jobs requiring equal amounts of skill and responsibility are of **comparable worth** to an employer, and that employees performing jobs of comparable worth should receive equal pay. Some state and local government agencies have explored and in a few cases implemented policies based on equal pay for comparable worth. The city of Colorado Springs, for example, determined that it was paying less for jobs held primarily by female workers, such as clerical work, than it was for jobs requiring a similar degree of responsibility (comparable worth) but filled primarily by male workers. The city then planned a way to bring the salaries more closely into line. It increased the salaries of the jobs held primarily by women faster than the salaries of the jobs held predominantly by men. Four years later, the differences were minimal. Figure 8.3 provides two examples of how salary gaps were narrowed.

Most private-sector (nongovernment) organizations have resisted the idea of comparable worth. Those who object to this policy argue about the difficulty and subjectivity involved in attempting to calculate the worth of different jobs. They also note that market forces influence compensation. For example, if there are a large number of applicants for a particular job (a large supply) and/or if there are very few openings (low demand) for a particular job, this market situation will affect the wages paid for the job. Thus, if there is an oversupply of, say, clerical workers, it is very difficult for a company to justify paying higher wages when there are plenty of people who will work for lower wages.

CHAPTER 8

Personnel and
Human
Resource
Management

Comparable worth The idea that jobs requiring equal amounts of skill and responsibility are of equal value to the employer and therefore should receive equal pay.

F I G U R E   8.3

Narrowing the Salary Gap between Jobs of Comparable Worth

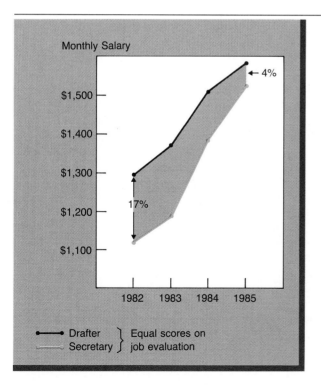

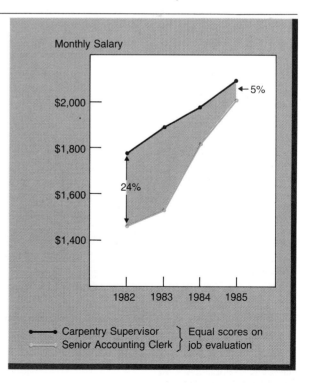

Nevertheless, some companies, including AT&T, are moving toward paying equally for work of comparable worth.

Performance-Based Compensation Besides paying wages and salaries, many companies offer their employees the incentive of performance-based compensation. During the last decade, pay linked to performance has become increasingly popular.

The compensation may reward individual or group performance. An **individual incentive payment plan** rewards a specific worker for high performance. The most popular such plan is **straight piecework,** in which employees are paid in direct relation to their output. For example, a plan that pays 40 cents per item will pay $4 to a worker who produces 10 items and $6 to a worker who produces 15 items. Besides piecework, which is associated with production workers, individual incentive plans can also be designed for salaried employees. For example, at General Motors they moved to a pay-for-performance plan. Under the old system, all salaried employees received about the same pay increases. Under the new plan, employees who are evaluated to have performed well receive big increases and those who performed poorly receive little or nothing. The vice president for personnel noted that, "A merit increase is something you have to earn. To treat people fairly you have to treat people differently."[14]

Although individual incentive payment plans are usually associated with manufacturing plants, other types of firms are also beginning to use this approach. At Union National Bank in Little Rock, Arkansas, 70 percent of 500 employees, from entry-level clerks to senior vice presidents are eligible for incentive pay. Teresa Lee, a 22-year-old teller at the bank, is a whiz at balancing her accounts at the end of the day, drumming up extra sales for the bank, and handling up to 500 transactions on a busy day. By doing so, she also adds up to $130 of incentive pay to her weekly paycheck.[15]

In addition to individual plans, a number of **group incentive plans** are also in operation today. These plans are designed to provide incentive pay to units, departments, and sometimes the entire organization when they meet or exceed a goal. Group incentives promote working for and with the group instead of against the group. That result is especially important in jobs requiring group cooperation and teamwork. For example, construction crews and many manufacturing jobs depend on group efforts and would benefit from group incentive programs.

Benefits and Services

Besides compensating employees, most companies offer employee benefits and services. Although during tight economic times some companies will cut back on benefits, most still offer a wide variety. Besides those required by law, the major categories of benefits are pensions, insurance, paid vacations and leave time, and employee services.

Legally Required Benefits Some benefits are required by law. The most important ones protect employees who are injured, disabled, retired, or between jobs:

> **Workers' compensation** provides compensation to those who suffer job-related injuries or illnesses.

Individual incentive payment plan Compensation that rewards a specific worker for high performance.

Straight piecework A compensation plan in which employees are paid in direct relation to their output.

Group incentive plan Compensation to units, departments, and sometimes the entire organization for meeting or exceeding a goal.

Workers' compensation A legally required benefit that provides compensation to those who suffer job-related injuries or illnesses.

Social security A legally required benefit that provides disability payments, old-age benefits, and survivors' benefits.

Social security provides disability payments, old-age benefits, and survivors' benefits.

Unemployment insurance provides subsistence payments to employees who have been laid off.

Pension Programs Many companies also offer pension programs, which are designed to provide employees with income for their retirement years. Today, approximately 60 percent of all hourly and salaried workers in the United States are covered by pension plans. In some cases, the employer makes the entire contribution; in other cases, the employer and the employee both contribute to the plan. Either way, the objective is to help the employee build up savings for retirement.

Insurance Programs Another major benefit is **insurance benefit programs.** Companies offer these programs to supplement government programs so that their employees have a sense of well-being and security. These programs provide various forms of coverage against accident, illness, or death. One of the most common insurance benefits is life insurance, which provides a stated benefit (for example, $25,000) if the person dies while the policy is in force. Today, most large and medium-sized companies and a growing number of small companies provide their full-time employees with a basic life insurance plan that is totally employer-financed.[16]

Another common form of coverage is health insurance. Most firms provide their employees with at least basic coverage, which pays (partially or totally) hospital-related expenses, surgical expenses, and physicians' expenses. Some firms also offer insurance that covers dental care, alcoholism treatment, drug abuse treatment, and vision care.

Other Benefits and Services In addition to pensions and insurance, companies offer many other benefits, often referred to as "fringe benefits." They include payment for time not worked, such as paid vacation, paid sick leave, payment for holidays not worked, and payment for time lost due to a death in the family.

Other fringe benefits are employee services. These include a variety of monetary and nonmonetary benefits, such as tuition assistance, company-provided cars, credit unions, financial counseling, and day-care centers. For example, almost one-third of Polaroid's employees take tuition-free courses for personal development on company time. Employees of Zale Corporation in Dallas can eat lunch with their young children at the company's on-site day-care center.[17] America West Airlines screens babysitters and their homes for its Home Caregivers program and reserves spaces for employees' children at a 24-hour facility.[18]

Flexible Benefits Because so many options are available, companies often give personnel some of the benefits and allow them to choose others up to a particular limit. This **flex benefits approach** allows each worker to tailor his or her own benefit package. For example, in addition to basic life and health insurance, employees may pick certain other benefits worth up to a maximum dollar amount, such as $5,000 annually. They may select the benefits that are of most value to them. Primerica and other users of this approach have received an enthusiastic reaction from their employees.[19]

Unemployment insurance A legally required benefit that provides subsistence payments to employees who have been laid off.

Insurance benefit programs Benefits designed to provide various forms of coverage against accident, illness, or death.

Flex benefits approach An employee benefit arrangement that allows each worker to tailor his or her own benefit package.

Zale Corporation was among the first U.S. companies to offer company-sponsored day-care facilities for children of employees. The growing number of single-parent and two-career families has made this employee benefit increasingly popular.

Source: Courtesy of Zale Corporation.

Checkpoint

1. What are the basic components of compensation and benefits?
2. Why do some companies offer group rather than individual incentives?

Managing Careers and Outplacements

A recently emerging concern for human resource management is managing the future of present employees on the one hand and the future of those who leave on the other. Careers have always been important to individual employees, and now companies are beginning to realize that systematic career management is also important to the effectiveness of the company.[20] Some companies are also acknowledging that employees who are terminated may require special types of assistance. They are using a more positive approach called outplacement, which can benefit both the person leaving and, in the long run, the company.

Career Management

Employees' careers are usually expressed in terms of promotion and transfer. A promotion is a move upward in one's career, and a transfer is a lateral move to another department or location. Career management actively plans and prepares employees for these changes through training and development efforts.

One way in which human resource managers take an active role in career management is through **career pathing.** This is the process of identifying a sequence of job assignments through which a person can move from one position to another laterally or up the hierarchy. Career paths have always existed in organizations, if only informally.[21] Working together, the human resource department and the targeted employee can map out a career path. In many firms, for example, operating employees who do well can move up to the supervisory ranks and then on to department manager and higher.

Career pathing The process of identifying a sequence of job assignments through which a person can move from one position to another laterally or up the hierarchy.

Outplacement Management

Employees leave the organization for different reasons. They may resign when they find what they think is a better job elsewhere. They may retire. They may die or become disabled. However, employees may also leave at the company's request. If the company is experiencing economic difficulties or is scaling back operations, which has been a fact of life in the 1980s in industries such as steel, oil, and automobiles, it may lay off workers. In this case, the human resource department may assist management in reducing the consequences of job loss. This is called **outplacement.**

Outplacement Human resource management efforts to help reduce the consequences of job loss.

The outplacement effort includes paying departing employees for a set number of weeks or months. A recent survey found that managers earning $50,000 to $150,000 per year receive an average 8 months' severance pay and those making between $150,000 and $200,000 receive an average 11 months' salary when they are pushed from their jobs.[22] They

233

CHAPTER 8

Personnel and
Human
Resource
Management

are also sometimes carried on the company's insurance plan for an extended period or assisted in finding another job. The human resource department may even provide trained experts to help managers break the bad news to their subordinates. Some companies also pay for outplacement consulting firms, which have grown in number from 80 to 160 in the 1980s, to provide a "transition center" for the departed employee. They provide secretarial help and counseling and offer seminars on assessing strengths and weaknesses, developing resume writing and interviewing skills, and building a self-marketing plan. As the head of one of these firms states, the goal of outplacement is to help the displaced employee overcome a "heavy sense of failure and loss."[23]

Checkpoint

1. What is involved in a career pathing approach to career management?
2. How do human resource managers assist in outplacing?

Issues Concerning Employee Rights

In recent years, employee rights have become a major area of concern in human resource management. Most attention has focused on three areas: sexual harassment, disability, and privacy.

Sexual Harassment

Sexual harassment consists of any unwelcome sexual advance. A typical incident might involve a supervisor promising a subordinate a more desirable task assignment or a positive evaluation in return for sexual favors. Harassment can also consist of unwelcome hugs or pats. Although usually thought of as a problem for women in the work place, some men are also experiencing harassment. Studies have found that 42 percent of American women and 24 percent of Finnish women reported experiencing sexual harassment. However, surveys have reported that 15 percent of American men and 26 percent of Finnish men felt sexual harassment as well.[24]

Title VII of the Civil Rights Act specifically outlaws sexual harassment. In recent years, a number of lawsuits have been filed by employees who charged that they were sexually harassed. The court decisions that followed have been instrumental in shaping company policies regarding how to handle complaints of sexual harassment. For example, in one case the court held that the employer is liable for the acts of its personnel. The only way for the firm to avoid being responsible is for it to have a written policy that specifically prohibits sexual discrimination and harassment and to show that the employee who violated the policy was aware of it. In another case, the court held that a company is responsible if it fails to investigate complaints of sexual discrimination.[25]

What can organizations do to prevent or stop sexual harassment? The many possible measures include:

Formulating and communicating an effective policy that defines what sexual harassment is and states that it will not be tolerated.

Sexual harassment Any unwelcome sexual advance.

Establishing a grievance procedure that employees can follow if they want to lodge a complaint.

Investigating all complaints thoroughly and objectively.

Making a decision regarding the offender based on the facts and following up to ensure that the decision is being carried out.

Disability

The law defines a handicapped person as anyone who has a physical or mental impairment that substantially limits one or more major life activities. But many people with a major physical or mental impairment prefer to characterize themselves as challenged, rather than handicapped, by a disability. They feel that labels such as handicapped prevent them from many job opportunities that they can effectively perform. Today's enlightened firms have a sense of social as well as legal responsibility to those challenged by a disability.

Contractors who do work for the federal government are legally required to develop recruitment efforts to attract qualified people who happen to have a disability and are not currently in the work force. They are also required by law to create and adapt the work environment to help accommodate these individuals. This may mean putting in special ramps that allow easy access to the building, locating parking facilities close to the building, and designing accessible rest rooms.

Research shows that many firms are meeting these legal requirements, spending thousands of dollars to make the facilities more accessible. One group of consultants found that the average cost of converting facilities ranges from 5 to 7 cents per square foot, a price that is easily within the budget of most firms.[26]

Best of all, many organizations are finding that employees challenged with a disability are excellent workers. A recent poll of 921 companies found that 88 percent of the department heads responded that disabled workers do a "good" or "excellent" job.[27] Research also shows that disabled workers often turn out to be more intelligent, more motivated, better qualified, and better educated than those without a disability. They also have lower accident rates.[28] Hiring people challenged by a disability is indeed good business.

Privacy

Another important employee right is that of privacy.[29] The federal government's Privacy Act of 1974 guarantees employees of federal agencies some degree of privacy with regard to information available to potential employers who are checking references. The act allows employees to determine which records the company collects, uses, and keeps. Since the 1974 law, there has been a great deal of interest in and legislation about employee privacy. Some states have enacted privacy laws, which allow employees to examine their personnel records.

Many companies are beginning to give more attention to employee privacy. For example, Cummins Engine's privacy policy extends to the desk files that supervisors keep on their subordinates. All performance review notes are discarded, and all disciplinary reviews are thrown out after the disciplinary period is over. At Northrop, a major government

235

CHAPTER 8

Personnel and
Human
Resource
Management

contractor, information gathered for federal clearances is kept separate from ordinary personnel records in order to maintain employees' privacy.[30] Chase Manhattan Bank has a formal privacy policy that assures that an employee's file will be seen only by those who need to know the information in it. Except for confirming employment dates, the bank will release other employee data to outsiders only after that individual has given permission.

Employment at Will

Fired employees often wonder whether the company had a right to force them to leave. "It wasn't fair!" they often exclaim. In fact, employers can usually fire anyone, unless the firing is based on unlawful discrimination or in retaliation for union activities or for reporting unlawful behavior on the part of the company (whistleblowing). The courts have long upheld the principle of **employment at will,** which means that the employer can retain or dismiss personnel as it wishes. If employees do not perform up to expectations, the employer may dismiss them.

Employment at will The principle that the employer can retain or dismiss personnel as it wishes.

However, in recent years, the courts have weakened this employer right.[31] In particular, the courts ruled that companies must act in good faith. For example, if a manager tells an employee, "We never fire anyone without giving a second chance," then the company may not fire this employee for making only one mistake. Likewise, the courts have held that employees cannot be fired to prevent them from collecting a sales bonus or to stop them from qualifying for the company's retirement program.

As of 1986, the right of companies to force personnel to retire on the basis of age is illegal. However, some companies, such as Polaroid Corporation and Bankers Life in Chicago, have never had a mandatory retirement policy. Anna Marie Buchmann, the vice president for human resources at Bankers Life, probably best summarized the whole modern perspective on personnel and human resource management when she stated: "Our policy toward older workers is the same as it is toward employees of any age. The ability to peform the job determines whether or not the individual is hired or retained."[32]

Checkpoint

1. What are two ways in which companies can minimize sexual harassment?
2. Why do some companies try to hire and accommodate workers challenged with a disability?

Closing Comments

This chapter explored the dimensions of human resource management. This function extends beyond hiring to planning, staffing, training, appraising performance, administering benefits, and managing careers and outplacement. In addition, many interesting and relevant issues face the human resource manager, including avoiding charges of discrimination and respecting employee rights.

Learning Objectives Revisited

1. **Describe human resource management.**

   Human resource management is the process of planning for, staffing, training, developing, appraising, and maintaining an organization's personnel. Supervisors used to handle this function, but since the 1930s, personnel and now human resource departments bear that responsibility. Today the human resource department also formulates human resource plans, manages careers and outplacements, and even advises top management in areas such as acquisitions and mergers.

2. **Explain the processes of human resource planning and staffing.**

   Human resource planning begins with a forecast of the number and kinds of employees needed to run the operation over the next year or two. If additional positions must be filled, the plan addresses sources of recruits and ways to attract them. Planning also includes preparation of job descriptions and specifications. Staffing begins where the plan leaves off. It involves recruiting, screening, testing, and interviewing job applicants and orienting and placing newly hired employees. The new employees come from the pool of job applicants that survive the selection process. The actual hiring decision is usually made by the manager to whom the individual will directly report.

3. **Discuss employee training and development.**

   The most common types of employee training are on-the-job training and apprentice training. Mentors, experienced employees who act as sponsors for the new employees, can also be used in certain situations. Other types of training and development programs include job rotation, cross training, and the use of outside workshops and programs.

4. **Define and analyze the techniques for performance appraisal.**

   Performance appraisal is the systematic observation and evaluation of worker behavior. Some of the most commonly used types of appraisal are supervisory appraisals, in which the immediate superior evaluates subordinates; peer ratings, in which workers rate each other; subordinate ratings, in which the workers evaluate their superior; and self-ratings, in which workers evaluate themselves. Some common rating errors that cause problems in performance appraisals are the halo effect and the severity and leniency errors.

5. **Present the ways compensation and benefits maintain employees.**

   Compensation management combines wages and salaries with performance-based compensation. The wage and salary levels are usually tied to what other firms in the industry pay. Performance-based compensation includes individual incentive plans, such as straight piecework, and group incentive plans. In addition, companies provide benefits and services. Legally required benefits are workers' compensation, social security, and unemployment insurance. Other benefits include pension programs, insurance programs, and a variety of so-called fringe benefits.

237

CHAPTER 8

Personnel and
Human
Resource
Management

6. Identify the important issues surrounding employee rights.
Some of the most important areas that human resource managers must consider in their efforts to protect employee rights are preventing sexual harassment, hiring and maintaining employees challenged by a disability, ensuring employee privacy, and understanding the concept of employment at will.

Key Terms Reviewed

Review each of the following terms. For any that you do not know or are unsure of, look up the definitions and see how they were used in the chapter.

human resource management	halo effect
personnel managers	severity error
human resource planning	leniency error
valid	comparable worth
reliable	individual incentive payment plan
structured interview	straight piecework
semistructured interview	group incentive plan
realistic job previews	workers' compensation
on-the-job training	social security
apprentice training	unemployment insurance
mentor	insurance benefit programs
job rotation	flex benefits approach
cross training	career pathing
supervisory appraisal	outplacement
peer rating	sexual harassment
subordinate rating	employment at will
self-rating	

Review Questions

1. For what activities is the human resource department typically responsible? How has this changed since the beginning of this century?
2. Why do managers engage in human resource planning? How do they conduct this process?
3. The owner of a fictional manufacturing company believes that minority workers are less productive than other workers. He will hire them, but he pays them less than other workers and refuses to "waste my good money" on putting them through the training programs available for other employees. This owner claims, "I'm well within the law, because I'm providing equal employment opportunity. I hire them just like I have to." Is this owner in fact abiding by the fair employment laws? Explain.
4. Clarissa Lee, president of You Wreck—We Fix Auto Body, is considering using a personality test in selecting workers for her chain of automobile body shops. "Well," said a human resource management

consultant, "the information would be interesting. But you should know that while the test you're considering is reliable, it's not really valid for your purposes." What does the consultant mean by this?

5. James Hampton is head teller at Great National Bank. When orienting new employees, he likes to get them off to a positive start by giving them a glowing description of life as a teller at Great National. What's wrong with this approach? What should James do instead?

6. Because Stephanie Grant can't be at both of her flower shops at the same time, she instituted a system of performance appraisals. The manager of each shop rates the employees who work at that shop. In reviewing the appraisal forms, she noticed that the employees at the downtown shop consistently received higher scores than the employees at the shopping center store. Does this mean she has better employees at the downtown shop? Explain.

7. What is the difference between equal pay for equal work and equal pay for jobs of comparable worth? Why is the latter concept controversial?

8. How can human resource managers tie compensation to performance?

9. How can human resource managers manage careers? How can the company benefit from this?

10. What is sexual harassment? How can companies prevent and stop it?

11. Adapting the work environment to make it accessible to those with a disability can be an expense to a company. Why would they want to do it?

12. Doug Sanderson's boss fired him because they didn't get along very well. In Doug's opinion he always did a good job; his only problem was a personality clash with the boss. Did Doug's company have a right to dismiss him? Explain.

Applied Exercises

1. Look through a recent edition of *The Wall Street Journal* and pick two of the employment ads. What types of jobs are the ads for? Why would a company advertise rather than use an employment agency to help find applicants for each of these jobs?

2. Visit a local firm and get a copy of its job application form. What does the form look like? What types of information does it request? What additional information do you think it should gather? Describe the form and your suggestions for improvement.

3. Visit a local firm that has its own personnel or human resource department. Find out what types of employment tests the department administers to job applicants. Then write a brief paragraph describing each test and why the firm uses it.

4. Interview a senior-level manager at a nearby large firm and find out how they deal with sexual harassment problems. Also, ask what steps the firm has taken to protect its employees' right to privacy. Write a summary of your findings.

Your Business IQ: Answers

1. True. Present employees can be an important source of leads, and many companies pay a referral bonus of $350 or more to employees who recommend well-qualified candidates. Typically the company pays the bonus if a candidate is hired and stays on the job for a stipulated period, such as six months.

2. True. The test should also measure what it is supposed to measure, usually how well the employee will perform on the job. A test that consistently measures the wrong thing will be of no use. Consistency of measurement is reliability; what the test measures is its validity. Validity is the key for effective selection tests.

3. False. Background and reference checks are still a common way to verify information on the application blank, although concern about rights to privacy is causing some firms to re-evaluate releasing such information.

4. True. This training, called on-the-job training, is the most widely used approach.

5. False. Federal law prohibits discrimination involving employees performing the same job (equal pay for equal work), but no federal law requires equal pay for different jobs that are judged to have comparable worth. Some state and local governments are paying equally for jobs of comparable worth, but this is still a controversial policy.

Case

Lorena Weeks, Fair Employment Pioneer

Today it's easier to take fair employment practices for granted. Overt actions and policies of sex and race discrimination are rare enough that most black, Hispanic, Asian, and female workers have come to expect an equal opportunity to succeed in business.

But it was only about two decades ago that women were filing pioneering sex discrimination lawsuits. For example, that was when Lorena Weeks brought suit against her employer, Southern Bell Telephone Company. She was a clerk and applied for a higher-paying job as a switchman. The company refused, citing a state law barring women from jobs that involved lifting more than 30 pounds (about the weight of an average two-year-old child). While the law was ostensibly on the books to protect women, Weeks believed it was a way to reserve the best jobs for men. She recalls that a union official told her he didn't want women to get such jobs because men were the "breadwinners."

Southern Bell lost the lawsuit in a 1969 landmark decision opening to women all previously all-male jobs. Today, switchmen are called switching-equipment technicians, and 140 women hold that position at Southern Bell. Weeks herself held the job for nearly 20 years.

However, she learned that problems don't always end when the court battle does. During her time at Southern Bell, she had to cope with resentful superiors and fight for training and favorable job openings. When the company installed new equipment, Weeks reports, her supervisors tried to send her to an older facility rather than retraining her. She threatened to take the company back to court, and her supervisors gave in.

Today, Weeks is retired and lives quietly with her husband in Georgia. "That was a chapter in my life," she says, "and now I've gone on to other things."

Case Questions

1. From what you have learned about the recruiting process, why is it to a company's advantage to practice equal employment opportunity?
2. Weeks threatened to return to court during her time as a switching-equipment technician. What claim could she have made if she had?
3. If you had been the human resource manager at Southern Bell, how would you have handled the problems between Weeks and her supervisors? Explain any actions you would take.

You Be the Adviser: Hit the Ground Running

Business has been so good at the Waxler Corporation that the board of directors has decided to open a new plant. The company manufactures and wholesales small appliances designed for the do-it-yourself home repairer. This market has grown so much over the last five years, largely due to franchising, that Waxler has seen its business mushroom. In particular, the high quality of the firm's products and its ability to meet delivery deadlines have helped it increase market share.

The board would like to see the company take over and refurbish the facilities of a plant that has gone out of business. This will eliminate the time delay associated with building a facility from the ground up. Then the company will have to recruit a work force of approximately 325 blue-collar workers and 125 managers and other white-collar workers. A site selection committee has been formed and hopes to make a final decision within 30 days. The head of the human resource department, Pat de Vries, has been charged with recruiting the necessary personnel.

The president would like Pat to get started immediately by drawing up a proposed plan of action. "Put together a plan that can be implemented the moment we have made our final decision about where we are going to set up the new plant," the president told Pat. "Then as the refurbishing is going on, you can be making progress toward getting the work force put together. I want to start using those facilities at the earliest possible moment. Let's see if we can't hit the ground running." Pat has 30 days in which to work up an overall plan.

Your Advice

1. If you were advising Pat, what would you suggest about recruiting people for this new plant? Offer at least two practical recommendations.
2. What steps will Pat have to take in screening job applicants? What should the plan include at this stage?
3. If the president also wanted these new hires to have some training and development within the first six months after the plant opened, what should the plan include? Be as specific as possible in your recommendations.

Union-Management Relations

LEARNING OBJECTIVES

- Explain what a union is and why employees join unions.
- Discuss the history of the labor movement in the United States.
- Describe union structures and functions.

- Present the dimensions of the collective bargaining process.
- Identify ways unions and management resolve disputes.
- Relate the major challenges facing unions.

Your Business IQ

How much do you already know about union-management relations? Test your business IQ by labeling each statement *true* or *false*. Answers and explanations are at the end of the chapter.

1. Unionizing efforts during the 19th century were greatly aided by the fact that the Constitution permitted the lawful assembly of people, so employers had to be careful in their efforts to attack unions.
2. For a company to be unionized, two-thirds of the workers must vote for the union.
3. When union members have a disagreement with their supervisor, the initial step is to call for a strike or walkout.
4. Over the last 35 years, union membership among the nonfarm work force has been increasing slowly.
5. Employees in the service sector are currently an important target of unionizing efforts.

Successful union-management relations involve discussion and effort to arrive at mutually acceptable solutions.

Source: © Diana Walker 1984, Gamma Liaison.

Looking Back and Ahead

Samuel Gompers, the recognized father of the modern American labor union movement, is known for his demand of "More, more, more!" This famous phrase represents the way many people, including some owners and managers of today's business firms, feel about unions and what they are trying to get. They believe unions are unreasonable and always want more. Are these people right? Have unions pushed too far? Or, as many other people—including union members and their leadership—would say, unions have benefited not only working people, but also society at large. Samuel Gompers also said, "The worst crime against working people is the company that fails to operate at a profit." This little-known quote recognizes that profit making is important not only to owners and managers, but also to union members. But beneficial or detrimental, unions are an important part of modern business.

In many organizations, a large part of managing human resources involves union-management relations. Management's relationship with unions is often crucial to the success of modern business firms. If a company has a good relationship with its employees in general and the union in particular, operations are likely to move smoothly and both groups can prosper. In contrast, animosity and conflict, work slowdowns, contract disputes, and a steady stream of grievances mean that work gets bogged down, performance lags, and the parties on both sides will suffer.

Understanding unions and how to work with them helps managers avoid such problems. This chapter begins by discussing the overall nature of union-management relations and summarizing the history of the labor movement. The rest of the chapter describes union structure and function, including the union-organizing campaign, grievance handling, collective bargaining, dispute settlements, and the challenges confronting unions today.

Nature and Importance of Union-Management Relations

Union An organization of workers who have joined forces to achieve common goals, such as higher wages and improved working conditions.

A **union** is an organization of workers who have joined forces to achieve common goals, such as higher wages and improved working conditions. The underlying assumption is that if workers speak with one voice through union representatives, they will have greater power relative to management.

Extent of Unionization

In the United States, about 17 million workers belong to a union; this number represents about 17 percent of the work force.[1] The graph in Figure 9.1 shows that union membership has dramatically declined in recent years. In certain industries, such as the railroad, automobile, primary metals, and transportation equipment industries, a majority of employees belong to a union. In other industries, however, such as retail trade, insurance, and banking, less than 10 percent of employees are union members. Unions have had a difficult time breaking into the high-tech and service industries, and only a small percentage of the white-collar work force has become unionized. Nevertheless, unions are still an important group in the business arena.

Importance of Cooperation

Enlightened, successful management teams and union leadership know that cooperation between the two is necessary. In recent years, for example, the survival of many companies has depended on the willingness of unions to make concessions even to the extent of giving up earlier gains. In the early 1980s, many contracts in the auto, steel, and airline industries contained no wage increases for union members. More positive evidence of the cooperation between unions and management is the group profit-sharing plans many firms have instituted. Under these plans, workers get additional money if the company prospers. For example, Chrysler and National Steel agreed to give their employees stock in the company in exchange for concessions in their labor contracts. Today, the image of management and the union bosses openly fighting each other is frequently inaccurate. Both sides are realizing the benefits and necessity of give and take.

Why Employees Join Unions

The working conditions we take for granted were only a dream during the years of the Industrial Revolution. Employees worked from sunup to sundown, typically 60 hours, sometimes even 84 hours a week (seven 12-hour days). Conditions were often unsafe, and many factory laborers were children. Workers found that by joining together, they had more

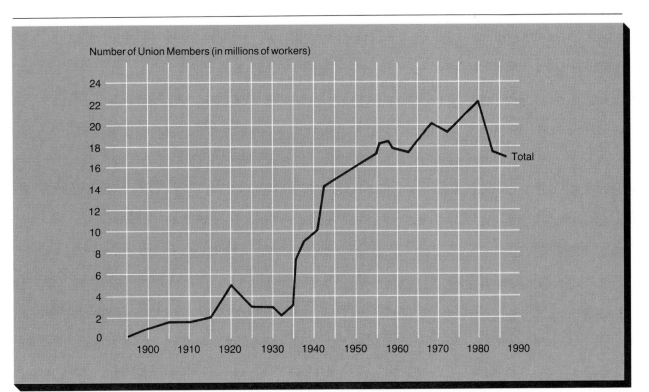

influence over management policies and public opinion and could gradually improve working conditions. Today, it is a rare manager who would propose returning to the conditions of the Industrial Revolution. Even though conditions and wages are far removed from the Indusrial Revolution, many workers still join unions for a number of reasons.

Wages, Benefits, and Security The primary reason employees join a union is very simple: They believe the union can help secure them higher wages, better benefits, and greater job security. Most union members feel that their union is aggressively pursuing these objectives for them.[2] The facts are that despite some slight shrinking of the wage gap in a few industries, union members, on average, still make a third more than their nonunion counterparts.[3]

Power and Influence Workers want to make their voices heard and to know that the company will listen. For an individual worker, especially in a large company, this is unlikely to happen. One way employees can counter the power of management is to join together in a union. Membership offers strength in numbers.

The union contract gives the workers specific rights and restricts management action. For example, when the union wins a 6 percent annual wage increase, it is exercising its influence over management. The union also exercises its power by challenging management's interpretation of the contract and demanding that any disagreements be settled through a prearranged grievance procedure.

Social Reasons Besides the obvious economic and political advantages of joining unions, workers also join for purely social reasons. Joining a union gives employees a common bond of friendship and draws them

Chrysler has found that when union members and managers meet to discuss ways to improve quality, both sides benefit. Teams such as the one shown here are part of the Quality Improvement Program, a joint effort of Chrysler and the United Auto Workers. The company credits these teams with contributing to substantial improvements in quality and productivity.

Source: Courtesy of Chrysler Corporation.

closer together. They become part of a social group as well as an economic and power group. This component of fellowship and good interpersonal relations helps sustain members' support of the union.

Limited Choice In some cases, workers join a union because they must if they want to work for a specific company or in a specific trade. Some states allow unions to require that all workers at a particular company be made members of the union. Workers who practice a trade such as carpentry or plumbing may find it difficult or impossible to get work without a union card. Some of these workers may not feel that the benefits of the union are worth the dues they pay, but they join to secure their livelihood.

Checkpoint

1. What are three reasons employees join unions?
2. How have unions and management cooperated in recent times?

History of the Labor Movement

Modern workers sometimes find it hard to avoid joining a union, but forming one was once extremely difficult. The earliest unions in the United States were groups of printers and shoemakers in Philadelphia and New York in the 18th century. Both managers and the courts were hostile to these early unions. In a celebrated 1806 case, a union of Philadelphia cordwainers (shoemakers) that went on strike for higher pay was found guilty of criminal conspiracy to restrain trade.

Water boys at a steel factory in Homestead, Pennsylvania, at the turn of the century. Boys like these kept the thousands of adult factory workers supplied with water by refilling their pails throughout the day. Today, federal laws greatly restrict the work that children may perform.

Source: Helena Frost Associates, Ltd.

Courts issued similar rulings for other strikes, and they also determined that boycotts, where union members or sympathizers refuse to buy or handle products of a targeted company, constituted illegal restraint of trade. To combat unions, companies used so-called "yellow-dog contracts," documents in which workers stated that as a condition of employment they would not join a union. Unions that tried to organize these workers were then found guilty of inducing breach of contract. Recurring economic depressions also took their toll in terms of unemployment and lowered wages. Despite these setbacks, workers continued to organize.

The Knights of Labor

Knights of Labor The most important federation of unions for skilled and unskilled workers in the years following the Civil War.

In 1869 a group of tailors met and secretly founded the Noble and Holy Order of the Knights of Labor. The **Knights of Labor,** which included unskilled as well as skilled workers, was the most important federation of unions of its time. By 1879, membership had reached 10,000, and the Knights ended the secrecy. By 1886, the federation had 700,000 members. However, rapid turnover in membership, lack of experienced leadership, lost strikes, and union violence that led to public disapproval brought about a rapid demise of the Knights. By 1890, membership had shrunk to less than 100,000. The organization finally disbanded in 1917.

The American Federation of Labor (AFL)

American Federation of Labor (AFL) The most important craft union federation in the United States.

Many of the craft unions looked for an alternative to the Knights of Labor. In 1881, under the leadership of Samuel Gompers, they formed the Federation of Organized Trades and Labor Union. Later they changed the name to the **American Federation of Labor (AFL),** the most important craft union federation in the United States.

The AFL organized only skilled trade or craft workers and focused on specific practical gains. Each union developed its own constitution and collective bargaining approach while remaining a member of the central AFL. This arrangement helped the AFL rapidly become a major force on the labor scene.

A Changing Climate

During the early part of the 20th century, employers continued to resist unionization. At the same time, they began to develop a new concern for the welfare of their employees. Often, this concern for improved employee relations was intended to reduce the likelihood of their employees joining a union.

Congress also began to demonstrate concern for workers. In 1926, Congress passed the Railway Labor Act, the first law guaranteeing the right of workers to bargain collectively as a union. During the Depression of the 1930s, public attitudes and the backing of the Roosevelt administration led to the passage of laws favorable to unions. Notable among these was the National Labor Relations Act (known as the Wagner Act), which established the National Labor Relations Board. This federal agency hears worker complaints of unfair labor practices and oversees the elections in which workers vote whether to have a particular union represent them. After World War II, the Taft-Hartley Act spelled out the rights of employers as well as those of unions. Table 9.1 describes these and other major laws affecting union-management relations.

The Congress of Industrial Organizations (CIO)

In the more favorable climate beginning in the 1930s, union membership grew rapidly. Notably, as mass-production and mining operations began to grow, unionization in these industries met with considerable success. These unions organized workers industrywide, rather than by specific skill or craft. The industrial unions initially formed a coalition called the Committee for Industrial Organizations within the AFL. However, the AFL was unsympathetic to union organization on an industrial basis; so, led by John L. Lewis of the United Mine Workers of America, the industrial unions left to form their own union federation, the **Congress of Industrial Organizations (CIO).** This became the most important industrial union federation in the United States. The CIO quickly became a major union force by organizing unskilled as well as skilled workers in the giant mining, steel, automobile, and rubber industries.

Congress of Industrial Organizations (CIO) The most important industrial union federation in the United States.

AFL-CIO Merger

In 1955 the AFL and the CIO took their own philosophy of strength in numbers to heart, set aside their differences, and merged under the leadership of George Meany. At that time the two groups collectively represented more than 16 million workers. Today the AFL-CIO is a confederation of semiautonomous labor unions representing over three-quarters of all union members. The confederation contains 100 national unions, including almost all the large unions in the United States. Even

TABLE 9.1

Major Legislation Affecting Union-Management Relations

Law	Date	Major Provisions
Railway Labor Act	1926	Gave railroad workers the right to unionize without fear of reprisal by the employer. Created the National Mediation Board to resolve disputes in the railroad industry.
Norris–La Guardia Act	1932	Prohibited courts from restraining nonviolent union activities. Outlawed yellow-dog contracts and contracts forbidding union activities.
National Labor Relations Act (Wagner Act)	1935	Gave workers the right to choose their own union and to engage in collective bargaining with the employer. Set forth unfair management practices. Created the National Labor Relations Board (NLRB).
Labor Management Relations Act (Taft-Hartley Act)	1947	Set forth unfair labor union practices such as the closed shop, which had required workers to be union members as a condition of employment. Swung the pendulum of labor regulation back to a more promanagement position.
Labor-Management Reporting and Disclosure Act (Landrum-Griffin Act)	1959	Regulated internal union activities. Provided a bill of rights for union members.

the large Teamsters Union (founded to represent truck drivers), which had not been a member for many years, rejoined the AFL-CIO in late 1987.

Checkpoint

1. Name three major pieces of labor legislation. What impact did these laws have on the labor movement?
2. How has the attitude of business toward unions changed during the 20th century?

Union Structure

An angry worker marching in a picket line carrying a sign demanding higher wages is the vision that many people have of what a union is all about. Although strikes, defiance, picket lines, and demands are part of unionism, it also must be remembered that there is an extensive organizational structure that backs up every union member. Employees at the local factory, professional athletes, the workers on the construction project across campus, or perhaps even some of your teachers are members of national and international unions that provide them with various types of support. However, it all begins at the local level.

Local Unions

Local union The basic unit of the union structure, representing members in a limited area.

The **local union** (the local) is the basic unit of the union structure, representing members in a limited area. Local unions usually operate democratically, that is, each dues-paying member has one vote and can participate in electing officials to run the union. Small unions typically have a president, a secretary-treasurer, and an executive board. Larger locals also have a business agent, a negotiating committee, and a grievance committee.

Steward An on-site union representative whose job is to protect the rights of members.

Regardless of their size, all locals have a number of stewards. A **steward** is an on-site union representative whose job is to protect the rights of members. For example, if a supervisor and one of the workers were to dispute schedules of pay rates, the worker could quickly contact the shop steward. The steward would then contact the supervisor and try to work out the problem. Usually they can reach an agreement, but if not, the contract spells out steps for resolving the dispute.

In small unions, the elected officials often serve without pay or for a small stipend (a few hundred dollars annually plus reimbursement for out-of-pocket expenses). Often the union president is directly responsible for leading the union team in negotiating the labor contract. In many large unions, the members elect a full-time salaried business agent. This individual helps negotiate and administer the employment contract and conducts the day-to-day business of the union. Because of the power of the position, the business agent often overshadows the union president in terms of authority, prestige, and influence.

National Unions

The **national union** (or international union if it has branches or locals in other countries) is the parent organization for the locals. While the local is concerned with day-to-day matters, the national union focuses on long-range considerations that affect all of the locals. In addition, the national provides a host of services to the locals, including:

Providing data on comparable wage and cost-of-living changes

Training local leaders in contract negotiations and grievance handling

Familiarizing local leaders with how to administer their union efficiently

At the national level, elected officials often consist of a president, secretary-treasurer, and several vice presidents. These national officers constitute the top policy making board for the union. For specialized assistance, they often appoint experts such as lawyers, economists, statisticians, and public relations personnel.

Checkpoint

1. What is the relationship between a local union and a national union?
2. How does a steward protect the rights of union members?

The Organizing Campaign

The national union is actively involved at the start of union-management relations during the organizing campaign. This campaign persuades workers in a company to join the union and to allow the union to represent them in bargaining over wages, hours, and conditions of employment.

Initial Efforts

The union strategy in organizing a firm starts with some quiet contacts. Union organizers contact a few selected employees at the work site and try to find out who is interested in unionizing and who is willing to help in the campaign. The union uses these volunteers to help recruit others. This initial activity may occur secretly.

Next, the organizers try to get the employees to sign an authorization-card. An **authorization card** is a request that the union represent the workers. If 30 percent of the employees sign this card, the union may petition the employer to become the bargaining representative or may petition the National Labor Relations Board (NLRB) for an election. However, to be assured of winning, most unions wait until they get at least 50 percent of the workers to sign these cards before asking for official recognition as the representative of the employees. If the NLRB is brought in, it determines whether the union has met all the requirements. If they have been met, an election will be held.

National union The parent organization for local unions which focuses on long-range considerations that affect all of the locals.

Authorization card A request that the union represent the workers.

A member of the United Steelworkers votes in an election in Pittsburgh. Each dues-paying union member has one vote to exercise in electing officials and ratifying contracts.

Source: © Fred Vuich 1984, Gamma-Liaison.

Campaign and Election

Before the election date, management and the union usually campaign vigorously. The pre-election period usually lasts 30 to 60 days. During this time, both sides bring up a number of campaign issues. For example, management may stress points such as these:

> Improvements in wages and job security do not depend on unionization.
>
> The cost of union dues far outweighs the benefits members will receive.
>
> If the union succeeds in the election, workers may lose benefits or have to go on strike.

The union may focus on the following issues:

> The union will bring better wages and benefits.
>
> The union will give employees a voice with management.
>
> The union will set up grievance and seniority systems.

The NLRB conducts the election. If more than half of the workers vote for union representation, the union will be certified by the NLRB and will become the official bargaining agent for the workers. If only half or less of the workers vote for union representation, the union is defeated and may not try again for at least one year. Figure 9.2 illustrates this process.

Over the last decade, unions have lost more than half of all elections supervised by the NLRB.[4] One possible reason for the reduced appeal of unions to workers may be management's use of consultants who suggest strategies to defeat the union organizing effort. There is growing evidence that companies are fighting harder against organizing drives.[5]

There also has been an increase in **decertification,** the process of dropping a union as the bargaining agent for the workers.[6] For decertification to take place, three criteria must be met:

1. At least half of the employees in the bargaining unit must ask for the union to be decertified.
2. The workers must file the petition at least one year after the union was certified.
3. The workers must file the petition within the time period established by law, which in most cases is 60 to 90 days before the current labor contract expires.

Decertification The process of dropping a union as the bargaining agent for the workers.

Checkpoint

1. What agency supervises an organizing election?
2. What steps are involved in a union-organizing campaign?

Collective Bargaining

Picture a smoke-filled room with union members on one side of a big oak table and managers on the other, glaring at each other and pounding their fists on the table. Is this collective bargaining? The answer is yes and no. **Collective bargaining** is a process in which management and employees, represented by the union of their choice, negotiate over the

Collective bargaining The process in which management and employees, represented by the union of their choice, negotiate over wages, hours, and conditions of employment.

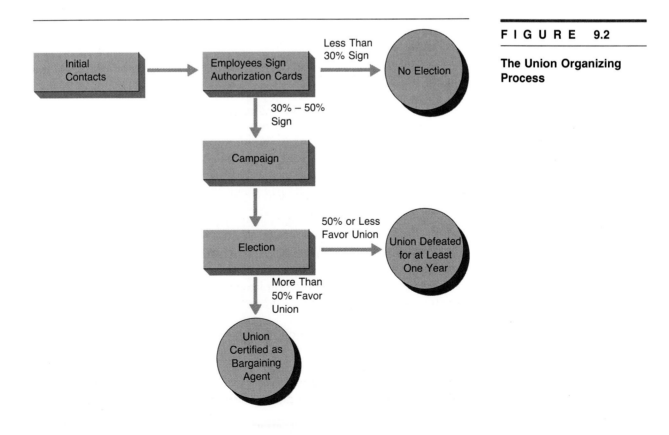

F I G U R E 9.2

The Union Organizing Process

wages, hours, and conditions of employment. Collective bargaining often involves tough negotiations between unions and management, and it often takes place in smoke-filled rooms with hostility on both sides. But there is also much more to collective bargaining. There are many basic issues that need to be resolved and many different bargaining strategies and techniques.

Bargaining Issues

The most important bargaining issues vary from one contract period to another. For example, during most of the 1970s, unions made wage increases their top priority. However, the major recession that began in the late 1970s put many firms, such as in the auto, meat-packing, and airline industries, in a financial crunch. Facing the threat of layoffs, most unions moved job security to the top of their list of demands.

Some issues raised during collective bargaining are simply invented to wring concessions from the other side. However, most of the bargaining issues are substantive. The most common and the most important involve union security, management rights, compensation, and job security.

Union Security Unions try to gain the security of being the sole bargaining agent for their members. Unions want to ensure that they will survive and prosper. To obtain such security, unions would ideally like to have closed shops, which would require that workers be union members in order to be considered for employment. Although the Taft-Hartley Act made closed shops illegal, the states are allowed to rule on other forms of union security. Thus, unions seek contract provisions for union or agency shops, maintenance of membership, and the checkoff.

A **union shop** is a company at which all employees, as a condition of employment, must join the union after a predetermind time period, usually 30 days. If employees fail to join within this time period, the company must let them go.

A **maintenance-of-membership provision** states that those who join the union must remain members. There is, however, a brief escape period just before the contract runs out (usually 10 to 15 days), during which members may leave the union. Additionally, those who are not members are not required to join.

An **agency shop** is one in which employees do not have to join the union but nevertheless have to pay union dues. The courts have ruled it is legal to assess dues for both union and nonunion members because members and nonmembers alike benefit from the services provided by the union.

The **checkoff** is a process by which the company deducts union dues directly from each member's paycheck and pays them to the union. The Taft-Hartley Act requires that employees sign a form authorizing the company to do this; the union may not demand that the company do this automatically.

These provisions are common in union strongholds in the industrialized Northeast, Midwest, and Far West. Many other states require an **open shop,** in which the workers do not have to join a union or pay union dues. Open shops exist in Sun Belt and agriculturally oriented midwestern states that have **right-to-work laws,** which prohibit union

Union shop A company at which all employees, as a condition of employment, must join the union after a predetermined time period.

Maintenance-of-membership provision A requirement that those who join the union must remain members.

Agency shop A company at which the employees do not have to join the union but nevertheless have to pay union dues.

Checkoff Deducting union dues directly from each member's paycheck.

Open shop A company at which the workers do not have to join a union or pay union dues.

Right-to-work laws State laws that prohibit union shops and other such union security arrangements.

shops and other such union security arrangements. However, they do allow for the checkoff. Figure 9.3 shows which states have right-to-work laws.

Management Rights While unions often strive during collective bargaining to obtain increases in wages and security, management tries to protect and clarify its rights. Any rights not given to the union in the contract are usually assumed to belong to management. These are called *management prerogatives.* In an effort to protect these prerogatives more formally, management often tries to spell them out in the contract. In particular, the company tries to protect its right to set production schedules, assign jobs, schedule work, impose disciplinary penalties, and subcontract work outside the facility.

Especially in recent years, businesses have become increasingly concerned with the motivation and productivity of their workers, and they have been willing to give up more authority and control over jobs. At General Motors' Saturn plant in Tennessee, for example, the labor contract calls for close cooperation between workers and management.

F I G U R E   9.3

Right-to-Work States

States having right-to-work laws

Workers are employed in units of 6 to 15 people each, and these units are directly responsible for operating a specified part of the plant, including setting schedules and helping to maintain the machinery.[7]

Compensation While allowing workers to play an increasing role in the design of work, management still carefully negotiates the wage package. The reason is that labor is a major cost in most organizations. The wage bill in today's firms often ranges from 30 to 90 percent of total costs, depending on the industry. This includes across-the-board wages, cost-of-living adjustments, various wage incentives, and benefits such as pensions, health insurance, supplemental unemployment benefits, and life insurance.

Bumping An arrangement permitting employees laid off from one department to go to another department in the company and replace, or bump, someone there who has less seniority.

Job Security A major concern to both management and employees is job security. If the company must cut back, who will it let go? Many contracts call for a "last hired, first fired" or seniority approach specifying that the newest employees are laid off first. Some contracts also allow for **bumping,** which means that employees laid off from one department may transfer to another department in the company and replace someone there who has less seniority.

Grievance Procedures Both parties are also concerned that they have a procedure for settlement of contract disputes. For example, if someone is disciplined with a two-day layoff, the union may argue that the penalty was too severe and file a grievance contending that the action violated the labor contract. Management wants to make sure that the agreement provides for a way to handle such grievances.

Working Conditions Union negotiators also try to obtain agreements that will promote safe and pleasant working conditions for union members. These agreements may include safety standards for employees working with video-display terminals or with heavy machinery in factories. They may prevent the company from expecting workers to work faster than a mutually agreed-upon standard.

In addition, work rules specify what tasks a particular employee may perform. For example, in some situations, a company may only require a welder to do welding; no one else may perform the job, and the welder may not perform other jobs. However, managers at many companies have complained that such restrictions seriously hurt efficiency, and unions have recently made concessions in this area.

A customer service representative looks up customer and product information on a video-display terminal. Employees of some companies have been concerned about the possible health dangers of spending hours in front of such terminals. Some companies go to great lengths to make conditions safe and comfortable; in other cases, employees have turned to unions for bargaining power over working conditions.

Source: Courtesy of Dow Corning Corporation.

The Negotiation Process

To negotiate these issues, management and the union each puts together a negotiating team. The management team usually consists of the company president, key executives, a lawyer, and members of the personnel, human resource, or labor relations department. If management expects bargaining to be difficult or if the firm is very large, they may also bring in an outside specialist in labor law and a professional negotiator.

The union team usually consists of the local union president, other members of the local leadership, and a representative from the national union. If the union anticipates problems or if it is bargaining with a big company, its team may also include a lawyer and a negotiating specialist from the national union.

Once each side has assembled its negotiation teams, the bargaining process begins. Traditionally, this process has followed an "us against them" approach. In recent years, however, this combative relationship has been slowly changing.

Preparation and Initial Demands Both sides begin the negotiation process by gathering as much information and relevant data as possible. The union wants to find out what its membership wants to see in the next contract and what terms arc in new contract agreements in the industry as a whole. By looking at other settlements, the union can gauge how far it can go in demanding wages, salaries, and benefits. Management checks with relevant personnel (such as first-line supervisors and specialists in the personnel or human resource department) to determine what changes these people would like to see in the new contract. Managers also examine the newly negotiated contracts of other firms in the industry. Both sides review the language of the current contract to see what clauses they want amended, modified, or removed.

Based on this pool of information, the two groups set forth their initial demands. These demands give each party an idea of the direction in which the other party will be moving. The initial demands also set the overall tone for the bargaining that will follow.

Bargaining Approaches Two major bargaining approaches are commonly used: distributive and integrative. **Distributive bargaining** occurs when a gain to one side is a loss to the other. Figure 9.4 provides an example. As shown, the union intends to make an initial wage demand of $6.80

Distributive bargaining
Bargaining in which a gain to one side is a loss to the other.

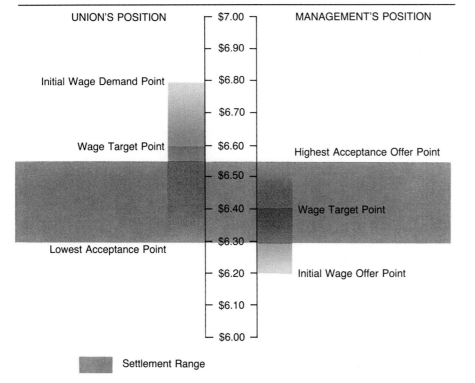

UNION'S POSITION — $7.00 — MANAGEMENT'S POSITION

- $6.90 -
- $6.80 - ← Initial Wage Demand Point
- $6.70 -
- $6.60 - ← Wage Target Point / Highest Acceptance Offer Point
- $6.50 -
- $6.40 - Wage Target Point
- $6.30 - ← Lowest Acceptance Point
- $6.20 - Initial Wage Offer Point
- $6.10 -
- $6.00 -

Settlement Range

FIGURE 9.4

Distributive Bargaining in Action

an hour for the lowest job classification of its members. It hopes to get $6.60 and will accept no less than $6.30. Meanwhile, management intends to make an initial wage offer of $6.20, hopes to settle for $6.40, and will pay no more than $6.55 an hour. Given this information, the settlement range will be between $6.30 (the union's lowest acceptance point) and $6.55 (management's highest offer point). This process is used to settle a number of issues besides wage rates, including benefits, vacation time, and job security.

Integrative bargaining
Bargaining in which both sides work together to solve a mutual problem.

Another common bargaining approach is **integrative bargaining,** in which both sides work together to solve a mutual problem. An example is below-industry-average productivity. This is a mutual problem because if a company can't compete in its industry in terms of productivity, it will not make a profit or even survive. If the company doesn't make profits, no money is available for wage increases; if the company doesn't survive, then, of course, the workers lose their jobs. Through an integrative bargaining process, management could agree to give workers more control over the design of their tasks, and in return the workers could give up seniority rules that govern the rehiring of laid-off workers, agree to work changes that eliminate costly rehandling of goods, and accept longer working hours in order to increase productivity.[8]

New Bargaining Strategies Over the years, the predominant bargaining strategy has been the relatively combative distributive bargaining approach. In recent years, more cooperative strategies have emerged. These approaches include concessionary and continuous bargaining strategies.

A struggling company may be able to persuade the union to engage in concessionary bargaining, in which unions agree to give back some of the previously won gains. For example, managers of some companies have been able to convince labor to accept reduced benefits or even wage cuts. In recent years, Chrysler and Eastern Airlines have used concessionary bargaining to help them survive, and wage and benefit concessions have become common throughout the meat-packing industry.

In combination with any of the preceding strategies, labor and management may conduct continuous bargaining, which involves regularly scheduled meetings between their negotiators. Rather than waiting for the contract period to roll around, commonly up to three or four years, the two sides discuss and attempt to overcome problems on an ongoing basis. As a result, a more cooperative relationship evolves, and bargaining becomes a less adversarial undertaking, free from the pressure of deadlines.

Resolution Methods

Resolution methods
Approaches used to overcome union-management disagreements.

Despite the variety of negotiating techniques available, unions and management cannot always reach an agreement. Nevertheless, it is still in the best interests of both sides to resolve differences harmoniously. **Resolution methods** are approaches used to overcome union-management disagreements. The two most commonly used methods of resolving these disputes are mediation and arbitration.

Mediation When the parties use **mediation,** a neutral third party helps both sides reach a settlement. A mediator has no formal authority to order either side to do anything, but instead recommends solutions in an effort to bring the parties together. Most mediators try to reduce the problems by first instructing both sides to identify their differences. Then each side is required to focus on these actual differences and make counterproposals for dealing with the demands of the other side. Each party is encouraged to accept reasonable accommodations by the other and to compromise. This no-nonsense approach that emphasizes comprise often resolves the dispute to the satisfaction of both parties.

Mediation A resolution method in which a neutral third party with no formal authority helps both sides reach a settlement.

Arbitration In some cases, a neutral third party listens to both sides and then directs each side in what to do. This process is called **arbitration.** Under **binding arbitration,** both parties agree to follow the decision of the third party (the arbitrator). Under final-offer arbitration, both sides make their final offers, and the arbitrator chooses one.

Arbitration has a number of benefits:

It may save time and money.

The parties in the dispute do not have to resort to drastic actions, and both can save face.

The resolution is rendered by an impartial, qualified third party, so it is as fair as possible for both union and management.

Arbitration A resolution method in which a neutral third party listens to both sides and then directs each side in what to do.

Binding arbitration Arbitration in which both parties agree to follow the arbitrator's decision.

Checkpoint

1. What are three major bargaining issues?
2. How can union and management reach an agreement when bargaining alone is not enough?

Grievance Handling

Jim Adams was told by his supervisor the first day on the job at Purity Ice Cream Company that so many employees had been stealing boxes of novelty products to take home to their kids that the company had just passed a strict rule that the first time anyone was caught stealing they would be docked a day's pay, and the second time they would be fired. Jim noticed that when his co-workers took breaks they would grab a couple of ice cream bars off the line and eat them in the lounge. The first time Jim ate an ice cream bar during the break, his supervisor ran up to him and said, "Jim, you know the rule about stealing. Since this is the first time, you will be docked a day's pay, but if I catch you again, you're fired!" Jim was shaken. He did not consider this stealing and filed a grievance with his union steward.

The contract that results from collective bargaining generally contains procedures for handling complaints brought by employees such as Jim who believe they have been treated improperly. These complaints are called **grievances.** Most labor contracts spell out the specific steps to follow if an employee files a grievance.

Grievance A complaint brought by an employee who feels that he or she has been treated improperly.

Grievance Procedures

The specific steps in the grievance procedure vary from contract to contract. Figure 9.5 illustrates the steps of a typical procedure, which are as follows:

1. An employee who has a grievance simply tells the supervisor. If the supervisor does not resolve it on the spot, the employee informs the union steward, who contacts the supervisor. If this does not resolve the grievance to the satisfaction of both parties, then the grievance moves to the next step.
2. The department head or the industrial relations manager and the steward, supported by a union official such as the president or the business agent, try to reach a compromise. Often they work out a solution at this point to prevent the process from going to the next level.
3. The plant or division manager or the human resource director reviews the grievance. The local negotiating committee, supported by top local officials and in some cases a representative from the national union, will represent the union. Grievances that reach this step may have far-reaching implications for union-management relations and may be costly. Only rarely would the grievance go beyond this step.
4. A neutral arbitrator reviews the evidence on both sides and renders a decision that is binding on both parties.

F I G U R E   9.5

A Typical Grievance Procedure

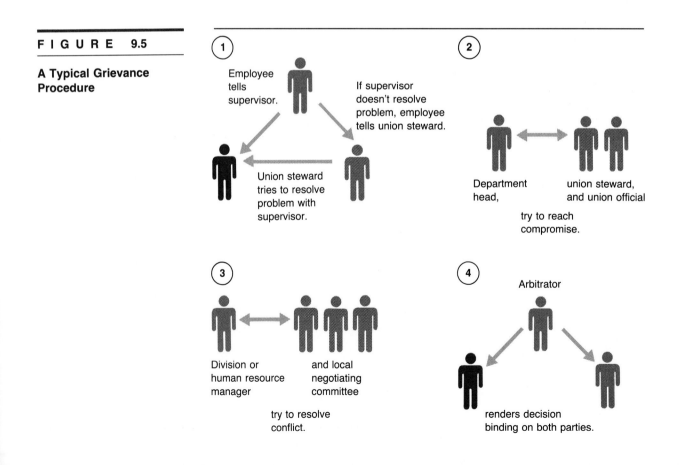

In addition to formal grievance procedures in unionized firms, some union and nonunion companies have tried alternative procedures such as allowing workers to participate more directly in the process. General Electric, Borg-Warner, and Control Data use such an approach. For details, see "Social Responsibility Close-Up: Worker Involvement in Grievance Resolutions."

Checkpoint

1. What is a grievance?
2. What are the steps in a typical grievance procedure?

Responses to a Breakdown in Negotiations

Although minor grievances are settled according to a specified procedure, other major disputes, especially those occurring during negotiations over wages, may lead the union and management to take drastic action against one another.

SOCIAL RESPONSIBILITY   **CLOSE-UP**

Worker Involvement in Grievance Resolutions

At General Electric's Appliance Park East plant in Columbia, Maryland, labor relations had never been very good. Whenever workers voted on unionizing, the union garnered about 40 percent of the total ballots. In an effort to convince the workers that management was interested in their welfare and wanted to work with them, the company introduced a new idea: an appeals panel with three hourly employees and two managers. A complaint that cannot be resolved at the lower levels of the hierarchy now finds its way to this committee.

The idea has succeeded. During its first four years, the panel heard almost 80 decisions on matters ranging from discipline to performance appraisal. Both sides feel that the arrangement has gone a long way toward

diffusing support for unionizing and building trust in management.

GE is not alone. Borg-Warner has instituted similar panels at 11 of its plants, and Control Data uses them so supplement its current grievance procedures. Honda of America has a similar committee, which reviews appeals of employees who have been discharged.

Many companies see labor-management grievance panels as a way to show their concern for employees. The employees view them as a means of ensuring that they are not discriminated against. Consequently, many experts in labor relations predict that these panels will receive more and more use during the 1990s.

Members of the United Auto Workers picketing in Detroit. When unions cannot resolve disputes through bargaining and negotiating, they may pressure the employer by calling a strike. The workers walk off their jobs and usually form a picket line. The union schedules the workers to picket in shifts and often provides signs explaining the purpose of the picket.

Source: UPI/Bettmann Newsphotos.

Strike   A collective refusal to work until a dispute is resolved.

Picket   An assembly of workers stationed outside the premises for the purpose of calling attention to their grievances.

Boycott   An organized effort to convince people to refrain from buying goods or services from a targeted business.

Union Actions

When the union cannot resolve a major problem with management, it may resort to a strike. A **strike** is a collective refusal to work until a dispute is resolved. Strikes occur only as a last resort and are usually damaging to both parties involved, the local economy, and sometimes even the nation as a whole. Some strikes, such as an airline strike, inconvenience the public at large. Others drag out and become violent, as happens periodically in the meat-packing industry. In 1986, manufacturers lost about 5.8 million worker-days to strikes.[9] The big steel company USX had the most costly strike, but extended walkouts also hit such well-known companies as Deere, Weyerhaeuser, General Electric, and Timken.

Workers may combine a strike with a picket. A **picket** is an assembly of workers stationed outside the premises for the purpose of calling attention to their grievances. Often the picketers carry signs or posters describing the reason for their actions. Sometimes union picketers will attempt to prevent nonunion workers from entering a company that is being struck. Members of other unions generally respect the striking unions and do not cross their picket line.

Another union technique is the boycott. Mentioned in Chapter 2, a **boycott** is an organized effort to convince people to refrain from buying goods or services from a targeted business. Unions have organized boycotts against clothing manufacturers such as Farrah and J. P. Stevens. When the union urges its members not to do business with a company, the action is a primary boycott and is legal. However, if the union attempts to influence others to boycott the company's goods, the action is a

secondary boycott, which is illegal under the provisions of the Taft-
Hartley Act.

Unions can also bring pressure on an employer through their influence on others. They can stir public pressure by providing information
to and making appearances in the mass media. They also can use some
of their financial resources to support the campaigns of political candidates who take prounion positions. Under pressure from public opinion
and government officials, the company may give in to union demands.

Management Actions

Management also has techniques that it can use in countering the union.
Under certain conditions, a company will resort to a **lockout,** which is a
refusal to allow workers to enter a facility. For example, if wage negotiations break down because management feels that the union is making
unreasonable demands, management may lock out the employees. For
this to be legal, the contract must have expired and the company must
not interfere with the rights of their employees or their union activities.
In combination with a lockout, managers may try to run the company on
their own.

If management wants to counter a union strike without the financial
risk of a lockout, it may try to get a court order that directs the strikers
to return to work. In some cases, such as a business whose operation is
vital to national security, a judge may issue such an order in an attempt
to get the parties back together.

If all attempts at settling a strike fail, management may eventually
turn to the use of **strikebreakers,** nonunion workers hired to do the
jobs of striking union employees. Strikebreakers are called "scabs" by the
union members. A widely publicized use of strikebreakers occurred
when members of the Professional Air Traffic Controllers Organization
(PATCO) went on strike several years ago and refused to return to work
after a court order directed them to do so. President Reagan, who determined that the strike was illegal, had the striking air controllers fired
and the union decertified. Strikebreakers were used to fill in for PATCO
members and were trained to ensure air traffic control and safety. This
broke the union, and the media exposure surrounding this action caused
the union movement in general to suffer a severe blow. Recently, however, the air controllers have begun organizing a union again.

A more recent example was the professional football players' strike in
the fall of 1987. Replacement players ("scabs") played for the striking
players, and some star players such as Tony Dorsett then of the Dallas
Cowboys and Joe Montana of the San Francisco Forty-Niners crossed the
picket lines and played during the strike. Although attendance dropped
considerably, the owners did not respond to the players' demands, and
the strike was broken when all the players returned to their teams after
three games. As with the air traffic controllers' strike, the tremendous
amount of publicity surrounding the football players' strike and its outcome undoubtedly hurt the union movement.

To counter the unions' influence, companies can also use **employer associations,** which are employer-sponsored lobbying and public relations
organizations primarily designed to promote promanagement legislation.

Lockout A company's
refusal to allow workers to
enter a facility.

Strikebreaker A
nonunion worker hired to
do the job of a striking
union employee.

Employer associations
Employer-sponsored
lobbying and public
relations organizations
primarily designed to
promote promanagement
legislation.

Checkpoint

1. What are two actions unions can take when collective bargaining breaks down?
2. What are two ways management can respond?

Challenges Facing Unions

Unions face tremendous challenges in managing the present and planning for the future. In recent years, they have been struggling. For over 35 years, union membership as a percentage of the nonfarm work force has been declining. From 1979 to 1988, there has been a 20 percent plunge in union ranks. At about 17 percent of the work force currently, union membership is projected to be under 14 percent by the year 2000. One reason is that unions have been having a difficult time winning elections. Their record among firms with 50 or more people has been especially dismal. Unions may be more successful in organizing and getting their demands met in small businesses, as described in "Small Business Close-Up: Union Success against the Little Guy."

SMALL BUSINESS   **CLOSE-UP**

Union Success against the Little Guy

Most often unions are associated with big manufacturing and mining concerns. Recently more and more small businesses are finding themselves targets for union organization and power moves. Consider the following two cases:

Publishers Group West, Inc., of Emeryville, California, had such a low profit margin that the company began instituting efficiency measures designed to run a tighter ship. The employees rebelled and voted, 14 to 7, to join the Teamsters Union. The management reports that the family atmosphere that prevailed before unionizing has vanished entirely.

Jerry Goldstein ran a quiet art supply store in Queens, New York, for 20 years. Suddenly, the Teamsters truck drivers, upon whom he depended to deliver his art supplies, struck. A three-week strike brought him to the bargaining table. During this time, he reports, his warehouse docks were filled with glue, his building was spray-painted, and his trucks were vandalized. The result: his employees won a salary increase, and his annual operations showed a loss.

Why are the Teamsters spending time and money to organize Mom-and-Pop operations and flexing their muscles with small firms? The answer is that union membership and power are slipping, and unions are now seeking out new targets. Moreover, while the average union wins less than half of its elections, the Teamsters have been winning more than half of those in small firms. They have a better chance of winning against the small firms. As one labor relations specialist put it, "Unions are seeking new targets these days, and one of their primary ones is small business."

Loss of Unionized Jobs

One reason for the decline in union membership are the job losses being experienced in heavily unionized industries, such as the steel and automobile industries. Unions have traditionally appealed to blue-collar workers, and this segment of the work force has seen the greatest decline in employment in recent years.

The employment decline has stemmed from a number of sources. Some companies have found that it is cheaper to have work done overseas. Thus, they may transfer some or all operations to developing countries such as Thailand, where wages are lower and union activity virtually nonexistent. Others have had to shut down plants because they have let them become old and inefficient. In some cases, a merger or acquisition may mean that the company can continue operations more efficiently with fewer employees. Or the company may install robots to replace workers or discontinue producing a product that no longer has sufficient demand. Whatever the reason for these cutbacks and plant shutdowns, unions face the challenge of stemming the loss of existing members' jobs.

Declining Public Image

Many Americans have lost confidence in unions. While they may still admit that unions can improve wages and working conditions, they have reservations regarding their overall value. In particular, many young people today doubt that unions are working for their best interests. This attitude differs markedly from that of workers entering the job market in the past.

Union members in New York demonstrating against imported clothing. Such protests are one way unions have attempted to stop losing members to industry cutbacks. Lower-priced imported clothing has reduced the demand for clothes produced by U.S. workers, leading to layoffs of union members. Through its message that imported clothing costs less because foreign workers are underpaid, the union hopes to convince consumers to buy American, causing union jobs to be restored.

Source: © Harvey Lloyd 1987/The Stock Market. All rights reserved.

One national poll among workers found that

> 63 percent would not vote for a union if the election were held tomorrow.
>
> 58 percent believe that employees do not need unions in order to get fair treatment from their employers.
>
> 54 percent believe that unions stifle individual initiative.
>
> 50 percent believe that unions increase the chances of the firm going out of business.[10]

Unions are aware of these image problems and are taking steps to solve them. One way is to take opinion polls among the rank and file to learn more about what the membership really wants. Many unions are finding that their people are concerned about losing their jobs to what they see as unfair trade practices of Japan and other countries. Unions are responding to such feedback by demanding that the government act to restrict imports.

Attracting Women and White-Collar Service Workers

Women are a particularly important target of the union movement because of their growing number in the work force and the fact that many are underpaid and, in some cases, still discriminated against. White-collar workers in service industries are another important target because they constitute the fastest-growing segment of the work force. Of the 12.6 million new jobs created from 1982 to 1987, 85 percent were in white-collar service industries, such as insurance and health care, as opposed to blue-collar manufacturing industries.[11] To date, unions have

Teachers are often members of a union. In fact, with over 1.4 million members at latest count, the National Education Association is much larger than either the United Auto Workers (over 900,000 members) or the United Steelworkers (less than 500,000). In recent years, white-collar workers such as teachers have been an important target of unionizing efforts because they represent a growing sector of the work force.

Source: © 1986 Jon Feingersh: CLICK/Chicago.

had only moderate success in their efforts to organize this growing area of the work force. For example, union membership among health-care workers increased 6 percent from the beginning to the middle of the 1980s. However, only 20 percent of this industry is unionized, and there continues to be a decline in unionization of other private-sector industries.[12] In addition, union membership has actually declined among women (who generally hold white-collar jobs) and black men.[13]

Unions must meet the important challenges of stemming the loss of unionized jobs, enhancing their public image, and organizing women and white-collar workers if the union movement is to remain a viable force in the economy and in American society. There are a few encouraging signs for union leaders that this may be happening. For example, unions have recently won some key organizing efforts, and some surveys indicate that workers are more receptive to unions than at any time since 1979.[14]

Checkpoint

1. What are three major challenges facing unions today?
2. How are unions trying to rebuild their declining membership?

Closing Comments

Most business managers either attempt to work with the union if their work force is organized or attempt to keep the union out if it has not yet gained a foothold. By understanding the background and structure of unions and the various dimensions of collective bargaining, managers can build a harmonious and constructive relationship with unions or with employee groups in nonunionized organizations. In such a relationship, workers and management can both be winners and can accomplish two concerns of one of the union movement's pioneering leaders, Samuel Gompers: "more" for the employees and "profits" for the employers.

Learning Objectives Revisited

1. **Explain what a union is and why employees join unions.**
   Unions are organizations of workers who have joined forces to achieve common goals. Employees join unions because they believe the union can improve their wages, benefits, and job security; gives them a more influential voice with management; and promotes friendship and good relations among one another. Sometimes workers join unions because it is their only real choice.
2. **Discuss the history of the labor movement in the United States.**
   Unions have existed in the United States since the 18th century. As the labor movement began to grow in the 1800s, many unions were hampered in their efforts to organize. The courts often ruled them to be illegal conspiracies acting in restraint of trade. Nevertheless, during the 1880s the Knights of Labor had membership of 700,000. Although this early federation of unions had a rapid demise, it was soon replaced by the American Federation of Labor (AFL), which

brought together craft unions from all over the nation. Legislation passed in the 1930s that was favorable to labor helped spur union membership. One result was that the Congress of Industrial Organizations (CIO) became the largest industrial union federation in the nation. In the 1950s, the AFL and CIO merged; today most of the large unions are part of the AFL-CIO.

3. **Describe union structures and functions.**

   Each union member may vote for those who will run the local, typically the president, secretary-treasurer, and executive board. Large locals also have a business agent, a negotiating committee, and a grievance committee. The union negotiates and administers the labor contract. The worker's day-to-day contact with the union occurs through the steward. The locals are members of large national unions, which in turn may be members of the AFL-CIO.

4. **Present the dimensions of the collective bargaining process.**

   Before collective bargaining occurs, the firm must be organized. If at least 30 percent of the workers sign authorization cards calling for a vote, the NLRB reviews the cards and schedules an election. If over half of the workers vote to unionize, the union becomes the workers' bargaining agent. During collective bargaining, management and the union negotiate over wages, hours, and conditions of employment and administering the labor contract. The two most commonly used strategies are distributive and integrative bargaining; some newer approaches are concessionary and continuous bargaining. When the parties need help in reaching an agreement, they may turn to mediation and arbitration.

5. **Identify ways union and management resolve disputes.**

   The contract provides for a specified procedure for minor grievances. Typically, the first step is for the supervisor and union member, along with the union steward, to resolve the problem. If this fails, the grievance then moves to the department head or industrial relations manager and the local union president or business agent. If necessary, top management and union officials become involved. If the grievance still is not settled, a neutral arbitrator issues a decision. With major unresolved disputes, labor may resort to striking, picketing, or boycotting. Management may use lockouts, court orders, or strikebreakers. Both sides may attempt to influence public opinion and government policy through lobbying and public relations efforts.

6. **Relate the major challenges facing unions now and in the future.**

   The major challenges facing unions are stemming the loss of union jobs, enhancing a declining public image, and organizing nonunionized segments of the work force, particularly women and white-collar workers in service industries.

Key Terms Reviewed

Review each of the following terms. For any that you do not know or are unsure of, look up the definitions and see how they were used in the chapter.

union
Knights of Labor
American Federation of Labor (AFL)
Congress of Industrial Organizations (CIO)
local union
steward
national union
authorization card
decertification
collective bargaining
union shop
maintenance-of-membership provision
agency shop
checkoff

open shop
right-to-work laws
bumping
distributive bargaining
integrative bargaining
resolution methods
mediation
arbitration
binding arbitration
grievance
strike
picket
boycott
lockout
strikebreaker
employer associations

Review Questions

1. Why do employees join unions?
2. How has the legal climate for unionizing changed since the early part of the 20th century? In your answer, identify specific laws where possible.
3. What is the role of the union steward?
4. What are the usual responsibilities of a national union?
5. A union wants to organize the sales clerks at a local chain of supermarkets. What steps should the union plan to take?
6. What are some arguments the union in Question 5 could make in its organizing campaign? What are some arguments that the store owners could make?
7. How do unions try to maintain security for themselves?
8. How do unions try to improve working conditions?

9. Central States Steel Company is attempting to increase work efficiency. What bargaining strategy should the company adopt? Explain how this strategy works.

10. Do you think a union should seek to engage in concessionary bargaining? Why or why not?

11. What is the difference between mediation and arbitration?

12. When Alice Hiller was returning from lunch, the vice president stopped her in the parking lot to ask her how things were going in her department. Consequently, Alice was late getting back to her desk, and her supervisor docked her for an afternoon's pay. Alice thinks her supervisor's action was unfair. As a union member, what can she do?

13. The union contract has expired at Blue Sky Aviation Company, and management has announced that it will not negotiate. "We are in a holding pattern around here; you can have what you had last time—take it or leave it," said the personnel manager to the union business agent. What actions can the union resort to? Why should Blue Sky try to avoid such a scenario?

14. What challenges are currently facing unions? Add any you can think of to those described in the chapter.

Applied Exercises

1. Interview a current member of a union (use relatives or friends if you wish). What can this member tell you about the history and current status of his or her union? Does this person believe the union has helped him or her? In what ways? Report your findings to the class.

2. At the library, get the latest statistics related to the current size of the AFL-CIO. How many unions are members of this federation? How many total members does the federation have? Based on your answers, what value does the federation offer to its members?

3. Visit a local company that is unionized and find out how its grievance procedure works. How closely does the company's procedure follow the one described in the chapter? Explain.

4. What has happened to unionization over the last five years? At the library, gather data on the specifics of union growth (or decline) during this time period. You can use *Employment and Earnings*, published by the U.S. Department of Labor. The January issue usually contains these statistics. Write a paragraph on what you learn.

Your Business IQ: Answers

1. False. The courts didn't interpret the Constitution in this way. In fact, they were basically antiunion and often ruled that strikes and boycotts constituted illegal restraint of trade.

2. False. A simple majority (more than half) of the workers must vote for the union in order for it to represent them.

3. False. If the worker has a disagreement with the supervisor, the normal procedure is for the worker to first contact the shop steward, the union representative at the work site. Only as a last resort will a strike or walkout occur.

4. False. During this time period, union membership among the non-farm work force has decreased.

5. True. Service-sector employees are important to unions because they are the segment of the work force that is growing fastest. However, unions so far have had only moderate success in their efforts to organize these workers.

Case

A New Union for Air Traffic Controllers

A 1981 strike brought about the demise of the Professional Air Traffic Controllers Organization (PATCO). As the text discussion mentioned, the union's 11,000 striking members were fired, the union was decertified, and new workers were brought in.

Now the controllers consist of workers who refused to strike in 1981 plus those who were willing to come in and help break the strike. Having weathered the difficult task of keeping the nation's airlines aloft during the strike, the Federal Aviation Administration (FAA) has presumably learned — or at least tried to learn — to maintain better relations with employees. Consequently, controller-FAA relations should be positive, but in fact, that may not be the case.

A new air controllers' union, the National Air Traffic Controllers Association, has been organizing the controllers with the backing of the AFL-CIO. Nearly half of the controllers have signed election petitions, and the government has authorized elections. The union promises to abide by the law forbidding strikes by air traffic controllers, but it does intend to use lawful means to improve controllers' jobs.

With experienced controllers making as much as $60,000 a year before overtime, why would they want to join a union? Some controllers say they want more voice in the air control system. Another clue may lie in a study by the General Accounting Office showing widespread dissatisfaction among controllers and their supervisors over the perceived inability of the FAA to deal with its employees on a human level from day to day. According to the survey, employees and first-line supervisors think that the FAA is paying little more than lip service to their concerns.

Controller Steve Bell, who works at the busy Terminal Radar Control Facility in Westbury, New York, may be a case in point. For the last several years, Bell has been working a lot of six-day weeks but would rather skip the overtime to be with his family. He can't take the time off, though, because the FAA hasn't trained enough controllers to eliminate heavy overtime at its busiest centers. Nor will the FAA let Bell rotate to a less demanding center. According to Bell, "FAA management tells us things like, 'If you don't like it, quit the job. They're hiring at Burger King.'"

Case Questions

1. Compared to most American workers, air traffic controllers earn a lot of money. Why are they dissatisfied? (In answering, you may want to review the material you learned in Chapter 7.) How can the union help improve the situation?
2. If the air traffic controllers' union can't call a strike, what means does it have to attain its goals?
3. How can the FAA build better relations with the air traffic controllers? Why should it want to?

You Be the Adviser: Getting Prepared

The Rivers Company has been a family-run operation for over 15 years. The company was extremely profitable until around six years ago, when industry competition increased dramatically and profits hit an all-time low. Since then, Joe Rivers, the president, has been cutting the budget to the bone. In the process, wages and benefits have dropped below what competitors offer.

Last week Joe learned that a union is trying to organize his workers. While he believes that this would be a mistake for the workers, he is equally certain that the union will win the election. Joe estimates that the organizers will be in a position to call for an election within 30 days. Rather than wait, he has decided to start planning for the labor contract negotiations. He has spoken with the head of the accounting department and the company lawyer. Both of them will join him on the management negotiating team. The heads of production and marketing will round out the group.

When asked why he was in such a hurry to get organized, Joe explained, "I'm just getting prepared for the inevitable. I know that the union is going to win, and if they get their way, they'll bankrupt us in the process. The only way to fight back is to have a strong negotiating team in place and have our strategy worked out ahead of time. In this way, we can save ourselves from getting steamrolled by the union." Joe then proceeded to assign tasks to everyone on the team. The group agreed to meet again in one week to begin hammering out their strategy.

Your Advice

1. What types of issues do you think the management team should be prepared to deal with? Identify and describe three.
2. What would you recommend that the management team include on their list of objectives? Identify and describe three items. What will the union want? Identify and describe three items.
3. If the bargaining reaches an impasse, what would you recommend that Joe do? Why?

Production and Operations Management

LEARNING OBJECTIVES

- Describe the nature of the production process.
- Examine the specifics of production planning and scheduling.
- Identify the important factors of plant location and layout.

- Discuss the automatic factory.
- Explain the important dimensions of purchasing and inventory control.
- Discuss quality control in manufacturing and service industries.

Your Business IQ

How much do you already know about managing production and operations? Test your business IQ by labeling each statement *true* or *false*. Answers and explanations are at the end of the chapter.

1. The major difference between service and manufacturing businesses is that manufacturers have a production or operations function, whereas services do not.
2. A business's fixed costs cannot be reduced by management.
3. Important criteria for the location of a factory are nearness to labor and transportation facilities.
4. Because robots have been so helpful in reducing costs, their use in American industry has skyrocketed during recent years.
5. A modern system of inventory is to keep a bare minimum of parts and supplies and to replenish them at the last minute.

This highly automated General Electric factory produces dishwashers. The worker in the foreground is seated in a computer control center that monitors robots, lasers, programmable controls, and other automation systems.

Source: © William Strode. All Rights Reserved.

Looking Back and Ahead

Stimulated by the need for increased productivity, greater competitiveness, and better quality, all types of companies, big and small, in heavy industry and in the service sector, are emphasizing management of the way they produce goods and services. Even though many industries are still suffering and relatively few jobs have been created in the manufacturing sector, most companies are turning out more products at a relatively lower cost than ever before.[1] Over the past several years, the output of manufacturers has risen by nearly 30 percent.[2] Manufacturers have accomplished this by cutting costs and using effective production and operations management.

An example would be Xerox's delivery-system goal of ensuring that downtime of about two million machines due to lack of availability of parts would not exceed, on average, 30 minutes. The company designed and implemented a highly responsive, economical parts-supply system. The Xerox service representatives stock the most common and compact parts and tools in their automobile trunks. Inventory is determined by a computer analysis of Xerox's repair experiences. If it is determined that the repair job requires a part not in the automobile, the representative phones into a Xerox stocking point and either picks up the part or has it delivered by cab. This system accomplishes Xerox's goal and provides the company with its most important competitive edge.[3]

In addressing operations management, this chapter moves beyond the previous three chapters' focus on the human side of management. One theme stressed in that discussion was the importance of people in enhancing a company's productivity and competitiveness. This chapter emphasizes the important role that the production process — planning and scheduling, laying out the facility, use of advanced technology and robotics, effective purchasing and inventory management, and quality control — plays in keeping American businesses productive and competitive.

Nature of the Production Process

The Industrial Revolution, which began around the turn of the 19th century in the textile mills of Great Britain, revolutionized the way goods were produced and dramatically altered the way people lived. In particular, the factory system of work employed millions of people and provided mass-produced, standardized, inexpensive goods. Today, the economy of every developed country depends heavily on **production,** the process of transforming inputs such as raw materials and labor into outputs, or finished products.

Production The process of transforming inputs such as raw materials and labor into outputs, or finished products.

Components of the Production System

As illustrated in Figure 10.1, a production system has three distinct components: input, transformation process, and output.

Production starts with inputs. An **input** is any resource needed to produce a desired good or service. Figure 10.1 shows some typical inputs for a restaurant (chefs, equipment, and food) and a manufacturing plant (raw materials, workers, and managers). In a bank, inputs include

Input Any resource needed to produce a desired good or service.

money, managers, tellers, computers, and a building. In a college, inputs consist of professors, students, administrators, a library, and classrooms. In general, the inputs consist of raw materials and other resources.

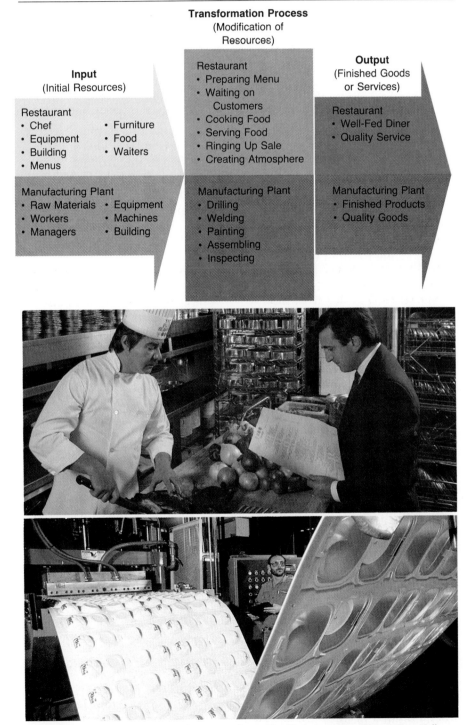

Transformation Process
(Modification of Resources)

Input
(Initial Resources)

Restaurant
- Chef
- Equipment
- Building
- Menus
- Furniture
- Food
- Waiters

Manufacturing Plant
- Raw Materials
- Workers
- Managers
- Equipment
- Machines
- Building

Restaurant
- Preparing Menu
- Waiting on Customers
- Cooking Food
- Serving Food
- Ringing Up Sale
- Creating Atmosphere

Manufacturing Plant
- Drilling
- Welding
- Painting
- Assembling
- Inspecting

Output
(Finished Goods or Services)

Restaurant
- Well-Fed Diner
- Quality Service

Manufacturing Plant
- Finished Products
- Quality Goods

Note: The top photo shows the chef and manager of a top New York restaurant. Photo © Tom Hollyman, 1987. All rights reserved. The bottom photo is an Amoco manufacturing plant that makes fast-food containers. Courtesy of Amoco Corporation.

Transformation process
Those activities that change inputs into the desired outputs.

When the inputs enter the production system, they undergo a change. The **transformation process** consists of those activities that change the inputs into the desired outputs. This is the heart of production. In Figure 10.1, some of the activities included in the transformation process for a restaurant are waiting on customers and cooking and serving food; for a manufacturing plant, drilling, assembling, and inspecting. In a bank, this process includes waiting on customers, accepting deposits, making loans, investing funds, and keeping records. At a college, this process involves registering students, giving lectures, assigning work to students, administering tests, and carrying out student-professor interactions.

Output The finished good or service that results from the production process.

The outputs complete the production system. An **output** is the finished good or service that results from the production process. Figure 10.1 shows that the output of a restaurant is a well-fed diner; for a manufacturing plant it is a finished product. For a bank, the output is a satisfied depositor and/or borrower. For a college, it is an educated student. In each of these cases, the output is the final step in the production process.

The output of one business may be the input of another. For example, a steel company might convert iron ore (input) into steel auto bodies (output). This output for the steel firm will become an input for the auto manufacturer, which is producing a totally assembled car. Unfortunately, another output of the steel company may be air pollution. As Chapter 2 discussed, socially responsible firms attempt to minimize such undesirable outcomes of their production processes.

Technological Development

Technology and research and development are modifying the production process. Engineers are designing new machines that can do the work of many people and do it more cheaply and efficiently. Recently, a number of businesses have adopted computer-integrated manufacturing, in which machines and robots perform many of the activities previously carried out by people. The robot frame can do the work of a human arm, and its microprocessor (a computer) can substitute for a human brain. For example, in automobile manufacturing, robots have been programmed to weld, assemble, paint, lift, dip, inspect, and carry parts.[4]

Most manufacturing facilities are quite small, and advanced technological developments such as robotics will have less of an impact on their operations. Nevertheless, even these small firms will be able to profit from using some of the latest developments on a piecemeal basis; they need not rip out all of the machines and replace them with state-of-the-art technology.

Checkpoint

1. What are the three components of a production system?
2. Does the production process apply to services, or only to goods produced in a factory?

Production Planning

Just as the human resource function of a business organization starts with planning, so does the production function. Through **production planning,** managers determine the most profitable way to produce the goods and services the company will sell. As you have already learned, long-term profitability depends on keeping productivity and quality high and costs low.

Profitability and Breakeven Analysis

Whether a good or service is new or already part of the firm's offerings, management must determine how much it can produce profitably. One way to determine this is to calculate the breakeven point. The **breakeven point** is the level of production at which total revenues from selling the products equal total expenses incurred in making them. The firm neither makes nor loses money at the breakeven point.

Determining the breakeven point for a particular product requires knowledge of fixed costs, variable costs, and selling price. The product manager has cost information and can obtain price information from the marketing department.

In the short run, certain expenses remain the same, regardless of how many units the firm produces. These expenses are *fixed costs*. An example is insurance on the building. Whether the company operates 80 percent of its machines or all of them, and no matter how much raw material it uses, it must still pay its insurance premium. The same is true for property taxes; they do not depend on how many units the firm produces.

The expenses that change in relation to output are *variable costs*. If production goes down, these expenses drop; if production goes up, these expenses rise. An example of a variable cost is raw material. The more units the firm produces, the greater its expense for raw material. The same is true for labor. If the firm adds individual workers or a second shift to produce more, its labor expenses will rise.

The price at which the firm sells the goods is the selling price. The higher the selling price, the fewer goods the company has to sell to reach breakeven.

Calculating the Breakeven The production manager enters this information into an equation to compute the breakeven point. As an example, assume that the total fixed cost for a particular product line is $100,000, the selling price per unit is $50, and the variable cost is $25. Here's how to arrive at the breakeven point in units:

$$\text{Breakeven point} = \frac{\text{Total fixed cost}}{\text{Selling price} - \text{Variable cost}}$$

$$= \frac{\$100,000}{\$50/\text{unit} - \$25/\text{unit}}$$

$$= \frac{\$100,000}{\$25/\text{unit}}$$

$$= 4,000 \text{ units}$$

Production planning The process whereby managers determine the most profitable way to produce the goods and services the company will sell.

Breakeven point The level of production at which total revenues from selling the products equal total expenses incurred in making them.

The company must sell 4,000 units to break even on this product line. At this level of production, it has revenues of 4,000 units × $50/unit, or $200,000. Its expenses are 4,000 units × $25/unit in variable expenses plus $100,000 in fixed expenses, or a total of $200,000. Thus revenues and expenses are equal. Figure 10.2 graphs the relationship of these variables to the breakeven point.

Of course, a business is unlikely to produce a good or service just to break even; a business needs to make a profit in order to grow, to provide a decent return to the owners, and, as Chapter 1 pointed out, to survive in a free enterprise economy such as that existing in the United States. In the above example, forecasted demand will thus have to be greater than 4,000 units for the company to profit. Perhaps the firm will set 4,400 as the minimum for this product line. At this point, the company will make a total profit of $10,000 (4,400 units at the selling price of $50 per unit minus the $100,000 fixed cost and the variable cost of $25 per unit times 4,400 units).

How Companies Use Breakeven Analysis In recent years, Chrysler has effectively used breakeven analysis to bring itself back from the edge of bankruptcy. Under the leadership of Lee Iacocca, this company dramatically reduced its costs by closing inefficient factories, reducing wages and salaries, laying off personnel, and reducing its inventory levels. The result: Chrysler was able to break even at a lower sales level, build up its momentum, and come roaring back into the marketplace as a full-fledged competitor in the volatile automobile industry. Other well-known U.S. firms such as AT&T, IBM, United Airlines, Exxon, CBS, and Union Carbide have reduced their costs by laying off personnel and closing facilities.

FIGURE 10.2

Finding a Breakeven Point

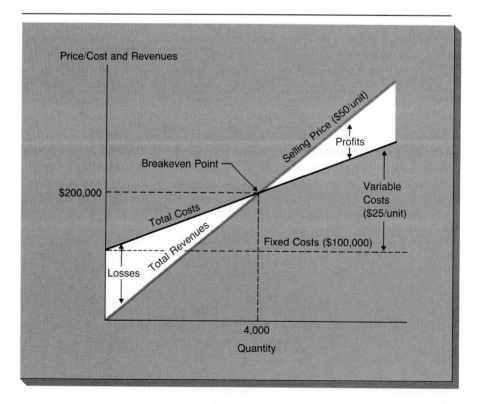

Fortunately, layoffs and cutbacks aren't the only way to keep costs down. Most production managers try to keep control over costs with efficient designs for products and improved production facilities and techniques.

Product Design

Besides helping the company plan how much it can produce profitably, production managers participate in the design of products. Based on information about what customers want, production department personnel determine how to make a product that meets the demand. Some companies design new products infrequently; others, such as Hewlett-Packard, design several a week.

Product design is the process of deciding the specific physical dimensions of the good or service to be produced. For example, restaurant managers would design the menu, the decor, special services such as valet parking or a wine steward, and standards for the food and service. Designers of waterbed liners would take into account size, durability, and the functions the liners perform. A well-designed product can save management millions of dollars in product recalls or changes.

The two areas of design that many successful firms emphasize today are value engineering and value analysis. **Value engineering** is the evaluation of new products and the application of research and development

> **Product design** The process of deciding the specific physical dimensions of the good or service to be produced.
>
> **Value engineering** The evaluation of new products and the application of research and development to design the highest-quality, lowest-priced output.

TECHNOLOGY   CLOSE-UP

Factories in Space

Many companies are interested in developing new products. Some are taking their ventures into outer space! Although this sounds far-fetched, some products can be developed better and more cheaply in a zero-gravity environment than they can on earth. Consider the following examples.

A McDonnell Douglas engineer who flew in the space shuttle *Discovery* produced 700 times more of the drug erythropoietin (EP) than could be made on earth with the same amount of solution, and it was four times purer. EP stimulates the production of red blood cells and can help people who have kidney diseases or who suffer from anemia.

The 3M Company is planning to make crystals in outer space. When crystals form on earth, gravity often causes imperfections in their molecular structure. The perfect crystals made in space can be used to make

semiconductor chips that work much faster than conventional silicon chips. The crystals can also be used in an optical computer that relies on light rather than electrical current to process data at high speed.

Deere & Co., the giant manufacturer of farm equipment, wants to conduct a shuttle experiment in which the researcher melts iron, adds other ingredients, and watches how the molecular structure solidifies in zero gravity. The objective is to learn how to make tractor parts stronger in factories back on earth.

These are only three examples, but firms are working on thousands more. In fact, the future of space-produced products is so great that the Center for Space Policy, Inc., predicts that U.S. industry will be selling $18 billion of space-made products by the year 2000.

282

Value analysis The evaluation of current products to determine how they can be improved.

to design the highest-quality, lowest-priced output. Value engineering is extremely important when a new product is on the drawing board.

Value analysis is the evaluation of current products to determine how they can be improved. For example, manufacturers of liquid detergent have recently designed their containers with a handle so that they are much easier to carry. Brewers now use snap-top beer cans and twist-off caps on bottles, making the can opener obsolete. Honeywell reports that for every $1 it spends on value engineering and value analysis, it saves $18.10 in costs of production.[5]

Another development in product design is computer-aided design (CAD). Using CAD, engineers are now able to produce blueprints by drawing directly on the computer screen and then ordering the computer to provide them with a copy of the design. They can also leave the design on the screen and have the computer rotate the drawing, stretch it out, produce a three-dimensional version of it, or even color or shade it in. Designers in many high-tech firms such as Hughes, TRW, and IBM use CAD, as do large and intermediate-sized architectural firms that produce blueprints daily.[6]

Checkpoint

1. What is a breakeven point?
2. What are two techniques that help production department personnel design quality products?

Engineers at Lockheed use computer-aided design to prepare custom designs of wiring assemblies — combinations of electronic components linked by wires. When printed onto circuit boards, these assemblies are what make electronic devices do their intended tasks. The computer simplifies the design process by enabling the engineer to make revisions or try out alternatives without starting over. It also can test whether the designs will perform as intended.

Source: Courtesy of Lockheed Corporation.

Production Scheduling

Once they have planned what to produce, production managers formulate a master production schedule. A **master production schedule** coordinates all of the raw materials, parts, equipment, manufacturing processes, and assembly operations necessary to produce the goods. This schedule helps everyone involved keep track of what is to be done and when. It also provides a basis for making changes should something go wrong. For example, if there is a power outage in one area, can the materials be sent to another area and processed on those machines? The answer is on the master schedule. It will tell whether the other area can accommodate the extra work.

In developing and maintaining a production schedule, managers often depend on specific production-scheduling techniques. Two of the most widely recognized and used are Gantt charts and PERT networks.

The Use of Gantt Charts

While many types of charts and graphs are suitable for production scheduling, the oldest and still most popular is the Gantt chart. Developed by Henry Gantt, a pioneering expert in scientific management, the **Gantt chart** is a tool for production scheduling and control that keeps track of projected and actual work progress over time.

Figure 10.3 provides an example of a Gantt chart. One of the reasons such charts are so popular is that they allow management to determine the status of work progress merely by looking at the chart. Based on this feedback, the operations manager can decide how to make up lost time on those jobs that have fallen behind and what new jobs to assign to those who have finished their current job orders.

Networking Techniques

When a project becomes more complex, requiring simultaneous scheduling, Gantt charts are no longer adequate. The manager needs to use networking techniques linking the activities of many areas. One of the best known is the **program evaluation and review technique (PERT).**

Master production schedule A plan that coordinates all of the raw materials, parts, equipment, manufacturing processes, and assembly operations necessary to produce goods.

Gantt chart A tool for production scheduling and control that keeps track of projected and actual work progress over time.

Program evaluation and review technique (PERT) A planning and control tool useful on complex projects requiring coordination.

F I G U R E   10.3

A Gantt Chart

Order Number	Quantity Desired	January					February				March				April			
		3	10	17	24	31	7	14	21	28	7	14	21	28	4	11	18	25
100	5,000																	
160	3,750																	
244	2,600																	
319	4,000																	
376	2,500																	

This planning and control tool is useful on projects requiring considerable coordination. For instance, if five or more different jobs must be coordinated in producing a finished product, it may be difficult to determine the overall status of the entire project. PERT enables the manager to do this.

Figure 10.4 shows a sample PERT chart in which five parts (A through E) must eventually be assembled into a finished product. You may have followed a similar scheduling process yourself if you've ever made a Thanksgiving dinner. You identify the tasks you need to do: roast the turkey, bake the pies, prepare the side dishes. Then you try to start each one of them at the right time to have everything ready to eat at a specified time. If you want to eat at 4:00 p.m. and the turkey will take six hours, you know you have to have it stuffed and in the oven by 9:30 a.m. (allowing it half an hour for cooling and slicing). That means you have to start making the stuffing even earlier, say, at 9:00 a.m. Then perhaps you make a salad at 2:30 p.m., start the potatoes at 3:00 p.m., and cook some peas at 3:30 p.m. Working within a specific time frame, you have juggled many tasks to create a finished product— Thanksgiving dinner. Production managers follow a similar, though more complex, process to schedule the manufacture of many products.

An important piece of information managers uncover with PERT is the **critical path.** This is the longest possible time the project will take. To determine the critical path, simply add up the time required to follow the longest sequence or path. In Figure 10.4 the critical path is the one that runs through the middle of the project and begins with making part C. (You can check this by adding all of the other paths and compar-

Critical path   The sequence of activities that identifies the longest possible time a project will take.

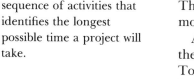

A Simple PERT Diagram

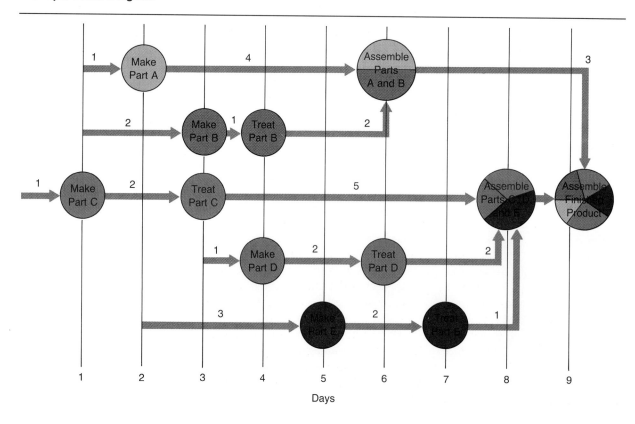

ing the time totals.) In the case of preparing Thanksgiving dinner, the critical path is the seven hours required to stuff, roast, and slice the turkey. Notice that you planned your other tasks around this one.

As long as this critical path takes no more time than is allowed for the overall project, the project will be completed on time or ahead of schedule. If progress along the critical path falls behind, the manager can take people off the shorter paths and have them help out with the activities along the critical path. Thus PERT helps management keep control over the project and reallocate equipment, materials, and people should it be necessary to prevent the project from coming in late.

Checkpoint

1. What are the two major production scheduling techniques?
2. If you were in charge of a complex project requiring simultaneous scheduling, what production scheduling technique would you use?

Plant Location

The location of the facility is another important variable in the operations function. Location of a manufacturing plant or other business facility can often mean the difference between profit and loss. For example, a company that makes bricks should be located near its customers, because the cost of shipping such a heavy but inexpensive product is great. Aluminum and chemical companies should locate in areas where there is sufficient electric power, because they need a great deal of energy to make their products.

There are three location factors that are especially critical: proximity to customers, raw materials, and a labor supply. Proximity to customers is a key consideration for most businesses. For example, Ford assembly plants are placed near population centers so that the finished cars can be shipped only a short distance to the dealers. Most service businesses try to locate near customers because production of a service usually involves interaction with the customer. If you need a tooth filled, you cannot simply request the dentist to ship you a filling via UPS.

A second key location factor is raw materials. If the raw materials are very heavy, the company will tend to locate near them. For example, steel mills have located in the Pittsburgh area because the coal needed to process the iron ore is near there. The same is true of perishable raw materials. For example, fruit and vegetable canneries must locate near the fields and fish canneries near the harbors.

Producers who need a large or specialized trained labor force may locate near the labor supply. For example, high-tech firms have tended to set up business in California's Silicon Valley, in the Boston area, or around Austin, Texas, because these areas are sources of engineers and scientists. It is easier to attract these well-educated technical people by moving into their area than it is to try to persuade them to move across the country. In order to attract workers, many businesses locate in or near a community that is pleasant to live in. Businesses look for an environment that will provide their employees with good educational, cultural, religious, and medical facilities.

Other location considerations include proximity to sources of power and water, the availability of transportation facilities, and the rules and policies of the community. If the operation draws heavily on power and water, the company may decide to locate near those resources. For example, companies that make chemical fertilizers need to be near abundant, cheap sources of power. Paper companies locate near rivers because of the tremendous amount of water needed to produce paper.

Transportation is another location factor that must be considered. Companies depend on transportation facilities to ship raw materials to the plant and finished goods to customers. When many sources of transportation are available, the competition between them is likely to keep prices down. Even a company with its own trucks needs to consider

To encourage businesses to locate in South Carolina, the state's Development Board ran this advertisement in business magazines. By describing the research being conducted at South Carolina's universities, the ad portrays the state as an attractive environment for high-tech businesses. Such companies often benefit from the resources of good universities, such as their libraries, faculty, and graduates.

Source: Courtesy of South Carolina State Development Board.

From the textile capital of America, designer genes.

Some of the most exciting work in America is being done in some of the most surprising places: South Carolina's historic universities.

At the University of South Carolina, Clemson University and the Medical University of South Carolina, research projects are under way that may one day feed the world, unlock the cure for cancer and provide products that immeasurably enhance our quality of life.

At the University of South Carolina, for example, genetic engineers are attempting to alter the genes inherited by certain species of animals. The long-range implications could dramatically influence the world's food supply.

At the Medical University, specialists in molecular genetics are building synthetic particles of genes, in an attempt to discover how white blood cells recognize and attack malignancies. An entire new generation of vaccines may be developed in that manner.

And at Clemson, scientists in the department of chemistry and geology are recognized internationally for substituting molecules of fluorine for other elements, thereby creating new man-made compounds. Products such as Teflon® and Scotchgard® for instance, are the beneficiaries of this type of research.

Not unexpectedly, all this excitement has not been lost on the private sector. More and more astute technology-based companies are exploring the merits of locating research and manufacturing facilities in the shadows of our universities.

Our coordinated statewide network of research parks—already in place and unique in America—could well hold the key to your company's future.

To discover exactly how, write J. Mac Holladay, Director, State Development Board, Suite 7000, P.O. Box 927, Columbia, S.C. 29202. Or call 803-734-1400.

We believe you'll find that a state long known as the textile capital of America is now reweaving the very fabric of American business.

South Carolina

whether it has easy access to highways. Businesses that provide services try to locate near parking facilities and public transportation.

The rules and policies of various communities also influence the location decision. Zoning ordinances restrict where commercial and industrial enterprises may operate. Some cities or townships have policies discouraging growth. However, the vast majority of cities and states have tried to attract businesses. Sometimes the government offers to let the business pay low (or even no) taxes for a period of time to help finance the operation. The government may even provide free or very inexpensive land for the facility. With all communities and states interested in creating jobs, the location alternatives are becoming increasingly attractive.

Checkpoint

1. What are three factors that should be considered in locating a facility?
2. What considerations might apply more specifically to service businesses?

Plant Layout

Once located, the company must next decide how to lay out the facility. The layout depends on the type and sequence of manufacturing processes used and determines the flows that the goods take through the plant.

Manufacturing Processes

In determining an appropriate plant layout, the production manager considers how the goods are to be produced. The two most common manufacturing processes are analytic and synthetic.

Analytic Process An **analytic manufacturing process** is one that reduces a raw material to its component parts for the purpose of obtaining one or more products. Texaco, Phillips Petroleum, Exxon, and other big oil refiners use an analytic process in converting crude oil into gasoline and a host of other oil-related products. "Cracking" the crude, as shown in Figure 10.5, produces a number of by-products. The same type of process is used in meat-packing firms such as Wilson and Iowa Beef Processors, where cattle are slaughtered for food. The company obtains animal hides, which can be used for making clothing and sporting goods (baseball gloves, for example), as well as hooves and horns, which can be used for making glue. Mining firms also employ an analytic production process to separate ore from dirt and other useless materials.

Synthetic Process A second manufacturing process relevant to how the plant is laid out is the **synthetic manufacturing process.** This process converts a number of raw materials or parts into a finished product. It often uses fabrication or modification. **Fabrication** is the combining of materials or parts in order to form or assemble them into a finished

Analytic manufacturing process A process that reduces a raw material to its component parts for the purpose of obtaining one or more products.

Synthetic manufacturing process A process that converts a number of raw materials or parts into a finished product.

Fabrication Combining materials or parts in order to form or assemble them into a finished product.

Modification The process of changing raw materials into a product.

product. A Chevrolet assembly plant uses fabrication when it takes the components shown in Figure 10.6 and creates a finished car. **Modification** is the process of changing raw materials into a product. An example is when USX takes iron ore and changes it into steel rods or pipes.

Production Sequences

In addition to the manufacturing processes, efficient plant layout also depends on the sequence in which the production activities are carried out. For example, the product being built may move along a conveyor belt to the workers, or it may stay in one place while the workers move. Each sequence requires a different type of layout. The two most common types of production sequences are continuous and intermittent.

At Fast Food Merchandisers, Inc., specially designed equipment produces Hardee's quarter-pound hamburgers. This is a continuous production sequence; the meat flows steadily along a conveyor. Such a sequence is appropriate for producing a large volume of goods of consistent size, shape, and quality.

Source: Courtesy of Imasco Limited.

F I G U R E   10.5

The Analytic Process: Crude Oil and Its Products

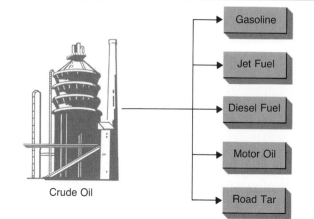

Crude Oil

Gasoline

Jet Fuel

Diesel Fuel

Motor Oil

Road Tar

Continuous Production Firms producing a standardized, high-volume good use **continuous production,** which is the steady, constant flow of materials. The automobile production line is perhaps the best example. In these plants, autos just keep coming down the line, hour after hour, day after day. Many General Electric plants use the same production process in producing consumer products such as washing machines. White Consolidated uses this process in turning out refrigerators. Companies use this production sequence when producing for immediate demand or when warehousing the goods to meet future demand.

Continuous production A production sequence in which the flow of materials is steady and constant.

Intermittent Production In the second type of sequence, **intermittent production,** the flow of materials is noncontinuous. This production sequence is used for making one-of-a-kind products or small batches of output. A one-of-a-kind item would be a communications satellite that is

Intermittent production A production sequence in which the flow of materials is noncontinuous.

F I G U R E   10.6

The Synthetic Process: Auto Assembly

Frame

Engine

Windows

Doors

Wheels

Tires

Radio

Air Conditioning

Gas Tank

Headlights

Taillights

Bumper

Steering Wheel

Interior

Seats

Dashboard

Brakes

Paint

Assembled Automobile

specially designed to handle certain types of communication transmissions. An example of small batches is production of ten locomotives designed to haul freight. The intermittent production sequence is used for handling specific customer orders.

Materials Flow

After production management determines the production processes and sequences, they lay out the flow the materials will take. There are two major possibilities, downward processing and horizontal flow.

Downward processing A materials flow in which different parts of the same product are produced on different floors.

Downward Processing In **downward processing,** different parts of the same product are produced on different levels or floors of the facility. Where possible, the lightest parts of the product are assembled first at the top level, and the heavier parts are added as the unit moves closer to the ground floor. This makes it easier to transport the unit from one level to the next. The unit is then shipped out from the ground floor.

Horizontal flow A materials flow in which all production takes place on the same floor.

Horizontal Flow In a **horizontal flow,** all production takes place on the same floor. The specific movement of the goods varies. Some firms use an I flow, in which goods move from one end of the factory directly to the other end. If the building is L-shaped, the production flow often follows this pattern. Sometimes companies use a U flow, in which the raw materials and parts come in one end of the building and the finished goods are shipped out from the same end. Which form of horizontal materials flow the company uses will depend on the type of product and the space available.

Common Forms of Layout

In planning the layout, the production management considers the ways of combining movements of workers and products. The result is generally one of three common forms of layout: process, product, or static.

Process layout A production layout that groups machines and equipment on the basis of function.

The company can group machines and equipment on the basis of function. This is called a **process layout.** A company using this layout might place welding machines in one area, lathe machines in another, and painting equipment in another. Under a process layout, the goods being produced move around the factory to the machines and equipment that will be used for the various operations. Job shops that produce small-batch orders often use a process layout because it gives them the greatest flexibility.

Product layout A production layout in which all machines are set up along a product-flow line, and the units to be manufactured move down this line.

In a **product layout,** all machines are set up along a product-flow line, and the units to be manufactured move down this line. The auto assembly plant is a good example. As the auto frame moves down the line, workers attach parts to it until it reaches the end of the line as a completed car.

Static layout A production layout in which the product stays in one place and the workers come to the product.

Under a **static layout,** the product stays in one place and the workers come to the product. Sometimes called *fixed position layout,* this approach is common when the product is extremely heavy or bulky. For example, in building a large aircraft or a locomotive, it is easier to move the workers than the product.

Checkpoint

1. What do managers consider in laying out a plant?
2. What are three forms of plant layout?

The Automatic Factory

The procedures discussed so far have enabled managers to operate production facilities efficiently. Now, however, as in all areas of business, procedures are rapidly changing. Over the last ten years a technological revolution has taken place in American factories. New manufacturing systems and ideas are enabling the production of better-quality goods faster and at lower cost. Unfortunately, this does not necessarily lead to the creation of new jobs or to improvement in the factory environment for workers. As described in "International Close-Up: Paying a Stiff Price," companies in Japan, where advanced technology is widely used in the work place, often do not have very desirable conditions for workers. Despite such problems, however, the use of robotics and flexible and computer-integrated manufacturing are having an impact on production and are the wave of the future.

Boeing uses a static product layout for building aircraft. These fuselages remain in one location, and workers move to them to perform their assigned tasks. The equipment needed to keep these components moving along an assembly line would be enormous and prohibitively expensive.

Robotics

When most people think of the automatic factory, they envision characters such as R2D2 or C3PO from the movie *Star Wars* making cars on the assembly line, but robots come in many shapes and forms. In general, **robots** are machines capable of doing a variety of tasks based on computer-programmed manipulations of materials and tools.

Robot A machine capable of doing a variety of tasks based on computer-programmed manipulations of materials and tools.

INTERNATIONAL CLOSE-UP

Paying a Stiff Price

Many critics of the American production line system argue that both output and working conditions would improve if American workers would more closely follow the Japanese. Why don't they? One reason is that working conditions in Japan are much different from those in the United States, and the average American worker would not put up with them. Consider the case of Hisashi Tomiki, a welder and team leader for the Toyota Motor Company in Toyota City, Japan.

Tomiki has worked for Toyota for over 20 years. For the first nine years, he earned so little money that he had to live in a company-owned dormitory room where no female guests were allowed. Only after he married did the company find him larger quarters. He eventually bought a $120,000 house that, by American standards, is quite small. The down payment exhausted the semiannual bonuses that he and his wife had saved over the years.

On a typical day, Tomiki gets up at 6 a.m. and leaves for work at 7 a.m. By 7:20 he is at the factory, having beaten the rush-hour traffic. He gets a good parking spot, has a cup of tea, and gets into his work gear. At 8 a.m. he and his team begin. The group is responsible for building cowls, which are steel chambers onto which the windshields and steering columns fit. Every two minutes he personally fits 24 metal pieces into designated slots on three welding machines, runs two large metal sheets through each of the machines, and fuses the two sheets together with 11 spot welds. If one of the team members

has a problem, as team leader he must run over and help fix it. The group must then hurry to catch up again with their output. He gets two 10-minute rest breaks and a 30-minute lunch break. At 5 p.m. the work day ends, but there is usually an hour of overtime. By 7 p.m. Tomiki is home with his family. He turns in at 11 p.m. in order to be well rested for the next work day. It is grueling work, and every other week he must switch and work the night shift.

The benefits that Japanese workers get are also not what they are cracked up to be. For Tomiki there are 20 vacation days and 10 holidays each year, but there is no sick leave; thus, some vacation time has to be saved in case of illness. On vacation, Tomiki and the family can stay at one of 14 Toyota guest houses around the country for a nominal sum. However, so many workers want to do this that every room is booked by lottery. Tomiki and his family can only stay overnight. Vacations are at best a one-day excursion.

For all of this work, Tomiki earns $26,250 a year before taxes, pension contribution, health insurance, and home mortgage payments. His monthly net is about $1,000. This is not a great deal of money, especially when prices on food and consumer products are skyrocketing. After reviewing these facts, one American worker noted, "It's a heck of a way to have to earn a living. I sure wouldn't want to do it." Undoubtedly, he is speaking for many, if not most, other American production-line workers.

Industrial robots are programmed to perform specific motions. The robot's computer "brain" allows it to remember what motions have been programmed in order to perform a job. The programs can be changed to have the robot perform a variety of tasks. What is most important, the robots' arms never get tired or make a mistake, they are not distracted by the heat or noise, and they never have any problems at home or with the supervisor.

The use of robots in American industry is falling short of earlier predictions. To date, about 25,000 have been installed in American factories.[7] This compares to the 118,800 used in Japan. Many big companies such as Westinghouse and GE have cut back their plans to produce robots because of the lack of demand. Tax incentives for buying such equipment have been eliminated under present law and they have turned out to be more expensive than anticipated. The exception has been the auto firms, who have purchased 50 percent of robots used in the United States. Auto factories have successfully used robots in the first stages of assembly such as welding and painting. For example, robots perform more than 98 percent of the spot welding on Ford's successful Taurus and Sable cars.

Whether robots move beyond doing relatively routine jobs and what the consequences will be for society are topics still open for debate and are discussed further in Chapter 16. Although robots can free humans from dangerous or boring tasks, they undoubtedly will also eliminate many needed jobs.

Flexible Manufacturing Systems

While robots are not as widely used as once predicted, other features of the automated factory such as computers in general and electronically controlled industrial machinery in particular are widely used by companies today. Robots account for only 2 percent of the $24 billion factory-automation business.[8] For example, a **flexible manufacturing system (FMS)** involves the use of computer-controlled machining centers that produce complicated metal parts at high speed.

Benefits of FMS The greatest benefit of a flexible manufacturing system is its ability to produce small quantities of goods at low prices. Before the use of FMSs, a small batch of goods would cost more per unit to produce than a large batch because the setup costs would have to be spread over fewer units. FMS allows firms to manufacture a few units or a few thousand units at the same basic cost per unit. This is good news for manufacturing firms, since 75 percent of all machined parts today are produced in batches of 50 or fewer.[9]

FMS also allows companies to change from producing one part to another quickly. For example, IBM used FMS at its Lexington, Kentucky, plant to make printers for its personal computers. It makes the 12 different models on the same line. Computers channel the various parts to the correct area for robots to assemble. The system is flexible because this same line could also produce toasters, videocassette recorders, and other products of the same size. FMS allowed IBM to introduce new models more quickly and helped them to regain their share of the market from the Japanese, who had held 80 percent of the computer printer market before IBM installed FMS at its Lexington plant.[10]

Flexible manufacturing system (FMS) A manufacturing system in which computer-controlled machining centers produce complicated parts at high speed.

Uses of FMS The Japanese have successfully used FMS in their automated factories, which rely heavily on computer-controlled machine tools. These plants are operated by much fewer personnel than would be needed in a conventional facility. For example, at Yamazaki Machinery Works, Ltd., only a dozen employees are at work in the $32 million plant during the day. At night the total staff consists of one guard with a flashlight. A conventional machining system would require 215 workers and four times as many machines.

Few firms can afford to spend the millions of dollars needed to completely change over to a flexible manufacturing system. However, they can introduce FMS gradually. For example, IBM, General Electric, Ford Motor, and General Motors have revitalized parts of conventional plants by installing flexible manufacturing systems where they will do the most good.

Computer-Integrated Manufacturing

Computer-integrated manufacturing (CIM) A manufacturing system that automates all of the factory functions and links them with company headquarters.

Closely related to robotics and FMS is **computer-integrated manufacturing (CIM),** which automates all of the factory functions and links them with company headquarters so that both groups are working as a team. Figure 10.7 illustrates how the process would work in a factory of the future.

At the present time, CIM is only beginning to emerge. Some of the things it will be able to do include:

Conceive new products on a computer-aided design (CAD) system

Pass information on to a computer-aided engineering system to verify that the design will do the intended job

Take the information needed to make the product and send it directly to the automated equipment on the shop floor, where it will be produced

Coordinate all of the information with a computerized inventory control system, which ensures that all the necessary parts and materials are available

A CIM factory will allow the company to switch from manufacturing one product to another automatically. It will also drastically cut labor costs. General Electric has announced plans to invest $1 billion to automate 14 appliance plants. Other large manufacturers intend to do the same. Industry estimates project that the sale of factory computers will rise to approximately $13 billion in 1990, in contrast to $4 billion in 1986, and the total CIM market will rise to $38 billion in 1990 in contrast to $13 billion in 1986.[11] Clearly, American manufacturing facilities are going to undergo dramatic changes in the near future.

Checkpoint

1. What are two ways in which businesses are automating factories?
2. What are two benefits of flexible manufacturing systems?

Purchasing and Inventory Control

Some companies find a more efficient alternative to producing parts or materials internally; they find that the time and cost involved make it wiser to buy from an outside supplier. In deciding whether to make or buy, the firm considers the costs and benefits of each alternative. Companies that buy from the outside are carrying out the purchasing function of production and operations.

Purchasing is the process of buying inventory and other assets. In most business organizations, managers of individual departments can directly buy whatever they need up to some limit, such as $200. Anything over this stated amount is handled through a central purchasing department. There are two reasons for this. One is that when buying large amounts of goods, the company often can get a quantity discount from the supplier. For example, Dunkin Donuts uses centralized purchasing to benefit its franchises.[12] By centralizing the purchases, the firm ensures that it is able to get quantity discounts. Another reason is that management is better able to coordinate and control what is going on if all large

Production and
Operations
Management

Purchasing   The process
of buying inventory and
other assets.

F I G U R E   10.7

**Computer-Integrated
Manufacturing**

Factory management oversees and coordinates production.

Top management decides to make a new product or modify an existing one.

Computer-aided engineering designs the product and programs production robots.

Computer-aided manufacturing produces parts.

Computer-aided assembly puts the parts together.

Manufactured Parts
Raw Materials

Manufactured Parts
Purchased Parts
Finished Product

Automated warehouse uses robot vehicles to shuttle raw materials, parts, and products from and to the warehouse.

DELIVERIES   PICK-UPS

Raw Materials

Purchased Parts

Finished Product

orders come through one central unit. Company management can better monitor costs and quality and build relations with suppliers and vendors.

The purchasing department buys the needed equipment and inventories and then, along with production management, controls the inventory costs and makes sure the right amount of inventory is on hand.

Equipment Purchasing

An organization occasionally needs to purchase equipment, from office equipment such as laser printers, personal computers, and photocopiers to production equipment such as lathes, welding equipment, and robots. In most cases, the purchases are handled through the central purchasing unit. For example, Domino's Pizza Distribution Company purchases the dough makers and other equipment for their more than 1,200 franchises in order to obtain better prices and control the large expenses.[13] Also, centralizing results in better records on the reliability of the vendors and the quality of their products.

Inventory Purchasing

The business must also purchase inventory when supplies begin to run low. For a manufacturer, this means keeping a supply of parts and raw materials; for a wholesaler or retailer, this means keeping a supply of the goods or services it sells. Most companies monitor their stock through the use of perpetual and physical inventory techniques.

Perpetual inventory A system for keeping track of inventory by subtracting what the company uses up or sells and adding what the company purchases.

Perpetual inventory is a technique for keeping track of the amount of inventory by subtracting whatever the company uses up or sells and adding whatever the company purchases. This technique is called "perpetual" because inventory records are updated as changes occur.

At a company using perpetual inventory, items are reordered whenever stocks hit a predetermined level. For example, if a company buys 100 units of a part that will be installed in product A and estimates that two units will be installed each day, the company will be out of this inventory in 50 working days. Under a perpetual inventory system, it will set a reorder level of, say, 20 units. When inventory reaches this level, the purchasing agent will reorder 100 more. If the reorder point is correct, the new units will arrive before current inventory is depleted, but not so soon that the company will spend a lot to store the extra inventory.

Physical inventory The process of counting the amount of inventory on hand.

Another inventory procedure is **physical inventory,** which involves counting how many units are on hand. Small firms conduct this process by literally sending someone to the storeroom or warehouse to count the inventory. Larger companies and many retail stores use a computer in this process. An example would be the local supermarket, where the clerk rings up groceries via an optical scanner that sends a computer information about what has been sold. The computer keeps track of the exact number of units on hand at any given moment. At some point, however, these firms supplement the computer information with a physical count of inventory. This procedure enables the store to adjust for errors that result from pilferage from shoplifters or employees and for items that the clerks charged without using the scanner or let slip by.

Controlling Inventory Costs

Maintaining an inventory constitutes an expense for businesses. Inventory expenses fall into two categories: order costs and carrying costs. **Order costs** are the expenses associated with ordering inventory. This includes typing up the order, mailing it, filing a copy, checking to see that the delivered inventory matches the order, and cutting a check for payment to the seller. **Carrying costs** are the expenses associated with keeping the inventory on hand. This includes the costs of storing or warehousing the goods; insuring them against theft, fire, and damage; and any losses associated with obsolescence.

In controlling these two usually significant costs, the company must take into account that order costs are greatest with frequent ordering, while carrying costs are greatest with infrequent ordering. Thus, there is a tradeoff involved. For example, if a law firm were to order enough office supplies to last an entire year, its order cost would be very low but its carrying cost would be very high. Conversely, if it ordered every day, the order costs would go up and the carrying costs would go down; the company would also run the risk that a delivery would be late and the firm would run out of supplies.

Maintaining the Right Amount of Inventory

What is the right amount of inventory to carry? The answer must weigh the costs of carrying the inventory against the risks of running out. Purchasing agents have traditionally done this by using quantitative methods such as the **economic order quantity (EOQ) model.** These methods maintain the right amount of inventory by estimating the probability of running out at various levels.

Although such quantitative approaches have been effective, the success of Japanese manufacturers with carrying very small, if any, supply inventories has led many American firms to begin re-examining their approach to inventory control. Many have arrived at a solution that allows them to carry very small amounts of inventory and thus reduce their costs. They restock continuously. This system of receiving inventory just before it is needed in the production process is called **just-in-time (JIT) inventory.**[14]

Production and
Operations
Management

Order costs The expenses associated with ordering inventory.

Carrying costs The expenses associated with keeping inventory on hand.

Economic order quantity (EOQ) model An inventory-ordering model that balances order and carrying costs and reduces the likelihood of running out of inventory.

The materials inventory of Campbell Soup Company includes many food items. For example, tomatoes are an ingredient in several varieties of Campbell's soup. With such perishable materials, careful planning is a crucial part of inventory control. The company can't keep crates of tomatoes sitting around for months while it builds production capacity or demand for tomato soup.

Source: Courtesy of Campbell Soup Company.

Just-in-time (JIT) inventory A system of receiving inventory just before it is needed in the production process.

Small firms are just beginning to make use of JIT, but the big manufacturers are widely using the approach. The Big Three automakers (General Motors, Ford, and Chrysler) all use just-in-time inventory on the assembly line. For example, the Chrysler Windsor plant receives sheet metal parts almost hourly from nearby plants; engines come from as far away as Mexico and Japan twice a week and sometimes every day; and, depending on their sizes and quantities, trim parts are received hourly to weekly.[15] Thanks to JIT inventory, the plant has been able to cut hundreds of millions of dollars from its costs.

The JIT system shifts a lot of the problems and pressures onto the suppliers, who have been forced to carry more inventory and be more responsive to the automakers' demands.[16] Those suppliers who are unable to provide the necessary parts when needed, where needed, and with an acceptable quality level are quickly dropped in favor of those who can. These new, rigorous demands by the automakers are sending ripples through the $85 billion auto parts industry. Suppliers are now realizing that they must increase their quality and lower their price if they hope to hang on to their share of Big Three business.

Checkpoint

1. What activities are involved in the purchasing function?
2. How are companies benefiting from using the just-in-time (JIT) approach to inventory?

Quality Control

Quality control The process of ensuring that goods and services are produced or provided within predetermined specifications.

Besides controlling costs, production managers must control quality. **Quality control** is the process of ensuring that goods and services are produced or provided within predetermined specifications.

Many firms today are concerned about the quality of their products and services. In the words of W. Edwards Deming, the quality-control expert who has been credited with teaching the Japanese about quality, "We in America will have to be more protective or more competitive. The choice is very simple. If we are to become more competitive then we have to begin with quality."[17] Companies often control quality through simple inspection and sampling techniques.

Inspection Techniques

Inspection takes place in service as well as manufacturing industries. For service businesses, inspection is an easy, practical way of checking on quality. For example, in many restaurants the owner comes around to the tables and asks the patrons whether everything is satisfactory. This is one way of ensuring that quality is up to standards. Another way is to examine the amount of repeat business in the establishment. If customers come back again, this is an indication that the quality is good. If few ever return, this indicates that something is wrong. Restaurants also closely monitor product quality. For example, McDonald's has strict quality standards such as the requirement that unsold Big Macs must be discarded after ten minutes and french fries after seven minutes so the products are always fresh.[18]

In manufacturing, managers want to conduct an inspection before the products are out in the marketplace. For example, a firm does not want to find out after the fact that the product has a safety problem. "Social Responsibility Close-Up: Is It Really the Customer's Fault?" discusses one company's recent possible quality-control problem that has potentially disastrous results in terms of human lives and huge liability lawsuits. A similar concern applies to all manufactured goods. For this reason, quality-control inspection is often carried out in the factory. If relatively few units are being produced, the company may inspect every one of them. For example, at Perdue Farms, a $750 million chicken business, inspectors are at work at every stage of production. This company believes that because customers inspect chickens one at a time, the company should do it that way, too.[19]

Inspection is part of quality control in publishing, especially for publications such as *National Geographic* that have built a reputation for quality production. These inspectors are checking to make sure that the printing and paper are up to standards. In buying paper, *National Geographic* maintains quality by providing suppliers with detailed specifications.

Sampling Techniques

Sampling The process of inspecting some of the goods and using the results to judge the overall quality of all the goods.

For companies manufacturing in large quantities, inspection can be very costly. These companies often rely on sampling techniques. Applied to quality control, **sampling** is the process of inspecting some of the goods and using the results to judge the overall quality of all the goods. For example, at General Electric it is too expensive to test every light bulb coming off the line. However, the firm takes a sample and tests it in order to generalize the results to the whole batch. For example, if the firm has found that it is cheaper to allow one defective unit per 100, it will take no action if 1 percent or less of these units are defective. If more than 1 percent are defective, the company looks for the problem and corrects it.

SOCIAL RESPONSIBILITY   CLOSE-UP

Is It Really the Customer's Fault?

When customers complain about a product malfunction, is it unethical for the manufacturer to refuse to conduct a product recall? This ethical issue has been posed by what some people now refer to as the "runaway Audi."

Beginning in 1978, some owners of the Audi 5000 began to report that when they shifted the gears from park to drive or reverse, the vehicle would suddenly accelerate and race off wildly. Sometimes the car would not respond to braking and, until it hit something, it was impossible to stop the vehicle. Audi doubted these claims and believed that the problem was with the drivers. In the company's opinion, the driver would accidentally hit the accelerator instead of the brake, thus propelling the car forward. By mid-1987, over 1,640 incidents of unintended acceleration have been reported by Audi 5000 drivers. Of these, 402 have resulted in injury and 5 in death.

Customers who believed that the company was building an unsafe car began to take legal action against the firm. In the meantime, the National Highway Traffic Safety Administration began to look into the possibility that there was a serious defect in the car. In an effort to deal with the problem, Audi announced that it was installing a shift lock that would prevent a driver from shifting into drive or reverse unless the individual was also pushing down on the brake.

After installing over 250,000 of these locks on the 1978–1986 models, the firm still had trouble. Some of the Audi 5000 owners continued to report problems with sudden acceleration. Specifically, a study by the New York Public Interest Research Group found that there were 125 sudden-acceleration incidents within six months of the time that Audi had begun installing the automatic shift locks. The executive director of the group reported, "The shift lock doesn't work." A spokesman for Audi of America, Inc., disagreed, claiming that, "The shift lock is working as designed. It is successfully preventing the typical cases of unintended acceleration."

The critics of the Audi 5000 remained unconvinced. They argued that the firm was refusing to admit that there was an error in the 5000 series because it did not want to face the costly legal consequences that would result. They believed that Audi's refusal to admit the problem and correct it was unethical because it showed a lack of concern for consumer safety. For its part, Audi continued to argue that there was nothing wrong with the basic design of the car and the critics were wrong.

Sampling is an important part of quality control because it helps the firm stay within the limits that it has established as "acceptable." However, with pressure from customers now demanding "zero defects" from products and some Japanese companies often reaching this level of quality, many American firms are making a new commitment to improve the quality of their products and services.

Quality-Control Circles

Managers and engineers do not have all, nor necessarily the best, answers on ways to improve product quality. Effective managers try to draw on the insights of their front-line workers. One way they do this is by forming quality-control circles. As described in Chapter 7, quality-control circles are a way to motivate employees by giving them a more participative role. This technique also benefits the company by improving products and production processes.

Commitment to Quality

Effective managers realize that while special techniques are important to quality control, management commitment to quality is the real key. For example, Ray Kroc, the founder of McDonald's, reportedly found a single fly while visiting a Winnipeg franchise. The owner lost the franchise two weeks later. Similar anecdotes from other successful companies reinforce the fact that such companies share this trait: "senior and middle managers alike who live the quality message with passion, persistence and, above all, consistency."[20] The head of Campbell Soup Company remarked, "Above all, we've got to teach our people to focus on quality first, cost second."[21]

Focus on Quality in Manufacturing Whole industries in America have recently taken up the quality challenge. Autos, high-tech, textiles, steel and major appliance industries are heavily committed to improving quality.[22] Manufacturing firms in these industries are not just talking about quality or putting out catchy slogans such as Ford's "Quality Is Job One" for advertising purposes. They are training their workers to be quality conscious and to "do it right the first time." A recent survey found that 8 out of 10 corporate executives believe that quality plays a very important role in making U.S. companies more competitive with foreign firms and that the quality of U.S. goods must be improved.[23]

In the early 1980s, Ford was an example of what had gone wrong in American manufacturing. Then, when they started to stress quality (along with other factors such as a new product design), they turned things around. For example, in 1986 Ford had higher profits than their rival General Motors for the first time in more than half a century. In 1987 Ford earned almost as much as GM, Chrysler, and American Motors combined. Ford President Harold Polling attributed the success to a carefully crafted plan "to be known as the producer of high-quality products with low cost and value for money for the consumer."[24]

How do the successful manufacturers actually implement such a quality focus? At Kawasaki Motors in Lincoln, Nebraska, production workers on the line making jet skis have the authority to request help or to stop the assembly line. When they get behind, they push a yellow button to get help so no sloppy work goes through. When they spot a defect, they push a red button to stop the line so that the problem can be fixed on the spot. Traditionally in American industrial plants, no one would ever dare stop the line. It would be considered sabotage, and the worker would be fired. But companies such as Kawasaki put quality ahead of quantity.

Focus on Quality in the Service Industry The commitment to quality exists not only in manufacturing but also in the mushrooming service industry. In fact, some experts are proclaiming that we now live in a new economy, a service economy, where service and performance are becoming more important than physical products. One observer noted that "McDonald's has more employees than U.S. Steel. Golden Arches, not blast furnaces, symbolize the American economy."[25]

The commitment to "quality service," currently a popular phrase in the business world, is exemplified by the following companies.[26] Nordstrom Department Stores, a rapidly expanding chain of stores based in the Northwest, has about double the industry average sales per square foot (the standard measure of performance in retail sales). This phenomenal performance is attributed to the quality of service Nordstrom offers to customers. For example, a clerk in the Seattle store personally ironed a customer's newly bought shirt so that it would look fresher for an upcoming meeting.

Mini Maid Services has 900 employees at 96 franchises in 24 states. The operation offers a menu of 22 basic daily cleaning chores that its four-member crews will efficiently perform in an average of 55 minutes for a fee of $39.50 to $49.50. The founder, Leone Ackerly, says the success of the company is based on the quality of customer service. "We arrive with a smile, we have knowledge, we deliver what is asked of us,

Retail firms such as Walgreens depend on quality service to keep customers. When Head Cosmetician Rosalie Saverino was transferred to Walgreens' North Michigan Avenue store in Chicago, loyal customers followed her there from her previous location further south in the city. She has received more "fan mail" from customers than any cosmetician in the company; the customer shown here is one who wrote.

Source: Courtesy of Walgreen Company.

and we call back new clients the next day to see what could be done better."

Amica Mutual Insurance, a top-rated small insurance company based in Providence, Rhode Island, made $13 million in profit on a relatively small $400 million in sales because it focuses on quality customer care. Amica does no advertising and uses only company-employed agents, adjusters, and underwriters. It prides itself on answering all customer mail within one day of receipt and responds to claims in the same speedy manner. When one policyholder was unable to get any government agency to remove a 10-ton tree that had fallen onto her house from a hurricane, she called Amica, and an adjuster came out the same day and arranged for a construction company to haul the tree away.

Checkpoint

1. What are two ways in which production managers control quality?
2. How can managers demonstrate a commitment to quality?

Closing Comments

Production and operations management underlies the efficient functioning of most manufacturing firms and, as this chapter indicated, is also part of running a service business. Production managers plan how to make products and where. They schedule work and make sure the necessary materials and equipment are available. The production process involves increasingly sophisticated computerization techniques, but in the end still comes down to people (who can produce quality products or deliver quality service) and ideas (such as just-in-time inventory in a manufacturing plant or calling back new customers the next day to get feedback on what could be done better in a service business).

Learning Objectives Revisited

1. **Describe the nature of the production process.**
   Production is the process of transforming inputs into outputs. A production system has three phases: an input, which is any resource needed to produce a desired good or service; a transformation process, which changes the inputs into the desired outputs; and an output, which is the finished good or service.
2. **Examine the specifics of production planning and scheduling.**
   Production planning involves determining the most profitable way to produce the goods and services the company will sell. A major planning technique is breakeven analysis, which identifies the level of production at which total revenues equal total expenses. Another part of planning is product design, or deciding the specific physical dimensions of the good or service to be produced. Production scheduling is based on the master schedule, which coordinates all of the raw materials, parts, equipment, manufacturing processes, and assembly operations. Two techniques for this are Gantt charts and PERT analysis.

3. **Identify the important factors of plant location and layout.**

   The key factors for location are proximity to customers, raw materials, a labor supply, power and water, and transportation. Location should also take into consideration community regulations and quality of life. The plant layout depends in part on the type of manufacturing process used. An analytic manufacturing process reduces a raw material to its component parts in order to obtain one or more products. A synthetic manufacturing process converts a number of raw materials or parts into a finished product. Plant layout also depends on the direction of material flow. In downward processing, different parts of the same product are produced on different floors of the factory. In horizontal flow, all production takes place on the same floor, and the material often flows in the shape of an I, L, or U.

4. **Discuss the automatic factory.**

   The automatic factory uses robots, machines capable of doing a variety of tasks based on computer-programmed manipulations of materials and tools. Another feature of the automatic factory is a flexible manufacturing system (FMS), in which computer-controlled machining centers produce complicated metal parts at high speed. Still another feature is computer-integrated manufacturing (CIM), which automates and links together all of the factory functions with company headquarters, so that factory and headquarters are working as a team. Although CIM is much more sophisticated and costly than an FMS, it enables the company to slash labor costs and to switch from one product to another automatically.

5. **Explain the important dimensions of purchasing and inventory control.**

   Purchasing is the process of buying equipment and inventory. Perpetual inventory is a system that calls for reordering inventory whenever stocks hit a predetermined level. Physical inventory involves counting how many units are on hand. Every firm does this occasionally to ensure that its inventory on the books is in line with the actual inventory in the warehouse. Quantitative techniques such as the economic order quantity (EOQ) model have been helpful to operations managers in deciding what is the right amount of inventory to carry. However, based on the experience of Japanese firms, companies have been moving to innovative techniques such as just-in-time (JIT) inventory.

6. **Discuss quality control in both manufacturing and service industries.**

   Quality control is the process of ensuring that goods and services are produced or provided within predetermined specifications. Manufacturing and service businesses very often use inspection, an easy, practical technique of checking on quality. Some companies require that every product be inspected, but companies that produce large numbers of goods find it too expensive to check every item. These firms use the technique of sampling, in which only a small number of units per batch are inspected. If the quality is sufficient, the firm assumes that the rest of the uninspected units are also acceptable. In recent times, however, consumer demand for "zero defects" has led some manufacturing firms to increase their commitment to quality. The same is true in the service industry, where "quality service" may be the difference between success and failure.

Key Terms Reviewed

Review each of the following terms. For any that you do not know or are unsure of, look up the definitions and see how they were used in the chapter.

production	continuous production
input	intermittent production
transformation process	downward processing
output	horizontal flow
production planning	process layout
breakeven point	product layout
product design	static layout
value engineering	robot
value analysis	flexible manufacturing system (FMS)
master production schedule	computer-integrated manufacturing (CIM)
Gantt chart	purchasing
program evaluation and review technique (PERT)	perpetual inventory
	physical inventory
critical path	order costs
analytic manufacturing process	carrying costs
synthetic manufacturing process	economic order quantity (EOQ) model
fabrication	just-in-time (JIT) inventory
modification	quality control
	sampling

Review Questions

1. Identify the input, transformation process, and output for each of the following production systems: a pickle factory, a movie theater, and a writer of mysteries.
2. How can production departments improve the design of products?
3. You are the production manager for a company that makes washing machines. To schedule production, would you use a Gantt chart or a PERT network? Explain your choice.
4. In deciding where to locate a plant, what factors are important?
5. Miracle Processors Inc. is a company that makes sweet-and-sour sauce, puts it into small plastic packets, and sells it to Chinese restaurants to give out with egg rolls. Does this company use continuous production or intermittent production? Explain.
6. Blue Streak Boat Company has just leased a three-story factory. The production manager wants to take advantage of the factory's height to use downward processing. In laying out the factory, where should the manager try to have the heaviest parts of the boats installed?
7. How does a process layout differ from a static layout? For what production processes would each layout be most suitable?

8. How can companies automate their factories?
9. What is computer-integrated manufacturing? How can companies benefit from using it?
10. Why would a store want to conduct both a perpetual inventory and a physical inventory?
11. Because Ted's Drive-In-and-Thru uses just-in-time inventory, it has on hand a minimal supply of menu items and risks running out if many more customers show up than expected. Why do you think Ted doesn't order a lot of these items so that he can be sure not to run out?
12. What is the difference between inspection and sampling? What are the advantages of each?
13. How can managers demonstrate a commitment to quality? If you think of ideas in addition to those mentioned in the chapter, add them to your answer.

Applied Exercises

1. Research the use of computer-aided design (CAD). Who is using these techniques and for what purposes? Write a brief summary of your findings and report them to class.
2. Visit a local manufacturing or construction firm that uses the Gantt chart and/or PERT. Find out why and how the firm uses them. Report your findings to the class.
3. Visit a local manufacturing or print shop. Find out if the firm uses continuous production or intermittent production. Also look at their materials flow and their plant layout. Report your findings to the class.
4. Read up on industrial robots, flexible manufacturing systems (FMS), and computer-integrated manufacturing (CIM). Who is using these recent developments? For what purposes? Write a one- to two-page summary and report your findings to the class.
5. Visit a large local retailer (a supermarket, discount store, or department store). Find out whether the firm uses perpetual and/or physical inventory. Also, does the store use the economic order quantity (EOQ) model or some similar quantitative approach for balancing order and carrying costs? Write a two-page summary of your findings and report them to the class.

Your Business IQ: Answers

1. False. Manufacturing goods and providing services both involve a production or operations function. In general, this is the conversion of resources such as raw materials, time, and employees' skills and talents into a finished good or service.

2. False. Fixed costs are the costs that remain the same regardless of whether the quantity produced changes. Managers can cut fixed costs by, for example, selling a factory or a piece of equipment or by laying off workers. However, this could make it difficult or impossible to produce a greater quantity in the future.

3. True. These are two of several criteria that a company would consider when deciding where to locate a production facility.

4. False. Although automakers have started to use robots extensively, the overall use of robots by American manufacturers is less than was once predicted. Robots have turned out to be more expensive than companies had anticipated. Many businesses are, however, finding that robots are worthwhile for some applications.

5. True. This approach keeps down the cost of stocking and warehousing supplies and is called just-in-time inventory.

Case

GM Starts from Scratch

It has been years since any of the American automakers built a new production plant. Thus, when General Motors decided to do so a few years ago, industry analysts were both surprised and relieved. Many believed that this new plant, designed to produce the Saturn, a subcompact car that would compete against the Japanese imports, was just what the industry needed.

In contrast to other American auto assembly plants, all of the work at the Saturn plant is to be done in one place. Raw materials will come in one end of the building, and cars will go out the other.

While the new plant was originally projected to cost $3.5 billion, that figure has now been trimmed to $1.7 billion. It still will be one of the largest industrial setups in the United States. Using new technology and management techniques, many of which emulate those of the Japanese firms, GM hopes to turn out 250,000 cars per year and gain a strong foothold in the small-car market. As one auto expert noted, "If we let the Japanese have the small-car market without a fight, they'll move up to the medium-sized cars, and we'll be left building just Cadillacs." Clearly, GM does not intend to let this happen.

The major problems that Saturn seems to be having are that initial estimates of demand have been trimmed down by 50 percent, and the assembly apparently will utilize less high technology, such as robots, than originally planned. As one Saturn official explained, "GM can't produce the kind of miracle everybody has been expecting. No one can produce that kind of miracle." One thing that has not changed, however, is that the car will use parts that require less energy and materials in the manufacturing process. These two components account for approximately half the cost of production and are critical in keeping the auto's price competitive.

Case Questions

1. What type of plant layout would you expect to find in the Saturn operation? Explain.
2. When it comes to inventory control, what techniques would you expect GM to use? Give an example.
3. Would you guess that the plant will use flexible manufacturing systems or computer-integrated manufacturing? Why do you suppose they have cut back from their original intent to use robots extensively?

You Be the Adviser: From the Bottom Up

Pedro Ramirez has run a small factory for over 15 years. Recently he decided to expand his operation and to start bidding on more subcontracting work. To ensure that his factory is as up-to-date as possible, Pedro has decided to build a new facility from the bottom up. He plans on a one-story building that will be highly automated and will be capable of handling both small- and large-batch orders.

Some of the work he will be doing will call for receiving finished parts, assembling them into finished goods, and then shipping everything to the major contractor. Most of the work, however, will require Pedro's company to take raw material and convert it into the finished products. In either event, all of these jobs will involve making various kinds of small and intermediate-sized industrial equipment.

Right now Pedro is in the process of looking over all of the production-related activities that will be handled in the factory and completing plans for plant layout and operations. His local banker has promised to lend him all of the necessary money, and Pedro is determined to build the most efficient plant possible.

Your Advice

1. What type of materials flow would you suggest to Pedro? Why?
2. What type of plant layout (process, product, or static) would you recommend? Why?
3 What advice would you give Pedro regarding inventory control? Be as complete as possible in your answer.

Career Opportunities

Many different types of career opportunities are available in the area of managing people and operations. These include public relations specialists, operations supervisors, personnel specialists, and training specialists.

Public Relations Specialists

Public relations specialists help organizations build and maintain positive relationships with the public. In this role, they perform a wide number of functions, including handling relations with the press, community, and customers. They may also be involved in fund raising and employee recruitment. The specific roles will depend on the needs of the organization. For example, a public relations director of a small private college may spend most of the time recruiting a student body and trying to raise funds from alumni or the community. Working for a large corporation, the public relations specialist may work with stockholders, government agencies, and customers. Public relations workers put together information that keeps the public aware of the organization's policies, activities, and accomplishments. Their job also entails keeping management aware of public attitudes.

At present there are approximately 90,000 public relations specialists, and the Department of Labor estimates that this career field will see a much faster than average growth through the 1990s. A college education combined with public relations experience is good preparation for public relations work. Most newcomers have a college major in journalism, communications, or public relations, although some employers prefer training in a field related to the firm's business. Public relations specialists earn approximately $32,000, although the range extends from $15,000 to over $55,000.

Operations Supervisors

Operations supervisors, at the first level of management, direct the activities of operating employees by telling them what has to be done and making sure the work is done correctly. In manufacturing, for example, supervisors inspect products during and after the production process to ensure that they conform to customer needs and company quality standards. Supervisors at a truck terminal would assign workers to load trucks, and then check to see that the material is loaded correctly and that each truck is fully used. Operations supervisors also prepare work schedules and keep production and employee records. They plan employees' activities, teach safe work habits, enforce regulations, demonstrate time-saving techniques, and ensure that employees are properly trained. Other duties include telling subordinates about company plans and policies, recommending good performers for raises, and improving performance by retraining workers and, when necessary, issuing warnings or recommending discipline or dismissal.

At present approximately 1.5 million operations supervisors are employed in the United States. They work in all types of organizations, including construction, manufacturing, wholesale and retail trade, public utilities, transportation, and government agencies. With recent cutbacks in the middle-management ranks of many organizations, more first-line supervisors will probably be needed to handle the work that will be delegated downward.

Traditionally, supervisors rise through the ranks. They start out as operating employees, and the outstanding ones are made supervisors. Recently, however, companies have been hiring more and more college graduates as supervisors because they are judged to be more effective in managing the workers. This is particularly true in the aerospace, oil, and electronics industries. Most supervisors earn $25,000 to $35,000 per year, although newly hired supervisors make $18,000 to $23,000 and more experienced supervisors make as much as $50,000.

Personnel Specialists

Personnel specialists perform jobs in a number of different areas. Many interview and recommend applicants for job openings. They may also be involved in wage administration, pensions, benefits, or employee assistance programs. Recruiters maintain contacts with community employment agencies and may travel to college campuses to search for promising job applicants. They also may administer tests and check references. EEO (equal employment opportunity) representatives or affirmative-action coordinators investigate and resolve EEO grievances, examine corporate practices for possible violations, and compile and submit EEO statistical reports. Compensation specialists conduct job analyses and devise ways of ensuring fair and equitable pay rates.

Most personnel specialists are college graduates and have studied personnel and labor relations. At present approximately 150,000 people are employed as personnel specialists, and opportunities in this area should grow at about the same rate as the economy in general. Salaries vary depending on the size of the organization and its geographic area. Personnel specialists, recruiters, and compensation specialists earn approximately $26,000–$28,000 annually, and EEO specialists earn around $37,000.

Training Specialists

Training specialists develop courses, workshops and other programs tailored to the training needs of an organization and its employees. They consult with managers and supervisors about specific training needs, prepare manuals and other materials for use in training sessions, and inform employees about training opportunities. Overall, they are responsible for planning, organizing, directing, and evaluating a wide range of training activities. They often conduct orientation sessions and arrange for on-the-job training for new employees. They help rank-and-file workers maintain and upgrade their job skills. To prepare employees for future responsibilities, they may set up individualized training and career plans to strengthen existing skills or teach new ones. Training specialists in some companies set up programs designed to develop executive potential among employees in lower-level positions.

At present approximately 65,000 people hold jobs as training specialists in industry and government. Most training specialists have college degrees in business administration with a specialization in personnel or organizational behavior. Other popular majors for these jobs include psychology, sociology, or communication. Starting salaries are in the $18,000 to $20,000 range, and experienced training managers may earn $50,000 or more.

Marketing Goods and Services

Few companies can successfully sell their goods and services without an effective marketing effort. Whether the business simply needs to let people know about a good or service or must try to persuade them that its product is better than the competition's, marketing is important. Part IV shows how companies carry out their marketing activities.

Chapter 11 examines what marketing is and how managers devise a marketing strategy. Years ago, managers were almost solely concerned with producing goods; today, however, successful managers start by finding out what the customer wants.

Chapter 12 addresses the important marketing dimensions of product planning and pricing. Most products last no more than five years in the marketplace. Therefore, marketers must replace them with new offerings.

Chapter 13 examines promotional strategies, the primary one being advertising. The most effective type of advertising depends on the nature of the product and its competition. Advertising strategy typically shifts as the product moves from introduction to heavy competition to slowdown and decline.

Chapter 14 addresses how marketers distribute products and services to customers. It describes the paths the products take, as well as the intermediaries — wholesalers and retailers — that help distribute the products.

When you have finished studying Part IV, you should understand the strategies and basic functions of marketing. You should know how new products are planned and the various pricing strategies that marketers use to help sell them. You should also recognize the important role of advertising and personal selling in the promotion effort and the various forms of intermediaries and distribution channels that move products from producer to consumer.

Source: Courtesy of AMD Industries Incorporated.

Marketing: Functions and Strategies

LEARNING OBJECTIVES

- Define the overall nature of marketing.
- Describe the basic functions of marketing.
- Discuss the nature and importance of marketing research.

- Present the various types of market segmentation
- Explain how a marketing manager identifies a target market.
- Identify the "four Ps" of marketing.

Your Business IQ

How much do you already know about marketing? Test your business IQ by labeling each statement *true* or *false*. Answers and explanations are at the end of the chapter.

1. Most businesses today build their marketing approach around the adage that "a good product or service will sell itself."
2. The marketing process consists of the various stages of selling.
3. Consumers are not necessarily conscious of their motives for buying something.
4. Small businesses generally use telephone surveys as their major tool for researching what customers want.
5. Marketers at large companies often divide the total market into segments and develop a strategy to meet the needs of one or more of these segments, rather than trying to please everyone with the same strategy.

Designing sunglasses and developing a quality image for its Wayfarer and Ray-Ban brands are part of Bausch & Lomb's marketing activities. The company has prospered in the market for sunglasses by treating them as a fashion accessory and not merely as protection from the sun.

Source: © Ted Kawalerski.

Looking Back and Ahead

It used to be that businesses rarely had any trouble selling what they produced. Consumers had a pent-up demand for goods and services, and they pretty much bought whatever business could supply. Production ruled supreme. But the production experts did their job almost too well. Business's inventories began to build up, and managers began to wonder, "How will we get rid of this stuff?" Enter the marketing function.

Henry Ford is a good example of someone who emphasized production over marketing. Starting out at around the turn of the century, his company soon dominated the auto business. In 1914 Ford produced 270,000 cars, while the other 299 auto firms in America manufactured a total of only 287,000 cars. However, Ford failed to change with the times. Once supply met demand, suppliers had to identify and provide for customer desires. For example, when Ford's dealers came to him and complained that General Motors was turning out cars in many different colors, Ford told them, "You can have them any color you want, boys, as long as it's black." Quite clearly, Ford did not understand that marketing had become an integral part of business. As a result, General Motors, which under the leadership of Alfred P. Sloan had a marketing philosophy of "a car for every purse and purpose," eventually captured the largest share of the auto market. Ford Motor Company has only recently been able to recover from the strategic error of ignoring the marketing function.

The history of American business is full of such stories. Another example concerns the invention of photocopying. The inventor, Chester Carlson, was looking for a company to take over the new invention, but IBM and DuPont turned him down. They did not think there would be a market for this type of product. The Haloid Corporation did see the benefits, struck a deal with the inventor, eventually changed its name to Xerox, and the rest is history.

While Part III focused on managing people and operations, this chapter begins the study of marketing. It first defines the overall nature of the marketing concept and process and then examines the marketing functions. Then it turns to the basis for planning a marketing strategy: information. Marketing managers need to understand how to conduct marketing research to discover how consumers behave and what kinds of buyers make up the total market. The chapter ends by discussing how managers use this information to formulate a marketing strategy.

The Nature of Marketing

American business has come to recognize the customer as king. Although Henry Ford himself may not have recognized this, a current vice president of Ford Motor Company observed, "There's one central objective in our business, and that's to earn a return on our investment. I think we've now learned there's something else that's central . . . serve the customer."[1] Serving the customer is the basis of the marketing function of the modern business firm. More specifically, **marketing** is the process of identifying the goods and services the customer wants and providing them at the right price and place.

Marketing Identifying the goods and services the customer wants and providing them at the right price and place.

The Modern Marketing Concept

Over the last 50 years, the marketing concept in American business has changed significantly. In particular, the emphasis has shifted from production-oriented marketing to consumer-oriented marketing.

Production-Oriented Marketing Fifty years ago, companies typically engaged in **production-oriented marketing.** This approach to the marketing concept is based on the belief that a good product or service will sell itself. This belief certainly has merit and has worked for many companies. For example, when Edwin Land first introduced the Polaroid camera, he was convinced that people would buy it once they saw what it could do, that is, produce instant pictures. He was right; his unique product sold itself. However, success from production-oriented marketing has turned out to be more the exception than the rule.

The goal of production-oriented marketing has been to "build a better mousetrap." The business must always have the best product, so it will sell itself. Some time ago, a company called Woodstream actually built a better mousetrap. In contrast to the typical, cheap wooden trap, which the user could throw out with the mouse, this one was made of metal and could be cleaned and reused. The trap was more efficient and easy to set. Although it cost more than the wooden version, it was more economical because it could be continually reused. The company shipped thousands of these traps to hardware stores across the country—and there they sat, gathering dust. Why? People were unwilling to take the dead mouse out of the trap. The metal trap may have been a better designed product than its wooden competitor, but there was no demand for it.[2] Thus, the old adage may need to be rephrased: American consumers may not always *buy* the better mousetrap. Had Woodstream's managers depended on a consumer-oriented marketing concept, they would not have been stuck with thousands of technologically superior but unsalable mousetraps.

Consumer-Oriented Marketing In contrast to the production-oriented approach, **consumer-oriented marketing** is based on the belief that a company must find out what the customer wants before providing a good or service. This approach underlies the modern marketing concept and holds that the consumer is the most important part of the business.

McDonald's Corporation is an excellent example of effective consumer-oriented marketing. Every year, McDonald's tries out a host of new products to see which ones customers like. Those that prove popular are added to their menu; those that receive little acceptance are dropped. For example, a few years ago, the company offered a pork sandwich that oozed with barbecue sauce. Many people tried McRib—one time.[3] Customers just did not like the sloppiness or the taste. The company soon dropped it from the menu. Other products such as McNuggets have met with great success.

The Role of Quality and Price

The quality and price of the products also play a key role in modern marketing. Some companies focus more heavily on one of these than the other, although most consider both product characteristics. For example,

Production-oriented marketing Based on the belief that a good product or service will sell itself.

Consumer-oriented marketing Based on the belief that a company must find out what the customer wants before providing a good or service.

every year, the Harris corporation sells millions of dollars in sophisticated computer equipment to the federal government. The government is more interested in the performance of this equipment than in getting the lowest possible price. For this reason, Harris uses a marketing approach that emphasizes product quality. Other high-tech firms employ the same approach. For example, when selling to business, IBM and Hewlett-Packard both emphasize what their machines can do to help the company operate more efficiently.

In contrast, many firms emphasize price. Although Sears is well known for the quality of its merchandise, most people shop there because of its competitive prices. They feel they get more "bang for the buck" at Sears than at, for example, Lord & Taylor, a store with a reputation for high-quality, expensive merchandise. The same is true for Penney's, K mart, and Wal-Mart, which most often attract customers on the basis of their prices.

Business executives often fly first class because they need the extra seating space and comfort for doing their work en route, for relaxing, and for knowing that someone will take care of all their needs (a cup of coffee, a cocktail, an attractive meal, a newspaper, or a magazine). To carry this quality service a step further, some airlines in the near future will run a computer program, send a telex, or make hotel and rental-car reservations for a passenger from an on-board computer.[4] Quality ground transportation and lodgings are also important to business executives. Often, senior-level executives have a limousine take them to the hotel, where they have reservations for first-class accommodations.

On the other hand, most consumers are neither interested in nor willing to pay the price for first-class service. They would rather fly coach and put up with some inconvenience than pay a higher price. In fact, the airlines have found that many travelers, especially vacationers, will bear the inconvenience of flying at off-peak hours or in the middle of the week for cut-rate fares. Of course, there are limits to what consumers will take, as described in the "Social Responsibility Close-Up: The Angry Fliers." When they arrive at the airport, they will wait for the hotel minibus or public transportation to take them to the hotel, and they will have reservations for comfortable and clean, but not lavish, accommodations.

Checkpoint

1. How is production-oriented marketing different from consumer-oriented marketing?
2. What roles do quality and price play in modern marketing?

Marketing Functions

Marketing involves more than just selling. The marketing process involves eight basic functions: buying, selling, transporting, storing, standardizing and grading, financing, risk taking, and obtaining marketing information. Figure 11.1 illustrates these marketing functions. Some firms use all of them, but most carry out only some.

The Angry Fliers

When travelers buy an airline ticket, they expect on-time, efficient, and courteous service. On the other hand, in order to accommodate millions of fliers every month, the airlines must rely on rules, policies, and procedures for efficiently managing their operations. The result is that customer expectations are not met. The airlines contend that many fliers fail to follow instructions or simply misunderstand the terms under which their ticket is issued.

A growing number of airline passengers feel that some carriers are not treating them fairly and have questionable ethics when it comes to certain practices. There is support for these charges. For example, a recent investigation found that many carriers take months, and even years, to refund unused tickets. Others tack on unexplained charges for prepaid tickets. Still others refuse to honor passengers' claims for lost baggage unless they have the original purchase receipts for the goods that were inside. These are only a few, less-publicized complaints. Frequent airline passengers have occasionally run into the following types of problems:

The Check-In Rule Hassle If passengers are bumped off a flight (they have a confirmed reservation but the flight is overbooked and they can't get on the plane), they are entitled to some form of compensation. Typically the bumped passenger is given a free ticket on the next flight. However, if the individual misses check-in time, the airline does not have to give the person anything. And when is check-in time? For most airlines, it is 10 to 30 minutes before departure. And when is departure? That depends on whether the plane is on time or late. If it is on time, the passenger should be checked in at least 10 minutes before flight time. If the individual calls from home and finds that the flight is delayed an hour, when is flight time? Many airlines still use the original time of departure, and if someone checks in late because

the flight was delayed and misses the flight because of overbooking, the airline may refuse to award any overbooking compensation.

Fly Standby for Free When a flight is overbooked, airlines will ask for volunteers to give up their seats in return for a guaranteed seat on the next available flight to their destination and a travel certificate for free round-trip fare to any domestic city served by the airline. Sounds like a great deal. However, some airlines only honor these certificates if the individual makes the reservation *less than* 24 hours in advance. Simply put, the travel certificate is little more than a standby ticket.

Missed Connections Many passengers traveling at night find, to their chagrin, that if their plane arrives late and they miss a connecting flight, the airline will not always put them up for the night and pay for the expenses. All hotel and food expenses have to be paid by the passenger.

These are not the only complaints against the airlines, and not all airlines are constantly guilty of these practices. But they happen frequently enough that many travelers feel that some airlines are being unethical in their treatment of their customers. Some people are fighting back by taking the airlines to court. Congress has also enacted legislation requiring the airlines to report each month on how frequently their flights are cancelled or late, baggage is misplaced, and passengers are bumped. The law also forces carriers to state in their advertising if discount fares apply to a limited number of seats. On the other hand, the airlines argue that many of these problems are the result of overbooking by travel agents, bad weather, and passengers' failure to read the terms and conditions of the ticket. The airlines believe that they are highly ethical and are being made the scapegoat by angry passengers and politicians.

264

Buying

When applied to marketing, the purchasing function is called **buying** and involves deciding the type and amount of goods to be purchased. Managers typically base such decisions on a forecast of consumer demand. In the case of giant retailers such as Macy's in New York, Bullock's in Los Angeles, or Rich's in Atlanta, buying involves thousands of merchandise orders that vary in quality and quantity. In the case of a small boutique in a college town, the decision is much more limited and is likely to involve purchases that are but a fraction of those made by a giant retailer.

Buying Deciding the type and amount of goods to be purchased.

Selling

The selling function is probably most closely associated with marketing and really is its central activity. **Selling** includes identifying buyers, developing a promotional campaign to attract their business, and concluding the sale. Notice that the process involves much more than simply handing over the merchandise and ringing up the sale. In fact, marketers usually spend more time and effort identifying potential buyers and figuring out how to entice them to seek out the company's goods and services than they do giving a sales pitch and then closing the sale. Selling can occur through the written media. Advertisements in magazines and newspapers are part of selling as are catalogs.

Selling Identifying buyers, developing a promotion campaign to attract their business, and concluding the sale.

Transporting Moving goods from where they were manufactured or purchased to where they are needed.

Transporting

For selling to take place, the company must also engage in **transporting,** the process of moving goods from where they were manufactured or

FIGURE   11.1

Marketing Functions

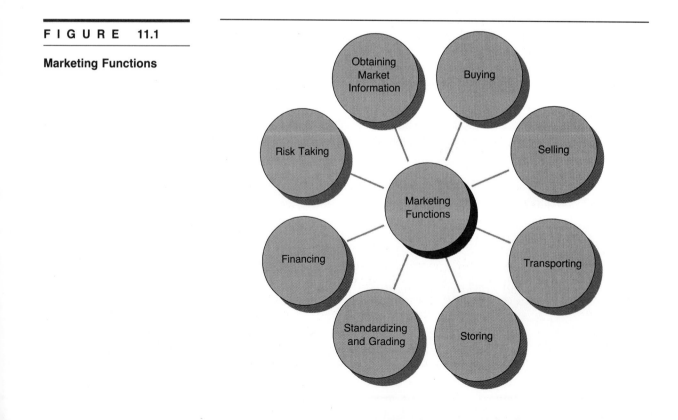

purchased to where they are needed. In many instances, the manufacturer performs this function by shipping the goods to wholesalers. The wholesaler, in turn, breaks up the shipment into smaller lots and transports them to retailers. Customers then visit the retail store to purchase the merchandise.

Although the manufacturer-wholesaler-retailer sequence is the most common, it is not the only way to carry out the transportation function. For example, some wholesalers buy in large quantities from the manufacturer and then sell directly to customers, while some manufacturers ship directly to retailers. In some cases, the manufacturer also owns and operates a direct retail outlet. For example, Pendleton has a direct factory outlet for its fine woolen apparel at Bemidji, Minnesota. Some companies, such as L. L. Bean and Domino's Pizza, take orders through the mail or over the phone and then transport goods directly to the customers. However the business does it, transportation is an important marketing function because it gets the goods or services to a location where customers buy them.

Storing

Following transporting comes the process of **storing,** or warehousing, goods. Few firms operate hand to mouth; instead, most firms store goods until they are demanded. Even small retail stores have large back rooms where they keep additional merchandise. If they need more room, they rent space from a public storage company. Large firms typically have their own warehouses, although they also rent or purchase storage space if they run out of room. While companies that sell services rarely can keep an inventory, they might address this need by hiring more workers for busy periods.

Because storing goods is expensive, managers have to weigh the benefits of having the goods on hand against the expense. The procedures are similar to the ones described in Chapter 10 for managing inventories of raw materials.

Storing Warehousing goods.

Standardizing and Grading

When you go to a hardware store to buy 100-watt light bulbs, you don't want to bother with testing each bulb until you find enough 100-watt bulbs. Likewise, if you need a shirt, you don't want to try on every shirt in the store looking for one that fits. Companies meet this need by standardizing. **Standardizing** is establishing specifications or categories for products. For example, when General Electric makes a light bulb, the company makes it to certain specifications, such as 100 watts. Clothing manufacturers make shirts to certain size specifications. The company then labels the product with this information. Standardization is important in helping customers identify the specific characteristics they are looking for—such as size, weight, height, texture, ingredients, or color.

Closely related to standardizing is **grading,** which involves sorting goods into classes on the basis of quality. For example, eggs and dairy products are graded. Meat, fruit, and farm produce are also sorted by quality. Grading goods make it much easier for the consumer to decide what to buy.

Standardizing Establishing specifications or categories for products.

Grading Sorting goods into classes based on quality.

When you shop for light bulbs, you don't have to test them to see how bright they are. The marketer simplifies the job by standardizing wattages, and you select 60-, 75-, or 100-watt bulbs. By necessity, standardizing limits the variety available; you won't find 63-, 72-, or 106-watt bulbs. The company offers a wide range of products to fill a variety of customer needs. General Electric, for example, doesn't sell 72-watt bulbs along with the 75-watt bulbs because a need has not been established; other products are viable alternatives. Costs of development, production, packaging, and marketing would be prohibitive for a company having countless variations of a product. When GE develops a new product to fill a specific need, such as a long-lasting bulb for hard-to-change places, the company test-markets the product to determine reactions to it.

Source: Photo © Steve Dunwell 1986 for GE Lighting, General Electric Company.

Financing in Marketing

As a marketing function, financing is paying for merchandise to sell and arranging for credit to buyers. Part VI of this text covers all aspects of financing. Applied to marketing, this process has two major parts: financing the purchase of the goods and financing the sale of the goods.

In the first case, many marketers pay for their merchandise at the end of the month. When this time rolls around, they issue a check to the seller. If the marketers cannot afford to pay for the goods out of current revenues, they will typically arrange for a short-term loan with the local bank and draw on these funds. When marketers sell goods, they sometimes offer financing terms to buyers. For example, large firms like General Motors, Ford Motor, General Electric, and Sears all offer their customers financing arrangements.

If consumers buy a General Motors automobile, they can arrange financing for it through General Motors Acceptance Corporation (GMAC). The buyer can pay the bill in monthly installments. In recent years, this has been an important marketing approach for the automobile industry. The auto dealer can offer loans at interest rates that are usually below what local lending institutions would charge—often as low as 1.9 percent—to make it easier to buy a new car. The buyer need not come up with ready cash.

Many manufacturers and wholesalers also provide financing arrangements to the businesses that purchase their merchandise. This ranges from giving the buyer 30 days to pay for the merchandise (in essence, a month of free credit) to allowing the buyer to pay for it over an extended period of time. A good example of the latter occurs when the manufacturer has a great deal of inventory and is willing to ship it to the seller under an arrangement whereby the customer pays for it as it is sold. This agreement permits both sides to come out ahead.

Risk Taking in Marketing

As a marketing function, risk taking is the process of assuming potential liability. When marketers take possession of merchandise, they run the risk that the goods will be destroyed by fire, be stolen, or (perhaps worst of all) have no market demand and not be sold. Some marketers reduce this risk by purchasing insurance against such calamities as fire and theft. Others limit their risk by assuming ownership of no more merchandise than they believe they can sell over the next 30 days. Still others, like brokers, never take possession of goods. They simply try to identify buyers and sellers, and then bring the two groups together. In this case, the risk is that of losing a lot of time trying to put together a deal that eventually falls through. For virtually all businesses, risk taking is an inherent part of the marketing function. In this sense, marketing resembles entre- or intrapreneurship (discussed in Chapter 3).

Obtaining Market Information

Market information helps businesses identify and address consumer needs. Businesses need answers to many types of questions, from how consumers behave to what the most effective advertising is to where to sell the merchandise. Large companies spend millions of dollars each year obtaining market information. AT&T wants to know how well it is providing telephone service and what additional services customers would like. Swanson's wants to know if there are a growing number of vegetarians, so they can develop new frozen dinners. American Express wants to know what new services they can offer their customers. To a large degree, then, marketing effectiveness is based on accurate information.

Checkpoint

1. What are three functions of marketing?
2. How do businesses use financing to make it easier for customers to buy their products?

Understanding Markets

Applying the eight functions of marketing is a complex process. Each company's situation requires a unique approach. To make the marketing functions part of a successful strategy, marketing managers must prepare themselves by developing an understanding of the market to which they must appeal. A **market** consists of a group of customers who have the money and desire to purchase goods and services.

There are two basic types of markets: industrial and consumer. Goods and services that are used to produce still other goods are called **industrial goods or services.** For example, a chain saw in a lumber camp is an industrial good because it is used to produce other goods. However, if a consumer bought a chain saw to cut firewood on his acreage, the saw would not be considered an industrial good. In other words, it is the use to which a good is put rather than any intrinsic qualities that classifies it. Temporary secretarial help is another example of an industrial service. The primary purpose of hiring temporary help is to produce some other output. Other common examples are tools, personal services, office equipment, supplies such as chemicals and building materials, and raw materials such as coal and iron.

Goods and services destined to be used by consumers are **consumer goods or services.** The chain saw used by a homeowner to cut firewood is considered a consumer good. There are many examples; for purposes of clarity, they can be categorized into the following four groups:

1. A *convenience good or service* is one that consumers tend to purchase quickly and with a minimum of effort. Typically low-priced items, convenience goods include newspapers, bread, milk, chewing gum, candy, and toothpaste. A service such as a shoeshine could also be considered in this category. The success of convenience stores such as 7-Eleven and Kwik Shops attests to the market that exists for these goods. The stores have become extremely popular in recent years as consumers have become less patient and society has grown increasingly fast paced.
2. A *shopping good or service* is one that consumers buy only after comparing the various models or approaches. In this process, they consider price, style, quality, service, and so forth. Examples include

Market A group of customers who have the money and desire to purchase goods and services.

Industrial good or service A good or service used to produce still other goods or services.

Consumer good or service A good or service destined to be used by a consumer.

automobiles, furniture, refrigerators, microwave ovens, and TVs. Services such as photo finishing or hairstyling could also be included.

3. A *specialty good or service* is one that consumers are willing to spend extra effort to locate and buy. Consumers often buy these goods on the basis of brand name and/or quality. Because consumers are so different, a specialty good for one person may not be a specialty good for another. For example, if Sally Rogers buys only designer clothes, then clothing is a specialty good for her. If Al Jones believes that clothes are all alike, and he buys strictly on the basis of price, clothes are a shopping good for him. A physical fitness/health spa would be an example of a specialty service.

4. An *unsought good or service* is one that customers do not initially want or are unaware that they can afford or practically use. Examples of the first category often include encyclopedias, life insurance, and cemetery plots. Examples of the second category might be products such as a riding lawn mower or a satellite dish. Travel packages to exotic places would be an example of a service in this category.

Checkpoint

1. What are the two basic types of markets?
2. What are some examples of consumer goods?

Consumer Behavior

Whether they are selling industrial or consumer goods and services, marketers need to understand how buyers behave. For example, why do some consumers say they are concerned about price but then buy an expensive brand of shampoo that cleans hair no better than a generic brand? Why do some people go to college upon graduating from high school, while others begin full-time jobs to buy cars and stereos? Possible answers to such questions come from an understanding of the nature of consumer behavior.

Consumer behavior The way consumers go about making their purchase decisions.

Consumer behavior is the way consumers go about making their purchase decisions. This complex psychological process typically follows the steps shown in Figure 11.2. First, the prospective buyer or customer recognizes a problem or opportunity. For example, a young mother may conclude that she needs to place her three-year-old son in a day-care center if she wants to get a good job and contribute income to her family. The buyer searches the available options and evaluates each one of them. The mother might visit the various day-care centers and compare programs, meals, facilities, and costs. Based on the evaluation, the consumer decides whether and what to buy and enters into a transaction. The mother might decide to enroll her child in one of the centers on a trial basis. The experience with this center provides feedback. She might decide this center isn't for her child, or she might decide that she likes it so much she will enroll him and take a full-time job. Thus, the feedback from a transaction influences future decisions.

Buying Motives

The consumer's ultimate decision depends on a variety of motives. Family and friends may encourage certain decisions; for example, parents or friends who value nutrition highly may encourage their children or friends to buy certain types of foods. The consumer's own attitudes and beliefs also influence a buying decision. For example, a consumer who values projecting an image of being wealthy will buy a different car than one who values saving money.

Consumers are more aware of some of these motives than others. Applied to consumer behavior, **conscious motives** are the reasons for buying that people are willing to express. For example, many consumers have consciously decided that they prefer AT&T long-distance service over that of US Sprint because they feel AT&T provides more comprehensive and better-quality service.

People are often unwilling to express some of the reasons they have for buying. These reasons are called **suppressed motives.** For example, many consumers buy products that give them prestige, such as an expensive car (a Cadillac, Mercedes, or BMW) or a Rolex watch. They often explain such a purchase in terms of the performance of the automobile, the quality of the watch, or the fact that both are likely to hold their resale value. They do not want to say, "I'm trying to impress people."

People also buy in response to **unconscious motives,** reasons they are unaware of. Many people are influenced by advertising but do not know it. When they go to the supermarket, they may purchase some products without giving their choices a second thought. Sometimes this undetected influence comes from family, friends, or co-workers. For example, a young man whose favorite uncle drives a Pontiac Firebird may also buy one without realizing that he is emulating his uncle. He may explain the purchase in terms of sale price or car performance, but his real reason is that he wants to be like his uncle.

Conscious motives The reasons for buying that people are willing to express.

Suppressed motives The reasons for buying that people are unwilling to express.

Unconscious motives The reasons for buying that people are unaware of.

Reasons for Understanding Consumer Behavior

To effectively sell goods and services, marketers have to know *why* people buy their products or can be influenced to buy them. However, marketers have come to realize that what people say is not always a reliable

FIGURE 11.2

How a Consumer Makes a Purchase Decision

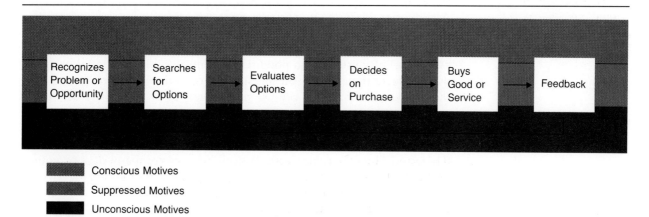

Recognizes Problem or Opportunity → Searches for Options → Evaluates Options → Decides on Purchase → Buys Good or Service → Feedback

■ Conscious Motives
■ Suppressed Motives
■ Unconscious Motives

indicator of what they will do. For example, a number of years ago, a farm equipment firm researched the behavior of its potential consumers and found out that farmers liked multicolored machinery. However, the company's dealers reported that the farmers resisted buying machinery that had bright, eye-appealing colors. Apparently, the farmers liked the eye-appealing machinery, but were unwilling to admit it.

The company overcame the problem by successfully tying the bright color scheme to product safety and ease of operation. The company painted red any parts of the machine that tended to get hot and were never to be touched without wearing gloves, yellow parts were for operating the machine, and so forth. Once farmers heard this explanation, they consciously accepted what they unconsciously wanted. This example shows how understanding consumer behavior can help marketers develop products and sales messages that will appeal to buyers' real needs and wants.

Checkpoint

1. What are three types of motives that buyers may have?
2. Why is understanding consumer behavior important to marketers?

Marketing Research

Marketing research
Investigating marketing problems and identifying market opportunities.

To move beyond general principles and apply them to specific situations, companies conduct **marketing research.** This is the process of investigating marketing problems and identifying market opportunities.

Marketing research has many applications. It typically addresses questions such as the following:

Why do customers buy our products? (Or why don't they?)

How good is our quality vis-à-vis that of our competitors?

What do people like most (or least) about our advertising campaign?

Would people buy more of our products if we lowered our price?

What effect would a price increase have on the demand?

What do our customers want that we are not currently providing?

One important objective of marketing research is to find out why some consumers are buying the company's products and others are not. A firm often learns as much from those who are not buying as from those who are. For example, new salespeople often learn that when a customer says, "I don't want the product," the correct response is to ask "Why not?" By listening to potential customers explain why the product will not meet their needs, the salesperson can identify important information that the company can use in redesigning or improving the product. Many large makers of office equipment, including NCR, Xerox, and IBM, make extensive use of this approach.

The marketing department gathers information in a variety of ways. These techniques involve using existing internal company data or going outside the firm for secondary and primary sources of data.

Company Data

The marketing research effort typically begins with gathering information currently contained in company records. Collecting and analyzing this information is called *internal research*. Many firms have data from questionnaire cards accompanying their product that instruct the buyer to fill out and mail back the card. Such cards typically ask the buyer's occupation, age, income level, and reason for buying the product. This information helps marketing researchers identify who buys the product and why.

Secondary Research

Researchers also conduct *secondary research,* information gathered from external sources such as newspapers, books, magazines, and government reports. This information often provides a better understanding of the market and the customer. For example, market researchers in the home appliance industry are particularly interested in numbers of new-housing starts. People building or buying new homes are likely to want new appliances; therefore, this is a major source of product demand in the appliance industry. Firms that manufacture other home-related products such as carpets, building materials, windows, and air conditioners also rely heavily on this information to help them estimate customer demand.

Other information available from secondary research includes economic trends, plans and activities of competitors, new technology that might be applicable to the company's products, and changes in customer needs. A pet store might want to change its offerings if it learns that homeowners are becoming concerned about thefts in their area of town, and a travel agency might want to shift its emphasis in travel packages if it learns that the local population is aging.

Marketing managers often find it most efficient to begin research with an investigation of information that already exists within the company

One way to conduct primary research is with a focus group, a panel of potential users that meets to discuss issues related to a product. In this focus group at Compaq Computer Corporation, a researcher asks the group about the merits of several portable computers. This type of research can give marketers insight into what features or benefits potential buyers are looking for. Participants sometimes bring up concerns researchers wouldn't think to ask about in a questionnaire.

Source: Courtesy of Compaq Computer Corporation.

and in outside publications. This is because the company can save a lot of money by building on existing information rather than duplicating it unnecessarily.

Primary Research

Sometimes the marketing department also conducts *primary research,* which is research conducted to gather information for the first time. Interviewers who conduct surveys in person, over the phone, or by mailed questionnaires are doing primary research.

Surveys are not the only way to conduct primary research; marketers also learn a lot by directly observing behavior. For example, researchers at Arizona State University sent out students to visit trailer campgrounds in metropolitan Phoenix and count the trailers. The students calculated that 47,000 trailers and recreational vehicles spent much of the winter in the campgrounds. Assuming that each unit averaged two residents and that a typical couple spent $1,000 a month for four months, the researchers concluded that visitors to the campgrounds pumped about $188 million into Phoenix's winter economy.[5]

Primary research is generally not the most important source of information, but many companies spend the money because it is most adaptable to specific information needs. While large companies, especially consumer product firms, often have their own in-house marketing staff do primary research, many firms hire outside marketing research firms to collect information for them. Other market research firms conduct research and then sell the information to interested businesses. Some consumer advocates are questioning the ethics of this type of research. For example, one data-gathering concern will go to 70 million homes with a questionnaire asking for preferences on consumer products, as well as the occupant's name, address, telephone number, occupation, and family income. However, as a spokesperson for an ethics-in-marketing group points out, "They're saying they're doing a survey, but in essence, they're offering to give your name, address and phone number to anyone who wants it."[6]

Uses of Marketing Research

Small firms tend to rely most heavily on internal research and possibly also on secondary research. Large companies use all three techniques. For example, while the Big Three automakers (General Motors, Ford, and Chrysler) all conduct internal and external research on car buying, they also read and study published reports in the area. One such report is the *Power Report on Automotive Marketing,* published annually by J. D. Power & Associates, an independent automotive marketing research firm. The company ranks new car quality and consumer satisfaction and also provides insights into automobile-purchasing trends.[7] Table 11.1 describes some of the major categories of car buyers Power & Associates has recently identified through their research.

Checkpoint

1. What are the three sources of data used in marketing research?
2. How can marketing research be used by marketers?

Market Segmentation

Marketing research and an understanding of consumer behavior helps marketers conduct **market segmentation,** the process of dividing markets into groups that have similar characteristics. Market segmentation gives marketers a clearer picture of the kinds of buyers that constitute a market and what they are looking for.

Marketers divide up markets in several ways. The most common are demographic, geographic, psychographic, and benefit segmentation. Figure 11.3 gives some examples of these.

Marketing:
Functions and
Strategies

Market segmentation
Dividing markets into
groups that have similar
characteristics.

T A B L E   11.1

Categories of Car Buyers

Buyer Category	Percentage of the Market	Description	Type of Car Owned
Autophiles	24%	Know a lot about cars and enjoy working on them	Dodge, Pontiac
Sensible-centrists	20	Prize practicality	Volvo, AMC
Comfort-seekers	17	Favor options and luxury models	Jaguar, Mercedes, Lincoln
Auto-cynics	14	View cars as appliances	Porsche
Necessity drivers	13	Prefer an alternative way of traveling	AMC
Auto-phobes	12	Care most about safety	Oldsmobile, Mercury

F I G U R E   11.3

Market Segmentation: Some Examples

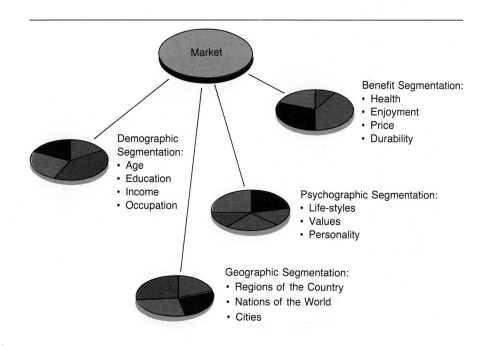

Demographic Segmentation

Under **demographic segmentation,** the company segments the market on the basis of socioeconomic characteristics. These characteristics, such as age, income, sex, education, and occupation, describe a person's place in society and in the economy. These characteristics are the subject of demographics, the statistical study of populations.

Marketers of toys, for example, are interested in demographic information such as the birth rate, the number of children in each age category, and income level of parents. This helps the marketers determine the size of the market and what parents can afford to buy. They also try to learn what kinds of toys parents and children in the different groups tend to like. By comparing preferences to the demographic information, they are able to segment the toy market. This helps them decide what types of toys are most popular and why. From here, the marketer can develop the appropriate strategy to appeal to its chosen segments.

Marketers select demographic segments according to various criteria. Some marketers attempt to appeal to certain income groups. Others focus on different age groups. For example, Petticord Swimwear sells a line of swimwear specifically for women between the ages of 25 and 45. Levi Strauss markets one line of jeans to adults by advertising how the jeans are made to give a little extra room where it is needed. Marketing research has recently found that 13- and 14-year-olds may have considerable influence on the purchase decision for high-priced items such as VCRs, TVs, computers, and boats.[8]

Geographic Segmentation

Markets are also divided using **geographic segmentation,** which is dividing up a market on the basis of where people live. Over the last 20 years, the population of the United States has shifted. Between now and the turn of the 21st century, this shift will continue, with the Sun Belt (Florida, Texas, and Arizona in particular) and western states (for example, Nevada) gaining population and other states, such as Iowa and West Virginia, losing population.[9]

Sears sportswear buyers of the company's Los Angeles regional buying office meet with a California manufacturer to review designs. A key strategy for Sears is to market products in tune with regional lifestyles. This marketing strategy combines geographic and psychographic segmentation.

Source: The Sears, Roebuck and Co. 1988 Annual Report. Photographer, Jay Silverman, Hollywood, CA.

Geographic segmentation often takes into account more than population concentration and state boundaries. In the example in Figure 11.4, the geographic segments are determined by criteria such as ethnic composition and economic status. These data help firms determine what to sell and where to sell it.

Geographic segmentation helps marketers refine their product lines. For example, a clothing manufacturer will sell warmer clothing in the North than in the South. Given the population trend toward the Sun Belt, the company may be well advised to focus on lighter clothing. For auto manufacturers, a car heater is more important to northern customers than to southern customers. On the West Coast, buyers are accustomed to purchasing fully loaded automobiles, because this is how the Japan automakers tend to ship them in, and 30 percent of all new car sales in this region are imports. Consequently, American manufacturers tend to put extra features on the cars they market there.

Psychographic Segmentation

Another way to divide the market is by **psychographic segmentation,** which is segmentation of a market on the basis of the customer's life-style, values, or personality. Based on an understanding of consumer behavior, the objective of this type of segmentation is to understand how the buyer's life-style influences overall purchasing habits. For example, college-educated people are more likely to buy encyclopedias for their children than are people with less education. Why? Because education is part of their life-style.

Marketers find many applications for psychographic data. For example, people with children are more likely to purchase cable TV because it provides more channels for the children's enjoyment. Medical doctors tend to purchase large, expensive cars if only to maintain an image of success and let their clients know that they are in good hands. Miller beer attempts to attract the working person with its beer commercials. Showing a group of hard-working lumberjacks or commercial fishermen who relax after the end of the day with a Miller beer fits into the life-

Psychographic segmentation Dividing up a market on the basis of the customer's life-style, values, or personality.

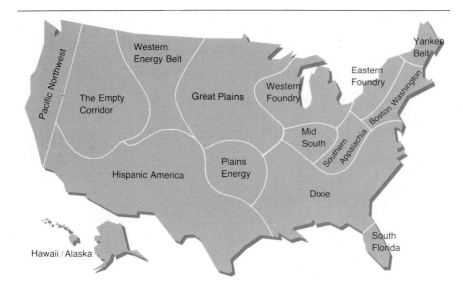

F I G U R E   11.4

Market Segments by Geographic Area

style of people who work with their hands, mainly construction workers, maintenance workers, and blue-collar factory workers. McDonald's targets children with its commercials because hamburgers have now become a part of many kids' regular diets. It's part of their life-style. Psychographic segmentation is becoming more popular today because it goes further than many other types of segmentation in identifying and appealing to specific consumer tastes.

Benefit Segmentation

Benefit segmentation

Dividing up a market on the basis of the benefits that people seek.

A final type of market segmentation is **benefit segmentation,** which is the dividing up of a market on the basis of the benefits that people seek. Under this approach, a company will identify the reasons why certain people would want to buy their product—how they would benefit from it—and they try to target this group. For example, for years Jergens hand lotion had been marketed to older people. The company then applied benefit segmentation by pointing out that the product also helped protect the skin of young people. The advertising showed young people using the lotion to soften their skin from the weather and make them more attractive. In short, the hand lotion was beneficial to everyone, not just older people. The result: Jergens' revenues rose as young people began buying the product. Table 11.2 provides other examples of benefit segmentation.

Marketers often use benefit segmentation in conjunction with other forms of segmentation. For example, marketers of presweetened cereal know that children, the ultimate consumers of their products, value sweet taste and prizes. However, those who actually purchase the cereals are the parents, who often are more concerned about nutrition. Based on this combined benefit and demographic segmentation, makers of cereal also proclaim—in advertisements and packaging—that their cereals contain vitamins as well as a sweet taste and prizes.

T A B L E   11.2

Benefit Segmentation

Product or Service	Benefit Promoted	Target Market
Gleem toothpaste	Reduces cavities and keeps your teeth white	Parents and young people
Certs mints	Keeps your breath smelling fresh	Adolescents and young adults
All Bran cereal	Provides the daily fiber needed to keep you healthy	Middle-aged and older people
One-a-Day vitamins	Gives all the vitamins you need for a healthy body	Active young people
The Wall Street Journal	Gives timely business information you need to keep up with trends in your industry	Young executives and those in the investment business
AT&T long-distance phone service	Provides reliable phone service anywhere in the country	Businesses and households

Kodak uses benefit segmentation in this advertisement for
batteries. The ad explains that
Kodak Ultralife lithium power
cells last twice as long as competing 9-volt batteries. It also
notes that the battery is tipped
with gold to provide a good
contact.

Source: Reprinted courtesy of Eastman Kodak Company.

Segmenting Industrial Markets

The types of segmentation described so far apply not only to consumers,
but also to the buyers of industrial products. For example, when selling
oil-drilling equipment, manufacturers use geographic segmentation.
They note the areas where drilling is to occur and design their equipment to handle that type of terrain. The equipment needed in a Texas
oil field must meet different specifications than that employed in the
Gulf of Mexico or in Saudi Arabia.

Virtually all industrial marketers use benefit segmentation. They continually ask themselves, "How can our product meet the customer's
need?" A good example is provided in the recent case of a major Miami
boat builder. This builder's craft are well known for their sleekness and
speed, so drug dealers were buying his boats and outrunning the Coast
Guard's slower boats. Now the builder is designing and building even
faster craft for the government so that they can catch up with the drug
runners. This is marketing in action!

Checkpoint

1. What are three kinds of market segmentation?
2. How can segmentation be used in industrial markets?

Formulating a Marketing Strategy

Based on the information gathered through marketing research and market segmentation, as well as general knowledge of consumer behavior, the marketing manager formulates a marketing strategy. The variables and steps involved in formulating a marketing strategy are shown in Figure 11.5. First, the manager determines whether the company should sell to the entire market or target certain groups. Then the manager decides which segments of the market the company can serve most effectively. Based on this information, the manager puts together a marketing mix, which brings together strategies for product, price, place, and promotion. In the marketing strategy, the markets the manager has targeted influence the marketing mix.

Basic Approaches

As shown in Figure 11.5, before the marketing manager can devise a strategy, he or she must select one of three basic marketing approaches:

Concentrated marketing
Focusing marketing efforts on a single market segment.

Differentiated marketing
Selling a range of related products to specific market segments.

1. **Concentrated marketing** occurs when a firm focuses on a single market segment. The Limited clothing stores are a good example. The company directs its marketing effort toward teenage girls and young women who want trend-setting clothes.
2. **Differentiated marketing** involves selling a range of related products to specific market segments. For example, Coca-Cola offers Classic Coke, new Coke, Diet Coke, and other brands. Many people drink one of these products but not the others. A differentiated marketing approach allows a firm to appeal to many parts of the overall mar-

F I G U R E   11.5

Formulating Marketing Strategy

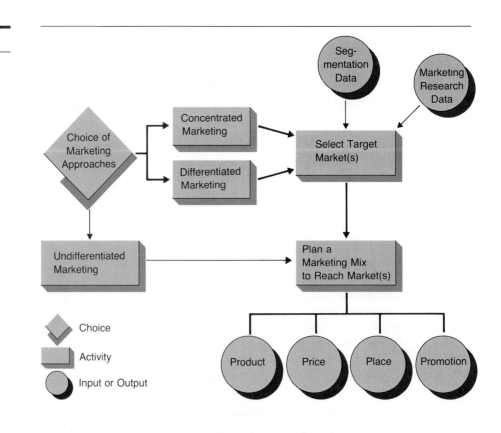

ket. However, as Miller Brewing and Coors found out, companies have to be very careful in their differentiation strategy. Both of these firms are now associated with light beer, and their regular beer sales have suffered. They probably should have used an entirely different name for their light beers; they must now depend on advertising to more clearly differentiate their light beers from their regular beers.[10]

3. **Undifferentiated marketing** involves selling a single product to all customers. Dry cleaning is a good example. This service is appealing to consumers regardless of age, income, sex, or geographic locale. Most dry-cleaning establishments offer the same basic service to all customers.

Undifferentiated marketing   Selling a single product to all customers.

In selecting one of these approaches, the company considers the needs of the various types of markets. Research shows that businesses, especially small ones, do best if they identify a market to serve and stay with it rather than trying to change from one group of customers to another. For some examples of how this works, see "Small Business Close-Up: Stick to the Knitting."

Target Markets

If the manager decides to use concentrated or differentiated marketing, the next step is to identify target markets. A **target market** is a group of customers who are likely to buy a company's goods or services. For example, a target market for health clubs is young professionals in the 25 to 45 age bracket; a target market for home-cleaning services is families with two working spouses.

Target market   A group of customers who are likely to buy a company's goods and services.

Determining a target is more complex than simply identifying the business the company is in. Each business has certain strengths and advantages. A business that produces a high-quality, state-of-the-art product tries to determine which market segments value such a product. A business that manufactures products in large quantities and at a low price targets segments that value low price. A tax preparation company with many outlets may try to identify customers who value convenience. A competitor with a famous, respected name may try to identify customers who want the reassurance of dealing with a familiar and trusted business. In every case, the business determines its target markets by analyzing its particular areas of strength. The manager uses the available research and information on market segments to select the appropriate markets to target. Those markets selected should be ones the company can serve profitably.

The Marketing Mix

When the marketing department has a clear picture of whom it is selling to—its target market—it is ready to complete its strategy by planning a marketing mix that will effectively reach the target market. The **marketing mix** is the combination of a firm's strategies for product, price, place, and promotion. Figure 11.6 depicts these four elements, often referred to as the "four Ps."

Marketing mix   The combination of a firm's strategies for product, price, place, and promotion.

Product   In determining the optimal marketing mix, the marketing manager starts with the **product,** the good or service that the firm offers to

Product   Any good or service that the firm offers to the customer.

the customer. The company may sell an existing product, modify it, or develop a new product. An example of a modified product is the pumpkin-patch crew, which was a take-off on the highly successful Cabbage Patch dolls. Called the OH Lantern family, more than 1 million of the ugly pumpkin heads sold for as much as $17 apiece only two months after their debut.[11] An example of a new product is Simplesse, a low-calorie substitute for fat produced by the NutraSweet Company. Early speculation is that this new product may have a revolutionary impact on diets.[12] However, research shows that for every 100 new product ideas, only two ever become products, and only one succeeds. Yet it is important for business firms to continue developing new goods and services because most become obsolete in less than ten years. Many of the elec-

SMALL BUSINESS   CLOSE-UP

Stick to the Knitting

What do successful small businesses have in common? Recent research reveals that one of their secrets seems to be finding a specialty and sticking with it. Firms that "stick to the knitting" tend to have higher returns on investment than their competitors that don't. For example, at one point the successful franchise Dunkin' Donuts diversified into fast foods and even considered hat shops and educational programs. Profits suffered until they got back to the coffee and donut business and got rid of unrelated businesses.

Mylan Laboratories manufactures patent and generic drugs. Its patented antihypertensive drug, Maxzide, grosses approximately $5 million a month and holds about 25 percent of the market. The firm also manufactures a wide array of generic drugs. When asked about plans for the future, the chairman of the board noted that the firm will stay in the health-care field. This focus on doing what it knows best has paid off handsomely for the Pittsburgh-based company. During the first half of the 1980s, it achieved a 33.9 percent average annual return; in other words, someone investing $1,000 in the firm at the beginning of that period would have seen that investment grow to $20,833.

Dreyer's Grand Ice Cream has set its sights at becoming the country's distributor of "premium" ice cream. The product is priced below the Haägen-Dazs and Früsen Glädjè brands and above the more common brands such as Sealtest and store-labeled ice creams. How well has it done? During the first half of the 1980s, Dreyer's has had an average return on investment of 25.3 percent, meaning that during this time period, the value of $1,000 invested in the firm would have grown to $3,405.

Postal Instant Press is another successful small enterprise. With over 1,100 franchised centers throughout the country, the firm holds a 5 percent share of the $4 billion instant printing market. During the first half of the 1980s, the company has had an annual return on investment of 20.9 percent; $1,000 invested in the firm during this period would have grown to $1,987. What does the company intend to do in the future? "More of the same," says founder William LeVine. "We are in the printing franchising business."

Commenting on the importance of staying with what one does best, *Forbes* recently noted that $1,000 invested in each of the 14 best small companies in America, including the three above, for a period of five years would have returned a total of $76,521 — clear evidence that companies that know what they are doing and focus exclusively on that specialty often come out ahead.

tronic products on the local retailer's shelf were not there a decade ago. Those that are may be obsolete before the end of this century.

This reflects the fact that products go through a life cycle. A typical cycle begins with the introduction of the product, followed by growth, maturity, and decline. In some cases, companies have been able to stave off decline by taking a product that is in the mature stage of its life cycle and finding new uses for it. For example, DuPont initially made nylon for parachutes. When the company found additional uses for nylon, such as in stockings, the product returned to the growth stage and continued to generate revenues and profits for the big chemical company. Figure 11.7 provides some examples of products at different stages of their life cycles.

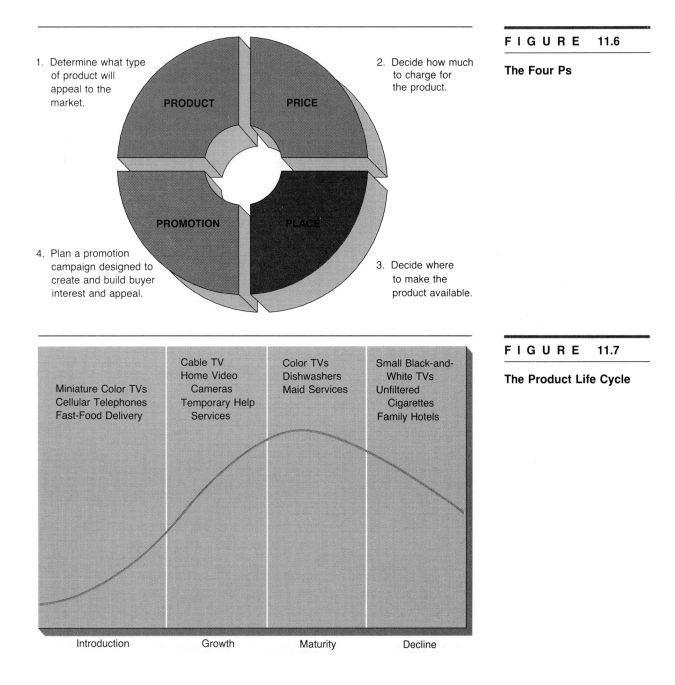

F I G U R E   11.6

The Four Ps

1. Determine what type of product will appeal to the market.
   PRODUCT

2. Decide how much to charge for the product.
   PRICE

4. Plan a promotion campaign designed to create and build buyer interest and appeal.
   PROMOTION

3. Decide where to make the product available.
   PLACE

F I G U R E   11.7

The Product Life Cycle

Miniature Color TVs
Cellular Telephones
Fast-Food Delivery

Cable TV
Home Video
Cameras
Temporary Help
Services

Color TVs
Dishwashers
Maid Services

Small Black-and-
White TVs
Unfiltered
Cigarettes
Family Hotels

Introduction   Growth   Maturity   Decline

Price The cost of the
product to the purchaser.

Price The second component of the marketing mix is **price,** which is
the cost of the product to the purchaser. In the case of manufacturers,
price is the charge to the wholesaler or retailer. In the case of a retail
store, it is the charge to the final customer.

Price strategy typically depends on industry and company practices. At
the industry level, for example, businesses often give discounts to customers who pay their bills within ten days of receipt. However, in some
industries, such as auto supplies, it is equally common to find firms taking the discount even when they pay 30 days later. The practice is so
widespread that auto supply companies have learned to accept the discounted payment.

At the individual consumer level, many stores, such as supermarkets,
refuse to discount. Their advertised or posted price is their final price.
However, among many small businesses and stores such as those selling
jewelry, furniture, or autos, there is almost always room for price negotiation. Additionally, regardless of its initial pricing strategy, just about
every firm makes a point of meeting the advertised prices of their competitors.

Place The location where
a good or service is available
for purchase.

Place The third ingredient in the marketing mix is **place,** which is the
location to which customers go to buy a particular good or service. Most
consumers know where to find goods that have been on the market for
some time. For example, they get their hamburgers at a fast-food franchise, their medicine at a drugstore, and the latest best-selling novel at a
bookstore. In recent years, however, place strategy has gained in importance because businesses have been changing their approach to providing goods and services.

For example, a decade ago, a person with a toothache went to a local
dentist's office. Today, large dentist offices, such as Dental Land, are located in shopping malls all around the country. The facilities are larger,
a number of dentists are on hand to provide both general and specialized services, and the price is often less than that charged by the local
dentist. These new locations, often referred to as McDentists, are having
a major impact on the field. So are small medical offices set up to provide such services as general physical examinations and minor surgical
procedures. These offices are competing vigorously with hospitals for
the high-profit, easy-to-handle outpatient business. Popularly known as
"Doc in the Box," they usually locate in suburban areas and eliminate
the need for people to drive a distance to the hospital.

Place is also an important strategy for people trying to break into a
market or gain market share. For example, Coca-Cola and Pepsi have
long dominated the supermarket soft-drink shelf. Since there is limited
space, other soft drink brands such as Shasta and Diet-Rite have had a
more difficult time getting on the shelf, a major problem that has stifled
their opportunity for growth.

However, a change in place strategy can backfire. If people are unac-
customed to going to a particular locale to buy a product, it may be impossible to lure them to it. For example, when IBM entered the personal
computer market and saw how popular its IBM PC was, it decided to
open IBM Service Centers through which it could sell them. However,
the firm was unable to dislodge the computer stores that were already
selling the product. Most people were accustomed to going to stores like
ComputerLand and Computer World to look for a personal computer.

IBM also lacked the sales staff to deal directly with the noncommercial consumer. As a result, its place strategy proved to be ineffective, and IBM sold the service centers to NYNEX.

Promotion The final component of the marketing mix is **promotion,** the process of stimulating demand for a company's goods and services. Advertising and personal selling are the most common techniques used by companies. Other promotional techniques include packaging, branding, point-of-purchase displays, coupons, and premiums. Chapter 13 provides an in-depth examination of promotional techniques and strategies.

A company develops a promotional strategy for one of two reasons: to maintain or to increase its share of the market. IBM entered the personal computer market and then spent a considerable amount on advertising its PCs because it wanted to maintain its share of the total computer market. Although the market for computers had been growing annually, IBM's share had been slowly declining. Once it saw Apple take off in the personal computer market, IBM knew it had to enter this market and effectively promote its product or lose more overall share.

In other cases, firms want to increase their market share. A good example can be seen in the pasta market. Despite all their efforts, no national firm has yet managed to dominate this market.[13] The market is splintered, with regional brands dominating individual geographic locales. For example, Ronzoni, a General Foods product, holds a 36 percent market share in New York City. This good showing in New York helped General Foods claim 8 percent of the total national pasta market. Borden, with its Creamettes and Ronco brands, has approximately 13 percent of the national market. CPC International holds over 15 percent of the national market, thanks to its Mueller pasta. The largest share is held by Hershey (best known for its chocolate), which has six separate

Promotion The process of stimulating demand for a company's goods and services.

Workers at AMD Industries assemble a point-of-purchase display for Brach's candy (*inset*), made by Jacobs Suchard/Brach, Inc. The colorful graphics on the display, are intended to catch the consumer's eye. The combination of wood grain and brass is designed to evoke pleasant childhood memories. The easy access and variety are meant to stimulate customers to buy several kinds of candy.

Source: Courtesy of AMD Industries Incorporated.

regional brands of pasta that account for over 17 percent of the national market. Each firm continues to promote its products vigorously in hopes of increasing the national market share. This marketing effort has undoubtedly helped fuel the overall sales growth of the industry. Over the last decade, the average American's consumption of pasta has more than doubled, making it a $10 billion business.

The Marketing Mix in Action The marketing mix will vary depending on the product's life cycle. For example, when a product is first introduced, the company often sets a high price. The firm will want to recover quickly some of the costs of getting the product launched. Later, as other firms enter the market, it will lower the price to meet the competition. Price strategy will change as the good moves along its life cycle.

The same is true for place strategy. Initially, the company may offer the product only in certain locales. However, as the item enters its growth and maturity stages, the firm will offer it in any store where it can generate sales. When the product reaches the decline phase, distribution will again be selective as the company phases out unprofitable outlets.

Promotional strategy follows a similar pattern. Initial advertising, for example, will be aimed at early adopters, those who first buy a product. However, as the product enters the growth phase, the ads will be focused on making the mass market aware of the item's benefits. By the time the product enters the decline phase, the firm will have switched to an ad strategy that emphasizes low price.

Checkpoint

1. What are the four Ps?
2. How do marketing managers formulate a marketing strategy?

Closing Comments

This examination of marketing functions and strategies began by noting the importance of marketing and how Henry Ford's failure to understand its value caused Ford to lose ground to General Motors. Successful managers know that marketing involves more than just selling and more than just intuition regarding what will sell. Managers also must conduct marketing research and, where possible, segment the market. Based on knowledge of the target market, the manager formulates the marketing mix—the combination of strategies for product, price, place, and promotion.

Learning Objectives Revisited

1. **Define the overall nature of marketing.**
   Marketing is the process of identifying what goods and services the customer wants and providing them at the right price and place. A

production-oriented approach to marketing assumes that if a firm provides a good product or service, it will basically sell itself. A consumer-oriented approach assumes that a company must find out what the consumer wants before deciding what to provide. Marketing can emphasize two dimensions of a product, quality and price. Most firms emphasize a combination of the two, although they tend to favor one over the other.

2. **Describe the basic functions of marketing.**

The major functions of marketing are buying, or deciding the type and amount of goods to be purchased; selling, or identifying buyers, developing a promotional campaign, and closing the sale; transporting, or moving the goods to where they are needed; storing, or warehousing the goods; standardizing and grading, or establishing specifications or categories for the goods and sorting them into classes based on quality; financing, or paying for the merchandise and arranging for credit; risk taking, or assuming potential liability; and obtaining market information, or gathering information on the customer's needs.

3. **Discuss the nature and importance of marketing research.**

Marketing research lies at the very heart of formulating marketing strategy. It involves gathering information to help managers investigate marketing problems and identify market opportunities. This research can draw on internal, secondary, and primary sources. Most large firms rely on all three sources; many small firms use just the first two.

4. **Present the various types of market segmentation.**

Market segmentation is the process of dividing markets into groups that have similar characteristics. Some of the most common forms of segmentation include: demographic segmentation, which divides the market on the basis of socioeconomic characteristics; geographic segmentation, which divides the market on the basis of where people live; psychographic segmentation, which divides the market on the basis of the customer's life-style; and benefit segmentation, which divides the market on the basis of the benefits people seek from products.

5. **Explain how a marketing manager identifies a target market.**

When the manager has decided to engage in concentrated (a single market segment) or differentiated (range of related products to specific market segments) marketing rather than undifferentiated (single product to all consumers) marketing, the first step is to review information gathered from marketing research and segmentation. Based on this information and an assessment of the company's strengths, the manager selects a target market the company can profitably satisfy.

6. **Identify the "four Ps" of marketing.**

The four Ps of marketing are product, the good or service that the firm offers to the customer; price, the cost of the product to the customer; place, the location where the product is available for purchase; and promotion, the process of stimulating demand for the good or service. The company uses all four Ps in developing an overall marketing strategy.

Key Terms Reviewed

Review each of the following terms. For any that you do not know or are unsure of, look up the definitions and see how they were used in the chapter.

marketing

production-oriented marketing

consumer-oriented marketing

buying

selling

transporting

storing

standardizing

grading

market

industrial good or service

consumer good or service

consumer behavior

conscious motives

suppressed motives

unconscious motives

marketing research

market segmentation

demographic segmentation

geographic segmentation

psychographic segmentation

benefit segmentation

concentrated marketing

differentiated marketing

undifferentiated marketing

target market

marketing mix

product

price

place

promotion

Review Questions

1. How does production-oriented marketing differ from consumer-oriented marketing? Is a company guaranteed to succeed if it has the best version of a product? Explain.

2. Sea Sweets, Inc., makes salt-water taffy. The company mails out bright-colored catalogs showing the various flavors of taffy and the attractive gift packages they come in. Buyers can mail in an order or call a toll-free number, and Sea Sweets will ship out the order via UPS or, for an extra charge, Express Mail. The company accepts MasterCard and Visa. Based on this description, what marketing functions does Sea Sweets engage in?

3. What marketing functions would be especially important in selling unsought goods? Why?

4. How do consumers make buying decisions? If Ron Hall receives information stating the advantages of resort condominiums, but doesn't think owning resort property is an opportunity or the solution to a problem, how will this information affect his decision of whether to buy?

5. Phil Victor is a marketing consultant. One of his clients, Lucy Green, called him in to investigate the market potential of the new line of diet doughnut shops she was thinking of opening. "I'm eager to get started," said Lucy. "Let's get going on a survey." What type of marketing research do surveys fall under? If you were Phil, what would you do next?

6. What are some ways in which marketers divide the market into segments? How do they use this information?

7. How do marketing managers formulate a marketing strategy?
8. What might be an appropriate target market for each of the following businesses? Explain your choice.
   a. A chain of law offices that specializes in handling routine documents and legal matters
   b. A passenger railroad company
   c. A maker of high-fashion but inexpensive sportswear
9. What are the elements of the marketing mix? Define each.
10. How do marketing managers adapt the marketing mix to the product's stage in the product life cycle?

Applied Exercises

1. Visit a local manufacturing company and discuss with the appropriate manager the marketing functions that this firm carries out. Identify and describe these functions. How do they compare with those discussed in the chapter?
2. Go to a shopping mall or popular shopping area and browse through the stores. After you have left, write down examples of what would be convenience, shopping, specialty, and unsought goods for you. Compare your list with those of others in the class.
3. Visit a firm that you think relies heavily on marketing to sell its goods or services. Discuss with the manager how, if at all, the company uses the four Ps in its marketing effort. Write a two-page paper on your findings.
4. Look through the advertising section of the Sunday newspaper and choose six advertised products. Place each on the product life-cycle curve (see Figure 11.7). Compare your list with those of others in the class. Then discuss ways in which promotion can help sell each of the six products you have identified.

Your Business IQ: Answers

1. False. Many business people believe in this saying, and it sometimes has proved to be true. However, most businesses gear their marketing efforts to consumer needs, not product design.
2. False. Selling is but one important function of marketing; others include buying, storing, transporting, standardizing and grading, financing, risk taking, and obtaining marketing information.
3. True. Some buying motives are suppressed or unconscious. Successful marketers try to identify motives at all levels.
4. False. Small firms rely most heavily on internal records and published information. Telephone surveys and other types of primary research are generally too expensive for a small business.
5. True. This approach is called market segmentation. Even companies that sell nationwide may alter their product, its price, where they sell it, or how they promote it to meet the needs of different segments.

Case

Richmond, Indiana, Finds Winning Marketing Strategy

Many cities in the United States have adopted a marketing approach to attract businesses. For example, big cities and small towns in Indiana are selling themselves as attractive places for businesses to locate. The specific target market: Japanese companies. As a result, in recent years, Japanese investment in Indiana has totaled over a half-billion dollars and has accounted for almost 96 percent of foreign investment in the state.

One city that has scored a notable success is Richmond, Indiana. In 1981, this blue-collar community of 40,000 developed a plan to build a cultural bridge with Japan. At the time, Richmond was losing jobs, key businesses, and its young people. The town examined its resources and concluded that one thing set it apart from other towns: Earlham College, located in Richmond, had ties with Japan that dated back nearly a century. In the 1890s, Quaker missionaries from the college had started a student exchange program with the prestigious Waseda University in Tokyo.

The town built on a reservoir of talent that included Japanese-speaking faculty and students. Jackson Bailey, a local Japan scholar, put together a program to educate local citizens about the Japanese and to eliminate existing prejudices. With his students, Bailey prepared a bilingual brochure about Richmond and made a videotape, narrated in Japanese by a community leader, promoting Richmond as a place to do business. Even the banks prepared brochures in Japanese. "It's not that the Japanese can't read English," explains Bailey. "But making the gesture means that you have given it thought to get ready."

After several failed attempts to woo businesses, Richmond struck success. Sanyo Manufacturing Corporation agreed to locate two divisions in Richmond. One Sanyo plant makes refrigerators and another, high-technology factory makes compact discs. The CD plant is the first of its kind in the area. Sanyo officials publicly state that their decision to locate in Richmond was a purely financial one, but according to some city leaders, Sanyo officials privately credit the city's cultural-based approach as influential.

Case Questions

1. At the beginning of the case, at what stage of the product life cycle was Richmond as a place to locate a business? At the end of the case?
2. Based on the information given, what was Richmond's marketing strategy? Identify the elements of the marketing mix that the city used. What additional elements could the city have used? Explain.
3. How can the city use a marketing approach to continue building investment in the geographic area?

You Be the Adviser: Branching Out

Phil Krantz was a computer programmer for seven years before he broke away last year to start his own business. Phil has been writing software for three large insurance companies that want special programs designed to meet their needs. They have been pleased with Phil's efforts, and it looks as if he will be able to keep them as customers for at least another two years. However, Phil would also like to branch out and start writing software for other customers.

Recently, Phil has been toying with the idea of writing educational software. In particular, he believes that there could be a massive market for software teaching mathematics and science. Over the last three months, he has developed a science package designed to help students tutor themselves in high school physics. The program contains a number of different subject areas. Phil was able to identify these areas by reviewing the ten leading high school physics books in the country. For each subject area, he wrote a module that presents information and then tests the student on it. If the student enters a wrong answer, the program gives him or her a chance to try again or to simply ask for the right answer and the explanation. In either case, the program explains the correct answer before moving on. At the end of the module, the program gives the student a score based on the number of right answers the student gave on the first try.

Phil has shown the program to a number of teachers in the local high school system, as well as to the head of the board of education. Everyone appears interested in the project, and Phil believes it will be worth his time to pursue the marketing and sale of this product.

Your Advice

1. Is Phil production-oriented or consumer-oriented? Based on your answer, what advice would you give to him regarding how to proceed?
2. What types of market information does Phil still need to gather? What would you recommend? Explain your answer.
3. How can market segmentation help Phil develop a strategy? What approach would you suggest? Why?

Product
Planning and
Pricing

LEARNING OBJECTIVES

- Describe the steps involved in development of new products.
- Explain how business use product analysis.
- Discuss the use of brands and trademarks.

- Describe the value of packaging and labeling.
- Present the dimensions of product-pricing strategies.
- Identify product-pricing techniques.

Your Business IQ

How much do you already know about product planning and pricing? Test your business IQ by labeling each statement *true* or *false*. Answers and explanations are at the end of the chapter.

1. In recent times, the typical life cycle of a new product is only 25 years.
2. By registering a trademark with the U.S. Patent and Trademark Office, a company guarantees that it will have the exclusive right to its use.
3. The government requires that labels on food list the ingredients of the food, beginning with the largest percentage of the product on down to the smallest.
4. Successful companies emphasize high quality, not low price.
5. Many businesses receive cash discounts if they pay their bills quickly.

As part of Dow Chemical's efforts to increase soybean yield, a soybean pod is injected with a plant hormone to determine the hormone's effect on seed growth. New regulators for plant growth are one of three targets of Dow's global research; the others are new herbicides and insecticides. These formal research targets help Dow keep its idea generation on track with company goals.

Source: Courtesy of The Dow Chemical Company.

Looking Back and Ahead

In northern climates, the consumption of fruit and vegetable products drops dramatically every winter, and it's no wonder. Produce, most of which is picked green and shipped in from southern climates, is typically tasteless and has an unappealing texture. How are produce companies responding? Some are putting their researchers to work studying the ripening process and trying to identify the function of specific genes. Other growers and processors are experimenting with packaging techniques that can slow ripening, enabling them to pick riper fruits and vegetables. So far the new techniques have resulted in some success, but prices for produce using the techniques are higher. In the meantime, the experts keep working on ways to produce appealing products that northern consumers will buy in the winter.[1]

From the neighborhood grocer to the big automakers, businesses depend for their survival on having appealing goods and services to sell. To survive and grow, companies must plan what to sell and at what price. This effort is part of the marketing function, described in Chapter 11. Chapter 12 takes a closer look at the product and pricing aspects of marketing. We begin by examining the various product strategies, including branding and packaging, employed in today's successful marketing efforts. The chapter ends with a discussion of pricing strategies and techniques.

New-Product Development

In the 1960s, people played music on "record players"; a decade later, music lovers found their new stereos to be a big improvement. Today, some music fans think that CDs (compact discs) and digital audio tapes will make records themselves obsolete. Whereas young people of the previous generations talked about their 45s, today most young people do not even know what 45s are.*

Customer wants, needs, and expectations are continually changing, so marketers must keep up. The typical life cycle is only five to ten years. Unless a company develops new products, it may find its total sales declining. Large and small companies avoid this problem by making new-product development an important part of their making effort. New products help companies achieve sales growth, meet competition, and round out the product line.

The Development Process

Companies can add new products in two ways. The easiest way is to acquire them from another firm and simply add them to the existing product line. A company's product line is the group or line of products that it offers. In recent years, many companies have done this through acquisitions or mergers. For example, when R. J. Reynolds merged with Nabisco, it acquired Oreo cookies, Ritz crackers, and many other products.

The other way to add new products is to develop them from the ground up. The process of developing new products typically involves

*They are the small records that play at the speed of 45 revolutions per minute.

six steps, shown in Figure 12.1. Management reviews the idea at each step of the process and may terminate the project at any time.

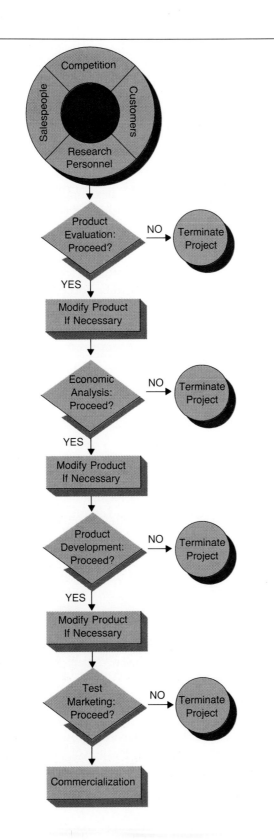

F I G U R E   12.1

**The Process of New-
Product Development**

Idea Generation New-product development begins with the formulation of an idea that can be translated into a new product. Marketers primarily formulate ideas in two ways. The most popular is to gather suggestions from salespeople, customers, and in-house personnel who have knowledge of the market. The marketer supplements this information by reviewing what the competition is doing.

The other approach is to develop the entire idea in-house. This commonly takes place in firms that are committed to research and development. These companies are usually part of industries where new technology is an important advantage. For example, ITT, General Electric, AT&T, GTE, and Hewlett-Packard spend millions of dollars every year conducting research to develop new and better electronic equipment.

Product Evaluation The purpose of the next stage, product evaluation, is to determine whether the product fits with the company's long-term objectives. Will the proposed product be compatible with the current product line? Can the firm promote it using existing promotion efforts? Can the company produce it with its existing production facilities? Can the company distribute it through existing channels? Sometimes a firm will find that a proposed product is likely to be successful but does not fit with the company's image or the firm's ability to manufacture and market it.

Economic Analysis The next stage is economic analysis. At this stage, the manager evaluates the overall profitability of the product. How much demand will there be for it? How much will it cost to produce? What is the likely selling price? The answers to such questions will help the manager evaluate how profitable the product is likely to be and decide whether to proceed.

Product Development The fourth stage, product development, involves building a model, mockup, or prototype. Many manufacturers have production design engineers to do this. In a small concern, this process might be much simpler. For example, a restaurant's chef might try out a new type of soup or an exotic dessert. The value of a prototype is that it helps everyone understand what the product will be like. The production people can find out how hard it will be to make and whether it actually does what it is intended to, and the marketing people can show it to prospective customers.

Test Marketing Test marketing involves taking the product into the marketplace to see how selected customers respond to it. A national company often chooses one or two cities in which to sell the product. Based on consumer response, the company decides whether or not to go forward with the product. Examples of products that have recently fizzled when tested include catfish and Oriental fast food. It was found that consumers perceived catfish as "muddy tasting," and the Oriental fast food did not coincide with the popular image of local mom-and-pop Chinese operations.[2] On a smaller scale, the chef who made the new soup or dessert might ask a few regular customers to try it. Their reactions would influence whether the restaurant adds the soup or dessert to the menu.

Commercialization At the final stage, commercialization, the company makes the product available to the entire target market. Large companies selling consumer goods usually sell the good in one particular region and then expand coverage to the national market. For example, an orange-picking robot developed in Florida was taken to Sicily for commercial development.[3] Smaller companies usually start with local distribution and gradually expand to a regional market. In both cases, the firm starts small and seeks to identify the sales strategies that work best. Then, as the company increases distribution, it can better handle any marketing problems that happen to arise.

Why Products Fail

Using the stages of new-product development helps ensure successful new products, but most new products still fail. A number of reasons account for this. Three of the most common are inadequate market analysis, ineffective sales effort, and problems or defects in the product.[4] Recent research indicates that product quality often has more to do with a new product's success or failure than does price.[5] This is particularly true for high-tech goods such as computers and cameras and for luxury products such as automobiles. For example, after brisk initial sales, Kodak withdrew its disc cameras because of the fatal flaw with its minuscule

In Procter & Gamble's test kitchen, a technician uses a new product called Olestra to prepare various foods. Olestra is a substitute for cooking fats that provides the rich taste and cooking properties of traditional shortenings and oils but with fewer calories and less fat and cholesterol. Before Procter & Gamble tries to sell Olestra, it runs tests to make sure that the product performs as expected. The company also must obtain approval from the Food and Drug Administration.

Source: Courtesy of The Procter & Gamble Company.

negatives, which tended to produce grainy snapshots.[6] This defect became even more glaring with the arrival of simple and inexpensive 35 mm cameras.

Another important reason why new products fail is that it costs too much to produce them. In other words, the problem results from ignoring or inaccurately doing the economic analysis. Detroit automakers have been wrestling with this problem for years and seem to be finally getting costs under control. As a result, cars of the 1990s are going to be different from those of the 1980s. By using new materials such as ultra-high-strength plastics, aluminum, and electrogalvanized steel, manufacturers will be able to build more durable and cheaper-to-produce automobiles.

Besides cost, another critical variable is how long it takes to get a new product developed. A few years ago Xerox was shocked to learn that Japanese competitors could develop new copiers in half the time it took Xerox. Today, after a sweeping reorganization and millions of dollars in investment, Xerox can develop and produce a new copier in two years, as opposed to four or five years.[7] This is still behind the Japanese, but the timing gap for new-product development is beginning to narrow.

Checkpoint

1. What are the steps in the process of new-product development?
2. Why do some products fail?

Product Analysis

Once a company develops a product and makes it available, the marketing manager must decide how to price, package, distribute, and promote it. One way of planning these strategies is to analyze an existing product's current performance or the potential of a new product. It is or could it be a market leader? Is it just barely paying its own way? Or is it losing money? The results of product analysis determine what follow-up strategy to develop.

Portfolio Analysis

Portfolio analysis A method for developing a product strategy based on the attractiveness of a market and the product's share of that market.

Many firms use an approach to product analysis called **portfolio analysis.** This is a method for developing a product strategy based on the attractiveness of a market and the product's share of that market. The attractiveness of a given market depends on the degree of consumer demand, the amount of existing competition from other firms, and the potential for growth in the coming years. The widely used technique for portfolio analysis is the four-cell matrix developed by the Boston Consulting Group and illustrated in Figure 12.2.

A manager using this matrix considers two factors: the attractiveness of the market and the market share currently held by the product. Depending on these factors, the manager places the product into one of the four cells in Figure 12.2. The appropriate strategy depends on the cell into which the product fits. In general, companies using portfolio analysis employ a strategy that cultivates the stars, pushes the question marks, milks the cows, and drops the dogs. Of course, this is just a general guideline; companies try to take into account the unique characteristics of each product and market.

Life-Cycle Approach to Product Analysis

Not all firms use portfolio analysis. Some look at the product's place in its life cycle and develop a strategy based on this. Chapter 11 introduced you to the concept of the product life cycle. Table 12.1 shows the strategies that apply at each stage.

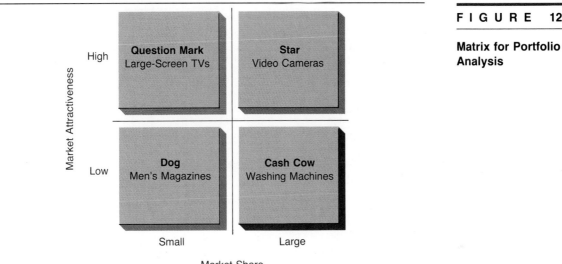

F I G U R E   12.2

Matrix for Portfolio Analysis

T A B L E   12.1   **The Product Life Cycle: Characteristics and Product Strategies**

	Introduction	Growth	Maturity	Decline
Characteristics				
Sales	Low	Increasing rapidly	Increasing slowly	Declining
Profits	Negligible or very low	Very high	Starting to decline	Low or negative
Customers	Early adopters	Mass-market adopters	Mass-market adopters	Loyal adopters
Competitors	Few	Increasing number	Many	Declining number
Product Strategies				
Objectives	Expand the market	Penetrate the market	Defend market share	Keep expenses down
Marketing expenditures	High	High but declining	Declining	Low
Marketing emphasis	Product awareness	Brand preference	Brand loyalty	Hold on to die-hard customers
Distribution	Selective	Many outlets	Many outlets	Selective outlets
Price	High	Lower	Lowest	Going back up

354

The strategy is tied to the characteristics of the life-cycle stage. When a product is in the introduction stage, sales tend to be low and profits are negligible. The firm's objective at this stage is to expand the market and make people aware of the product.

Unless the firm wants to gain entry to the market through a low-price strategy, it sets the initial price fairly high. As more and more people buy the product and it enters a growth stage, the company lowers the price and begins to seek greater market share. When the product enters the maturity stage, the firm tries to defend its market by lowering the price or developing persuasive promotional techniques. Finally, when

At this stage in the life cycle of alcoholic beverages, consumer sentiment favors lighter drinks consumed in moderation. This reflects a general health and safety consciousness among the public. Anheuser-Busch appeals to that preference with this ad advocating moderation and featuring its popular Spuds McKenzie mascot and cans of light beer. Anheuser-Busch takes the position that socially responsible promotion of alcoholic beverages is ultimately to the company's greatest advantage.

Source: Courtesy of Anheuser-Busch Companies, Inc.

the good enters the decline stage, the company tries to cut its expenses and remain profitable as long as it can. Sometimes the company can combat a decline in sales by modifying existing products or introducing a new mix of products. For an example, see "Social Responsibility Close-Up: Appealing to a Lighter Taste."

Checkpoint

1. What are two techniques for conducting product analysis?
2. What kind of product strategy would be appropriate for a growing market?

Brands and Trademarks

For products at all stages of the life cycle, marketers are interested in finding ways to make their products stand out from competitors' offerings. One way is to use brands and trademarks. A **brand** is a name, term, symbol, or combination thereof used to identify a firm's products and differentiate them from competing products. Brands can include names such as Levi's, Jiffy Lube, and Xerox. They can also incorporate visual symbols such as NBC's peacock and McDonald's golden arches.

Brand A name, term, symbol, or combination of these used to identify a firm's products and differentiate them from competing products.

SOCIAL RESPONSIBILITY · CLOSE-UP

Appealing to a Lighter Taste

At the turn of the century, many people drank their liquor straight. In the post–World War II era, this trend changed as more and more customers mixed their alcohol with tonic, soda water, or a soft drink. Today the trend toward lighter drinking continues, and distillers are realizing that the era of heavy drinking may be at an end. Today more people than ever drink for the taste rather than for the alcohol. Light drinks, fruit-flavored beverages, and nonalcoholic offerings are gaining a larger share of the market.

Several developments are supporting this trend. In part, it is the result of social pressure. Many young people no longer feel it is the "in" thing to go out and get drunk. Drunk-driving laws and enforcement are also getting stricter. In their advertising, distillers are urging their customers to drink in mod-eration and not to drink and drive. These social and legal developments have resulted in a host of new drinks that taste sweeter and contain less alcohol than their predecessors.

Does this trend mean that the distillers are going to lose money? Surprisingly, perhaps, it may mean just the opposite. Sweet drinks are not only bolstering sales, but they have higher profit margins. For example, distillers earn 20 to 30 cents more on each dollar they spend selling flavored cordials than on each dollar spent selling bourbon. Brandy and rum are also highly profitable, as are some of the newest concoctions to reach the market, including peach-flavored and grapefruit juice drinks. Distillers are learning that selling low-alcohol drinks does not have to mean a decline in profits. They can be socially responsible and profitable at the same time.

Marketers try to build sales and market share by developing a positive association between a brand and a product benefit. McDonald's hopes that hungry travelers will stop when they see the golden arches. Levi Strauss hopes that people shopping for jeans will look for Levi's. Two products for which branding has been particularly successful are Coca-Cola and Pepsi. In blind taste tests, cola drinkers generally have trouble telling the two apart; nevertheless, most consumers are very loyal to one brand or the other.

The owner of the brand may be the manufacturer or the retailer of the product. For example, Chrysler, General Electric, Westinghouse, AT&T, and Goodyear all manufacture products bearing their own brand names. In contrast, Sears purchases appliances from many manufacturers and markets them under the Kenmore brand. A&P, the giant supermarket chain, buys canned goods, jams, jellies, household cleaning products, and an assortment of other commodities and offers them for sale under the Ann Page, A&P, and Jane Parker brand names.

Types of Brands

Marketers can use a number of different types of brands. Figure 12.3 illustrates the major ones. They are:

Private brand A brand owned by a retailer.

Private brands, which are owned by the retailer. An example is Sears's Craftsman brand for tools.

National brand A brand owned by a manufacturer.

National brands, which are owned by the manufacturer. Ford and Nike are examples.

Family brand A brand used with all of the products a firm sells.

Family brands, which are used with all of the products a firm sells. For example, all of Kellogg's, Post, Nabisco, or Keebler products carry the brand name. These companies hope that by building a good reputation for their names, they can persuade buyers of one of its products to look for its name when buying other products.

Individual brand A brand used exclusively for one of the products a firm sells.

Individual brands, which are used exclusively for one of the products a firm sells. For example, General Motors manufactures the Chevrolet, Pontiac, Oldsmobile, Buick, and Cadillac brands of automobiles. Companies use individual brand names when customers prefer a particular product or product line rather than just any one manufactured by that corporation. This preference may be based on differences in price, quality, style, prestige, or other features.

F I G U R E   12.3

Types of Brands

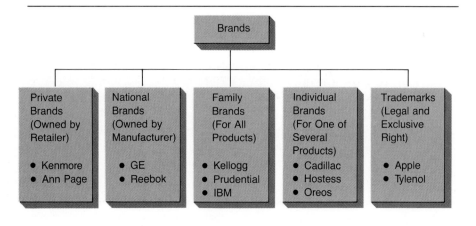

Trademarks

A **trademark** is a brand that the owner has the legal and exclusive right to use. Trademarks are registered with the U.S. Patent Trademark Office. Common examples include the McDonald's arches, the Prudential rock, the NBC peacock, and names such as 7-Up, Buick, and Memorex.

The owner of a trademark must protect its rights to the trademark, or it may become a generic term, unprotected by law. In that case, competitors can trade on a company's brand name by using a similar one. For example, a few years ago, a firm offered a board game called Anti-Monopoly. Parker Brothers, owners of the trademark Monopoly, which identified their own board game, sued. The court held that because the name of the Parker Brothers board game had passed into common usage, it had become a generic name and was no longer protected by law. Thus, manufacturers of the Anti-Monopoly game were free to market their product. Nestlé's Toll House cookies have met a similar fate. The courts have ruled that this is another generic name, and the company no longer has an exclusive right to its use.

Product Planning and Pricing

Trademark A brand the owner has the legal and exclusive right to use.

There are two R's in Xerox.

One is right in the middle.

But the really important one is the one you probably never notice.

It's the little R in a circle—like the one you see at the bottom of this ad—that tells you that Xerox is a registered trademark.

And it reminds you that our name—which is also our trademark—should only be used in connection with the products and services of our corporation.

Including everything from Xerox copiers to workstations to laser printers.

So as you can see, our trademark is a very valuable one.

To us. And to you, too.

Because it ensures that when you ask for something you can be sure of what you're going to get.

Of course, we don't expect you to use the second R every time you use our name.

But we do hope you'll give it a second thought.

Team Xerox. We document the world.

XEROX ® is a trademark of XEROX CORPORATION.

Xerox Corporation uses this advertisement to protect the trademark status of the term *Xerox.* The two Rs referred to are the r in the middle of the word and the r in the trade mark symbol ®. The ad explains that the word *Xerox* may be used only in connection with a product or service of Xerox Corporation.

Source: Courtesy of Xerox Corporation.

One way in which companies protect their trademarks is by advertising the special status of these words and symbols. Companies also print the symbol ® next to the name to show that it is a registered trademark. If a company believes its trademark has been violated, it can take court action. For example, a judge recently granted a request to block the sale of actress Elizabeth Taylor's perfume called Passion to large department stores because a French firm has a fragrance by the same name.[8]

Branding Alternatives

In recent years, a special form of branding has become popular: licensing. Under this arrangement, a company pays the creator of a character for the right to use that character to help promote the company's products. For example, if a movie or TV character becomes popular, manufacturers try to license the name of the character and use it to sell toys, food, clothing, or whatever products the name might be associated with. Popular movie characters, such as Rambo, have been used in this way in promoting toys.

Generic product A product with no brand and simple packaging.

Some marketers avoid branding altogether in favor of generic products. A **generic product** is one with no brand and simple packaging. Many generics are on the market today. Most supermarkets, including national chains such as Jewel Company, A&P, and Safeway, stock generic paper towels, facial tissues, bleaches, coffee creamers, plastic bags, cooking oil, ice cream, and a host of other products. Even generic alcoholic beverages simply labeled "beer," "vodka," "bourbon," and so on are available.

Generics have grabbed a large share of the market among products that do not vary much by quality. For example, most people feel that paper towels are all basically the same, and generics have done well in this market niche. However, many consumers believe that when it comes to food, the quality of the generics is sometimes below par, and branded foods are more reliable. As a result, generic foods have done poorly compared to other generic products.

Product Packages and Labels

One place a product's brand appears is on the product's package. Marketers have found that labeling and the packages themselves can be important marketing tools.

Objectives for Packaging

Over the last 25 years, packaging has begun to play a greater role in the marketing process.[9] As a result, packaging has become one of the largest industries in the country, accounting for annual sales exceeding those of either steel or textiles. By designing convenient and safe packaging, marketers can make the package a product benefit. Marketers can also evaluate and try to minimize the effects of packaging on the environment.

Convenience If you bought a dozen unpackaged eggs and carried them home in a paper bag, you would have a mess before long, because some of the eggs would inevitably break and leak all over. An egg carton makes it easy to transport them. Likewise, carrying home a large jar of liquid laundry detergent might be a burden. However, today you can buy detergent in a lightweight plastic container with a convenient handle that makes it easy to carry. Frozen dinners are another product for which the package provides benefits. Until a few years ago, they were all packaged in aluminum wrap in order to keep the food fresh. With the advent of the microwave oven, manufacturers are now offering frozen foods packaged in a special cardboard and plastic wrap that still keeps the product fresh, but can be put right into a microwave.

Safety Besides offering convenience, packaging helps preserve and protect products such as foods and pharmaceuticals. In the case of food, it prevents contamination. In the case of drugs (and some food products), it provides protection from tampering. In 1982, when seven people died after ingesting cyanide-laced Extra-Strength Tylenol capsules, Johnson & Johnson, the manufacturers of Tylenol, redesigned and reinforced its packages to discourage tampering. Regrettably, in 1986, another cyanide incident occurred, and the company recalled all capsules and has now completely stopped offering Tylenol in capsule form. However, companies continue to seek ways to improve tamper-resistant packaging.

Pollution Control A drawback of packaging is that it is often a source of pollution. For example, plastics cannot be recycled and are not biodegradable. In fact, some emit dangerous gases when burned. In addition, glass and plastic bottles and aluminum cans litter the streets and countryside and create millions of tons of garbage each year. Some makers of glass bottles recycle their products and urge retailers to stock their products because glass-packaged goods usually have a longer shelf life than other packaged products. However, aluminum- and plastic-packaged goods are usually easier to stock, and more of them can fit into the same space. Some states have enacted — often over industry protests — laws in which customers are charged a deposit (typically 5 cents) on all soft drink and sometimes beer products that is refundable only when the empty bottles or cans are returned to the store. However, because the number of states with such laws are few, and because both bottles and cans are still widely used, pollution will continue to remain an area of social concern to marketers and package designers.

One hopeful development is a new plastic that disintegrates in the sun. When ultraviolet rays from the sun strike a disposable cup or tray made of the plastic, the container gradually becomes brittle and breaks apart. Eventually, after two months to five years, it degrades into water and carbon dioxide. (This doesn't happen in a store or home because ultraviolet rays don't pass through glass.) The maker of the plastic, Ecoplastics of Toronto, reports that the material adds about 5 percent to the cost of manufacturing a cup or tray. In one year, however, sales of the new plastic rose from 30 metric tons a year to 20 metric tons a month, mostly to companies in Canada and Italy.[10]

Labeling

Most packages contain labels. A **label** is the part of a package that presents information about its contents. The label may include a wide variety of information including the following:

Label The part of a package that presents information about its contents.

Brand name and logo. This helps distinguish products from competing offerings. Putting the company's name on the product also tells consumers that the company is putting its reputation on the line for the product's quality.

Registered trademark symbol (®). This symbol indicates that the company has exclusive rights to its trademark. This is one way a company can protect its trademark rights.

Package size. This information helps buyers make informed decisions on the price they are paying for a given amount.

Materials or ingredients. The buyer may be attracted to a product based on its materials or ingredients. The buyer of a shirt may like the comfort of cotton or the easy care of polyester. The buyer of cereal may look for high calcium or fiber content. A recent controversy has erupted in the fruit-drink business over whether the label must show the exact juice content. Marketers who have 100 percent juice in their products want the Food and Drug Administration to enforce the rule requiring the percentage to be listed, but others are fighting the rule. Ocean Spray Cranberries, Inc., with only 27 percent juice in their product, claims that it is impossible to sell pure cranberry juice because it is too tart. They contend that they would be penalized because consumers would automatically think their product was less nutritious and less juice for the money.[11] Their argument probably will not hold up in the drive to give the consumer as much information as possible.

Directions for using the product. A buyer who can't figure out how to use a product will be disappointed with it. Consequently, many labels contain directions.

Safety precautions. Companies include safety precautions for the same reasons they include directions. In addition, their social responsibility and their fear of lawsuits leads them to include this information.

Name and address of the manufacturer. Some manufacturers include their name, address, and a toll-free phone number to encourage questions or comments from customers.

Universal Product Codes (UPCs) Today most products sold in the United States include universal product codes on their labels. At the checkout counter, an electronic scanner reads this bar code to identify the product and ring up the price. This enables the store to automatically keep track of inventory and speed up the checkout process.

Today, the uses of UPCs extend far beyond the grocery or department store checkout counter. As technology continues to develop, these systems are becoming cheaper and more flexible. Libraries use bar codes to keep track of their books. Clinical laboratories put the codes on containers of blood and urine samples for accurate identification. Airlines use them to keep track of luggage. And Alamo Rent A Car has labeled its 60,000-car fleet with bar codes.[12]

Checkpoint

1. What objectives do marketers aim for in designing a package?
2. What kinds of information are found on food labels?

Product
Planning and
Pricing

These labels identify the brand, the type of product, its price, and tracking numbers for computerized inventory control. In addition, a universal product code (the series of vertical bars) makes it possible for an electronic scanner to read information more quickly than a checkout clerk can type in numbers. Soabar Service Bureaus, the company that prints the price tags, has a computer linkup with stores; store employees use phone lines to send Soabar the data to print. With this arrangement, Soabar can quickly meet a store's specific needs for price tags.

Pricing Strategies

While most everyone associates product strategies with marketing, they less often think of pricing strategies as a marketing approach. Yet understanding and using an effective pricing strategy can give a company a distinct advantage in the marketplace.

Businesses use many different pricing strategies in their marketing efforts. The best strategy depends on the customers. For example, research has shown that at one time, personal computers that sold for *less* than $1,000 encountered market resistance. Customers believed that the machines were not powerful and sophisticated enough to do "real" computer work. The market viewed them as merely low-quality, expensive toys. On the other hand, personal computers priced above $3,000 also ran into market resistance, because consumers believed these machines were too sophisticated and expensive for the intended use.

Marketers can't predict exactly how each customer will respond to a given price. Consequently, in determining the best pricing strategy, they consider the economic environment and the company's profitability objectives.

The Economic Environment

Supply The amount of a good provided at a particular price.

Demand The amount of a good purchased at a particular price.

Price level The price being charged in the industry.

Supply and demand play a vital role in a competitive economy. Briefly defined **supply** is the amount of a good provided at a particular price, and **demand** is the amount of a good purchased at a particular price. Supply is greatest at high prices, while demand is greatest at low prices. Between these extremes is the equilibrium or market price, where supply and demand are equal — $20 in Figure 12.4. (For further details, see Appendix A, "Fundamentals of the Economy.")

Implications for Marketers

What supply and demand and equilibrium mean for marketers is that in a competitive market, they must set a price at the overall **price level,** the price being charged in the industry. All other things being equal (for example, service, convenience, reputation, and so forth), a company that charges more than the equilibrium price may lose customers to competitors who charge less. A company that charges less than the equilibrium price may shortchange itself; in a competitive market, that doesn't make good business sense.

Sometimes, marketers may seem to violate this pricing arrangement by trying to shift the price downward. For example, a gas-station owner might try undercutting a competitor across the street. Soon the competitor cuts prices to match, and price wars rage for a while. But this cuts into profits, and before long the prices creep back up to the equilibrium point.

Sometimes, companies seem to be charging different prices for the same product. For example, different stores may charge different prices for the same merchandise. But when customers buy something at a

F I G U R E   12.4

Supply, Demand, and Price for Shirts

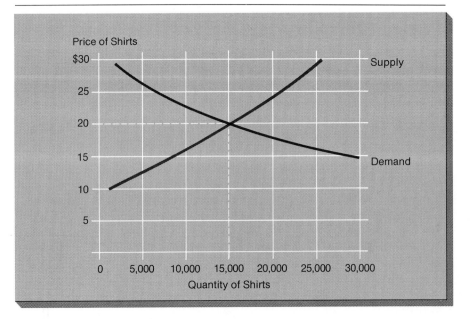

store, they are buying more than just the item itself. Recall the discussion in Chapter 11 of the tradeoffs customers may use when buying a product or service. The store may be making the product available in a convenient location at convenient times. In addition, some stores offer more services than others. For example, some shoppers may derive greater enjoyment from shopping in the quiet, carpeted aisles of Nieman-Marcus, where they can easily obtain sales assistance, than they do from shopping for the same products at K mart, and they are willing to pay more for this additional benefit.

Profitability

Most businesses have profit goals. Therefore, marketers must consider how the price of the product will enable the company to earn a profit. To determine profitability, or in less competitive environments, to set the price, the manager computes costs, then adds a markup to reach profit goals. Only in the short run can the seller afford to sell below cost in the hopes of creating a loyal customer base or, perhaps, driving out the competition.

The major issue for the seller is how far above its costs it can price the product. For example, many car dealers will sell to customers on the basis of dealer's invoice (their cost) plus an agreed-upon amount. The size of this amount depends on the degree to which customers will be influenced by price. In general, if customers can easily find the same thing somewhere else, the seller is limited to a small markup. If the product is difficult to obtain or is prestigious, the markup can be larger.

Quality and Price

The price a company charges also depends on whether it has chosen to please a few quality-conscious customers by emphasizing quality or to sell a lot of a product by emphasizing low price. Companies can earn the highest profits by focusing on quality or price. Emphasis on quality pays off because the relatively few customers who will pay for high quality and special service will usually pay more than the additional cost to the supplier for providing the extras. Emphasis on price works because the low price should enable the company to capture a large market share; additionally, selling in quantity usually gives the company a cost advantage. Companies that don't adopt either focus are sometimes referred to as "stuck in the middle."[13] Their profits tend to be relatively low.

Consider an example. Häagen-Dazs charges an above-average price for its ice cream, but some customers are willing to pay extra for the quality ingredients. In contrast, Sealtest—which doesn't boast of the same quality, but costs less than premium brands like Häagen-Dazs—sells a lot more ice cream.

Profitable small companies often focus on quality at higher prices rather than quantity at lower prices. The reason is that a company must produce and sell more of a low-priced item in order to make a profit. This entails larger-scale production capabilities, which small companies often lack. For examples of some companies that have profited by emphasizing quality, see "Small Business Close-Up: Getting Fat on Staying Slim."

While some large companies, such as IBM, emphasize quality and service, others emphasize price. A large company can also offer some products in each category. For example, General Motors has a strategy of offering a variety of brands; Chevettes compete on the basis of price, while Corvettes compete on the basis of quality.

Keep in mind that companies with high-quality products also evaluate the importance of price in their marketing strategy. Likewise, low-cost producers are interested in production quality. However, each has a primary focus.

Checkpoint

1. What basic concerns do marketers consider in setting a price strategy?
2. What would be a suitable price strategy for a small bookstore?

SMALL BUSINESS   CLOSE-UP

Getting Fat on Staying Slim

Over the last decade, Americans have grown increasingly interested in improving their physical fitness. Most go to a gym or health club, but there is a growing market for home exercise equipment. Many exercise buffs find it easier to buy the necessary equipment and work out in the comfort of their own homes than to go out.

Many entrepreneurs who have responded to this demand are getting fat on the profits they earn helping America slim down. Perhaps the best known equipment manufacturer is Nautilus, Inc., which for a long time marketed its equipment solely to health clubs. The company now is offering home machines. The first ones were for the abdomen and lower back, and Nautilus has followed with five additional specialized machines. Another company is Precor, which has developed stationary bicycles, treadmills, and rowers. Soloflex has been extremely successful in marketing its one-piece workout machines. Livingwell, Inc., sells Powercise machines, which are programmed to talk to users and are proving to be the hottest sellers on the market. And for those who feel that riding a stationary bicycle is boring, one firm now offers a $50, 60-minute videotape that simulates a grueling cycle tour of Yellowstone National Park. The rider can sweat while enjoying the scenery—all without ever leaving home.

These products have one thing in common: They are designed for people who want quality equipment in their homes and are willing to pay for it. The market may be limited to executives and professionals who have the extra income to spend on workout equipment, because costs are high: $600 for a rower that also keeps track of the amount of calories burned; $500 for a machine that helps slim the abdomen in only five minutes a day, three days a week; $300 for a wristwatch that monitors pulse rate. But despite the limited market, this line of business can be quite profitable. Some of these businesses are earning profits as much 15 cents out of every sales dollar.

Pricing Techniques

Based on the pricing strategy adopted, the manager selects pricing techniques from a variety of options. The major kinds of techniques are traditional pricing, discounts, and special techniques to stimulate sales.

Traditional Pricing

Pricing starts with the **list price.** This is the price announced for a good. At a supermarket, the list price is usually found on the product itself and on the shelf. At an auto dealership, the list price is found on the sticker attached to the car window. In a college bookstore, it is often on a label attached to the cover or stamped on the inside cover of each book. The list price of clothing appears on tags attached to it.

The traditional approach is to sell only at the list price. Under this **fixed-price technique,** the marketer sells at the announced price. In the supermarket, for example, if one can of tuna is priced at 60 cents, then two cans will cost $1.20 and three cans will cost $1.80. The seller does not negotiate. Restaurants and retail stores like Dillards or K mart also use a fixed-price strategy; they do not negotiate from their announced price. Hair stylists charge twice as much for two haircuts as they do for one, and the price is set in advance.

Discounts

Many businesses find that they can profitably boost sales by deviating from the fixed-price technique. Managers at these companies have strategically chosen or have been forced by the competition to use discounting. A **discount** is an amount subtracted from the list price. As illustrated in Figure 12.5, some common forms include trade, quantity, cash, and seasonal discounts.

List price The price announced for a good.

Fixed-price technique A pricing technique in which the marketer sells at the announced price.

Discount An amount subtracted from the list price.

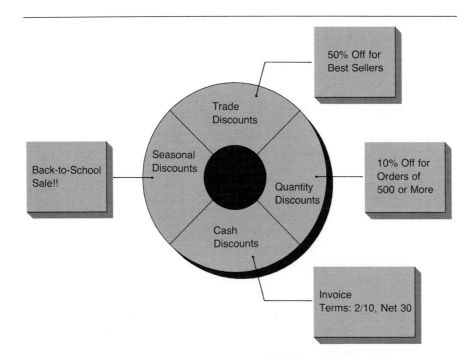

FIGURE 12.5

Types of Discounts

Trade discount
A discount given to merchants in the distribution channel.

Quantity discount
A discount given to buyers who place larger-than-average orders.

Cash discount   A discount given for paying a bill within a predetermined time period.

Seasonal discount   A discount given during particular times of the year.

Some businesses sell below list price to merchants in the distribution channel. Such a price reduction is called a **trade discount.** Manufacturers often give wholesalers a trade discount. In turn, wholesalers give retailers a discount. In publishing, bookstores such as Waldenbooks and B. Dalton, the two largest in the industry, typically pay half of list price for a best seller. They, in turn, may pass on some of the discount to customers. Sellers also may give a price reduction to buyers who place larger-than-average orders. This price reduction is a **quantity discount.** Such discounts are typically based on the number of units purchased. The larger the order, the greater the discount.

Some businesses reward their customers for paying their bills on time. A **cash discount** is a price reduction given for paying a bill within a predetermined time period. One common cash-discount term is "2/10, net 30," pronounced "two ten, net thirty." This means that if the buyer pays the bill within 10 days, the seller grants a 2 percent discount, but that in any case, the bill must be paid in 30 days. Under these terms, a buyer who gets a bill for $100 can settle it for $98 by paying within 10 days; otherwise, the entire $100 is due in 30 days.

Finally, a seller that wants to stimulate buying before or after peak periods may offer a **seasonal discount.** This is a price reduction given during particular times of the year. For example, swimsuit manufacturers offer discounts to retailers in the Midwest for buying before the peak summer months. Most bathing suits are sold between May and August, so manufacturers offer seasonal discounts in March and April. These discounts do more than help the manufacturer increase sales. They also save the company the cost of warehousing the inventory.

Many retailers also offer seasonal discounts. Using the same example, swimsuits are heavily discounted in the late summer and early fall. By this time, the retailer knows that anyone who needs a bathing suit for the summer already has one; the only way to get buyers to consider another is with a sale. Many merchandisers also have post-holiday sales, and mark down candy on February 15 and Christmas decorations, cards, and wrapping paper during the last week of December. In an effort to generate even higher sales, some retailers have begun changing these holiday sale periods and offering discounts *before* the holiday. Christmas sales on the Friday and Saturday after Thanksgiving have, to the distress of many people, become the norm.

Other Pricing Techniques

While discounts stimulate sales, they are not the only pricing techniques that businesses use. Other popular approaches include loss leaders, odd pricing, and flexible pricing.

Loss leader   A product that is priced below cost to attract people into a store.

Loss Leaders A **loss leader** is a product that is priced below cost. This pricing method is designed to attract people into the store, where, the retailer hopes, they will buy other goods as well. To ensure that the first group of customers to arrive doesn't buy up all the loss leaders, most stores limit purchases, such as "one to a customer."

Examples of loss leaders appear in the newspaper every week. Many supermarkets, for example, run ads for loss leaders such as coffee, soft drinks, and toothpaste in an effort to generate heavier-than-usual traffic. The store that placed the ad in Figure 12.6 may take a loss on corn and peaches. These are products that appeal to many consumers, so the prices are likely to build traffic. Note that "large" peaches are selling for more than twice as much as the featured price. The store managers may be hoping that many customers will decide that "medium-size" peaches

An Advertisement Using Special Pricing Techniques

Source: Copyright by Dominick's Finer Foods, Inc., 1988.

are too small and will switch to the bigger, more expensive ones. Department stores often run sales featuring loss leaders on weekends in order to attract customers at the time of the week when they are most likely to go shopping.

Odd Pricing A second pricing method is **odd pricing,** which is setting a price just below a round number for psychological reasons. An item may be priced at $98.95 instead of $100, or $2,995 rather than $3,000. This type of pricing is often referred to as "psychological pricing," because it tends to get people's attention and to suggest they are getting a good deal. At first glance, a price of $98.95 may seem to be a lot less than $100. More importantly, people feel that they are getting a bargain at $98.95 instead of $100. Odd pricing is an old technique that probably still works on many buyers.

A possibly mythical story involving Marshall Field suggests another basis for odd pricing. The founder of the Chicago retailing giant suspected that some cashiers were pocketing money from customers rather than putting it into the cash register. That was relatively easy to do when sales were for round amounts, such as $2. By changing to odd pricing, Field forced cashiers to ring up the sale in order to open the cash register, deposit the money, and give the customer back some change. According to this story, the store's receipts increased after Field instituted odd pricing.

Flexible Pricing Some sellers are willing to negotiate on price. These sellers use **flexible pricing,** in which the price of a product is negotiable. For example, flexible pricing is in effect on Saturdays at the farmers' market in Detroit. Especially toward the end of the day, when the choice produce is gone and the farmers are eager to return home, buyers haggle with sellers over the prices of the goods for sale. Many farmers will cut prices in order to sell off what they have. Some haggling also takes place at flea markets and garage sales around the country.

Auto dealers are also known for flexible pricing. They typically set the initial price as high as they can, figuring in every cost they possibly can. Their hope is that customers will be more likely to make a purchase when they see the price come down than they would if the price were fixed. If you've ever tried to sell your car to a dealer for cash, you might have found that the amount offered is considerably less than the dealer would offer for the same car as a trade-in allowance. That's because a generous trade-in allowance is one way dealers bring down the price of the car they are selling; it isn't necessarily based on the value of your car.

Odd pricing Setting a price just below a round number for psychological reasons.

Flexible pricing Selling a product at a price that is negotiable.

Checkpoint

1. Name two kinds of discounts marketers use.
2. What two pricing techniques do marketers often consider when introducing a new product?

Closing Comments

This chapter examined some of the basics of product planning and pricing. A case in point is the efforts of growers and processors to provide more appealing fruits and vegetables in the winter to customers in northern climates. They are considering ways to improve the produce itself, as well as the influence of packaging. They are also concerned about keeping control over the price of the improved produce.

In general, marketing managers develop a product strategy plan using techniques such as portfolio analysis and life-cycle analysis. They also consider proper branding, packaging, and labeling. These elements often spell the difference between success and failure. In addition, marketing success depends on pricing strategies and techniques. The right price depends on the economic environment, the company's profit goals, and consumer expectations.

Learning Objectives Revisited

1. **Describe the steps involved in development of new products.**
   New-product development involves six steps: idea generation, coming up with ideas and concepts that can be turned into new products; production evaluation, looking over the proposed products to see whether they fit with the firm's long-range objectives; economic analysis, evaluation of the project's overall profitability; product development, the construction of a model, mockup, or prototype of the product; test marketing, taking the product into the marketplace to see how well it does; and commercialization, making the product available to the market at large.

2. **Explain how businesses use product analysis.**
   To decide on a strategy for pricing, distributing, and promoting a product, the company analyzes the product's performance. Two common ways of doing this are portfolio analysis and analysis of the product's life-cycle stage. Portfolio analysis bases product strategy on market attractiveness and market share. Companies generally promote their stars, push their question marks in hopes of making them stars, milk their cows, and get rid of their dogs. Life-cycle analysis bases product strategy on the product's current life-cycle stage. For a product in the introduction stage, the company focuses on achieving product awareness and expanding the market. During this stage, the company sets the price and marketing expenditures high. When a product reaches the growth stage, the focus shifts to achieving brand preference and increasing market share. In the maturity stage, the firm focuses on brand loyalty and keeping its present market share. Finally, when the product enters the decline stage, the firm focuses on holding on to the product's most loyal customers and keeping its expenses down.

3. **Discuss the use of brands and trademarks.**
   A brand is a name, term, symbol, or combination of these used to identify a firm's products and differentiate them from those of the competition. A trademark is a brand that the owner has the legal and exclusive right to use. Businesses use brand names and trademarks in advertising and packaging so that the consumer will identify a particular type of product with their brand.

4. **Describe the value of packaging and labeling.**

Packaging is of value in marketing products because it often is part of the product itself. Effective packaging makes a product convenient and safe to use. Labeling tells what is in the product, provides information related to the product's use, and often carries an advertising message as well.

5. **Present the dimensions of product-pricing strategies.**

In competitive markets, businesses must sell at the equilibrium price. In a less competitive environment, a company may be able to set a price that covers costs plus a markup. Firms that price high and focus on quality often have small market shares but generate relatively large profits. At the opposite extreme, firms that charge a low price can often achieve market share and relatively large profits.

6. **Identify product-pricing techniques.**

Some companies accept only their list price, but many offer trade, quantity, cash, or seasonal discounts. Store owners may use loss leaders, which are goods priced below cost in an effort to draw customers. Another technique is odd pricing, which attempts to attract customers by setting a price just below a round number, say, $19.95 rather than $20.00. Some sellers use flexible pricing, in which the price of a product is negotiable.

Key Terms Reviewed

Review each of the following terms. For any that you do not know or are unsure of, look up the definitions and see how they were used in the chapter.

portfolio analysis	price level
brand	list price
private brand	fixed-price technique
national brand	discount
family brand	trade discount
individual brand	quantity discount
trademark	cash discount
generic product	seasonal discount
label	loss leader
supply	odd pricing
demand	flexible pricing

Review Questions

1. Why do companies need to be concerned about developing new products?
2. Louise Radcliffe is president of a company that produces paper products. So far, her company has made only familiar products such as cups, plates, and napkins, but Louise thinks that it is time the company set up a formal process for developing new products. What activities should Louise plan for?

3. Identify each of the following products as a star, a question mark, a cash cow, or a dog. Explain why you chose each category. What implications does the product's category have for the way the company should market it?
   a. Reynold's Wrap aluminum foil
   b. VHS videocassette recorders
   c. A locally owned health club
   d. Adler manual typewriters
4. For each of the products in Question 3, identify the product's stage in its life cycle. What does this tell you about how each product should be marketed?
5. What is the difference between a brand and a trademark? Which of the following terms are trademarks? (If you aren't sure, try consulting a recent edition of a dictionary.)
   a. Kleenex
   b. Toll House cookies
   c. Ping-Pong
   d. Vaseline
6. For the items in Question 5 that are trademarks, how can the owner protect its rights to the trademark? What will happen if the company fails to do so?
7. Why do you think marketers spend money on improving packaging? Isn't it the product inside the package that counts? In improving packaging, what concerns do marketers take into account?
8. What information would you recommend go on the label of each of the following products? Why would you include each item?
   a. A bag of corn chips
   b. A portable power drill
   c. A paperback novel (*Hint:* What functions as the label on a paperback?)
   d. A winter coat
9. In a competitive market, what can a marketer do if the company can't afford to produce at a low enough cost to sell at the equilibrium price?
10. Why do companies that focus on either quality or price achieve the greatest profitability?
11. What pricing techniques might help the owner of a bookstore build business?
12. What pricing techniques do companies typically use for introducing new products?

Applied Exercises

1. Pick out a product advertised in the local newspaper. Briefly describe each of the steps in the product development process that must have occurred as this product made its way from idea generation to commercialization. Share your answers with other students in the class.
2. Go to the supermarket and identify five generic products. Which do you think is the best-selling product of the five? Which is the poorest? Support your choices using principles discussed in the text.

3. Interview a manager from a local manufacturer or food processor on new-product development. What steps does the business person take in this process? Compare what you were told with the steps discussed in the chapter. Write up the results of your comparison.

4. Interview a manager from a local department store, discount store, or auto dealership. Ask him or her to explain how prices are set. In writing up your findings, identify the techniques that were used.

Your Business IQ: Answers

1. False. The typical product life cycle is only five to ten years. Innovation and new product planning is therefore crucial to the success of modern businesses.

2. False. Registration is the required first step in having a trademark, but does not in itself guarantee continuing rights. The owner of a trademark must protect its rights by making them known and, if necessary, enforcing them in court. If the trademark passes into common usage, as have the names Monopoly and Toll House cookies, the company may lose its rights.

3. True. This is a requirement of the federal government.

4. False. The most profitable companies specialize in either high quality or low price. Companies that lack either emphasis tend to be less profitable.

5. True. Businesses in most industries offer manufacturers and, in turn, some retailers and individual customers a small discount if they pay their bill within a stated few days.

MTV Seeks New Vitality

When it was launched in 1981, MTV was a quick success. The cable channel's exciting, imaginative video clips set to music influenced performers, movies, and TV commercials. Attracted by the channel's popularity, a number of imitators entered the market, including NBC's *Friday Night Videos* and WTBS's *Night Tracks*.

The initial success eventually waned. Ratings fell to 0.6 percent of the potential audience, from a peak of 1.2 percent. Viewers complained that the quality of the videos was slipping and becoming predictable. One problem for MTV is that it has no control over video quality, since the channel receives the videos free from the record companies.

Despite these problems, MTV is far from dead. It is available in almost 36 million cable homes, up from 2.5 million when it started. Advertisers continue to use MTV to reach the teenage audience, and revenues have risen steadily. Popular performers still depend on the channel for exposure. For example, MTV has been credited for the success of such groups as Bon Jovi and Poison.

MTV has tried to improve its position by diversifying. First the channel tried to appeal to a broader audience by adding pop music artists such as Lionel Richie and Billy Joel. That didn't work, so the channel tried diversifying its format. It now broadcasts situation comedies and reports on rock groups along with music videos. Explains MTV's entertainment president, Tom Freston, "We have changed directions from focusing on music alone to including life-style, the way people look, feel, dress. The challenge is to maintain freshness."

Case Questions

1. At what stage of the product life cycle is MTV? Explain.
2. How do marketers' price-versus-quality choices apply to MTV? Does the company currently have the most advantageous focus? Why or why not?
3. Can MTV improve on its performance? If so, how? If not, what can it do to keep from sliding further?

You Be the Adviser:
Helping Them Do It

Product Concepts, a small company located on the East Coast, has done extremely well over the last five years. The company is a research and development firm that investigates, researches, develops, and sells new products to large, national firms, which in turn market them. Over the last three years, Product Concepts has begun marketing some of its own discoveries, although only in the New England area.

Recently, the firm's product development scientists have told the president that they have discovered what might be a revolutionary product. It is a process that will allow a ballpoint pen to be used for five to seven years. The process involves a new method for generating ink, so that as ink is used, it is replaced within the cartridge.

The president believes that this idea could change the entire ballpoint pen industry. In particular, he is thinking about developing and marketing the pen with a five-year guarantee. If at any time during this period the pen runs out of ink, the company will replace it free.

As far as the president is concerned, the new product idea merits serious consideration. However, the firm has never entered an industry in direct competition with major, well-entrenched firms. Because this new venture will be risky and require a large investment, the president would like to examine the situation closely and be sure that the company is not biting off more than it can chew.

Your Advice

1. What steps would you recommend that the president take in developing this product? Identify and describe what to do at each step.
2. If the company introduces a five-year ballpoint pen, what pricing strategy and techniques would you recommend that the president use when it is first introduced? Explain your reasoning. Would you recommend a change in pricing if the product enters a growth phase? Why or why not?
3. Does this product idea seem to have a good chance of success? Why or why not?

Promotional Strategies

LEARNING OBJECTIVES

- Define advertising and its basic types.
- Identify the various advertising media.
- Explain how marketers analyze the effectiveness of advertising.

- Describe the types and process of personal selling.
- Discuss the basic techniques of sales promotion.
- Relate the roles that publicity and public relations play in promotion.

Your Business IQ

How much do you already know about advertising, personal selling, and sales promotion? Test your business IQ by labeling each statement *true* or *false*. Answers and explanations are at the end of the chapter.

1. Each of the top ten advertisers spends more than $500 million a year in advertising.
2. Advertisers in the United States spend more for television advertising than for any other form.
3. The initial step in the personal selling process is to present the product's strengths.
4. Many companies are finding that using coupons is too expensive a method for promoting their products.
5. Publicity is free advertising; there are no costs involved.

Wolf Brand Chili uses a successful promotional strategy that draws on many elements of the promotional mix.

Source: Courtesy of Wolf Brand Chili.

Looking Back and Ahead

Dallas-based Wolf Brand Chili wanted El Paso customers to start eating its chili, so it hired the Retail Merchandising Group (RMG), a Chattanooga, Tennessee–based company that specializes in promoting products. RMG recommended that Wolf Brand focus on radio; although newspapers are important for advertising food products, the company believes that radio can be effective in building local awareness of a brand.

So Wolf Brand bought a series of radio advertising slots. The company offered local retailers free ad time if they stocked up on Wolf Brand chili and featured it in special displays. The radio stations staged singles nights at supermarkets, with on-scene announcers talking up the chili and holding sweepstakes for free trips. They hosted on-air games, and one show even held a howling contest. The brand manager for Wolf Brand heralded the campaign as a success.[1]

Of course, the ultimate success of Wolf Brand chili will depend in part on the quality and price of the product. As you learned in Chapter 12, product and price are two key parts of the marketing mix. But unless customers know about a product and its benefits, all the product design and pricing strategies will go to waste. Consequently, this chapter focuses on promotional strategy as part of the marketing mix. Although the term *promotion* commonly refers to moving ahead in an organization, applied to marketing it means moving or selling products and services. Thus, promotion may involve a variety of marketing activities, ranging from selling products face-to-face (personal selling) to indirect efforts such as advertising and publicity.

Promotional Strategy

Before a company starts promoting a product, the managers must decide on an overall strategy for doing so. They consider what they want the promotion to accomplish, whom they want to reach, and the nature of the product they are selling. They also evaluate the various methods of promotion in order to decide which will best accomplish their objectives.

Objectives for Promotion

Promotion is not an end in itself; it is used as a tool to achieve marketing and company objectives. If the company has an effective procedure for setting goals, the manager will have a clear sense of what the promotion is intended to achieve. (Chapter 6 described procedures for goal setting.) Typical goals are achieving a certain profit level or attaining a particular market share (the percentage of all product buyers that buys the company's product).

In deciding how to achieve goals, the marketer takes into account the nature of the product or service. If it is radically new, the promotion will probably have to explain to potential buyers what it is and why they would want it. If the product or service has many competitors, the promotion will have to give potential buyers reasons to prefer the company's brand or approach to a service. For a complex product, buyers may need visual information to help them understand it. Buyers of an expensive product or service may be hesitant to make a commitment without the influence of a personalized approach.

Likewise, marketers consider the nature of the target market. Approaches that are suitable for a consumer market may be ineffective with an industrial market. For example, the percentage of people viewing the evening news who might buy an industrial robot would be very small; thus a TV ad would be an expensive way to reach customers of industrial robots.

Sometimes marketers promote to an industrial market consisting of their wholesalers or retailers. In this case, they are using a *pushing strategy* — they are trying to make wholesalers and retailers want to sell their product and therefore push consumers to buy it. This is the strategy Wolf Brand used when it offered stores free advertising time.

Marketers can also use the opposite approach: they can convince consumers to ask retailers to stock the product. This strategy, called a *pulling strategy,* is intended to get retailers to order more of the product. Wolf Brand used this strategy, too, by staging contests and games.

Marketers also need to know whether people in their target market read a lot and, if so, what publications. Do they watch television a lot? Do they drive to work or ride public transit? Do they buy on the basis of facts or the way the product makes them feel? Answers to such questions help marketers decide what to say and what methods to use.

The Promotional Mix

When marketers select the methods through which they promote their products, they are planning a promotional mix. This mix consists of the types of promotion available to marketers. Figure 13.1 illustrates the elements of the promotional mix and the relationship of the promotional mix to the marketing mix.

The elements of the promotional mix are advertising, personal selling, sales promotion, and publicity and public relations. The marketer selects which elements to use based on how well they help the company achieve its objectives. Most companies use sales promotion, publicity, and public relations to supplement their advertising and personal selling efforts. The rest of this chapter describes some of the information marketers consider in developing an overall strategy and implementing specific promotional techniques.

Checkpoint

1. What is the difference between a pushing promotional strategy and a pulling strategy?
2. What are the elements of the promotional mix?

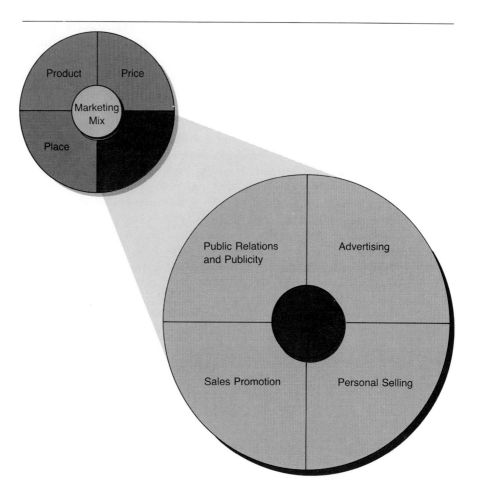

Advertising

Advertising A nonpersonal form of promotion in which a firm attempts to persuade someone to a particular point of view.

For most companies, the focus of the promotional effort is **advertising.** Advertising can be defined as a nonpersonal form of promotion in which a firm attempts to persuade someone to a particular point of view. It is so much a part of our culture that it literally affects the way we think and talk. For example, as a result of product advertising, just about every American understands and associates an image with the following words: Coke, Mickey Mouse, Pontiac, and Xerox. Some brands are even part of the vocabulary of foreign countries. In South America, for example, Raton Miqueto (Mickey Mouse) is familiar to every child. Table 13.1 shows America's ten leading advertisers; Table 13.2 shows annual advertising spending in various industries.

Types of Advertising

Advertising can take many different forms. One of the most common in modern times is a TV ad designed to persuade customers to buy a particular product. Another is a newspaper ad announcing a giant sale at a local retail store. The form a marketer selects depends on the promotional strategy.

Regardless of the form advertising takes, its ultimate objective is to sell more goods and services. To do this, the ad may introduce a new product or encourage people to buy the good or service more often. Sometimes companies use ads that attempt to create a positive image of the firm, in the hope that customers will be more inclined to buy from a company they admire.

Primary-Demand Advertising Some advertising is designed to increase the total demand for a good or service, rather than for a particular brand. This is called **primary-demand advertising.** Associations often use this approach to promote their members' products. For example, the American Dairy Association promotes the healthfulness of milk and the benefits of real butter. The American Dental Association encourages proper

Primary-demand advertising Advertising designed to increase the total demand for a good or service, rather than for a particular brand.

Rank	Company	Ad Spending in 1986 (thousands)	Ad Costs (% of sales)
1	Procter & Gamble	$1,435,454	N/A
2	Philip Morris	1,364,472	7.8%
3	Sears, Roebuck	1,004,708	N/A
4	RJR Nabisco	935,036	5.9
5	General Motors	839,000	.9
6	Ford	648,500	1.3
7	Anheuser-Busch	643,522	N/A
8	McDonald's	592,000	19.2
9	K mart	590,350	N/A
10	PepsiCo	581,309	7.2

TABLE 13.1

Ten Leading Advertisers

Rank	Industry	Ad Spending in 1986 (thousands)
1	Automotive	$3,754,443
2	Food	3,307,079
3	Business and consumer services	2,148,935
4	Travel, hotels, and resorts	1,776,037
5	Retail	1,731,586
6	Entertainment	1,686,243
7	Toiletries and cosmetics	1,671,306
8	Beer, wine, and liquor	1,413,720
9	Drugs	1,245,424
10	Snacks and soft drinks	1,053,038

TABLE 13.2

Advertising Expenditures by Industry

There's more to wool than meets the eye or hand. Wool is comfortable because it breathes, one of the reasons it feels so good. Wool tailors so well and keeps its beautiful appearance, wearing after wearing...season after season. Whatever your style, you'll enjoy dressing more when you wear wool.

BETTY HANSON & CO.

PURE WOOL

A primary-demand advertisement for wool clothing. The beneficial characteristics of wool are being advertised, not the maker of the clothes. The advertiser wants to increase demand for all clothing made of wool.

Source: Courtesy of The Wool Bureau Incorporated.

Selective advertising
Advertising designed to increase the demand for a particular brand of product.

Institutional advertising
Advertising designed to create goodwill and build a desired company image.

dental care (including, of course, regular checkups). An ad for wool clothing is another example of primary-demand advertising.

Selective Advertising More typically, advertisements are designed to increase the demand for a particular brand of product. Advertising with this objective is called **selective advertising.** Most advertising fits into this category, and more money is spent on selective advertising than on any other type.

Selective advertising attempts to set the advertiser's product apart from the competition. When Visa says, "It's everywhere you want to be," the company is suggesting that other credit cards might be less widely recognized. When AT&T calls itself "the right choice," it is implying that other long-distance carriers might not be such a good choice. The advertisers hope that by establishing a particular identity for their product or service, they can persuade more customers to buy or use it.

Institutional Advertising Companies also use advertising to create goodwill and build a desired company image. Such advertising is called **institutional advertising.** This advertising includes ads that tell of a company's concern for quality or dedication to environmental protection. A company may sponsor cultural programming on TV or radio and even buy print ads promoting that fact. For example, Mobil Oil has underwritten the costs of producing Masterpiece Theater on public television for years.

Companies use institutional ads so that people will think positively of the firm when they are looking for products that the company offers. For example, if someone who wants to buy a car thinks favorably of General Motors, GM's institutional advertising has done its job. Institutional advertising can also help keep people informed about changes that the company is making that will result in better goods and services. Some companies promote themselves in business publications. They may hope that creating a better corporate image will help them raise funds from lenders or potential investors if needed and attract and keep management talent.

Cooperative Advertising Sometimes manufacturers and retailers share the costs of a joint advertising campaign. This is called **cooperative advertising.** This approach encourages customers to buy a product, while also encouraging merchants to push the product. Large manufacturers often use cooperative advertising when they introduce a new product or want to stimulate sales. At the present time, companies spend about $9 billion annually for cooperative advertising.

Typical examples of cooperative advertising are arrangements between auto manufacturers and local dealers, computer makers and local outlets, and cosmetics firms and department stores. Franchises also use a form of cooperative advertising. The local franchisees pay a fee to the franchisor, who uses part of these funds for advertisements that complement the promotion efforts of the local operators.

Advertising Media

In deciding where to place their promotional messages, advertisers can select from among an ever-growing variety of advertising media. Figure 13.2 shows how U.S. advertising expenditures are distributed among the media. The most popular media today are newspapers, magazines, radio, TV, and direct mail. Table 13.3 summarizes the major advantages and disadvantages of these media.

Newspapers Marketers spend more money on newspaper advertising than on any other medium. One reason is that newspapers reach so many people. With total daily circulation exceeding 60 million, newspapers reach two-thirds of American adults during the week and almost three-quarters on Sundays.[2]

Because the circulation of most newspapers is geographically concentrated, marketers find newspapers an effective way to target local markets. Stores advertise sales, and movie theaters announce their current offerings. A restaurant or hairdresser in a particular suburb can take out an ad in the suburban newspaper. Marketers can also target geographically by buying an ad in certain editions of a newspaper that serves a relatively wide geographic area. For example, the suburban restaurant or hairdresser can place ads in the suburban edition of the city newspaper. It wouldn't make sense for these businesses to spend the money to

Cooperative advertising
Advertising for a product in which the manufacturer and merchant share the costs.

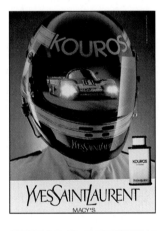

A cooperative advertisement for a cologne. The brand of cologne is Yves Saint Laurent, and the store is Macy's. The two companies share the cost of the ad because they both hope to benefit from it.

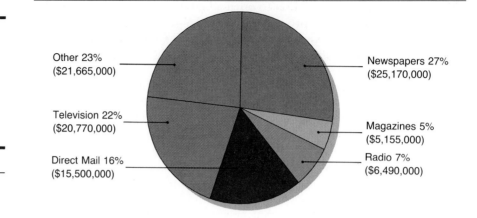

reach a national audience, since people visit restaurants and hairdressers that are reasonably close to home.

One disadvantage of newspaper advertising is that people usually throw away the newspaper once they have read it. This means that they are unlikely to see an ad more than once. They also are unlikely to pass the newspaper along to someone else who would also see the ad.

Magazines Millions of Americans read magazines, and ads are an integral part of each issue. Subscriptions and counter sales do not begin to cover the expenses of producing most magazines. To make money and even to stay in business, publishers need to generate ad revenue.

T A B L E   13.3   Advantages and Disadvantages of the Major Advertising Media

Medium	Advantages	Disadvantages
Newspapers	Reaches many people Geographically concentrated to target local markets Can place ads to catch the eye of those not looking for ads Can place ads in classified section for those wanting to buy	Read only once Not passed on to others Poorer quality paper than magazines
Magazines	Can generate considerable revenue for publisher Reach a large audience Can reach target markets Relative permanence of message because people keep and pass on to others	Needs advance preparation High cost
Radio	Can be targeted to specific location Can be targeted to specific audience Effective with products where sound is as or more important than appearance	Cannot see the product or service Short life of message Not passed on to others
Television	Reaches a large audience Can be targeted to specific location Can be targeted to specific audience Allows the product or service to be shown and demonstrated Allows creative input for big impact	Very expensive Short life of message Needs advance preparation
Direct Mail	Covers a wide territory Can focus on a particular market	Can be expensive to deliver Difficulty in obtaining relevant mailing list Consumer resistance

Many companies rely heavily on magazine advertising because of the large audiences these publications serve. General-interest publications such as *Time* and *People* reach millions of readers nationwide. This makes these publications suitable for advertising products with a broad appeal, such as lawn mowers, automobiles, and insurance.

Magazines also allow advertisers to reach target markets effectively. Like newspapers, many magazines offer regional editions for targeting geographically. The subject matter of magazines also enables advertisers to target groups with special interests and needs. For example, a marketer of makeup and high-fashion clothing might advertise in *Cosmopolitan*, while a marketer of software for IBM-compatible personal computers

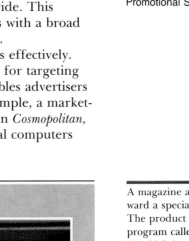

A magazine ad directed toward a specialized audience. The product is a computer program called Unigraphics II, which is used for designing products by creating three-dimensional images on a personal computer. This is something that technical personnel would use, so the maker, McDonnell Douglas, placed this advertisement in a magazine called *Managing Automation.*

Source: Courtesy of McDonnell Douglas.

UNIGRAPHICS II
GIVES HUFFY A FRAMEWORK FOR SUCCESS

When it comes to bicycles of all kinds, Huffy is America's first choice. But the largest bicycle manufacturer in the United States still needed a way to stay in high gear and remain ahead of the pack. "Foreign competition is heavy," says John Mariotti, Huffy Bicycle Division President and General Manager. "It created the demand for us to be able to develop product designs quickly."

Huffy needed a CAD system to eliminate the time-inefficient trial and error design process. "We're marketing driven and model year sensitive. Things have to happen fast," says Bill Leppak, Product Engineering Manager. "We have to translate marketing's needs into a product. We don't have the time to lay it out, make a sample, put it together, experiment and then cut the tools. With Unigraphics II from McDonnell Douglas, we lay out the design, use the same data for the assembly drawing, for the detail drawing, right on down the line. We chose Unigraphics because of its growth capabilities and because we can use its design data to build something rather than just for designing."

Huffy is happy with the results. "Unigraphics II has given us dramatic time savings and accuracy improvements. In some areas we've seen productivity grow by as much as 5:1. And we're estimating an overall productivity increase of up to 3:1 within the next year," noted Leppak.

Unigraphics II has met Huffy's current needs and is opening up new opportunities for growth in the future. Now, Huffy is picking up the pace, staying far ahead of the competition. If you're ready to put your design and manufacturing productivity on the fast track, shift to McDonnell Douglas. For more information, call 1-800-325-1551.

MCDONNELL DOUGLAS
MANUFACTURING INDUSTRY SYSTEMS COMPANY
ON THE INFORMATION FRONTIER

could reach the owners of such computers by advertising in *PC Magazine.*

Another advantage of magazine advertising is that people tend to keep magazines around for some time before throwing them away. They also pass them along to family members and friends, which increases the chance of the ads being read many times.

Besides the relatively high cost, perhaps the major disadvantage of magazine advertising is that ads usually have to be submitted six to eight weeks before publication. Current events or business conditions may change making the ad less relevant before it is seen by the buying public.

Radio Contrary to popular belief, advertisers are increasingly turning to radio advertising. One of its biggest advantages is that it lets the advertiser choose both the territory and the market to which the message is directed. Multicultural cities are a good example. In Miami, Florida, businesses selling to the Cuban-American market can advertise over Spanish-language stations. The same is true when selling to Mexican-Americans in Los Angeles or Puerto Ricans in New York.

Within a particular radio station's overall market, business can also target specific audiences. For example, those selling to teenagers or young adults can advertise on stations that feature the latest in rock music. Those selling to business people can run their ads during commuting times in large urban centers. Those selling to retired persons can advertise on programs that appeal to this particular audience.

As with newspaper ads, a major disadvantage of radio advertising is that the message is short-lived and not passed on to others. Another drawback is that the audience cannot see the product being advertised. This means that those who produce the ads must use their creative talent to draw on the listener's imagination. For example, 7-Up ran a series of commercials in which the fizzy, gurgly sound of the drink being poured into a glass was used to demonstrate 7-Up's refreshing nature. Also, radio advertising is effective in promoting products for which sound is more important than appearance. These products include records, concerts, cassette tapes, and car stereos.

Television Over the last decade, TV advertising has increased dramatically. Perhaps a major reason is that TV advertising allows for an actual demonstration of a product or service, along with delivery of the advertising message. Because it combines sight, sound, and motion, television offers great opportunities for advertisers to make a big impact. An example is the ad campaign described in "Competitiveness Close-Up: Bank Ads Blast Off." In terms of disadvantages, TV ads are very expensive, have a short life, and need considerable lead time to prepare.

TV advertising varies according to the breadth of the audience. There are three basic types of advertisements: network, spot, and local. A TV ad directed at a major audience around the country is a **network ad.** A common example is an ad carried during network evening news. Everyone watching NBC Evening News will see the same national ads at the same time. The same is true of ads carried during a blockbuster miniseries or a major sports event such as the Super Bowl. These programs are seen by a big portion of the national TV audience, so they are very expensive, as shown in Figure 13.3. However, the cost per viewer may

Network ad A television ad directed at a major audience around the country.

actually be similar to that of other shows, and to reduce costs network ads in general are moving from 30 to 15 seconds in length.[3]

A **spot ad** is a message broadcast over one or more stations at various times. An example would be a short commercial for Godfather's Pizza that is run on station breaks over several stations in the Midwest. Each station sends out the ad separately. Advertisers who use spot ads can choose the station, program, and time for their message.

A **local ad** is a message carried only in the immediate area. These are popular among local merchants. For example, the local furniture store may be running a big sale on TVs and appliances, so it advertises during the broadcast of local news.

Direct Mail When consumers and business people collect their mail, they usually find direct-mail advertisements among their letters and bills. This type of advertising ranges from circulars put out by the local grocery store to letters offering a credit card or magazine subscription to brochures describing the latest machine tool or stereo component. Doctors receive information on drugs, salespeople receive literature on training and motivation cassettes, and computer owners receive a stream of offers for supplies and software. People in all lines of work get direct-mail ads for related books and magazines.

One of the major advantages of direct mail is that it helps the marketer cover a wide territory while simultaneously focusing on a particular target market. Marketers can buy mailing lists that contain the names

Spot ad A television ad broadcast over one or more stations at various times.

Local ad A television ad carried only in the immediate area.

COMPETITIVENESS CLOSE-UP

Bank Ads Blast Off

The biggest news among banks these days is the ever-growing competition they face. Banks are responding to the competition by trying to improve their marketing efforts. Part of this effort goes to developing advertising that sets banks apart from their competitors.

One bank that has done this dramatically is New York's Chemical Bank Corp. Chemical used to favor image advertising, trying to build a good reputation in the community. Unfortunately for Chemical, everyone else was using the same strategy. So Chemical decided to tell consumers why it is different. Specifically, the bank decided to challenge a mistaken consumer impression that the competing Citibank Corp. offers more outlets.

Along with representatives from their advertising agency—Della Femina, Travisano &

Partners—Chemical's management settled on the theme "Chemical Is Everywhere I Go—Even When I Don't Know Where I'm Going." The creative people at the ad agency tried to come up with the most bizarre and visually striking circumstances under which someone might find the bank. As a result, television ads show an actor parachuting from a plane, ejected from a car, and shot from a cannon. In every case, the actor lands in one of Chemical's banks.

The creativity of the ads and the action emphasis of television gave the ads an explosive impact. Chemical managers are hoping that these dramatic scenes will cause consumers to remember the ads—and therefore the bank—when they are looking for convenience.

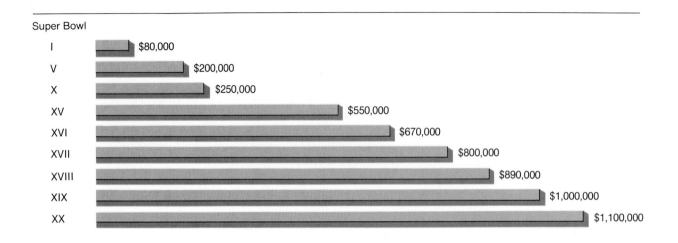

Super Bowl

Super Bowl	Rate
I	$80,000
V	$200,000
X	$250,000
XV	$550,000
XVI	$670,000
XVII	$800,000
XVIII	$890,000
XIX	$1,000,000
XX	$1,100,000

F I G U R E   13.3

**Super Bowl
Advertising Rates**

Most football fans try to watch their favorite teams every weekend. However, regardless of which specific games they do watch, there is one most fans never miss—the Super Bowl. This game attracts such a huge viewing audience that the advertisers have raised the cost of a 60-second commercial to new heights. Here is how much a 1-minute ad has cost, beginning with Super Bowl I.

and addresses of people whom they have identified as likely to purchase their product. These may consist of people who subscribe to a certain magazine, support some charity, buy from a particular catalog, or belong to a trade or professional association. Selecting the right mailing lists is central to the success of direct-mail advertising.

One of the major drawbacks of direct mail is that this type of advertising can be expensive compared to other forms of promotion. Much of the expense comes from the labor costs associated with hand-delivering circulars or the postage expense associated with mailing the materials. Also, many people throw away this type of mail without even opening it. One way advertisers try to overcome this problem is by designing the piece to look like a personal letter, a telegram, or, more recently, a Federal Express package or letter. These look-alikes attract attention and may at least get opened. Of course, the ethics of this misrepresentation may be called into question. The ethical considerations of generating and selling mailing lists were discussed in Chapter 11.

Other Media Besides the major advertising media, marketers look for other ways to get their message across. One way is with outdoor advertising such as billboards and signs. These ads must be simple because viewers seldom have much time to take in the message, but they can be useful for reinforcing awareness of a product. Marketers of cigarettes and liquor are heavy users of billboards because they have few ways to reach nonreaders; the law forbids them from advertising on radio and television. Radio stations also use this approach to advertise themselves. They post ads along heavily traveled routes, in the hope that commuters who see the ads will tune in the station on their car radio right away. Public transit systems often sell signs on the outside and inside of buses, trains, and stations. These have the advantage of advertising to a captive audience. Advertisers can reach target markets by choosing stations and routes in selected neighborhoods.

Advertisers are always on the lookout for new ways to advertise their products. They have tried skywriting, neon signs, and the Yellow Pages. Visitors to sports stadiums may see corporate or product logos posted near the field as well as ads on electronic scoreboards. Electronic displays print messages to people standing in line at post offices and supermarkets. Some marketers have even found it helpful to put ads on videocassette tapes. Video Information Network distributes 20- to 25-minute "FreeVee" video brochures and catalogs in video stores nationwide. Store customers can take home a FreeVee at no charge along with a paid rental. Customers are taking the FreeVees home even when clerks warn them that they're merely commercials. Evidently, they can't pass up the opportunity to get something for nothing.[4] Another innovative approach that is becoming an increasingly popular way to advertise products is to have them appear in movies. Companies pay the filmmakers to include their products, such as Huggies diapers in the movie "Baby Boom" and Miller beer in the movie "Dragnet."[5]

Evaluating Advertising Effectiveness

Advertisers want to know whether their ads are working. Are the business revenues being generated sufficient to offset the cost of the ads? Advertisers also try to minimize the risk of spending money on ineffective ads. To do so, they evaluate ideas before running the ads. To evaluate print ads, many advertisers use consumer pretests. A **consumer pretest** asks people to examine ads and rank them on their ability to capture and retain interest. Advertisers use this method in deciding which of several ads to run.

To test print ads they are already using, advertisers use readership reports. A **readership report** asks people to look at ads that have appeared in publications and to identify those that they recognize and those that they have read. Marketers want to prepare ads that readers will read as well as notice.

Consumer pretest A test of advertising effectiveness that asks people to examine ads and rank them on their ability to capture and retain interest.

Readership report A test of advertising effectiveness that asks people to look at ads that have appeared in publications and identify those that they recognize and those that they have read.

An unusual medium for advertising is this television on wheels. Called a MoboTRON, it contains two, 300-watt built-in speakers as well as a Sony JumboTRON large color video screen. MoboTRON units are on the road in Japan and the United States.

Source: Courtesy of Sony Corporation of America.

Similar tests rate TV ads. For example, every year Video Storyboard conducts interviews that ask consumers to name the most outstanding commercials they have watched in the last month. While the average person sees over 2,000 ads during this time period, one-third of the respondents are unable to identify even one.

The Video Storyboard research does not merely indicate which ads are the best-remembered. It also computes how much the advertiser spent for every 1,000 people who remembered the ad. The lower this number, the greater the ad's overall efficiency, because the advertiser was able to receive more attention for less money.

Another method used to test the effectiveness of radio and TV advertising is to call people's homes at random and ask them what channel they are watching or what station they are listening to. Advertisers assume that if people are watching or listening to a program, they are also watching or listening to the advertising that accompanies it.

People-meter An electronic instrument attached to a TV that records the channel to which the set is tuned.

The A.C. Nielsen Company has taken this idea a step further with the use of people-meters installed in TV viewers' homes. The **people-meter** is a complex electronic instrument that records who is watching which television programs. There are 3,000 of these meters randomly distributed around the United States. When a family member turns on the TV, the individual uses a special keypad to indicate who he or she is. (There is even a way of indicating if the person is a visitor to the home.) The meter then proceeds to record what the individual watches. Using this information, combined with diaries in which other families record their viewing habits for every TV set in the house, the company releases its famous Nielsen ratings. These ratings tell the networks and local stations how popular their programs are and help them decide how much to charge for a TV ad.[6]

Criticisms of Advertising

Many people profit from advertising. Consumers use it to learn about goods and services. Businesses use it to create, build, and sustain demand for their products. The general public benefits by getting free radio and television programming and reduced prices for newspapers and magazines. Yet some important criticisms have been launched against advertising. Chapter 2 identified advertising abuses such as the "bait and switch" tactic as a consumerism issue. Other common criticisms are that advertising is misleading, increases the price of a product, and encourages materialistic values.

Is advertising misleading? Opinion polls continue to report that many people think so. Sometimes they have good reason to feel this way. Over the years, the Federal Trade Commission (FTC) has forced advertisers to modify or drop many ads. For example, the FTC made a baking company admit in its ads that about as many calories were in a loaf of their diet bread as in regular bread. The major difference was that the so-called diet bread was sliced thinner and thus had fewer calories per slice. FTC also required a company that sells mouthwash to stop claiming that its product cured colds and sore throats, and it stopped the manufacturer of an engine oil additive from claiming that the additive was equal to an engine tune-up. In an effort to prevent children from being misled, the FTC also carefully watches ads directed at this impressionable market.

Besides being misleading, many people argue that advertising merely runs up the price of a product. After all, if a firm spends $50,000 in advertising to sell 50,000 units, the sales price must somewhere reflect this $1 per unit. Thus, consumers pay for the advertising costs in the form of higher prices. Additionally, critics contend, advertising does nothing more than switch buyers from one product to another. The final result is that prices go up but no one is really any better off as a result of advertising.

Another criticism of advertising is that it creates materialistic values. It makes people want what is being advertised, affecting their purchasing habits and, in the process, altering their life-styles. For example, many people today feel compelled to buy brand-name merchandise and to have the latest-model car. This, decry the critics, is a result of advertising, which in the final analysis, traps and imprisons people. It creates expectations for material possessions that, especially for poorer people, can never be met. The result is frustration, despair, and possibly crime.

How accurate are the criticisms of advertising? On the one hand, there is undoubtedly some truth in them. On the other hand, advertising also has value for business and the society at large. It not only helps generate a demand for goods and services, but also informs buyers and helps them make more intelligent purchasing decisions.

Checkpoint

1. What are the five major advertising media?
2. How do companies measure the effectiveness of their advertising?

Personal Selling

For some products and services, advertising alone is not enough to persuade people to buy. Few people buy cars or insurance on the basis of an advertisement, and institutional buyers are equally reluctant to order major equipment or expensive services such as corporate tax-preparation assistance based on an ad. In these cases, marketers turn to personal selling.

The mix of advertising and personal selling depends upon the marketing strategy. For example, it takes considerable effort to persuade many buyers that they would be better off with a new car. Rather than pay a salesperson to make repeated calls on each potential buyer, Chrysler runs advertising to stir interest. Then salespeople at the dealership close the sale on a particular car with particular options. In contrast, Mary Kay Cosmetics relies entirely on personal selling. It may take only one selling effort to persuade a customer of the desirability of a new shade of lipstick, and the decision to buy is typically more emotional and less dependent on gathering information about the product or on comparing prices.

Types of Personal Selling

Depending on the nature of the product and the customer's needs, the salesperson may engage in order taking, missionary selling, or creative selling. Most salespeople do each of these at least occasionally.

Order taking Processing orders from customers who have decided they want to buy.

Missionary selling A type of personal selling in which one salesperson supports the sales efforts of others.

In the Original Equipment Group of Donaldson Corporation, the sales force uses creative selling. Here sales and engineering representatives concentrate on solving a customer's problem involving filtration. The solution will probably utilize products from the Original Equipment Group. This team approach to selling can be effective, because customers like to do business with companies that help them solve problems.

Source: Courtesy of Donaldson Company, Incorporated.

Order Taking The simplest type of personal selling is **order taking,** which involves processing orders from customers who have decided they want to buy. This is the major portion of the job of a retail store salesperson. It also is the task of salespeople who call on retailers, checking the store's inventory and finding out what additional products the store wants to order to replenish its shelves.

The selling function comes in when the salesperson suggests some other item to go along with the order. For example, after you have placed your order while driving through a fast-food establishment, the order taker asks, "Would you like some fries to go with that?" or "How about a hot apple pie to go with that?" This "suggestive selling" can greatly increase sales. In addition, the salesperson can build repeat business by being courteous and helpful.

Missionary Selling Salespeople who engage in **missionary selling,** which is a type of personal selling in which one salesperson supports the sales efforts of others. The objective of missionary selling is to win over supporters for the product; the supporters then buy it from other salespeople or encourage others to do so. Missionary selling is the primary activity of pharmaceutical salespeople who make calls on doctors. Such a salesperson explains the benefits of the company's medications and en-

courages the doctor to prescribe them. The salesperson also provides the physician with free samples. At the same time, other salespeople are calling on pharmacies to convince them to stock the medicine. The success of the missionary salesperson helps generate sales at the retail level; if doctors prescribe a certain brand, pharmacies will have to carry it. Similarly, a computer salesperson who tells a customer about the benefits of having the machine serviced at the company's store is generating future sales for the service department.

Creative Selling The most complex type of selling is **creative selling,** which involves determining the buyer's needs and matching them with the products for sale. For example, many buyers of computers are uncertain what to ask for. A creative salesperson starts by asking, "What do you want to do with the computer?" and then suggests a system that can handle those applications.

Sometimes creative selling involves steering buyers from their current request to a substitute that the firm has on hand. If someone comes into a store to buy a shirt or blouse and the requested style or size is not in stock, the salesperson may say, "Let me show you what we have," or "Have you thought about this style? It is very popular." In this way, the salesperson is persuading the buyer to accept a substitute. Such creative personal selling is a large part of an effective salesperson's job.

Creative selling
Determining the buyer's needs and matching them with the products for sale.

The Process of Personal Selling

Salespeople can improve their performance by making sure they are proficient at each of the six steps of the personal selling process: prospecting, approaching, presenting, handling objections, closing, and follow-up. Figure 13.4 illustrates each step in sequence.

Prospecting Personal selling begins with **prospecting,** which involves researching potential buyers and choosing those who are the most likely customers. A salesperson in a department store may try to spot shoppers

Prospecting Researching potential buyers and choosing those who are the most likely customers.

F I G U R E   13.4

The Personal Selling Process

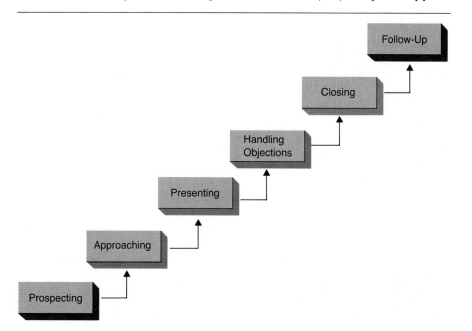

who seem to want help. Brokerage houses such as Merrill Lynch and Lehman Brothers identify high-income people, such as physicians, dentists, and other professionals, who are likely to have money to invest or need financial planning. The company prepares a financial program and presents it in such a way that it will appeal to the potential client's needs. Insurance firms such as New York Life and Prudential do the same. In many cases, salespeople identify current customers as prospects for additional products from the company.

Approaching the Prospect Armed with background information, the salesperson approaches the prospective customer. A salesperson in a retail store simply walks up to a customer who looks interested and asks, "May I help you?" Sometimes, approaching the customer is much more difficult. For example, salespeople at brokerage and insurance firms, who typically identify prospects by telephoning, may have to make repeated phone calls before getting through to the prospect. If the prospect initially shows little interest, the salesperson may have to call back several more times before being able to set up an appointment to make a presentation. Technological developments have made some salespeople more effective at this and other stages of the selling process. For an example, see "Technology Close-Up: Cellular Phones and Selling."

Cellular Phones and Selling

Many people view cellular phones as just another gimmick for status-conscious consumers. But writer Jack Falvey discovered that B. F. Goodrich has put the technology of cellular phones to work for the company's sales force. Falvey spent a day with Mike Rowland, a B. F. Goodrich sales representative, and saw the phone technology in action. As Rowland started off in the morning, he pressed a preprogrammed button that automatically dialed a customer service representative for Rowland's territory. Rowland had the customer service rep confirm his first appointment, check on the shipping status of an order for that customer, and set up an appointment for the following week with another customer.

When Rowland and Falvey pulled in for the first appointment, coffee and three engineers representing the company were ready for them. While Rowland knew from his phone call that the company's order had arrived toward the end of the preceding after-noon, the engineers hadn't yet learned of this and were impressed to find the salesperson so on top of things. The sales call proceeded smoothly.

Back on the road, Rowland called in a new order to the customer service rep and requested that some specifications be sent out. He called a restaurant to make reservations for lunch. (He had to stop the car to look up the number for that one.) Another call by the customer service rep prepared the way for the next appointment.

The rest of the day proceeded along these lines. By using cellular phones to link field sales reps such as Rowland with a central customer service rep, B. F. Goodrich is making efficient use of its sales personnel. The field sales rep can keep abreast of customer-related concerns while remaining free from doing the paperwork. Not only is this approach efficient, but the smooth service pleases customers and results in increased revenues for the company.

Making the Presentation If the prospect is interested, the salesperson then makes the presentation. The nature of the presentation depends on the good or service. In the case of financial planning, the salesperson will describe the past performance of various investments and show the prospect why it is wise to begin a particular investment program immediately. The retail salesperson will let the customer examine the product and can demonstrate how it works and discuss its attractiveness or value. An automobile salesperson will suggest that the prospect take a test drive.

To present complex and expensive products, the salesperson may rely on the support of various presentation aids. For example, insurance is an abstract concept, so a salesperson often uses charts, graphs, and even photos illustrating the benefits of insurance. To convince a prospective client to buy consulting services, a consultant brings a proposal, often bound in a handsome binder, describing what the company intends to do and what its qualifications are. To convince a group to hold a convention in its city, representatives from the city government may show the convention committee slides or a videotape describing the city's features and try to convince the group that this is the place to hold the convention.

Handling Objections Usually the salesperson handles objections after making the sales pitch. This forces the customer to focus on the sales pitch and leaves the salesperson in charge of the situation. If the customer interrupts the salesperson every few seconds with questions, the rhythm of the pitch is lost. Ideally, the sales pitch addresses and resolves commonly raised objections or questions before the prospect can raise them.

Closing After handling objections, the salesperson is ready to close the sale. Closing involves asking the prospect for the order. This is the key to any sale; everything else is preliminary. Salespeople have a number of ways of closing. One is simply to ask for the sales. For example, a salesperson may ask the customer, "Would you like to buy this TV?" A second approach is to offer a choice: "Would you like to take it with you or have it delivered?" This approach implies that the customer has already decided to buy and sometimes serves as a final nudge in helping the buyer make the purchase. Often, salespeople who are reluctant to make a closing simply start writing up the order. If the individual does not object, the sale is completed. This can be a difficult step, because the salesperson walks a fine line between losing the sale by being pushy and making the sale by being assertive.

Following Up Once a sale is completed, the salesperson must follow up on the order and ensure that the customer is satisfied. This includes making sure that delivery was on time, the goods were in proper condition, and the customer had no problem in using the purchase. The follow-up lets the customer know that the salesperson is interested in the buyer's satisfaction. It also gives the salesperson a chance to reinforce the buyer's decision. This, in turn, increases the chances the buyer will return. For example, successful car salespeople know that a key ingredient is to follow up by calls and mail to make sure the new owner is satisfied.

396

Checkpoint

1. What are the types of personal selling?
2. What steps must a salesperson take before closing a sale?

Sales Promotion

For prospects who need a nudge to make up their minds, many companies supplement advertising and personal selling with sales promotion techniques. **Sales promotion** consists of promotional activities, other than advertising and personal selling, that stimulate consumer purchasing and dealer effectiveness. This definition, drawn from the American Marketing Association, shows that sales promotion is open-ended, comprising a variety of techniques from trade shows to coupons to free samples.

Attention-Getting Techniques

One way in which marketers use sales promotion to stimulate sales is to get customers' attention. The customer may notice the product at a trade fair or on a special display. In addition, a contest or a novelty item may attract a customer to a product.

Trade Shows, Fairs, and Conventions One popular approach to sales promotion is the use of trade shows, fairs, and conventions. Often an industry organizes trade fairs in conjunction with its conventions. The industry group invites producers to display their products so that potential customers can see what is available. For example, at computer conventions, hardware and software manufacturers rent booths and display their products. At academic conventions, textbook firms display their latest offerings for professors to examine for adoption in their classes. Res-

Sales promotion
Promotional activities other than advertising and personal selling that stimulate consumer purchasing and dealer effectiveness.

One way the Paint Applicator Division of Thomas Industries tells prospective customers about its new products and merchandising displays is to exhibit at trade shows. This photo shows the division's exhibit at the National Decorating Products Show, held in St. Louis, Missouri. The prospects browsing at the exhibit include dealers for home center, hardware, and paint stores.

Source: Courtesy of Thomas Industries/Ott Photography.

taurant and food-service conventions are filled with the smells of the new products that company representatives are cooking and passing out to attendees. The companies displaying their products also send their salespeople to the convention, where they are able to make contacts with potential customers.

Point-of-Purchase Displays Marketers enlist the help of retailers to promote products by using **point-of-purchase (POP) displays.** These are in-store displays of a product that draw attention by setting the product apart and putting it in an eye-catching holder. For example, Hanes displays L'eggs pantyhose on 7-foot egg-shaped units placed in supermarkets and drugstores. Publishers often design POP displays for books that they expect to become best sellers. These cardboard stands typically use bright graphics and attention-getting headlines. POP is particularly effective in promoting unplanned purchases. Research shows that people make almost two-thirds of their buying decisions for consumer goods when in the store.

Contests Firms also generate interest in their products with contests. One of the best known is the Publishers Clearing House Sweepstakes. Another is the Reader's Digest Sweepstakes. Both of these contests offer thousands of dollars worth of prizes and prize money.

Many radio stations have their own versions of contests. For example, four times a day, a station may ask listeners to call in with the answer to a particular question, and the tenth caller with the right answer will win a prize. In other cases, the contest calls for members of the audience to send their name to the station. At various intervals during the day, the disc jockey announces the winning person's name, and if that person calls the station within a predetermined time period, such as ten minutes, the caller gets all of the money in the jackpot. If there is no winner, the station adds a certain amount to the jackpot, and the contest continues. The higher the jackpot goes, the greater the number of people who stay tuned, listening for their name.

Specialties Marketers also create awareness by giving away specialties, useful items on which the company's name is imprinted. Typical specialties are pens, hats, T-shirts, drinking glasses, coffee cups, note pads, and calculators. Specialties such as buttons and bumper stickers are usually part of the promotion effort for political candidates. In some cases, certain items have become popular enough that the company sells them rather than giving them away. For example, for the first Farm Aid concert, organized by Willie Nelson, they gave away bumper stickers or asked for a donation. For Farm Aid III, the bumper stickers cost a dollar. When the recipient uses the specialty, it serves as a reminder of the product or service and generates goodwill or, in the case of bumper stickers, publicity for the company.

Discounts and Giveaways

Marketers can also interest customers by making their product look like a good deal. A customer considering a product might be swayed by the savings from a coupon, rebate, or premium. A free sample might entice the customer to give the product a try.

Point-of-purchase (POP) displays In-store displays of a product that draw attention to it.

Couponing Marketers also use **couponing,** a sales promotion technique that offers buyers a specified discount if they redeem a coupon. Couponing is useful for persuading buyers to try a new product. It also can help build and maintain market share and ward off the competition. Customers who see two brands as similar are more likely to buy the brand for which they have a coupon. Coupons are most commonly distributed in newspapers, magazines, and direct mailings. Another technique is to print the coupon on the package of the product.

Some companies avoid using coupons because they have found that the cost of printing and processing them can be extremely high. Additionally, coupon fraud has been on the rise in recent years. In one case, federal agents arrested supermarket employees who were submitting cents-off coupons, without ever having sold the products, and keeping the refunds for themselves. Despite such ethical problems, however, couponing remains a popular sales promotion technique.

Couponing A sales promotion technique that offers buyers a specified discount if they redeem a coupon.

Refunds and Rebates Some manufacturers find that refunds or rebates are an effective way of promoting their products. One of the most common approaches is a money-back offer, such as $1 for five proofs of purchase of a certain product. On big-ticket items such as automobiles, some manufacturers have offered rebates of $500 to $1,000. These rebates have become so common that many auto buyers now seem to expect a rebate and refuse to buy a car until one is offered.[7] To avoid such situations, marketers must use rebates with care. If the rebate becomes a customer expectation, then it is no longer an effective way to promote the product.

Samples Still another form of sales promotion is the use of samples that the company gives away to customers or sells for nominal prices. Typically, the sample is a smaller version of the regular-sized good. If it is toothpaste, the tube is perhaps 20 percent of the size of a regular tube; if it is a candy bar, it is a miniature of the average size. In the case of a newspaper, magazine, or textbook, the company offers a sample in the hope that the recipient will buy a subscription or adopt the textbook for a class. Often, the company mails the samples to customers or distributes them at the store where the product is being offered.

Premiums Goods offered to potential customers as an incentive to purchase a product.

Premiums Companies can also give away **premiums.** These are goods offered to potential customers as an incentive to purchase a product. A common example is a bank that gives a free coffee percolator or toaster on all new accounts of $2,000 or more. Manufacturers and retailers of personal computers may give away certain software with the purchase of a machine so that the buyer can begin using the computer immediately.

Checkpoint

1. What are two ways in which marketers use sales promotion to get attention?
2. What are two ways in which marketers use sales promotion to make products or services seem more affordable?

Publicity and Public Relations

Seldom can a company convince the public that it is a responsible organization producing a fine product just by saying so. Most organizations find it necessary to cultivate good relations with the general public and persuade other sources to spread positive messages about the company. Consequently, companies make publicity and public relations part of their promotional strategy.

Publicity

Although advertising and publicity closely resemble one another, there are major differences between them. Both are messages about a company or its products communicated by the mass media. However, **publicity** is product- or company-related information that the firm does not pay the media to carry and that the firm does not control.[8] When new fat substitutes came on the market, the popular press compared and contrasted NutraSweet Company's Simplesse product with Procter & Gamble's Olestra.[9] The writers of the news stories, not the companies, controlled what was said about each product.

In an effort to get as much favorable publicity as possible, most large firms provide the media with news releases. These releases are typically a page or two long and describe some new development or decision by the firm. For example, a local newspaper recently ran a half-page story and accompanying picture about the very successful game Pictionary. As the head of the firm that promotes the game noted in the news story, "The thing that really got this game going was public relations."[10] All the stores in town sold out of the game after the story ran.

Publicity is especially important to small, local firms. Typically, the business's owner or a top manager makes a personal telephone call to the business editor's desk at the local paper or radio station and relates what the firm is doing and why it is newsworthy. Small firms need to take more advantage of publicity than most of them do.

One challenge of generating publicity is that most media outlets are inundated with press releases. Marketers cannot hope that every new product or promotion will receive television or newspaper coverage. Consequently, marketers try to stage events that will draw attention. For example, Austin, Minnesota, drew national attention when it celebrated the 50th year of Spam. Events in the town, where Spam was first canned, include a "hog jog," a Spam cook-off, and a parade.[11]

Public Relations

Another way in which a company indirectly communicates information about itself is through **public relations,** which comprises all activities directed toward creating and maintaining a favorable public image. Public relations activities include sponsoring events, handling consumer and press inquiries, and supporting charities. For example, to improve its public image, General Motors recently spent $20 million to set up an exhibit at the Waldorf-Astoria hotel in New York with elaborate videos and displays of its technology and arranged for its chairman to tout the company in network television interviews. GM also put eight-page advertising inserts in such publications as *Reader's Digest.* The purpose of this

Publicity Product- or company-related information that the firm does not pay the media to carry and that the firm does not control.

Public relations All activities directed toward creating and maintaining a favorable public image.

costly effort was to counteract some of the bad news surrounding the company by convincing its own people and the public that "GM still leads America's leading industry."[12] Unlike publicity, the company does have direct control over its public relations efforts.

Sponsoring charitable events is a popular method of public relations. Coca-Cola, for example, often provides free soft drinks to charities that are attempting to raise money for worthwhile causes. Tony Roma's, a national chain of spareribs restaurants, donates all of the food for the annual Miami Spinal Cord Research picnic.

Other firms sponsor sports or cultural events, or public television or radio programs. The objective of these activities is to provide enjoyment and assistance to the community at large. At the same time, the company gets its name and, in turn, its products in front of the public and is associated with being a responsible member of the community.

Checkpoint

1. What is publicity?
2. What are two common public relations techniques?

Part of Mobil's public relations program includes sponsorship of the Big Apple Games. This effort gives the company recognition while it is working on fulfilling its social responsibility. Here, as part of the Big Apple Games, football player Hershel Walker demonstrates his sprinting form for inner-city children.

Source: Courtesy of Mobil Oil Corporation.

Closing Comments

This chapter examined the elements of the promotional mix: advertising, personal selling, sales promotion, and publicity and public relations. Companies combine the use of these according to the nature of their product and the market for it. For example, Wolf Brand Chili used advertising and publicity tactics along with point-of-purchase displays to stimulate interest among consumers and retailers.

Recently, a successful businessperson observed: "I know half of my promotional dollars are wasted, but since I don't know which half, I'm not willing to cut back on my expenditures." A major challenge for marketing managers is to make sure the company is getting its money's worth out of the promotional effort. But whether or not marketers have a dependable way to do so, they know that a promotion strategy and specific techniques are necessary to make buyers aware of the products that are available.

Learning Objectives Revisited

1. **Define advertising and its basic types.**
   Advertising is a nonpersonal form of promotion designed to persuade someone to a particular point of view. Primary-demand advertising is designed to increase total demand for a particular good or service. Selective advertising is designed to increase the demand for a particular brand of product. Institutional advertising is designed to create goodwill and to build a desired image for the company. Cooperative advertising jointly promotes manufacturers and merchants, who share the advertising costs.

2. **Identify the various advertising media.**
   The five most common types of advertising media are newspapers, which continue to be the most popular form; magazines, which provide the opportunity for both national and regional coverage; radio, which helps advertisers target their market audience; TV, which allows advertisers to describe and demonstrate the product; and direct mail, which allows advertisers to cover a wide territory while focusing on a particular target market.

3. **Explain how marketers analyze the effectiveness of advertising.**
   To analyze the effectiveness of advertising, marketers use aids such as consumer pretests, which ask people to examine and rank ads based on their ability to capture and retain interest; readership reports, which ask people to look at ads that have been run and to identify those which they recognize and have read; and the Nielsen audimeter, which records the channel to which the viewer's TV is tuned.

4. **Describe the types and process of personal selling.**
   The three basic types of personal selling are creative selling, which is determining the buyer's needs and matching them with the products for sale; missionary selling, which is personal selling in support of the sales efforts of others; and order taking, which is the processing of orders from customers who have decided what they want to buy. Personal selling involves prospecting, approaching the prospect, making the presentation, handling objections, closing the sale, and following up on the sale to ensure that the customer is satisfied.

5. **Discuss the basic techniques of sales promotion.**

The basic techniques of sales promotion include attention-getting techniques such as trade-show and convention displays, point-of-purchase (POP) displays, contests, specialty items, and discounts and giveaways such as coupons, refunds, samples, and premiums.

6. **Relate the roles that publicity and public relations play in promotion.**

Publicity is product- or company-related information that the company does not control and does not pay the mass media to carry. Companies rely on publicity to help keep their name in front of the public and to create a positive image. Public relations comprises all activities whose objective is to create and maintain a favorable public image. Business firms do this in many ways, such as sponsoring sports and cultural events, public television, and so forth. Along with bringing the company's name and products to the public's attention, these activities provide enjoyment and assistance to the community at large and show the company to be a responsible member of the community.

Key Terms Reviewed

Review each of the following terms. For any that you do not know or are unsure of, look up the definitions and see how they are used in the chapter.

advertising	order taking
primary-demand advertising	missionary selling
selective advertising	creative selling
institutional advertising	prospecting
cooperative advertising	sales promotion
network ad	point-of-purchase (POP) displays
spot ad	
local ad	couponing
consumer pretest	premiums
readership report	publicity
people-meter	public relations

Review Questions

1. If a manufacturer of snow skis wants to increase sales, to whom should the company promote the product: retailers or consumers? Explain.
2. Of the basic types (not media) of advertising, which is used most? Why do you think it is?
3. Which kind of advertising do you think the Florida Citrus Commission would use most? Why?
4. If stories about a car's defects were hurting the reputation of its maker, which kind of advertising do you think it would use? Why?
5. Ultimate Bike Company has just introduced a programmable bicycle. How should the company's advertising message change as its product moves through its life cycle?

6. Which media would you use for advertising each of the following products? Explain your choices.
   a. Used cars
   b. Xerox copiers
   c. The latest concert series at the local auditorium
   d. Diet Pepsi
7. Marketers spend more for newspaper ads than for ads in any other medium. What benefits of newspaper advertising help account for its popularity?
8. If you were targeting a local market, would television advertising ever be appropriate? If so, explain what circumstances would make it appropriate.
9. How do advertisers evaluate print ads? How do they evaluate broadcast ads?
10. What criticisms have been leveled against advertisements? What benefits does advertising offer?
11. Roger Mills sells business forms. His employer prints and sells standardized forms or will print forms to the client's specifications. What type of selling should Roger engage in? Explain.
12. Eloise Churchman thinks that because she only sells dresses in a clothing store, she doesn't need to bother with presenting the product. However, sales in her department are not meeting expectations. How can Eloise use the presentation step in the personal selling process to boost sales?
13. What sales promotion techniques would you recommend for each of the following situations? Explain your choices.
    a. A record company wants to boost sales of an album by a popular rock group.
    b. A small Mexican restaurant in a suburb of a large city wants to build business among neighborhood residents.
    c. A national food company wants to introduce a new line of tea.
14. What is publicity? How do managers go about getting publicity for their companies?
15. Why are business firms interested in public relations?

Applied Exercises

1. Look through recent issues of *Time, Newsweek, Business Week, Fortune,* or *Forbes.* Identify examples of primary-demand advertising, selective advertising, and institutional advertising. Explain how you were able to identify each ad.
2. Visit a firm that advertises and find out how the managers evaluate the effectiveness of the ads. Compare your answers to those of others in the class.
3. Visit a company that relies heavily on personal selling. Interview two of the salespeople and write down examples of how, if at all, they use creative selling, missionary selling, and order taking. Find out how they carry out each step in the personal selling process. Compare your answers with those of others in the class.
4. Choose a large local firm and interview a top manager regarding how the firm uses publicity and public relations to promote itself and its products or services. Report your findings to the rest of the class.

Your Business IQ: Answers

1. True. The top ten advertisers each spend more than half a billion dollars annually. Over 100 firms spend more than $100 million a year to advertise.
2. False. Although TV advertising expenditures have increased greatly in recent years, advertisers still spend more on newspaper advertising than on any other type.
3. False. The first step in personal selling is to prospect — to research potential buyers and choose the ones most likely to become customers. The seller then approaches those prospective buyers and presents the product's benefits.
4. True. Many companies are discovering that printing and processing coupons can be extremely costly. Fraudulent redemption of coupons for products not sold also adds to the cost of couponing. Nevertheless, this promotional technique has remained popular.
5. False. Companies that use publicity do not pay the media to carry the message, but they do bear other costs. For example, a business may have to pay someone to write a press release, or the company may incur expenses to create a newsworthy occasion. Compared to advertising, however, publicity is an inexpensive way to spread a message.

General Mills Launches the Oatmeal Wars

For years, Quaker Oats Company has dominated the market for oatmeal, and its current share is about two-thirds of the market. Despite this intimidating competition, General Mills has launched a new product: Total Oatmeal.

General Mills decided to attack the competition by advertising that its product has "more nutrition than any other hot cereal." Unlike Quaker Oats, Total Oatmeal is sprayed with a mixture of vitamins and minerals that gives it 100 percent of the recommended daily allowance of ten vitamins and minerals. The company spent $12 million and distributed 175 million coupons in a six-month advertising and promotional campaign. The company is also promoting to grocers, using a promotional piece in which a box of Total Oatmeal towers over a tipped and leaking box of Quaker Oats.

Quaker was quick to plan retaliatory strategy. It developed a "sensible nutrition" advertising campaign budgeted at $35 million for the first year. Quaker made plans to give away 12.5 million packages of its instant oatmeal in boxes of its cold cereal and to use a game promotion with prizes of microwave ovens and cookware. Quaker fortified its Apple Raisin Walnut flavor of instant oatmeal to match the nutrition in Total Oatmeal. Quaker also took General Mills to court for using its Quaker Man logo on the Total Oatmeal box and for claiming that Total Oatmeal is more nutritious than Quaker Oats.

In its promotion to grocers, General Mills announced, "We're about to set the hot cereal category on its ear." If General Mills can win the tough battle, it will do what no other company has yet been able to do in the hot cereal market.

Case Questions

1. Based on the description, which elements of the promotional mix discussed in this chapter is General Mills using to introduce Total Oatmeal? Which elements is Quaker Oats using in its counterattack?
2. What type(s) of advertising has General Mills used so far for Total Oatmeal? How does this fit with the promotional strategy for this product?
3. How can General Mills improve its promotional mix to stand up to Quaker Oats?

You Be the Adviser: Helping Bill Get Started

Bill Hartack is in the process of opening a hardware store. Bill has had 20 years of experience in this business, most of it working for a large hardware chain in the Northeast. Last year, for health reasons, Bill moved to a southwestern state. Drawing on his early-retirement income and his savings, Bill has more than enough money to start a store of his own.

Bill's location is on the west side of town. This area is not densely settled, but the rent is quite low and if Bill can attract a clientele drawn from throughout the town, he can make the operation profitable. Bill will have four salespeople working with him, and two others will staff the back office.

Right now Bill is in the process of doing two things. First, he is trying to write interesting, effective ads that will attract customers and acquaint the community with his store. Second, he has to train the salespeople in selling techniques, since none of them have had much experience in this area.

Bill has three weeks before his store is scheduled to open. During this time, he intends to devote his efforts to the advertising and personal selling activities. The biggest problems confronting him are that he has no experience in writing ads and that although he feels he knows a lot about selling, he has never received formal instruction on how to sell. Nevertheless, Bill is determined to deal with these two issues.

Your Advice

1. What type of advertising media would you recommend that Bill use? Why?
2. How can Bill determine the effectiveness of his advertising efforts? What would you suggest that he do? Explain.
3. What type of training in personal selling would you recommend that Bill give to his people? What do they need to know? Briefly describe what Bill should teach his sales staff.

Wholesaling, Retailing, and Physical Distribution

LEARNING OBJECTIVES

- Define the nature and types of channels of distribution.
- Explain the benefits of using wholesalers.
- Identify the types of wholesalers.

- Describe the types of retailers.
- Discuss the nature and functions of physical distribution.
- Present the major modes of transportation.

Your Business IQ

How much do you already know about wholesaling, retailing, and physical distribution? Test your business IQ by labeling each statement *true* or *false*. Answers and explanations are at the end of the chapter.

1. Wholesalers and retailers (sometimes called intermediaries) help producers in a variety of ways, but unfortunately for consumers, they add to the final price of goods without adding to their value.

2. Small producers are less likely to sell through wholesalers and retailers than are large businesses.

3. In recent years, more and more manufacturers have been opening stores that sell directly to consumers.

4. Railroads carry more freight than any other mode of transportation.

5. Pipelines are one of the least costly ways to transport goods.

This truck is part of the wholesale food distribution business of a subsidiary of IU International Corporation. The subsidiary buys from food producers and sells to retailers such as this restaurant. It delivers at night so the restaurant will have fresh food when it opens for business the next day.

Looking Back and Ahead

The Izod alligator was once an emblem of high fashion on polo shirts; then, in the mid-1980s, sales took a dive. Now Izod is trying for a comeback. Besides making changes in product design and manufacturing, the company is taking a hard look at who sells the company's clothing. Izod's problem stems from losing its original elite image by allowing its shirts to be sold in discount stores. Says the company's chairman, "You no longer wanted to go to your country club in an Izod shirt when your chauffeur was wearing the same shirt." To upgrade the brand's image, the company is trying to withdraw from discount stores and regenerate interest among upscale department stores.[1]

As the Izod story illustrates, developing and advertising a product do not guarantee its success. Therefore, marketers supplement the promotional activities described in the preceding chapter with a strategy for distributing their products. This strategy includes decisions about using wholesalers and retailers as well as about the physical means of moving goods from producer to consumer.

To address these concerns, this chapter examines the channels through which products move and the outlets that sell the products. The heart of the chapter describes the two major marketing outlets: wholesalers and retailers. The chapter concludes with a discussion of physical distribution, especially the ways companies transport goods.

Placement or Distribution: Making Products Available

In Chapter 11, you learned that marketing adds utility to products by making them available at convenient times and in convenient locations and by providing a way for customers to obtain ownership of them. A marketer's efforts to do this constitute one of the four Ps in the marketing mix: placement, also called distribution. Thus, when Wendy's arranges for franchisees to sell its hamburgers at conveniently located outlets, it is fulfilling its distribution function. When Wendy's sets up a test project to let customers in selected locations pay for their hamburgers with electronic banking cards,[2] it is also carrying out this function.

When business people think of distribution, they usually focus more narrowly on how companies move their products from where they are produced to where they are sold to the final customer. This decision has two parts: identifying the most effective path of intermediaries for distributing the product and, in the case of tangible goods, determining the most efficient way to physically move and store the goods. The first part of the chapter describes selecting a path for distribution; the last part discusses moving and storing goods.

Channels of Distribution

Channel of distribution
The path a product follows from production to final sale.

Wholesaler An intermediary that normally purchases goods and sells them to buyers for the purpose of resale.

The path a product follows from production to final sale is the **channel of distribution** for that product. Besides the manufacturer and the ultimate user, the channel may contain one or more intermediaries: wholesalers and retailers. A **wholesaler** is an intermediary that normally purchases goods and sells them to buyers for the purpose of resale. A **retailer** is an intermediary that sells goods and services to the final consumer.

Consumers sometimes complain that intermediaries increase the price of the products. However, despite the often-heard cry to "eliminate the middleman" (another term for an intermediary), intermediaries serve an important role in business. They simplify and make more efficient the exchange process between buyer and seller.

Figure 14.1 shows a simple example of how this works. Suppose an apple grower, a baker, a butcher, and a dairy farmer want to sell their products to four households. Without intermediaries, the sales would require 16 (four times four) exchanges. To buy their groceries, the households would have to chase around from seller to seller. But with a grocer acting as intermediary, only 8 exchanges are required. With more sellers and buyers, the use of intermediaries becomes considerably more important.

Retailer An intermediary that sells goods and services to the final consumer.

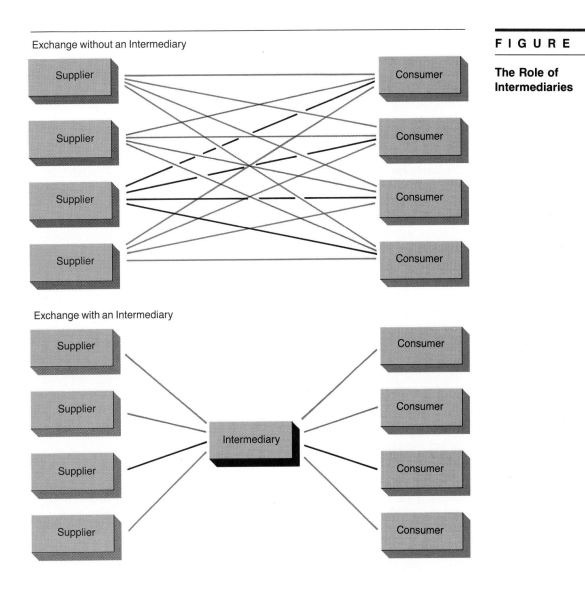

Exchange without an Intermediary

Exchange with an Intermediary

F I G U R E 14.1

The Role of Intermediaries

Today, enormous variety in the types of intermediaries brings great diversity to marketing channels. Customers may buy from tiny boutiques, giant department stores, sidewalk vendors, factory outlets, warehouses, hypermarkets, catalogs, and more. But the basic patterns of the channels are more limited. The choices available depend on whether the marketer is selling industrial or consumer goods.

Channels for Industrial Goods Industrial goods, as defined in Chapter 11, are those used in the production of other products. Machinery and office supplies are examples. Businesses commonly purchase them for use in operations or in providing goods and services to their own customers. Figure 14.2 shows the two common types of distribution channels used for industrial goods.

Direct channel A distribution channel that bypasses all intermediaries.

Most often, marketers of industrial goods use a **direct channel,** which bypasses all intermediaries. The company that produces the product sends out salespeople or catalogs to sell it. For example, a company that builds custom machinery might receive an order for a particular type of lathe, build it to customer specifications, and then ship it directly to the buyer. Most aircraft manufacturers use a direct channel. For example, United might order 50 aircraft from Lockheed, which will manufacture and deliver the planes directly to the airline.

In other cases, the manufacturer uses a wholesaler to distribute the product. This is common when the producer does not want to go through the bother of building a sales force or is just getting into the business and has, at best, only a few customers. The manufacturer needs someone to sell the product and turns to a wholesaler.

Channels for Consumer Goods Slightly different choices are available to marketers of consumer goods—products that are destined to be sold to the final consumer. In moving from manufacturer to consumer, these goods typically take one of the three routes illustrated in Figure 14.3.

Some manufacturers use a direct channel, selling to consumers themselves. For example, some producers set up their own retail outlets. Goodyear Tire and Rubber sells its tires through company-owned tire outlets.

Other manufacturers sell to consumers through a retailer. A good example is a discount chain such as Wal-Mart that purchases directly from manufacturers and then passes the savings along to customers. Auto dealers also buy from manufacturers.

Some situations call for a more complex channel: manufacturer to wholesaler to retailer to consumer. Many retailers use this channel be-

FIGURE 14.2

Distribution Channels for Industrial Goods

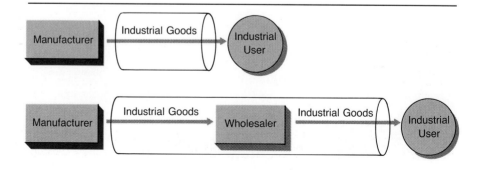

cause they cannot afford to buy in large quantities from the manufacturer. They have to rely on a wholesaler to supply them with smaller shipments as well as other services. Companies that sell their product through many stores also find wholesalers helpful.

Many businesses use more than one channel. Magazine publishers use routes such as selling to subscribers through direct channels (subscriptions) and to single-copy buyers through retailers (over-the-counter sales). Large general-merchandise retailers such as Sears and J. C. Penney use different forms of a direct channel: mail-order catalogs and retail outlets. General Motors sells cars directly to the government and to rental car companies (Hertz, Avis, National, and Budget), while using its dealers to handle retail sales to the average single-car buyer. Issues related to a novel channel for prescription drugs are stirring controversy, as described in "Business Ethics Close-Up: New Channels for Pharmaceuticals."

F I G U R E   14.3

Distribution Channels for Consumer Goods

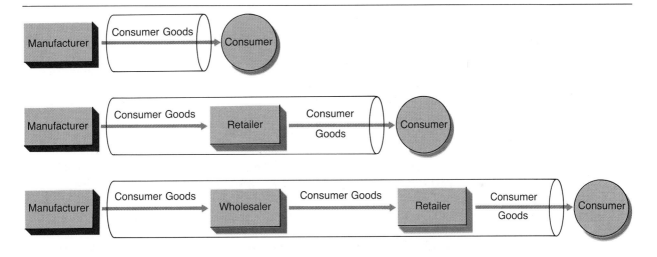

The jet fuel Citgo sells to airlines is an industrial good. The company uses a direct channel, delivering it in trucks to 21 major airports. In this way, Citgo supplies 6 percent of the nation's aviation turbine fuel.

Source: Courtesy of CITGO Petroleum Corporation.

Channel Strategies

Why do some companies use one type of channel, while others use a different channel or a combination of channels? The answer depends on the company's strategy. Marketers develop a strategy by considering the nature of the product and customers and the extent of the company's resources.

Product Considerations Companies that make complex products for which quality and service are important tend to use the shortest channels. For example, a consulting firm will sell its services directly to clients, so that company representatives can discuss how the firm can meet the client's specific needs. A company that sells computers may choose a direct channel because customers will expect the company to service the products and answer questions. The closeness to the customer provided by a direct channel gives the manufacturer more control over the service accompanying the product.

BUSINESS ETHICS   CLOSE-UP

New Channels for Pharmaceuticals

Over the last few decades, pharmaceuticals companies have adopted a two-pronged approach to selling prescription drugs: convincing doctors to prescribe them, and convincing pharmacists to carry them in their drugstores. The doctor writes a prescription, and the patient has it filled in a pharmacy.

More recently, a new approach with ethical implications is being tried. Under this approach, intermediaries, called repackagers, buy drugs in bulk and resell them to doctors in convenient, patient-size dosages. The doctors then sell the drugs directly to their patients, rather than having them make a trip to the pharmacy.

In some cases, it is argued, this does patients a big favor. For example, certain cancer patients have had to go to the drugstore to purchase drugs and then return to the doctor to have them injected. In this case, buying drugs from the doctor saves extra running around. Furthermore, doctors often charge less for a drug than a pharmacy does. Patients may also be more likely to get their prescription filled; surveys showed that about 20 percent of prescriptions are never filled under the current system.

Nevertheless, this new marketing channel has raised ethical questions. For example, the National Association of Retail Druggists complains that profits from selling drugs will tempt doctors to overcharge, overprescribe, or prescribe whatever the doctor has on hand instead of what will be most effective. Druggists also maintain that they serve as a check on physician mistakes and can help prevent harmful combinations or excessive dosages by keeping records of all the medications a patient is taking. Consequently, druggists have tried to persuade Congress and state legislatures to pass laws forbidding physicians from selling drugs or limiting the circumstances in which they can do so.

In fact, doctors may never become the major dispensers of drugs. For example, visiting a doctor can be an inconvenient and expensive way to get a refill. Also, doctors seldom keep the long hours of most pharmacies. Thus, it may come as no surprise that dispensing through doctors now accounts for only one-tenth of 1 percent of the market for prescription drugs.

If they use an intermediary, companies that sell expensive and complex products may allow only one intermediary to distribute the product in a given area. This approach is called **exclusive distribution.** For example, General Motors arranges for Buick, Cadillac, and Chevrolet dealers to sell these products exclusively in one area. This allows each dealer to sell an acceptable number of cars without cutting into another dealer's sales. Limiting the number of distributors is another way the manufacturer can keep more control over distribution and maintain its reputation for quality.

For products that are less complex but that do have quality and style differences, companies use distribution channels that help them set the product apart. Companies that want to differentiate their products also limit the number of intermediaries that handle their product. The example at the beginning of this chapter showed that selling Izod shirts only through selected stores is an important part of maintaining the image of the brand. Likewise, until recently, the ice cream shops licensed to use the Häagen Dazs name could sell the entire line of flavors, while grocery stores were limited to only a few flavors. Allowing only a few intermediaries to distribute a product is called **selective distribution.**

In the case of products of standard quality, customers look for convenience as well as low price. Customers will not travel to the other side of town to buy a particular brand of milk or paper clips. For these products, companies use **intensive distribution,** in which the producer sells its goods through every available outlet. Milk is available in grocery stores, convenience stores, and vending machines. Paper clips can be purchased in office-supply stores, drugstores, department stores, and

Wholesaling, Retailing, and Physical Distribution

Exclusive distribution
A channel strategy in which only one intermediary distributes a product in a given area.

Selective distribution
A channel strategy in which only a few intermediaries distribute a product.

Intensive distribution
A channel strategy in which the producer sells its product through every available outlet.

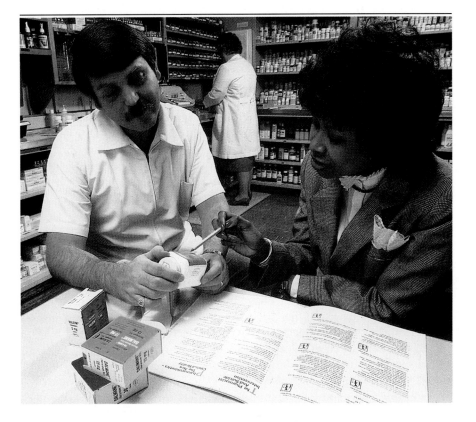

A representative for Hoffman–La Roche discusses a product with a hospital pharmacist.

hardware stores, and through catalogs. Companies using intensive distribution often depend heavily on wholesalers to get their products into these various outlets. In fact, the company may use several wholesalers.

Companies that produce services instead of goods usually employ direct channels. The reason is because the customer must be present when services are produced.

Customer Considerations The nature of their customers also gives marketers some clues about the most appropriate distribution channel. For example, if a company's customers are clustered geographically, the company may use a direct channel. If the customers are widely dispersed, intermediaries become more important. Likewise, companies with several target markets may use several channels, while companies with one specific target market will more likely use a single, possibly direct channel.

Changes in markets lead companies to take a new look at their marketing channels. For example, households today are less likely to have someone home during business hours than was the case 30 years ago. Fuller Brush Company traditionally sold its brushes and home-cleaning products through door-to-door salespeople. However, it has responded to the change in customer habits by opening test stores in Texas. The company also sells its products through direct-mail catalogs.[3] Another trend is that American incomes increasingly can be classified into extremes of high and low. This means that stores with a reputation for low prices, such as Wal-Mart or K mart, and high-status retailers, such as Neiman-Marcus or Lord & Taylor, currently tend to prosper at the expense of midlevel department stores. Manufacturers often find they must choose a strategy that is either very selective or very broad.

Company Considerations In selecting a distribution channel, the company also has to consider its own strengths and limitations. A large manufacturer may find that selling directly to retailers or through its own stores enables it to pass along to customers the savings gained in bypassing a wholesaler. In contrast, small or young companies are often unable to afford the sales force necessary to get the product to all interested buyers.

A well-known brand name is another company strength. One reason that Fuller Brush has done well with catalogs is that many consumers already recognize and trust the name. In contrast, a buyer might be reluctant to order an unknown brand sight unseen from a catalog. In that case, the name of a reputable distributor might be helpful.

Vertical Marketing Systems

In the past, most marketing channels evolved over time and were basically unplanned. As producers and intermediaries realized the need to open a more direct channel to have more control over distribution or to expand volume by extending the present one and involving other intermediaries, they took a more proactive approach and changed the marketing channel. In recent years, however, some managers have established planned distribution systems in which all levels are brought under unified control. Such a system is called a **vertical marketing system (VMS).** The producer of the product may own the distributors in

Vertical marketing system (VMS) A planned distribution system in which all levels are brought under unified control.

the VMS (an example would be Firestone), or it may establish contractual agreements with channel members (an example would be a franchisor such as Burger King or a wholesaler-sponsored chain of retail stores such as Western Auto).

Checkpoint

1. What is a channel of distribution?
2. What do companies consider when deciding what intermediaries to include in a channel of distribution?

Wholesalers

When most people think of wholesalers, they think of the intermediaries that provide a link between producers and retailers. However, wholesalers may also sell to industrial users or to other wholesalers. Wholesalers are an important part of the marketing function because of the benefits they provide to manufacturers and to the intermediaries (mostly retailers) that follow them in the marketing channel.

Benefits of Wholesalers

Producers or manufacturers use wholesalers because they perform functions that the producers cannot perform as efficiently or at all. The producer may turn to the wholesaler for help with some or all of the following activities:

Carrying inventory. Wholesalers buy inventory, which they in turn sell to retailers or other customers. Without wholesalers, manufacturers would bear the burden and, more importantly, the expense of keeping all of this inventory on hand.

Providing a sales force. Wholesalers can serve as the manufacturer's sales force. This frees the manufacturer from the substantial time and effort required to recruit, train, and maintain salespeople.

Providing marketing information and support. Wholesalers deal with hundreds of retailers and generally have a clear idea of what the marketplace wants. By feeding this information back to the producers, wholesalers help producers decide what to produce and in what quantities. Wholesalers also assist producers in the marketing effort. They may design store displays or advertise the product.

Retailers and industrial customers often would rather buy from wholesalers than from producers. The reason is that they, too, benefit from some of the services wholesalers provide. Wholesalers' customers turn to them for some of the following services:

Breaking bulk. Wholesalers can help both large- and small-volume retailers by breaking large shipments into smaller ones that meet each retailer's particular demand. For example, a paper company might ship out pallets stacked with 10-ream cartons of copier paper. A wholesaler could buy a few pallets and then sell offices a single carton or even a few reams.

Providing credit. Wholesalers often give their retail customers better credit terms than they could get if they purchased directly from the manufacturer. They keep closer tabs on the retailer and are thus willing to take higher risks. Small retailers, in particular, often need this break in order to survive.

Providing marketing information. Wholesalers, thanks to their contacts with competitive retailers, often know what is selling and what to stock for the upcoming season. These insights are extremely valuable to retailers, many of whom have limited access to such sources of information.

Choosing a Wholesaler

Producers that decide to include wholesalers in their channels of distribution need to consider which wholesaler services they require and which services will be important to their customers. Different wholesalers provide different combinations of services, such as breaking bulk or providing marketing information. This means that a producer can select a wholesaler based on marketing objectives. However, industry tradition sometimes makes it harder for a producer to choose a type of wholesaler. To ease this problem, Wal-Mart Corporation has created Sam's Warehouse Clubs (named after the founder and head, Sam Walton), to serve as an intermediary for small retail merchants. Small retailers can shop at Sam's Warehouses and take advantage of buying a small amount of merchandise at a relatively low price. Also, because the Wal-Mart buyers know what will be in high demand, the small retailer can also take advantage of this marketing knowledge when shopping at a Sam's Warehouse. However, clothing manufacturers have typically not used this method of wholesaling, and whether it will be successful remains to be seen.

McKesson Corporation helps retailers with ordering and inventory control. This store employee is using McKesson's Econoscan ordering equipment. The electronic pen in the man's right hand reads the bar codes on the shelf labels. The employee can then add an attachment to the calculator in his left hand, connect it to a telephone receiver, and send ordering information to McKesson's central computer center. McKesson then fills the order, delivering it to the store along with automatically printed labels for the products.

Source: © John Blaustein 1987 for McKesson Corporation.

To make informed choices, marketers need to be aware of the major types of wholesalers. These fall into three general categories: merchant wholesalers, manufacturer-owned wholesalers, and agent intermediaries. Figure 14.4 illustrates these categories.

Merchant Wholesalers The largest group of wholesalers, accounting for approximately 80 percent of all wholesale business, are **merchant wholesalers.** These intermediaries actually buy, or take title to, goods. After purchasing merchandise, the merchant wholesaler sells it to retailers. Producers usually prefer this approach because a wholesaler that buys the merchandise is assuming the risks of ownership and immediately owes money to the producer.

Some merchant wholesalers provide a wide variety of services to customers. Typical services include storing the goods and then delivering them to the customer as needed, restocking the shelves as required, and providing financial assistance in helping the retailer pay for the goods. Other merchant wholesalers carry out only some of the wholesaling functions. For example, many do not offer financial arrangements to the buyer. Others may own the goods but never physically take possession of them.

Manufacturer-Owned Wholesalers Some manufacturers prefer the control of owning their own wholesaler. While manufacturer-owned wholesalers account for only 10 percent of wholesale business, they are common among some of the largest corporations in America. For example, rather than have an independent wholesaler handle their output, the major automakers each have their own wholesale arm. So do most of the large companies in the chemical and petroleum products industries.

While owning a wholesale operation means that the company must incur the effort and risks of the wholesale business, some companies are large enough to cut distribution costs this way and pass the savings along to their customers. Manufacturer-owned wholesalers are also advantageous to companies selling a product for which service is important. Construction and farm equipment producers are examples. These firms often find that their own outlets provide faster and more reliable service to customers. In addition, if customers need technical assistance or advice, the manufacturer can provide it better than anyone else.

Merchant wholesalers
Intermediaries that take title to the goods they distribute.

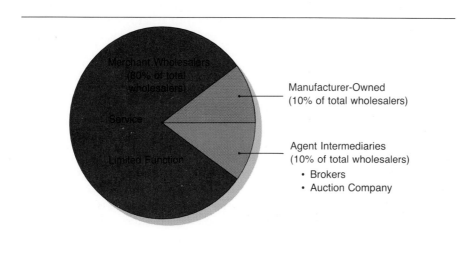

F I G U R E   14.4

Common Types of Wholesalers

Agent intermediaries
Wholesalers that do not take title to the goods they distribute.

Broker An agent intermediary that brings buyers and sellers together.

Agent Intermediaries Some wholesalers do not take title to (do not own) the goods they exchange. Although the producer would like to sell to the intermediary and thus reduce risk, this is not always possible. Such a wholesaler, called an **agent intermediary,** provides other services to the buyer or seller, in exchange for which this intermediary receives a commission or fee.

A common type of agent intermediary is the **broker,** who brings buyers and sellers together. In the real estate business, brokers help people buy and sell houses. Not all salespeople in real estate are brokers, but only brokers have the necessary license to buy and sell. Brokers also work in the financial securities markets, where they buy and sell stock for customers. In some cases, brokers receive their commission from the buyer, as in the case of a business person who uses a broker to purchase some used machinery. In other cases, the broker receives a commission from the seller, as in the case of a couple who use a real estate broker to sell their house.

Agent intermediaries can take many forms. Some represent several noncompeting manufacturers, while others specialize in, say, grocery products. Some agent intermediaries handle the company's entire marketing job in a particular geographic area, from pricing to advertising to selling the product. Sellers of tobacco, livestock, used cars, and art often turn to auction companies, which provide a common place for buyers and sellers to come together. Companies that do not have a salesperson in a particular locale to handle a transaction there may turn to an agent intermediary that sells goods on commission. Thus, even companies with limited means can usually find a suitable wholesaler.

Checkpoint

1. What are the three broad categories of wholesalers?
2. What are three ways in which wholesalers benefit producers?

Retailers

Producers of consumer products often rely on retailers to make those products available at convenient times and locations. Consequently, as Figure 14.5 shows, there has been a slow but steady increase in retail sales in the 1980s, reaching over $125 billion in recent years. Besides large and well-known retailers such as Sears, J. C. Penney, Wal-Mart, and K mart, many small retail outlets provide opportunities for people interested in sales, management, and entrepreneurship.

Choosing a Retailer

Companies that decide to channel their goods through retailers must answer some seemingly basic questions that are becoming increasingly complicated. Managers of goods-producing firms must decide whether to sell through stores, nonstore retailing, or both. Then they must decide which stores will make their products convenient enough, maintain the desired image, and sell at the right price. Choosing stores is also complicated by changes resulting from scrambled merchandising and strategy shifts.

Scrambled Merchandising Years ago, producers had an easier time identifying the right retailer for their product. People bought groceries at grocery stores, fabric at dry-goods stores, and medicine at pharmacies. However, this has changed over the last two decades because of scrambled merchandising. **Scrambled merchandising** consists of diversifying the store's selection of products in order to increase sales volume. For example, grocery stores became supermarkets, and many now offer a variety of drugs, toiletries, alcoholic beverages, small appliances, and more. Today's average supermarket shopper is exposed to 17,000 products in a shopping visit that lasts less than 30 minutes.[4] Sears, which started off selling general merchandise, now offers optical, legal, real estate, financial, and insurance services as well.[5] Today Coldwell Banker, which is part of Sears, is the largest real estate company in the country, and Sears's long-range plan for Dean Witter Reynolds, Inc., should soon make it the country's third-largest stock brokerage.[6]

Strategy Shifts Besides adding merchandise, stores often adjust their marketing strategies over time. Like other businesses, many stores start out by attempting to establish a foothold with a low-price strategy. However, as they encounter competition and the market matures, these stores begin offering more services and upgraded products. For example, K mart originally started as a low-price outlet, but in recent years has tried to upgrade its image and set itself apart from other low-price retailers by changing the decor of its stores and using personalities such as Jaclyn Smith and Martha Stewart to promote some of its merchandise.[7] In other cases, stores use special promotional strategies to differentiate their units from those of the competition.[8] For example, Burger King stresses "having it your way" in their ads to differentiate their burgers from those of McDonald's.

Types of Retail Stores

Not only is retailing changeable, but there are a wide variety of stores. Sometimes the types of stores overlap and the distinctions may be blurry. One way to understand the different types of retail stores is to divide them into categories by what they offer consumers: variety, specialty, and low price. Figure 14.6 illustrates the types of stores in each category.

Scrambled merchandising
Diversifying the store's selection of products in order to increase sales volume.

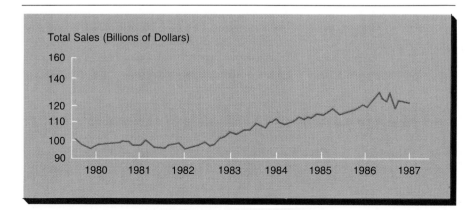

F I G U R E   14.5

Growth in Retail Sales

Total Sales (Billions of Dollars)

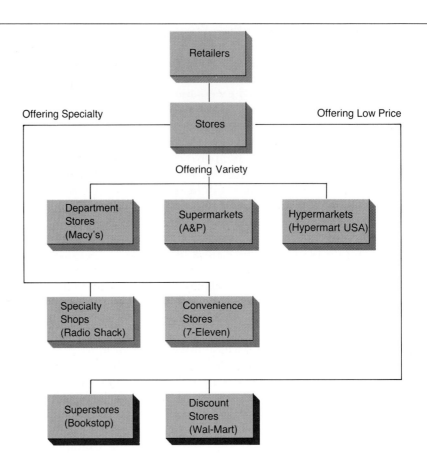

Stores Offering Variety Some stores offer a variety of food and personal-care items; other stores offer a variety of more expensive goods. The broad selection attracts many customers from all walks of life. This makes the stores important for producers with a mass-merchandising strategy.

Most common today are **department stores,** which are relatively large and offer a wide variety of merchandise grouped into departments, such as housewares, electronic equipment, men's clothing, and cosmetics. These stores are popular because they allow the customer to do a great deal of shopping under one roof. Consequently, developers of shopping centers or malls try to get at least one department store such as J. C. Penney or Macy's to locate there and draw customers.

People who want variety in food offerings shop at **supermarkets,** large stores that sell a wide variety of food products as well as some non-food items. Unlike the original grocery stores, supermarkets operate on a self-service basis. They emphasize low price and customer convenience. Because the markup on food is so low, many have added nonfood items that have large markups, especially **impulse items,** which are goods that consumers buy on the spur of the moment, such as magazines, razor blades, and gum. One marketing research firm concludes that 60 percent of supermarket purchases are unplanned.[9] In recent years, super-market managers have found that some of the most profitable products are those that offer freshness and convenience, so they have set up in-store bakeries, delis, and seafood counters.[10]

Department store A large store that offers a wide variety of merchandise grouped into departments.

Supermarket A large store that sells a wide variety of food products as well as some nonfood offerings.

Impulse items Goods that consumers buy on the spur of the moment.

Competition among supermarkets has become fierce. In response, some supermarkets try to differentiate themselves from their competitors by offering gourmet foods, check-cashing services, extended hours of operation, and free carryout service. In St. Louis, for example, Dierbergs Markets offer FTD florists, full-service banks, post offices, and videocassette rentals. The grocery chain was the first to provide motorized shopping carts for the handicapped. The store's managers have found that educating shoppers about food increases sales, so several of the stores have home economists on the premises to answer shoppers' questions. Dierbergs also provides information through a quarterly newsletter titled "Customer Club News," demonstrations of recipes featuring in-season produce, and five cooking schools. According to Dierbergs' consumer services director, people who learn quick and easy methods of cooking will eat at home more.[11]

Taking the expansion of supermarkets one step further are **hypermarkets,** giant stores selling a combination of grocery items and general merchandise, from fresh shrimp to stereos. These stores, which originated in Europe a quarter-century ago, emphasize convenience because they offer so much under one roof. They are also able to offer low prices because their enormous size gives them bargaining leverage with suppliers. One French-based chain, Carrefour, even sells insurance through a subsidiary and is considering branching into other financial services as well.[12] Wal-Mart has recently launched into the hypermarket concept, sometimes called "malls without walls." Their Hypermart USA is a combination discount store and supermarket in 200,000 or more square feet.

Hypermarket A giant store selling a combination of groceries and general merchandise at low prices.

Stores Offering Specialty Some stores target specific market segments by offering specialized goods or services such as high-fashion shoes, quality stereo components, or fast service. The targeted approach of these stores often makes them appropriate outlets for producers that want to maintain a quality image or reach customers with special interests.

An example of a retail outlet that specializes in fast service is a **convenience store.** Many of these stores sell only fast-moving merchandise such as bread, beer, milk, cigarettes, and snack foods. 7-Eleven and Kwik Shops are good examples. In recent years, gasoline retailers have begun to emulate this approach by setting up stations that sell fast-moving grocery products in addition to gasoline. Consumers patronize convenience stores for their long hours as well as their quick service.

Convenience store A limited-line store that specializes in fast service.

Many find specialty retailing an attractive way to start a business because it is suitable for small stores. However, to compete with the broad appeal of stores offering variety, specialized stores often have to use ingenuity to attract customers. Sunglass Huts, for example, locates its kiosks (a type of open booth) in the busy aisles of shopping malls or under mall escalators. Specially trained salespeople convince shoppers of the benefits of Sunglass Huts' quality sunglasses, which cost from $35 to $80 a pair. This strategy has paid off: At the oldest outlet, sales run $5,200 per square foot—a retailing record.[13]

Stores Offering Low Prices As you learned in Chapter 12, many companies adopt a marketing strategy emphasizing low price. This strategy is not limited to manufacturers; a variety of retail outlets feature a low-price strategy. Such stores are particularly suitable for products targeted

Discount store A retail store that offers lower prices and fewer customer services than other retailers.

to a broad segment of the population: customers interested in prices.

While many kinds of retailers can keep prices down, discount stores and catalog stores really focus on low price. A **discount store** is an outlet that offers lower prices and fewer customer services than other retail stores. When these stores first emerged, they limited their offerings to hard goods, such as radios, TVs, cameras, and typewriters. Today, they offer a wide variety of merchandise, including clothing, toys, sporting goods, office supplies, and home and garden supplies. K mart and Wal-Mart, for example, offer a variety of products at low prices. New retailers such as the Texas-based Bookstop Inc. bookstore chain, an example of what are being called "superstores," carry large inventories (Bookstop stores have three times the industry average) and feature low prices (all books are discounted up to 45 percent).[14]

Some stores keep prices down by storing most of their merchandise in a backroom warehouse, with only one sample of each item displayed in the showroom. Customers look through a catalog they receive in the mail or find in the showroom. They fill out an order form for the items they want, and employees fill the order from the backroom warehouse.

VideoConcepts stores are single-line stores. They specialize in name-brand video products, including portable and console televisions, large-screen and projection televisions, and video recorders. Because these stores specialize, they can offer a great variety of video products.

Source: Courtesy of Tandy Corporation.

This type of retail store is called a catalog showroom. These stores—such as Best Products and Service Merchandise—attract buyers willing to make a little extra effort in their shopping in exchange for lower prices.

One retailer that has successfully combined several discounting techniques is IKEA. To learn more about this Scandinavian company, see "International Close-Up: Swedish Discounter Expands to America."

Nonstore Retailing

While most people associate retailing with stores, many retailers have found other effective ways to sell the consumers. Through mail, telephones, television, and other means, such retailers are able to reach consumers in their homes and workplaces. In many cases, nonstore retailing enables companies to focus their efforts on those consumers most likely to buy a particular product. Figure 14.7 shows the types and some examples of nonstore retailers.

INTERNATIONAL CLOSE-UP

Swedish Discounter Expands to America

When he was only 17, a Swede named Ingvar Kamprad started a store he named IKEA, combining his initials with those of his family farm (Elmtaryd) and his home town (Agunnaryd). The store did so well that the company expanded to 76 stores, stretching from Norway to Australia and recently including the United States.

IKEA sells Swedish-designed furniture and other household goods at low prices. One way IKEA keeps prices low is by selling unassembled merchandise. Buyers take kits home and assemble their purchases with the aid of drawings, a screwdriver, and a special hexagonal wrench that IKEA supplies to install its special bolts. The company features the wrench in its promotional displays where the wrench talks in cartoon balloons, giving information about policies and services. Besides selling furniture unassembled, IKEA keeps costs down by buying an entire year's supply of goods in advance for all its stores, betting that its sales projections are correct.

An IKEA shopper starts by picking up a catalog, note pad, pencil, and measuring tape. Walking through the store, shoppers view displays of furniture from over 1,500 suppliers. Altogether, the store carries about 13,000 items. Customers who want some time to think about what to buy can stop in IKEA's restaurant, located just off the showroom floor. After deciding what they want, customers then head for the self-service warehouse. There, they help themselves from rows of shelves. Thus, the store further cuts costs by reducing the need for display space (most merchandise is in the warehouse) and warehouse employees (customers help themselves).

American consumers are evidently pleased with IKEA's retailing strategy. In its first 15 months of business, the IKEA in Dale City, Virginia, sold about $40 million in merchandise. The company has another store outside of Philadelphia and is expanding across the country.

426

Selling over the telephone is often called "telemarketing." This telemarketing representative for Westinghouse Furniture Systems responds to customer inquiries and follows up on the efforts of the field sales staff. She talks on the phone through the headset she is wearing. This frees her hands to check company catalogs and to look up information on her computer.

A company can achieve a personal touch by using **door-to-door retailers,** salespeople who sell products house to house. While this used to be a popular retail channel, the high costs associated with direct selling have led many companies such as Fuller Brush to look for alternatives. However, door-to-door retailers still sell vacuum cleaners and encyclopedias in this fashion, and go into people's homes to sell Avon and Amway products and Tupperware.

Many companies find that selling through the mail is a more efficient way to approach customers. A **mail-order house** is a merchandiser that sells goods through a mail-order catalog. Sears is still the leading mail-order retailer in the United States, although hosts of increasingly popular retailers, such as L. L. Bean, also use this approach. For companies that also operate stores, items in catalogs generally carry lower prices than the same merchandise sold in the company's store. Mail-order retailing is a popular way to start retail selling, because the seller avoids the expense of setting up a store. Taking the lead of mail-order merchandisers, even some banks such as Bank of America and insurance companies are beginning to use catalogs to sell their financial services.[15]

Companies selling impulse items often use **vending machines,** mechanical retail outlets that store products and dispense them directly to customers. The vending machine makes products widely available at low selling cost. Typical vended goods include candy, cigarettes, coffee, and stamps. Some stores are even dispensing videos and fresh-cooked French fries through vending machines. Jukeboxes, pinball machines, and automatic teller machines are vending machines that dispense services. Vending machines are located in facilities such as hotel lobbies, airports, service stations, and company cafeterias.

A relatively new approach to nonstore retailing involves selling products by displaying them on cable television, along with a toll-free number for viewers to call and place an order. This type of retailing, called

Door-to-door retailer A salesperson who sells products house to house.

Mail-order house A retailer that sells goods through a mail-order catalog.

Vending machine A mechanical retail outlet that stores products and dispenses them directly to customers.

F I G U R E   14.7

Major Types of Nonstore Retailers

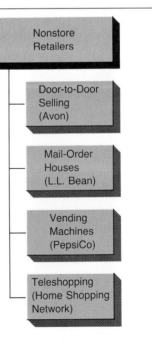

home shopping or teleshopping, combines the convenience of door-to-door selling with the great efficiency of catalog selling. One of the major teleshopping retailers is Home Shopping Network (HSN), which sends out 60,000 pieces of merchandise from liquidators and overseas manufacturers at tantalizing prices. Lured by HSN's success, operators of traditional retail stores, such as J. C. Penney and Sears, are getting involved in the home-shopping trend.[16]

Trends in Retailing

Besides teleshopping, a number of trends reflect retailers' efforts to find new ways of differentiating themselves and attracting customers. These developments include citylike complexes, vertical shopping malls, theme plazas, drop-in professional clinics, and greater use of direct channels.

Citylike Complexes Consumers have traditionally traveled some distance from their home to get to work and to go shopping. However, they now have a new alternative with the emergence of citylike complexes, which typically contain apartments and condominiums, business offices, and facilities for shopping and entertainment. Today these complexes exist in all parts of the country. They allow residents to meet most of their needs within one high-rise building or series of large interconnected buildings. Examples include the Renaissance Center in Detroit, the Broadway Plaza in Los Angeles, the Crown Center in Kansas City, and the Venetia in Miami.

A new development in vending machines is this French-fry vending machine. For 75¢ or $1, it adds water do dehydrated potatoes, cooks them in hot oil, and delivers a 3½-ounce serving in 35 seconds. Ore-Ida originally introduced this machine to test markets in the Chicago area, with plans to expand nationwide.

Source: Courtesy of Ore-Ida Foods, Inc.

Vertical Shopping Malls With land becoming more expensive, some developers are building shopping malls tall rather than wide. In some cases, they are including these malls in the citylike complexes noted above. Sometimes, these vertical malls are built into landmark buildings, such as the Jax brewery in New Orleans.

Theme Plazas Small, outdoor shopping centers often take on themes. Rather than leasing the units to anyone who is willing to pay the rent, developers can match the businesses with a central theme. In one plaza, there may be a certain ethnic theme such as Hispanic or Greek that features restaurants and food and even clothing stores. In another, there may be a wellness theme featuring a health-food store, a spa, a sporting goods store, and an exercise equipment retailer.

Convenient Professional Services Drop-in professional clinics, where no appointment is necessary, are becoming popular. These facilities may bring together lawyers, accountants, and financial planners to handle basic financial and legal matters, such as planning a retirement fund or drawing up a will. In medical facilities, dentists and doctors of various specialties can conduct tests and carry out minor surgery within a few hours and without an appointment. The cost of these services is often lower than in a traditional office, because the professionals share expenses for the facility and administrative work.

Direct Channels More and more manufacturing firms are opening their own retail outlets. By eliminating the expenses of intermediaries, the manufacturer may be able to pass some cost savings on to the consumer

428

and reap greater profits. In recent years, Tandy, Xerox, Texas Instruments, and IBM have done this. Other manufacturers, especially in the clothing business, are opening factory outlet stores. These factory outlets are usually located in smaller towns a short distance from large cities so they do not directly compete with their regular retailers. For example, Formfit Rogers has a factory outlet selling women's intimate apparel and sportswear in Nebraska City, Nebraska (located between Omaha and Kansas City). The cities of Freeport, Maine (a couple of hours north of Boston), and Reading, Pennsylvania (a few hours outside of Philadelphia), each have numerous factory outlets. The outlets do not advertise in the media (again, so they do not appear to compete with their retailers), but tell you upon entering that the merchandise is highly discounted.

Checkpoint

1. Name three types of retail stores.
2. How can retailers sell products without opening a store?

Physical Distribution

When they have decided on distribution channels, marketers of tangible goods still have to figure out how to move the goods physically through the channels to the users. The activities necessary to move goods from the producer to the final user are known collectively as **physical distribution.** These activities, illustrated in Figure 14.8, are order processing, inventory management, packaging and materials handling, warehousing, and transporting.

Physical distribution The activities necessary to move goods from the producer to the final user.

Order Processing

Before the company can ship goods to customers, it must be determined what they want. Therefore, the manager sets up a system for **order processing.** This involves taking sales orders, checking them, and then seeing that the product is shipped to the customer. Employees accomplish these tasks through some combination of face-to-face communication, telephone conversations, memos, and letters. For example,

Order processing Taking sales orders, checking them, and then seeing that the product is shipped to the customer.

FIGURE 14.8

Physical Distribution

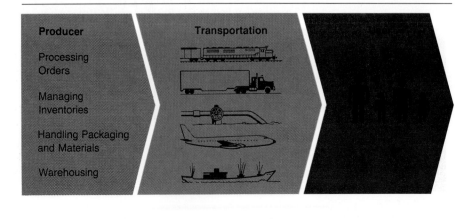

employees at L. L. Bean, the highly successful general store that specializes in outdoor clothing and equipment, process mail-order forms worth over $300 million per year and take 28,000 telephone orders a day during the peak season.[17] These employees ensure that each order is filled and shipped as specified. To prepare them for this important task, L. L. Bean provides 40 hours of training before the employees take their first order. Many firms rely increasingly on computers to help them carry out this order processing function.

Inventory Management

To be able to fill orders, the company needs an inventory of finished goods. However, carrying extra inventory may be unnecessarily expensive. To resolve this conflict, effective firms use **inventory management,** which involves efficiently balancing inventory with sales orders. Ideally, the company should have a lot of inventory on hand just before its peak selling season and little on hand during its slowest selling season. This requires that inventory managers study previous consumer buying habits, evaluate the firm's current promotional efforts, and forecast economic conditions.

Inventory management
Efficiently balancing inventory with sales orders.

Packaging and Materials Handling

Whether or not the order was processed and filled promptly, the customer will be upset if it arrives damaged. Such mistakes are costly to the seller and the buyer. Therefore, physical distribution also involves ensuring the goods are properly packaged so that they are not damaged in

Order processing is a major undertaking at Blair/New Process Company, which receives most of its orders for clothing and home furnishings through the mail. More than 65,000 pieces of mail arrive at the company each day. One department opens the orders, another checks them for completeness, and still another types the ordering data into the computer. Employees in other departments process payments.

Source: Courtesy of New Process Company.

Materials handling
Overseeing the movement
of goods within the
company's facilities.

Warehousing Storing
goods until they are ready
to be shipped.

Private warehouse A
storage facility owned or
leased by the company
whose goods it stores.

Public warehouse A
public storage facility
whose owner is not the
company storing goods
there.

the warehouse or in transit. Packaging experts decide what materials the
package should be made of and whether the goods should be placed in
individual packages, large boxes, or sealed containers.

Protecting the goods also involves **materials handling,** overseeing the
movement of goods within the company's facilities. This includes moving
finished goods directly from the production line to the shipping dock or
to the warehouse and then, at some later time, to the shipping dock.

Warehousing

While the company theoretically could avoid inventory costs by transporting goods directly to the customer, this is often impossible or impractical. To get a head start on meeting orders, most companies
produce goods in advance. They warehouse the products, make arrangements for shipment, and send the goods so that they reach the customer
on the desired delivery date. The storing of goods until they are ready
to be shipped is called **warehousing.**

A company's size influences its choice of a warehouse. Large firms use
a **private warehouse,** which is a storage facility owned or leased by the
company. If the amount of inventory is too great or the firm has no private warehouse, it typically rents space in a **public warehouse,** which is
a public storage facility owned by someone outside the company.

Once Blair/New Process Company's employees have re-
corded orders and payments,
employees at the company's
distribution facility go to work.
The company's newest and
larest warehouse is located
seven miles from its main
headquarters in Warren,
Pennsylvania, and covers over
400,000 square feet. During
peak periods, the facility holds
more than five million pieces
of merchandise.

Source: Courtesy of New Process
Company.

Transporting Goods

The transportation of goods from the warehouse to the customer lies at the heart of physical distribution. Transportation is the largest single expense associated with the distribution of most goods. Managing the transportation of goods starts with selecting a carrier. To do this, the manager must match the company's needs and resources with the types of carriers and modes of transportation available.

Companies that need relatively few special services and want to minimize cost often use a **common carrier.** This type of transportation company performs transportation services within a particular line of business for the general public. For example, Eastern Airlines flies people and certain types of freight on its many routes. The Union Pacific Railroad carries freight along its rails. These companies follow timetables, so a company that wants to use them must have the goods ready on time. Similarly, a trucker for a common carrier starts out with a list of stops. The company wanting to transport goods must wait for the trucker to come around.

Companies that prefer to pay for special service might turn to a **contract carrier.** Such a company performs transportation services called for by an individual contract. The carrier works exclusively for a particular customer; when the contract is completed, the carrier moves on to another job. Most contract carriers are in the trucking business, where the truckers may own their own rig and work on a "for hire" basis.

Sometimes a company ships in such volume that it finds a **private carrier** to be most efficient. This type of carrier is owned by the company whose goods it transports. For example, Exxon owns oil tankers, Federal Express owns airplanes, and Safeway owns delivery trucks. This arrangement requires a substantial investment in equipment and wages but gives companies the greatest control over transportation practices.

Common carrier A transportation company that performs services within a particular line of business for the general public.

Contract carrier A transportation company that performs services called for by an individual contract.

Private carrier A transportation company owned by the company whose goods it transports.

Manufacturers Railway Company, an Anheuser-Busch Companies, Inc., subsidiary, operates a fleet of over 500 insulated and cushioned railcars used exclusively for transporting Anheuser-Busch beers. The company also operates hopper cars and boxcars for use by Anheuser-Busch and other companies, trucking and warehouse services, and a 17,000-ton molasses terminal on the Mississippi River.

Source: Reproduced with permission from the 1986 Anheuser-Busch Companies, Inc., annual report.

432

Companies with small shipments may turn to a **freight forwarder.** This is a common carrier that leases or contracts space from other carriers and resells it to small-volume shippers. Freight forwarders do not own any of the transportation equipment that hauls the merchandise. They simply pick up the goods from the shipper, see that these goods are loaded on the carrier and transported to their destination, and take care of all the billing involved. Freight forwarders help small shippers by selling them space on common carriers such as ships or airplanes. They also help common carriers by taking care of all the minor details associated with small shipments.

Freight forwarder A common carrier that leases or contracts space from other carriers and resells it to small-volume shippers.

Transportation Modes

Managers must also select an appropriate mode of transportation. The options include: railroads, trucks, water carriers, pipelines, and air carriers. Figure 14.9 compares the advantages of these five modes.

The two biggest questions marketers must answer in deciding what transportation modes to use are how quickly must the goods be delivered, and how much will it cost. After balancing the time and expense involved, the company selects the modes it will use.

Piggyback service The shipment of a fully loaded truck trailer on a specially designed railroad flatcar.

Railroads As shown in Figure 14.10, the railroads carry more freight than any other transportation mode. They are particularly cost-effective in transporting bulk commodities over long distances. In recent years, the railroads have responded to vigorous competition from motor carriers by introducing a number of new services, including the following:

Piggyback service, which involves the shipment of a fully loaded truck trailer on a specially designed flatcar. The merchandise does not have to be taken out of the truck, loaded into a railroad car, and then reloaded into a truck at the final destination. The simplicity of this arrangement greatly reduces shipping costs.

F I G U R E 14.9

Advantages of the Major Modes of Transportation

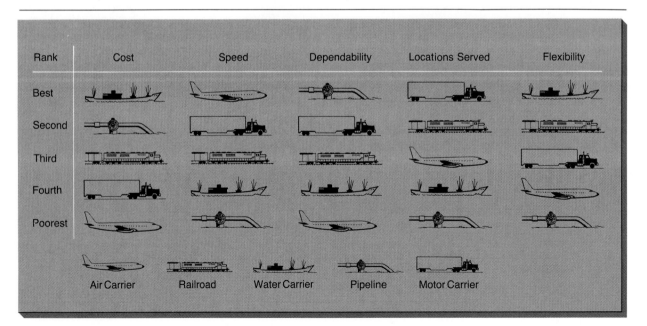

Rank	Cost	Speed	Dependability	Locations Served	Flexibility
Best	Water Carrier	Air Carrier	Pipeline	Motor Carrier	Water Carrier
Second	Pipeline	Motor Carrier	Motor Carrier	Railroad	Railroad
Third	Railroad	Railroad	Railroad	Air Carrier	Motor Carrier
Fourth	Motor Carrier	Water Carrier	Water Carrier	Water Carrier	Air Carrier
Poorest	Air Carrier	Pipeline	Air Carrier	Pipeline	Pipeline

Air Carrier Railroad Water Carrier Pipeline Motor Carrier

Fast freight, which is the rapid conveyance of perishable goods. The train bypasses congested freight yards, stays on the main track, and races great distances in delivering the goods rapidly. This gives railroad companies an edge in competing for business when speed is important.

In-transit privileges, which allow shippers to stop a shipment along the way in order to perform a function such as an assembly task on the product being transported and then continue the shipment.

Motor Carriers Motor carriers — almost always trucks — account for about a quarter of all domestically shipped freight. These vehicles are efficient for moving small shipments over short distances. Trucks are flexible and can operate anywhere there is a road. For shipments traveling less than a few hundred miles, trucks are almost always cheaper than the railroad.

Economic and political forces are keeping trucking rates down. In recent years, the trucking industry has been deregulated. This, combined with the fact that many of the common carriers are independents who own their own rig and trailer, means that prices have become extremely competitive. Some firms have further cut costs by using truck transportation to cut out intermediaries by delivering goods directly to the final consumer.

Water Transportation Transporting by water is an inexpensive way of shipping goods. However, it is also a slow way of getting the goods to their destination. The two most common forms of water carriers are inland or barge lines and deep-water, ocean-going vessels. Barges work the Great Lakes, major rivers, and inland canals across the country. Ocean-going vessels also operate on the Great Lakes and between port cities of the United States and other nations.

Pipelines Transportation via pipelines is primarily used to carry oil and natural gas. A good example is the Alaskan pipeline, which carries crude oil from the north slope of Alaska to the southern Alaskan city of

Fast freight The rapid conveyance of perishable goods by train.

In-transit privileges Permission to stop a train shipment along the way in order to perform a function and then continue the shipment.

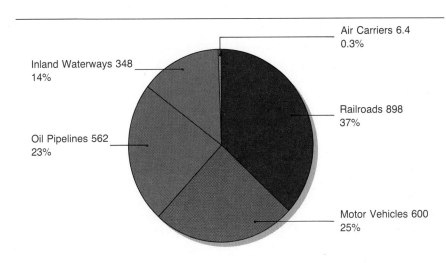

Air Carriers 6.4
0.3%

Inland Waterways 348
14%

Railroads 898
37%

Oil Pipelines 562
23%

Motor Vehicles 600
25%

F I G U R E   14.10

Domestic Freight Traffic by Major Carriers (in Billions of Ton-Miles)

A ton-mile is the movement of 1 ton (2,000 pounds) of freight for the distance of 1 mile.

Valdez, where it is loaded on tankers and transported to oil refineries. Pipelines are one of the lowest-cost forms of transportation, but can handle only limited types of products.

Air Carriers Air transportation is the fastest mode now available. It is also the most expensive. Therefore, companies tend to use air carriers only when speed far outweighs cost considerations. For example, air carriers transport millions of tons of mail that must be delivered overnight or within a few days. However, as Figure 14.10 shows, air carriers handle less than 1 percent of all freight.

Combined Modes Not all products are distributed by a single mode of transportation. Often a company uses two or more modes. For example, Alaskan crude oil is carried by pipeline and then by oil tanker to the refinery. Goods arriving at a seaport are typically transferred to a motor carrier and then, perhaps, to a railroad. Trains may deliver goods to the buyer's factory, but often a motor carrier picks up the freight at a railroad terminal and delivers it to the buyer. In fact, some railroads have their own trucking line. Motor carriers complement air carriers in a similar fashion. The ability to combine transportation modes gives marketers great flexibility in moving goods to their customers.

Checkpoint

1. What are the five basic modes of transportation?
2. Besides transportation, what do marketers have to plan for in arranging physical distribution?

Pier 1 Inc. uses combined modes of transportation. Here a company truck heads to a warehouse with a containerized shipment removed from the ship in the background. The ability to move containers from ships to trucks makes combined modes of distribution more efficient than ever.

Source: Courtesy of Pier 1 Imports, Inc.

Closing Comments

As the makers of Izod shirts have discovered, the way a company distributes its product can make the difference between marketing success and failure. This chapter explained how companies manage this important function, from choosing marketing channels to planning a means of physical distribution. Often producers turn to intermediaries — wholesalers and retailers — for help in carrying out these activities. Consequently, wholesaling and retailing are an important and growing part of American business.

Learning Objectives Revisited

1. **Define the nature and types of channels of distribution.**
   The channel of distribution is the route that goods take in moving from producer to user. Different channels are used for industrial goods and consumer goods. Industrial goods commonly move through direct channels or through wholesalers. Consumer goods take one of three different routes: through direct channels, through retailers, or through both wholesalers and retailers.
2. **Explain the benefits of using wholesalers.**
   Manufacturers benefit because wholesalers can take inventory off the producer's hands, assume the risk associated with carrying inventory, provide a sales force, and provide marketing information and support. Retailers and industrial customers benefit because wholesalers can break bulk for them, provide better credit terms, and provide marketing information.
3. **Identify the types of wholesalers.**
   Merchant wholesalers are intermediaries that take title to the goods. These wholesalers may provide a variety of services or carry out only some of them. Manufacturer-owned wholesalers handle the wholesale function for the parent company. Agent intermediaries are wholesalers that do not take title to the goods. For example, brokers specialize in bringing together buyers and sellers.
4. **Describe the types of retailers.**
   Retail stores that offer variety include department stores, supermarkets, and hypermarkets. Stores that offer specialization include convenience stores. Stores offering low price include discount stores and catalog showrooms. Nonstore retailing includes door-to-door retailers, mail-order houses, vending machines, and teleshopping.
5. **Discuss the nature and functions of physical distribution.**
   Physical distribution consists of the activities necessary to move goods from the producer to the final user: order processing (taking sales orders, checking them, and seeing that the product is shipped to the customer); inventory management (the efficient balancing of inventory with sales orders); packaging and materials handling (packaging the goods properly and moving them within the company's facilities); warehousing (storing the goods until they are ready to be shipped); and transporting goods (moving the goods from the company's warehouse to the customer).
6. **Present the major modes of transportation.**
   The five major modes of transportation used to convey goods through the distribution channel are railroads, motor carriers, water

carriers, pipelines, and air carriers. Railroads are particularly cost-effective when shipping goods long distances and offer many special privileges, such as piggyback service, to shippers. Motor carriers are often the most efficient mode when shipping goods short distances. Water carriers are an inexpensive, but slow, way to move goods over great distances. Pipelines are highly efficient in transporting certain products, such as petroleum. Air carriers are a good choice when speed, not cost, is of the essence.

Key Terms Reviewed

Review each of the following terms. For any that you do not know or are unsure of, look up the definitions and see how they were used in the chapter.

channel of distribution	door-to-door retailer
wholesaler	mail-order house
retailer	vending machine
direct channel	physical distribution
exclusive distribution	order processing
selective distribution	inventory management
intensive distribution	materials handling
vertical marketing system (VMS)	warehousing
merchant wholesalers	private warehouse
agent intermediaries	public warehouse
broker	common carrier
scrambled merchandising	contract carrier
department store	private carrier
supermarket	freight forwarder
impulse items	piggyback service
hypermarket	fast freight
convenience store	in-transit privileges
discount store	

Review Questions

1. What is a channel of distribution? Based on the "International Close-Up" box, describe the channel of distribution that includes IKEA stores. What role does IKEA play in this channel?
2. What do producers consider when deciding on the appropriate type of distribution channel?
3. What is a vertical marketing system? Why would some companies use this system?
4. Sam Tobias is setting up a new company, Tobias Restaurant Supply, which will sell huge ovens and refrigerators to restaurants. Sam figures he can keep more of the profits if he doesn't use wholesalers, but he wonders whether wholesalers might benefit him in the long run. How might wholesalers benefit Sam's business?
5. What type of wholesaler provides the widest variety of services?

6. Francine Quinn wants to sell a parcel of land to a developer. She thinks it is in an ideal location for development as a shopping mall. What kind of wholesaler will be interested in helping Francine sell the land? Describe this type of intermediary.

7. Why are retailers hard to classify?

8. Identify and describe types of retailers that appeal to a broad cross-section of consumers. Why did you select each?

9. What kind of retail outlets would a publisher of college textbooks use? Why?

10. How are some retail outlets able to offer consistently lower prices?

11. What are some ways in which retailers sell to consumers without using a store?

12. Green Lawn Mowers sells its products through hardware stores nationwide. What physical distribution activities does this involve? Briefly describe each.

13. Which modes of transportation do you think would be most appropriate for Green Lawn Mowers (Question 12)? Why?

14. Why do you think UPS (United Parcel Service) owns its own trucks, while some manufacturers ship through common carriers?

Applied Exercises

1. Find out about and then visit a company that markets to two different types of customers (for example, the government and private consumers). Then compare the ways this firm markets these two types of customers. Describe and contrast the types of channels that are used.

2. Interview a manager from three retailers: a department store, a convenience store, and a discount store. Report to the class why each of these retailers uses its particular form of distribution.

3. Visit a local truck company or railroad office. Interview the owner or a manager to find out what types of goods they mainly transport. What are the major problems or issues they are faced with? Write up your report and share it with the class.

4. Identify a nonstore retailer in your community or on television. What products do they sell? What are the major problems or issues they are faced with? (In the case of teleshopping, you may have to do some library research.)

Your Business IQ: Answers

1. False. Wholesalers and retailers add value to goods by making them available to customers at convenient times and in convenient locations. Without these intermediaries, customers would have to chase around from producer to producer to buy the things they want.

2. False. Most small companies are less likely to be able to sell directly to the final customer, since doing so often requires a large sales force and widespread appreciation of the company's reputation.

3. True. An increasing number of manufacturers have been opening such stores, often called factory outlets.

4. True. Railroads carry the most freight, in part because they are cost-effective in transporting bulk goods over long distances.

5. True. Pipelines are inexpensive. However, they can handle only a few products, such as oil and natural gas.

Competing Channels for Ralph Lauren

Mention the name Ralph Lauren, and many people immediately recognize him as the famous designer who sells fragrances, women's and men's apparel and accessories, home furnishings, luggage, shoes, swimwear, and eyeglasses. Including sales by licensees, Polo/Ralph Lauren, Inc., grosses over $600 million annually.

Lauren used to market his goods solely through upscale retailers such as Saks Fifth Avenue, Bloomingdale's, and Macy's. Then he created a string of franchise stores that stock Lauren products exclusively. These stores stretch from Palm Beach on the East Coast to Beverly Hills on the West Coast. Lauren recently opened his own 20,000-square-foot retail emporium in the Rhinelander mansion on Madison Avenue in Manhattan.

Why is Lauren opening up a retail outlet that clearly competes with the prestigious retailers that currently carry his lines? One reason is increased profit. By eliminating the intermediary for his goods, Lauren is able to reduce his distribution channel costs. A second is that he feels retailers will eventually get tough with designers and begin making lower-profit deals with them. Lauren wants to be in a position that does not require him to rely heavily on these retailers. By striking out on his own, Lauren reduces the chances of his being replaced by a different clothing line. With many retailers introducing their own upscale clothing lines, Lauren's decision may have a great deal of merit.

How do the large retailers with whom he is currently doing business feel about Lauren's strategy? They do not like it. Some are tactful in their response. For example, the president of Bloomingdale's publicly made diplomatic statements while privately he gritted his teeth. Others, like the senior vice president at Saks, believe that, "It's got to come out of our hides." On the other hand, these retailers realize that there is nothing they can do about it. If they drop Lauren's line, they will lose the customers who come into their stores to buy Lauren's products, and they will be replaced by competitors that will happily sell Lauren's products. As one retail consultant put it, "Stores could win their battle on principle — by dropping the collection — but what about servicing the customers who buy Lauren's clothes? [The retailers] have nobody to replace Lauren." Customers seem to agree. During the most recent year Lauren's franchised units have grossed over $200 million. Customers seem willing to buy his products anywhere; and as long as this remains true, Lauren will be able to get away with using competing channels.

Case Questions

1. How did Lauren initially distribute his goods? Describe his distribution channel.
2. When Lauren began setting up franchise units, what type of distribution was he using: intensive, exclusive, or selective? How did this distribution strategy differ from the previous one?
3. In what way does Lauren's decision to open his own store change the distribution channel he is currently using? Do you think this idea will be successful? Why or why not?

You Be the Adviser:
A Host of New Channels

A large company headquartered in the central United States is famous for its high-quality industrial machinery. The firm manufactures this machinery on a to-order basis. This means that when a customer places an order, the firm builds the machine to the client's specifications.

Over the last five years, the company has concluded that it needs to expand its customer base and start selling more products. As a result, it bought a firm that makes gourmet foods and another that manufactures pastas, sauces, and related products. The company then acquired a firm that produces snack foods. Next, it purchased a company that makes office equipment, including file cabinets, metal desks and chairs, and related accessories. More recently, it acquired a firm that manufactures high-quality electric lawn mowers (both riding and nonriding types). At the same time, the corporation has decided to complement its to-order approach to producing machinery by manufacturing and selling some selected types of machinery through a newly created sales force. These latest developments promise to make the firm twice as large as it was five years ago.

The president of the company would like to attain some coordination between these new acquisitions in terms of distribution channels. For example, where possible he would like to use the same channels to move goods to the customer. "If we are selling a number of different types of food, we have a host of different market niches, but we can reach these people by using the same distribution channel. The same is true of other products we ship to our customers," he explained to one of his major stockholders. "For example, our gourmet foods, pastas, and snack foods all use the same channel. So despite the fact that we have a number of different product lines, distribution channels for many of them will be the same."

Your Advice

1. Through what marketing channels would you recommend that the company market its gourmet foods? Its pasta products? Its snack foods? In each case, explain your answer.
2. What marketing channels would you recommend for the office equipment line? The lawn mowers? Why?
3. How would you recommend that the firm market the industrial machinery that it is going to sell through its newly created sales force? Why?

Career Opportunities

Marketing offers many career opportunities, especially for those who enjoy working with people. Possible jobs range from buying and selling to developing a promotional strategy to carrying out marketing research. The following are just a few of the possibilities.

Wholesale Salespeople

Wholesale salespeople help move goods from the manufacturer to the consumer. They call on and try to sell to buyers for retail stores, industrial firms, and institutions such as schools and hospitals. They provide catalogs or bring samples of items their company sells. They may also show buyers how their products can save money or improve productivity. They also keep records of sales, forward orders to their wholesale firms, prepare reports and expense accounts, plan work schedules, draw up lists of prospects, make appointments, and study background information describing their products.

In addition, these salespeople often perform many services for retailers, including checking the store's stock and showing how to order items that will be needed before the next visit. Some wholesale salespeople help retailers with their advertising, pricing, and window and counter displays.

The necessary background for being hired in wholesale sales depends on the product line and the market. Complex products require technical backgrounds. Drug wholesalers, for example, seek people with a college degree in chemistry, biology, or pharmacy. Many wholesalers of nontechnical products prefer graduates with a major in business that emphasizes marketing and sales.

The opportunities are great. At the present time, about 1.2 million workers are wholesale salespeople, and the number of such jobs is expected to increase faster than the average for all occupations through the mid-1990s as the volume and kinds of goods produced in the economy expands. Salaries are highly variable because the job may be based on commissions tied to the amount the person sells. Usually, however, incomes range between $22,000 and $26,000, with newcomers earning less. Experienced salespeople can earn as much as $45,000 and up.

Retail Salespeople

Retail salespeople provide service to customers, from answering questions about products to selling the items to the customer. Typical responsibilities include ringing up orders and making out sales slips, receiving cash payments, giving change and receipts, handling returns and exchanges of merchandise, helping stock racks and shelves, marking price tags, taking inventory, and preparing displays.

This field is large and growing. Today, there are about four million retail salespeople. They are employed, in the main, by department stores; general merchandise stores; apparel and accessories stores; food, drug, and furniture stores; and car dealers. Employment is expected to grow about as fast as the average for all workers through the mid-1990s.

A college education is not necessary for this work, but some stores require that their management trainees fresh out of college have selling experience on the floor before they assume supervisory positions. Most full-time retail salespeople earn between $10,000 and $19,000 annually, although some, thanks to commissions and bonuses, can make more.

Travel Agents

Travel agents are specialists who have the information and know-how to make the best possible travel arrangements within their clients' tastes and budgets. When making travel arrangements, they consult a variety of sources for information on airline departure and arrival times, fares, and hotel ratings and prices. In the case of international travel, agents also typically provide information on customs regulations, required papers (passports, visas, and certificates of vaccination), and the most recent currency exchange rates. Travel agents also do considerable promotional work in putting together travel tours and making special arrangements with hotels, airlines, and rental-car firms.

Many agents are self-employed and secure contracts with companies to be their exclusive agent for all travel arrangements. Before going into business for themselves, however, most have worked in travel agencies and gained important job-related experience. No particular educational background is required to secure a job in this business, but a business degree or diploma in hotel and restaurant management probably provides the best base.

The travel agency business is expected to grow much faster than the average for all occupations through the mid-1990s. Depending on the annual dollar volume of the agency, salaries will vary. Most travel agents make between $25,000 and $60,000 annually, not counting all the extra benefits that often accrue to them, such as free or discounted travel and lodging.

Purchasing Agent

Purchasing agents are responsible for seeing that goods, materials, supplies, and services purchased for internal use by the organization are of suitable quality and sufficient quantity and that they are delivered when and where they have been promised at the agreed-upon price. Purchasing agents typically buy raw materials, machinery, parts and components, office furniture, business machines, vehicles, and office supplies. These agents use a variety of means to choose suppliers, including comparisons of price, quantity, quality, and reliability.

Skill in working with people is important. Purchasing agents typically meet with suppliers to discuss future purchasing needs and to invite bids on large orders, which, other things being equal, they give to the lowest bidder. Purchasing agents must develop a good working relationship with suppliers in order to obtain cost savings, favorable payment terms, quick delivery, responsiveness to emergency orders, and help in securing scarce materials. They also work closely with personnel in various departments in their own organization.

About 200,000 purchasing agents are employed in the United States. As the volume of goods and services produced increases, employment in this area is expected to increase about as fast as the average for all occupations through the mid-1990s. Although there are no universal educational requirements for entry-level jobs, most large organizations require a college degree and prefer applicants with a master's degree in business administration or management. Beginning salaries are about $22,500, but the top 10 percent of purchasing agents earn more than $40,000.

DECISION-MAKING TOOLS AND TECHNIQUES

Business managers constantly make decisions, such as what raw materials to purchase, how much to produce, what prices to charge, what kind of employees to hire, and what promotional strategy to use. To make these decisions and to weigh the outcomes, the managers rely on various decision-making tools and techniques. Although business people seldom need to be accountants or computer scientists or even programmers, they do need enough grasp of these areas to apply them as tools for making decisions.

Chapter 15 addresses how business people use accounting information to make decisions. The chapter explains basic accounting procedures and describes the major accounting reports: the balance sheet, the income statement, and the statement of cash flows.

Chapter 16 discusses the use of information systems and computers to collect, analyze, and disseminate information to support decision making. As the flow of data continues to build, business people increasingly need a way to manage it so that they receive timely and relevant information. Typically, the solution includes using a computer. The chapter describes the changes in computer technology that have led to increased capacity, power, and flexibility at much lower costs. The chapter concludes with a description of some advantages and disadvantages of computers and the basic applications of computers in the business environment.

When you have finished studying Part V, you should be familiar with the fundamentals of accounting and computers. You should have a sense of how business people draw on them for assistance in making effective decisions. You should also be able to identify some of the kinds of information business people seek as a basis for their decisions.

Source: Courtesy of Campbell Soup Company.

Accounting Information for Decision Making

LEARNING OBJECTIVES

- Define accounting and the types of accountants.
- Discuss the nature and types of budgets.
- Explain the accounting equation and double-entry bookkeeping.

- Describe the balance sheet.
- Present the income statement and the statement of cash flows.
- Identify ratios used to analyze financial statements.

Your Business IQ

How much do you already know about accounting? Test your business IQ by labeling each statement *true* or *false*. Answers and explanations are at the end of the chapter.

1. Both certified public accountants (CPAs) and certified management accountants (CMAs) can officially express an opinion and have final authority to say whether a firm's financial statements are accurate and have been reported fairly.
2. Financial transactions require two bookkeeping entries.
3. For accounting purposes, the federal government begins its annual operations on October 1, not January 1.
4. A business's "bottom line" is the profit or loss shown on its income statement.
5. In evaluating the information on a financial statement, business people should take care to stick to the numbers and not be prejudiced by external influences on the company's performance.

A major role of accounting is to prepare the financial statements that appear in a company's annual report. The annual report tells investors and other interested people about the company's financial condition.

Looking Back and Ahead

Financial accounting reports for General Electric Company show that during John F. Welch, Jr.'s, first five years as chief executive of the company, revenues have grown from $30 to $40 billion, and profits from $3 to $5 billion.[1] Information such as this is interesting to a variety of business people, including job applicants, competitors, and potential lenders. Investors would also be interested to learn that the company's earnings per share of stock have been growing faster than those at other major companies. And all of this information—examples of accounting information—helps Mr. Welch and other GE managers make important decisions more effectively.

Both outsiders and insiders are interested in the financial condition of a company. Outsiders such as investors want to know whether stock in the company is a good buy. Applicants interviewing for jobs with the company want to know what its growth prospects are and whether they are likely to be laid off as soon as the economy slows down. Competitors try to learn the company's strengths and weaknesses for ideas on how to gain a competitive advantage. Lending institutions want to know whether the company will be able to repay a loan. Inside the company, managers want to evaluate whether their efforts are working and pinpoint where they need to modify their approach. In order to make effective decisions, both outsiders and insiders turn to accounting information.

This chapter focuses on the generation and analysis of basic accounting information. After presenting an overview of the accounting profession and the budgeting process, the chapter describes the major accounting statements: the balance sheet, the income statement, and the statement of cash flows. The rest of the chapter discusses the most common ways to analyze these financial statements.

Accounting and the Accounting Profession

Accounting The process of measuring, interpreting, evaluating, and communicating financial information for the purpose of effective decision making and control.

Accounting is the process of measuring, interpreting, evaluating, and communicating financial information for the purpose of effective decision making and control. The role of accounting in business firms has changed considerably over the past few decades. Years ago, a bookkeeper systematically entered the company's financial transactions in a ledger book. For example, if the company bought a new piece of equipment, the bookkeeper would see that the purchase was correctly entered on the books.

Today's accountants provide services that go far beyond mere bookkeeping. Financial accountants measure and analyze financial data for legal purposes. The focus of financial accounting is to provide accounting information to users such as lenders, investors, and the government that are outside the firm. Managerial accountants, on the other hand, provide information for internal purposes. Managerial accounting data makes an important contribution to decision making and control. Both financial and managerial accountants help managers analyze and evaluate the firm's financial position and participate in planning for the future. Figure 15.1 summarizes the major responsibilities of accountants today. Sometimes the ethics of how these responsibilities are carried out are called into question,[2] as in the case discussed in "Social Responsibility Close-Up: Where Were the Accountants?"

Small firms seldom employ a full-time accountant. Instead, they use a bookkeeper to handle the day-to-day financial activities and periodically hire an outside public accounting firm to balance the books, provide financial statements that reflect the financial condition of the firm, and prepare the tax returns. Large companies, on the other hand, usually employ a full-time, in-house accounting staff to carry out these activities.

Public Accountants

Accountants who are employed by an accounting firm and provide financial services to clients are called *public accountants*. They are independent of the business or enterprise they serve. As such, they are expected to be objective and follow generally accepted accounting principles (GAAP) in evaluating a company's financial statements. The importance of objectivity has led accountants to set and follow professional standards, such as refusing to be paid a fee based on the company's profits[3] and limiting advertising by members of their profession.

Many public accountants have become certified. A **certified public accountant (CPA)** has met the state certification requirements of education and job experience and has passed a comprehensive examination. In recent years, most states have been increasing the requirements for the CPA. For example, some states now require five years of accounting education and two more of practice, in addition to passing a rigorous CPA exam.

Certified public accountant (CPA) A public accountant who has met state certification requirements of education and job experience and has passed a comprehensive examination.

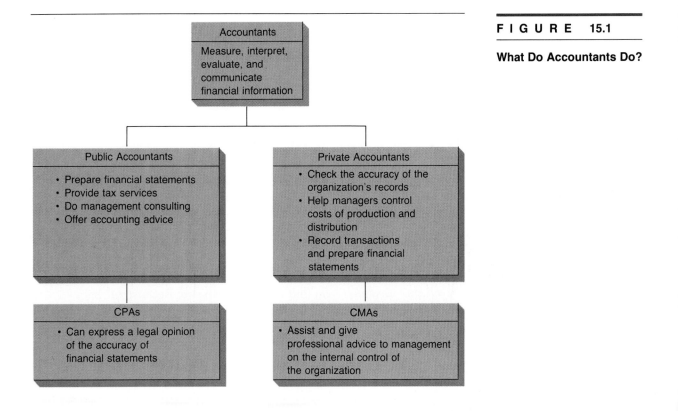

F I G U R E   15.1

What Do Accountants Do?

CPAs have professional status in their field the same way that physicians or attorneys do within their respective fields. As such, there are some activities only they can perform. For example, only CPAs may officially express an opinion on whether a firm's financial statements are accurate and have been reported fairly. The annual reports of firms that have had their accounts reviewed by a CPA firm contain a statement from the accounting firm that reads something like this:

> In our opinion, the consolidated financial statements that appear in this report present fairly the financial position of [company's name]. Our examinations of these statements were made in accordance with generally accepted auditing standards and accordingly included such tests of the accounting records and other auditing procedures as we considered necessary in the circumstances.

SOCIAL RESPONSIBILITY   CLOSE-UP

Where Were the Accountants?

When a certified public accountant (CPA) certifies that a firm has a net worth of $67 million, investors have a right to rely on this information as accurate. In fact, outsiders have a right to believe that the accountant is aware of the company's financial position and is openly and candidly reporting this information. Unfortunately, this is not always the case. The Wedtech Corporation of the South Bronx, New York, provides a recent example that has serious ethical implications.

Wedtech was a minority-owned firm that was able to secure large government contracts. It has been revealed that the company got some of these contracts through kickbacks to politicians and that its financial statements were often inaccurate or incomplete. For example, when outside public accountants found that the company was faking millions of dollars of invoices so that the firm could speed up progress payments from the government, they alerted top management. However, the accountants never mentioned this when the company filed the necessary papers for issuing stock for sale to investors. Moreover, a few days before the stock was sold to the public, Wedtech hired the outside accountant who was in charge of the prestock audit. This individual eventually was paid $2.5 million in cash, loans, and stock for eight months of work.

Nor did the unethical behavior end there. Two years later the company again sold stock to the public. This time it said that it was on schedule in meeting all outstanding contracts. In truth, the firm was seriously behind schedule on its biggest contract (building pontoons for the U.S. Navy), and the auditors could have determined this from the financial records. Later that same year the company sold more stock in order to pay off bank loans. What the investors were not told was that these loans were called in by the banks and had to be paid. Again, the accountants said nothing.

How much could the accountants have done to identify and reveal these events? Many investors, and some prosecutors, think the accountants could have at least ensured that the public was given more information about what was really going on in the firm. There is also concern over the fact that the accountants were well paid. The two outside public accounting firms received a total of $3 million for three years of work. Investigators who have reviewed this case say that the accountants should have seen what was going on and blown the whistle. Because of their failure to do so, the accountants are now one of the targets in a federal investigation that is being prosecuted in U.S. District Court in Manhattan.

The CPAs at public accounting firms can perform a wide range of services for their clients. In addition to auditing financial statements, they provide tax services, management consulting, and professional accounting advice to companies ranging from small businesses to multinational corporations. Because of the increasing number of fraud cases, like the one involving ZZZZBest Co. in California, and an increase in the number of malpractice suits against accounting firms, a new service specializing in detecting fraud is in high demand. One of these so-called forensic (as in crime detection) accountants describes his job as follows: "When the death of a company occurs under mysterious circumstances, forensic accountants are essential. Other accountants look at the charts. But forensic accountants actually dig into the body."[4]

Most of the corporations listed on the New York and American Stock Exchanges have their books examined by one of the "Big Eight" public accounting firms. These prestigious firms include Arthur Andersen & Company; Arthur Young & Company; Coopers & Lybrand; Ernst & Whinney; Deloitte Haskins & Sells; Peat Marwick Main & Co.; Price Waterhouse; and Touche Ross & Company.

Private Accountants

Some organizations employ their own accountants. These *private accountants* perform a number of different jobs. For example, internal auditors check the accuracy of the organization's records and accounting methods. Managerial accountants help management control the cost of manufacturing and distributing goods. General accountants record all business transactions and prepare reports and financial statements for the firm.

Some private accountants are also certified management accountants. A **certified management accountant (CMA)** has met certain educational and professional requirements and has also passed a series of exams from the National Association of Accountants. These exams are comparable in length and difficulty to the CPA exam. The CMA was created in 1972, and today thousands of private accountants hold this certification. Although holding the CMA does not give any special privileges, it does designate a level of competency and professionalism for private accountants.

The Budgeting Process

Accountants often help managers through the budgeting process that is a part of the planning function discussed in Chapter 6. A **budget** is a financial plan that specifies revenues and expenses for a given time period. Budgeting puts data into management planning. Most budgets are for one year, and many are revised quarterly (every three months). Effective managers, especially in large firms, use budgets to make sure that the goals of the various divisions are in harmony. The budget is also an excellent method of controlling the operation (discussed in Chapters 6 and 10). Most supervisors and managers provide information for preparing the budget and work with the accountant or someone familiar with the accounting process.

Managers use different types of budgets, depending on their needs. Most companies must plan for and control sales income, production

An audit team from Ernst & Whinney, one of the Big Eight accounting firms. Such teams often work in client offices for weeks at a time, going over records to make sure they accurately represent the company's financial position.

Source: Courtesy of Ernst & Whinney/Lawson Products.

Certified management accountant (CMA) A private accountant who has met certain education and professional requirements and has passed a series of exams.

Budget A financial plan that specifies revenues and expenses for a given time period.

costs, and cash requirements. Consequently, the most common budgets address these concerns:

The *sales budget* predicts sales revenue based on a forecast of unit sales and selling price.

The *production budget* forecasts the number of units to be manufactured in order to meet sales demand and desired ending inventory levels.

The *cost of goods sold budget* estimates the cost of materials, labor, and overhead expenses that will be used in manufacturing the goods.

The *cash budget* forecasts cash receipts and disbursements. The purpose of this forecast is to prevent the company from running out of daily operating funds. It usually covers a period of 30 to 60 days.

Checkpoint

1. How do public accountants differ from private accountants?
2. What kinds of budgets do managers use?

Foundation for Accounting

Although different accountants specialize in different activities, modern accounting is built on a common set of principles and procedures. Understanding these is the basis for effectively applying accounting information to specific situations.

The Accounting Equation

A basic concern of a company's owners (whether proprietors, partners, or stockholders in a corporation) is the worth of their investment. How much do they own, and how much does the company owe to others? To get a picture of this, business people use the **accounting equation:**

$$\text{Assets} = \text{Liabilities} + \text{Owners' Equity}$$

Assets are everything of value owned by the enterprise. Examples include cash, accounts receivable (money due to the company), inventory, and machinery. **Liabilities** are creditors' claims on the enterprise's assets. These claims may be for credit purchases, wages, salaries, taxes that are as yet unpaid, and long-term debt. **Owners' equity** is the owners' claim on the assets of the enterprise. This is often referred to as a "residual" claim because it consists of whatever is left over after the liabilities have been satisfied.

If you can determine any two of the numbers in the accounting equation, you can compute the third. For example, if the company has assets of $1,000,000 and liabilities of $700,000, then owners' equity is $300,000. Similarly, if the company has liabilities of $400,000 and owners' equity of $200,000, then assets are worth $600,000.

Accounting equation The relationship stating that assets equal liabilities plus owners' equity.

Assets Everything of value owned by an enterprise.

Liabilities Creditors' claims on an enterprise's assets.

Owners' equity The owners' claim on the assets of an enterprise.

Making chicken broth at
Campbell Soup Company. The
machinery and soup are assets
of the company, and the obligation to pay the worker is a
liability. The difference between the company's assets
and its liabilities constitutes the
owners' equity in Campbell.

Source: Courtesy of Campbell Soup
Company.

Double-Entry Bookkeeping

From the accounting equation, you can see that a change in one category means that the same or some other category must change to keep
the equation balanced. For example, if an asset increases, then another
asset must decrease or liabilities and/or owners' equity must increase by
the same amount. To maintain this balance, accountants use **double-
entry bookkeeping,** or the use of two entries for every transaction.

The actual entries start by recording a financial transaction in a journal. These are chronologically listed and represent changes in account
balances. These journal entries are then transferred to a ledger that contains separate accounts for items such as accounts receivable, inventory,
salaries, and sales. The data from these ledgers are then used to prepare
the financial statements. Traditionally, this process was done by hand by
bookkeepers. Today, much of this process is done by computers. For example, when a sale is made or an item is taken from or added to inventory, this information is inputted into the computer and stored until
called on for calculating financial statements.

As an example of double-entry bookkeeping, if a company buys
$7,500 of computer equipment, it has increased its assets by that
amount. However, it also has acquired the obligation to pay for the purchase within 30 days. This is a liability called "accounts payable." The
two changes to the equation are as follows:

Assets	=	Liabilities	+	Owners' Equity
$7,500	=	$7,500	+	$0
(equipment)		(accounts payable)		

**Double-entry
bookkeeping** The use of
two entries for every
transaction.

As shown, assets increase by $7,500 and this is counterbalanced by liabilities increasing by $7,500. Owner's equity is not affected.

Under double-entry bookkeeping every transaction requires two entries. Sometimes these involve a change in each side of the accounting equation; in other cases, they affect only one side. For example, if one of the assets increases, then one of the following occurs:

Another asset decreases by an equal amount. For example, the company could sell some machinery (decrease in assets) in exchange for cash (increase in assets).

Liability or owners' equity increases by an equal amount. For example, the company could sell some stock (increase in owners' equity) in exchange for cash (increase in assets).

Some combination of the two above will occur. For example, the company could buy a new facility (increase in assets) in exchange for a cash down payment (decrease in assets) plus an agreement to pay the balance in monthly installments (increase in liabilities).

In this way, the accounting equation remains in balance.

Accounting Statements

Over the years, accountants have developed basic formats for accounting statements. These formats give managers and others a basis for comparing the financial positions of different departments or companies. The accounting statements most commonly used for measuring a company's current profits and position for earning future profits are the balance sheet, the income statement, and the newly created statement of cash flows.

Checkpoint

1. What is the accounting equation?
2. How does double-entry bookkeeping work?

Balance Sheet

Balance sheet A financial statement showing the position of a firm as of a particular date.

The accounting equation serves as the basis for the **balance sheet,** which is a financial statement showing the position of a firm as of a particular date. It is akin to a snapshot of the enterprise. The balance sheet is commonly prepared as of the close of business on December 31. This makes it possible to compare how the balance sheet has changed from year to year. For example, how much has cash gone up over the last year, or how much have accounts payable declined?

Fiscal year The 12 months that constitute an organization's annual operation.

In some cases, organizations use a different **fiscal year,** which is the 12 months that constitute their annual operation. Some companies, and many governmental bodies, operate on a fiscal year from June 1 to May 31. The federal government's fiscal year runs from October 1 to September 30. Regardless of the specific 12 months involved, the annual balance sheet reflects the organization's financial position as of the end of the fiscal year.

The balance sheet describes the three elements of the accounting equation: assets, liabilities, and owners' equity. Each category contains a number of accounts. In examining these accounts, we will use the balance sheet of a fictitious company, the Sunrise Manufacturing Corporation, which appears in Table 15.1. The first column of data is taken from the ledger categories; the second column represents the totals for the categories (for example, there is $80,000 in cash assets); and the third column is the totals for assets, liabilities, owners' equity, and the grand total ($880,000).

T A B L E 15.1

SUNRISE MANUFACTURING CORPORATION
Balance Sheet
December 31, 19XX

Assets

Current Assets		
Cash		$ 80,000
Marketable securities		10,000
Accounts receivable	$170,000	
Less: Allowance for doubtful accounts	10,000	160,000
Notes receivable		15,000
Inventory		210,000
Prepaid expenses		5,000
Total current assets		$480,000
Fixed Assets		
Machinery and equipment	$310,000	
Less: Accumulated depreciation	50,000	$260,000
Office furniture and equipment	$ 30,000	
Less: Accumulated depreciation	10,000	20,000
Building	$ 70,000	
Less: Accumulated depreciation	20,000	50,000
Land		30,000
Total fixed assets		$360,000
Intangible Assets		
Patents	$ 30,000	
Goodwill	10,000	
Total intangible assets		$ 40,000
Total assets		$880,000

Liabilities and Owners' Equity

Current Liabilities		
Accounts payable	$ 80,000	
Notes payable	20,000	
Payroll and benefits payable	40,000	
Accrued taxes	70,000	
Accrued interest	40,000	
Total current liabilities		$250,000
Long-Term Liabilities		
Mortgage payable	$ 70,000	
Notes payable	20,000	
Long-term bonds outstanding	100,000	
Total long-term liabilities		190,000
Total liabilities		$440,000
Owners' Equity		
Common stock	$120,000	
Retained earnings	320,000	
Total owners' equity		440,000
Total liabilities and owners' equity		$880,000

Assets

The balance sheet usually divides the company's assets into three separate categories: current, fixed, and intangible assets.

Current assets Assets that the company will use or convert into cash within the year.

Current Assets It is often important to know which assets will be used or converted into cash within the next year. This gives an indication of the company's ability to generate cash. Therefore, balance sheets separate out these assets, called **current assets.** For the Sunrise Corporation, these include:

Cash. Funds that are on hand in the company or are in bank deposits and can be withdrawn as needed.

Marketable securities. Temporary investments of surplus funds in forms that can be quickly converted to cash when the need arises. Examples are stocks and bonds, described in Chapters 18 and 19.

Accounts receivable. Money due from customers who purchased goods and have not yet paid for them. In some cases, such as bills that are long overdue, managers expect that they will never be paid. To correct for this expectation, they subtract, or write off, the debt through an allowance for doubtful accounts ($10,000 for Sunrise).

Notes receivable. Money owed to the firm by someone who has been given funds and, in turn, signed a written document acknowledging the debt. An example is a loan made to a major supplier who wants to expand operations and provide better service to the company.

Inventory. Merchandise on hand, usually in the warehouse or out on the sales floor, which is available for sale, as well as raw materials, component parts, and goods that are in the manufacturing process.

Prepaid expenses. Goods and services that the company has paid for but not yet received or used. Examples include insurance premiums that are paid before the coverage goes into effect and supplies that are paid for before delivery.

Fixed assets Assets that the company intends to keep for more than one year and use in the operation of the business.

Depreciation A deduction from the value of a fixed asset to account for its gradual wearing out.

Fixed Assets The remaining tangible assets are **fixed assets,** which are assets that the company intends to keep for more than one year. These assets are used in the operation of the business. Examples of fixed assets include machinery, equipment, furniture, fixtures, buildings, and land.

Machines, furniture, and other fixed assets are listed at the purchase price, but they lose value from year to year because they gradually wear out. To account for this, each year the accountant subtracts a percentage of the initial cost of an asset. This deduction is called **depreciation.** The specific procedure for calculating depreciation varies and depends on federal laws that frequently change. In general, the company either selects an equation or uses a table that indicates the percentage of the total value to subtract in a given year. The company usually depreciates all fixed assets except land. Land is not depreciable because it is not considered to wear out and in fact it often increases in value.

Intangible assets Assets such as patents or goodwill that do not have physical presence.

Intangible Assets Sometimes a firm owns assets that do not have physical presence. If it does not, then this category will not be included in the balance sheet. These **intangible assets** include patents and goodwill. Goodwill represents the firm's reputation and is generally entered on the

Eddie Bauer has three broad
categories of assets. The store's
merchandise and the cash in
its cash registers are current
assets. Its fixtures and equipment are fixed assets. Its name
recognition and reputation for
quality are intangible assets.

Source: © Steve Niedorf 1987 for
General Mills, Incorporated.

company's books only if the firm buys another company and, in the process, pays for the goodwill. In other words, the buyer is willing to pay
for the intangible asset of the other company's excellent reputation.

Liabilities

Liabilities usually appear on the balance sheet in the order in which they
will come due. Specifically, current liabilities are followed by long-term
liabilities.

Current Liabilities Financial obligations that will fall due within the next
year are **current liabilities.** Table 15.1 shows typical liability accounts:

> *Accounts payable.* Amounts that the firm owes to its suppliers and oth-
> ers who have extended it credit.
>
> *Notes payable.* Loans due in one year or less to be paid by the firm.
> The firm has signed a written document or a note acknowledging
> the debt. An example would be a loan from a bank or a supplier.
>
> *Payroll and benefits payable.* Money owed to employees plus contribu-
> tions to be made to the health insurance and retirement programs.
>
> *Accrued taxes.* Taxes the company owes but has not yet paid.
>
> *Accrued interest.* The amount of interest owed on outstanding loans.

Current liabilities
Financial obligations that
will fall due within the
year.

Long-term liabilities
Debts that will be due one or more years in the future.

Long-Term Liabilities After current liabilities, the balance sheet lists **long-term liabilities,** debts that will be due one or more years after the balance sheet is drawn up. Table 15.1 provides some typical examples:

Mortgage payable. The outstanding real estate loan on the enterprise's land and buildings.

Notes payable. Loans that will come due in more than a year (usually two to five years).

Long-term bonds outstanding. Financial obligations that carry a fixed rate of interest and come due on a stipulated maturity date.

Owners' Equity

Common stock An ownership share in a corporation.

Retained earnings Profits that have been reinvested in the company.

The difference between total assets and total liabilities is the owners' equity in the company. The last part of the balance sheet shows the different accounts that make up owners' equity. For corporations, such as Sunrise Manufacturing, this includes common stock and retained earnings. **Common stock** is the most basic type of stock ownership. It represents an ownership share in the corporation. This stock is described in detail in Chapters 18 and 19. **Retained earnings** are profits that have been reinvested in the corporation. When the firm has a profit at the end of the year and decides to use these funds to expand operations, the retained earnings account will increase by this amount. Conversely, if the corporation suffers an operating loss, retained earnings will decline by the amount of the loss.

For unincorporated businesses (proprietorships and partnerships), the owners' equity section will contain the direct investment of the owner or each partner in a capital account. This capital account includes the initial investment, subsequent additional investments, withdrawals, and retention of earnings. Unlike the corporate equity section, which lists common stock and retained earnings in separate accounts, the unincorporated business has everything combined into the single account. By looking at this section of the balance sheet the reader can determine the type of ownership of the company.

The Balance Sheet as a Management Tool

The balance sheet is an important financial statement for controlling operations and helping management make effective decisions. It reveals whether the firm is solvent (i.e., current assets are greater than current liabilities, the firm can pay its bills and wages) by providing a breakdown of all assets, liabilities, and owners' equity. It allows managers to compare balance sheets from one year to the next to see changes in assets, liabilities, and owners' equity. By analyzing the data in the balance sheet and comparing it with previous years, managers can identify trends and pinpoint potential problem areas.

The balance sheet and the other financial statements of publicly held firms are printed in the annual report and are thus available to everyone. There is a trend to make annual reports slimmer and easier for stockholders to read,[5] and some firms, such as London's Burton Group (a fashion retailer) use the report as a marketing tool. Burton's report looks like a fashion magazine, with the required accounting figures squeezed in among lavish photos of fun-loving models wearing stylish clothes.[6] Except for these innovative uses, management depends on the balance sheet as a financial statement to help lenders analyze the firm as a credit risk. Managers also compare their company's balance sheet with those of their competitors in order to identify their company's relative strengths and weaknesses.

Checkpoint

1. What are the three major categories of accounts on the balance sheet?
2. What are two uses for the balance sheet?

Income Statement

Managers want to know more than whether the company has sufficient resources; they also want to know whether the company is using those resources successfully. For this accounting information, they turn to the income statement. An **income statement** is a financial statement that summarizes the firm's operations for a given period of time, usually one calendar or fiscal year. The income statement indicates whether the company made a profit or a loss (the famous "bottom line" of business). This bottom line determines the very survival of business firms in a free-enterprise economy.

Income statement A financial statement that summarizes the firm's operations for a given period of time, usually one year.

Contents of the Income Statement

Like the balance sheet, the income statement is based on an equation. This equation is:

$$\text{Revenues} - \text{Expenses} = \text{Profit}$$

Table 15.2 presents a sample income statement for the Sunrise Manufacturing Corporation. As you can see from the table, the income statement includes four categories: revenues, cost of goods sold, operating expenses, and net income.

Revenues The income statement begins by listing the company's revenues. This entry shows all the money the company earned during the year. Normally this is from sales, but in a professional service such as a doctor's office revenues will come from fees. Sometimes this entry is called "gross sales" or simply "sales." If the firm allows customers to return merchandise because the goods are damaged or do not meet quality standards, the accountant deducts these returns from the overall revenue to arrive at a net sales figure. Sunrise Manufacturing deducted $20,000 from total revenue for this reason.

Cost of Goods Sold The next section of the income statement describes the first of two kinds of expenses: cost of goods sold. The **cost of goods sold** consists of the costs involved in producing or acquiring a product to sell. For a manufacturing firm, the cost of goods sold primarily consists

Cost of goods sold The costs involved in producing or acquiring a product to sell.

SUNRISE MANUFACTURING CORPORATION
Income Statement
Year Ended December 31, 19XX

Revenue from Sales	$2,820,000	
Less: Sales returns and allowances	20,000	
Net sales		$2,800,000
Cost of Goods Sold		
Beginning inventory	$ 230,000	
Cost of goods manufactured	1,900,000	
Total goods available for sale	$2,130,000	
Less: Ending inventory	210,000	
Total cost of goods sold		1,920,000
Gross margin		$ 880,000
Operating Expenses		
Selling expenses	$ 180,000	
Administrative expenses	220,000	
General expenses	120,000	
Total expenses		520,000
Net Income from Operations		$ 360,000
Less: Interest expense		40,000
Net Income before Taxes		$ 320,000
Less: Taxes		80,000
Net Income		$ 240,000

T A B L E   15.2

of expenses for production employees and raw materials. For a wholesaler or retailer, the cost of goods sold includes the money spent to acquire and stock the inventory it has sold.

To calculate the cost of goods sold, the accountant measures how the inventory changed from the beginning to the end of the year. The first step is to ascertain beginning inventory (often from the previous year's income statement). To this amount, the accountant adds cost of goods manufactured for a manufacturing firm or purchases for a wholesaler or retailer for the year; the sum is the total cost of goods available for sale during the year. This amount minus the ending inventory gives the total costs of the goods actually sold. Figure 15.2 illustrates this calculation for a wholesaler or retailer. In some cases, the financial statement does not show these calculations, but merely contains an entry for cost of goods sold.

Subtracting the cost of goods sold from net sales gives the gross margin. Managers are interested in this figure because it gives them infor-

F I G U R E   15.2

Calculating Cost of Goods Sold for a Wholesaler or Retailer

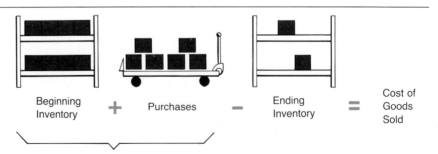

Beginning Inventory + Purchases − Ending Inventory = Cost of Goods Sold

Goods Available for Sale

mation on evaluating performance and, when compared to previous years, identifies trends that help in controlling the firm and making effective decisions.

Operating Expenses Besides spending money to produce what it sells, the company incurs other expenses to keep running and to sell its products. These operating expenses can be selling expenses, administrative expenses, or general expenses:

> *Selling expenses* are all costs directly related to the selling of goods and services. Examples include advertising, salaries and commissions paid to salespeople, sales supplies, delivery expenses, and other sales-related costs.

> *Administrative expenses* are costs incurred by the management and office personnel in running the company's operation. Examples are management salaries, secretarial wages, and rent.

> *General expenses* are all costs not charged directly to one department or unit because it is too difficult or time-consuming to determine their proper allocation. For example, property taxes, insurance, and utilities often fall into this category.

Companies that own fixed assets include a special kind of expense on their income statements: depreciation. Although the company doesn't actually spend any money on depreciation, this deduction is advantageous when calculating income for tax purposes. By using depreciation to reduce income, the accountant reduces the amount of taxes the company owes. This is the government's way of encouraging companies to invest in new facilities and equipment. In other situations, such as reporting the company's financial strengths to shareholders, the accountant tries to report as little depreciation as possible. Thus, within the guidelines of the law, which changes from time to time, accountants may consider the audience for their reports when selecting a method of calculating depreciation.

Net Income The last part of the income statement shows the computation of net income. Accountants specify income from operations and income before taxes to gain more information for effective decisions and to use in further analysis. First the accountant subtracts total expenses from gross margin to arrive at net income from continuing operations. Then the accountant deducts the interest expense on outstanding loans to arrive at net income before taxes. The interest expense is separated out from the other expenses to show the cost of borrowing and financing the operation. Finally, by deducting taxes, the accountant arrives at net income.

Income Statement Decisions

The income statement is more than just a series of numbers added and subtracted to arrive at net income. Accountants must exercise judgment in deciding how to present and evaluate various kinds of information. For example, you have learned that even though companies don't spend money on depreciation, the way it is calculated affects the amount of income the company reports. Other judgment calls involve ways of valuing inventory and handling inflation.

Rather than keeping track of every roll of paper towels and every can of corn, accountants for grocery stores and grocery distributors choose a standard method for valuing inventory. Either they assume that the last goods to arrive at the company are the first to be sold, or they assume that the first goods to arrive are the first to be sold. Albertson's, Inc., which distributes the merchandise shown here, uses the former method, known as LIFO, for most of its inventory. It reports that fact in a footnote to its financial statements.

Source: Courtesy of Albertson's Inc.

LIFO An inventory valuation system under which the last goods produced or acquired are considered the first ones sold (**L**ast **I**n, **F**irst **O**ut).

FIFO An inventory valuation system under which the first goods produced or acquired are considered the first ones sold (**F**irst **I**n, **F**irst **O**ut).

F I G U R E   15.3

Inventory Valuation Systems: LIFO and FIFO

Valuing Inventory Accountants have a choice in deciding how to value inventory. The reason for this is that it would be costly and difficult to keep track of exactly which costs are associated with the sale of which items. To take an extreme example, imagine a hardware store that sells nails the old-fashioned way, from bins. The last batch of number 10 common nails that the store bought cost 5 cents a pound; the store sells them for 25 cents a pound. These nails are popular, so the next month the store gets another shipment of nails at 6 cents a pound and dumps them in the bin with the nails left from the preceding month. During the following week, customers come in and grab nails by the handful. Which nails are they buying: the 5-cent nails or the 6-cent nails?

Obviously, the company can't keep track, so it has its accountant make assumptions. Either the company assumes that it always sells the oldest nails it has, or it assumes that it always sells the nails that it bought most recently. If the accountant assumes that the last goods received are the first ones sold (Last In, First Out), the inventory system is called **LIFO.** If the accountant assumes that the first goods received are the first ones sold (First In, First Out), the inventory system is called **FIFO.** Figure 15.3 illustrates the difference.

LIFO

Last-in (Green Items)
3 @ $120 each

First-out (Any 3 Items)
Cost $360

FIFO

First-in (Red Items)
3 @ $100 each

First-out (Any 3 Items)
Cost $300

In times of rapid inflation, LIFO produces higher cost of goods sold, a less valuable ending inventory, and lower profits. In contrast, FIFO brings about a lower cost of goods sold, a more valuable ending inventory, and greater profits. Many firms opt for LIFO in order to keep down their reported profits and, as a result, their cash payments for taxes. The choice of method is an important decision, because once set up, it takes government approval to change it. The financial statement should specify which method is used so that readers can take this into consideration in evaluating the firm's overall performance.

Handling Inflation Besides having an impact on inventory values, inflation affects a company's bottom line in various ways. Inflation can enable a company to charge higher prices for its products, but it can also cause expenses to rise. For example, if a fast-food outlet that sells hamburgers for $1.20 finds that inflation enables it to raise prices to $1.30, it will receive 10 cents more for each hamburger it sells. If it sells 1,000 hamburgers a week, this increase comes to $100 more a week. However, the company may also find that it has to pay more for wages, ground beef, and heating the restaurant. Thus, revenues may increase, but not necessarily by as much as the expenses.

In evaluating an increase in revenues or even profits, you need to keep in mind whether the increase is the result of effective management or simply inflation. If the change reflects inflation, the company may run into serious problems when inflation slows.

Benefits of the Income Statement

Like the balance sheet, the income statement can be an important resource for effective management control and decision making. Most fundamentally, it tells managers whether the firm is operating at a profit. By comparing income statements from one period to another, the managers can see which expenses are rising too quickly and take steps to control them. The statement also allows banks and other financial institutions to evaluate the firm's creditworthiness. It shows whether the business is able to generate a profit with its resources.

Checkpoint

1. What equation is the basis of the income statement?
2. How do accountants determine the cost of the goods the company sold?

Statement of Cash Flows

Besides a balance sheet and an income statement, accountants for most companies also prepare a **statement of cash flows.** This financial statement has just recently come on the scene and has replaced the funds statement or statement of changes in financial position. The older statement was mainly concerned with changes in working capital (current assets minus current liabilities). This newly accepted financial statement of cash flows provides information regarding a firm's cash receipts and cash

Statement of cash flows
Provides information regarding a firm's cash receipts and cash payments.

payments. It does so by an **activity format,** which classifies cash inflows and outflows in terms of operating, investing, and financing activities.

Operating activities relate to a firm's main revenue-generating activities; the cash flows from operating activities. Cash inflows from customer collections would be the major one. Investing activities include lending money, say, to a supplier, and collecting on those loans. Another example reflecting the outflow of cash would be purchases of equipment and the inflow would be the sale of equipment. Financing activities would include borrowing and repaying money from creditors, obtaining funds from owners, and paying dividends to stockholders. Table 15.3 shows an example of a statement of cash flows. This financial statement helps management better control and manage their cash flows, which are vital to their solvency.

Activity format Classifies cash inflows and outflows in terms of operating, investing, and financing activities.

Checkpoint

1. What is measured by the statement of cash flows?
2. What are the three major activities involved in the cash flow?

Analysis of Financial Statements

Over the years, accountants and managers have developed standard techniques for evaluating the information contained in the various financial statements. Generally, they start by putting the statement into context. Then they use techniques based on a variety of ratios.

T A B L E   15.3

SUNRISE MANUFACTURING CORPORATION
Statement of Cash Flows
Year Ended December 31, 19XX

Cash flows from operating activities:		
Operations: net income	$ 240,000	
Add (deduct) items not affecting cash:		
Depreciation expense	40,000	
Increase in accounts receivable (net)	(10,000)	
Decrease in inventory	20,000	
Decrease in accounts payable	(5,000)	
Net cash provided by operating activities		$ 285,000
Cash flows from investing activities:		
Sale of equipment	10,000	
Purchase of machinery	(100,000)	
Net cash used by investing activities		(90,000)
Cash flows from financing activities:		
Retirement of mortgage payable	(100,000)	
Dividends	(50,000)	
Net cash used by financing activities		(150,000)
Net increase in cash		$ 45,000

Putting the Statement in Context

When managers and others evaluate a company's performance and compare it to the performance of other companies, they must evaluate the context in which the accounting information appears. This requires an understanding of the environment in which the company has been operating. It also requires taking into account the various choices the accountant made.

A company's performance is colored by the economic environment. You have already learned that inflation can affect a business's profits. Likewise, companies typically suffer during an economic downturn. Some industries, such as real estate and oil, are particularly prone to business cycles. It would be misleading to evaluate an individual company's performance without taking these circumstances into account. If a company prospers during a time of growth or struggles during an economic decline, the evaluator must look for clues that indicate whether the performance reflects the position of the particular company or the nature of the economy in general.

The manager also needs to consider the accounting techniques used. As you have already learned, how depreciation was calculated or the technique for valuing inventory affect the business's financial statements. The person using accounting information must determine whether a change in the financial statement reflects a change in the company's health or merely the adoption of a new accounting technique.

Analysis Using Ratios

Calculating ratios is a popular method of analyzing financial statements. Ratios are calculated by dividing one item on a financial statement by another item. The ratio shows relationships between financial variables. Managers who use ratio analysis can pinpoint where the firm is doing well and where it is doing poorly. When compared with previous years, the ratios identify trends. Many different types of ratios can be calculated to measure a company's short- and long-run position and profitability.

Ratios Measuring Short-Run Position Ratios that measure the firm's short-run position investigate its liquidity. The short-run position is the firm's ability to pay currently maturing obligations, usually liabilities due within a year. **Liquidity** is the ease with which an asset can be converted into cash. For example, a firm with most of its assets in cash, stock, and accounts receivable is considered to be very liquid, because stocks are easy to sell and accounts receivable are likely to be paid before long. Conversely, a firm with most of its assets tied up in real estate and slow-moving inventory has very low liquidity. The two most common ratios that measure a firm's short-run position are the current ratio and the acid-test ratio.

The **current ratio,** the ratio of current assets to current liabilities, is a simple way to assess liquidity. For Sunrise Manufacturing (see Table 15.1), the current ratio is:

Liquidity The ease with which an asset can be converted into cash.

Current ratio The ratio of current assets to current liabilities.

$$\frac{\text{Total Current Assets}}{\text{Total Current Liabilities}} = \frac{\$480,000}{\$250,000} = 1.92 \text{ to } 1$$

This current ratio provides an indication of Sunrise's ability to meet its current liabilities.

Is 1.92 to 1 an adequate ratio? The answer will depend on the industry. Utilities have a lower current ratio than manufacturing firms. For a typical utility, 1 to 1 is adequate because the company has predictable sales, a high collection rate, and no product inventory. For most other kinds of firms, however, 2 to 1 or better is generally considered acceptable. Since Sunrise Manufacturing's current ratio is less than this, its managers may be a little concerned. On the other hand, they should withhold judgment until they compute the other liquidity ratio, the acid-test ratio.

Acid-test ratio The ratio of highly liquid assets to current liabilities.

The **acid-test ratio** (sometimes known as the quick ratio) compares highly liquid assets against current liabilities. While it resembles the current ratio, the acid-test ratio compares only highly liquid assets—cash, marketable securities, and accounts receivable—against current liabilities. It does not take inventory into account because of the time it will take to convert this asset into cash. Thus, it is a more conservative ratio than the current ratio. The acid-test ratio gives increased information on a firm's ability to pay short-term debts. For Sunrise Manufacturing, the acid-test ratio is:

$$\frac{\text{Cash + Marketable Securities + Accounts Receivable + Notes Receivable}}{\text{Current Liabilities}}$$

$$= \frac{\$80,000 + \$10,000 + \$160,000 + \$15,000}{\$250,000} = \frac{\$265,000}{\$250,000} = 1.06 \text{ to } 1$$

A generally acceptable acid-test ratio is 1 to 1. If the manager doubts that marketable securities and accounts and notes receivable can be converted dollar for dollar, then 1.5 to 1 is acceptable. Sunrise Manufacturing meets the guideline, so it should have no trouble covering its current liabilities.

Ratios Measuring Long-Run Position Managers who use financial statement analysis to control the firm are also interested in its long-run position. A representative ratio that measures long-run position is the debt-equity ratio.

Debt-equity ratio The ratio of total debt to total equity.

To calculate the **debt-equity ratio,** divide total debt by total equity. For Sunrise Manufacturing, this calculation is:

$$\frac{\text{Total Debt}}{\text{Total Owners' Equity}} = \frac{\$440,000}{\$440,000} = 1 \text{ to } 1$$

This calculation indicates that the firm is being financed equally by debt and equity. Many lenders avoid lending a greater amount than the owners have in equity. A total debt-equity ratio of 1 to 1 is thus the maximum. In the future, it is likely that Sunrise will begin paying off this debt or increasing its equity by selling more stock and retaining more profits.

Income Statement Ratios Business people also calculate ratios from the data on the income statement. These ratios provide a measure of current operating performance and efficiency. A common income statement ratio is the net profit margin ratio.

The **net profit margin ratio** compares net income to net sales. For Sunrise Manufacturing, this calculation is:

$$\frac{\text{Net Income}}{\text{Net Sales}} = \frac{\$240,000}{\$2,800,000} = 8.6\%$$

The net profit margin shows the company's overall profitability. By comparing this year's margin with those of the last three to five years, managers can see whether profitability is improving or declining. The 8.6 percent figure for Sunrise is fairly typical for modern firms. Profit margins are generally much lower than many people realize.

Combined Ratios Business people can gain additional insights from ratios that combine information from the balance sheet with information from the income statement. The most popular of these combined ratios are used to measure the level of activity known as the inventory turnover and to refine the profitability picture by analyzing the return on owners' equity and earnings per share in corporations.

   Inventory turnover indicates the number of times that inventory is replaced during the year. Managers keep track of this because inventory that sits unsold on the shelf of a store or in a warehouse costs the firm money. It takes up space, may wear out or become dated, and ties up funds the company could have invested in something more profitable. Consequently, managers try to keep inventory turnover relatively high.

   To compute inventory turnover, divide the cost of goods sold during the year by the average inventory. *Average inventory* is the average of beginning and ending inventory; to compute it, add those amounts and divide by two. For Sunrise Manufacturing, average inventory is calculated this way:

$$\frac{\text{Beginning Inventory} + \text{Ending Inventory}}{2} = \frac{\$230,000 + \$210,000}{2} = \$220,000$$

Then use average inventory to calculate inventory turnover:

$$\frac{\text{Cost of Goods Sold}}{\text{Average Inventory}} = \frac{\$1,920,000}{\$220,000} = 8.7$$

Sunrise is turning over its inventory 8.7 times a year. To determine the average number of days that inventory was on hand before being sold, divide 8.7 into 365, the number of days in a year:

$$\text{Average Number of Days to Turnover} = \frac{365}{8.7} = 42$$

   To determine whether 8.7 is a good inventory turnover figure, you need to gather data on what competing firms are doing. If competitors have a turnover of 6.0, Sunrise is doing well. If the competition has a turnover of 11.3, Sunrise is doing poorly and must take steps to increase its turnover. This might involve dropping slow-moving lines or increasing sales on credit.

   A more accurate financial picture of profitability requires a comparison of the income to the amount of investment that has been made. **Return on owners' investment** is the ratio of net income to total owners'

Net profit margin ratio
The ratio of net income to net sales.

Inventory turnover   The number of times that inventory is replaced during the year, expressed as the ratio of costs of goods sold to average inventory.

Return on owners' investment   The ratio of net income to total owners' equity.

equity. Commonly referred to as return on investment or simply ROI, this ratio tells the stockholders the return the company earned on their investment. For Sunrise Manufacturing, the calculation is:

$$\frac{\text{Net Income}}{\text{Total Owners' Equity}} = \frac{\$240,000}{\$440,000} = 55\%$$

This return is extremely high. The owners could not possibly get this type of return on their money from a bank or a government note. Sunrise is doing extremely well, and the stockholders should be pleased.

A final profitability ratio is the **earnings per share.** This popular ratio shows the amount of income or profits earned for each share of common stock outstanding. Outside investors obviously are very interested in this ratio. Management uses it to decide on dividends to pay stockholders and as an important measure of performance of the firm. For Sunrise, it would be calculated as follows:

$$\frac{\text{Net Income}}{\text{Common Stock Shares Outstanding}} = \frac{\$240,000}{\$120,000} = \$2.00$$

This $2.00 earnings per share can be compared to those of other years and to those of competitors in the same industry. Chapter 19 covers the topic of stocks in more detail.

Ratio Analysis in Perspective The ratios we have discussed are useful, but, as was stated earlier, anyone evaluating the numbers must put them in the context of the company's practices and the economic environment. Sometimes a company's prospects are brighter or gloomier than the ratio numbers would suggest. To see how observers of the banking industry put one company's performance into context, read "Business Communication Close-Up: The Numbers Don't Always Speak for Themselves." While ratio analysis is a useful tool for helping make more effective decisions, managers must be careful not to let the numbers alone make the decision.

Checkpoint

1. Define two ratios managers use to interpret a company's financial position.
2. How do business people decide whether the company is earning an adequate return on its assets or owners' equity?

Closing Comments

This chapter launched a discussion of the decision tools that lead to effective management. The particular focus of attention was on the generation and analysis of accounting information. Accountants construct the firm's financial statements and often participate in analyzing them to help managers make informed decisions. Managers inside the firm and other business people on the outside analyze financial information by determining how much of net sales covers expenses and how much goes to income, as well as by calculating a variety of ratios.

Earnings per share The ratio of net income to common stock shares outstanding.

Learning Objectives Revisited

1. **Define accounting and the types of accountants.**

   Accounting is the process of measuring, interpreting, evaluating, and communicating financial information for the purpose of effective decision making. The two main types of accountants are public accountants and private accountants. Public accountants, who may be certified, are accountants who are independent of the business they serve. Private accountants work for a business other than a public accounting firm. They include internal auditors, managerial accountants, and general accountants.

2. **Discuss the nature and types of budgets.**

   A budget is a financial plan that specifies revenues and expenses for a given time period. The budget helps managers plan and control

---

BUSINESS COMMUNICATION   **CLOSE-UP**

The Numbers Don't Always Speak for Themselves

Recently A. W. Clausen was appointed chairman of BankAmerica Corporation. An examination of the actions that followed his appointment illustrates the fact that business people must be careful in evaluating the numbers on a financial statement.

For example, under Clausen, BankAmerica began selling assets. This doesn't change balance sheet totals, because the company brings in cash, another asset. The company does generate revenue, however, thereby improving its bottom line. But what does this indicate about long-term performance? It means that the company has fewer assets to use in the future and might mean that its managers are having trouble generating money from the company's real business. The careful analyst notes the proportion of revenues coming from the sale of assets and tries to assess how much the company can generate from its operations.

Another tactic BankAmerica has adopted since Clausen's arrival has been to record total fees charged on new mortgages as income in the year in which the mortgages are created. The more conservative strategy adopted by most banks is to spread the fees over the 15- to 30-year life of the loan, recognizing

only part of the fees as revenue in each year. BankAmerica created as much as $70 million in annual profits by using the same strategy from 1979 to 1981. But in subsequent years, when the bank didn't have these fees to add to revenues, profits suffered.

BankAmerica has also been cutting costs, and computer systems and engineering have been hard hit. More than half of a skilled group of computer systems managers were fired or quit during Clausen's first six months. This will reduce salary expenses, but observers wonder whether the bank will be able to keep up with changing technology and hence keep costs down over the long run.

These examples suggest that someone looking at recent financial statements for BankAmerica should look beyond the numbers to consider whether a jump in profits reflects business strength or merely accounting practices. One industry observer noted, "After he runs out of assets to sell, Tom's going to have real trouble." Many are wondering whether Clausen's strategies are sacrificing the company's future in order to communicate business strength in the present.

operations by identifying objectives and then providing feedback regarding how well the company is doing in meeting these targets. Some of the most popular budgets are the sales budget, the production budget, the cost of goods sold budget, and the cash budget.

3. **Explain the accounting equation and double-entry bookkeeping.**
The accounting equation is assets equal liabilities plus owners' equity. Assets are everything of value that the enterprise owns. Liabilities are creditors' claims on the enterprise's assets. Owners' equity is the owners' claim on the assets of the enterprise. To keep the equation in balance, accountants use double-entry bookkeeping, the use of two entries for every transaction. If the total on one side of the accounting equation changes, then the accountant must make an offsetting entry to keep the sides in balance.

4. **Describe the balance sheet.**
The balance sheet describes the three components of the accounting equation: assets, liabilities, and owners' equity. The asset side of the balance sheet has two major categories: current assets and fixed assets. On the other side of the balance sheet are liabilities and owners' equity. The liabilities are current liabilities and long-term liabilities. The owners' equity section for a corporation lists stock and retained earnings and for an unincorporated business contains a single capital account.

5. **Present the income statement and the statement of cash flows.**
An income statement summarizes the firm's operations for a given period of time. It reports the revenue from sales after deducting returns and allowances, as well as the cost of the goods that were sold, the operating expenses, and the net income. The statement of cash flows provides information on cash receipts and cash payments. Using an activity format, it classifies cash flows in terms of the operating, investing, and financing activities of the firm.

6. **Identify ratios used to analyze financial statements.**
Some of the most important balance sheet ratios used in evaluating a firm's performance measure the company's short-run and long-run position. For the short run, these include the current ratio (current assets divided by current liabilities) and the acid-test ratio (liquid assets divided by current liabilities). For the long run, a representative ratio would be the debt-equity ratio (total debt divided by total owners' equity). An important income statement ratio used in evaluating a firm's performance is the net profit margin ratio (net income divided by net sales). Ratios that combine information from these statements are used to measure the level of activity such as the inventory turnover and refine the profitability picture by analyzing the return on investment or ROI (net income divided by owners' equity) and earnings per share.

Key Terms Reviewed

Review each of the following terms. For any that you do not know or are unsure of, look up the definitions and see how they were used in the chapter.

accounting

certified public accountant (CPA)

certified management accountant (CMA)

budget

accounting equation

assets

liabilities

owners' equity

double-entry bookkeeping

balance sheet

fiscal year

current assets

fixed assets

depreciation

intangible assets

current liabilities

long-term liabilities

common stock

retained earnings

income statement

cost of goods sold

LIFO

FIFO

statement of cash flows

activity format

liquidity

current ratio

acid-test ratio

debt-equity ratio

net profit margin ratio

inventory turnover

return on owners' investment

earnings per share

Review Questions

1. What is accounting? Why should anyone besides accountants be interested in this financial information?
2. What is the difference between a certified public accountant (CPA) and a certified management accountant (CMA)? How do their activities differ?
3. Ron Jacobs is business manager of a theater group that puts on plays in a small auditorium it owns downtown. In planning the group's finances for the upcoming season, what kinds of budgets should Ron use? What kinds of information should these budgets contain? Try to be specific.
4. What is the accounting equation? Describe how each of the following transactions would affect the elements of the accounting equation.
   a. A bakery sells doughnuts for cash.
   b. A car rental company acquires a new fleet of cars and agrees to pay for them within 90 days.
   c. An insurance company pays stockholders a dividend of $1 for every share of stock they own.
   d. A factory pays its workers their weekly wages.
5. What basic kinds of information appear on a balance sheet? Why are managers interested in this information?

6. Define the different categories of assets. Identify each of the following as a current, fixed, or intangible asset.
   a. A printing press
   b. The shoes in a shoe store
   c. The shoe store's reputation for quality
   d. The chairs in a doctor's waiting room
7. What is owners' equity? What forms does it take?
8. On what equation is the income statement based? What is the bottom line for a company that had total sales of $750,000 and spent $400,000 to produce the goods it sold and $200,000 on other expenses?
9. When Ann Wilson prepares the tax returns for Big T Manufacturing, she tries to depreciate the company's machinery as quickly as is legally possible. In other words, she tries to write off the maximum proportion of the total value in the first years of the machinery's life. Why would she want to do this? What effects does her approach have on the company's profits?
10. What are two ways in which accountants measure the value of inventory? Describe how each works.
11. What is the statement of cash flows? What can business people learn from reading one?
12. What general procedures do business people follow in analyzing financial statements?
13. What is liquidity? Why is it important? What are two ways to measure it?
14. At the Thrill-A-Minute Amusement Park, total assets come to $5.5 million, total debts are $3 million, and owners' equity is $2.5 million. Compute a ratio that measures the company's long-run position. How can you tell whether such a ratio is favorable or not?
15. What ratio can a manager use to analyze the information on an income statement? Describe how it is calculated.
16. Why is inventory turnover important? Why is turnover in accounts receivable important?

Applied Exercises

1. At the library, go through the appropriate *Moody's* manual and get a copy of the most recent balance sheets for Citicorp, PepsiCo, and USX. Compare the balance sheets in terms of the major categories. Based on your comparison, what conclusions can you draw? Write them down and share them with the class.
2. Compare the income statements of the three firms listed in Question 1. Based on your comparison, what conclusions can you draw? Write them down and share them with the class.
3. Interview an accountant from a large local firm. Does the company use FIFO or LIFO for its inventory? Why? Write down the accountant's explanation and report your findings to the class. Compare your accountant's answer with those of others in the class. Are the answers basically the same, or are there different reasons?
4. Interview a public accountant who holds a CPA. Ask what generally accepted accounting principles are the toughest to implement in actual accounting practice. Why? Compare what you find with others in the class.

Your Business IQ: Answers

1. False. Only the certified public accountant (CPA) is legally considered the final authority.

2. True. This procedure, called double-entry bookkeeping, keeps a balance between assets on one side of the accounting equation and liabilities and equity on the other.

3. True. The period beginning October 1 and ending September 30 is called the federal government's fiscal year. Like the federal government, some businesses select fiscal years that begin on a date other than January 1.

4. True. The company's profit or loss, which appears at the bottom of its income statement, is often called the "bottom line" of the business.

5. False. Part of evaluating a company's performance is to evaluate the context in which the information appears. The analyst should consider how the company has been affected by environmental influences such as business cycles and new laws, and how the company plans to respond to these influences.

Case

Sam's Success

The fastest growing retail chain in America over the past decade has been Wal-Mart Stores, Inc., of Bentonville, Arkansas. Founded in the 1950s by Sam Walton, who continues to be the company's chairman, Wal-Mart has seen annual sales growth of 30 to 40 percent in each of the last 10 years.

Most of Wal-Mart's stores are located in the central and southern part of the United States. The stores offer general merchandise at discount prices. In addition, Wal-Mart has wholesale clubs, a discount drug outlet, and is now opening hypermarts.

When Sam Walton first started his company, he made the decision to open outlets only in small towns. Major low-price retailers had bypassed this market because they believed there was not enough business to support their stores. In this way, Walton was able to avoid going head-to-head with firms such as K mart and Sears. His strategy has proven so successful that he is now opening over 100 new stores a year.

Bankers and investors alike agree that Wal-Mart is a phenomenal success story. Its financial statements show rapid sales and profit growth (see the following balance sheet and income statement), and its stock price has risen so phenomenally over the last 10 years that many of the employees who started out with Sam Walton are millionaires today. Wal-Mart plans to be the second largest retailer, behind Sears, within the next decade. Given its annual rate of growth, this appears to be an achievable goal.

WAL-MART STORES, INC., AND SUBSIDIARIES
Balance Sheet, January 31, 1986 and 1987

Assets	(Amounts in thousands)	
	1986	1987
Current assets		
Cash	$ 9,250	$ 8,527
Short-term money market investments	165,168	157,018
Receivables	57,662	90,380
Inventories	152,410	47,160
Prepaid expenses	1,388,168	2,030,972
Other	11,617	19,214
Total current assets	$ 1,784,275	$ 2,353,271
Property, plant, and equipment, at cost:		
Land	$ 103,514	$ 134,351
Buildings and improvements	314,325	402,845
Fixtures and equipment	474,769	655,253
Transportation equipment	44,131	45,346
	$ 936,739	$ 1,273,795
Less accumulated depreciation	192,380	267,722
Net property, plant, and equipment	$ 744,359	$ 970,073
Property under capital leases	652,003	832,337
Less accumulated amortization	92,912	126,128
Net property under capital leases	$ 559,091	$ 706,209
Other assets	15,920	19,539
Total assets	$ 3,103,645	$ 4,049,092

Liabilities and Owners' Equity	(Amounts in thousands) 1986	1987
Current liabilities		
Accounts payable	$ 695,439	$ 924,654
Accrued liabilities		
Salaries	49,698	62,774
Taxes, other than income	39,704	46,496
Other	107,158	159,985
Accrued federal and state income taxes	89,399	132,833
Long-term debt due within one year	1,605	1,448
Obligations under capital leases due within one year	9,680	12,101
Total current liabilities	$ 992,683	$ 1,340,291
Long-term liabilities		
Long-term debt	180,682	179,234
Long-term obligations under capital leases	595,205	764,128
Deferred income taxes	52,514	74,946
Preferred stock with mandatory redemption revisions	4,902	—
Common shareholders' equity		
Common stock	209,211	$ 220,075
Retained earnings	18,068,448	18,470,418
Total common shareholders' equity	$1,277,659	$ 1,690,493
Total liabilities and shareholders' equity	$3,103,645	$ 4,049,092

WAL-MART STORES, INC., AND SUBSIDIARIES
Income Statement, Year Ended January 31, 1986 and 1987

	(Amounts in thousands) 1986	1987
Revenues:		
Net sales	$ 8,451,489	$11,909,076
Rentals and other	55,127	84,623
	$ 8,506,616	$11,993,699
Costs and expenses:		
Costs of sales	6,361,271	9,053,219
Operating, selling, and general and administrative expenses	1,485,210	2,007,645
Interest costs	56,543	86,809
	$ 7,903,024	$ 846,026
Income before income taxes	603,592	395,940
Provision for federal and state income taxes	276,119	—
Net income	$ 327,473	$ 450,086

Case Questions

1. What was Wal-Mart's working capital during the two years presented in the financial statements? What conclusions can you draw as a result of your calculations?
2. What was Wal-Mart's net profit margin rate and return on investment (ROI) during the two years presented in the financial statements? What conclusions can you draw as a result of your calculations?
3. In addition to the financial calculations you have made already, what other accounting ratios would you compute in determining how well the firm is doing? Explain.

You Be the Adviser:
The Proposed Expansion

The Beldon Company is a large retail store that sells a wide variety of home appliances and convenience goods. Last year the company had a beginning inventory of $1 million, inventory purchases of $4 million, and an ending inventory of $1 million. The store sells its merchandise for double what it pays, and annual sales are approximately twice that of the competition. However, Beldon would like to expand.

For $2 million, the store will be able to double its warehouse and showroom floor space and, its managers hope, also double its annual sales. The competition currently turns its inventory over eight times a year, and Beldon would like to get its turnover up to ten times. At the present time, cash stands at $100,000, accounts receivable are $400,000, inventory is $1 million, and current liabilities are $2.5 million.

The president of Beldon believes that the company should expand operations as soon as possible. The accountant disagrees. She feels that, if anything, the firm should work on controlling inventory more closely.

Your Advice

1. From the information presented in the case, what is its present inventory turnover?
2. Based on your calculations in Question 1, what conclusions can you draw regarding inventory turnover? Explain.
3. Would you recommend following the president's desire to expand or the accountant's suggestion that the firm focus on controlling inventory? Explain your recommendation.

Information Systems and Computers

LEARNING OBJECTIVES

- Explain how information systems help managers make decisions.
- Describe the evolution of computers.
- Identify the hardware and software components of computers.

- Define the basic types of computers.
- Discuss how business people evaluate the merits of computers.
- Present the basic applications of computers to business.

Your Business IQ

How much do you already know about information systems and computers? Test your business IQ by labeling each statement *true* or *false*. Answers and explanations are at the end of the chapter.

1. Top managers typically need information for long-term planning, while first-line managers more often need information that helps them run day-to-day operations.
2. Although modern computers are much more compact and faster than their earlier counterparts, they cost significantly less.
3. Computers are useful for some routine tasks, but they will never be able to mimic human thinking.
4. The term *hardware* refers to the instructions, or programming, of computers.
5. Businesses use computers more for designing new products than for any other function.

Computerized reservation systems, such as this one installed by Unisys for Trans World Airlines, provide information about available flights and fares. The reservation agents can use the computer to update information to reflect ticket sales and cancellations.

Source: Courtesy of Unisys Corporation.

Looking Back and Ahead

The government is an enormous user of information. Government employees keep billions of records for identifying needs, locating fugitives, collecting taxes, and more. Most records are stored on computers, enabling the government to compare various sets of data to identify inconsistencies. This approach helps a variety of government workers, including police, social workers, and tax collectors.

However, as is also the case in the private sector, the information is only as good as the people entering and retrieving it and the system designed to handle it. The way information is entered influences the quality of data at the FBI's National Crime Information Center (NCIC). The information comes largely from local police agencies, and the quality varies widely from state to state. In Mobile, Alabama, three-quarters of the wanted persons were listed as weighing 499 pounds and standing 7 feet, 11 inches tall—the maximum entries. Investigation revealed that the person entering data in Mobile thought that only names, not weight and height, needed to be entered into the system.

Poor retrieval and analysis at another agency caused problems for California math teacher Frederick Harris. After running a match for delinquent student loans, the Department of Education billed Harris for a $5,814 college loan. He assured the agency that he had never taken out a student loan and was being confused with another Harris with a different social security number, address, and college. Nevertheless, the Department of Education sent Harris's record to a private credit agency; as a result, he was turned down for a car loan. Only when Harris's congressional representative intervened did the department admit its mistake.[1]

As these examples show, statistics are only a part of how managers use numbers to make decisions. For statistical and other information to help managers, it must be accurate and readily available. Therefore, most businesses have systems for collecting and organizing information and for making it available to the managers who need it. This chapter begins by describing what information systems are and some ways in which businesses use them. For help in generating and managing information, most businesses today rely on computers. The chapter therefore examines the evolution of computers, describes how they work, and identifies some benefits and disadvantages of using computers. It concludes with a discussion of basic applications of computers in business.

The Role of Information Systems and Computers in Business

We live in an information age. Many of the business activities discussed so far—personnel, operations, marketing, and accounting—both depend on and result in the generation of information. Thus most organizations are directly involved in producing information, whether they are part of the manufacturing sector or the service sector. For example, in their book *Re-inventing the Corporation*, Naisbitt and Aburdene note that,

> A large percentage of the half a million people working for GM in the United States get paid for processing information, not for making cars. There are the accountants, the managers, clerical and sec-

retarial staff as well as the data processing people. The same goes for most other industrial companies.[2]

In the service sector, employees in financial services, insurance, transportation, communications, health care, professional services, and utilities are heavily involved in generating and using huge amounts of information. With this information explosion, information systems are more important than ever.

Management Information Systems

Few businesses have a shortage of data. Rather, most are swamped by a daily inpouring of sales literature, news stories, press releases, customer comments, and internally generated production, sales, and financial reports. The decision maker's problem, therefore, has become not one of how to get data, but how to sift through it and make sense of it. This process consists of turning data into information, that is, data relevant to the decision maker.

To turn data into information, businesses use some form of a **management information system (MIS),** a method for collecting, analyzing, and disseminating timely information to support decision making. The MIS determines what information each decision maker needs, finds a source of that information, and reports the information to the decision maker. Although microfilm, television, and telephones can be used to collect and store information, computers are most closely associated with today's management information systems.

Management information system (MIS) A method for collecting, analyzing, and disseminating timely information to support decision making.

Computerizing the MIS

Because of the great volume of information that business decision makers must handle, they have found it helpful to rely on computers. Computers are a useful tool in an MIS because they can search through and manipulate data very quickly, making it more readily available than can be done manually. The kinds of information a computer can manipulate vary widely, from sales and population statistics to the words in this text.

The growing power and shrinking price of computers have brought about a computer revolution in business. Some have labeled it the Second Industrial Revolution. Not only are more firms buying computers, more computer firms are offering a wider selection of models. Large and small businesses alike are seeking niches in the industry (see "Small Business Close-Up: Computer Services"). As a result, millions of American households and businesses now have computers. In some cases, it is even proving to be a link between the home and the workplace. Every night and on weekends, thousands of business people across the country take work home with them and do it on their own computer. Some people, especially salespeople, have portable laptop models they can take on the road. Jetting across the United States at 35,000 feet, today's business person can process orders, write memos, and carry out financial computations.

To keep computers in perspective, however, remember that the most common use of these machines is as a tool for storing and manipulating data. Consequently, their benefits depend on the quality of data entered

Purchasing a lottery ticket by touching characters on a screen. On this computer system, the screen acts as the input unit. Because this form of input is simple and requires no training of the user, it has become an increasingly popular way to enable customers to make purchases.

Source: Courtesy of Bally Manufacturing Corporation.

and the skill of the user. In addition, the computer is most useful to decision making in a business if it is part of a system to organize the collection and dissemination of information.

Checkpoint

1. What is a management information system?
2. How do business people use computers to manage information?

SMALL BUSINESS CLOSE-UP

Computer Services

Small businesses find it extremely difficult to succeed at producing computers. The costs of entering the market are high, and the likelihood of success is slim. IBM, Apple, Digital Equipment, Hewlett Packard, Wang, and several other large firms already dominate the industry.

Small firms also find it difficult to sell personal computers. The retail end of the business has seen a great number of failures in recent years. Stiff competition comes from company-owned retail outlets and large retailers that buy in huge quantities and pass the savings on to their customers. New retailers have to build name recognition while keeping prices low.

However, small businesses are finding opportunities in a new industry: personal computer services. As more firms and individuals purchase computers or upgrade their current model, an increasing number need someone who can help them make the right choices. What type of computer should they buy? What kinds of software should they purchase? Should they have any software specially designed for them? Providing answers to these questions is a labor-intensive enterprise and thus suitable for a small business.

Another service area that is proving profitable for small businesses is rentals of computer equipment. These companies rent components by the day, week, or month. Cornell Fitch, owner of Comp-U-Rent in Arlington Heights, Illinois, is trying to create a nationwide network called American Eagle Computer Exchange, which would operate along the lines of the FTD (floral telegraph delivery) service. A customer would go to a local rental company, which would arrange for the equipment to be supplied by American Eagle outlets in cities where the customer wants to use the equipment. Another approach is that of PCR Corporation, which is developing a network of rental franchises. Although the cost of purchasing equipment and keeping an up-to-date inventory is high, the rental industry is approaching $1 billion a year and growing.

Of course, the big firms are not giving up on the service side of the business. They intend to profit from selling computer services to their large clients. However, many smaller markets are going unserviced or underserviced, and these offer the best opportunities for small businesses with computer know-how. As one expert put it, "Helping customers buy and use equipment may be unglamorous, but it can be a profitable business."

The Nature of Information Systems

A company's MIS provides management decision makers with information about both internal operations and external events. It applies to a wide variety of activities. For example, marketing research information, described in Chapter 11, is usually a vital part of a company's information system. Tying this data into the company's overall information system helps keep marketing activities in line with overall company objectives. The same is true of the other areas of the business.

Elements of an Information System

While each MIS is adapted to meet a company's specific information needs, all of these systems have the same basic components. These are information sources, users, information, and equipment. Figure 16.1 illustrates these elements for a typical manufacturing company.

Information Sources The information in an MIS comes from a variety of sources inside and outside the firm. One outside source is the federal,

F I G U R E   16.1

Elements of a Management Information System for a Manufacturer

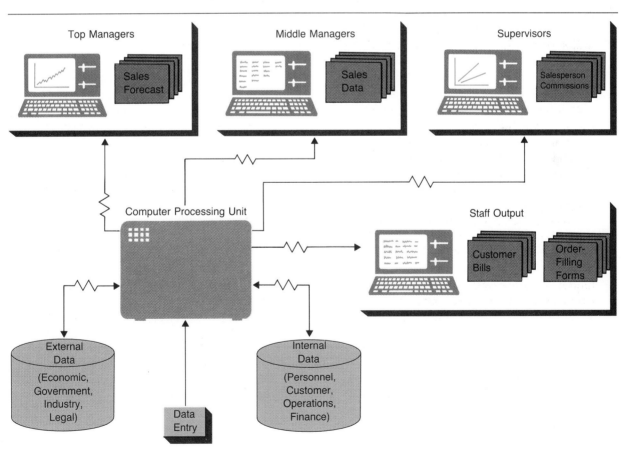

state, and local government, which provides data on regional and national economic trends, information on industry regulations and tax laws, demographic data, and much more. The bank and other organizations that help finance the business may also provide information on economic trends, and, especially for small businesses, advice on financial matters. The business's customers can provide information on their experiences with the company's and competitors' products. Vendors are often a good source of information about industry trends and activities.

Many important information sources are located within the company itself. Virtually every department conducts activities that affect decisions made in other departments. For example, when various departments request the purchasing department to buy supplies and equipment, they are generating information about where the company is spending its money. This information affects accounting and budgeting decisions.

Users The users of the information system are all the decision makers and those who support them (thus the term *decision support system* is sometimes used instead of *MIS*). This includes line managers as well as staff back-up personnel. A well-planned MIS should ensure that each type of information gets to those who need it, when they need it.

To get the right information to the right users, the information system must accommodate the different needs of users at different levels of management. For example, first-line managers are more likely to seek information that affects how to run daily operations in their particular area. They tend to be most interested in how they can influence the present and the immediate future. Middle managers, on the other hand, may look for information on the appropriate strategies for contributing to corporate objectives. They may focus more on the next year or two. Top managers tend to focus on information that helps them plan long-range strategies and overall policies for the organization.

Information The information in an MIS is data that have been organized in a way that is useful to decision makers and those who support them. Increasingly, the data are organized for rapid search and retrieval; this type of organization of data is called a **data base.** The resulting information often takes the shape of reports and forms. For example, an organization may transmit information through purchase orders, inventory reports, tax forms, and reports of earnings projections, among other means.

Data base An organization of data for rapid search and retrieval.

Equipment Companies used to store all their information in file cabinets and disseminate it manually by filling out forms and typing reports. Today, however, most companies rely on computers that are programmed to speed up the process of retrieving and disseminating information. An increasing number of companies are hiring MIS experts to help design and set up a computer system for their particular needs.

Applications for MIS

Although it is obvious that decision makers and those who support them in all departments of a business need information, the specific needs of some major MIS users bear a closer look. Examples of those that rely heavily on information systems are sales, production, and top-level and middle-level managers.

Information Systems for Sales Top sales managers need to know what the sales forecast is for the next couple of years, what products the company will sell, and which areas of the country are projected as having the greatest sales potential. These managers also need to know how well each sales region is doing relative to its sales forecast. They review general sales information that is designed to provide them with an overall picture of expectations and progress.

Middle- and lower-level sales managers need to know the sales quotas and goals for their regions and whether they are meeting these objectives. The information they receive tends to be specific (sales revenue by area, number sold of each product, and so forth) and provides a basis for measuring how well they are doing in each area of their overall sales territory.

Information Systems for Production Top production managers are interested in the number of units being manufactured each week and how this compares to the forecast. These managers need information related to the overall production picture.

Middle- and lower-level production managers are interested in day-to-day operations, such as machine downtime and repairs, quality problems and the reject rate, and worker tardiness, absenteeism, and turnover. This information helps the managers and supervisors resolve specific problems and clear up bottlenecks that affect production.

Information Systems for Top and Middle-Level Management Top-level executives use information systems for planning the organization's overall direction and measuring results quarterly, semiannually, and annually. To this end, they are interested in information related to strategic planning and policy decisions.

Middle- and lower-level managers use information systems for planning their department's direction and measuring results daily, weekly, and monthly. These managers are most interested in information related to controlling and operating decisions. For example, a manufacturing supervisor receives timely reports from quality control on the number of defects and from personnel on the absenteeism rates of his or her workers.

Checkpoint

1. What are the elements of an information system?
2. How do managers' information needs vary by their level in the organization?

The Emergence of the Modern Computer

As noted, computers play a major role in today's information systems. The rest of this chapter explores the development of computers, how they work, their various types, and how they are applied. One of the earliest examples of a type of computer is the abacus, which consists of a frame that encloses several columns of beads and a horizontal crossbar. Developed in ancient times by the Chinese, the abacus is still used in many parts of the world.

The computer as we know it today seems to have originated with the work of Charles Babbage, a British mathematician. In 1834, Babbage conceived of an "analytical engine." His plans for this machine called for it to add, subtract, multiply, divide, and store many numbers fed in on punched cards. Unfortunately, the machine was never built because the mechanical parts were too sophisticated to be machined and assembled, and, of course, it did not have the advantage of electricity. Nevertheless, Babbage's design of a machine that could take in information, store it, process it, and provide output contained all of the elements of the modern computer.

The First Electronic Computers

No one can say with certainty when the first electronic computer appeared. Some date it from 1930, when Vannevar Bush and his associates at the Massachusetts Institute of Technology developed and placed in operation the first "differential analyzer." This was the first fully automatic calculating instrument that could be programmed to do different types of problems. The controversy is over whether Bush's analyzer was really a computer. Therefore, some say the modern computer age began in 1944, when the U.S. Navy and IBM built the Mark I, an electromechanical computer that used punch cards and paper tapes and was capable of performing both arithmetic and logical operations. Still others believe that the first modern computer was the ENIAC (Electronic Numerical Integrator and Calculator) developed in 1946 at the University of Pennsylvania.

In the 1950s, computers began to catch on. In 1951, the Sperry Corporation came out with the UNIVAC I and sold it to the Census Bureau. In 1954, General Electric purchased one for its business. First

A farmer using an abacus at his stall in Moscow. The abacus is lying in front of the farmer, just left of the cash box. In the United States, pocket calculators are an inexpensive and convenient substitute for the abacus.

Source: Ricki Rosen/Picture Group.

large and then smaller organizations began installing computers. Now virtually all governmental, scientific, and business organizations have computers.

Generations of the Computer

The first computers were large, cumbersome, and slow compared to today's models. In fact, the popular personal computers of today hold more data and operate faster than most of the early models, which were much larger and more expensive. To arrive at this modern stage, the computer has moved through four recognized generations.

Evolutionary Development The first generation of computers, built from 1944 to 1959, operated with vacuum tubes. The machines were extremely heavy, took up a lot of space, and contained a large number of tubes. For example, the pioneering ENIAC weighed 30 tons and held 18,000 vacuum tubes. During the second generation (1959 to 1964), computer makers replaced the vacuum tubes with more reliable transistors, and high-speed card readers and printers were introduced to speed up input and output. From 1964 to 1974, the introduction of integrated circuits brought in the third generation of computers. An **integrated circuit** is a network of dozens of tiny transistors etched onto a silicon wafer. The result was a smaller, faster computer that required less electricity and provided greater storage. During this generation, remote terminals were also introduced so that users could gain access to the computer from various locales and at all levels and functions of the organization.

Integrated circuit A network of dozens of tiny transistors etched onto a silicon wafer.

The mid-1970s saw the emergence of large-scale integrated circuits, which some people call "superchips." These silicon-wafer chips are only about one square inch in area, but they can accommodate millions of integrated circuits and perform multiple applications, such as payroll, inventory, and economic forecasts. This miniaturization of the computer chip revolutionized the industry. With mass production of the chip, its price plummeted and the market for home microcomputers opened up. Consumers could now buy a small computer that performed more functions, worked faster, and cost much less than the large computers of the previous decade.

The Next Generation: Artificial Intelligence? Researchers continue to work on new computer technology; no doubt their efforts will usher in yet another generation. One likely source of change is called *artificial intelligence (AI)*. Sometimes called the fifth generation, this technology involves developing computers that can mimic human logic. Some of the earliest attempts at AI programmed computers to play chess, to help mechanics repair diesel locomotives, to track medical data and offer diagnoses and treatments, and to help salespeople by ordering complex computer components for customers. More recently, firms have been developing computer programs that allow the user to interact with the computer in English rather than "computerese."

An example of the application of AI is American Express's "expert system," called "Laurel's Brain." This AI system is named after Laurel Miller, a credit authorization manager. Her decision-making expertise was programmed into the computer system to screen out bad credit risks among the company's 23 million card holders. American Express has reaped increased productivity and profits from this application of artificial intelligence, and Laurel says, "There's no question it can do as good a job as I can."[3]

Other programs for AI and closely related "expert systems" are being developed for use in sales work, inventory control, and financial planning. In every case, the approach is the same—the programmer teaches the computer to think like a human. Some of the latest approaches involve teaching the computers to create their own solutions to problems.[4]

Checkpoint

1. What are the identifiable generations of computer technology so far?
2. Why do you think small firms have begun buying computers only in the last decade or so?

How Computers Work

Computers receive, manipulate, and store data based on the instructions they receive. The machinery and physical components of the computer that perform the tasks are called computer **hardware.** The series of instructions, or programming, that tells the computer what to do is called **software.** These instructions may be built into the computer or stored separately.

Hardware The machinery and physical components of a computer.

Software The series of instructions, or programming, that tells the computer what to do.

Basic Hardware Components

While the design and capabilities of computers vary substantially, the basic components of computers fall into the following categories: input units, central processing units (CPUs), secondary storage devices, and output units. These components are interrelated, in that the input unit passes data to the CPU, where the information is processed. The results then go to the output unit to be available to the user. The results also are usually stored. Meanwhile, the control unit of the CPU continuously monitors operations. Figure 16.2 diagrams the components and shows how they are linked.

Input unit A component that converts data into a form that the computer can understand.

Input Unit Before you can learn and apply the information in this text, you must translate the little marks on the pages into words and ideas. The computer, too, must translate data before it can store and apply it. The computer's **input unit** converts data into a form that the computer can understand.

Terminal A keyboard combined with a screen or printer and wired to a processing unit in another location.

Modern computers receive data from a variety of input units. A popular way to enter information is to type it in on a keyboard. The keyboard may be part of a **terminal,** a keyboard combined with a screen or printer and wired to a processing unit in another location. Computers can also read information from magnetic tapes or from diskettes, also known as "floppy disks." They may also receive data in the form of impulses transmitted through a telephone line. The device that enables computers to communicate with one another over telephone lines is called a **modem.** Some users can also enter information by moving a small box called a "mouse" around their desktop or on a pad.

Modem A device that enables computers to communicate with one another over telephone lines.

Central Processing Unit The **central processing unit (CPU)** controls what the computer does by storing and processing the information. The CPU has three basic parts: the memory, arithmetic/logic, and control units.

The memory unit stores information. This includes the data to be manipulated and the instructions for manipulating it. For example, to determine weekly paychecks, the memory unit would store each employee's social security number, wage rate, and withholding allowance, as well as instructions for calculating deductions and determining how much money each employee on the payroll should receive. The memory unit contains a primary storage unit, where all data are held until processed; a working storage unit, where the processing actually takes place; an output storage unit, where processed data are held until their release; and a program storage area, which holds the processing instructions.

The arithmetic/logic unit performs calculations, such as adding, subtracting, multiplying, and dividing. Once the calculation is complete, the computer transfers the information back to the memory unit.

The control unit interprets the program or instructions stored in the memory. It also commands the computer circuits to execute instructions and sees that the orders are carried out.

Secondary Storage Devices Most computer applications involve so much data and so many instructions that it would be impractical if not impossible for the computer to store everything in its memory unit. Looking for a single instruction or piece of data among all the possibilities would slow the system down unnecessarily. Consequently, most computer systems include secondary storage devices.

Users store data and instructions on these devices. The users assign each collection of related information, such as the software for running the inventory control system or the list of customer addresses, to a separate file with a unique file name. When a user wants the computer to do

Central processing unit (CPU) The component that controls what the computer does.

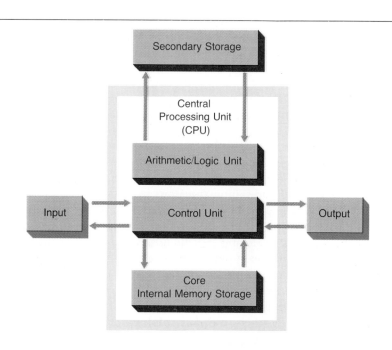

**Basic Components
of a Computer**

something with information in a file, he or she has the computer retrieve that file.

The commonly used storage devices include some that are also used as input units: magnetic tapes and floppy disks, for example. When the user stores information on them, they act as storage devices; when the user retrieves the information, they act as input units. Other storage devices with this dual role are hard disks and hard cards. These are rigid and larger than floppy disks, and are installed directly in a computer.

A more recent development in computer storage is the compact disk. These devices offer the advantage of condensing information into a small area. One compact disk can hold about 10,000 pages of text,[5] compared to a few hundred pages of text on a floppy disk.

Output Unit An output unit sends information from the computer to the user. Typically, this unit is a printer or a video screen. (Video screens are often called CRTs, an abbreviation for *cathode-ray tube*, the device that causes the characters to show up on the screen.) The computer may also use a modem to send information to another location. When the computer generates output, it also keeps the information in its memory. That way, the information becomes available for future reference or use.

Software: Programming the Computer

The fanciest computer hardware in the world cannot meet the business's information needs without instructions directing it what to do. The software that gives the machine its instructions comes in the form of computer programs. A **computer program** is a series of coded instructions that tell the computer what to do. Software quality is important because, except for some recent systems dealing with artificial intelligence, computers generally do what they are told to do—no more, no less. Therefore, if "garbage" (incorrect or useless information) is programmed into the computer, then "garbage" will be the output. This observation is commonly summarized as GIGO: garbage in, garbage out.

For most business people, learning how to program a computer is no more necessary to operating one than learning the intricacies of the internal combustion engine is to driving a car. Business people can hire computer programmers to create software for the company or to modify existing software, or they can buy ready-made computer programs. The companies that have full-time programmers on staff are typically very large firms with specialized needs. However, even large companies usually find that they can at least start with an existing program, modifying it if needed. One reason for this is that as more and more businesses buy computers, more and more software companies write and sell specialized software. For example, some programs are designed specifically to handle timekeeping and billing functions in business offices.

Most computer users are not computer programmers, but rather are nontechnical people who simply want to use the machine to perform some function such as retrieving specific information or preparing a report. Therefore, software companies try to make their programs "user friendly." A **user-friendly program** is one that is easy to understand and master. The dynamic growth of personal computers has done a great deal to stimulate the development of user-friendly programs. The development of computer graphics, the translation of print concepts to video,

Computer program A series of coded instructions that tells the computer what to do.

User-friendly program A computer program that is easy to understand and master.

is helping this process. For example, instead of tediously wading through numerical data bases on, say, medical information, the graphic software might create a form of a human body to speed the search. The user could glide over the model, magnifying specific organs and pushing a key to read data about a precise location. Such computer graphics are so user friendly that it is almost like playing a video game.[6]

Checkpoint

1. What are the basic types of computer hardware?
2. How do most business people go about obtaining software for their computers?

Types of Modern Computers

Today's computers provide a striking contrast to the large, cumbersome early machines. In addition, computers cost much less and offer versatility in size and power. There are three basic categories of modern computers: mainframe computers, minicomputers, and microcomputers.

Mainframe Computers

A **mainframe computer** is a large computer system with considerable storage capacity. It offers faster processing than smaller systems and may tie together a network of terminals. For example, a large chain of retail stores could have each of its units tied in directly to the mainframe at corporate headquarters. Each of the stores, via terminals, could feed expense and revenue information into the mainframe computer at headquarters and get back financial reports and other operating data that help the store manager make important on-site decisions. Large enterprises need a large central computer to coordinate data and provide a primary source of operating information. A mainframe computer performs this function.

Mainframe computer A large computer system with considerable storage capacity and fast processing capability.

Mainframe computers by IBM, Digital Equipment Corporation, and Wang support the information needs of the researchers and managers at SmithKline & French laboratories, a pharmaceutical company. Businesses often keep mainframes together in a single, climate-controlled room.

Source: Courtesy of SmithKline Beckman Corporation.

Minicomputer A medium-sized computer in terms of physical dimensions and storage capacity.

Minicomputers

A **minicomputer** is a medium-sized computer in terms of physical dimensions and storage capacity. The minis began making their appearance during the mid-1960s. Unlike the mainframe, the mini is about the size of a file cabinet, so it can be easily installed in a typical office or facility of a small business. In contrast to the mainframe, however, the mini has less storage capability and is slower in processing data. Another major difference is that fewer people can work on minis concurrently. However, some organizations tie minis directly to the mainframe. Thus, the mini can use the mainframe to help perform certain functions.

Microcomputers

Microcomputer A small desktop computer that relies on a microprocessor.

Microprocessor An integrated circuit on one chip that is the equivalent of the central processing unit in a larger computer.

A **microcomputer** is a small desktop computer that relies on a microprocessor. A **microprocessor** is an integrated circuit on one chip that is the equivalent of the central processing unit in a larger computer. The microprocessor was developed in 1971, and since then it has spawned a major market for computers: the personal computer (PC).

The personal computer has become very popular because of its size (it takes up little office space), processing power, and price. In recent years, the price of a PC has dropped to less than half of what it was a few years ago. Depending on its features, it can range from a few hundred to a few thousand dollars. Another attractive feature is that PCs can be tied to one another via a network in an office complex. Microcomputers allow small businesses to use computerized information to manage operations like large companies do.

The basic components required to operate a PC system are a system unit and a keyboard. In addition, the user adds other components, depending on the needs the computer is designed to fill. These components usually include diskettes, a video monitor (screen), and some type of printer, and sometimes a modem, a mouse, or extra storage devices. Figure 16.3 illustrates the components of a typical personal computer system.

Microprocessors made by Harris Corporation are used as the central processor—the "brains"—of the IBM PC Convertible, a portable personal computer. The microprocessors go inside the computer, but displaying them on the keyboard shows how small they are. In fact, the microprocessors are even smaller than they appear here; what you can see are the plastic and lead carriers that house the chips.

Source: Courtesy of Harris Corporation, Semiconductor Sector.

Because of the technological breakthroughs that have occurred over the last decade, the distinction between the mainframe, the mini, and the micro has become somewhat blurred in terms of what each can do. Generally, a mini costs around $15,000 to $100,000 or more; a mainframe can run up to several million dollars, depending on its size and capabilities. However, as microcomputers become increasingly powerful, the minis may become a less popular option for businesses.

Checkpoint

1. What are the differences between a mainframe computer and a minicomputer?
2. What is a microprocessor, and what role does it play in a personal computer?

Evaluating Computers

Although computers offer many benefits, business people must also consider their shortcomings in determining how computers can help meet the company's information-processing needs. Generally, evaluating computers boils down to weighing the efficiency they provide against the costs and risks they create.

Advantages to Business

Business people can use computers when they want to make a job faster, easier, and even more interesting.

Speed Computers are fast; they can make calculations in a fraction of the time it would take an individual. In fact, the person feeding the information into the computer is typically the slowest link in the process. The machine itself can carry out millions of instructions per second. For example, NASA's supercomputer system is currently capable of 250 million computations a second. Within a decade, the agency expects the system to achieve a mind-boggling 10 billion computations a second.[7] Also, by using computers in parallel (using many processors linked together so they can share the load, each working on a different piece of a problem at the same time), computer scientists have achieved speed-ups of problem solving by 1,000 times faster than a single processor from the same system.[8]

Accuracy Properly programmed computers are accurate, because, as noted earlier, computers do as they are programmed to do. If the machine is told to add 100, 200, 225, 406, and 911, the answer will be 1,842 every time. People get tired; computers do not. Some experts like

F I G U R E   16.3

A Typical Personal Computer System

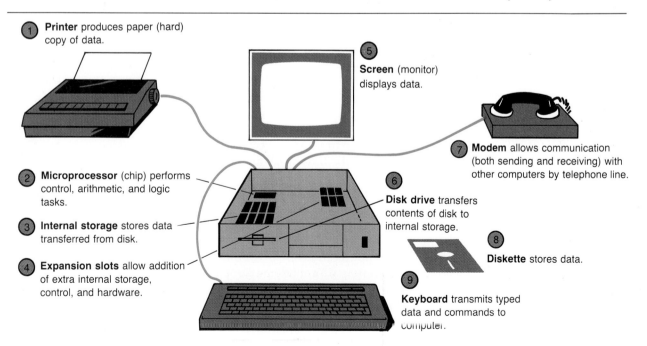

① **Printer** produces paper (hard) copy of data.

⑤ **Screen** (monitor) displays data.

⑦ **Modem** allows communication (both sending and receiving) with other computers by telephone line.

② **Microprocessor** (chip) performs control, arithmetic, and logic tasks.

③ **Internal storage** stores data transferred from disk.

④ **Expansion slots** allow addition of extra internal storage, control, and hardware.

⑥ **Disk drive** transfers contents of disk to internal storage.

⑧ **Diskette** stores data.

⑨ **Keyboard** transmits typed data and commands to computer.

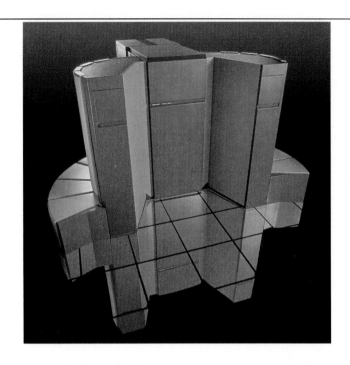

The CRAY-Y-MP supercomputer, made by Cray Research, which sells more supercomputers than any of its competitors. Supercomputers, which sell for $5 million to $25 million, are tremendously fast and powerful. Today's machines can perform billions of operations in a second's time, and the next generation is expected to be able to handle trillions of operations per second. Some applications for supercomputers include designing the arrangement of transistors on silicon chips, preparing complex investment strategies, locating oil deposits, and creating special effects for movies.

Source: Paul Shambroom, photographer. Courtesy of Cray Research, Incorporated.

Byte   A character of data.

to point out that "computers are too dumb to make mistakes," which means that mistakes typically result from improper programming, not machine errors.

Large Capacity   Computers are capable of storing huge amounts of information. The amount of a computer's memory is measured in terms of a unit called a *byte*. A **byte** is a character of data, such as 6, A, or +. For example, the word *help* takes up four bytes. Because most memories are so large, the common units are Kbytes (1,024 bytes) and Mbytes (1,048,576 bytes). You may find it useful to think of Kbytes as roughly a thousand bytes and Mbytes as roughly a million bytes. Most personal computers today have a minimum of 64K of memory. The cost to add memory to a PC is minimal.

Assumption of the Boring and Routine   Many business people appreciate computers because they handle boring tasks such as adding numbers, rearranging data, and performing routine computations. The computer performs these tasks quickly and accurately, thus freeing employees to devote their time to more creative work. As one computer firm put it, "Computers do the busy work and free people up to do the think work."

Increased Efficiency   Finally, computers help organizations increase their efficiency. They do so in a number of ways. One is by quickly retrieving information needed for decision making. People are able to interact via computers and work jointly on problem solving. Computers can also simplify communications by providing a place to leave and retrieve messages. Computers with modems can pass information across telephone lines, allowing managers and sales personnel on the road with a portable computer to send their information back to the office while still remaining out in the field. Finally, special software enables computers to increase the efficiency of business functions such as production and finance.

Disadvantages to Business

Some of the possible drawbacks to computers are that they can be expensive, can make mistakes, can be relied on too much, seem to be anti-people, and can be a security risk.

Expense Unfortunately, computers can be expensive, especially if the organization does not know how to use them efficiently. An expenditure of $35,000 for a minicomputer may produce daily sales reports and help the enterprise control its cash flow and inventory. However, if the employees have been doing this all along, the computer is merely speeding up an existing process. This may not merit a $35,000 expenditure.

Managers must weigh the benefits a computer can provide against its cost. A manager who buys out of awe at a computer's capabilities may purchase much more computer memory or power than is necessary. Some managers may blindly buy whatever their competitors are purchasing. The desire to have the best equipment or do exactly as the others do can override such down-to-earth criteria as profitability and efficiency. However, careful consideration of benefits may render even a high price worthwhile.

Some of the supercomputers currently under development are costing a lot more money than their producers initially estimated. As described in "International Close-Up: Japan Hits a Snag," Japanese companies encountered escalating costs in their development of a supercomputer. These expenses in computer development are sure to be passed on to the customer in the form of higher prices.

Mistakes Another potential pitfall of computers is errors. Computers do only what they are programmed to do; thus, programmers and operators can cause mistakes. And when an error is made, it often turns out to be a big one. As one critic lightheartedly remarked, "In a few minutes, a computer can make a mistake so great that it would take many men many months to equal it." For example, not long ago, a computer operator called up the wrong mailing list and sent out a letter to business people all over the country, thanking them for staying at the company's hotel. In reality, few, if any, had stayed at the hotel. Unfortunately, many of the managers' spouses read the letter and wanted to know what was going on at that hotel. The president of the hotel chain wrote a personal letter of apology to everyone who called to complain, including one complainer who said, "If you don't straighten out this problem immediately, my marriage is on the rocks!"

Vulnerability to Overreliance Computers also cause problems when managers overrely on them. Managers receive many different types of computer-generated reports. Sometimes information is wrong or incomplete, and if managers rely too heavily on the data, they will make a mistake.

Many managers attribute great credibility to computer-generated reports. A research study found this is especially true of managers with little or no computer experience. If they had little computer experience, their decision making was greatly influenced by the mere fact that the data was generated by a computer.[9] Other studies have found that even when computerized printouts contain erroneous data, the manager tends to accept the information. This overreliance is dangerous and shows that many managers use computers to make decisions, as opposed to using the machines to help them analyze the information on which to base their decisions.

People Problems Computers are sometimes viewed as "antipeople." One reason is that they simply do as they are told without taking into account what the ramifications might be. For example, some people have received computerized bills for goods either that they have not purchased or for which they have already submitted payment. In either case, every time they indicate this information on their computer bill, it is ignored and they receive increasingly more urgent letters demanding that they pay up or else. Their inability to get a human to intervene in the process makes it all the worse.

INTERNATIONAL   CLOSE-UP

Japan Hits a Snag

The American computer business has faced increasingly tough competition from Japan. In 1981, Japan announced a "Superspeed Project," which would receive $150 million in financial support from the government. The objective of this project was to build a super-computer that was 100 to 1,000 times faster than existing models. IBM, Hewlett-Packard, Cray Research, and other large American computer firms were concerned. Would the Japanese be able to make a giant leap forward in computer technology and seize a major share of the total world market for large computers?

So far, apparently not. In fact, so many problems have developed that computer experts now believe that the Japanese "Super-speed Project" will eventually be abandoned. The parties have yet to agree on a basic design for a prototype machine. Problems with computer chips have also slowed the project. One of the three exotic computer-chip technologies that was expected to give the machine its tremendous processing speed has been virtually abandoned. The other two technologies have developed so slowly and cost so much money that Japanese designers now believe they would be better off using conventional silicon chips for all but a few of the machine's components. Furthermore, the government has begun reducing its financing of the project; it has come to believe that the project may be an interesting research undertaking, but one unlikely to result in a competitive computer for the world market. The last, but perhaps most damaging, reason is that the costs of the project are now so high that the supercomputer would not be economically feasible. Business firms would save money by using slower machines that cost far less.

The Japanese have certainly made important breakthroughs in computer technology, including the very large-scale integrated circuit that helped them dominate the memory-chip market. However, their latest project hit so many snags that the Americans seem to be beating them. For example, computer scientists at Sandia National Labs in New Mexico recently announced they had broken records for speed-ups, a measure of the increased speed at which a problem can be solved on a multiprocessor parallel computer.

A second people problem is technological unemployment, which occurs when computerization leads to elimination of workers' jobs. As Chapter 10 pointed out, computerized robots have already been introduced into some factories. For example, in the auto industry, welders and other assembly-line workers are being replaced by robots. These high-speed, sophisticated machines can do some types of work faster, cheaper, and more efficiently than humans. Computerization also can affect white-collar jobs, in that computers can collect and analyze data more quickly and cheaply than staff personnel. For example, Wells Fargo Bank was able to function with two fewer layers of staff in the personnel department when a computer system was installed to process everything from salary increases to hiring.[10]

Security Risks The use of computers also raises the issue of security. The popular movie *War Games,* in which a young boy taps into a government high-security program and activates a war game, may be a little far-fetched, but the basic idea is not. In recent years, students have managed to gain access to computers at the government weapons research laboratory in Los Alamos, New Mexico, and the Sloan-Kettering Cancer Center in New York City. These stories made headlines. What have not made headlines are the bank computer thefts carried out by computer whizzes who know the correct codes to use to enter accounts in order to steal or manipulate money. Industry experts estimate that computer theft runs into the hundreds of millions of dollars each year.

Societal Implications of Computers

Besides the implications that computers have for business, computers also affect society at large. For example, many people fear that computers can result in an invasion of their privacy. Many businesses keep their payroll and personnel files on computers. Anyone with access to the company computer can easily obtain private information on the firm's personnel. Additionally, anyone who has used a credit card in the last year is in a computer file somewhere. If such a person were to apply for a home mortgage, the bank would have a credit agency carry out a credit check on the person. This agency would have little trouble getting the individual's outstanding credit card balances and other personal financial information. Most people, whether they know it or not, could have their privacy invaded by an individual with access to their computer file. If the file contains a mistake, the problems could be even worse.

   In an effort to prevent these abuses, many organizations are establishing tighter security measures. Some companies continually change the computer access code so that only those who are supposed to know the code can get into the files. Another approach is to install a "callback" unit, which checks to make sure that the person attempting to reach the computer through a telephone is calling from a company's authorized telephone number. The company may limit access to certain computer files to certain times of the day, thus preventing people from getting into these files when no one is around. The system might also alert security people if someone is trying to gain computer access.

   Another issue relating to privacy concerns the monitoring of employees in the workplace. A report released by the Congressional Office of

Ford's CreditNet system links participating dealers with Ford Credit, the automaker's finance subsidiary. Dealers such as this one can receive quick approval of customer loans by using the computer to communicate with Ford Credit's data base. The easy access to sensitive information like credit histories requires businesses to institute security measures to protect their data and their customers.

Source: Courtesy of Ford Motor Company.

Technology Assessment indicates that more than seven million employees have their daily work monitored by computers. At present, computer monitoring mostly affects clerical workers in areas such as computer data entry and insurance claims processing who sit at a computer work station. Activities being monitored include job production, use of telephones, presence at the work station, customer service calls, and frequency of errors. Besides the invasion of privacy issue, there is some evidence that computer monitoring leads to job stress and more frequent illness. Computer monitoring also seems to be spreading to those doing more complicated tasks. Critics are concerned that this is another example that the United States is becoming a "surveillance society" and that those companies that use computers to monitor their employees have become "electronic sweatshops."[11]

Checkpoint

1. What are two major advantages and two disadvantages of computers?
2. What societal issues must business people consider when setting up and using a computer system?

Computer Applications in the Business World

Businesses today use computers to handle a multitude of tasks. Some of these, such as handling deposits and withdrawals or booking airline reservations, are unique to a particular industry. But most business software performs one or more basic functions: word processing, desktop publishing, spreadsheets, data base management, telecommunications, electronic mail, and networking.

Word Processing

An application that has revolutionized business offices across the country is **word processing,** a system to store, retrieve, edit, and print text. Typically, the operator enters a report, letter, or other text by typing it on the keyboard or retrieving it from a file. Then the operator makes any changes desired and prints or saves the revised text. The two biggest advantages of word processing are that it reduces the time needed to revise documents and that it cuts back on the amount of storage space required for filing them.

Word processing offers many features that vary somewhat from program to program. However, most word processing programs offer the following:

Ease in correcting errors. Generally, the operator can back up and type over characters or delete words by pressing a few keys.

Assistance in catching errors. A "spell check" in the program can compare every word in the document with a dictionary file to make sure the words are correctly spelled. However, one problem is that a word in the document may match a word in the dictionary while not being the correct word for that context. For example, the operator may have typed *the* instead of *they*.

Ease in making revisions. Word processing programs allow the user to move chunks of text around. If users want to insert new material in the middle of a paragraph, they merely type it in the desired location, and the program automatically adjusts the text that follows it. This means that the operator can make a change without having to retype an entire page or report.

Flexibility in creating a format. The operator can specify margins, spacing, and usually type size. Depending on the printer's capabilities, the word processing program allows the operator to specify that some text be in boldface, italics, uppercase, or underlined. Special commands can also center text or align it at the right margin.

Capability for reusing text. The ability to save and retrieve files of information enables the operator to save time spent retyping the same information. For example, the user could retrieve files containing report formats or standard closing paragraphs, rather than retyping them each time a report or letter called for them.

Special features. Some programs can make an index out of words that the operator flags. Others can sort data alphabetically or numerically. Some programs make graphs out of quantitative data. Most word processing programs contain some of these features plus a wide variety of others.

These features make word processing useful for a variety of tasks, from typing letters and memos to creating reports, invoices, and other documents. The manuscript for this book was prepared on a word processor.

Word processing A system to store, retrieve, edit, and print text.

Desktop publishing A computer system that allows companies to publish newsletters, charts, brochures, and other printed material in-house.

Spreadsheets Data arranged in tables of rows and columns.

Desktop Publishing

A recent development that has taken word processing one step further is called **desktop publishing.** This allows companies to create and produce newsletters, charts, brochures, and other printed material in-house. What used to be sent out to professional publishers and printers can now be done on a desktop computer system consisting of a computer, laser printer, and software package. At present, such systems run about $7,500 to $10,000, and the costs for producing printed materials can be 50 to 65 percent below that charged by outside printing firms. Those familiar with word processing can learn the system with little effort.

Desktop publishing offers great potential for the future. Industry experts estimate that within a few years most companies will have such a system in place, enabling them to create high-quality printed material at a low cost and with little lead time. As one analyst noted: "The invention of movable type during the 14th century allowed the average person to become a printer; the invention of desktop publishing will allow everyone to become a publisher."[12]

Spreadsheets

While word processing programs help business people manage and present information in the form of text, decision makers also work with information in the form of numbers. For help with this quantitative information, they turn to **spreadsheets,** which are simply tables, such as the one shown in Table 16.1. Of course, it's possible to create such a table with a pen or typewriter, but spreadsheet software makes the job simpler and more flexible.

To use a spreadsheet program, you label the columns and rows that will contain information. You can also identify which amounts are calculated from other amounts, specifying how to calculate them. For example, in Table 16.1, you would have the computer add the quarterly amounts in each row to find the total for each row. Also, you would specify that income for each column is the difference between sales and total expenses. When you enter the amounts for sales and expenses, the computer automatically calculates the total for each item, total expenses, and income.

Spreadsheets have a variety of applications. A spreadsheet along the lines of the one shown in Table 16.1 might be useful for financial statements or in preparing a budget. Managers might use a spreadsheet for their department's budget. A related use would be to compare planned revenues and expenses with actual ones. The company could also use spreadsheets for preparing payroll. The spreadsheet could contain wage rates, hours worked, and deductions, and use this information to compute each worker's total pay automatically. Other uses of spreadsheets are for bank transactions and balances and for estimating the financial impact of proposed new projects. In fact, the application of spreadsheets is limited only by the user's imagination.

Data Base Management

As you learned earlier in this chapter, management information systems often store data in the form of a data base for easy retrieval. Computer programs called data base management software automate this task. Data base management programs store information labeled according to category. For example, in a customer list, the file may identify the customer's name, telephone number, address, zip code, and product purchased. The company can then use the computer to search the file for specific characteristics in any of these categories. For example, the company may want to send a mailing to everyone who bought a certain product or who lives in a certain area (identified by a range of zip codes). Using the computer to generate a mailing list and print out the

T A B L E   16.1   **Sample Spreadsheet**

	First Quarter	Second Quarter	Third Quarter	Fourth Quarter	Total
Sales	$101.2	$93.6	$75.3	$162.1	$432.2
Expenses					
Cost of Goods Sold	54.5	47.8	39.2	72.0	213.5
Salaries	10.2	10.2	10.2	10.2	40.8
Rent	5.0	5.0	5.0	5.0	20.0
Other Expenses	3.3	3.0	3.0	3.5	12.8
Total Expenses	$ 73.0	$66.0	$57.4	$ 90.7	$287.1
Income	$ 28.2	$27.6	$17.9	$ 71.4	$145.1

mailing labels is far simpler than searching through piles of receipts and hand typing mailing labels.

Data base management systems have other applications besides mailing lists. The company could use this software to keep track of marketing research information, such as reports on the company's various products. If the company has a library, it might want to keep its records on such a system. This software is also useful for preparing directories, glossaries, or other information that the user wants sorted alphabetically. In general, data base management programs are helpful for information that users want to organize, reorganize, and retrieve swiftly.

Telecommunicating

Telecommunicating
Using a modem to send information between two computers or between a terminal and a processing unit.

Besides using computers to manipulate and help interpret information, business people use them for communication—the sending and receiving of information. The basis for communicating is software designed for **telecommunicating,** or using a modem to send information between two computers or between a terminal and a processing unit. A recent court ruling allowing the seven regional Bell companies to use their telephone network to carry information services will greatly expand the availability and ease of using telecommunication. Everyone with a phone can now tap into the growing number of information services, ranging from voice mail (recording and sending out telephone messages) to pay-for-view cable TV (by dialing a phone number one can get a "menu" of channels and programs; to select a show the user will simply punch the corresponding number on the phone pad).[13]

Telecommunicating is an efficient way to send long or complex information. A company might telecommunicate with its sales force in the field by sending customer requests and feedback from managers, while the sales people could send sales reports and customer orders. Many decision makers use telecommunicating to link up with data bases produced by other companies. For example, a manager might telephone a data base service and look up information on stock prices or the latest research in a particular field. However, because telecommunication is more expensive for short messages than sending a letter or placing a phone call, business people have to establish which means of communication is most appropriate for a particular situation.

Telecommunicating is changing the nature of the workplace by allowing employees, ranging from clerical workers to staff specialists to top-level managers, to work at home while remaining in touch with the office through a computer hookup. Companies that adopt this approach with clerical workers can save themselves office space. Those employees who use this approach are given the opportunity to work on their own schedule. Parents who want to be home for their children in the afternoon are able to be there. These "telecommuting" employees must complete a minimum amount of work; in many cases, they actually end up doing much more than employees who commute to the office.

A relatively new application of communication by computer is **electronic mail.** This is a system for sending and receiving messages through computers. The process is quite simple. The sender normally types the message into the computer and tells the machine who is to receive it. The computer sends the message as soon as it can contact the recipient's computer. That computer saves the message in a special file. When people in the electronic mail system turn on their computer, they can ask the machine whether they have any messages. If they do, the computer then displays their mail on the screen. Many firms have found that they need two to three days to distribute a regular paper memo; with electronic mail, the same process takes only seconds. It also avoids the annoyance and wasted time of "telephone tag"—calling someone who is unavailable and who finds you unavailable when trying to return the call. With electronic mail, the entire message waits in the computer file until the recipient is free to read it.

Electronic mail A system for sending and receiving messages through computers.

Computer Networking

Especially if they use several of the applications described previously, companies with several users often have a comprehensive **computer network.** This is a system that allows for multiple users and multiple activities. A number of people can use the system simultaneously, and they can all be doing different things. Some may be communicating through the computer; others may be ordering the computer to print a letter or file, while still others are analyzing spreadsheet data. Each of these users, communicating with his or her computer or terminal, is able to draw on the computer's power.

Computer network A system that allows for multiple users and multiple activities.

In the future, this idea may expand into what Japanese companies call value-added networks. A **value-added network (VAN)** is a system providing electronic links between an organization and outside personnel. Figure 16.4 illustrates how this would work for an auto manufacturer. The VAN electronically links the dealer, company headquarters, and suppliers.

Value-added network (VAN) A system providing electronic links between an organization and outside personnel.

Japanese companies are using VANs to communicate over long distances, thereby linking manufacturers, suppliers, and customers.[14] As a result, goods are produced faster and more cheaply and are brought to market in record time.

Checkpoint

1. What are two major computer applications in business?
2. Which applications would be suitable for a small manufacturing firm? For a large insurance company?

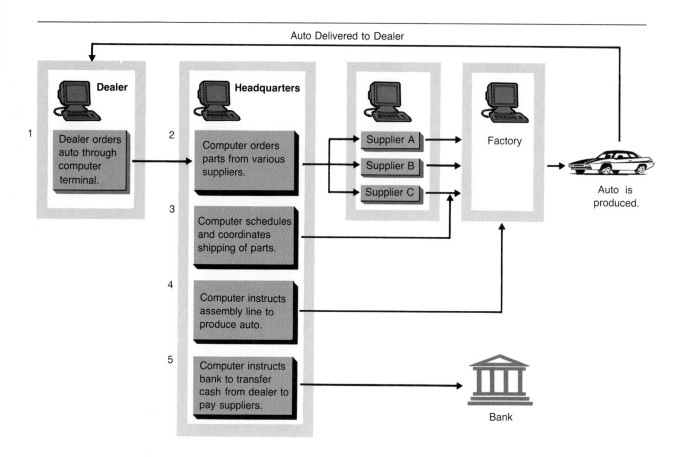

Auto Delivered to Dealer

Dealer

1 Dealer orders auto through computer terminal.

Headquarters

2 Computer orders parts from various suppliers.

Supplier A
Supplier B
Supplier C

Factory

Auto is produced.

3 Computer schedules and coordinates shipping of parts.

4 Computer instructs assembly line to produce auto.

5 Computer instructs bank to transfer cash from dealer to pay suppliers.

Bank

FIGURE 16.4

A Value-Added Network (VAN) for Auto Manufacturing

Closing Comments

This chapter examined how information systems and computers help business people generate, transmit, analyze, and use information. As numerous government agencies have discovered, managing the flow and accuracy of information is crucial to making well-informed, effective decisions. With careful data entry and programming, computers can be an immense help in the task of managing information. Their role will no doubt grow as they continue to become more powerful and versatile, thanks to hardware and software developments. In turn, this will open up many new uses for computers, complementing or even replacing those that were discussed in this chapter.

If the computer has as big an impact on business in the next 15 years as it has had on the past 15 years, students and practitioners of business must be knowledgeable about what they can expect from these machines. To address that need, this chapter explained what types of computers are available and the basic functions they perform in helping business people make better decisions.

Learning Objectives Revisited

1. Explain how information systems help managers make decisions.
A management information system (MIS) is a method for collecting, analyzing, and disseminating timely information to support decision

My E

America
ment (T
billion. '
paperw
there ar
required
tained e
vided by
better a

One
for T&
transmi
allows t
tion and
check tl
class in
the trip
nating
vices ar
issuers.
tion sys
control
both ac

Wha
inform
corpor;
up-to-c
its mer
that wi
frame
tion of
All tha
go and
will ha
from t
inform

Case

1. H(
   a (
2. In
   th
   fr
3. W
   bu

making. This system typically uses computers to link information sources with users, directing the appropriate types of information to each user. Managers at the upper levels of the organization need general information to help them formulate the enterprise's overall goals and long-range strategy. Middle managers look for information that helps them contribute to corporate objectives in the near future. First-line managers need more specific information for help in running day-to-day operations.

2. **Describe the evolution of computers.**
   The first generation of computers relied on vacuum tubes and were large, heavy, and expensive to operate. The second generation replaced tubes with smaller and more reliable transistors. The introduction of the integrated circuit ushered in the third generation, making computers smaller and faster. The fourth generation uses microprocessors containing millions of integrated circuits. This generation has brought computer power into the home as well as the business. The next generation is still in the development stage; one direction receiving attention is artificial intelligence, programming that would enable computers to mimic human thinking and logical reasoning.

3. **Identify the hardware and software components of computers.**
   Hardware is the machinery and physical components of the computer. These components consist of input, processing, secondary storage, and output units. The input unit, such as a keyboard or modem, converts incoming information into a form that the computer can understand. The central processing unit controls the computer system by using three basic parts: the memory unit, the arithmetic/logic unit, and the control unit. Secondary storage devices retain information when the computer is off, and include floppy and hard disks, tapes, and compact disks. The output unit sends the information from the computer to the user; typical units are printers and video screens. Software is the series of instructions, or programming, that tells the machine what to do. Most business people buy ready-made software designed to do specific tasks rather than writing or commissioning their own programs.

4. **Define the basic types of computers.**
   The basic types of computers are mainframe computers, minicomputers, and microcomputers. A mainframe is a large computer system that offers tremendous storage capacity and rapid processing of information. A minicomputer is a medium-sized computer that is often tied into a mainframe to link offices or departments with the main computer. A microcomputer, or personal computer, is a small desktop computer that relies on a microprocessor. The microcomputer typically includes a system unit, keyboard, video screen, and printer. Some systems also have a modem, a mouse, or extra storage devices.

5. **Discuss how business people evaluate the merits of computers.**
   Business people weigh business advantages and disadvantages, as well as societal implications. Some of the major advantages include speed, accuracy, large capacity, assumption of boring tasks, and increased efficiency. Some of the major disadvantages are expense, consequences of mistakes, vulnerability to overreliance, people problems, and security risks.

You Be the Adviser: Weighing the Benefits

Eileen Crespo owns an auto supply store. Eileen bought the store six months ago, just after she quit her job with a large oil company. While with the oil company for five years, Eileen had sold auto supplies to service stations and other retail outlets. During this time, she became familiar with the field and concluded that it has the potential for high profit. In particular, Eileen believes that over the next decade, more and more people are going to begin servicing their own cars. "A growing number of people want to save money on their cars," she recently told a friend. "It's going to be a lot like the home repair business in the mid-1980s."

When Eileen learned that Tony Rezazzo was looking to sell his auto supply store, Eileen went to talk to him. Within two days, they had struck a deal, and within a month, Eileen had taken over.

One of the first things she has done is to make a complete count of the inventory. She currently has $203,000 of auto supplies, including batteries, hoses, spark plugs, mufflers, windshield wipers, and various parts. Eileen believes that the key to success in this business is a small inventory that turns over rapidly. However, she is concerned that if the inventory is too small, she will continually be out of stock and will lose customers. Last week she had a visit from a computer salesperson. He suggested that Eileen purchase a microcomputer and accompanying software for $2,500 to maintain her financial records and control inventory. The idea sounds fine to Eileen, but she wonders whether the computerized information system approach is really necessary. It might be just as easy to control inventory by adding and subtracting the units purchased and sold from her physical count of how much she has. This would provide a running total of her inventory. When Eileen begins to run low on some products, she can reorder them.

Your Advice

1. What kinds of information does Eileen need? How can a computer help her manage this information?
2. Could Eileen control inventory manually? How would this compare to using a computer?
3. Would you recommend that Eileen buy a microcomputer? Why or why not? Be sure to consider the advantages and disadvantages.

Career Opportunities

Many different careers build on the knowledge of accounting, information systems, or computers. For example, in the accounting area alone, people hold jobs as public and private accountants, auditors, accounting clerks, and bookkeepers.

Accountants

Accountants can work for a public accounting firm or for any type of business. They prepare, analyze, and verify financial reports. They furnish information to their clients or managers to help them make better decisions. A special type of an accountant called an auditor verifies the accuracy of a firm's financial records and checks for waste and fraud. Other accountants specialize in tax matters, preparing income tax forms and advising management of the tax advantages and disadvantages of various business decisions. Others concentrate on consulting and offer advice on managerial matters. Of the approximately 900,000 accountants in the United States, roughly 300,000 are CPAs.

Most public accounting and business firms require applicants to have a bachelor's degree in accounting. Many prefer a master's degree in accounting or a master's degree in business administration or computer science.

Starting salaries for college graduates with an accounting major are in the range of $20,000 to $25,000. For those with a master's degree or accounting-related experience, the range is $25,000 to $35,000. Senior-level accountants in large firms or partners in CPA firms can expect to earn $100,000 or more. Opportunities in this field are expected to grow much faster than the average for all occupations through the mid-1990s.

Statisticians

Statisticians analyze quantitative information to help managers make better decisions. They are particularly helpful in applying statistical methods to a particular area such as economic, marketing, operations, personnel, or financial data. They often use these techniques to predict economic conditions, product demand, the current state of product quality, the causes of turnover, and other information that can be vital to effective managerial decision making.

Most statisticians have majored in a quantitative subject such as statistics, mathematics, economics, or finance. Starting salaries for a person with a bachelor's degree are around $17,000 annually. A master's degree can earn a person $22,000 to start, and a Ph.D. will command $30,000 or more. Although only large companies will hire statisticians per se, those with a statistical background could be hired in the areas of marketing research, production control, or accounting. Jobs in this area are expected to grow at the same rate as the economy at large.

Systems Analysts

Systems analysts use computer expertise to plan and develop programs for computerizing business tasks or improving computerized information systems already in use. Analysts determine the nature of the problem and break it down into its component parts. They design a system that will solve the manager's problem and prepare diagrams that describe it in terms that managers and other users can understand.

Approximately 350,000 systems analysts hold positions in business and government. Most work for manufacturers, banks, insurance companies, data-processing service firms, and governmental agencies. Most employers require majors in management, computer science, or engineering, because they are reluctant to spend the time and money necessary to train people from scratch. Starting salaries are in the $25,000 range, but average annual earnings are around $35,000, with the high end of the scale running up to $50,000 and above. Employment in this field is expected to grow much faster than the average for all occupations through the mid-1990s.

FINANCING THE ENTERPRISE

Every enterprise needs funds in order to operate. To meet these needs, business people look for interested lenders and investors. When a business has excess funds, it looks for ways to protect them. Part VI examines the financing function of modern enterprise. This activity extends from using the financial system to borrowing and selling stocks to managing risk through insuring.

Chapter 17 looks at the topics of money and banking. The chapter also discusses how the government regulates the money supply and insures bank deposits. The last part of the chapter examines recent developments in the banking field.

Chapter 18 focuses on financial management, giving specific attention to short-term and long-term sources of capital. Also important are investments for excess funds. The last part of the chapter discusses the role of financial intermediaries.

Chapter 19 discusses the ways in which investors buy and sell stocks. It also describes how investors try to make money by predicting market movements, interpreting the financial news, and picking successful strategies. The last part of the chapter addresses how the government regulates securities transactions.

Chapter 20 focuses on risk management and insurance. Business people manage risk by avoiding it, reducing it, assuming it, or shifting it. Shifting risk involves the use of insurance. The chapter describes the types of insurance that meet the need to shift risk.

When you have finished studying Part VI, you should have a solid understanding of how enterprises finance their operations and manage risk.

CHAPTER 17

Money and Banking

LEARNING OBJECTIVES

- Explain the nature and purpose of money.
- Describe the money supply and its components.
- Present the major financial institutions.
- Discuss the Federal Reserve System.
- Explain how government agencies protect deposits.
- Identify recent developments in banking.

Your Business IQ

How much do you already know about money and banking? Test your business IQ by labeling each statement *true* or *false*. Answers and explanations are at the end of the chapter.

1. Paper currency makes up the majority of the money supply.
2. In recent years, some banks have begun paying interest on checking accounts.
3. The services offered by financial institutions such as commercial banks, savings and loan associations, and credit unions are starting to resemble one another.
4. For help in balancing the budget, Congress turns to the Federal Reserve System.
5. Because of increasing competition, many banks are paying lower interest on savings accounts and charging smaller fees.

Money puts many kinds of business decisions into action.

Source: © 1986 Jon Feingersh: CLICK/Chicago.

Looking Back and Ahead

Suppose you need a car to travel between school and your job. Your job will eventually pay you enough to buy a car, but you need the car now. How can you buy it? You might ask your father or your aunt to lend you what you need; as you earn money, you would pay back the loan. This is an example of a simple financial transaction; your relative uses a supply of funds to meet your demand for funds.

Direct transactions such as your borrowing money to purchase a car play a minor role in the economy. If a big retailer wants to borrow several million dollars to build a new distribution center, the president doesn't go through the phone book looking for people with extra money. Moreover, consumers who have money to invest don't go looking for would-be borrowers such as new homeowners. This direct approach to financial transactions is usually much too inefficient.

Instead, the suppliers and demanders of funds use intermediaries in the form of financial institutions. Figure 17.1 shows how this works. Consumers and organizations that have money to save or invest lend it to financial institutions in exchange for payments of interest. Borrowers—businesses, the government, and consumers—then pay the financial institution interest for the privilege of using money.

Money is necessary to start a business and to make it grow and contribute to the economy. For this reason, many important business decisions concern the acquisition and use of money. This chapter begins a discussion of financing a business by considering the functions of money and banking. The chapter first examines the role of money in the U.S. economy. Then it describes the major institutions that act as financial intermediaries. It goes on to discuss a major force affecting the money supply: the Federal Reserve System. The chapter concludes by discussing some current developments in the U.S. banking system.

The Nature and Purpose of Money

In a simpler world, if John has a loaf of bread and Mary has a gallon of milk, John might exchange half the loaf for half the milk so that they can both eat and drink. Such a transaction is called *barter*—the trading of goods and services. However, today's world is not so simple. To address this issue, the parties in most exchanges use **money**—anything a society generally accepts in payment for goods and services. In the past, societies have adopted many kinds of objects as money, including cattle,

Money   Anything a society generally accepts in payment for goods and services.

FIGURE   17.1

Financial Institutions as Intermediaries

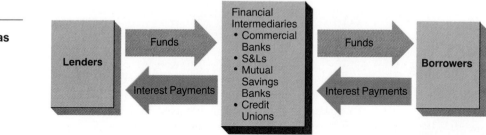

pepper, tobacco, animal hides, and, of course, gold and silver. Today, money usually takes the form of coins and specially printed pieces of paper.

The Functions of Money

Money is a medium of exchange. This means that a supplier of a product will accept money in exchange for the product, knowing that other suppliers will in turn accept that money for other products. For example, Attorney Mary Smith will accept money in exchange for drawing up a will, knowing that she can use the money to buy supplies for her law office and pay herself a salary for her personal needs.

Money is also a standard of value. In other words, it is a measure of the relative worth of goods and services. If a phone call costs 25 cents, a carton of yogurt costs 50 cents, and a dental checkup costs $25, then we know that a carton of yogurt is worth twice as much as a phone call and a checkup is worth 100 times as much as a phone call. This is easier to keep track of than remembering to bring 50 cartons of yogurt to the dental clinic.

Money also serves as a storehouse of value. If you don't need money right away, you can keep it or invest it until you are ready to use it. If you get paid twice a month, money enables you to spread out your expenditures from paycheck to paycheck and even into retirement.

Characteristics of Money

Money best performs these functions when it has certain characteristics: divisibility, portability, durability, stability, and security.

Divisibility To be flexible as a medium of exchange, money should be divisible into smaller units. Centuries ago, the Spanish government issued a gold doubloon. The coin was often carved into eight pieces, hence the term "pieces of eight." This allowed the owner of the coin to buy goods worth less than a doubloon.

Today, money is divisible in a symbolic sense; coins and bills are available in various denominations. The dollar is divided into pennies, the British pound into pence, and the German mark into *pfennigs*. If you buy a 25-cent newspaper with a 1-dollar bill, the seller can give you change.

Portability Money should also be easy to carry around. Imagine leading oxen or hauling silver ingots to the auto dealership at the other end of town. The bulkier or heavier the money, the more difficult it is to use. This is why governments eventually developed paper money. Bills with large denominations further increase portability. In the United States, bills have had denominations ranging from $1 to $100,000, but in recent years $100 is the largest bill issued.

Durability Money must be able to stand up to abuse and wear and tear; otherwise it will become worn out and useless. The importance of durability may explain the enduring popularity of precious metals as money. Over the centuries, gold coins have proved particularly effective in standing the test of time. Modern forms of money are less durable and

A train conductor making change illustrates a number of characteristics of money in modern economic systems. It is divisible; for example, a rider can pay a ninety-cent fare with a dollar bill and receive a dime or two nickels in change. It is portable; this conductor carries coins in the changer and probably paper money in a pocket. It is fairly durable; the change the conductor hands out will probably last through many transactions. In addition, money should be difficult to counterfeit, and its value should remain relatively steady.

thus are often replaced. New U.S. coins—pennies, nickels, dimes, and quarters—are issued every year, although they are in circulation 10 or more years. Paper money is replaced, on average, every 18 months.

Stability The value, or purchasing power, of money should remain relatively steady. This inspires confidence in the money and a willingness to continue using it as a medium of exchange. Because stability is important, governments try to keep inflation under control. Runaway inflation can rapidly erode the value of a country's money and lead people to look for other storehouses for their wealth. Governments also pursue stability in the international arena. For example, the U.S. government tries to maintain a stable dollar vis-à-vis the currency of other countries. For recent government efforts in this area, see "International Close-Up: Revamping Monetary Policy."

Security To preserve the value of their money, governments must make it difficult to counterfeit. After all, if anyone could produce money on the nearest photocopier, the money wouldn't be worth much. When countries relied on gold coins as their major source of money, counterfeiting was a minor problem. The value of the currency was in the gold itself. The only way to undermine its value was to mint a coin with less gold and pass it off as having full value, and the color and standard weight of gold made this difficult to accomplish. However, with the issuance of paper money, the problem of counterfeiting became much more serious. Today, the paper on which U.S. money is printed has small red and blue threads embedded in it. While this makes effective counterfeiting extremely difficult, it is still a problem. Other nations have followed similar approaches in ensuring that their monetary system is not undermined by counterfeiters who flood the market with phony paper money.

The U.S. Money Supply

M1 A measure of the money supply equal to currency and demand deposits.

Currency Coins and paper money.

Demand deposits Checking accounts.

Stability and security are two of the concerns that lead the U.S. government to try to measure the supply of money. Changes in the supply that indicate instability might lead the government to attempt corrective actions. Although economists and financial experts sometimes debate exactly what is included in the money supply, most refer to it as M1. **M1** is a measurement that usually consists of currency and demand deposits.

Currency Coins and paper money make up **currency.** Coins are the small change of the money supply. At present, approximately 2 to 3 percent of the total U.S. money supply is in the form of coins. Paper money makes up approximately 25 percent of the money supply. About $100 billion of paper currency is in circulation at any one time.

Demand Deposits A less obvious part of the money supply is **demand deposits,** which are the various types of checking accounts. A large percent of all financial transactions use a check. The reasons are quite simple:

Checks are versatile. You can make a car payment of $164.23 with one check instead of coming up with the right combination of bills and change each month.

Checks reduce the possibility of theft. You can specify who has a right to the money; this is especially important if you want to mail in a payment.

Checks provide a record of the transaction. This simplifies bookkeeping and provides evidence if you need to prove a bill was paid or want to claim a tax deduction.

The most common type of demand deposit is **regular checking,** an account that pays no interest but allows the depositor to write checks on the funds. Most such accounts assess a monthly service charge based on

Regular checking An account that pays no interest but allows the depositor to write checks on the funds.

INTERNATIONAL   CLOSE-UP

Revamping Monetary Policy

One of the biggest problems facing many countries is that of maintaining the stability of their currency. Every day, investors buy and sell the currencies of foreign nations in money markets throughout the world. This helps establish the value of the currency of one country against that of another. When the value of the yen decreases relative to the value of the dollar, Japanese goods become cheaper in terms of American dollars. When the value of the dollar drops, more dollars are necessary to buy foreign goods; at the same time, however, buyers with other currencies can afford more American-made goods.

The American government has been concerned because the dollar has taken a roller-coaster ride in recent years. For example, between 1981 and 1985, the value of the dollar climbed more than 50 percent when measured against the currencies of major trading partners. However, starting in February 1985, the dollar started to decline, and two years later the dollar lost all the gains it had made during the previous five years. This made the dollar seem less stable than it had been in the past. As a result, financial experts in the governments of the United States, Great Britain, Germany, Japan, and France made plans to revamp their monetary systems and try to stabilize the relative value of their money.

The United States has suggested that the governments cooperate further to ensure monetary stability and proposed establishment of a secret "target zone" within which currencies will fluctuate. For example, if the governments secretly agree to keep the exchange rate between the dollar and the yen at about 150 yen, they will support this rate. If trading in the money markets were to push the rate to 160 to 165 yen to the dollar, the American and Japanese governments would intervene to bring the rate back to 150. This would mean selling dollars in the money markets, thereby increasing the supply and driving down the price, or exchange rate. Conversely, if the dollar began to weaken and the exchange rate fell toward the target zone, the governments would begin buying dollars, increasing the demand for this currency and sending the rate back toward 150.

In advocating that world currencies be stabilized through a form of international agreement, the Americans are proposing that the governments do away with letting currency values be determined by the open market. Will this come about? It is too early to say, but monetary stability will certainly continue to concern the U.S. government.

the number of checks written or the average daily balance in the account. The more checks written or the lower the balance, the higher the fee.

An attractive type of demand deposit for those who are willing to forgo some privileges in exchange for earning a little money is the **negotiable order of withdrawal (NOW) account,** a checking account that pays interest. In recent years, the interest rate for NOW accounts has been about 5½ percent. However, these accounts are subject to some restrictions. In particular, the depositor sometimes may write only a limited number of checks in a stated period of time. In addition, the fees on NOW accounts sometimes exceed the interest paid. Depositors must therefore compare fees as well as interest when shopping for a checking account.

A special type of demand deposit is the **traveler's check,** which is a check that is sold with a preset value and is redeemable if lost. The price of the check is the value on the check plus a processing fee. The most popular brand is the American Express traveler's check, which is widely used by international travelers. As advertised, a buyer who loses one can often obtain a full refund within 24 hours.

Near Money: A Broader View of the Money Supply Sometimes observers of the economy want to measure not just the money supply in the strictest sense, but the total assets that owners can easily use to make purchases. As Chapter 15 pointed out, assets that can be converted into cash quickly are said to be *liquid*. Money itself, of course, is a liquid asset; if you have money during business hours, you can rush right to the store and convert the money to other assets by purchasing something. At the other extreme, real estate is not nearly as liquid; if your only asset is your house, you'd need a while to sell or mortgage it to pay your tuition.

To view this broader picture of the money supply, economists and financial experts measure **near money,** certain highly liquid assets that do not function as a medium of exchange.[1] These assets consist of noncheckable savings deposits and time deposits. They do not function as a medium of exchange because before you can use them, you have to go to the trouble and probable expense of converting them to money.

Savings Deposits There are several ways savers can keep their money. **Passbook savings accounts** are noncheckable interest-bearing accounts. These conservative investments tend to pay low interest rates. Years ago, they were popular because low inflation made the interest attractive and few alternatives were as readily available to small investors. Today, because of the higher interest rates available in other near-money investments, their popularity has waned. However, they are flexible and liquid, and their few restrictions appeal to small savers looking for a place to get started.

In recent years, depositors have been offered attractive alternatives to passbook savings accounts. One is the **money market mutual fund,** which consists of shares in mutual funds that make short-term investments in securities of the federal government and major corporations. These investments expire on specified dates, at which time the mutual fund gets the invested money back and purchases other short-term investments. Because the rate of interest is usually higher than that on a savings account and has relatively low risk, these funds have become very popular over the last decade and reached record levels after the stock market crash in 1987.[2]

In 1982, Congress allowed financial institutions to start offering their own money market accounts, because many of their customers were withdrawing deposits and investing them in money market mutual funds. These **bank money market accounts** are short-term, special deposit accounts that offer competitive interest rates. Banks typically put these deposits into high-yield investments that allow them to pay high interest. Often, depositors can write checks against these accounts. If they can, then it no longer is classified as near money.

Time Deposits Besides savings deposits, where depositors can withdraw money at any time, the other form of near money is time deposits. **Time deposits** are savings accounts that require the depositor to give notice before withdrawing funds or to pay a penalty for withdrawing funds before a specified date. Because the restrictions mean that depositors are likely to leave their funds in the account longer, the financial institution usually pays more interest for these deposits.

For example, depositors can usually earn more interest on **certificates of deposit (CDs),** which are fixed-term accounts that pay a predetermined rate of interest. The longer their deposit term and the greater the investment, the higher the interest rate. Terms range from 90 days to 5 years or more, but the average CD depositor usually purchases a CD for a year or less. In the early 1980s, a small ($1,000 or less) one-year CD was paying around 14 percent. By 1987, inflation had slowed and the annual rate had dropped to around 7 or 8 percent, depending on the amount and term of the CD. Because of these variable interest rates, some institutions are offering innovative techniques to attract long-term CDs. For example, to attract those saving for their children's college expenses, a New Jersey bank offers a CD with an interest rate tied to an annual index of higher education costs. As the chairman of the bank notes: "With us, families have shifted the risk of rising tuition and inflation from the household to the bank."[3] This is an instance of a family practicing risk management (discussed fully in Chapter 20).

Credit Cards: Short-Term Loans A comprehensive definition of money includes all near money, but it does *not* include credit cards, even though consumers use them to make purchases. A **credit card** is an instrument used for obtaining a short-term loan for a cash purchase. The term *credit* means these cards create loans that the borrower must repay with money; they are not money themselves. Visa and MasterCard are widely used credit cards.

Credit cards are enormously popular in the United States. Millions of the major cards are in circulation, and they account for billions of dollars of billings annually. Coupled with charges to the hundreds of other cards issued by oil companies and other retailers, credit card purchases run into the hundreds of billions of dollars each year. However, as Sears discovered with its Discover credit card, it is a very competitive and complex business. In the first two years of its existence, the Discover card lost $400 million.[4] Finally, in the First quarter of 1988 the firm reported a profit.

A less popular way to shop with plastic is to use a bank-issued debit card. The merchant uses these cards to deduct purchases directly from

Bank money market accounts   Short-term, special deposit accounts that offer competitive interest rates.

Time deposits   Savings accounts that require the depositor to give notice before withdrawing funds or to pay a penalty for withdrawing the funds before a specified date.

Certificates of deposit (CDs)   Fixed-term accounts that pay a predetermined rate of interest.

Credit card   An instrument used for obtaining a short-term loan for a cash purchase.

the buyer's bank account. Although consumers have preferred checks and credit cards for shopping, they do use the debit cards to obtain funds from automatic teller machines (ATMs). The user slides the card into the machine, types in an access code number assigned by the bank (which should be a secret to everyone except the user and the bank), and tells the ATM how much is to be deposited or withdrawn, and the machine takes care of the rest.

In the case of withdrawals, the machine dispenses the money right on the spot. Typically, the financial institution sets a maximum for withdrawals at any one time (often $100 to $200) and during any 24-hour period ($200 in many locales). ATMs are spreading to many locations, including college campuses across the country. Whether used in ATMs or for shopping, debit cards are not part of the money supply; they merely move money in the customer's checking account, which has already been counted as part of the money supply.

Students without a credit history can get a credit card on their parents' account to cover them in emergencies. However, establishing your own credit is usually wise in the long run. Department stores and other retailers are usually the easiest sources of credit for those who are starting out. If you have a car, an oil company company credit card is another possible way to begin. The companies that issue major credit cards are usually hesitant to establish an account until you have worked somewhere for a year or two. Keep making payments on time, and pay other bills promptly. Eventually you should qualify for a major credit card.

Checkpoint

1. What are the characteristics of money?
2. How does money differ from near money?

Smartcard International's Ulticard incorporates a tiny programmable microchip that turns the card into a wallet-sized computer. The Ulticard can be used in financial transactions, as a debit or credit card, or to permit access through a security system. Such cards could add a whole new dimension to shopping with plastic.

Source: Courtesy of General Instrument Corporation and Smartcard International. Photo by Franz Edson.

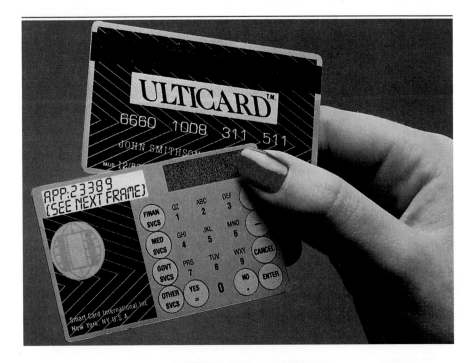

Types of Financial Institutions

In most cases, borrowers and lenders come together through some form of financial intermediary. These financial institutions typically pay interest on the money deposited by suppliers of funds; they then lend the funds to borrowers at a higher rate of interest. The difference between what the institution pays depositors and what it receives from borrowers goes to run the business and make a profit.

Several kinds of financial institutions provide money to borrowers. The major types of financial intermediaries in the United States are commercial banks, savings and loan associations, mutual savings banks, credit unions, and several kinds of nondeposit institutions. Some of these, such as commercial banks, lend the deposits they receive; others, such as life insurance companies and pension funds, invest money set aside to handle future contingencies such as death or retirement. Table 17.1 summarizes how each of these institutions serves as an intermediary. While the distinctions between them have blurred over the last decade because they have begun offering more similar services, all of these institutions continue to remain important.

T A B L E 17.1 **How Different Financial Institutions Serve as Intermediaries**

Financial Institution	Major Sources of Funds	Most Common Forms of Investments	Services for Customers
Commercial banks	Customer deposits, interest from loans	Personal loans, business loans	Checking and savings accounts; ATMs; loans; credit cards; some brokerage, insurance, and financial/estate planning services
Savings and loan associations	Customer deposits, interest from loans	Home mortgages, construction loans	Checking and savings accounts; ATMs; loans; credit cards; some brokerage, insurance, and financial/estate planning services
Mutual savings banks	Customer deposits, interest from loans	Home mortgages, construction loans	Checking and savings accounts; ATMs; loans; credit cards; some brokerage, insurance, and financial/estate planning services
Credit unions	Member deposits, interest from loans	Second mortgages, auto loans, short-term member loans	Share draft account (like checking account); savings accounts; ATMs; loans; credit cards; larger ones offer some brokerage, insurance, and financial/estate planning services
Insurance companies	Policyholder premiums, earnings on investments	Government bonds, commercial real-estate mortgages, long-term loans	Savings plans; loans; insurance; some financial/estate planning services
Pension funds	Contributions by employers and/or employees, earnings on investments	Corporate securities, government bonds	Savings plans; some loans; insurance and financial/estate planning services
Commercial and consumer finance companies	Short-term borrowing, interest earned on loans	Short-term business loans, short-term consumer loans	Loans; some insurance and financial planning services

Commercial Banks

The most common and readily identifiable financial institution is a **commercial bank.** This is a financial institution that accept deposits and provides a wide array of financial services, from loans to checking accounts to safe-deposit boxes. As Figure 17.2 shows, many of the largest banks in the country are commercial banks.

A commercial bank may be a national bank or a state bank. A **national bank** is chartered by the federal government. The charter spells out the articles of incorporation under existing laws. About one-third of all commercial banks fall into this national bank category. These banks tend to be large, holding approximately 60 percent of all commercial bank deposits. A **state bank** is chartered by an individual state. There are about twice as many of these smaller state banks.

Commercial banks are often referred to as "full-service" banks. This is because they offer their customers a wide range of financial services, including checking and savings accounts, business and personal loans, bank credit cards, safe-deposit boxes, the electronic transfer of funds to other banks, traveler's checks, and financial counseling. Today banks also have ATMs.

These services are not free. In one way or another, the bank charges for them, although many depositors are not always aware of it. For example, many banks assess a service fee if an account balance falls beneath a particular minimum, such as $200. Unless the depositor pays attention to the amount of interest earned and fees charged, the account can actually lose money. If the account is small enough, say, $50, the fees will eventually deplete the entire fund. Banks also charge a fee for overdrafts. If a depositor writes a check for $200 when only $180 is in the account, the bank may refuse to honor the check and impose a fee (often $5 to $10). Credit cards are another source of income for banks, since banks typically charge a fee of $20 to $35 a year per card in addition to charging interest on the balance. Borrowers also pay fees, usually based on the amount of the loan.

Commercial bank A financial institution that accepts deposits and provides a wide array of financial services.

National banks Commercial banks chartered by the federal government.

State banks Commercial banks chartered by individual states.

FIGURE 17.2

The Ten Largest Commercial Banks in the United States

Savings and Loan Associations

The original goal of **savings and loan associations (S&Ls)** was to encourage home ownership. These institutions originally used funds in families' savings accounts to make home mortgage loans. Today, S&Ls still emphasize this activity but also offer checking accounts and a variety of other types of loans.

Government regulations used to set the interest rates on S&L savings accounts slightly higher than comparable accounts at commercial banks. This enabled S&Ls to attract small savers who wanted to make the highest possible return without the risk of most investments. In turn, the S&L loaned these funds to home buyers at competitive rates. Since S&Ls specialized in home mortgages, they were often the first place people turned to when they wanted to finance a home.

In recent years, however, all of this has changed. Deregulation of the banking industry has allowed banks and S&Ls to set interest rates freely. Banks have matched the rates at S&Ls, thereby attracting depositors. At the same time, many S&Ls were stuck with mortgages paying relatively low interest while they had to pay higher rates to attract deposits. As a

**Savings and loan
association (S&L)**
Financial institution that
emphasizes savings
accounts and home
mortgage loans.

Many commercial banks offer their bigger customers personal attention in comfortable settings. This meeting is taking place at a luncheon club near Comerica Bank, a Detroit-based commercial bank.

Source: Courtesy of Comerica Incorporated.

result, an unusually large number of S&Ls went out of business in the early 1980s. Texas S&Ls were particularly hard hit. Hit first by the oil bust, then a real estate collapse, it is estimated that they lost $5 billion in 1987 alone.[5]

Many other S&Ls have sought creative ways to compete. Deregulation has freed S&Ls to offer services that used to be the exclusive domain of the commercial banks. These include such services as checking accounts, NOW accounts, home improvement loans, auto loans, certificates of deposit, cashier's checks, and traveler's checks. Some S&Ls have begun to make commercial loans. S&Ls have also sought ways to make their traditional involvement in mortgage lending more profitable. In the past, S&Ls offered only fixed-rate mortgages, loans on which the interest rate remained the same for the 20- or 30-year life of the loan. Today they also offer variable-rate mortgages, on which the interest rate fluctuates in relation to market conditions. If S&Ls continue to diversify, they may someday offer exactly the same services as commercial banks.

Mutual Savings Banks

Mutual savings bank
State-chartered bank that offers many of the same services as S&Ls.

Similar to savings and loan associations, but less common, are **mutual savings banks.** These are state-chartered banks that offer many of the same services as S&Ls. When these institutions were first formed in the early 1800s in the Northeast, they were strictly savings banks; they encouraged savings by individual households and helped these groups meet their borrowing needs. The names of some of these institutions reflect their origins: Dime Savings Bank, Emigrant Savings Bank, and Seaman's Bank of Savings. With the changes in banking regulations, mutual savings banks have left behind their conservative approach. Today they offer NOW accounts, home mortgages, and other services that make them particularly competitive with S&Ls.

Credit Unions

Credit union A savings cooperative that lends money to its members.

Sometimes the members of a group form a savings cooperative. They pool their funds and share ownership of the pool, each member in proportion to his or her investment. Representatives of the pool manage it for the group. A savings cooperative that lends money to its members is a **credit union.**

A typical credit union consists of members of a specific group, such as employees of a company or a university. Only those who belong to this group may join the credit union. Most credit unions require a minimum deposit such as $100 to join the credit union. In return for putting up the deposit, the members can earn interest on savings and apply for loans. In most cases, credit unions pay slightly higher interest rates than other financial institutions pay on similar accounts.

Like other financial institutions, credit unions have recently been expanding their financial services, offering life insurance and interest-bearing checking accounts. However, their ability to compete with other lending institutions is severely limited. For one thing, they accept deposits only from their members, which limits the funds they can accumulate. Also, they typically must limit the amount they can lend to any one person, making it extremely difficult for them to compete for large loans.

Nondeposit Institutions

Unlike those discussed so far, some financial institutions do not get their money through deposits. Funds for these "nondeposit" financial institutions come in three major forms: insurance premiums, contributions for retirement, and sale of bonds and short-term loans. Examples of such financial institutions include insurance companies, pension funds, and finance companies.

Insurance Companies Besides protecting their customers against risk, as we will describe in Chapter 20, insurance companies act as financial institutions because they receive billions of dollars in premiums (payments for coverage) every year. When covered individuals die or have a theft or fire, the companies use some of these funds to pay claims. However, in any given year, most of the people covered with insurance have no claims and will continue to have none for decades. This leaves a substantial amount of funds from premiums for the company to invest so that they will grow large enough to cover future claims and generate a profit for the company.

Pension Funds The desire to prepare for retirement has led to the creation of another type of nondeposit financial institution: the **pension fund.** This is a pool of money set aside and invested to take care of retirement obligations. The money may come from employers, employees, or unions. In many organizations, employees are entitled to a pension based on how long they have worked there and how much they were paid annually. If the employee makes contributions, the size of this contribution may also affect the size of the pension. Often, pension funds are managed by professional pension fund managers. Preset rules specify the income that each person is entitled to receive upon retirement.

Pension fund A pool of money set aside and invested to take care of retirement obligations.

With assets in the range of $1 trillion, these funds are a significant source of financing. Typical investments include high-quality stocks and long-term mortgages on commercial properties. These investments provide funding to the corporations that issue the stock and to the developers of the real estate.

Finance Companies Some nondeposit institutions, called finance companies, emphasize lending. They obtain funds to lend by borrowing themselves and by the sale of bonds. **Commercial finance companies** specialize in providing short-term, collateralized loans to businesses. A collateralized loan is backed with something of value that the lender can claim in case of default. **Consumer finance companies** do the same for individuals. The interest rate on these loans is generally higher than that charged by commercial banks. Because of this, borrowers usually turn to finance companies only after they have been turned down by a bank. These borrowers are riskier because they are young or otherwise unable to meet the strict requirements of a commercial bank's lending policies. Commercial Credit and CIT Financial are two of the major commercial finance companies, and Beneficial Finance and Household Finance are examples of consumer finance companies. In addition, a growing number of smaller finance companies have been attracted by the potentially high profits gained by lending to businesses and individuals that cannot qualify for loans at commercial banks.

Commercial finance company Lending institution that provides short-term, collateralized loans to businesses.

Consumer finance company Financial institution that makes short-term loans to individuals.

General Electric Credit Corporation (GECC), with over $25 billion in assets, is among the nation's largest finance companies. It lends to businesses as well as consumers. A $30 million loan from GECC helped finance renovations to Philadelphia's historic Packard Building, which includes this impressive bank lobby.

Source: © Lawrence S. Williams, Inc.

Checkpoint

1. What are three major types of financial institutions?
2. You started a small word-processing business last year, and you want to borrow $2,000 to upgrade your computers. Two banks have turned you down. Where might you turn for financing?

Regulation and Control of Financial Institutions

Until this century, when one lending institution needed money, it would borrow from others with available funds. If it had more than enough funds to meet its obligations, the institution would seek to lend them to those with shortage of funds. This worked well as long as the amount that banks wanted to borrow approximated the amount available for lending. However, when too many banks needed funds at the same time, the shortage of funds often led to panics and the failure of some institutions.

To create greater stability, the federal government has over the years introduced various controls affecting all types of financial institutions. The major ones, which primarily involve banks and savings and loan associations, are the Federal Reserve System and agencies that insure deposits.

The Federal Reserve System

To oversee the thousands of banks throughout the nation, the government in 1913 created the **Federal Reserve System** (commonly called "the Fed"), a network of regional banks that regulates banking in America. The Fed is jointly owned by the government and its member banks.

As Figure 17.3 shows, at the top of the Federal Reserve System is the board of governors, seven people appointed by the president of the United States and confirmed by the Senate. To help keep the board free from political pressure, each board member serves a 14-year term, none may be nominated for a second term, and the terms are staggered so that one member is replaced every two years. The board appoints a chairperson to a four-year term. The board members come from the 12 different Federal Reserve districts.

Within each district is a regional bank called a Federal Reserve bank (Figure 17.4). These, in turn, operate 25 branch banks throughout the United States. Each of the 12 Federal Reserve banks is owned by member banks in that district, and each has its own governing board of directors consisting of nine people. Three are bankers and are elected by the member banks in the district. Three represent the borrowers and they also are elected by the district member banks. The final three are selected as representatives of the general public and they are chosen by the board of governors of the Fed.

All national banks must be members of the Federal Reserve System. State banks are not required to join, and most do not. Member banks have a number of important privileges, including the right to:

Obtain funds by borrowing from their district reserve bank.

Use a variety of services provided by the system.

Obtain financial advice and assistance.

**Federal Reserve System
(Fed)** A network of
regional banks that
regulate banking in
America.

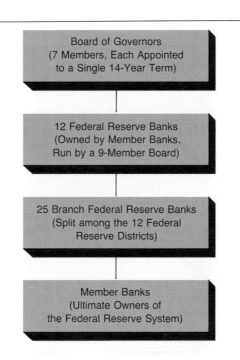

F I G U R E   17.3

**Organization Chart of the
Federal Reserve System**

Board of Governors
(7 Members, Each Appointed
to a Single 14-Year Term)

12 Federal Reserve Banks
(Owned by Member Banks,
Run by a 9-Member Board)

25 Branch Federal Reserve Banks
(Split among the 12 Federal
Reserve Districts)

Member Banks
(Ultimate Owners of
the Federal Reserve System)

Vote for six of the nine board members of the district bank.

Receive a dividend on stock owned in the district bank.

The Fed carries out five basic functions, four of which are designed to control the money supply and keep the economy on an even keel: (1) establishing reserve requirements, (2) conducting open-market operations, (3) setting the discount rate, and (4) using credit controls. Table 17.2 summarizes how the Fed's monetary tools heat up or cool down the economy. The fifth function of the Fed is check clearing.

Reserve Requirement The most powerful tool available to the Fed in controlling the money supply is the reserve requirement. The **reserve requirement** is the percentage of all deposits that a bank must keep on hand at the bank or on deposit with the Fed. The more the bank has on reserve, the less it has available to circulate through the economy by lending. If the Fed requires banks to keep 20 percent of all funds on deposit, then they can loan out the other 80 percent. Thus, if the banks

Reserve requirement The percentage of all deposits that a bank must keep on hand at the bank or on deposit with the Fed.

FIGURE   17.4

Regions of the Federal Reserve System

in your city had $100 million in deposits, they could lend $80 million of it to individuals, who will buy more goods, and to businesses, which can use the funds to expand. If the Fed were to raise the reserve requirement to 25 percent, the banks would be able to lend only $75 million. Individuals and companies would have $5 million less for buying goods and expanding business.

These Fed actions can affect interest rates and economic activity. In basic supply-and-demand analysis, when the supply of something increases, its price falls, and vice versa. The price borrowers pay for the privilege of using money is the interest rate. Therefore, when the reserve requirement goes down, making more money available, interest rates fall. When the reserve requirement rises, less money is available and thus interest rates rise. When interest rates are high and money is hard to come by, businesses put off borrowing and expanding, and consumers put off borrowing and shopping. Economic activity slows down. When interest rates are low, the opposite occurs.

The reserve requirement also controls bank actions. For example, a bank with $10 million in checking accounts might have $1.5 million on hand at the Fed to meet a 15 percent reserve requirement. If the Fed raised the requirement to 20 percent, the bank would have to come up with another $500,000. This would mean calling in some loans and not making any new ones until it had met the reserve requirement.

During the late 1970s, the number of Fed member banks began to decline sharply. The reason was that in order to keep up with rapid inflation, banks wanted to earn as much interest as possible on their funds. Deposits at the district federal reserve banks do not earn interest. Banks began withdrawing from the system and putting these funds into interest-bearing investments. The government responded by requiring *all*

T A B L E 17.2   **The Federal Reserve System's Tools for Monetary Control**

| | | | Intended Effects on the Economy | |
| | | Effect on the Money Supply | Interest Rates | Economic Activity |
Tool	Fed Action			
Reserve requirement	Decrease the requirement	↑	↓	↑
	Increase the requirement	↓	↑	↓
Open-market operations	Buy government securities	↑	↓	↑
	Sell government securities	↓	↑	↓
Discount rate	Lower the rate	↑	↓	↑
	Raise the rate	↓	↑	↓
Credit controls	Lower margin requirements	None	Purchases of securities increase; consumer buying increases	
	Raise margin requirements	None	Purchases of securities decrease; consumer buying decreases	

↑ Increase
↓ Decrease

banks and deposit institutions to keep a percentage of their deposits at the Fed, whether or not they are member institutions. As these changes have gone into effect, the distinction between member and nonmember banks has begun to fade.

Open-market operations
The buying and selling of government securities by the Fed.

Open-Market Operations The Fed also controls the money supply through **open-market operations,** which consist of the buying and selling of government securities (bonds). When the Federal Open Market Committee buys government securities, it increases the money supply by putting more money into circulation. Conversely, when the committee sells government securities, it decreases the money supply by taking money out of circulation.

Open-market operations are easier to use for making small adjustments in the money supply. With these operations, the Fed can fine tune the economy without shaking up the entire financial structure, which is what might happen if it continually announced changes in the reserve requirement.

Discount Rate The Fed is sometimes referred to as "the banker's bank," because it lends money to member banks. The banks borrow from their district bank, which determines its own interest rate, subject to approval by the Board of Governors of the entire system. This rate — the rate the Fed charges — is called the **discount rate.**

Discount rate The interest rate that the Fed charges member banks for loans.

When the Fed lowers the discount rate, member banks are more likely to borrow. When the rate goes up, they are less likely to do so. The banks, in turn, adjust the rates they charge their customers to cover what they pay the Fed. The amount of funds that commercial banks obtain through loans may be quite small, usually only about 3 to 4 percent of their total reserves. Nevertheless, the discount rate is an effective monetary tool because the Fed can use it to fine tune the economy and influence the rate at which banks lend to their customers.

Credit Controls The Fed also has the authority to use a series of selective credit controls. One of these is the power to establish the margin requirements on credit purchases of stocks and bonds. The margin is the percentage that credit customers must pay in advance. Before the stock market crash of 1929, this requirement was 10 percent. A person could buy stock worth $100 merely by putting down $10. If the stock started to drop into the low nineties, the stock broker would ask for more money; if the buyer was unable to come up with it, the broker would sell the stock before it reached $90 and keep the balance due. The investor would lose most, or all, of the investment.

In recent years, the Fed has set the margin requirement on securities at 50 percent. Even so, in the stock market crash in 1987, many investors lost tremendous amounts of money when the stocks dropped dramatically and the brokerages called in their margin accounts. Chapter 19 will give more attention to this and other aspects of investing in the stock market.

The Fed also has the power to influence consumer credit purchases. It sets rules for the minimum down payment and the length of the repayment period. The Fed has not exercised this power in recent years, but if it did, it could have a dramatic impact. For example, most new-car loans have terms of three to four years and require a small down payment, usually 10 percent. If the Fed required a 20 percent minimum down payment and a loan term of no more than two years, many people would be unable to buy a new car. This restriction on credit would cripple consumers' purchasing power. As consumers bought less, the economy would slow down.

Check-Clearing Services Besides its monetary functions, the Federal Reserve System also clears checks by moving them from the bank where they were deposited to the bank on which they are drawn. Figure 17.5 depicts how this works. The check travels electronically from the depositor's bank through the Federal Reserve bank in its district and the Federal Reserve bank in the district of the payer's bank to the payer's bank.

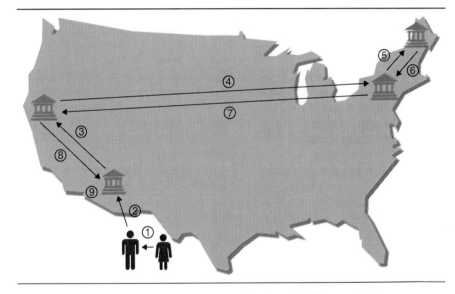

F I G U R E   17.5

How the Federal Reserve System Clears Checks

What the Numbers Mean:
1. While on vacation, Mrs. Adele Johnson of Bangor, Maine, buys a western painting in Phoenix, Arizona, and pays with a check drawn on her hometown bank.
2. Joe Garcia, the artist, deposits the check in his Phoenix bank.
3. The Phoenix bank electronically transfers the check (the check does not physically travel through the Reserve system) for credit in its account at its district bank, the Federal Reserve Bank of San Francisco.
4. To collect the funds, the Federal Reserve Bank of San Francisco transfers the check to the district bank for Bangor, the Federal Reserve Bank of Boston.

5. The Federal Reserve Bank of Boston transfers the check to Mrs. Johnson's bank in Bangor, which deducts the amount of the check from her deposit account.
6. Mrs. Johnson's bank authorizes the Federal Reserve Bank of Boston to deduct the amount of the check from its deposit account with the reserve bank.
7. The Federal Reserve Bank of Boston pays the Federal Reserve Bank of San Francisco the amount of the check.
8. The Federal Reserve Bank of San Francisco credits the Phoenix bank for the amount of the check.
9. The Phoenix bank credits Joe Garcia's account for the amount of the check.

Then the payer's bank sends the payment back through the same channel in the opposite direction. If a check is written and drawn on banks in the same Federal Reserve district, the Federal Reserve bank in that district handles the entire matter. For example, if a renter living in Manhattan writes a check to the landlord, who deposits it in a bank in Brooklyn, the Federal Reserve Bank of New York is the only Fed bank involved in clearing the check.

Insuring Deposits

Federal Deposit Insurance Corporation (FDIC) A federal agency that insures bank deposits up to $100,000 in case of bank failure.

The government is also involved in protecting deposits. During the depths of the Great Depression in the early 1930s, a run on a bank, in which masses of depositors demanded their money, was a common occurrence. In 1933 alone, almost 4,000 banks collapsed. To restore confidence in banks, Congress established the **Federal Deposit Insurance Corporation (FDIC)** in 1934. The FDIC is a federal agency that insures bank deposits up to $100,000 in case of bank failure. Besides the insurance, the FDIC also protects the public by now requiring the banks it regulates to give customers, on request, information about asset quality (bad loans), capital, and earnings. This should prevent customers from doing business with banks that are in trouble.[6] All commercial banks that are members of the Federal Reserve System pay for the insurance and are covered. Banks that are not members of the system may also join the FDIC. Most in fact do, and today fewer than 1,000 banks are not members.

Federal Savings and Loan Insurance Corporation (FSLIC) A federal agency that insures deposits up to $100,000 at savings and loan associations.

Other organizations insure deposits at other types of savings institutions. The **Federal Savings and Loan Insurance Corporation (FSLIC)** insures deposits up to $100,000 at savings and loan associations. The **National Credit Union Administration** insures deposits up to $100,000 at federal- or state-chartered credit unions.

National Credit Union Administration A federal agency that insures deposits up to $100,000 at federal- or state-chartered credit unions.

People who have more than $100,000 to deposit and want to be fully insured can establish a combination of accounts. For example, a married couple can open three accounts (two single and one joint), and each will be insured up to $100,000. Other combinations with children, grandchildren, or other relatives would have the same effect. Those who do not want to use joint accounts can open individual accounts in different banks. Using a little money management, a person can make sure that all deposits are insured.

Federal insurance coverage has become of great importance in recent years, because the number of bank and S&L failures has increased in the 1980s. A number of forces have brought this about, including deregulation, a large number of questionable loans, a slow economy (especially in agriculture), and a big drop in oil prices. In 1987 alone, there were 184 bank failures, the most recorded since the depth of the Great Depression in 1933.[7] Because the depositors in most banks had the FDIC to fall back on, they didn't rush to withdraw their funds. This has prevented a troublesome problem for the banks from becoming a runaway disaster for the economy at large.

Checkpoint

1. How does the Federal Reserve help control the money supply?
2. How does the government protect depositors?

Recent Developments in Banking

Technological developments and increased competition in the face of
deregulation have changed the face of American banking. Managers of
financial institutions are finding that today's environment requires more
than financial expertise; they also must be able to use human relations,
marketing, and computer techniques. In addition, they must be more
skilled than ever in responding to the needs and concerns of the public.

Bank Technology

Banks and other financial institutions are using computer technology to
help process billions of checks and keep records of a multitude of customer transactions. This technology is reducing the need for both individual customers or the financial institutions to carry large sums of
money.

One developing area is the use of the **electronic funds transfer system,** which is a computerized system for depositing and withdrawing
funds electronically. One of the most popular ways of doing this is
through the use of a push-button telephone. The user enters a personal
identification number and presses other buttons to indicate what
amounts the computer should transfer to pay certain bills (for example,
the monthly car payment, the telephone bill, or the electric bill). The
computer subtracts the amount from the customer's balance and adds it
to the creditor's balance. The customer's monthly bank statement lists all
of these telephone transactions, providing a record of what was paid and
to whom that takes the place of canceled checks. Some bank customers
have readily adopted this system, appreciating its convenience, while
many others have been reluctant to give up the float (the time between
the writing of a check and when it is withdrawn from the account) and
tangibility of checks.

Another example of bank technology is the **point-of-sale terminal,**
which allows a retail customer to pay for goods by using a computer terminal and a debit card to transfer funds from their bank account to that
of the merchant. A number of companies are now using these cards, including Publix supermarkets in Florida, Atlantic Richfield gasoline stations, and some Montgomery Ward retail stores. The procedure for
using these terminals is the same as that for debit cards, discussed earlier.

Deregulation and Competition

During the 1980s, the banking industry became less regulated, although
some states still prohibit branch banking (where a bank will have a number of locations), holding companies (where a large bank will own several smaller banks), and similar developments. Nevertheless, this
deregulation has stimulated mergers into regional banks, diversification
efforts, and service and price competition. Unfortunately, deregulation
may also be one contributing factor to the dramatic increase in bank
frauds. Because of the pressure of competition stemming from deregulation, there has been a frenzy of questionable loans to friends and insiders, phony asset appraisals, and other misdeeds. In Texas alone, some
experts estimate that fraud-related losses since deregulation may eventually top $5 billion.[8]

**Electronic funds transfer
system**   A computerized
system for depositing and
withdrawing funds
electronically.

Point-of-sale terminal   A
computer terminal that
allows retail customers to
use a debit card to transfer
funds from their bank
account to that of the
merchant.

First Nationwide Bank, owned
by Ford Motor Company, operates in eight states and has
government approval to expand into six more. Some of
its branches, like this one, are
located in K mart stores. Such
convenient locations are one
way financial institutions are
meeting increased competition.

Source: Courtesy of Ford Motor
Company.

Competitive Small Banks Many small banks are facing up to huge competitors by merging to form regional banks. These banks combine expertise to serve several local markets. Other small and medium-sized banks are competing by finding a special need and meeting it. They may offer longer hours and special services. For example, University Bank and Trust of Palo Alto, California, makes twice the profit rate as larger banks because of what they call "endless service," including free shoeshines with deposits, helping customers balance their accounts, selling postage stamps at cost, and, if teller windows develop long lines of customers, having the bank president wait on customers.[9] These small banks often develop strong ties to businesses and the general public in their own geographic area. Many of these local and regional banks are in better financial shape than some of their huge competitors from New York or California. Their profits are high, and they are well managed.

Diversification A number of financial institutions have used deregulation as an opportunity to diversify. For example, many banks are providing brokerage services to help their customers invest their money. Before deregulation, the investor would have had to go through a brokerage house, but now a customer who wants to buy 100 shares of stock or sell a bond can do it through the bank. Banks are also providing financial counseling and helping people set up retirement accounts. Other institutions, too, are diversifying. For example, most life insurance companies offer financial planning and a number of investment choices.

Service Competition Many financial institutions are meeting the deregulation challenge by competing on the basis of service. One approach is to diversify and offer more services; another approach is to provide better customer service. Some banks have tried assigning each of their major customers to a "personal banker." If a customer has a problem or wants a question answered, he or she simply calls the personal banker, who gives the problem or question personal attention. At University Bank and Trust, cited above, a customer who needs something, even when the bank is closed, merely calls his or her personal banker. The bank will open for the customer at any hour of the day.[10] Such personalized, quality service is becoming increasingly recognized as a major ingredient to successful organizations.

Price Competition Deregulation has made a greater array of choices available to the users of financial services. Today, more than ever, customers of financial institutions look around for the highest return on their savings or the lowest rate they can get on a loan. Because most customers find it easiest to make comparisons based on interest rates, financial institutions have tended to compete most heavily in this area.

However, offering competitive rates has meant some hard choices for the managers of these institutions. When the government set ceilings on the interest rates that banks and S&Ls could pay on savings, the institutions could use this cheap source of funds to pay for a variety of services. But now that the institutions have to pay more to attract funds, they find that many accounts and services are money losers. A small savings or checking account may not even give the bank enough funds to justify the bookkeeping costs of administering it. Other services, such as cashing checks or helping customers balance their checkbooks, are purely expenses. Consequently, banks and other institutions are finding it necessary to drop the unprofitable services or institute a way to recover the costs involved.

Dropping unprofitable lines of business has stirred controversy. Many fear that the young, the old, and the poor will be shut out of banking services altogether. For more on this issue, see "Social Responsibility Close-Up: Lifelong Banking."

SOCIAL RESPONSIBILITY   CLOSE-UP

Lifelong Banking

Commercial banking is generally considered to be very socially responsible and have high ethical standards. In fact, a recent comprehensive survey of the leading members of the business, government, and academic communities ranked commercial banking as having the highest ethical standards of any industry. Yet there are still some potential problems concerning the social obligations of banks. For example, most established, employed people have no trouble opening a bank account, getting a credit card issued by the bank, and obtaining services from a financial institution. However, some people cannot get even a checking account. One such group is people with a low annual income. Banks are reluctant to open small checking accounts, because they cost the institution more money than earnings on these funds can generate. Many financial institutions are also reluctant to open accounts for people without an established credit history. These limitations can be hard on young people, although some banks do cater to students, with the expectation that they have the potential to be big customers.

Some people without an account still need a bank's services. For example, those with low or fixed incomes may need to have their weekly or monthly checks cashed. But because they do not have an account with a bank, they are forced to cash their checks at check-cashing establishments, where the proprietor often charges up to 10 percent for this service.

These individuals, and others who are concerned about them, contend that everyone should have a right to a bank's services. This idea of "lifelong" banking has appealed to many among the general public and in Congress. Advocates say that people who cannot afford the fees for a checking account or a credit card should still be given one. Their reasoning is that banks have a social responsibility to help the needy, and one of the worst ways of depriving people in our society is to lock them out of financial services. Lifelong banking is thus akin to providing special utility rates for people who are too poor to pay their electric bills or providing free or discounted health care to people who are unable to pay for medical services.

Some enlightened banks that agree with the basic idea of lifelong banking have made basic services available under a no-frills package. Some of the most popular include providing people with free checking accounts, giving them use of an ATM so that they can draw their funds out as needed, and waiving monthly charges for small accounts. Congress has considered requiring banks to provide minimum services to the elderly and the impoverished. If this ever becomes law, it will be illegal for banks to deny services to anyone.

Vulnerability to Lawsuits

As banks become more cost conscious and customers shop around, there is a growing movement toward suing banks that customers believe offer poor advice or make decisions that harm them. Customers have sued banks for reducing or eliminating lines of credit and leaving the client short of funds and for cutting off funding after giving the impression that it would be forthcoming.

In recent years, a number of major banks have lost major suits to customer companies. For example, Jewel Company won a $26 million suit against Bank of America, Farrah Manufacturing got damages of $18.6 million from the State National Bank of El Paso, and KMC Co. received $7.5 million from a suit it brought against Irving Trust.[11] In an extreme case, Herbert and Nelson Hunt, brothers in the multibillion-dollar family empire that has recently hit rock bottom, are claiming that the banks conspired to drive them out of business. They are suing their bankers for a combined total of $3.6 billion.[12] The future is likely to see a number of such challenges facing banks as they try to balance their social obligations to treat their customers fairly and ethically with their profit objectives.

Checkpoint

1. What technological developments have recently affected banking?
2. How has deregulation influenced the banking industry?

Closing Comments

Every day, the banking system brings together suppliers and demanders of money, making possible a multitude of transactions—buying cars, building warehouses, earning interest. The financial institutions that make this possible include banks, savings and loan associations, mutual savings banks, credit unions, and nondeposit institutions. The government, too, plays a role. The Federal Reserve System regulates the money supply, and various agencies insure deposits. Together, financial institutions and the government try to ensure that a reliable supply of funds is available to meet the needs of business and consumers.

Learning Objectives Revisited

1. **Explain the nature and purpose of money.**
   Money is anything generally accepted as payment. It serves as a medium of exchange, a standard of value, and a storehouse of value. Money best performs these functions when it is divisible, portable, durable, stable, and secure.
2. **Describe the money supply and its components.**
   The money supply is often defined as money and near money. Money includes currency and demand deposits. Currency consists of

coins and paper money; demand deposits are checking accounts, including regular checking accounts, NOW accounts, and traveler's checks. Near money is certain highly liquid assets that do not function as a medium of exchange. These include savings accounts and time deposits such as money market mutual funds, bank money market accounts, and certificates of deposit. Unlike demand deposits, near money must be converted to money before you can use it.

3. **Present the major financial institutions.**

The major financial institutions are commercial banks, savings and loan associations (S&Ls), mutual savings banks, credit unions, and nondeposit institutions. Nondeposit institutions include insurance companies, pension funds, and finance companies. In recent years, the differences between these institutions have become blurred. For example, like commercial banks, many S&Ls and mutual savings banks offer checking accounts, NOW accounts, savings accounts, and various forms of time deposits, and credit unions offer checking and savings accounts.

4. **Discuss the Federal Reserve System.**

The Federal Reserve System (the Fed) is designed to control the nation's money supply and regulate the economy. A board of governors oversees 12 Federal Reserve districts, each of which has a Federal Reserve bank. The district banks operate 25 Federal Reserve branches. Each of the district banks is owned by the member banks in that district, and each has a governing board of directors. To regulate the economy, the Fed sets reserve requirements, conducts open-market operations to buy and sell government securities, determines the discount rate, and uses credit controls to increase or decrease the down payment needed to buy stocks, bonds, and consumer goods. The Fed also clears checks through the system.

5. **Explain how government agencies protect deposits.**

For all banks that purchase its insurance, the Federal Deposit Insurance Corporation (FDIC) insures deposits up to $100,000. The Federal Savings and Loan Insurance Corporation (FSLIC) provides a similar service for S&Ls. Credit unions can buy equivalent insurance from the National Credit Union Administration.

6. **Identify recent developments in banking.**

Most current developments in the banking industry stem from new technological developments and deregulation. Electronic funds transfer systems and other computerized systems allow customers to receive financial services without ever coming into the bank. Less regulation and competition are resulting in a decrease in the distinctions between commercial banks, S&Ls, mutual savings banks, and credit unions. To compete, institutions are merging, diversifying, featuring personalized services to attract major accounts, offering competitive interest rates, and charging fees to cover costs.

Key Terms Reviewed

Review each of the following terms. For any that you do not know or are unsure of, look up the definitions and see how they were used in the chapter.

money

M1

currency

demand deposits

regular checking

negotiable order of withdrawal (NOW) account

traveler's check

near money

passbook savings accounts

money market mutual funds

bank money market accounts

time deposits

certificates of deposit (CDs)

credit card

commercial bank

national banks

state banks

savings and loan association (S&L)

mutual savings bank

credit union

pension fund

commercial finance company

consumer finance company

Federal Reserve System (Fed)

reserve requirement

open-market operations

discount rate

Federal Deposit Insurance Corporation (FDIC)

Federal Savings and Loan Insurance Corporation (FSLIC)

National Credit Union Administration

electronic funds transfer system

point-of-sale terminal

Review Questions

1. What is the difference between money and currency?
2. People use credit cards to buy a wide variety of goods and services. Why aren't credit cards considered part of the money supply?
3. How does a commercial bank differ from a savings and loan association?
4. Ralph Burgess just took a job with a company that has a credit union. Why might Ralph investigate switching his savings account from his S&L to the credit union?
5. Some financial institutions get their funds from sources other than deposits. What are these institutions, and where do they get their funds?
6. What type of financial institution might be best suited for each of the following needs?
   a. The president of a company wants to set aside money for employees to retire on.
   b. A recent graduate wants a safe place to keep the earnings from her new job and a way to pay bills conveniently.
   c. A large and profitable corporation wants to sell stock to generate funds for expansion.
   d. A 20-year-old law firm with a steady flow of business wants to borrow funds to computerize its operations.

7. What privileges does a bank obtain by joining the Federal Reserve System?

8. Imagine that the economy is growing rapidly. Businesses are producing more and more, and consumer spending is keeping pace. Nevertheless, the members of the Fed's board of governors are worried. They fear that if the economy grows any faster, a dizzying inflation rate will result. How can they try to slow the pace of economic activity? Which approach or combination of approaches would you recommend? Why?

9. A sign in the window of Upright Savings and Loan Association reads "Deposits Insured by the FSLIC." What does this mean?

10. Annette Blasedell is a commercial real estate broker. She is single and lives alone in a comfortable apartment near her parents' home. A stupendous deal has netted Annette an impressive $300,000 commission check. Until Annette decides what to do with the windfall, how can she keep it all in an insured account?

11. How can a bank customer benefit from an electronic funds transfer system? Why are many bank customers reluctant to do their banking this way?

Applied Exercises

1. Visit a local commercial bank and find out the various types of demand deposits it currently offers. Write a brief paper identifying and describing these deposits. Report your findings to the class.

2. Visit a local savings and loan association and find out the various types of demand deposits it currently offers. Write a brief paper identifying and describing these deposits. Compare your answer to those for the first question. Report your findings to the class.

3. Visit a local bank and have a representative explain the role of the FDIC. Put this in your own words and describe it to the class.

4. Visit a commercial or consumer finance company and have a representative describe what they do. Where do they get their funds, and whom do they lend to? Write up your findings in a short report.

Your Business IQ: Answers

1. False. Paper currency makes up only around one-quarter of the money supply. Most of the money supply consists of demand deposits (checking accounts).

2. True. Changes in banking regulations have allowed banks to pay interest on checking accounts. Previous regulations prohibited interest payments on these accounts.

3. True. These institutions are offering similar services. Within a decade, the types of financial institutions will probably be difficult to distinguish between.

4. False. The Federal Reserve System (the Fed) has no direct influence on the budget. The Fed's role is confined to controlling the money supply and regulating banking.

5. False. Financial institutions have tended to compete by paying the highest possible interest on accounts and charging the lowest possible interest on loans. They have compensated for this by charging higher, not lower, fees on accounts.

Barnett Banks Blends
Old and New Styles

In a time when banks are trying to compete by branching and diversifying, Barnett Banks of Jacksonville, Florida, sticks with offering basic services close to home. Although Florida allowed branch banking beginning in 1976, Barnett remains a collection of 33 separate subsidiaries, about half of which operate as national banks and half as state banks. However, the subsidiaries do have branches, about 450 in all, with new ones opening at the rate of 25 to 30 a year. Except for one bank outside Atlanta, all the Barnett banks are located in Florida.

In recent years, the company has performed well. Barnett's assets and profits have risen more than sevenfold over the last decade. More than two-thirds of the company's offices were opened in the past ten years, capitalizing on the rapid growth of Florida's population. Barnett holds 22 percent of the bank deposits in Florida, more than double what it had in 1979.

One reason for this success is the bank's local touch. The board of directors of the subsidiaries consist of local people, and they are encouraged to develop new business. Knowledge of the area also helps the bankers evaluate whether loan applicants are good candidates for repayment, not an easy job in a fast-growing area. Also, the bank tries to stick to lending only to those who do business in Florida. This has kept Barnett away from the kinds of international loans that were the downfall of so many banks in recent years.

The company's chief executive officer, Charlie Rice, uses what he calls an "entrepreneurial system." The head of each subsidiary bank is responsible for that bank's operations and is left alone as long as he or she meets performance standards. Those who exceed their bank's goals for the year receive a hefty bonus. The result is highly motivated managers. To woo new customers, one bank's president even holds barbecues for people who are new in town.

The company's strategy is to become the dominant corporate bank in the state while retaining 30 percent of the retail market. The competition will be tough. Besides three interstate regional banks, Barnett may have to go up against Chemical Bank if state law permits the big New York bank to come into Florida. But the sunshine state is still getting 1,000 new residents every day, and Rice believes that these people are looking for a bank that sticks to the basics.

Case Questions

1. Is Charlie Rice missing an opportunity by not setting up an extensive system of branch banks? Explain.
2. Based on the information given, do you think that Barnett Banks is in a position to compete with the larger interstate banks and Chemical Bank? Why or why not?
3. How do you think Barnett Banks can continue to grow in the future? Will the company need a change in strategy? Explain.

You Be the Adviser: Profits and Problems

When Tina Rodriguez was hired as president of the bank, it was in poor shape. Approximately 5 percent of its loans had been made to countries south of the border that were unable to pay, and another 10 percent were held by businesses in the agricultural sector of the economy and were judged to be "marginal" in terms of collectibility. Tina set to work straightening things out.

Over the last three years, she has managed to collect 70 percent of the foreign loans and has written off the rest as uncollectible. She has also managed to collect 80 percent of the marginal farm loans. At the same time, she has tightened up the borrowing policies of the bank and now lends only to those who are considered good risks and have the appropriate collateral. The board was afraid that if the loan policies were made more stringent, the bank would have trouble finding borrowers. Thanks to Tina's efforts, however, the bank has loaned just about as much money as it has available. In fact, just last week, one of the directors said he heard that the Fed was going to raise the reserve requirement. "How would you handle this situation?" he asked Tina. She said that she would look for additional deposits rather than try to call in any of the outstanding loans.

Despite its high profitability, the bank is not without its problems. An analysis of customer accounts shows that 20 percent of those who have checking accounts with the bank keep an average daily balance of less than $100. Even with the monthly service charge, these accounts cost the bank more than it collects. Tina has also had a visit from the local representatives of elderly people in the area. The spokesperson for the group has demanded that the bank do something about providing free financial services to all retired people over the age of 70. Tina has promised to look into the matter.

Earlier this morning, Tina told the board that quarterly profits would be at an all-time high and this should continue for the rest of the year. "My biggest concern," she said, "is to keep small accounts and free services from eating up all of our profits. We have to draw the line somewhere and start making people pay for what they're getting. After all, we're here to serve the community, but we are also a profit-making institution."

Your Advice

1. If the Fed does raise its reserve requirement, what would you suggest that Tina do?
2. How would you recommend that Tina deal with the problem of people who carry small balances in their checking account and whose accounts end up costing the bank money?
3. What would you recommend that Tina do in response to the request for free services to the elderly in the area? Support your recommendation(s).

Financial Management

LEARNING OBJECTIVES

- Define the role of financial management.
- Identify ways entrepreneurs can finance the start-up of their business.
- Present the various types of short-term financing.
- Discuss the use of loans for long-term financing.
- Describe the use of bonds for long-term financing.
- Explain how companies use stocks for long-term financing.

Your Business IQ

How much do you already know about financial management? Test your business IQ by labeling each statement *true* or *false*. Answers and explanations are at the end of the chapter.

1. The overriding goal of financial management is to borrow enough money to meet the company's short-term and long-term needs.
2. The major source of start-up funding for most new businesses is the personal assets of the entrepreneur.
3. A business with substantial accounts receivable (money that customers owe the business) may raise funds by selling these receivables.
4. When investors buy $1,000 bonds at a premium of $100, they are getting them for only $900 each.
5. If a corporation declares bankruptcy, the preferred stockholders are first in line to share in the assets of the firm.

An important business responsibility is to make sure the company has enough cash to operate and expand. The most basic way to generate funds is to sell products. When companies need additional sources of funds, they often turn to a commercial bank.

Source: © Mark PoKempner: CLICK/Chicago.

Looking Back and Ahead

Consider these recent financial news items: TLC Group, an investment business controlled by Reginald F. Lewis, borrowed $450 million from the Manufacturers Hanover Trust toward the purchase of Beatrice International Food Company, an acquisition that will make TLC the largest black-owned business in the United States. Pulse Engineering, Inc., has decided to sell 2 million shares of common stock through a broker called Oppenheimer & Company. And a Danish energy consortium sold millions of dollars worth of bonds on the international market. What do these financial actions have in common? Each represents the efforts of a business to raise money.

As you learned in Chapter 17, money makes business transactions possible, and the banking system gets money from those who supply it to those who demand it. To make the most of this supply of funds, businesses require expertise in planning for financial needs and obtaining and investing money — the activities of financial management.

This chapter starts by describing the role of financial management in modern business. It then outlines the financing options available for starting a new business. The bulk of the chapter describes short-term and long-term financing, with emphasis on sources of funding. These include various types of loans, bonds, and stock. The chapter closes with a discussion of using financial intermediaries to help the company sell stocks and bonds.

The Role of Financial Management in Modern Business

In the past, financial management was rarely a major concern for a business. The company treasurer would establish a working relationship with a local bank; in return for the business, the bank would give the company a line of credit or a loan as needed. If the bank thought the firm was becoming overextended, it would take action to protect itself, but this was considered a last resort. To a large degree, the bank handled the financing, and the company took care of producing and selling.

Today, this has changed. Although a few small, local firms still operate this way, few businesses of any size sit passively and let their banker decide what is best for them. They have their own financial people who work with the bank, negotiating terms, comparing rates among competing financial institutions, and matching resources to the company's needs as determined by its strategic plan.

Skillful management of finances is critical to the survival of a company and, if done effectively, can contribute greatly to its profits. Financial management begins with creation of a financial plan, which identifies the timing and amount of funding needs and sources. It also includes carrying out the plan, monitoring the flow of funds to make sure it is adequate, and adjusting the company's financial strategy as necessary. Successful financial management ensures that the company has adequate funding to meet company objectives for current operations and long-term growth.

The Financial Manager

In intermediate-sized and large firms, the person charged with the management of finances is the **financial manager,** who is responsible for developing, implementing, and controlling the financial plan. This manager—who in large organizations heads a team of financial experts—generally has a formal education and practical experience in finance, accounting, and economics.

Today, financial managers often use personal computers to assist them with financial analysis and planning. "Computer Technology Close-Up: Spreadsheet Analysis" gives examples of how financial managers use popular computer programs such as Lotus 1-2-3 and Framework. This software is especially helpful in small businesses, where the owner-manager usually assumes the role of financial manager. Because the software is so easy to use, it can help a manager with limited financial experience get a feel for how various decisions will affect the business.

The Financial Management Process

An important goal of financial management is to maximize the wealth of the owners (stockholders in the case of corporations). To do this, financial managers must make sure that the company obtains, at the best possible

Financial
Management

Financial manager The person responsible for developing, implementing, and controlling the financial plan.

COMPUTER TECHNOLOGY — CLOSE-UP

Spreadsheet Analysis

Financial managers often forecast economic conditions and then analyze how the forecasted conditions might affect business operations. For example, the manager may estimate that at worst the economy will expand at a rate of 2 percent, and at best at a rate of 6 percent. To see the effects of slow growth, the manager has to calculate the company's revenues, costs, and profits if the economy expands by 2 percent. To see the effects of rapid growth, the manager has to recompute all these figures for the 6 percent rate. Years ago, this would have required hundreds of work hours spent on tedious mathematical computations of the different changes.

Today, however, computers make this process fast and simple. Software such as Lotus 1-2-3 and Framework is designed to create detailed spreadsheets that show the company's revenues, expenses, and profits. The program contains formulas to compute whatever changes the user specifies. If the financial analyst wants to see the effect of a change in economic growth, he or she merely enters the percentage into the computer. The machine performs the calculations and displays the results. Moreover, if certain costs increase faster or slower than economic growth, the user can have the computer adjust for the difference.

These computer programs are user-friendly and great time-savers. They can calculate the results of virtually any kind of forecast and print out a spreadsheet within minutes. Many managers are now using spreadsheet software to project costs and profits at various levels of sales activity. More and more business people are letting the computer do the busywork associated with financial management while they concentrate on the interesting part: examining the impact of various economic events and deciding how to respond.

price, the funding it needs to meet its strategic objectives. (The price of funds is measured in terms of interest rates.) Therefore, the financial manager's job starts and ends with the company's objectives. Figure 18.1 shows how the process of financial management works.

The financial manager begins by reviewing corporate objectives to determine the funding they require. Usually, the financial manager has participated with the other managers (such as those in personnel, operations, and marketing) in planning these objectives. The objectives should be familiar and financially achievable. The financial manager compares the expenses involved to the expected revenues. This information enables the financial manager to predict cash flow, the movement of funds illustrated in Figure 18.2. The available cash at any given time consists of beginning cash plus customer payments and funds from financing. This is the money available to the company for adding to its inventory and paying expenses.

The financial manager plans a strategy based on whether the ending cash is positive or negative. If cash inflows exceed cash outflows, the company will have cash to invest. The financial manager's job is to look for a reliable and flexible enough investment that will pay a satisfactory rate of interest.[1] If cash outflows exceed cash inflows, the company will eventually run out of cash for operations. One solution is to find a way to reduce outflows. The manager may investigate a variety of options. Can the company pay bills more slowly or persuade customers to pay faster? Can the company trim expenses in some area, perhaps by keeping a smaller inventory? For answers to such questions, the financial manager must consult with the other managers and staff experts. In addition, the financial manager typically looks for outside sources of financing that offer an acceptable combination of flexibility, timing, and interest rate.

Varying circumstances guide the financial manager in examining avenues to use for obtaining funds. The choices include long-term and short-term financing techniques. The manager selects short-term techniques when flexibility is important or needs are limited. The manager selects long-term financing for extended needs; it is less flexible but typically less costly.

Periodically throughout the year and at the end of the fiscal year, the financial manager reviews the company's financial status to see whether the company is keeping to the financial plan and meeting corporate objectives. If it is not, the manager seeks ways to bring the company back on course. This activity helps the manager plan the next year's financial strategy.

Credit Policies

The best financing techniques in the world cannot save a company without paying customers. Consequently, establishing and following an effective credit policy should be part of financial management. Many firms overextend credit and find that some of their customers are unable to pay their bills. By making credit too easy to obtain, the company ends up with uncollectible accounts. For example, Sears found this out when they issued their Discover credit cards and lost a tremendous amount on unpaid bills.[2] One way of reducing this problem is by investigating the credit rating of customers before allowing them to purchase on credit.

Small firms do this in a number of different ways, including asking new customers for credit references. The firm can check and find out how reliable the customer has been in the past. In recent years, a growing number of small businesses and practically all large firms have speeded up this process by combining computer credit checks at a local credit agency with computer verification of credit at a local bank.

Checkpoint

1. What information is the basis of a financial plan?
2. What is the financial manager's role in a month when cash inflow exceeds cash outflow?

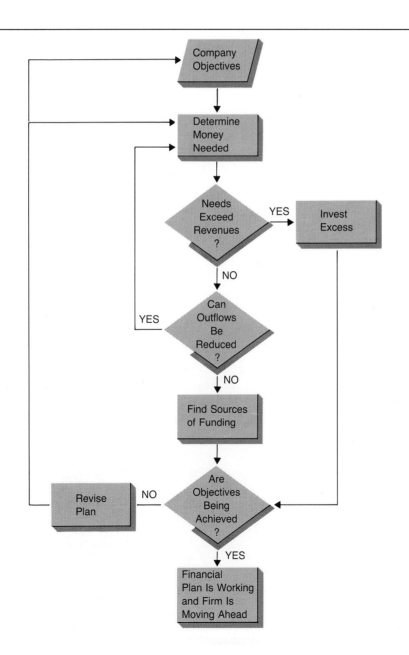

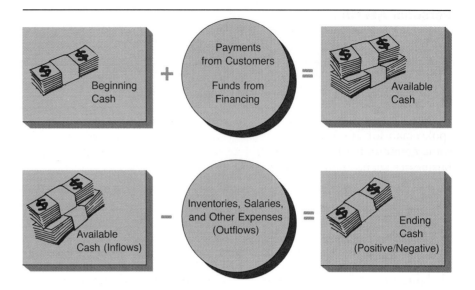

F I G U R E   18.2

Simplified Cash Flow

Start-Up Financing

Financial management starts from the beginning of the company. The entrepreneur must find sources of money that will last until revenue begins to exceed cash outflows. That time often comes much later than the owner initially anticipates, and as a result many new businesses fail.

The entrepreneur often must be creative in finding start-up funding. To learn about a creative funding source with Asian roots, see "Small Business Close-Up: Starting Up the *Kye* Way." Most new small businesses draw heavily on the entrepreneur's own assets. In addition, start-up financing may come from friends and relatives or, for larger businesses, from venture capital investors.

Kwon Sik Choi manages a shoe store now but plans to join a *kye* to raise money to open his own store.

Personal Assets

Most entrepreneurs invest personal assets in the start-up of their new small business. Other investors are understandably reluctant to put their money into a venture that an entrepreneur considers too risky for his or her own money. For example, small private investment firms made up of wealthy individuals and institutions insist that ventures they lend to have the management retain from 5 to 50 percent of the business. As a spokesman for one investment firm states, "It makes us feel we have some community of interest going forward."[3] Therefore, owners of new businesses spend money from their personal savings to cover business expenses, and they pledge assets such as a home or car as collateral when they borrow. If the new business goes bankrupt, the owner must sell these assets to meet the company's debts.

What types of personal assets can entrepreneurs use to help them raise funds for the business? One is their home. The value of the home that the owner has paid for is called the owner's equity in the home. By pledging this equity, the homeowner can obtain a second mortgage or a

---

SMALL BUSINESS   CLOSE-UP

Starting Up the *Kye* Way

After three years spent working in someone else's dry-cleaning establishment, Korean immigrant Linda Choi was ready to own her own business. But she speaks little English and is short on cash and bank credit. So Choi joined a *kye* (pronounced *gay*). She and 19 other present and prospective entrepreneurs each agreed to pool about $500 for 20 months. Each month, in an order determined by a lottery, one member of the *kye* gets $10,000 from the group—minus the cost of the dinner the recipient buys everyone that month. Those who collect early pay somewhat more each month than those who collect in the later months.

Choi was eighth in the drawing. By combining her funds from the group with the $12,000 her family had saved, she was able to buy her own dry cleaner in Chicago, just three years after her arrival in the United States. In addition, she has the friendship and monthly dinners of the *kye* members.

Like Choi, many Asian immigrants have been opening their own small businesses, such as dry cleaners, newsstands, import-export shops, shoe stores, restaurants, and light manufacturing plants. Recent immigrants usually find that it is virtually impossible for them to get bank loans, so many turn to one another and form *kyes*. Estimates suggest that one-third or more Korean businesses in the United States may have used *kyes* for financing.

This form of financing does have its drawbacks. The interest rate—the extra amount the early recipients pay in each month—is a little higher than a bank interest rate. Furthermore, the participants run the risk that the *kye* will collapse before they have collected if someone pulls out or takes off with the funds.

Despite those drawbacks, the *kye*—with its roots in Asia going back to the Middle Ages—continues to attract would-be immigrant entrepreneurs. For example, Kwon Sik Choi plans to use a *kye* to help him buy a shoe store. He estimates that he will need $70,000 to start the business, of which he has saved half. Anticipating that no one will lend him the rest, he says he can get it in "only two ways: a *kye* or a stickup, and I won't do that."

home equity loan. Many enterprising owners have borrowed all of the equity they have in their house and pumped it into their business. Managers who have been paying their original mortgage for ten or more years have often been able to borrow $25,000 and up.

Another common source of start-up funding is a life insurance policy. Many policies build up what is called cash surrender value. This is money that the policyholder can borrow at low interest rates (typically 5 to 8 percent). If the borrower does not repay the loan, the amount is simply deducted from the overall face value of the policy.

Finally, for those who need more cash or lack some of these other assets, banks offer the variable-rate installment loan. This is a personal loan with an interest rate tied to government securities, the prime rate (the rate the institution charges its best customers), or some other index. When the index changes, the interest rate moves in the same direction. Lenders may be more willing to make a personal loan with a variable rate than a fixed rate. The reason is that the ability to change the interest rate reduces the money-losing loan in a changing economy.

Family and Friends

Family members and friends can be an excellent source of start-up funds. They tend to be most helpful for financing small businesses, which often need only a small amount of funds ($25,000 or less). Many people can afford to lend this amount of cash. These lenders are also often willing to lend at a low interest rate. However, if the lender charges no interest or an unusually low rate, the Internal Revenue Service may assess taxes as if the lender had charged more. Professional tax advice can avoid unpleasant surprises. Another concern is that important relationships may be jeopardized if the business flounders and the borrower cannot repay the loan. Entrepreneurs may conclude that the feelings of family and friends are too precious to risk.

Entrepreneurs who do decide to draw on the resources of family and friends may want to compensate them by sharing ownership of the business. The lender could become a partner or a shareholder in a corporation. Chapter 5 described the basic options available for sharing business ownership.

Venture Capital Firms

Venture capital firms
Financial intermediaries that specialize in funding ventures with special promise.

In some cases, new or young companies can receive funding from **venture capital firms.** These are financial intermediaries that specialize in funding ventures with special promise. Typically, venture capital firms invest in enterprises expected to generate high profits within five years. The businesses receiving funding have tended to be in high-tech industries, but venture capital firms have been broadening their base, especially to the health care field.[4] These companies typically finance only a small percentage of the projects they examine.

Every week, new venture capital deals are put together. These funds are typically used for one of four types of financing: (1) seed money to get the company started, (2) funds for helping the venture grow and gain market share, (3) money for taking advantage of lucrative market opportunities, and (4) funds for buying out a business.

Checkpoint

1. Where can an entrepreneur get money for starting a small business?
2. What kinds of companies are venture capital firms typically interested in funding?

Short-Term Financing

Once a business is under way, the financial manager must meet the company's needs for short-term and long-term financing. **Short-term financing** consists of raising funds to meet obligations that will come due within the next 12 months and investing funds that the company doesn't immediately need. Quite often a firm's receipt of funds does not directly match up with its outflow of funds. Firms can obtain short-term financing to fill the gap in a number of ways. The most popular sources of short-term funds include trade credit, loans from commercial banks, factors, sales finance companies, commercial paper, and government sources.

Trade Credit

The most popular source of short-term financing is **trade credit** — the purchase of merchandise on an open account. Under this arrangement, the seller lets the buyer use the goods immediately, and the buyer promises to pay at the end of a given time period, such as 30 days. A typical trade credit arrangement is 2/10, net 30, which is a cash discount pricing technique described in Chapter 12, whereby if buyers pay within 10 days they get a 2 percent discount. The availability of this discount depends in part on industry practices.

A company that takes advantage of the trade credit can reap considerable savings that can be used as a source of short-term funds. For example, if the company purchases $1,000 of merchandise and pays within 10 days, it saves $20 on its bill. Assuming that it takes the same discount each month, the company is actually getting a 24 percent discount on an annual basis (2 percent × 12 months) for the purchase of $1,000 of goods. These terms are so favorable that many companies borrow the money from a bank (at, say, 10 to 15 percent) in order to take advantage of the trade discount.

Funding from Commercial Banks

Perhaps the most sought-after source of short-term funds is commercial banks. As Chapter 17 pointed out, banks provide loans to businesses. Business loans fall into three categories: unsecured loans, secured loans, and lines of credit.

If the business doesn't put up collateral when it borrows, the loan is an **unsecured loan.** Banks usually restrict unsecured loans to customers with an excellent credit rating. Businesses usually apply these funds to inventory purchases and pyaing bills that will be coming due in the near future. They usually repay unsecured loans within a year's time.

Short-term financing
Raising funds to meet obligations that will come due within the next 12 months.

Trade credit The purchase of merchandise on an open account.

Unsecured loan A loan that requires no collateral.

Using a computer-generated order document, McKesson's Debbie Pruitt stocks a tote box by merchandise category. McKesson Drug has a 95 percent delivery rate, one of the highest in the distribution industry, providing customers with the products they order, usually by the next day.

Source: © 1987 John Blaustein for the McKesson Corporation.

When the company wants to borrow a large amount of money or has an unsatisfactory credit rating, it pledges collateral to back up the loan. Such a loan is a **secured loan.** The business's managers sign an agreement to turn over pledged assets if they do not repay the loan. In the railroad business, for example, collateral often takes the form of rolling stock — railroad cars and locomotives. Manufacturing firms use their plant and equipment to secure the loan. In retailing, accounts receivable and inventory often serve as collateral.

Secured loan A loan backed up with collateral.

A particularly flexible lending instrument is a **line of credit,** which is a stated cash reserve available whenever the business wants to draw on it. Companies with a solid financial position prefer lines of credit to normal loans for a number of reasons. One is that a bank charges interest on the entire loan from the day it turns over the funds to the company. However, on a line of credit, the bank charges interest only on the amount of money the company has borrowed. Lines of credit also tend to be open-ended. When the firm needs cash, it draws on its line of credit; when it has extra cash, it repays part or all of the outstanding balance. Moreover, as the company gets larger, it usually can have the bank increase the credit line, ensuring an adequate source of short-term funds.

Line of credit A stated cash reserve available whenever the business wants to draw on it.

Factors

Less widely known than commercial banks are factors. A **factor** is a financial institution that purchases accounts receivable. A business with a large amount of accounts receivable may find itself in a cash bind until customers pay the amounts due. Selling these receivables gives the business cash for continuing its operations. The factor buys the right to collect the money due; because collection is uncertain, the factor pays only a percentage of the amount due.

Factor A financial institution that purchases accounts receivable.

The percentage that the factor pays depends on the quality of the receivables and the conditions under which they are sold. The quality depends on how long the receivables have been outstanding and who owes them. In examining the length of time the receivables have been outstanding, the factor considers the terms under which the goods were sold. If the terms were 2/10, net 30, no receivables should be over 30 days old. The older the receivables, the less likely the factor will want to buy them.

Many industries use factoring, including the garment and furniture businesses, as well as small retailers in general. These firms sell on credit to generate high sales and then factor the accounts to get money. In recent years, some large companies have also turned to factoring, including Coca-Cola, which used it to collect the receivables owed to Columbia Pictures, one of its acquisitions.

Sales Finance Companies

For financing similar to that offered by factors, a firm may turn to a **sales finance company,** which is a financial institution that purchases installment sales contracts. Many merchants allow their customers to pay for purchases on a time payment schedule. For example, a consumer might buy a stereo and pay for it in 12 monthly installments. The merchant, in turn, can sell the installment contract to a sales finance com-

Sales finance company A financial institution that purchases installment sales contracts.

pany. The finance company may give the merchant the principal immediately, and then collect the interest and principal from the buyer. Merchants get their funds immediately, but considering that many installment loans cost 15 to 21 percent annually, the sales finance company can also benefit handsomely. In fact, profits have proved so lucrative that many large retailers have begun financing their own sales and profiting on both ends of the deal: the sale and the financing. For example, General Motors sells cars through its dealers and finances the sales through General Motors Acceptance Corporation (GMAC).

Commercial Paper

Some big firms obtain funds by selling **commercial paper,** which is an unsecured promissory note. In some cases, the company can use drafts and checks in the same way. Because commercial paper has no collateral behind it, only firms with a solid reputation, usually major corporations like General Motors or Exxon, are able to sell it. Businesses known as commercial paper houses buy these notes from the issuing company and sell them to investors and other financial institutions.

Companies pay commercial paper obligations in the short term, typically 60 to 180 days. For major firms that need to raise working capital for day-to-day operations, commercial paper can be an important source of short-term financing. Conversely, for companies with idle cash, purchasing short-term paper is often a good investment because it usually provides a higher interest rate than is available elsewhere.

Commercial paper An unsecured promissory note.

Government Sources

In special cases, a business may obtain short-term funds from the federal government. For example, the Small Business Administration (SBA), discussed in Chapter 4, lends directly to small businesses and works with banks to guarantee small-business loans. This assistance is available to small businesses that are unable to get financing any other way and can meet SBA loan requirements. In addition, the Department of Defense sometimes grants cash advances to firms engaged in defense-related work.

Checkpoint

1. What are three sources of short-term funding?
2. Besides acquiring funds, how do financial managers handle short-term financing?

Long-Term Financing

Businesses that are expanding or upgrading facilities have long-term funding needs. Firms meet these needs by increasing the company's debt or its equity. Debt financing consists of taking out long-term loans or selling bonds. Equity financing involves the sale of stock. Figure 18.3 illustrates these alternatives.

Long-Term Financing Instruments

Characteristics of Long-Term Debt

Whether loans or bonds, long-term debt instruments have a number of characteristics in common. The debt requires interest payments and provides the lender with a claim on assets. Both types of debt require repayment, and both offer tax advantages and leverage.

Interest Most long-term debt instruments carry an interest rate. These rates vary based on risk and interest rates on other investments competing for lenders' funds. For example, during the early 1980s, bonds were considered to be a poor investment. Many of them with face value of $1,000 were selling at $300 to $500, reflecting the low interest at which they had been issued and the fact that many people felt other investments were much safer. By the mid-1980s, the bond market had recovered quite a bit. The perception of investors was that bonds were not a high risk and were considered to be a good investment alternative. Annual returns were in the range of 9 to 10 percent, and bonds were once again proving to be an important avenue for raising long-term capital.

Claim on Assets If a company declares bankruptcy, its assets will be sold to cover the debts. Under this arrangement, creditors are first in line for repayment. Unpaid vendors who have provided the firm with goods and services are often among the first to be paid. After these creditors, come the bondholders. This means that in the case of bankruptcy, the bondholders may get only 10 to 50 percent of their money back. However, this is better than nothing; stockholders in most cases would end up getting nothing.

Repayment At some time, long-term debts must be repaid. In the case of bonds, the company may set aside money in a special reserve fund. When the bonds reach maturity, the fund contains enough money to pay off the debt. The company can also refinance the entire long-term debt by obtaining a new loan or floating new bonds to replace the old ones. In this case, if the company had set up a fund for retirement of the debt, the company might use it for improvements such as new machinery, equipment, or facilities.

Tax Advantages Interest payments on loans and bonds are treated as expenses. This means that the company subtracts them from its revenues to find taxable income.

Leverage Long-term debt also provides a benefit that helps businesses grow: **leverage.** This is the use of borrowed funds to increase the return on the owner's own funds, or equity. Just as a mechanical lever lets users get more power out of their muscles, financial leverage enables users to get more financial power out of their cash. For example, if a firm can earn 15 percent on $10,000 of its own cash invested in a new piece of equipment, then the return is $1,500. But if it can borrow $30,000 at 10 percent in order to buy three more machines that also earn 15 percent, then it can realize an additional return of $1,500 ($4,500 return − $3,000 interest cost). Thus, by leveraging (using borrowed funds), the

Leverage The use of borrowed funds to increase the return on equity.

Bristol-Myers' pharmaceutical research center in Wallingford, Connecticut. This building represents the largest capital expenditure in the company's history. Extensive projects such as this require long-term financing.

Source: © Norman McGrath 1986.

firm can greatly magnify its return. In other words, it takes money to make money. The key, of course, is that the cost of borrowing (the interest on the loan) must be less than the return realized. In other words, leveraging works best during good economic times.

Entrepreneurs can also use the leverage concept to their advantage. For example, Bill Stoecker, a former Chicago construction worker, initially bought up dilapidated real estate properties that banks had foreclosed on. He was able to obtain 100 percent loans from banks because they were glad to get rid of these properties any way they could. He then would fix up the properties, sell them during a good real estate market, and make substantial profits. He declares that when starting off he was "always 100 to 115 percent leveraged" which means he had more borrowed funds than the worth of his properties.[5] Today, at only 30 years of age, Bill has leveraged his way to the top, becoming one of the wealthiest people in America. One of his latest deals was a $157 million buyout of Fruehauf Corporation's aerospace division.

The major drawback, of course, is that no matter how much money the entrepreneurs or firms make from the borrowed funds, they must repay these loans with interest. Bill Stoecker made money because the real estate market was booming, and he got out before it went sour. The interest charges might outweigh the benefits of leverage. For this reason, many borrowers still prefer to obtain long-term financing through equity rather than through debt.

Long-Term Loans

Long-term loan A loan that has a term of at least one year.

A **long-term loan** is a loan that has a maturity of at least a year — typically one to ten years. During this time, the firm is required to pay interest on the debt and to abide by any other agreements associated with the loan. For example, the lender often protects its financial position by requiring that the company obtain the lender's permission before taking on any additional long-term debt. In addition, the lenders often require that the company either make periodic payments on the principal or establish a fund for paying off the loan in a lump sum at maturity. If the lender regards the loan as particularly risky, it may even require the firm to limit or eliminate dividends to stockholders. This increases the cash available for repaying the loan.

Whether the borrower will accept these conditions often depends on what funding options are available. If the lender's terms are stringent and the company can obtain funds elsewhere, it may turn to other sources. Companies that are in good financial shape can be more particular; other firms may have to accept the conditions laid down by the borrower. When Chrysler got into financial trouble several years ago, the federal government agreed to provide a $1.5-billion loan guarantee. However, the government required Chrysler to operate under a very tight budget. One of the government's conditions was that Chrysler sell its corporate aircraft, even though Chrysler's managers believed that the plane used executives' time efficiently and therefore ultimately saved time and money. Following the government's restrictions, Chrysler executives often ended up sitting in airport terminals waiting for their flights.

Bonds

If the financial manager wants to use debt financing but wants a longer term and freedom from lenders' restrictions, the company might issue **bonds.** These are long-term debts with a maturity date 20 to 30 years in the future that are sold to raise funds. Federal, state, and local governments issue government bonds. Corporations issue corporate bonds, which may be secured or unsecured. Figure 18.4 shows a typical corporate bond.

Whether the bond is secured or unsecured depends on the condition of the firm. When a company that has had financial problems wants to sell bonds, it often offers some collateral. For example, companies may sell mortgage bonds, which are backed by real or personal property, and firms in the transportation industry, such as the railroads or airlines, may secure their bond issues with rolling stock (their equipment). Without collateral, it is often difficult, if not impossible, to find investors who are willing to buy the bonds. Unsecured bonds, called **debentures,** have rarely been used in recent years. The corporations that have successfully used them in the past tended to be huge companies such as AT&T. But even AT&T now has problems because of the turmoil in the telephone industry, so debentures are seldom used.

Most bonds carry a face (sometimes called par) value of $1,000 and pay a predetermined interest rate, sometimes called the coupon rate. The rate is a percentage of the face value. The company pays this interest quarterly, semiannually, or annually, as agreed upon in advance.

The Indenture Agreement The terms of a bond issue are specified in an **indenture agreement.** For example, the indenture agreement may specify the amount and frequency of interest payments. It also may identify any assets that are pledged as collateral for the bonds.

Bonds Long-term debts with a term of 20 to 30 years that are sold to raise funds.

Debenture An unsecured bond.

Indenture agreement A document that sets forth the terms of a bond issue.

FIGURE 18.4

A Sample Bond

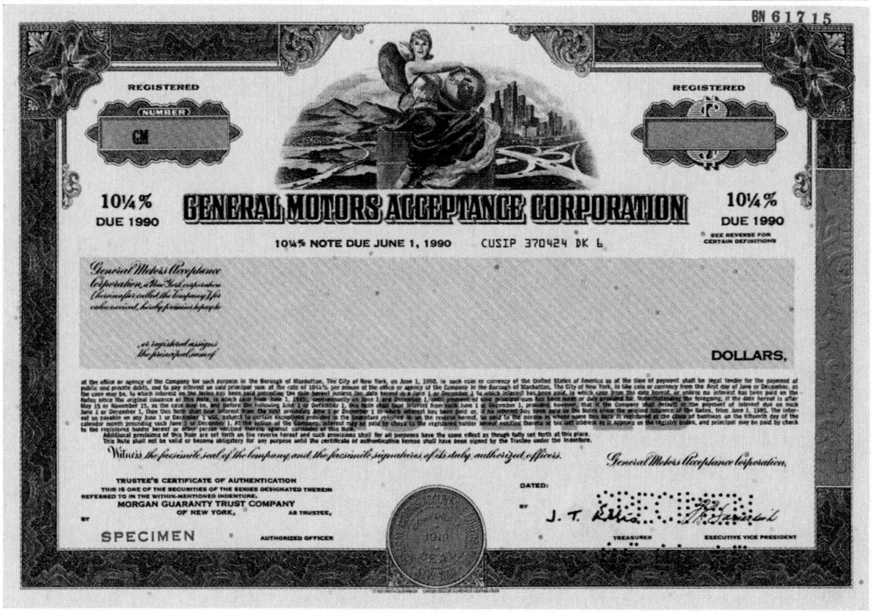

Source: Courtesy of General Motors Acceptance Corporation.

Call provision A bond provision that allows the firm to repurchase the bonds before maturity.

Redemption premium A bonus the company pays bondholders for early redemption of bonds.

Conversion privilege A provision permitting conversion of bonds into a stated number of shares of common stock.

Premium The price paid for a bond above its face value.

Discount The amount by which a bond's price is less than its face value.

Retiring Bonds Depending on the terms of the agreement, the issuer may retire bonds before they mature. If the indenture agreement contains a **call provision,** the firm may repurchase the bonds before maturity. For example, if a firm issued 20-year $1,000 bonds at 10 percent in 1986, the company would redeem them in 2006 at $1,000 per bond. However, if by 1996 other companies were paying only 7 percent, the company might want to call in its 10 percent bonds and replace them with a 7 percent issue. When a firm exercises this option, it also pays the bondholders a **redemption premium,** a bonus paid for early redemption of bonds.

Another flexible feature in some indenture agreements is the **conversion privilege,** which allows bondholders to convert their investment into a stated number of shares of common stock. This privilege gives the bondholders some flexibility. For example, if the price of the company's common stock is going up, the investors can profit from conversion.

If the price of the stock remains steady or is going down, the investors can hang on to their bonds. Moreover, the investors know the price at which they may convert, so they can wait until the exchange is favorable to them. For example, if a bondholder paid $1,000 for the bond and can convert this to 100 shares of common stock, any rise in the stock above $10 makes conversion profitable. If the stock goes to $12 and levels off, the bondholder can convert or simply wait and see what happens. If the stock falls back, the bondholder has lost nothing; if the stock suddenly zooms to $20, he or she can convert and have an investment valued at $2,000. The main reason for offering convertibility is to make the bond issue more attractive to potential investors.

Bond Prices Bonds do not always sell for their face value. Sometimes they sell at a **premium,** a price above face value. At other times, they sell at a **discount,** an amount below the bond's face value.

One determinant of a bond's actual selling price is its interest rate. If a newly issued bond pays the same interest rate as most bonds, it will probably sell for close to its face value. However, if interest rates begin to rise, bondholders can get more money by selling their bonds and investing in something else. As they begin to sell their bonds, the market price for them begins to drop. The result is that the effective interest rate on the bonds will rise. For example, if a bond that has a face value of $1,000 and pays $100 a year in interest sells for $900, it will provide the investor with an annual return of 11.1 percent ($100 ÷ $900). If the price were to drop to $800, the effective rate of return would go to 12.5 percent ($100 ÷ $800), because bondholders would now be earning $100 annually on an $800 investment.

Conversely, if interest rates on other investments started to drop, more people would begin buying bonds. This would cause the price to rise and the effective interest rate to drop. For example, if a $1,000 bond initially paid 10 percent a year and its price rose to $1,100, the effective interest rate would fall to 9.0 percent ($100 ÷ $1,100). As the price rose to $1,200, the effective interest rate would fall to 8.3 percent ($100 ÷ $1,200). The price of the bond would level off when the effective interest rate was equal to the rate investors could earn on investments with a similar risk.

Besides the interest rate, time until maturity causes a bond's price to fluctuate. If investors bought $1,000 bonds paying $100 annually for

$800, they would be receiving an effective interest rate of 12.5 percent. However, this does not take into account the fact that upon maturity, the investors will receive $1,000, or $200 more than they paid for the bond. This increases the value of the bond, and the closer the bond is to maturity, the more the value rises. Therefore, as bonds get closer to maturity, their prices tend to move closer to the face value.

If the company is judged to be a poor risk, however, this may not happen. Investors will think that the firm is unable to redeem the bonds, and they will end up settling for less than the face value. In these cases, the bonds continue to sell at a discount.

Common Stock

Sometimes the company's managers want to avoid increasing the company's debt obligations. In that case, they turn to **equity financing,** the sale of ownership in a firm. The two basic instruments of equity financing for corporations are common stock and preferred stock. Chapter 5 described the rights and privileges of common stock ownership, and Chapter 19 describes preferred stock and the market for stock. This section focuses on how stocks help the firm meet its needs for long-term funding.

By far the most common form of equity financing is the sale of **common stock,** which is ownership shares in a corporation. Most people who own stock in a corporation hold common stock. (See Figure 5.3, page 127, for a sample common stock certificate.) Chapter 5 listed the technical rights of stockholders, but it can be simply said that most investors buy common stock because it gives them the right to share in the company's earnings.

Share in the Earnings As you learned in Chapter 5, common stockholders receive their share of the company's earnings in the form of a dividend for each share of stock they own. Large firms usually pay dividends quarterly. Firms that declare minimum dividends, such as 25 cents per year, usually pay them annually.

As Table 18.1 shows, some companies have not missed a dividend in years. Most investors regard dividends as guaranteed payments. However, this is not really an accurate assumption. The board of directors

Equity financing The sale of ownership in a firm.

Common stock Ownership shares in a corporation.

Company	Year in Which Dividend Payments Began
Bank of New York Company, Inc.	1784
Citicorp	1813
J. P. Morgan & Company, Inc.	1840
Chase Manhattan Corporation	1848
Continental Corporation	1853
Travelers Corporation	1866
American Express	1868
Cincinnati Bell, Inc.	1879

T A B L E   18.1

Some Firms That Have Never Missed a Dividend in Over a Century

declares a dividend based on the earnings and expected growth of the corporation. If the company runs into hard times, it may cut or eliminate the dividend. A firm may also use its profits for new-product development or to expand or upgrade its facilities, leaving little for dividends. For example, IBM has followed such a policy for many years. In the mid-1980s, the firm was paying $4.40 annually, which represented a return of less than 4 percent on the value of the stock. IBM's philosophy is similar to that of many successful high-growth firms. Spending profits on research and development or on equipment and facilities may enhance the value of the company, benefiting the stockholders in the long run as the price of the stock rises to reflect the greater worth of the company.

Voice in Management As you learned in Chapter 5, common stockholders have the right to vote on certain corporate matters, including the election of the board of directors. Consequently, financing through the sale of stock means that the original owners risk sacrificing control. That risk often influences the decision whether to finance with debt or equity.

Claim on Assets If the corporation dissolves or goes bankrupt, the common stockholders, as owners, have a claim on its assets. However, this claim is usually of little value, because the claims of so many others usually take priority over those of the common stockholders. The order of priority is determined by law. As noted earlier, those who come before common stockholders include creditors, lenders, bondholders, and preferred stockholders. As a result, if the corporation goes bankrupt, the common stockholders seldom receive much, if anything.

Permanent Ownership The corporations may not recall common stock. It can, however, get the stock back in two ways. One is to purchase it from the existing stockholders. Widely recognized firms such as Beatrice, Levi Strauss, and Denny's have bought back all their stock, an action called *going private*.

The other way of getting the stock back is to merge with another firm and trade the company's common stock for the merged firm's stock. For example, under this arrangement, stockholders in Company A will receive three shares of stock in Company B for every share of common stock they currently hold in Company A. When the exchange is complete, there is no longer any outstanding common stock in Company A; only Company B's stock remains in the marketplace. In recent years, many acquiring firms have swapped their stock for stock in the firm being purchased. For example, when USX recently took over Texas Oil and Gas, for every share of Texas Oil and Gas the shareholders received 0.633 of a share of USX.

Preferred Stock

Preferred stock Stock that provides preferential treatment in the payment of dividends and the distribution of assets.

Less often used than common stock in equity financing is **preferred stock,** which is stock that provides preferential treatment in the payment of dividends and the distribution of assets. Many people liken this form of stock to a combination of bonds and common stock, because it has characteristics of both. For example, preferred stock is like a bond in that it has a fixed dividend. However, it is unlike a bond because the board must declare the dividend, and it is paid before anything is distributed to the common stockholders. On the other hand, preferred stock is like common stock in that under specified conditions, the preferred stockholder may have a voice in management. Although preferred stockholders may not vote for the board of directors, they may be able to vote on corporate matters when the corporation fails to pay the preferred dividends.

Another way in which preferred stockholders can obtain a voice in management is through the conversion privilege, which allows the investors to convert their holdings to common stock. This privilege has two advantages: it helps make the stock offering more attractive, and it gives the stockholders a chance to be heard by the board of directors.

After converting to common stock, the preferred stockholders can vote for the board of directors at the annual meeting. If the company has issued a large block of preferred stock and its owners convert a majority to common stock, they can hold a large percentage of the common stock. This, in turn, would ensure them a voice, and they may even obtain some seats on the board of directors. Aware of the consequences of such action, most board members try to see that the corporation is managed effectively, in order to prevent dissatisfaction among the preferred stockholders.

Investment bankers often want a first-hand look at a business's activities. Here, an engineer escorts two representatives of Shearson Lehman on the site of a roadway and railroad tunnel being constructed under Hong Kong's harbor. Shearson Lehman not only arranged the financing for this project, but also assembled the group of international businesses that won the franchise to build and operate the tunnel.

Investment bank A
financial intermediary that
purchases and resells
bonds and stocks.

Help in Issuing Bonds and Stocks

Companies that want to issue bonds and stocks usually turn to financial intermediaries that help the company reach potential investors. The major intermediary for bond and stock sales is the **investment bank.**[6] For example, if Consolidated Edison wanted to raise money by floating a $25 million bond issue, it would turn to investment banks. These firms, which include such prestigious names as Merrill Lynch, Morgan Stanley, Salomon Brothers, Drexel Burnham, and Goldman Sachs, will typically form a group or syndicate that agrees to sell the bonds.[7] For this service, these investment bankers receive a fee that depends on the interest rate the bonds will pay and the utility's credit rating at the time. The higher the company's credit rating, the lower the risk associated with repayment and the more likely that the investment bankers will be able to generate sales interest.

Organizations that analyze the financial shape of companies determine credit ratings for bond issuers. The two best-known ratings are those by Standard & Poor and the Moody's Investor Service. Table 18.2 shows their rating scales and describes what each rating means.

In the case of a stock issue, the arrangement with the investment banker is similar. The banks that form the syndicate will attempt to sell the stock to their clients or to other organizations such as retirement funds or investor groups that are looking to invest in the stock market. If the company issuing the stock is considered a good risk, the syndicate often agrees to take the issue at a discounted price, rather than charging a fee. For example, the banker may pay $9 million for 1 million shares of stock to be sold at $10 each. The $1 million profit is used to cover the expenses associated with reselling the stock, as well as the risk that the banker won't be able to sell all of the issue at the intended price and will have to hold on to it for a while or sell it for less.

TABLE 18.2

Bond Ratings

Ratings by Moody's Investor Service, Inc.	Meaning	Ratings by Standard & Poor Corporation	Meaning
Aaa	Prime quality	AAA	Highest grade
Aa	High grade	AA	High grade
A	Upper-medium grade	A	Upper-medium grade
Baa	Lower-medium grade or speculative	BBB	Medium grade
Ba	Lower-medium grade or speculative	BB	Lower-medium grade or speculative
B	Speculative	B	Speculative
Caa		CCC	
Ca	Range from very speculative to in or near default	CC	Very speculative
C		C	
		DDD	
		DD	In default; rating based on relative salvage value
		D	

Checkpoint

1. What is the difference between long-term debt financing and equity financing?
2. Why are some managers reluctant to use equity financing?

Closing Comments

Financial management is a complex responsibility that begins with evaluating how funding will help the company achieve its objectives. The financial manager must ensure that the company has money for its short-term and long-term needs and that it makes wise use of the money on hand. Funding may come from trade credit, the sale of assets, the acquisition of debt, or the sale of stock. A well-designed financial plan is often necessary not only for profit and growth, but also for the firm's very survival.

Learning Objectives Revisited

1. **Define the role of financial management.**
   Financial management consists of creating a financial plan, carrying out the plan, monitoring the flow of funds, and making adjustments as needed. The financial plan identifies the timing, amount, and sources of funds needed to achieve company objectives. In a large company, the person charged with these responsibilities is the financial manager, who may head a team of financial experts.
2. **Identify ways entrepreneurs can finance the start-up of their business.**
   Entrepreneurs usually draw on their own assets to start up a small company. They may use money they have saved or pledge personal assets to obtain a loan. Sometimes an entrepreneur's friends and relatives are willing to invest their money in the company, in exchange for interest payments or perhaps part ownership. If the company has potential for rapid growth and large profits, venture capital firms may be willing to invest in it.
3. **Present the various types of short-term financing.**
   Short-term financing consists of raising funds to meet obligations that will come due within the next 12 months and investing funds that the company doesn't immediately need. Some of the most common ways of securing this type of financing include utilizing trade credit, commercial banks, factors, sales finance companies, and commercial paper. In some cases, a company may receive government assistance. When seeking investments for idle cash, the financial manager weighs the interest rate against the risks involved.
4. **Discuss the use of loans for long-term financing.**
   A long-term loan is a loan that has a maturity of at least a year. It normally carries an annual interest rate and requires repayment at the end of a predetermined time. The company may make payments of principal and interest, or it may pay the interest in installments and the principal in a lump sum at the end of the loan's life.

5. Describe the use of bonds for long-term financing.

A bond is a long-term debt instrument with a maturity date typically 20 to 30 years in the future that are sold to raise funds. Most bonds carry a face value of $1,000 and pay a predetermined interest rate. Some bonds include a call provision, which allows the firm to retire the bonds before their maturity, and a conversion privilege, which allows the bondholders to convert their investment into common stock.

6. Explain how companies use stocks for long-term financing.

The company may issue common stock or preferred stock. Common stockholders are entitled to share in the company's earnings; they have the right to vote on corporate matters, including the election of the board of directors; in case of bankruptcy or liquidation, they have a claim on the assets; and their stock cannot be recalled by management. Preferred stock provides preferential treatment in the payment of dividends and the distribution of assets in the case of bankruptcy. Under certain conditions, preferred stockholders can have a voice in management. For help in selling stocks and bonds, companies turn to investment banks.

Key Terms Reviewed

Review each of the following terms. For any that you do not know or are unsure of, look up the definitions and see how they were used in the chapter.

financial manager	bonds
venture capital firms	debenture
short-term financing	indenture agreement
trade credit	call provision
unsecured loan	redemption premium
secured loan	conversion privilege
line of credit	premium
factor	discount
sales finance company	equity financing
commercial paper	common stock
leverage	preferred stock
long-term loan	investment bank

Review Questions

1. What does a financial manager do?
2. How does a credit policy serve as a financing technique? What are the risks of a liberal credit policy? What are the risks of a strict credit policy?

3. Bruce Russo is the financial manager for National Surgical Supply, a company that distributes surgical supplies, some of which it also manufactures. One of the company's objectives for next year is to increase sales 8 percent by adding several new products and increasing sales of current products. Based on this objective, what are some funding needs that Bruce might identify? List as many as you can think of.

4. Jane Rivera is a loan officer at National Bank. In reviewing a loan application from Greg Glasgow, who wants to start a photography studio, Jane observes that Greg wants to obtain all his start-up funds through an unsecured loan from National. When Jane suggests that Greg obtain part of the financing by taking out a home equity loan, Greg looks shocked. "No way!" he exclaims. "If the business doesn't work out like I hope it will, I could lose my home." Do you think Jane is likely to approve the loan request? Why or why not?

5. What kinds of companies typically are able to obtain funding from a venture capital firm?

6. How does trade credit serve as a source of funding?

7. Why do banks offer more favorable interest rates on secured loans than on unsecured loans?

8. Linda Turner is the financial manager for a chain of coffee shops called Lucky Breaks. Last month, revenues exceeded expenses, and Linda expects this pattern to continue for another month or two. Does this situation require action from Linda? Explain what Linda should do or why she need not act.

9. If the company looked like it might fail, would you rather be one of its bondholders, one of its stockholders, or one of its vendors? Why?

10. How does a long-term loan differ from a bond?

11. Why might a company want to include a call provision in a bond's indenture agreement? Why might it want to include a conversion privilege?

12. Golden Rent a Car is issuing $1,000 bonds, each paying $80. Most bonds on the market are currently providing a return of 9.25 percent. Do you think Golden's bonds will sell at a premium, at face value, or at a discount? Why?

13. How does common stock differ from preferred stock?

14. Gradgrind Machining handles small, specialty machining jobs. Because of intense competition, the company has gone through some difficult times. The company's managers believe that their best chance for a rebound lies in careful investment in high-technology machinery and equipment, making the plant a model of efficiency. The company may have to sustain losses for several years, but ultimately it will be more profitable than ever. Do you think the company should finance this plan through the sale of stock? Why or why not? If you think equity financing is wise, would you recommend common or preferred stock? Explain.

15. How do investment banks serve as financial intermediaries?

Applied Exercises

1. Try to find a local company that sells its accounts receivable to a factor. Find out the process that this firm uses. Report your findings.

2. Visit a retailer that offers credit to customers, and discuss its credit policies with a manager. How are these policies determined? How stringent are they? Does the manager seem to be happy with these policies, or does he or she believe that the company may need to be more selective in giving credit? Write a short report on your findings.

3. Find a local corporation that has issued stock in the last five years (a stockbrokerage firm should be able to help you). Visit with a representative to find out why they chose to raise funds this way. Write a short report of your findings.

4. Visit a local bank and ask about lines of credit. Find out who gets these and why? Report your findings to the class.

Your Business IQ: Answers

1. False. The goal of financial management is broader: to maximize the wealth of the owners. This often involves borrowing money, but not necessarily.

2. True. Most entrepreneurs invest personal assets in the start-up of their business. A new business is too risky an investment for most outsiders.

3. True. Some financial institutions, called factors, specialize in purchasing accounts receivable for a percentage of the amount due.

4. False. When investors buy bonds at a premium, they pay more than the face value of the bond, not less.

5. False. The preferred stockholders are ahead of the common stockholders, but the company's creditor's and bondholders are ahead of the preferred stockholders.

Fast Lane Proves to Be Too Fast

When James Bildner opened his first supermarket in Boston in 1984, he thought he would soon achieve his childhood dream of becoming rich. The store, equipped with antique brass fixtures and imported marble tiles, catered to an upscale clientele and sold everything from paper goods to gourmet foods. Sales grew, and Bildner soon announced plans to open 24 more stores in 15 months. By 1985, Bildner was already saying, "I'd like to be the head of a multinational corporation."

That's when the investment bankers of Kidder, Peabody & Company entered the picture. They saw an opportunity for a big stock offering, and they began telling Bildner he should take his company public—selling stock so that others could share ownership by investing in the company. Eventually, Kidder analysts convinced Bildner that a public stock offering was the road to a quick fortune. In September 1986, the company went public as J. Bildner & Sons Inc., with stock selling at $13 per share. The offering raised $18.8 million.

From there, the company's future darkened considerably. The new stores experienced unexpectedly high start-up costs and other problems. Earnings slumped, and seven months after the initial stock offering, in May 1987, the funds were depleted. With Kidder's help, the company sold $27.5 million in convertible bonds. By the end of the summer, half of that money was gone as well. Although 18 stores had been opened, the company had lost $2.6 million from operations. The value of the company's stock slid 40 percent.

Evaluating his company's experience so far, Bildner concludes that he was pushed to grow and didn't resist the temptation. His banker at Kidder agrees that the expectations underlying the stock sale were unrealistic. Bildner says, "All I want now is to run a well-managed company."

Case Questions

1. Were Bildner's financing techniques at the heart of the company's problems? Explain.
2. What do you think were Kidder, Peabody's goals with regard to Bildner's company? How did these mesh with Bildner's own goals?
3. What do you think Bildner should do to improve the company's performance? What financial goals does this involve?

You Be the Adviser: An Expansion Plan

Mike Sherral owns 14 fast-food outlets located in a 50-mile radius of Los Angeles. Mike opened his first one three years ago, and his restaurants have been extremely profitable from the beginning. Mike wants to keep expanding and sees only two avenues available: franchising or selling stock. Mike would like to retain control of the enterprise and believes that he can best accomplish this by selling stock and using the proceeds to expand.

He has put together two expansion proposals:

1. Issue 500,000 shares of common stock and sell 200,000 of them. A representative of a large investment banking firm has told Mike that the bank will take the shares off his hands at $9 each and will sell them for $10. To make the offer appealing, the investment bank wants Mike to declare an annual dividend of $1 payable quarterly.
2. Issue 300,000 shares of common stock and keep them all, and issue 20,000 shares of preferred stock. The investment bank is willing to buy these $100 par shares of preferred stock for $88 each. To make the offer appealing, the banker believes that Mike should pay a 7 percent dividend and allow the shares to be convertible at seven shares of common stock for each preferred share. The banker also feels that the stock should be callable with a 6 percent premium if the company exercises this option.

Both of these proposals are equally appealing to Mike, although he has continued to emphasize the importance of maintaining control of the firm. He also wants to ensure that if business continues to be as good or better, he can obtain more long-term funds for additional expansion. The investment banking people have told him that if his business continues to grow as it has in the past, this should be no problem. For the moment, however, the question is which of the two financing alternatives to pursue.

Your Advice

1. What are the benefits associated with issuing the common stock?
2. What are the benefits associated with issuing the preferred stock?
3. Which of the two alternatives would you recommend to Mike? Why? Defend your answer.

C H A P T E R 19

Investments and the Stock Market

LEARNING OBJECTIVES

- Identify the types of investors and their major objectives.
- Describe securities exchanges.
- Relate the mechanics of buying and selling stock.

- Discuss how investors try to make money in the stock market.
- Explain how to read and understand financial news.

Your Business IQ

How much do you already know about investments and the stock market? Test your business IQ by labeling each statement *true* or *false*. Answers and explanations are at the end of the chapter.

1. Twenty years ago, personal (individual) investors accounted for most stock market transactions, but today large institutional investors account for most of them.
2. Bonds are regarded as a safer investment than preferred stock, which in turn is regarded as safer than common stock.
3. While stock exchanges like the New York Stock Exchange trade stocks of large national or multinational corporations, regional stock exchanges generally trade the stocks of lesser-known firms that do business in their geographic area.
4. Since the Great Depression in the 1930s, the Federal Reserve has required that investors pay for 90 percent of the value of a stock in cash. The stockbroker may extend credit for only 10 percent.
5. Stock market averages have tended to move up in years that an original National Football League team has won the Super Bowl and to move down in years that an original American Football League team has won.

The floor of the New York Stock Exchange, where brokers trade stocks and a variety of other securities.

Source: © David Ball/The Stock Market. All rights reserved.

Looking Back and Ahead

The changing fortunes of Federal Express show how views of a company's strength affect the price of its stock. Although Federal Express dominates the business for overnight letter delivery, the company faces stiff competition. United Parcel Service is offering lower prices, and the growth of the overall market for overnight delivery is slowing as business people turn to faster telecommunications techniques using computers and facsimile machines. Before the 1987 stock market crash, investors had bid higher and higher prices for Federal Express stock, causing the price to rise from $3 a share in 1978 to a high of $75. During the crash, the stock's price fell to $46 a share. The company's problems may deter investors from bidding the price back up. Says one observer, "I'm not saying this isn't a great company, this just isn't a great stock any more."[1]

Opinions of investors are important to corporations, because these individuals and organizations are the necessary second party in the financial management process described in Chapter 18. Businesses seeking funding need investors willing to buy stocks and bonds from them. While Chapter 18 emphasized financial transactions from the operating business's point of view, this chapter focuses on financial transactions from the institutional or personal investor's standpoint.

This chapter begins by examining the types of investors and their objectives. The discussion then turns to the investment process. Because stock markets are the most visible and popular form of investment, they are the focus of attention. This section describes the marketplaces in which investors buy and sell stock and other investments, outlining the procedures involved in buying and selling stock. The last part of the chapter describes how investors try to make money in the stock market, a skill that depends on having enough knowledge of a given industry, a particular company, and economic changes.

Investors: Who and Why

Most of us are investors at some time in our lives; we spend money in ways that we hope will generate additional money. For example, a college education is in one sense an investment. When you spend money on tuition and books, you are increasing your eventual earning power. Recent statistics indicate that households headed by college graduates have median incomes 54 percent greater than those of high school graduates.[2] This figure suggests that spending money for your education is a wise investment.

Most businesses depend on the goodwill of investors. These people often supply the funds a business needs to operate and grow. When investors believe a company is strong, they will pay a higher price for its stock or accept a lower rate on its bond offerings. In this way, a firm's financial performance helps dictate its ability to raise additional funds. For example, if the price of the company's stock rises, investors will look forward to buying future stock issues. Business people therefore need to understand investing and the markets for investments. This chapter focuses on the kind of investments that are easiest to exchange: **securities,** or evidence of ownership (stocks) or debt (bonds). In other words, as

Securities Evidence of ownership (stocks) or debt (bonds).

Chapter 18 pointed out, securities can simply be thought of as stocks and bonds.

Types of Investors

Investors may be organizations or individuals. Organizations that buy securities with their own funds or with funds held in trust for others, such as pension contributions or insurance premiums, are called **institutional investors.** Major institutional investors include insurance companies, pension funds, and university foundations. An insurance company wants its investments to generate profits and funds for paying future insurance claims. A pension fund wants to make money on its investments so that it can pay off pensioners. A university foundation is interested in making money so that it can draw on these funds to support research, erect buildings, and ensure the survival of the institution. Institutional investors undertake huge transactions, for example, buying or selling 10,000 shares of stock. In recent years, institutional investors have accounted for approximately 80 percent of all trading carried out on regulated stock exchanges.[3]

Institutional investors
Organizations that buy securities with their own funds or with funds held in trust for others.

The other type of investors, called **personal investors,** are individuals who trade securities for their own account. In fact, even though institutions carry out most of the volume on stock trades, individuals control nearly two-thirds of all stocks. And their presence is growing: During the first half of the 1980s, the number of personal investors grew by more than 55 percent, to 47 million.[4] The majority of personal investors have relatively small stock portfolios (collections of stock), usually valued at less than $50,000. They often use these funds as the down payment for major purchases such as a home, as supplemental retirement income, or as a source of cash should an emergency arise. Figure 19.1 compares the relative size of institutional and personal investors.

Personal investors
Individuals who trade securities for their own account.

Objectives of Investors

Most institutional buyers are consistently conservative in their investment objectives. They want securities that will provide a predictable return. Personal investors have a wider range of investment objectives. While many personal investors are moderately conservative in their objectives, others are extremely conservative or much greater risk takers. The extremely conservative investors look for guaranteed income; the risk takers try to make a quick fortune. To be more precise, the objectives of

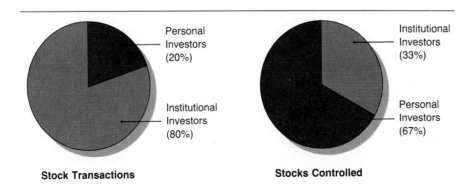

Personal
Investors
(20%)

Institutional
Investors
(80%)

Stock Transactions

Institutional
Investors
(33%)

Personal
Investors
(67%)

Stocks Controlled

F I G U R E   19.1

**Relative Size of
Institutional and Personal
Investors**

investors can be identified in terms of speculation, growth, income, and safety. Table 19.1 summarizes how well the three major types of securities meet these investment objectives.

Speculation The assumption of large risks in the hope of large returns.

Speculation Most investors, especially institutional investors, prefer being fairly certain that their investment will make money or at least not lose money. Because the demand for risky investments is low, these investments pay a high return—when they succeed. Some investors set an objective of achieving big payoffs. They engage in **speculation,** or assuming large risks in the hope of large returns. Many investors made considerable sums of money speculating on stocks in the middle 1980s, when the market was on an upswing. Of course, they may also wind up with a big loss. In the crash of the stock market in October 1987, many investors suffered big losses.

Speculators can pursue many different avenues. One is to purchase "penny stocks," highly speculative stocks that typically are shares in new ventures and sell for less than $5. The investor is hoping the price of the stock will rapidly soar. A $1 stock that is suddenly in great demand might quickly run up to $3, thus tripling the initial investment. On the other hand, few penny stocks actually see such a rapid rise. Speculators who make a killing in one of these stocks often lose it all when others they hold go down.

Blue-chip stocks Stocks of large, high-quality companies with a proven track record.

Growth More investors are interested in long-term growth in the value of their investment. When they cash in their securities, they want to have a sizable pool of funds. Investors interested in steady growth often choose blue-chip stocks. **Blue-chip stocks** are those of large, high-quality companies with a proven track record. Examples of such companies are IBM, General Electric, General Motors, Coca-Cola, and American Express. Investors with a growth objective are typically interested in the long run and believe that regardless of what happens in the economy over the next five to ten years, the firms they invest in will prosper. Often the dividend for blue-chip stocks is relatively low. This is because blue-chip firms reinvest their profits in research and development in order to remain competitive and growing.

Income Some investors rely on securities to provide them with income. A good example is a retired couple living on a small pension and social

---

T A B L E 19.1

Investment Objectives Related to Type of Security

Type of Security	Investment Objectives: Opportunity For			
	Speculation	Growth	Income	Safety
Common stocks	Moderate	Very good	Moderate	Least
Preferred stocks	None	Very little	Steady	Moderate
Bonds	Very little	Very little	Very steady	High

security. If the couple invests in the stock market, they probably will seek stocks that pay generous dividends.

Investors with income objectives are interested in a stock's yield. **Yield** is the percentage return from stock dividends, or the dividend divided by the selling price per share. Utility stocks (Commonwealth Edison or Kansas Gas and Electric) typically have higher yields than industrial stocks such as those of computer firms (IBM), manufacturing firms (General Electric), and financial service companies (American Express). The reason utility stocks have a high yield is that they have minimal risk. Also, because they are closely regulated and thus cannot rapidly grow, utility stocks must have a high yield in order to attract investors.

Safety All investors have at least some interest in safety. They will take a risk but only within certain limits. Preferred stock is regarded as safer

Yield The percentage return from stock dividends, or the dividend divided by the selling price per share.

Even the relatively stable, regulated utilities have begun to encounter competition in recent years. For example, Northern Illinois Gas used this advertisement to persuade businesses to generate electricity with gas-fired systems as a money-saving move.

Source: Courtesy of Northern Illinois Gas Company.

than common stock, because preferred stockholders receive dividends before any are paid to the common stockholders. In the case of common stock, utilities are considered safer than high-tech stocks. For example, Commonwealth Edison has paid quarterly dividends since 1890. However, even utilities have risks; today, especially, independent power producers are introducing competition, and nuclear power plants are causing problems related to costs and safety. The accompanying ad illustrates the competition electric utilities face from gas companies.

Government bonds are the safest type of security because they are backed by the government, but even corporate bonds offer the security of their face value. As Chapter 18 pointed out, no matter how low the price of the bond falls, the company will pay the face value upon maturity. Sometimes it is just a matter of holding on until the bond matures. Of course, if the company goes bankrupt, it may be unable to pay.

Checkpoint

1. What are three major objectives of investors?
2. If you sat on a committee charged with investing $500,000 that had been willed to an orphanage, what types of stock would you recommend?

The Securities Exchanges

Securities exchange A marketplace where securities such as stocks and bonds are bought and sold.

A **securities exchange** is a marketplace where securities such as stocks and bonds are bought and sold. It simplifies the selling process. Theoretically, if investors wanted to purchase 100 shares of AT&T stock, they could advertise in the newspaper for sellers. Similarly, if sellers wanted to get rid of 100 shares of AT&T, they could advertise for buyers. However, with a centralized marketplace, investors and their representatives know where to go to find interested buyers and sellers. It must be emphasized that security exchanges do not buy and sell securities; they simply provide the location and services for the brokers who buy and sell.

Stockbroker An individual who has demonstrated knowledge by passing a series of exams on buying and selling securities and who, for a fee, performs this function for clients.

In most cases, personal investors use a stockbroker to handle stock transactions. A **stockbroker** is an individual who has demonstrated knowledge by passing a series of exams on buying and selling securities and who, for a fee, buys and sells securities for clients. Most stockbrokers are associated with a brokerage house, the ten largest of which are listed in Table 19.2.

Stock exchange An organization whose members provide a trading place for buying and selling securities for clients.

Acting on the client's orders, the broker has the order executed at a stock exchange where the particular stock is traded. A **stock exchange** is an organization whose members provide a trading place for buying and selling securities for clients. Most stock exchanges are physical entities, and each of the larger ones occupies its own building. To trade on the exchange, a "seat" must be purchased on the exchange. There are only a limited number of seats, so the cost is highly variable. For example, in 1976 the high was $105,000 and the low was $40,000. In the spring of 1987, a seat on the New York Stock Exchange sold for a record $1 million.[5] A seat is a membership; the members actually stand and move around to make contact with those interested in completing a transaction.

The members represent stockbrokers. When a stockbroker calls in an order to sell, the member representing that broker seeks a buyer at the price requested. A joke going around brokerage houses after the stock market crash of 1987 points out this selling function: A panicked investor called his broker with an urgent order. "Sell! Sell!" he shouted. "To whom? To whom?" the broker replied.[6] When a broker calls in an order to buy, the exchange member seeks a buyer at the price offered. Often, the member keeps an inventory of certain stocks and may fill orders with that inventory if the price is right.

The New York Stock Exchange

The largest and best-known exchange in the United States is the **New York Stock Exchange (NYSE).** It is often referred to as the "Big Board" because of a large board on the stock exchange wall that was formerly used to summon brokers from the floor and relay messages to them. When the brokers were on the trading floor, they would continually look at the board to see if their number was showing. If it was, a message was waiting for them, and they would hurry to find out what orders were being sent over from their brokerage house. Today all of this is handled automatically by telecommunication technology (for example, linking computers at the brokerage with those at the exchange).

There are 1,366 seats on the NYSE, and on average approximately 2,000 stocks and 3,400 bonds are traded daily. The record volume occurred in the hectic days of October 19 and 20, 1987, when over 600 million shares were traded each day. Securities on the NYSE represent 90 percent of the market value of all outstanding stocks in the United States.

Most of the stocks of major corporations are traded on the NYSE, including American Express, Chrysler, General Electric, IBM, PepsiCo, McDonald's, and Xerox. In order to be listed on the NYSE, a firm has to meet certain requirements:

Pretax earnings of at least $2.5 million in the previous year

Tangible assets of at least $16 million

New York Stock Exchange (NYSE) The largest and best-known exchange in the United States.

Merrill Lynch

Salomon Brothers

Shearson Lehman[a]/American Express

Dean Witter

E. F. Hutton[a]

Goldman, Sachs

Paine Webber

Prudential-Bache

First Boston

Bear, Stearns

T A B L E   19.2

The Ten Largest Stockbrokerages

[a]Shearson Lehman has agreed to acquire E. F. Hutton. See Anthony Bianco, "Can Cohen the Consolidator Make Shearson-Hutton Work?" *Business Week,* December 21, 1987, pp. 96–98.

At least 1 million shares of stock publicly held

At least 2,000 shareholders who each own 100 or more shares of stock

A minimum market value of publicly held shares of at least $16 million

The American Stock Exchange

American Stock Exchange (AMEX) The second-largest exchange in the United States.

The **American Stock Exchange (AMEX)** is the second-largest exchange in the United States. Located in downtown Manhattan, it has approximately 500 full members and 400 associate members. The AMEX operates in the same way as the NYSE, but smaller companies qualify for listing. Some of the firms whose stocks are listed on the AMEX include Husky Oil, Hormel, the New York Times, and Texas Air. To be listed on the AMEX, a firm has to meet the following requirements:

Pretax earnings of at least $750,000 in the previous year

Tangible assets of at least $4 million

At least 400,000 shares of stock publicly held

At least 800 shareholders who each own 100 or more shares of stock

A minimum market value of publicly held shares of at least $3 million

Other Stock Exchanges

Most people associate the stock market with the NYSE and possibly the AMEX. However, regional exchanges, the over-the-counter market, and foreign exchanges are also important for trading stocks.

Regional stock exchanges Exchanges that trade the stocks of firms that serve regional markets.

Regional Exchanges The NYSE and the AMEX primarily trade in stocks of companies with national operations. Firms that serve regional markets usually trade on **regional stock exchanges.** Examples of these exchanges include the Midwest Exchange in Chicago, the Cincinnati Stock Exchange, the Pacific Coast Stock Exchange in San Francisco and Los Angeles, the Philadelphia Stock Exchange, the Boston Stock Exchange, and the Spokane Stock Exchange. In recent years, large national firms have had their stock listed on regional as well as national exchanges. If a broker in Chicago wants to buy 100 shares of USX (formerly U.S. Steel) for a customer, he or she might well purchase it at a regional exchange rather than sending the order to the NYSE for execution.

Over-the-counter (OTC) market A marketplace for unlisted securities that trade outside of the organized securities exchanges.

Over-the-Counter Market One marketplace for stock is intangible: The **over-the-counter (OTC) market** trades unlisted securities outside of the organized securities exchanges. The OTC market is difficult to describe because trading does not take place at any particular locale. Rather, the nearly 60,000 securities in this market are traded among about 5,000 brokers scattered throughout the country. They buy and sell unlisted stocks and bonds by phone and keep in regular contact with one another. A stockbroker wanting to buy an OTC stock for a customer will get in touch with a dealer firm that in essence acts as a securities wholesaler. If the dealer firm does not have an inventory of the desired stock, they will call around to find out who does and arrange for the transaction.

Although being listed on the NYSE gives stock a certain credibility in the eyes of most investors, not all firms want their stocks so listed. Many firms prefer to be listed in the OTC market because these stocks are actively traded by brokers all across the country. In the minds of many investors, selling in multiple markets better reflects the real market price of stocks.

The prices of the OTC securities are established by supply and demand, just as they are in the major stock exchanges. Electronic screens located in the offices of brokerage firms display OTC transactions, so brokers can continually keep customers up-to-date on the latest prices. Some well-known stocks traded over the counter include Apple Computer, Adolph Coors Company, MCI, Intel, and Safeco.

Foreign Exchanges International trading is growing in importance. Foreign exchanges are located in many of the major cities of the world, including Toronto, London, Paris, Hamburg, Hong Kong, and Tokyo. The October 1987 crash brought out the interdependence between these foreign markets and the U.S. markets. When stocks crashed in the United States, they did the same in these foreign markets. During the hectic days following the crash, American investors closely watched the foreign exchanges that opened earlier in the day to guide their buying or selling decisions for the coming day's session. At one point, Hong Kong closed trading and may pay dearly for the move in the future because the world financial community then lost confidence in the stability and security of the Hong Kong market.

Major U.S. firms that do substantial business abroad often have their stock traded on the international exchanges. For example, IBM is traded on both the London and Tokyo stock exchanges. Similarly, the stock of large foreign multinationals such as Sony (Japan) and Royal Dutch/Shell (Holland) is traded on the NYSE. A recent development in international stock exchanges such as the London Stock Exchange is the replacement of face-to-face buying and selling of securities with telecommunication technology, especially computerization, paralleling what is happening in the U.S. OTC market.

Automation and the Stock Exchanges

Telecommunication is helping the OTC market. For instance, the National Association of Securities Dealers Automated Quotation (NASDAQ) has linked together the computers of the major OTC dealers into a nationwide electronic network that communicates OTC trades within 90 seconds of the time they take place. As a result, no matter where a share of Apple Computer stock is sold in the OTC market, it is in the electronic network in less than two minutes. Companies like MCI, Intel, and Apple like the computerization of NASDAQ because it is directly in line with their own high-tech operating philosophy. The OTC market quotations (sometimes referred to as the NASDAQ national market quotations) appear in the daily stock sections of many national newspapers, including the *New York Times* and *The Wall Street Journal*.

The NASDAQ System of the National Association of Securities Dealers handles most of the trading in national and international stocks sold on the over-the-counter market. In 1987, Jaguar was the most active overseas security in the system, trading more than 204 million shares.

Computerization has also had a major effect on the other stock exchanges. In recent years, all exchanges, including the NYSE and the AMEX, have spent millions to implement computerized information systems as discussed in Chapter 16. This eliminated the pencil-and-paper record keeping that they used for years. In the early 1960s the AMEX would have been unable to handle trading of 5 million shares a day without causing a monumental backlog of paperwork. By the mid-1980s computers were enabling the AMEX to handle volume in excess of 100 million shares a day. However, when the record volume of over 600 million shares were traded in October 19 and 20, 1987, there were up to two-hour backlogs of orders on the NYSE and AMEX. Many brokers during these hectic days were uncertain whether the computers were registering their sell orders so they just kept selling to make sure, and this fueled the plunge.[7]

Some personal investors are also taking a lead from the stock exchanges and using computers to help them carry out their own stock transactions. Both personal and institutional computerized selling greatly magnified the 1987 crash, and many experts attributed the extent and quickness of the plunge to automatic computer programs being triggered to sell in a type of domino effect. For more information on how this all works, see "Computer Technology Close-Up: The Computer Goes to the Stock Market."

These fiberoptic cables link data terminals of traders for Shearson Lehman Brothers at the World Financial Center. Through these cables, which offer far more capacity than conventional metal cables, the traders can execute transactions and gain quick access to data on current market activity, economic statistics, and general news.

Source: Courtesy of American Express Company.

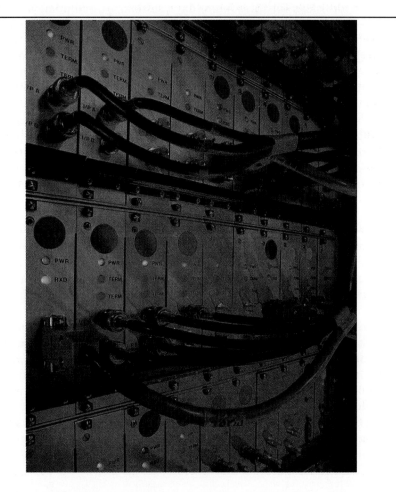

Markets for Other Securities

Besides the major marketplaces for corporate stocks and bonds and government bonds, other specialized markets handle certain types of securities. For example, some trading involves financial instruments called options, described later in this chapter. Options are traded on the major stock exchanges, and also on another important marketplace for options, the Chicago Board Options Exchange (CBOE).

COMPUTER TECHNOLOGY   **CLOSE-UP**

The Computer Goes to the Stock Market

Many personal investors rely on their brokers to handle their accounts. If the broker thinks a stock's price has risen as much as it can, the broker will sell the stock for the client. If another stock has dropped five or six points and the broker thinks it will go even lower, the broker will sell it also. If the broker identifies some stocks that seem ready to move up, the broker will advise the client to buy. As long as investors want to rely on brokers, this arrangement works just fine.

In recent years, however, an increasing number of institutional and personal investors have begun taking command of their own accounts. They figure out what to buy and sell and give the broker specific instructions. They often do so by using a computer. For an investor to be able to decide what to buy and sell, the investor needs timely feedback about the latest stock prices. In the past, this has meant calling the broker, sometimes two and three times a day. However, for a small hourly fee, investors with a personal computer can get the latest prices of all stocks in their portfolio from a database. Popular databases include Dow Jones News/Retrieval, Compuserve, and The Source. A typical charge for this service is $10 for the first hour of usage each month and $20 per additional hour. Moreover, if the broker has the necessary computer system, an investor who decides to buy or sell can transmit this order to the broker by hooking the computer up to a telephone and sending the desired instructions to the broker's computer.

Many brokerage firms can receive computerized orders to buy and sell stock, bonds, options, and even Treasury securities. After the order is carried out, the broker's computer sends information to update the client's account by showing revised totals of cash and securities. The broker will then call the investor and confirm the transaction. A client without access to the computer during working hours can call up closing prices after work, decide what to sell or buy, and then forward the order to the brokerage. The broker will execute the order the next business day.

Computer trading benefits investors in several ways. It saves a minute or two on transactions. Commanding a computer to order the sale of 100 shares of AT&T is faster than calling the broker and asking for the same service. Also, some brokers offer discounts for computer orders because the costs involved in processing these orders are very low. However, the October 1987 Crash pointed out the flaws in the use of computers. Shut downs occurred in almost every component of the computerized system, from the printers on the exchange floors to the minicomputers that do the bulk of the work. The designated order turnaround system, which transmits orders from brokerage firms to the floor of the exchange stopped four times, and an unidentified software problem temporarily misplaced transaction reports involving 4.3 million shares on the day of the crash.

Some business people are interested in the prices of certain commodities, such as corn, soybeans, hogs, cattle, copper, and silver. They may trade contracts to buy or sell these commodities at a specified price in the future. These so-called futures contracts trade on commodities exchanges; one of the largest is the Chicago Board of Trade. Note that the exchange members don't sell the actual commodities, but only the contracts for them. Business people who buy the commodities for their company, such as food processors, watch prices on the commodities exchange to get an idea of their future expenses.

Checkpoint

1. What are the two largest stock exchanges?
2. Who may conduct a transaction on a stock exchange?

Buying and Selling Stocks

Many investors have traditionally put their money into stocks because they view them as a more attractive investment than bonds and safer and less trouble than dealing in real estate or precious metals. In the mid-1980s, the stock market boomed while bonds sagged, many real estate investments went sour, and gold and silver leveled off. Then came the Crash of 1987, when on October 19 the Dow Jones Industrial Average plummeted an astonishing 508.32 points or 22.6 percent. In comparison, in the Crash of 1929, which preceded the Great Depression of the 1930s, the market declined by 12.8 percent.

Almost all financial experts as well as the general public were puzzled by the dramatic turn of events. Amidst lingering fears of inflation, rising interest rates, and a weakening dollar, and the facts that the United States had become the world's largest debtor nation and had a huge

Brokers in the trading room of Chemical Bank.

trade deficit, economic indicators were relatively strong. While stock prices tumbled, gold prices soared to their highest level in five years. The lessons to be learned are that history has a way of repeating itself and that all investments can be risky. As economist John Kenneth Galbraith reportedly observed with mischievous delight, "In both cases, in 1929 and 1987, a large number of investors were feeling they were blessed with original financial genius. They were going to get out before the crash. Somehow, they didn't quite make it."[8] Although the optimism of the mid-1980s was certainly dampened by the Crash of 1987 and its aftermath,[9] the stock market remains a major investment vehicle for both individuals and institutions.

Placing an Order

Most investors have their brokers buy and sell stock on one of the major exchanges. The general pattern of this transaction is the same regardless of where the actual purchase or sale occurs. The investor begins by placing an order, that is, informing the stockbroker what stock and how much to purchase or sell. For example, an investor might call the broker and say, "Buy me 100 shares of General Electric." In this case, the investor is buying at the best current price for GE stock. This is called a **market order,** which is an order to purchase or sell a stock at the best possible price at the present time. The broker who receives the purchase order will have it conveyed to an exchange member on the trading floor. If the stock brokerage has a seat on the stock exchange, an exchange member affiliated with the brokerage will carry out the order. If the brokerage is a small company, it will have its order executed by a member affiliated with a larger brokerage.

In either event, if the most recent sale of GE's stock was at $47\frac{1}{4}$ ($47.25), the broker on the floor attempts to get a better price for the buyer by offering a little less. For example, the broker might offer $47\frac{1}{8}$ and see if someone will sell at this price. Depending on the number of buyers and sellers at that particular time, the broker will settle on a final price. If the investor were selling, the broker would attempt to get a slightly higher price, by offering, say, $47\frac{3}{8}$.

Whatever price is worked out, the final sale will then be electronically relayed by an employee on the trading floor back to the broker who placed the order. Within minutes, the investor knows the stock's purchase or selling price.

Limit Orders In some cases, investors are not willing to issue a market order because they have a specific price in mind. The investor will place a **limit order,** which is an order that specifies the highest price at which the broker may buy or the lowest price at which the broker may sell. The broker on the trading floor will attempt to accommodate the investor immediately. If this is not possible, the broker will place the investor's order in a sales book and execute it in order of priority.

For example, if a buyer is willing to pay no more than 45 for GE and the current price is $47\frac{1}{4}$, no one may be willing to sell for the lower price. Perhaps the stock will rise to $50 per share. However, if it comes down to 45, everyone who has a limit order at this price will be sold the stock, in the order in which the requests came in. If the buyer in our example is fifth in line, the broker will fill this order after the first four

Market order An order to purchase or sell a stock at the best possible price at the present time.

Limit order An order that specifies the highest price at which the broker may buy stock or the lowest price at which the broker may sell stock.

buyers are accommodated. Conversely, if the investor wants to sell at 47 and the current price is 46¼, the seller must wait and hope that the price goes up. If it does, the first person to place a sales order at this price gets to sell the stock, and this continues as long as there is remaining demand for GE stock at this price.

Limit orders are good only for one day. An investor who wants to keep the order on the books must issue an open order. An **open order** instructs the broker to leave the order on the books until it is executed or the investor cancels it.

Open order An order that instructs the broker to leave it on the books until it is executed or the investor cancels.

Discretionary Orders Sometimes the broker on the trading floor has a better idea of what is going on than does the investor at home. The investor may therefore want that broker to exercise judgment in making money. In that case, the investor will give the broker a discretionary order. A **discretionary order** is one that gives the stockbroker the right to execute it immediately or wait for a better price. For example, the broker on the trading floor might determine that the price of GE is going to rise dramatically over the next three hours of trading. If buying, the broker will therefore complete the transaction right away. Conversely, if selling the stock, the broker would wait, because in a few hours the stock will reach a much higher price.

Discretionary order An order that gives the stockbroker the right to execute it immediately or wait for a better price.

Brokers on the floor of the New York Stock Exchange. Each broker is looking for buyers and sellers of the securities he or she wants to trade. The process typically becomes chaotic, with the brokers all shouting for attention. Of necessity, traders have developed a set of hand signals to indicate the transactions they wish to make.

Round Lots and Odd Lots Many people buy and sell 5, 10, or 20 shares of stock at a time, while institutions may trade 10,000 shares at a time (sometimes called a block sale). An **odd lot** is any number of shares less than 100. A **round lot** is 100 shares of stock. To facilitate purchases, brokers usually trade stocks in lots of 100, although some will handle odd lots at a slightly higher price per share. Most often, however, when an investor orders a broker to buy 15 shares, this odd-lot order will be combined with a series of other small orders to form a round lot, at which time the broker executes the order.

Odd lot Any number of
stock shares less than 100.

Round lot 100 shares of
stock.

Paying for Stock Transactions

In addition to the price of the stock, the investor pays the broker a commission for buying or selling the securities. Commissions vary among brokers. In recent years, a number of discount brokers have emerged. These firms charge lower commissions than the major brokerages but provide fewer services. Schwab & Company and Quick & Reilly Inc. are two well-known discount brokers.[10]

Sometimes investors pay less than the full amount when they buy stock. Buying stock without putting up the full value of the transaction is called **margin trading.** The Federal Reserve determines the minimum margin required. For example, if an investor bought 100 shares of General Electric at 47, the total price would be $4,700. In recent years, the stock margin has been around 50 percent, so the investor could buy the 100 shares by paying only $2,350. The investor would then pay interest on the amount borrowed (in this case, the other $2,350).

To ensure that the investor does not sell the stock and abscond with the funds, the broker keeps stock certificates of margin accounts at the brokerage as collateral. Also, if the stock were to plummet, the broker would act to protect its interests. Before the stock reached $23.50 a share, the broker would call the investor and request that he or she put up more money or have the stock sold.

Margin trading Buying
stock without putting up
the full value of the
transaction.

Bulls and Bears

Investors who are active buyers of stock are called bulls. A **bull** is an investor who believes the prices of stocks are going to rise. Bulls follow the old Wall Street adage of "buy low, sell high." In a "bull market," many investors think the stock market is on the upswing. The heavy demand for buying stocks keeps the prices high. The mid-1980s witnessed a very long bull market. Investors kept the prices of stocks going steadily upward for reasons such as favorable interest rates and a slowing of the previous inflationary spiral. Some individual stocks, however, move counter to the trend.

As the Crash of 1987 attests, even bulls become bears. A **bear** is an investor who believes that stock prices are going to fall. In a "bear market," the majority of investors believe the stock market is on the downswing. For example, bears dominated the market in October 1987, when stock values plunged. Bears follow the adage "sell high, buy low." One high-risk strategy the investor can use to do this is called *selling short.*

Bull An investor who
believes that stock prices
are going to rise.

Bear An investor who
believes that stock prices
are going to fall.

Selling Short

An investor who expects the price of a stock to decline may sell short.
Selling short involves selling stock that one does not own (it is borrowed
from the broker) in the hope of later buying it on the open market at a
lower price.[11] At some point, the borrowed stock has to be returned to
the broker. Investors make money selling short if the price of the stock
goes down; they make the difference between what they sell the borrowed stock for and what they paid for the stock on the open market.
The broker makes money on the commissions charged for the transactions.

For example, suppose the investor closely followed AT&T and, because of declining revenues, predicted that the company was going to
declare a cut in its dividend and that the price of the stock would therefore drop. The investor would be better off selling now, when the price
is higher, and buying later, when the price will be lower. If AT&T's
stock is selling at 47 now but will drop to 44 after the company announces a cut in the dividend, the investor could borrow 1,000 shares
from the broker and sell them now for $47,000. When the price went
down, he or she could purchase the shares for $44,000 on the open
market, give back the 1,000 shares to the broker and make $3,000. Of
course, if the investor is wrong about the reduced dividend or if other
circumstances cause the price of a share to rise, the investor could lose
as much or more.

During the stock market crash of 1929 and 1987, a few investors
made a fortune selling stocks short. For example, in the 1929 crash,
President John Kennedy's father, Joseph Kennedy, made millions in the
market because he realized the wisdom of selling high, buying low. Had
he misjudged the market, the Kennedy fortune might well have been totally wiped out. Such risks are the biggest danger of selling short. A
$100 stock that is sold short can, at its best, give the investor a gain of
$100. (The stock can only drop 100 dollars.) However, there is no limit
to which the stock can climb. The more the stock goes above $100, the
more the person selling short loses.

Options

Options are contracts that permit an investor to either purchase or sell a
particular security at a predetermined price and within a certain time
period. The investor pays for the option but does not have to exercise it
by buying or selling the security. Depending on the investor's expectations, he or she may buy a put option or a call option. Figure 19.2 illustrates how these work.

Why would anyone want to buy or sell an option? The answer is that
this can be an inexpensive way to play the market.[12] If the price of a
stock does not change enough to warrant exercising an option, its owner
will let the option expire and lose only the cost of the option. On the
other hand, if the price of the stock changes dramatically in the expected direction, the option owner can make a great deal of money with
a small investment. Selling options can also be profitable, although the
seller must have the stock on hand if the option sells a right to buy. If
the option's owner does not exercise it, the seller gets to profit from the
payment for the option. Despite the risk, options are popular among
speculators.

Put Options An option that grants the owner the right to sell a security is a **put option.** An example of a put option is a $500 option to sell 100 shares of PepsiCo at $47 a share within 90 days. An investor might buy this option if he or she believes that the price of PepsiCo will drop over the next 90 days. If it does, the investor will benefit from selling the shares at the option price to the person who sold the option. The put option therefore guarantees that the shares will be worth at least $47 a share. But because the investor has paid $500 for this right; the put will not generate a profit unless the stock drops below $42. If the price of PepsiCo drops to 36 during the 90-day option period, the investor can force the person who sold the option to buy 100 shares of PepsiCo at $47 a share.

Put option An option to
sell a specific security.

Call Options If investors predict that the price of a stock will rise in the near future, they will buy a call option. A **call option** grants its owner the right to buy a specified amount of a stock at a predetermined price within a designated time period. For example, if investors believe that the price of PepsiCo will rise during the next 90 days, they could buy a 90-day option that allows them to call 100 shares of the stock away from the seller of the option. If this option costs $500, then the buyer will profit if the stock price rises enough to earn the investor more than $500. For every dollar the stock rises, the investor makes $100. If the

Call option An option to
buy a specific security.

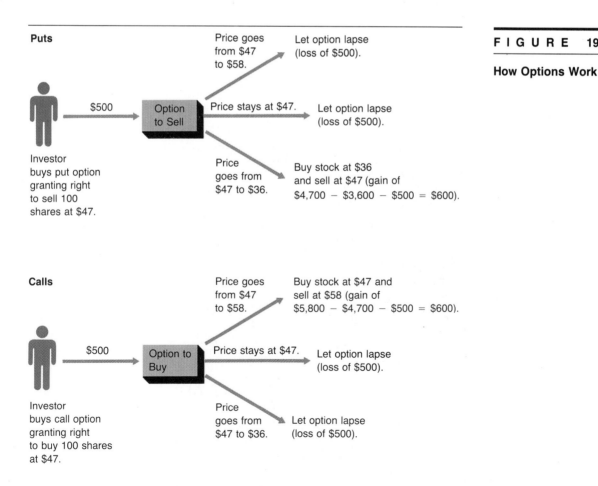

Puts

Investor buys put option granting right to sell 100 shares at $47.

$500 → Option to Sell

Price goes from $47 to $58. → Let option lapse (loss of $500).

Price stays at $47. → Let option lapse (loss of $500).

Price goes from $47 to $36. → Buy stock at $36 and sell at $47 (gain of $4,700 − $3,600 − $500 = $600).

Calls

Investor buys call option granting right to buy 100 shares at $47.

$500 → Option to Buy

Price goes from $47 to $58. → Buy stock at $47 and sell at $58 (gain of $5,800 − $4,700 − $500 = $600).

Price stays at $47. → Let option lapse (loss of $500).

Price goes from $47 to $36. → Let option lapse (loss of $500).

F I G U R E   19.2

How Options Work

exercise price is $47, then at $52 the price difference covers the cost of the option. Everything above $52 is profit. If the price of the stock rises to $58, the holder of the option can buy 100 shares of a $58 stock for only $47 a share. Even if the price of the stock rises to less than $52, the investor can cut his or her losses by exercising the option. Of course, if the stock drops below $47, the investor will not exercise the option and will lose the cost of the option.

Mutual Funds

Mutual fund An investment company that pools the contributions of investors; the fund is carefully managed by buying and selling securities to meet the investment objectives.

Many people today purchase stock indirectly; they buy shares in mutual funds. A **mutual fund** is an investment company that pools the contributions of investors; the fund is carefully managed by buying and selling securities to meet the investment objectives. No-load funds do not have sales charges. Mutual funds are particularly well suited to small investors without a lot of money to invest, because it enables them to buy a variety of stocks; when one stock does poorly, another might be making up for the loss. Mutual funds also attract investors who do not want to manage their holdings closely.

A mutual fund typically buys large blocks of stock in many different types of firms. Sometimes the fund invests in any type of company that appears to be a good investment.[13] In other cases, the fund limits itself to specific types of firms such as growth companies or enterprises that promise a high yield. Other funds stick strictly to money market investments, which do particularly well when interest rates are high, as they were during the early 1980s.

Checkpoint

1. What are put and call options?
2. An investor wants to buy a specific stock but not at more than $25 per share. How can the investor place such an order?

Making Money in the Stock Market

While the approaches to investing in stocks are varied and often complex, investors buy stock for one simple reason: to make money. Most investment experts would agree that the surest way to earn money from stocks is to create as diverse a portfolio as possible and hang on to it for a long time, preferably decades. Investors who jump from stock to stock seeking quick profits have more opportunities to make mistakes. Even when they manage to avoid mistakes, the brokerage fees can eat up most or all of the profits. Nevertheless, enough investors have reaped sizable gains from selective investing to attract others to the idea of beating the market. To succeed at this, investors need good sources of information.

Using a Broker

Much information about the market comes from stockbrokers. Brokers devote a considerable amount of time and resources to studying market reports and getting information on the forecasted financial performance of companies. Large brokerage houses, in particular, have in-house research departments that carry out these investigations and keep company brokers alert to potential market developments. Having this type of information does not guarantee that brokers will pick a winner every time. In fact, some studies indicate that, when they manage their own money, brokers from prominent brokerage houses perform below average.[14] In contrast, another recent comprehensive study found that the top brokerage houses fared much better than average on their list of recommended stocks.[15] The best was Thomson McKinnon's "Long Term Investment" list of stocks that had an average return of over 15 percent, even during the Crash year of 1987. Having as much information as possible to pass on to their customers undoubtedly increases the brokers' chances that they will be right. What the individual investor reads in the business section of the morning paper is often information that brokers have acted on the day before.

The amount of assistance an investor can expect is reflected in the broker's fees. Some brokers are more than willing to discuss the market and recommend opportunities, but their fees may be heavy. Others provide special services such as newsletters; another special service is the one described in "Business Communication Close-Up: Broker's Skills Tap Underserved Market." At the other extreme are discount brokers. These brokers charge small fees, but their services are generally limited to executing orders.

Going It Alone

Many investors prefer to avoid high brokerage fees. They pay a small fee to a bank to buy and sell securities but plan and implement their own investment strategy. Most successful approaches to investing on one's own depend on getting good information and avoiding common pitfalls. Serious investors often subscribe to investment newsletters from brokerage houses and financial experts that carefully study the stock market. Such newsletters provide insights about specific stocks or the market in general. To the degree that the newsletter is accurate, investors can do quite well. Some investors are very loyal to such a service.

One way investors can get ahead of the crowd is to become an expert in a particular industry. Investors might study an industry such as telecommunications or machine tools and identify the firms that appear to be the strongest and most likely to grow over the next couple of years. If the industry looks healthy and one of the companies is superior to the others, it may be a good investment. Another way to obtain expertise is to watch developments in one's own field of employment. Companies the person has first-hand knowledge of that have introduced new technology or competitively advantageous techniques may be good candidates for investment. However, this investor must be careful to avoid illegal insider trading (obtaining advantageous information that is not available to the public at large in order to make investment decisions).

A simpler investment strategy is to choose a handful of reliable blue-chip stocks that have performed well in the past and stick with them. Examples include American Express, Disney Productions, General Electric, and IBM, which have been popular among investors in recent years. This technique may not make a quick fortune for the investor, but it is relatively safe and over the long run can earn money.

Investors using any of these strategies should also recognize common mistakes so that they can avoid making them. Here are the ones that seem to occur frequently and some suggestions on how to avoid them:[16]

Failure to diversify, or spread the risk over several different investments. Depending on one's financial goals (growth or income), it is usually wisest to divide investments up into bonds and various types of stocks. The 1987 Crash made believers out of many investors who had not followed a diversification strategy. Those who held bonds and precious metals saw some gains in these investments that partially offset heavy losses incurred in the stock market.

Paying too much for a stock with the mistaken belief that it will continue to go up. This can be avoided through careful research of industry and company performance and trends in the overall economy.

Not knowing when to sell, or hanging on to a stock and then riding it down. This can be avoided by setting a selling price and sticking to it.

Buying fad stocks. Stay away from fads and stick with the long-standing quality stocks.

BUSINESS COMMUNICATION   **CLOSE-UP**

Broker's Skills Tap Underserved Market

As a first-year student at the University of Arizona, Janice Goldman signed up for a course called "manual communication," thinking she would learn how to type. She was wrong; the class was about sign language for the hearing impaired. Goldman was curious and stayed in the class, and today she has put that communication skill to work in her career as a stockbroker.

Today Goldman is a senior financial consultant in the Chicago suburb of Northbrook, Illinois, office of Merrill Lynch, Pierce, Fenner & Smith. Building a clientele was easy, because she knew many deaf adults from her earlier work. A number of her clients transferred their accounts from other brokerages to Goldman because they found it easier to communicate with her. Explains Goldman, "When they first came to me, they showed me these thick pads of paper that they had used [in communicating] with other brokers.

They had to write everything down and pass the pad back and forth."

To communicate with deaf clients who are outside her office, Goldman uses a teletypewriter. This electronic machine combines a typewriter and a telephone. As one person types in a message, the receiver's machine instantly prints it out. Before Goldman began offering her special brokerage services, deaf clients had to travel to a broker's office every time they wanted to initiate a transaction.

With roughly 20,000 hearing-impaired people living in the Chicago area, Goldman has a ready source of clients. Few brokers are skilled at communicating in sign language or have teletypewriters. But, says Goldman, "Deaf persons have the same financial concerns as the rest of us. They want to know about individual retirement accounts and college funds and so on. The key is being able to speak their language."

Buying on the basis of a "hot tip" without realizing that it is old news to insiders. Rumors and tips usually are cold, not hot; it is best to ignore them.

The mistaken belief that an investor can identify the market's peaks and troughs while they are occurring. Imagine the surprise of those who believed that after three days of record losses on October 14 to 16, 1987, the market had bottomed out and therefore bought stocks. The following Monday the market crash occurred. Most small investors are a step behind; relying on such intuition is difficult if not impossible.

Techniques and Strategies for Predicting Stock Market Activity

If investors could predict where a stock's prices were heading before anyone else could, they would make a killing in the market. As the 1987 Crash made abundantly clear, no surefire methods exist for predicting the stock market's future. However, many investors—especially the professionals—try to improve on chance alone by becoming experts in techniques and strategies used for making predictions about the market. Two common approaches used by knowledgeable investors are fundamental analysis and technical analysis, and two more unique but maybe as effective approaches, the random walk theory and contrarianism.

Fundamental Analysis To evaluate an individual company's stock, most serious investors begin with **fundamental analysis,** which is the process of comparing a company's current financial position and future prospects with those of other firms in the same or different industries. For example, an investor might compare the financial and managerial prospects of Ford, General Motors, and Chrysler in deciding which has the brightest outlook for the next two to three years. The ratios discussed in Chapter 15 are often part of a fundamental analysis. Conducted properly, this type of analysis can help an investor decide whether the price of a particular stock is likely to go up or down based on estimates of future sales and profits.

Fundamental analysis
The process of comparing a company's current financial position and prospects for the future with those of other firms.

Technical Analysis Some investors, called "chartists," select stocks based on patterns they identify in the movement of stock prices. This approach is called **technical analysis.** Chartists spend a great deal of time charting the prices of specific stocks over time and then deciding whether these securities are ready to move up or fall back. By looking at the pattern of a stock's price, these analysts try to identify the stock's "behavior" and use this as a basis for predicting future price movement.

In recent years, some financial experts have challenged this approach, arguing that one can select better stocks by throwing darts at the financial pages than by using technical analysis. Nevertheless, some market analysts still firmly believe that a stock's price follows a set pattern of behavior and that watching a stock closely enough makes it possible to forecast what is going to happen next.

Technical analysis The process of using the pattern of a stock's price over time to predict the stock's future price movement.

Random Walk Some investors not only doubt that stock prices follow patterns, they believe that the prices are random. The **random walk theory** holds that future stock prices are independent of past stock prices. Therefore, investors who hold this view say that stock prices follow a

Random walk theory An investment strategy holding that future stock prices are independent of past stock prices.

random walk, as opposed to a predictable pattern. Based on this theory, technical analysis is a waste of time. To choose stocks that are about to move up, investors might simply identify what brings about increases in stock prices, such as sound management and favorable government policies, and hold on to stocks in companies that meet these criteria.

Contrarianism A group of investors has adopted an unusual approach, **contrarianism,** which holds that the market will move in the direction opposite to that predicted by the general public. This view is based on an assumption that the average investor is usually wrong. Most investors get information too slowly, so they buy just as a stock's price is topping out and sell just before the stock starts to go up. A favorite motto of contrarians is "buy on bad news, sell on good news." In other words, these investors do the opposite of what the general public does.

Supporters of contrarianism defend their position by noting that most investors cannot make big profits in the stock market; in the end, only a small minority comes out ahead. Once the public hears an idea or fact, it acts on it, and then its usefulness is at an end. For example, if word gets out that a company has just developed a new product with great potential, the sudden surge of interest in that company's stock will drive up the price before most investors can get in on the ground floor. Contrarians therefore believe that the little guy always winds up losing. Fortunately, such a view is not totally accurate. Small and large investors can both make money in stocks, but investing takes hard work, skill, and, perhaps, a dose of luck.

Understanding the Financial News

A key to any investment strategy is to keep as informed as possible. Every day financial news is broadcast over radio and TV and is published in the newspapers. Investors can find out which stocks have moved up, which have fallen back, and what new developments are taking place that are likely to affect security prices. Detailed feedback is also available through electronic data services (see the earlier presentation of "Computer Technology Close-Up: The Computer Goes to the Stock Market"). In addition, serious investors should review stories and forecasts about particular companies and the market in general in such financial papers as *The Wall Street Journal* and *Barron's.*

At the heart of this information are price quotations. Prices for a variety of securities are published in the business section of most newspapers following every business day. This information is important to investors because it shows how well their investments are performing and provides a basis for detailed comparison with other securities. In addition, managers of companies that issue publicly traded securities follow price quotations to see how investors view their company's prospects.

Stock Prices Regardless of what paper lists them, stock prices appear in the basic presentation shown in Figure 19.3. To understand the entries, consider Textron, the seventh stock down. The price is stated in dollars and eighths of a dollar. This stock had a high price of $65.25 and a low of $44.125 during the previous 52 weeks. It paid a dividend of $1.80, which is a yield of 3.5 percent (dividend divided by the stock price) on its current selling price of $52.00. The stock's price-earnings (P-E) ratio

---

Contrarianism An investment strategy based on the belief that the market will move in the direction opposite to that predicted by the general public.

is nine, meaning that the stock is selling for nine times the company's earnings per share; and on this particular trading day, 91,200 shares were traded. During this day, the stock sold at a high of $52.00 and a low of $51.75, and it closed the day at $52.00. This closing price was the same as it was on the previous business day.

Any additional information supplementing this list appears in a footnote or explanatory table. For example, in Figure 19.3 there is a letter "e" after the $5.35 dividend of the first stock listed. This letter is explained at the bottom of the stock page, as are any other letters or symbols.

Over-the-Counter Stocks Listings for over-the-counter stocks are easier to read than most other because they provide less information; specifically they do not show dividends, yields, or P-E ratios. Figure 19.4 provides an example. Taking the third stock reported in the figure, Apple Computer had 52-week high and low prices of $39.125 and $14.25, respectively. On the trading day reported in Figure 19.4, 670,000 shares were traded, with the high and low for the day being 31¾ and 31⅛, respectively. The stock closed at 31⅜, which was ⅛ of a dollar higher than the closing price on the previous business day.

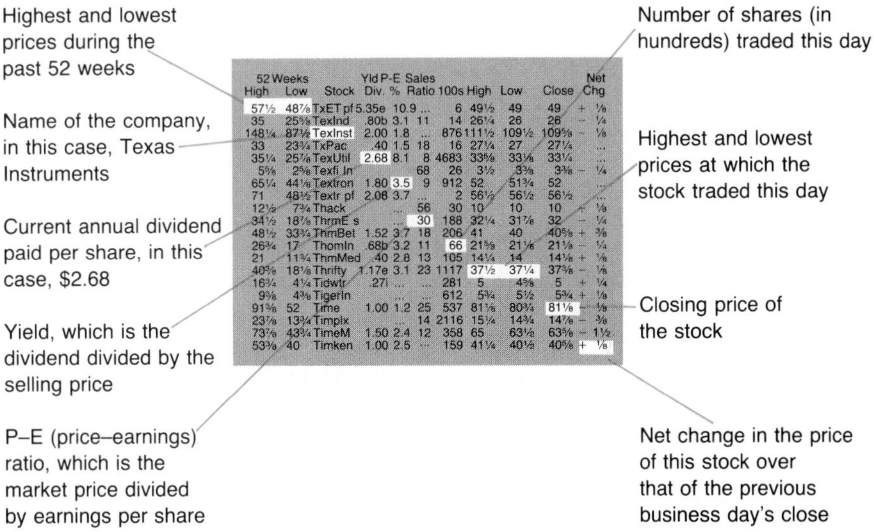

Highest and lowest prices during the past 52 weeks

Name of the company, in this case, Texas Instruments

Current annual dividend paid per share, in this case, $2.68

Yield, which is the dividend divided by the selling price

P–E (price–earnings) ratio, which is the market price divided by earnings per share

Number of shares (in hundreds) traded this day

Highest and lowest prices at which the stock traded this day

Closing price of the stock

Net change in the price of this stock over that of the previous business day's close

FIGURE 19.3

Reading a Stock Market Quotation

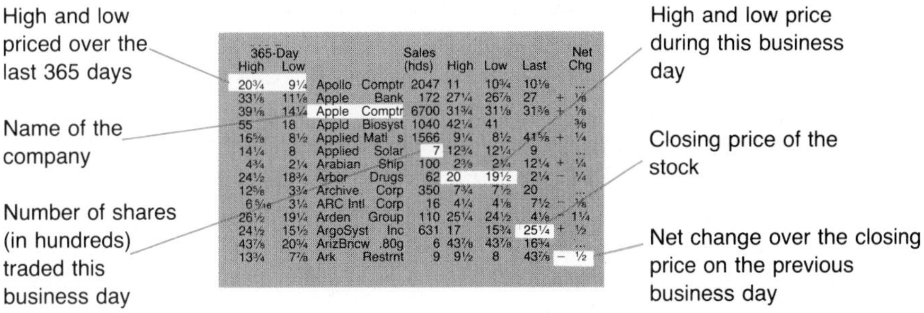

High and low priced over the last 365 days

Name of the company

Number of shares (in hundreds) traded this business day

High and low price during this business day

Closing price of the stock

Net change over the closing price on the previous business day

FIGURE 19.4

Reading an Over-the-Counter Quotation

Stock Averages Some investors are as interested in the stock averages or indexes as they are in what has happened to a particular stock. Three stock averages are most widely recognized and quoted. The most popular is the Dow Jones, which is really three different indexes based on the market prices of 30 industrial, 20 transportation, and 15 utility stocks. The Dow Jones industrials include a host of popular blue-chip stocks, including AT&T, General Electric, Eastman Kodak, IBM, and Sears.

While individual stocks may go up or down, the index provides a general gauge of market activity for a given time period. For example, the Dow was below 1000 in 1981 and reached well above 2000 in 1988. This indicates that the market made a major advance in recent years and that investors were in a bullish mood.

Two other popular averages are the Standard & Poor's Index and the New York Stock Exchange Composite. The Standard & Poor's Index is based on 400 industrial, 40 financial, 40 utility, and 20 transportation stocks. This index almost tripled in a six-year period in the mid-1980s. The New York Stock Exchange Composite includes every stock traded on the Big Board. Like the Dow Jones averages, these two indexes serve as a guide to overall stock market performance and can be found in the daily financial section of all major newspapers.

Will these averages go up or down this year? Some investors who are less than thrilled with the accuracy of sophisticated forecasting techniques propose, with tongue in cheek, that the easiest way to predict this is to find out who won the last Super Bowl. Some observers have found a correlation between whether a team from the original National Football League or a team from the original American Football League wins and the direction stock indexes head during the years. Specifically, when a team from the original NFL wins, the stock market indexes that year are usually higher than they were the previous year. When a team from the original AFL wins, these averages tend to drop. As shown in Table 19.3 on page 596, over the Super Bowl's first 22 years, this pattern has held in all but two cases, leading many market analysts to wonder if they should not be spending less time conducting stock market analysis and more time reading the sports pages.

Bond Prices Bond quotations are stated as percentages of par or face value. The prices are quoted in hundreds of dollars. Thus, on a bond with $1,000 face value, a quotation of 66⅛ means $661.25, not $66.125. Figure 19.5 describes what each of the entries means. The last bond is a Consolidated Edison bond that pays 9⅛ percent on a $1,000 bond that is due to expire in 2004. The current yield on the bond is 9.1 percent ($91.25 interest ÷ $1000 selling price), and 34 of these bonds were traded on this day. Because bonds are issued in denominations of $1,000, the prices in the last four columns are shown without the last decimal place. Thus, the highest price paid was $1,000, and the lowest was $997.50. The bond closed at $1,000, which was an increase of $1.25 over its closing price on the previous business day of trading.

Mutual Fund Prices Figure 19.6 provides a newspaper report of a mutual fund quotation. Information on these funds is provided in a manner similar to that of bonds and over-the-counter stocks. In the Dreyfus mutual fund, the growth fund is one of many in the group. The net asset value (NAV) of 11.37 is the value of one share of the growth fund and

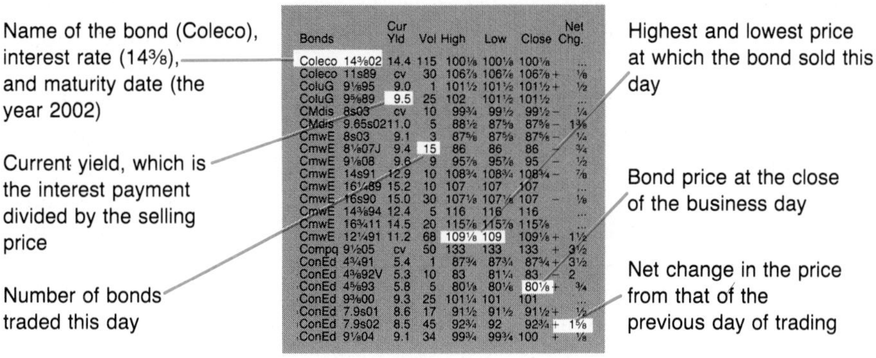

Bonds	Cur Yld	Vol	High	Low	Close	Net Chg.
Coleco 14⅜02	14.4	115	100⅛	100⅛	100⅛	...
Coleco 11s89	cv	30	106⅞	106⅞	106⅞	+ ⅛
ColuG 9⅛95	9.0	1	101½	101½	101½	+ ½
ColuG 9⅝89	9.5	25	102	101½	101½	...
CMdis 8s03	cv	10	99¾	99½	99½	− ¼
CMdis 9.65s02	11.0	5	88½	87⅝	87⅝	− 1⅜
CmwE 8s03	9.1	3	87⅝	87⅝	87⅝	− ¼
CmwE 8⅛07J	9.4	15	86	86	86	− ¾
CmwE 9⅛08	9.6	9	95⅞	95⅞	95	− ½
CmwE 14s91	12.9	10	108¾	108¾	108¾	− ⅞
CmwE 16¼89	15.2	10	107	107	107	...
CmwE 16s90	15.0	30	107⅛	107⅛	107	− ⅛
CmwE 14⅜94	12.4	5	116	116	116	...
CmwE 16¾11	14.5	20	115⅞	115⅞	115⅞	...
CmwE 12¼91	11.2	68	109⅛	109	109⅛	+ 1½
Compq 9½05	cv	50	133	133	133	+ 3½
ConEd 4¾91	5.4	1	87¾	87¾	87¾	+ 3½
ConEd 4⅜92V	5.3	10	83	81¼	83	− 2
ConEd 4⅝93	5.8	5	80⅛	80⅛	80⅛	+ ¾
ConEd 9⅜00	9.3	25	101¼	101	101	...
ConEd 7.9s01	8.6	17	91½	91½	91½	+ ½
ConEd 7.9s02	8.5	45	92¾	92	92¾	+ 1⅝
ConEd 9⅛04	9.1	34	99¾	99¾	100	+ ⅛

Name of the bond (Coleco), interest rate (14⅜), and maturity date (the year 2002)
Current yield, which is the interest payment divided by the selling price
Number of bonds traded this day
Highest and lowest price at which the bond sold this day
Bond price at the close of the business day
Net change in the price from that of the previous day of trading

FIGURE 19.5

Reading a Bond Market Quotation

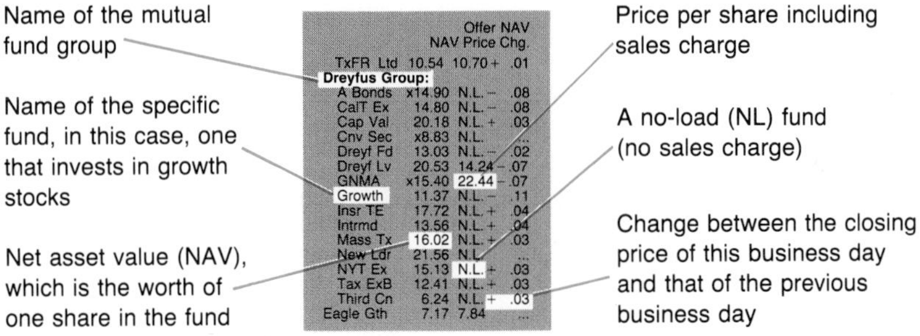

	NAV	Offer Price	NAV Chg.
TxFR Ltd	10.54	10.70	+ .01
Dreyfus Group:			
A Bonds	x14.90	N.L.	− .08
CalT Ex	14.80	N.L.	− .08
Cap Val	20.18	N.L.	+ .03
Cnv Sec	x8.83	N.L.	...
Dreyf Fd	13.03	N.L.	− .02
Dreyf Lv	20.53	14.24	− .07
GNMA	x15.40	22.44	− .07
Growth	11.37	N.L.	− .11
Insr TE	17.72	N.L.	+ .04
Intrmd	13.56	N.L.	+ .04
Mass Tx	16.02	N.L.	+ .03
New Ldr	21.56	N.L.	...
NYT Ex	15.13	N.L.	+ .03
Tax ExB	12.41	N.L.	+ .03
Third Cn	6.24	N.L.	+ .03
Eagle Gth	7.17	7.84	...

Name of the mutual fund group
Name of the specific fund, in this case, one that invests in growth stocks
Net asset value (NAV), which is the worth of one share in the fund
Price per share including sales charge
A no-load (NL) fund (no sales charge)
Change between the closing price of this business day and that of the previous business day

FIGURE 19.6

Reading a Mutual Fund Quotation

the price is what buyers are willing to pay per share, including sales charge. The N.L. stands for no load, which means there is no sales charge when shares of this fund are bought or sold. The +.02 under the NAV Chg column for the growth fund is the change between the present buy price and the previous day's buy price. By following price changes, an investor can evaluate a fund's performance and decide whether to stay with that fund or switch to another.

Checkpoint

1. What are three strategies for investing in the stock market?
2. Many small investors believe that it is wisest to invest in mutual funds rather than in specific stocks. What do you think is the logic behind this investment strategy?

	Original NFL Team	AFL or AFC	DJIA[a] Stock Market Index
1. Green Bay	✓		+
2. Green Bay	✓		+
3. Jets		✓	−
4. Kansas City		✓	+[b]
5. Baltimore	✓		+
6. Dallas	✓		+
7. Miami		✓	−
8. Miami		✓	−
9. Pittsburgh	✓		+
10. Pittsburgh	✓		+
11. Oakland		✓	−
12. Dallas	✓		−[b]
13. Pittsburgh	✓		+
14. Pittsburgh	✓		+
15. Oakland		✓	−
16. San Francisco	✓		+
17. Washington	✓		+
18. Raiders		✓	−
19. San Francisco	✓		+
20. Chicago	✓		+
21. Giants	✓		+
22. Washington	✓		+

T A B L E   19.3

The Super Bowl and the Stock Market Indexes

[a]DJIA = Dow Jones Industrial Average.
[b]Exception.

Closing Comments

This chapter examined the process of investing, with emphasis on the stock market. Buyers and sellers of securities are both affected by price changes, so they need to know how to read and interpret financial news. These investors are also interested in the various investment strategies and how well they work. The famous humorist Will Rogers gave the following advice for those investing in the stock market: "Don't gamble; buy some good stock, hold it till it goes up, and then sell it. If it doesn't go up, don't buy it." Unfortunately, this type of advice may work about as well as the more sophisticated advice on investing in the stock market. Yet, by understanding the mechanics of the stock market, being as informed as possible, and following the guidelines provided in this chapter, investors may be able to improve their chances of achieving their investment objectives.

Learning Objectives Revisited

1. **Identify the types of investors and their major objectives.**
   Institutional investors are organizations that buy securities with their own funds or funds from pension contributions or insurance premiums held in trust for others. Personal investors are individuals who trade securities for their own account. Investors pursue large profits through speculation, steady growth, a flow of income, and safety in the form of relatively low-risk investments.

2. **Decribe securities exchanges.**
   A securities exchange is a central marketplace for the trading of securities. Its purpose is to provide a place where securities are bought and sold. Most exchanges are physical entities. To trade on the exchange floor, brokers become members by buying a seat. These exchanges include the New York Stock Exchange, the American Stock Exchange, and the Chicago Board of Trade. In addition, securities trade on regional and international exchanges. The over-the-counter market has a large network of brokers but no physical location.

3. **Relate the mechanics of buying and selling stock.**
   The purchase begins when a client places an order with a stockbroker. This can be a market order, a limit order, or a discretionary order. Most orders are in round lots of 100 shares. The broker who receives the order communicates it to an exchange member affiliated with the brokerage, who executes the order on the floor of the exchange. The results are then reported back to the client, usually within minutes. The client pays the price of any stock bought plus the broker's commission. Variations on this basic approach include selling short, buying options, and investing in mutual funds.

4. **Discuss how investors try to make money in the stock market.**
   The most certain approach to making money from stocks is to buy a variety of stocks and hold them for a long time. But to do better, many investors attempt to gain an edge by having good sources of information. Some investors try to keep up-to-date by relying on a stockbroker for advice. Others prefer to reduce their expenses (commissions to brokers) by conducting their own analysis of particular stocks or the market in general, and may use fundamental analysis, technical analysis, the random walk theory, and contrarianism.

5. **Explain how to read and understand financial news.**
   Stock market quotations typically list the highest and lowest prices during the past 52 weeks, followed by the name of the company, the dividend paid, the yield, the price-earnings (P-E) ratio, the number of shares (in hundreds) traded that day, the highest and lowest prices of the day, the closing price, and the amount by which the closing price differed from that of the previous business day. Over-the-counter quotations are similar, except that they do not show dividends, yields, or P-E ratios. A bond quotation lists the name of the bond, the interest rate, the maturity date, the current yield, the number of bonds traded that day, the highest and lowest price that day, the closing price, and the amount by which the closing price differed from that of the previous business day. A mutual fund quotation gives the name, the net asset value per share, the price per share including the sales charge for load funds, and the change between the day's closing price and that of the previous business day.

Key Terms Reviewed

Review each of the following terms. For any that you do not know or are unsure of, look up the definitions and see how they were used in the chapter.

securities

institutional investors

personal investors

speculation

blue-chip stocks

yield

securities exchange

stockbroker

stock exchange

New York Stock Exchange (NYSE)

American Stock Exchange (AMEX)

regional stock exchanges

over-the-counter (OTC) market

market order

limit order

open order

discretionary order

odd lot

round lot

margin trading

bull

bear

selling short

options

put option

call option

mutual fund

fundamental analysis

technical analysis

random walk theory

contrarianism

Review Questions

1. Which type of investor has a greater impact on stock market activity — institutional investors or personal investors? Why?
2. Which investment objective — speculation, growth, income, or safety — would each of the following investors have? You may indicate a combination of objectives if that seems most appropriate. What securities might best meet these objectives?
   a. Cathy Brown is a 25-year-old salesperson. Every year, she has received a bonus, which she has saved with the goal of accumulating enough to travel extensively some day. But Cathy is tired of watching her funds grow slowly in the bank.
   b. Arnold Gray is a 55-year-old welder. Through conscientious budgeting and careful investing, he has been able to accumulate almost enough funds to provide him with a comfortable retirement.
3. What are blue-chip stocks? Are they typically a good source of income? Why or why not?
4. Why do the managers of some companies prefer to have their stocks listed in the over-the-counter market, rather than on the more prestigious large exchanges?

5. How are computers automating stock transactions?

6. How can an investor rely on a stockbroker's judgment about the best price at which to sell a stock? How can an investor use his or her own judgment about the best price?

7. How can an investor use leverage (described in Chapter 18) in stock purchases?

8. Why do investors buy options? When would an investor buy a put option? When would an investor buy a call option?

9. Mutual funds charge a fee or a percentage of earnings in return for their services. What services do they provide? Why would investors use a mutual fund rather than investing directly in the stock market?

10. Where do investors get information about the stock market?

11. What are some common mistakes investors make? How can they avoid these mistakes?

12. Stock in All Things Enterprises rose steadily for ten years and then declined for ten years. The price has just begun rising again, and investors are growing interested in the company. How would you expect each of the following to respond to this news?
   a. Fundamental analysts
   b. Chartists
   c. Adherents of the random walk theory
   d. Contrarians

13. To answer this question, refer to the following stock quotations:

52 Weeks High	Low	Stock	Div.	Yld %	P-E Ratio	Sales 100s	High	Low	Close	Net Chg.
20¼	12½	RLI Cp	.32	2.2	6	40	14⅜	14¼	14⅜	+ ⅛
7	1¾	RPC	...	...	259	7	6⅝	6¾	− ¼
39	22¾	RTE	.68	2.3	18	72	29¾	29⅜	29⅜	− ⅜
10¼	4½	Radice	...	238	116	4⅞	4⅝	4¾	...
94	60	RalsPur	1.24	1.5	16	2179	85¼	83¾	83⅞	− 1⅝
9¾	6	Ramad	...	27	2203	7⅞	7⅝	7¾	− ⅛
6¾	3¾	RangrO	...	84	323	5⅞	5¾	5⅞	...
156	69⅝	Raycm	.44	.3	22	140	148	144¾	146	− 1
25¾	10⅝	RjamFn	.16	.9	10	26	17¾	17⅝	17¾	...
26	18⅝	Rayonr	2.60	12.8	8	58	20½	20¼	20⅜	...
13	4⅞	Raytch	...	11	231	12½	12	12	− ¾
84⅞	60	Raythn	1.80	2.2	15	1315	81⅞	80¾	80⅞	− ⅞

   a. On this trading day, what was the closing price for stock in Ralston Purina?
   b. How does this price compare to the closing price on the preceding day? To the highest and lowest prices in the preceding year?
   c. What is the stock's price-earnings ratio? What does this tell you about the company?

14. To answer this question, refer to the following bond quotations:

Bonds	Cur Yld	Vol	High	Low	Close	Net Chg.
Chvrn 5¾92	6.5	44	88⅝	88¼	88½	+1⅝
Chvrn 7s96	8.3	35	84⅛	84⅛	84⅛	+1⅛
Chvrn 8¾05	9.8	23	89¼	89¼	89¼	+1⅜
Chvrn 8¾96	9.3	45	93⅞	93⅞	93⅞	...
ChckFul 7s12	cv	25	94	94	94	+1
ChCft 13s99	12.7	5	102¼	102¼	102¼	...
Chrysl 8⅞95	9.2	29	96	96	96	− ⅛

a. What is the interest rate on Chrysler bonds?

b. In what year do these bonds mature?

c. What was the closing price of Chrysler bonds on this trading day? What was the closing price on the preceding business day?

Applied Exercises

1. Look through a recent day's stock market quotations on the NYSE and the AMEX, and choose three stocks that a young professional might purchase. Then choose three more that a retired person might purchase. When you are finished, write a short explanation of your choices for each of the two stock portfolios.

2. Visit a local stockbrokerage office and have a broker explain how stocks are bought and sold. Write a brief paper on what you have learned and present your findings to the class.

3. How do options work? When would someone buy a put option? When would someone buy a call option? Why would anyone be interested in selling either of these two types of options? After you have written down your answers, visit a local brokerage office and ask a broker the same questions. Have the broker comment on your answers, then rewrite your paper.

4. At the library, get a copy of *The Wall Street Journal* for this date two years ago. (You may have to get it on microfilm.) Using an imaginary fund of $100,000, invest the money in as many stocks as you would like. List the stocks you pick and the price of each. Then look up stock quotations in today's paper. How much would your investment be worth today? Compare your results with those of others in the class. On what basis did you choose your stocks? What principles from this chapter were you able to use?

Your Business IQ: Answers

1. True. The personal investor has been displaced by the institutional investor in terms of the volume of transactions. Institutional investors now make about 80 percent of all stock market transactions. However, individuals still control two-thirds of the stock; they just don't trade it as often.
2. True. This is the generally accepted ranking in terms of safety.
3. True. Regional firms are often unable to meet the requirements for listing on the major exchanges, but their stock is traded through regional exchanges.
4. False. Although the Fed does limit how much credit the broker may extend, the percentage of cash required has tended to be around 50 percent, not 90 percent.
5. True. Someone discovered that when an original NFL team wins, the market averages that year tend to be higher than the year before, and when an original AFL team wins, the stock market averages tend to be lower than those of the previous year. Strange as this may seem, it is true for all but two cases (the year Kansas City, an AFL team, won in 1970 the average went up, and the year Dallas, an NFL team, won in 1978 the average went down).

Investments That Could Be Chicken Feed

In the chicken business, profits can swing widely. The reason is that the volume of chicken production is hard to control. If the supply of chickens begins to outstrip demand, all the producer can do is to cut prices, even if that eats into profits.

The result has been a three-year cycle for chicken companies. In general, chicken producers have experienced a year of good profits, then a year of expanded output and declining profits, and then a year of losses and cuts on production. That pattern held until the boom that started in 1982, which lasted about five years. Producers were so happy about the rising demand for chicken that they expanded the supply faster and faster. Aiding the demand were an increasing preference for chicken over beef, innovations in fast-food items (Chicken McNuggets and Chicken Littles), and new marketing techniques. But these developments were not enough. In 1986, when production jumped a huge 8 percent, demand fell behind. By the following spring, the boom had ended.

The issue for investors is which companies can best ride out the slump. The top five chicken producers are Tyson Foods Inc., ConAgra Inc., Holly Farms Corporation, Perdue Farms Inc., and Gold Kist Inc. Perdue's stock is closely held (a relatively few stockholders own the company), and Gold Kist is traded only through a relatively small subsidiary, Golden Poultry Company, which only recently went public.

Analysts' opinions of the other three vary. ConAgra is widely diversified in other agricultural businesses, such as red meat and frozen foods. Tyson has a bigger share of the food-service market than the other companies do. It sells much of its production to the fast-food chains. Holly Farms is considered to be the most conservative of the five companies. Consequently, the company is less diversified but may be in a better position to withstand an industry downturn.

Analysts do agree that the key to investing will be determining what is ahead for the industry. Observers concur that the boom has ended but are unsure of how long the decline will last. However, they are optimistic. Consumption of chicken continues to rise, with industry observers predicting that it will outpace beef consumption by the 1990s. Specialty products such as marinated breast fillets are boosting profits, because they are priced at four to six times the cost of plain cut-up chickens. Perdue Farms pioneered marketing under a brand name, which also can boost profits. Today, all large companies sell under brand names.

Case Questions

1. If you were a chartist investor in the mid-1980s, what strategy would you have used for investing in the stock of chicken producers? Would this have been a profitable strategy? Explain.
2. Based on the information given, what would have been the best approach to investing in chicken producers? Which companies offer the best investment opportunities? Explain specifically.
3. What other information do you need for a final decision?

You Be the Adviser: The Personal Investor

Over the last six months, Andy Farr, a retired machinist, has done extremely well in the stock market, earning approximately 18 percent on his money. His broker, Charles Bentley, certainly knew what he was talking about when he put together a list of securities Andy should buy. Andy followed this advice to the letter and has never regretted it.

This past week, Andy called Charles and asked if they could meet for lunch. During their meeting, Andy explained that he had been doing a great deal of reading about securities markets and how they work. "I think I know a lot about the stock market and how to make money. That's why I wanted to talk to you. I have about $19,000 in savings at my bank. I'd like to draw out half this amount and begin playing the market on my own. I'd have two stock portfolios: you'd manage the large one, and I'd manage the small one."

Charles told Andy that his idea sounded fine. Andy was a reasonable investor and should have no trouble picking some good stocks on his own. "What do you have in mind as a strategy?" Charles asked. Andy outlined two specific plans of action that he had been thinking about. The first involved oil stocks: "I've been doing a lot of research on the oil firms," said Andy, "and I think I know when they are going up and when they are coming down. I've been playing with them on paper and have already made over $10,000 on a fictitious $25,000 investment. I have bought a couple and sold a few more short. In each case, I have made money. I'd like to put about $6,000 in about four selected oil stocks. The rest of the money I'd like to put into entertainment or movie stocks like Disney Productions and MCA. I read every issue of *Variety*, and I think I can pick out blockbuster movies the minute I've seen them. I've been playing these stocks on paper, too, and I've made almost 70 percent on my money in the last four months."

Charles listened carefully. When Andy was done, he congratulated him: "I never realized how much time and attention you were giving to the securities markets. You certainly seem to know a lot. I'm particularly impressed by your knowledge of the entertainment business. Maybe I can call on you for advice sometime. But about the oil stocks, let me warn you about going short. That can be a lucrative strategy, but you can also end up losing a pile of money. Watch out, and if you do go short, promise yourself that if the stock goes up more than three or four points, you will go back in and take your losses." Andy agreed and promised to follow Charles's advice. Before they parted company, Charles wished him luck and told Andy to call if he needed any assistance.

Your Advice

1. Should Andy put more of his money into oil or entertainment stocks, or should he divide it evenly? Why?
2. What do you think of Charles's advice regarding how to handle short sales? Is it good advice? Why or why not?
3. What investment pitfalls should Andy be concerned about?

Risk Management and Insurance

LEARNING OBJECTIVES

- Specify the types of risk and ways to manage each.
- Describe the criteria of insurability and sources of insurance.
- Identify the major types of property and liability insurance.
- Discuss the key types of health insurance.
- Present the major types of life insurance.
- Relate the special insurance needs of international businesses.

Your Business IQ

How much do you already know about risk management and insurance? Test your business IQ by labeling each statement *true* or *false*. Answers and explanations are at the end of the chapter.

1. The most common way companies avoid risks is by purchasing insurance.
2. An individual may not buy insurance on another person's life without first informing that person.
3. To fund the social security program, employees and self-employed workers pay a tax that averages about 25 percent of their income.
4. If a company's building burns, the firm's fire insurance will pay for the damaged property but not for the revenues the company loses while it is shut down to clean up.
5. The major difference between term and whole life insurance is that term is less expensive and whole life accumulates cash value.

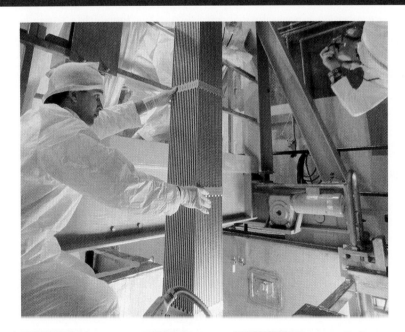

Georgia Power Company workers lower a fuel bundle into the Plant Vogtle Unit 1 nuclear reactor. There are serious risks associated with such jobs, and the company tries to manage these risks through insurance and other means.

Source: Courtesy of Georgia Power Company.

Looking Back and Ahead

For centuries, insurance for businesses consisted primarily of fire protection and coverage of seaborne cargo. But as American business grew, so did the demand for other types of coverage. At first the insurance industry was slow to respond. When an independent agent from Kansas wrote to one insurer regarding the availability of windstorm coverage, he received the following reply:

> We beg to say the Wind Storms being entirely foreign to the business of fire insurance in which we are engaged, we have nothing to do therewith. Neither do we suppose that any other reputable fire Co. does, but only such Companies as must resort to some ludicrous method or worse in order to get any business . . . . If against Wind, why not against Rain, Hail, Crushing by snow, accidents caused by faulty construction of buildings, etc. etc. etc. The proposition is too absurd for any strictly legitimate fire insurance company to consider for a moment.[1]

Today, insurance companies sell packaged policies that include these and many other types of protection.

When businesses invest in their operations (Chapter 18) or in securities (Chapter 19), they take a risk of losing money or earning less than they could have with a different strategy. This chapter discusses other kinds of risks that businesses incur and describes how insurance helps the organization manage them. Because businesses are subject to many risks, managing them is a challenging and important task.

The chapter begins with a broad look at risks and the possible approaches to risk management. It then identifies the kinds of risks that insurance may cover and examines the structure of the insurance industry. The remainder of the chapter describes the many different types of insurance available to companies and individuals.

Risk and How to Manage It

The existence of risk—uncertainty about a loss—is a fact of life for individuals and businesses. For example, if a company has a communications satellite put into orbit, any number of things could go wrong, destroying the satellite or causing it to malfunction. No matter how often a manufacturer stresses safety, someone is injured on the job eventually. At any type of company, a key employee could die, leaving the firm scrambling for new talent. A company that produces consumer goods may someday be sued for injury caused by the product. These are only some of the risks businesses face today.

Types of Risks

Speculative risk The threat of a loss coupled with the chance of a gain.

Notice that none of the risks just mentioned involves investing. An investment is a **speculative risk,** one in which there is a chance of either gain or loss. Betting on a racehorse is a speculative risk. So is gambling that the value of a stock is going to go down. So is taking a chance on backing a new rock group and sponsoring a national tour for them. Investors can increase or decrease speculative risk by adjusting their investment strategy.

This chapter discusses pure risk. **Pure risk** is the threat of a loss without the possibility of a gain. For example, if a K mart warehouse burns down, the company may lose millions of dollars in inventory. If no fire occurs, however, the lack of a fire will not add millions of dollars to the company's earnings. The risk of a fire involves a possible loss but no expectation of a gain. Figure 20.1 shows the possible outcomes of these two kinds of risk.

Risk Management

Because every company is subject to risk, business people practice **risk management,** the reduction of loss caused by uncontrollable events. There are four ways to manage pure risks: avoiding, reducing, assuming, or shifting them.

Avoiding the Risk If the possibility of a loss is great enough, a company may avoid it altogether. For example, a retailer may choose not to open stores in Beirut because of the unstable political climate there. When an airline cancels flights during a blizzard, it too is avoiding a risk. The airline is eliminating the uncertainty over whether one of its planes will crash and cause a substantial loss. It is certain that no planes will crash when parked. Of course, the airline has eliminated the possibility of producing revenue. Customer service also suffers, since customers get upset when their plane is grounded.

Businesses cannot avoid every risk, however. To eliminate all risk of property damage, the company would have to eliminate all property. To eliminate all risk that employees will become ill, sustain an injury, or die, the company would have to eliminate all employees. Any line of work carries risks. Most companies do, however, avoid the risk of high-frequency, high-severity losses.

Reducing the Risk When they can, business people try to reduce or prevent unavoidable risks. For example, managers may promote plant safety by training personnel and instituting safety rules and procedures. To reduce the risk of uncollected accounts, the financial manager might tighten up credit or offer incentives for prompt payment. The company might also deny further credit to customers who are constantly delinquent in paying. These actions do not eliminate the possibility that accidents will occur or customers will fail to pay, but they do reduce the likelihood of these losses.

In deciding whether to reduce a risk, business people may weigh the cost of doing so and their social responsibility against the size of the risk.

Pure risk The threat of a loss without the possibility of a gain.

Risk management The reduction of loss caused by uncontrollable events.

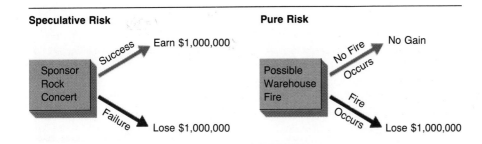

Speculative Risk

Sponsor Rock Concert — Success → Earn $1,000,000

Sponsor Rock Concert — Failure → Lose $1,000,000

Pure Risk

Possible Warehouse Fire — No Fire Occurs → No Gain

Possible Warehouse Fire — Fire Occurs → Lose $1,000,000

F I G U R E   20.1

Risk: Possible Outcomes

For example, a store might find that the additional sales that result from a generous credit policy outweigh the expected losses from bad debts. In that case, the company probably would not try to reduce the risk. But even though making a product or workplace safe can be costly, many companies bear the expense in order to fulfill their social responsibility.

Assuming the Risk When a company decides that a particular risk is worth taking, it assumes the risk. If the risk seems likely to result in an occasional, moderately serious financial loss, the firm may set up a self-insurance fund. In some instances companies are forced to self-insure because they cannot get insurance coverage from the outside. A self-insurance fund is a fund into which the company periodically sets aside cash, called reserves, to cover financial losses. The company pays for its own losses, but the fund enables it to spread out the expense.

Shifting the Risk Another way to manage a worthwhile risk is to shift it. The most popular way to shift risk is to buy **insurance.** This is a financial arrangement under which the cost of unexpected losses is distributed among those who are insured. Insurance spreads the losses incurred by a few over an entire group, thereby substituting average loss for actual loss. Each party desiring insurance pays a **premium,** which is a fee to cover the costs of the insurance policy. In exchange for this fee,

Insurance A financial arrangement under which the cost of unexpected losses is distributed among those who are insured.

Premium A fee to cover the costs of an insurance policy.

Paulette Fernholz and her staff at Pillsbury's Redemption Center reduce the company's risk of losses from coupon fraud — mainly coupons redeemed when no purchase was made. Fernholz built a system to detect coupon fraud and refuse payment on fraudulent submissions. In one recent year, the Redemption Center saved the company $3 million. Today, Fernholz is considered a national expert on coupon fraud.

Source: Courtesy of The Pillsbury Company.

the insurance company will pay the agreed-upon amount if the insured suffers a specified loss. For example, if a store buys a policy insuring it against losses from theft up to $10,000 and suffers a $4,000 theft loss, the insurance company will pay the store $4,000 minus the deductible. A **deductible** is the amount that a policyholder must pay before the insurance company pays for any part of a claim. If the store suffers a $4,000 loss from fire, the insurance company will not pay.

Buying insurance can be the easiest way to manage risk; the business merely pays a premium, and the insurance company covers any insured loss. Especially when used alone, however, insurance can be a costly approach to risk management. Most companies use some combination of risk management techniques. For example, a supermarket might refuse to carry dangerous products, carefully screen employees to minimize the likelihood of pilferage, and buy fire insurance.

Deductible The amount that a policyholder must pay before the insurance company pays any part of a claim.

Checkpoint

1. How does a pure risk differ from a speculative risk?
2. What are four ways to manage risk?

Criteria for Insurability

No matter how much a business is willing to pay, an insurance company will assume a risk only under certain circumstances. More specifically, the coverage must be for an insurable interest and must cover an insurable risk.

Insurable Interest

A person or business wanting coverage must have an insurable interest. This means that the person or business would suffer a financial loss if the event being insured were to happen. For example, a company can buy life insurance on its key managers; if one or more of them were to die, the company would suffer a financial loss. Even if another manager could do the job well, the company would incur expenses in hiring a replacement. If there were no chance of financial loss, there would be no risk to insure. For example, if the fan of a movie actor thought the actor seemed to be in poor health, the fan could not purchase a life insurance policy on the actor's life. Although the fan might feel sad if the actor died, he or she would suffer no financial loss. Therefore, no insurable interest is present. The actor's dependents could, however, insure the actor's life.

Insurable Risk

Besides having an insurable interest, the other criterion for insurability is that there must be an insurable risk. Specifically, an insurable risk involves prerequisites such as a lack of control, calculable losses, economic feasibility, and widespread coverage. These criteria enable insurers to manage their own risks involved in issuing insurance.

Workers leaving Cyprus Minerals Company's Plateau underground coal mine in eastern Utah. The risks that workers could be injured or company property damaged during the course of mining are insurable risks. Nevertheless, the company does not rely entirely on insurance for managing its risks. For example, it tries to reduce the risk of injury by posting safety information such as signs reading "Danger," "Slow," and "Safety Rules Apply to *You*."

Source: Courtesy of Cyprus Minerals Company.

Lack of Control The peril that is being insured against cannot be under the policyholder's direct control. Any losses must happen by chance or be accidental. For example, if a retailer insures his store against fire, he cannot burn down the building and collect. If an investigation finds that the retailer is implicated in the fire, the insurance company can refuse to pay the claim. Life insurance policies operate the same way. For instance, people may not take out $1 million of insurance and then commit suicide immediately in order to leave their estate with a large sum of money. However, on the assumption that few people plan their own deaths years in advance, most life insurance policies do pay off if the insured commits suicide after a predetermined time, such as two years.

Calculable Losses For a risk to be insurable, the losses related to it must be calculable. This means that the insurer must be able to predict how many losses will occur and how big they will be. The insurance company determines this by hiring **actuaries,** people who collect statistics about losses and use this information to make predictions. For example, actuaries calculate statistics that give average life expectancies for various groups of people, as well as the number of deaths likely to occur in each group during the course of a year. These expectancy figures do not show the likelihood that you or any other individual will die this year; They only show the proportion of deaths in the population.

Actuaries Experts in collecting statistics about losses and using this information to make predictions.

In recent years, some people have criticized insurance companies for determining premiums for certain types of insurance on the basis of sex. For example, women may pay higher premiums than men for the same health insurance coverage, but may pay lower premiums than men for an equal amount of life insurance. On the surface this may appear to be discriminatory, but as the accompanying ad points out, the insurance companies are charging premiums according to the risks associated with each group. Whether they have a social responsibility to charge men and women the same, regardless of the statistical risk, is still being debated.

To be calculable, a loss must also be measurable. For this reason, insurers cover only risks that involve a financial loss. For example, fire insurance covers the cost of the assets—building, furniture, and other belongings—lost in a fire. Life insurance replaces the income policyholders might have earned or the expenses of a funeral. Most insurance policies specify a maximum amount they will cover, which also helps the company predict the extent of losses it must cover.

Economic Feasibility The insurance company uses the information its actuaries gather to decide whether risks are economically feasible. Employees called underwriters decide what insurance the company can offer profitably. For example, if the company sells 1,000 insurance policies, each paying $50,000, and expects two deaths per thousand, the company can expect to pay out $100,000 in a year. It will sell the policies if it can charge more than $100 for each. If customers won't pay that much, the insurance company cannot make a profit and will look for other risks to insure.

Besides premium size, the insurance company considers the size of the potential loss. Most losses are small enough that the insurer can sell enough policies to cover the claims filed. But liability claims in some industries (such as those that made, sold, or installed asbestos) have been so large that insurers refuse to provide liability insurance to them. And the damages of war are so great that insurers won't cover the risk of a war.

Economic feasibility is linked to the insurer's profits. If an insurer predicts that product liability lawsuits will cost $5 million to defend and pay but that the company can raise only $4 million from selling the policies, it won't sell the insurance. However, if an insurer can make up the difference by investing the premiums until it has to pay out losses, the company may sell the insurance even if the premiums themselves fall short of expected payouts.

Widespread Risk Linked to the other criteria is the requirement that an insurable risk be widespread. To calculate the expected frequency of losses, the insurer must have a large number of cases to compare. For

An insurance industry advertisement supporting the practice of charging different rates for men and women. As this ad explains, the risks in each group are statistically different; women tend to live longer and, before age 55, tend to use health care services more than men. Thus, women typically pay less for life insurance and more for health insurance (until they are 55). However, critics contend that the distinction is artificially imposed, and the debate continues.

Source: Courtesy of ACLI (American Council of Life Insurance) and HIAA (Health Insurance Association of America).

example, in determining the frequency with which office buildings are struck by tornadoes, an insurer must be able to weigh the experience of more than a handful of office buildings. Because damage from tornadoes is widespread, the insurer can calculate this risk and sell enough policies to spread the risk widely and lower the cost borne by each customer.

Another dimension of widespread risk is that for many risks to be economically feasible, the insurer needs to spread them geographically. In the case of fire insurance, an insurer would not want to insure 25 large buildings in the lower Manhattan financial district and no others; a fire in this locale might wipe out all of the buildings. For example, when the Philadelphia police fire-bombed a house a few years ago, and the entire neighborhood burned down, if the same company had insured all these homes, they could have been wiped out, unless they could have recovered money from the city. However, if the insurer has covered buildings spread out across the state or country, a fire in one location will damage only a small percentage of all the insured buildings. Similarly, a life insurance company would not want to limit coverage to people in one city, because a calamity in this city, such as a tornado or hurricane, could wipe out the insurer's revenues.

Table 20.1 provides some humorous examples of requests for insurance. Can you identify which requests are insurable and which are not? In deciding, think of these risks as being insured today, even though some of these people lived hundreds of years ago.

Checkpoint

1. What is an insurable interest?
2. What makes a risk insurable?

The Insurance Industry

The insurance industry consists of two basic types of companies: public and private. The best known are privately owned. However, public insurers provide a wealth of benefits and services to millions of people.

Public Insurance Companies

A public insurance company is a governmental agency established to provide insurance protection. These agencies exist at both the federal and state levels and provide a wide range of coverage.

Old Age, Survivors, Disability, and Health Insurance (OASDHI) A federal insurance program that provides retirement, medical, disability, and death benefits.

Medicare A federal program providing hospital and medical insurance to the elderly.

Federal Protection At the federal level, perhaps the best-known insurance program is **Old-Age, Survivors, Disability, and Health Insurance (OASDHI),** commonly known as social security, which provides retirement, medical, disability, and death benefits. This insurance program was established by the Social Security Act of 1935. It was originally intended to be a retirement benefit program, but Congress has added other coverages over the years. For example, in 1965 Congresss added **Medicare,** a form of hospital insurance for the elderly.

Many people think of social security as a kind of retirement savings plan, but it actually operates under a "pay as you go" approach. In 1988, employees paid 7.51 percent of the first $43,800 of their pay to social security and the employer contributed another 7.51 percent. Self-employed persons, on the other hand, paid 13.02 percent of $43,800 to social security in 1988. In other words, employees, employers, and enterpreneurs contribute funds to finance the benefits currently provided to the elderly, the infirm, and others covered by this form of insurance. In turn, when those workers retire, they will receive benefits financed by those who remain in the work force.

Which of the following requests for insurance are acceptable and which are not? Consider whether each involves an insurable interest and an insurable risk. The answers appear below the table.

Person Requesting Insurance	Insurance Requested	Acceptable or Unacceptable?
1. Lee Iacocca	Fire insurance on the headquarters of General Motors	
2. Owner of the *Titanic*	Insurance covering loss of ship on the high seas	
3. Jessie James	Robbery insurance for a bank	
4. Leonard Bernstein	Broken baton insurance	
5. George Burns	Personal life insurance	
6. Noah	Flood insurance on his home	
7. Carl Sagan	Insurance to cover kidnapping by aliens from another planet	
8. Johnny Carson	Earthquake coverage on his Malibu home	
9. Houdini	Accident insurance in case he is injured during one of his escape tricks	
10. Steven Spielberg	Business interruption insurance covering his filming of *ET II*	

Answers:

1. *Unacceptable.* Iacocca lacks an insurable interest because he works for Chrysler. If GM were to have a fire at its headquarters, Iacocca would not suffer a loss.
2. *Acceptable.* Statistics would indicate the likelihood of the ship sinking, so an insurance company would be able to quote a premium on this type of risk. Insurers can spread the risk over the many oceangoing vessels in operation.
3. *Unacceptable.* There is direct control. Jessie James was a famous bank robber and might well rob the bank that he is insuring. He also has no insurable interest.
4. *Unacceptable.* It is not economically feasible. The cost of a baton with which to direct an orchestra is so small, given the possibility of breaking it, that the company would spend more money processing claims than it could collect in premiums.
5. *Acceptable.* Statistics are available on the life expectancy of people. The comedian George Burns is in his 90s, so an insurance company could have made a lot of money selling him life insurance.
6. *Unacceptable.* If the insurance company believed the world was about to be inundated with water, they would refuse to sell flood insurance. Of course, if the insurance company did not know this, then the insurance is acceptable; figuratively speaking, the insurance company is going to take a bath.
7. *Unacceptable.* The loss is not calculable; the insurance company cannot estimate the likelihood of Mr. Sagan being kidnapped by aliens from another planet.
8. *Acceptable.* The company would have statistics related to the risk associated with earthquakes in California and would issue a policy based on these data.
9. *Acceptable.* The insurance company would estimate the likelihood of an accident. Of course, if the trick is considered dangerous, the premium might be very high and Mr. Houdini might consider self-insurance.
10. *Acceptable.* Business interruption insurance is a common type of coverage. It is based on the likelihood of such perils as storms and strikes by workers.

Other forms of federal insurance protect individuals in diverse ways:

The Federal Deposit Insurance Corporation (FDIC) and Federal Savings and Loan Insurance Corporation (FSLIC) insure deposits in financial institutions (see Chapter 17).

The Federal Housing Administration (FHA) provides mortgage insurance to protect lenders against default by homeowners.

The National Flood Insurance Association protects property owners against floods and mudslides.

The Federal Crop Insurance Corporation provides farmers with crop insurance, protecting them against losses from crop failure.

Federal crime insurance is available to people who have property in high crime areas and are unable to purchase this coverage from private insurance firms.

State Protection At the state level, the two basic types of insurance are unemployment insurance and workers' compensation insurance. **Unemployment insurance** provides benefits to workers who have been laid off. These weekly payments typically extend for 26 to 39 weeks, although in some states this time period is much shorter and in others it runs for a year or more. For the duration of the time they receive these benefits, the unemployed are supposed to be actively seeking work. Many states offer placement services. Unemployment insurance is funded from employer contributions, and the more workers a company lays off, the higher its contribution.

Workers' compensation insurance provides benefits to workers who suffer a job-related injury or illness. This compensation generally covers a percentage of wages or salaries, medical care costs, rehabilitative services, and, for certain types of injuries such as a loss of an arm or foot, a lump-sum payment. The employer pays the premiums, which are based on the company's record of past claims. Today, every state has workers' compensation laws requiring companies to carry this type of insurance. Even though required by state law, companies normally contract with private insurers to provide this benefit.

Private Insurance Companies

Most of the insurance in the United States is provided by private firms. These firms may be stock insurance companies or mutual insurance companies. A **stock insurance company** is a corporation operated for profit. As with any other corporation, those who invest by purchasing shares expect a return in the form of dividends or an increase in the value of the stock.

A **mutual insurance company** is a type of cooperative; the policyholders become shareholders of the company. Any profits the company makes go back to the policyholders in the form of dividends or reductions in premiums. Most mutual insurance companies sell life insurance. As Table 20.2 illustrates, more than half of the ten largest life insurance companies in the United States are mutual companies.

Private insurance companies offer many different types of insurance relevant to modern business, and these are basically the same types that individuals would buy to insure against risk. Most companies specialize in property and liability insurance, health insurance, or life insurance.

Unemployment insurance A state program that provides benefits to workers who have been laid off.

Workers' compensation insurance A state program that provides benefits to workers who suffer job-related injury or illness.

Stock insurance company A corporation that sells insurance for profit.

Mutual insurance company A type of cooperative in which the policyholders become shareholders of the insurance company.

Checkpoint

1. What types of benefits are provided by social security?
2. Who receives the dividends paid by a stock insurance company? A mutual insurance company?

Property and Liability Insurance

Businesses risk losses from damage to their buildings and equipment, from theft or other crimes, and from lawsuits resulting from negligent actions or faulty products. They shift the risk of these losses by purchasing property and liability insurance. These insurance policies include fire, fidelity and surety, business interruption, marine and aviation, public liability, and automobile insurance.

Insuring against Loss of Property Due to Fire

The property component of property and liability insurance most commonly provides protection against loss of property due to fire. In the United States, about five fires happen every minute, and many of these damage business property. This makes fire insurance coverage very important. The policies for fire insurance can and usually will be expanded to cover other perils such as losses stemming from wind, ice, water, and smoke. These policies pay the value of the loss or the amount of the policy, whichever is lower. For example, if a corporation carried a $10 million fire insurance policy on its headquarters building, but the building was valued at $8 million, the insurance company would pay only $8 million if the structure were completely destroyed by fire. If the structure were valued at $11 million, the insurance company would pay the maximum $10 million.

Few buildings are completely gutted by fire. A typical fire does only partial damage to a structure. For example, a building worth $10 million

Company	Assets (in $ billions)
Prudential[a]	$103.3
Metropolitan[a]	81.6
Equitable Life Assurance[a]	48.6
Aetna Life	43.0
New York Life[a]	29.8
Teachers Insurance & Annuity	27.9
John Hancock Mutual[a]	27.2
Travelers	27.2
Connecticut General Life	24.8
Northwestern Mutual[a]	20.2

[a]Indicates a mutual company. The others are stock companies.

T A B L E   20.2

The Ten Largest Life Insurance Companies

might suffer $1 million in fire damage. To prevent firms from underinsuring their buildings and taking a chance that the fire will not destroy the entire structure, insurance companies put a coinsurance clause in the policy. This clause requires the firm to cover at least 80 percent of the value of the building in order to receive full coverage for any loss.

Insuring against Income Loss

Another form of property and liability insurance is to protect against income loss. There are several types of this insurance.

Fidelity and Surety Bonds When employees handle money, the company risks losing some of the money to a dishonest employee. The company can insure against such a loss by purchasing **fidelity bonds,** which provide coverage against loss caused by employee embezzlement or theft. If a bonded employee were to abscond with funds, the bond would cover the loss up to its face value. The insurance company will then try to recover the funds. As with other risks, companies combine insurance with other forms of risk management. "Computer Technology Close-Up: Reducing Employee Theft" describes some modern techniques.

A **surety bond** provides coverage against the risk that someone will fail to perform on a contract. For example, a corporation that is having a new headquarters built might want to insure itself against the risk that the builder will not finish on time or will walk away from the job. If either of these does happen, the bond provides the funds necessary to hire someone else to complete the project.

Crime Insurance Employees are not, of course, the only people who might steal from a business. To protect against losses arising from theft by outsiders, a company can buy crime insurance, also called theft insurance. This policy may cover robbery, which is taking property from someone by force or threat of force, and burglary, which is taking property by forcible entry into the premises.

Business Interruption Insurance A number of problems, such as a strike or flood, may cause a business to shut down temporarily. To protect themselves, companies buy **business interruption insurance,** which is designed to cover losses from temporary business closings. Without this protection, many temporary closings would become permanent ones. For example, if a store has a fire, it may need a week or two to clean up the mess and replace its inventory. Fire insurance would pay for the damage but not the lost revenues. Business interruption insurance can cover that loss.

Many movie production firms buy this insurance to handle losses caused by the injury or death of a lead actor. The production has costs for the crew and other actors and for the set or location that are normally committed and cannot be put on hold. Should such a calamity occur, the entire crew would have to either wait for the actor's recovery or hire a replacement. In either case, business interruption insurance would help minimize the financial losses.

Marine and Aviation Insurance Companies that transport cargo or passengers take on special kinds of risks. To protect against losses involving their boats, ships, trucks, railcars and engines, planes, and their cargo,

Fidelity bond Coverage of losses caused by employee embezzlement or theft.

Surety bond Coverage against the risk that someone will fail to perform on a contract.

Business interruption insurance Coverage of losses from temporary business closings.

Marine insurance Coverage of losses to boats, ships, trucks, railcars and engines, and planes.

Ocean marine insurance Coverage of losses that occur to ships or their cargo on the high seas or in port.

companies buy **marine insurance.** As transportation modes expanded beyond ships, the word *marine* became too limiting. **Ocean marine insurance** covers losses that occur to ships or their cargo on the high seas or in port. **Inland marine insurance** covers damage to or loss of goods shipped by rail, truck, airplane, or inland barge.

Aviation insurance provides coverage of airliners and passengers. Airlines carry aviation insurance to cover the liabilities arising from damage to the aircraft or the passengers. A typical policy provides $500 million of liability insurance on small-body aircraft and $800 million on wide-body craft, and has a deductible of $250,000.

Credit and Title Insurance Buying and selling goods also carry risks. When a company sells goods on credit, it risks not receiving full payment. The debtor may die before the total payment is due, leaving the seller to bear the loss. To protect against this risk, many sellers buy credit insurance or require that borrowers pay for such insurance when they take out a loan.

Inland marine insurance
Coverage of damage to or loss of goods shipped by rail, truck, airplane, or inland barge.

Aviation insurance
Coverage of losses involving airliners and their passengers.

COMPUTER TECHNOLOGY ## CLOSE-UP

Reducing Employee Theft

Employee theft accounts for almost 70 percent of retailers' losses to all kinds of crime, and store owners are understandably concerned about this problem. Studies suggest that three out of four retail employees know at least one colleague who is stealing, and only one out of seven employees is willing to tell management about a dishonest co-worker. Fidelity bonds are a way to shift the risk, but store managers also try to reduce the risk. They are responding to the problem by educating employees and putting computer technology to work wherever they can.

One approach uses data base software. Participating retailers provide private companies with data on workers caught stealing and people caught shoplifting. For example, Stores Mutual Association of Illinois, Inc., has a data base of more than 50,000 names of shoplifters, dishonest employees, and credit card imposters. Participating stores can then use this information to help screen job applicants and thus avoid hiring any of these people.

In addition, stores use surveillance techniques to apprehend dishonest employees.

These techniques, too, are making increasing use of computer technology. Electronic cash registers, for example, can be a helpful source of information. For example, Marshall Field's uses sales terminals to add a clerk's cash sales, refunds, and voided sales checks. If a clerk makes an unusually large number of refunds, managers may suspect fraud; the money may be going to the clerk or to friends. Having many voided sales or few cash sales also suggests dishonesty.

Computers are also working in tandem with cameras. While a security officer is using closed-circuit cameras to watch a clerk ring up an order on an electronic cash register, a nearby computer can identify what items the clerk is ringing up. The security officer can compare the information to make sure the clerk is not slipping extras into a friend's or relative's bag.

Computer technology is thus an important part of managing the risk of employee theft. However, most retailers still emphasize finding employees who are honest and keeping them that way.

Buyers of real estate risk finding out that someone other than the seller has an interest in the real estate. For example, a buyer may find out one day that the seller was an imposter or that the seller had a spouse who now says that he or she never wanted to transfer ownership of the property. To cover the costs of any resulting lawsuit and possible loss of the property, buyers of real estate often purchase a title insurance policy.

Insuring against Loss from Liability

Large losses can arise if a court finds that a business is liable for causing personal injury or property damage. Even if the company is found innocent, the costs of legal defense are often substantial. To protect against these losses, businesses buy personal or public liability insurance, which is designed to protect individuals and businesses from lawsuits arising from injuries or property damage. This form of insurance covers many different types of liabilities.

Personal Liability Insurance Many homeowners' policies include personal liability insurance to protect the owners from claims by individuals who injure themselves on their property. In addition to their regular coverage, many individuals with considerable risks, such as parents who are responsible for teenage drivers, or people in the public eye who are exposed to suits such as for slander, buy an umbrella liability policy, which extends coverage to $1 million or more.

Cargo is often transported in heavy-duty semitrailers such as this one. To protect themselves against losses from damage to or loss of cargo, businesses buy inland marine insurance.

Professional Liability Insurance A special type of personal liability insurance is professional liability insurance, which covers professionals against lawsuits arising from accusations of malpractice. Doctors, lawyers, architects, and even college professors have been sued in recent years by irate clients or students. Professional liability insurance helps protect the insured from financial losses resulting from successful lawsuits. To learn how doctors, the Canadian government, and insurers handle physicians' liability, see "International Close-Up: Malpractice in Canada."

A special kind of professional liability insurance is **directors' and officers' liability insurance,** which provides coverage to board members and senior corporate executives in the case of lawsuits arising out of their actions. For example, as Chapter 5 pointed out, stockholders have recently sued some directors and officers, claiming that negligence on the part of directors resulted in needless corporate losses.

Directors' and officers' liability insurance Coverage of the costs of lawsuits against board members and senior corporate executives arising out of their actions.

INTERNATIONAL   CLOSE-UP

Malpractice in Canada

In the United States, thousands of malpractice lawsuits are filed every year. Consequently, some physicians have malpractice insurance premiums that are greater than the average income of most Americans. For example, while a general practitioner in a small town in Arkansas may pay about $4,000 for malpractice insurance, a Miami neurosurgeon can expect to pay in excess of $100,000. However, Canada has found an alternative to soaring malpractice insurance costs.

In personal injury cases, the Canadian Supreme Court limits damage awards for pain and suffering to $128,000 plus punitive damages. In U.S. courts, similar suits can result in settlements of a million dollars or more. Moreover, Ontario province bans contingency fees, under which the lawyer takes a percentage of the overall settlement, and a number of other provinces restrict them. These restrictions on fees reduce the likelihood that lawyers will try for huge settlements, because their fees are not tied to the size of the award. However, on the other hand, some good lawyers may now be reluctant to take on personal injury cases.

Another interesting development in Canada is that frivolous suits can end up being

expensive for the party that brings the action. In the United States, some people will sue their doctor for $1 million in the hopes of getting $10,000 for some relatively minor claim. In Canada, if the individual loses this suit, the person can be liable for up to two-thirds of the doctor's legal fees.

Because of the different approach taken to malpractice insurance, doctors in Canada pay much less for their insurance than do their counterparts in the United States. High-risk specialists, such as neurosurgeons or obstetricians, typically pay around $3,500 for protection that costs a U.S. doctor $90,000 or more.

Most Canadian physicians are insured with the Canadian Medical Protective Association (CMPA), which provides legal defense and pays malpractice claims. The annual fees for doctors range between $300 and $3,500. Best of all, perhaps, is the reputation of the CMPA. If it feels a patient is bringing a claim that is unjustified, the association will fight it to the bitter end. As one lawyer put it, "They'll spend $15,000 to fight a $15,000 action." Clearly, there is a big difference between American and Canadian views regarding malpractice suits.

Product Liability Insurance To protect themselves from lawsuits related to their products, companies buy a form of personal or public liability insurance called product liability insurance. Product liability claims can pose a serious problem for companies. For example, a number of women sued the A. H. Robbins Company resulting in claims totaling millions of dollars for damages caused by the firm's Dalkon Shield intrauterine contraceptive device. Merrell Dow Pharmaceuticals withdrew Benedectin from the market after a jury awarded $750,000 to a family who claimed that the drug, designed to fight morning sickness, caused their child to be born with a birth defect. Union Carbide continues to face millions of dollars in product liability claims from the toxic-gas leak in its plant in Bhopal, India, which resulted in the death of several thousand people.

Although the crisis in liability insurance, which saw premiums skyrocket in the mid-1980s, now appears to be over except in a few high-risk areas such as ski resorts and medical malpractice, the insurance world may never be the same.[2] Some insurance companies are facing charges that they illegally got together to offer liability policies with less coverage for more money.[3] In addition, more businesses than ever are self-insuring (up to about one-third of the product liability market and growing). For example, Hardee's Food Systems now pays for losses up to $2 million itself and just buys insurance against catastrophes. Hardee's believes the key to this approach is to manage risk in ways other than insurance by taking steps such as installing nonskid floors to minimize falls.[4] Other companies such as DuPont and Control Data have helped create new insurance companies to stabilize the market. As a result of these efforts and good old supply and demand at work, insurance companies are once again offering better policy terms.

Automobile Insurance

Combining elements of property and liability coverage is automobile insurance, which provides protection from such perils as theft, fire, collision, and personal injury in the operation of an auto. Private individuals as well as firms that own autos almost always carry insurance on them, and an increasing number of states require proof of insurance before they will register a vehicle and issue a license plate. A number of important types of coverage are available:

Comprehensive insurance covers damage to the car from a variety of mishaps, including fire, theft, falling objects, earthquakes, broken glass, and malicious vandalism. This coverage also often includes the cost of renting a car in case of theft or disabling damage.

Collision insurance covers damage to the car if it collides with another car or object. Most policies have a deductible of at least $100 for collision. Thus, in the case of a $500 claim, the insurance company would pay only $400. If the damage was less than $100, the insurance firm would not pay.

Liability insurance provides coverage for bodily injury and property damage. Bodily injury liability insurance provides coverage against claims by anyone inside or outside the car who suffers bodily injury because of the driver; property damage liability insurance provides protection against claims or damage to other people's property in an accident. The policy sets liability limits, or maximum amounts of coverage. These are typically expressed as three numbers, such as 100/300/50, which means that up to $100,000 for bodily injury is payable to any one victim of an accident, up to a total of $300,000 is payable to all victims of the accident, and up to $50,000 may be paid in settlement of property damage caused to another person's car or personal property.

Medical payments insurance provides a wide range of coverage for reasonable medical or funeral expenses that occur within a year's time of an auto accident. The bodily injury liability insurance may pay for damages beyond medical bills, for example, for loss of earning power because of resulting loss of time or a disability. The insurer usually pays for the medical expenses, regardless of who caused the accident.

Uninsured motorist insurance covers expenses from injury to anyone in the car when an uninsured motorist or a hit-and-run driver causes an accident.

No-fault insurance provides for compensation regardless of who was at fault during an auto accident. The insurance company pays for financial losses suffered by anyone involved in the accident. However, the insurance also limits the right of victims to sue. As Figure 20.2 shows, 25 states require no-fault insurance, and the number is growing. Although these no-fault laws were passed to put a rein on spiraling auto insurance premiums, some states (for example, Nevada and Pennsylvania) found that costs kept rising rapidly and have repealed their no-fault laws.

No-fault insurance
Coverage providing compensation regardless of who was at fault in an auto accident.

Checkpoint

1. What are three types of property and liability insurance?
2. What type(s) of insurance coverage would you purchase for your brand new automobile?

Health Insurance

The great majority of Americans carry some form of health insurance. Health care costs have risen so high that this type of insurance has become a necessity (See Figure 20.3). Most employees receive group coverage through their employer, who pays part or all of the premium. The insurance typically covers medical expenses arising from illness or injury.

Major Types of Health Insurance Coverage

The basic components of most health care coverage are hospitalization, surgical and medical, and major medical insurance. Hospitalization insurance covers the expenses of a hospital stay up to a coverage limit. Typically included are a semiprivate room, food, routine nursing care, and medication. Extras such as a TV or a private room are seldom covered. Surgical and medical insurance covers the costs of surgeons and medical specialists. In addition to any operating expenses, this coverage includes in-hospital visits by the doctor as well as office visits or house calls after the patient's release.

Hospitalization and surgical and medical coverage often carry limits. When a person exceeds those limits, major medical takes over. Major medical insurance covers health care expenses that exceed the coverage limits of other insurance.

Other Types of Health Insurance Coverage

Sometimes health insurance policies include dental and vision insurance, which covers a fixed percentage of expenses for dental and optical care. This insurance typically covers periodic checkups by a dentist, plus routine fillings and other dental work. The vision portion usually covers eye exams, eyeglasses, and medically prescribed contact lenses. The insurance seldom covers cosmetic work such as capping all of the teeth or providing orthodontic care for purely aesthetic reasons, nor does it cover corrective eye surgery undertaken to eliminate the use of glasses.

Many companies are now beginning to offer their employees some form of mental health insurance. Mental health insurance provides cov-

F I G U R E   20.2

States with No-Fault Auto Insurance

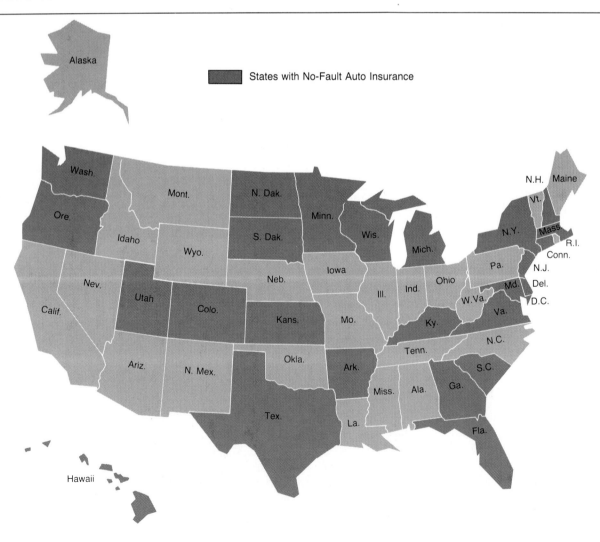

erages for psychiatric care and sometimes counseling. This coverage varies widely. Some firms have programs with little if any deductible and cover the individual up to a predetermined limit such as $50,000; other programs require the insured to bear more of the costs. Mental health coverage is becoming more common as the importance of such care gains recognition.

In addition to medical expenses, being sick for more than a few days can lead to lost income. Disability income insurance provides income to those who are unable to work because of a disabling illness or injury. These policies generally have a waiting period of a week or more before payments begin. The payments are usually a percentage of the worker's former earnings. Many employers provide this insurance, although individuals can also buy it themselves if they are not covered by their employer or want to supplement what the employer provides.

Checkpoint

1. What are the major sources of health insurance coverage?
2. What losses does major medical insurance cover?

Life Insurance

Millions of Americans have life insurance. This coverage provides money to the insured's beneficiary (the person or persons, usually family members, whom the policy owner names to receive the insurance benefits) upon the insured's death. In addition, some types of life insurance

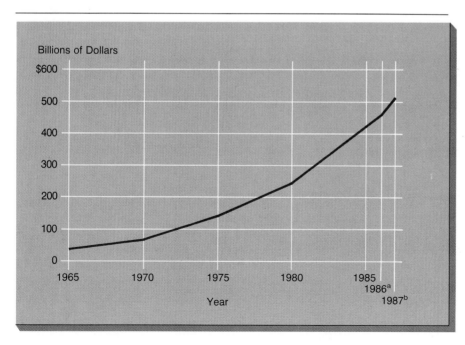

FIGURE 20.3

The Cost of Health Care in the United States

[a]Estimate by U.S. Department of Commerce.
[b]Forecast by U.S. Department of Commerce. Percentage figure not available.

function as a form of investment. The purchaser's risks and objectives determine the most appropriate type of life insurance to buy. While the most common forms of life insurance are term life and whole life, insurance companies are offering an increasing number of alternatives.

Term Life Insurance

Term life insurance
Coverage for a death benefit during a stated number of years.

The least expensive type of coverage is **term life insurance,** which provides coverage for a death benefit during a stated number of years; if the insured dies during this time, the insurance company will pay the stated or face value of the policy. Term insurance can be purchased for a term of 1, 5, 10, or 20 years and may have a fixed or declining death benefit. With a fixed benefit such as $100,000, the premium will increase every year or two. With a declining or decreasing benefit, the benefit declines every year while the premium is fixed. For example, the premium might buy $100,000 of coverage the first year, $99,000 the second, $97,000 the third, and so forth.

The cost of term insurance is based on the insured person's age. The older the insured, the greater the premium, with rates tending to rise rapidly beginning at around age 50. For this reason, it is most popular among young people who want to buy as much insurance as possible at as low a price as they can.

Whole Life Insurance

Whole life insurance A combination of a death benefit and tax-deferred savings.

Cash value The amount of money in a life insurance policy that the insured can borrow or obtain by canceling the policy.

Whole life insurance combines a death benefit with savings. Premiums remain the same from year to year and, usually, beginning in the second year, the policy begins to accumulate cash value. The **cash value** of life insurance is the amount of money in a policy that the insured can borrow or obtain by canceling the policy. If the insured borrows the cash value, he or she must pay interest (usually at a variable rate); if the insured dies, the company subtracts the borrowed amount from the face value of the policy before paying the death benefit.

Whole life used to be the most common form of life insurance, but it has recently accounted for less than half of all policies sold. The reason is that it is expensive compared to other forms of insurance. Fewer people find the accumulating cash value worth the additional cost. Many other attractive investment opportunities are vying for people's savings, and rarely charge the investors interest when they want to borrow some of their investment.

Limited-Pay Life Insurance

Limited-pay life insurance Whole life insurance that limits the number of years the insured must pay premiums.

Some whole life insurance, called **limited-pay life insurance,** limits the number of years the insured must pay premiums. A typical limit is 20 years; such a policy is commonly referred to as "20 pay life." The major benefit of this type of policy is that the insured can limit premium payments to the years when he or she expects to be making the most money. However, this form of insurance provides less protection for the money than does whole life.

Endowment Life Insurance

A policy that combines a death benefit with a great deal of savings is **endowment life insurance.** The premium on this type of policy is greater than that of whole life or limited-pay life, but the cash value also increases a lot faster. In fact, at the end of a stated time period, such as 20 years, the cash value is equal to the face value of the policy, and the insured can cash it in. If the insured dies before this time, the company pays face value of the policy to the beneficiary named in the policy. This form of policy has diminished in popularity in recent years because there are easier ways to save money.

Endowment life insurance Life insurance that combines a death benefit with a great deal of savings.

Universal Life Insurance

Recently very popular, **universal life insurance** combines term insurance with a tax-deferred savings plan. By the mid-1980s, universal life was accounting for almost 40 percent of all life insurance sales.[5] This form of insurance is even growing in popularity as a benefit offered by companies to their employees. A recent large survey indicated that over one-fifth of the companies offered their workers group universal life policies.[6] Premiums are used to cover losses, just as they are in a term insurance policy. However, any remaining funds are invested at competitive rates of interest. As a result, the cash value of the policy may, depending on interest rates, go up faster than that of a whole life policy. Some of these policies also allow the insured to change the premium or the coverage or to withdraw savings from time to time. This kind of flexibility makes it different from whole life and has made the universal policy attractive to buyers. However, the interest earned on the savings is subject to tax when it is withdrawn.

Universal life insurance Life insurance that combines term insurance with a tax-deferred savings plan.

Universal life was developed by the insurance industry to meet changing customer needs. Other products such as variable life insurance, which allows the policyholder to designate a certain amount of premium dollars to investments in stocks, bonds, or a money-market mutual fund, are also available. As in other industries, the insurance industry is offering an increasing number of alternatives. Businesses and individuals need to be aware of their options when considering their life insurance needs.

Business Life Insurance

As with health insurance, many businesses buy life insurance as an employee benefit. Typically, they provide group life insurance, which is term life insurance on all members of a particular group, such as the employees of a company. Unlike most individual life insurance policies, a group plan does not require the employees to take a physical exam. The death benefit goes to the insured's estate, and its size is usually tied to the insured's salary.

To protect themselves, businesses buy **owner or executive insurance,** also called key employee insurance, which reimburses the organization upon the death of a key employee. Often, small partnerships buy key employee insurance on the life of the owners, so that if one dies, the

Owner or executive insurance Life insurance that reimburses an organization upon the death of a key employee.

others can buy out the deceased's interest in the firm. In larger enterprises, the funds from this insurance compensate for the contribution a senior executive or vital manager would have made and to cover the costs of finding and hiring a replacement.

Checkpoint

1. What are three types of life insurance?
2. What risks does a company shift when it buys owner or executive insurance?

Special Insurance for International Business

As more and more businesses enter the international arena, they develop special insurance needs. For example, businesses operating in other countries run a greater risk of losses from actions such as the kidnapping of an employee or nationalization of the company's overseas operations. To protect themselves, many international businesses buy kidnap, ransom, and extortion insurance, and expropriation and inconvertibility insurance.

Kidnap, ransom, and extortion insurance covers costs associated with these criminal acts. Firms sending their personnel into risky overseas areas, such as the Middle East, are particularly interested in this form of insurance. The coverage typically reimburses the business for extortion payments, ransom paid to kidnappers, and expenses associated with negotiating a victim's release. Also covered are medical, legal, travel, and other costs related to activities conducted before and after a victim's release.

Expropriation and inconvertibility insurance covers losses associated with the nationalization of property and conversion of currency. If a foreign government seizes a firm's plant and equipment (as when Castro took over Cuba), expropriation insurance compensates for the assets. If a company is unable to convert its foreign currency back into U.S. dollars, inconvertibility insurance helps the firm cover any losses or pay for the costs of negotiating a solution. In most cases, the insurer delays reimbursement for at least 30 days, during which time the company tries to work out the problem. If these efforts fail, the insurer reimburses the company based on the exchange rates prevailing on the day the period of inconvertibility began.

Kidnap, ransom, and extortion insurance Political risk insurance that covers costs associated with these criminal acts.

Expropriation and inconvertibility insurance Political risk insurance that covers nationalization of property and conversion of currency.

Checkpoint

1. Why do international companies need special forms of insurance?
2. What risks are covered by expropriation and inconvertibility insurance?

Closing Comments

Modern businesses encounter a variety of risks, such as damage to their property, losses stemming from crime, lawsuits over faulty products, and the loss of a key employee. Businesses manage these risks in one or more of several ways: avoiding, reducing, assuming, and shifting the risks. When the risk is insurable, risk management almost always includes insurance. The major types of insurance are property and liability insurance, health insurance, and life insurance. International companies buy special insurance to protect them against political risks.

Learning Objectives Revisited

1. **Specify the types of risk and ways to manage each.**
   Pure risk is the threat of a loss without the possibility of a gain, while speculative risk involves the uncertainty of a loss or a gain. Risk management is the reduction of loss caused by pure risk. The four ways of managing such risk are avoiding the risk, reducing the risk, assuming the risk, or shifting the risk. The most common way to shift risk is to buy insurance.

2. **Describe the criteria of insurability and sources of insurance.**
   Insurability requires an insurable interest and an insurable risk. An insurable interest means that a person or business would suffer a financial loss if the risk being covered were to happen. An insurable risk is outside the control of the insured, involves calculable losses, is economically feasible to cover, and is widespread. Insurance is available through public insurance companies (government agencies) and private insurance companies, which may be stock companies or mutual companies.

3. **Identify the major types of property and liability insurance.**
   Property insurance includes fire insurance and protection against loss of income in the form of fidelity and surety bonds, crime insurance, business interruption insurance, marine and aviation insurance, and credit and title insurance. Personal or public liability insurance protects individuals and businesses from lawsuits and includes personal and professional liability insurance and product liability insurance. Automobile insurance combines property and liability coverage for risks associated with the ownership and operation of an auto.

4. **Discuss the key types of health insurance.**
   Health insurance includes hospitalization insurance, surgical and medical insurance, and major medical insurance. It also may cover dental and vision care and mental health care. Disability income insurance provides income to an insured person who is unable to work because of a disabling illness or injury.

5. **Present the major types of life insurance.**
   The major types of life insurance include term life insurance, whole life insurance (which includes limited-pay life insurance), endowment life insurance, and universal life insurance. Businesses often buy group life insurance, which provides term life insurance on all employees, and owner or executive insurance, which reimburses the organization for the loss of a key employee.

6. Relate the special insurance needs of international businesses.
International businesses buy kidnap, ransom, and extortion coverage to protect against costs related to these risks. Expropriation and inconvertibility insurance covers nationalization of property and conversion of currency. These political risks are encountered more often by businesses operating overseas.

Key Terms Reviewed

Review each of the following terms. For any that you do not know or are unsure of, look up the definitions and see how they were used in the chapter.

speculative risk	marine insurance
pure risk	ocean marine insurance
risk management	inland marine insurance
insurance	aviation insurance
premium	directors' and officers' liability insurance
deductible	
actuaries	no-fault insurance
Old Age, Survivors, Disability, and Health Insurance (OASDHI)	term life insurance
	whole life insurance
	cash value
Medicare	limited-pay life insurance
unemployment insurance	endowment life insurance
workers' compensation insurance	universal life insurance
stock insurance company	owner or executive insurance
mutual insurance company	kidnap, ransom, and extortion insurance
fidelity bond	
surety bond	expropriation and inconvertibility insurance
business interruption insurance	

Review Questions

1. Identify each of the following as a pure risk or a speculative risk, and explain why you made each choice.
   a. An investor's risk that the price of stock might fall
   b. The risk to a company that someone might kidnap an employee and demand that the company pay ransom
   c. The risk of a retailer's security guard detaining a suspected shoplifter who turns out to be innocent of any wrongdoing
2. What approaches are available for managing each of the risks in Question 1? Be as specific as you can.

3. Why might a company avoid a risk rather than buying insurance to cover it?

4. Which of the following are insurable interests? Explain.
   a. A manufacturing firm's interest in its machinery
   b. The plant manager's interest in the machinery
   c. The plant manager's interest in his job
   d. The manufacturing firm's interest in the plant manager's life

5. If State Farm Mutual Automobile Insurance Company makes a profit this year, what can it do with the profits?

6. What are the differences among fidelity bonds, surety bonds, and crime insurance?

7. Pat Blount buys an auto insurance policy that includes comprehensive and collision insurance, each with a $100 deductible. The liability coverage is described as 100/300/25. What risks has Pat shifted? What risks has Pat retained?

8. If a store is fully covered by a fire insurance policy, why would it also want business interruption insurance?

9. How can an appliance maker protect itself from lawsuits concerning its products? How can a law firm protect itself against lawsuits over poor advice?

10. If you were to buy insurance today, which of the types described in the chapter do you think you would select? Why?

11. How can international businesses protect themselves against the special risks of doing business overseas?

Applied Exercises

1. Talk to the risk manager or someone who handles insurance in a local firm that self-insures some of its risks. (If you have trouble finding such a firm, talk to a representative of a local insurance agency and ask that person for some local companies that use this approach to handling risk.) Discuss with the risk manager or insurance person why the company self-insures and report your findings to the rest of the class.

2. If your location has a stock insurance company and/or a mutual insurance company, ask a representative to tell you about how they differ and how they are the same. Does there seem to be a good business reason for this difference? Write a report on your findings.

3. Talk to managers at two local businesses of any type and find out the types of property and liability insurance coverage that each carries. How is this coverage similar between the two? How does it differ? What accounts for the differences?

4. Arrange to meet with an insurance agent. Tell him or her you have an assignment to find out what advantages universal life has over whole life. What new types of insurance does his or her company offer or plan to offer? Write a short report on your findings.

Your Business IQ: Answers

1. False. Buying insurance is the most common way businesses *shift* risks. The risks still exist, but the businesses are paying insurance companies to assume them.
2. False. An individual may buy insurance on another person's life without telling that person, but only if the buyer has an insurable interest — that is, if the buyer will suffer an economic loss if the insured person dies. Those with insurable interests in a person's life include dependents and employers.
3. False. Employees and the self-employed pay a social security tax, but the 1988 rate was 15.02 percent of income for employees, and 13.02 for the self-employed. However, employers paid half the contribution of employees (that is, employers and employees each contributed 7.51 percent).
4. True. Fire insurance covers only property damage. To shift the risk of losing revenues after a fire, companies must buy business interruption insurance.
5. True. These are the major differences. Term insurance provides coverage for a death benefit during a stated number of years at a relatively low premium. Whole life combines a death benefit with savings at a relatively high premium.

Big Risks at Acmat Corporation

Case

After a career as a jazz pianist, Henry Nozko founded Acmat Corporation (short for "acoustical materials") in 1950. The business originally specialized in soundproofing rooms for radio stations, restaurants, and corporate boardrooms. The most popular acoustical material was asbestos spray, because it worked well and looked attractive. In a few years, Acmat became the leading acoustical contractor in New England.

Years later, however, scientists discovered that asbestos is a potential cause of cancer. In 1970, Nozko switched to using other materials, and three years later, the EPA banned asbestos. In 1976, Acmat began offering asbestos-removal services. Seven years later, half of Acmat's sales were for asbestos removal, a business that proved highly profitable.

Unfortunately for Acmat, some large liability verdicts were scaring insurance companies away from covering asbestos liability. In the fall of 1984, Acmat received a call from an agent of its insurer, CIGNA. According to Nozko, the agent said, " 'Suppose you're doing the Pan Am building,' which we were, 'and suppose one of your people goes mad and bursts all the windows and you infect all of New York.' " Nozko told the agent that smashed windows and flying asbestos were an unlikely scenario, and he reminded the agent that CIGNA had a $1 million limit on its liability coverage. Nevertheless, CIGNA canceled the liability insurance. Eventually, Acmat's other insurance policies were canceled. Clients canceled contracts because they didn't want to do business with an uninsured firm. Acmat's earnings plunged from a $1.1 million profit to a $4.3 million loss in one year.

Nozko resisted advice that he file for bankruptcy. Instead, he borrowed $10 million to keep the company alive. Then he went looking for insurance. On his 80th try, he found someone to insure him — American Empire Surplus Lines, which held a near-monopoly in selling liability coverage to asbestos abatement firms. Acmat bought a policy, paying $2.8 million, compared to $480,000 two years earlier. By charging and receiving these sky-high premiums, the value of American Empire had grown from $2 million to $124 million in less than a decade.

American Empire's success gave Nozko an idea. After researching the industry and finding a partner, he started an insurance company of his own. The new company — United Coastal Insurance — specializes in writing asbestos liability policies. United Coastal writes only "claims made" policies, which pay only for claims made during the policy period. "As it's turned out," Nozko says, "United Coastal is a money machine." Much of that money is going back to Acmat.

Case Questions

1. When Acmat specialized in soundproofing rooms, what risks did the company have to manage? How could it do so?
2. When Acmat began offering asbestos-removal services, did its risks change? What about its needs for risk management? Explain.
3. When CIGNA canceled Acmat's insurance, how did Acmat subsequently manage its risks? What do you think of Acmat's actions?

You Be the Adviser: Reviewing the Plan

In the past, managers of the Wolfson Company gave a very superficial, informal annual review of its insurance coverage and decided what changes were needed. Now, however, insurance costs and potential liabilities have reached the point where the company has appointed a full-time risk manager. Chuck Stevens, who had previously worked in employee benefits, was given the job. Chuck does not yet know a lot about insurance, but whatever recommendations he makes to the insurance company that handles the firm's business, as well as any recommendations they make to Chuck, must be submitted to the board of directors for final approval.

The insurance company representative has made a number of recommendations to Chuck, who intends to pass them on to the board for review. The recommendations fall into two major categories:

1. The company owns a large warehouse in which chemicals are stored. The warehouse has a value of $20 million and is insured for 80 percent of its value. The insurance firm has recommended that fire coverage be extended to the full $20 million, because a fire near these highly flammable chemicals would undoubtedly burn the entire structure to the ground.
2. The firm intends to start manufacturing a product that will be distributed by a large pharmaceutical marketing firm. The insurance company feels that Wolfson should purchase product liability insurance to protect itself from any problems arising from the potential side effects of the product.

Before passing these recommendations on to the board, Chuck wants to evaluate them. He would like to develop basic knowledge in the subject and determine whether he agrees or disagrees with each recommendation. He is also concerned that these recommendations come from a source that would profit from selling the company more insurance.

Your Advice

1. If you were advising Chuck, would you agree that the fire insurance policy should be extended to cover 100 percent of losses? How can Chuck decide which level of coverage is wisest?
2. Should the firm buy product liability insurance? Why or why not? Besides buying insurance, how can the Wolfson Company manage its product liability risk?

Career Opportunities

The financial industry offers a variety of strong career opportunities. These include positions in banks, stockbrokerages, and insurance companies. This description focuses on four especially promising careers.

Bank Managers

Banks have relatively more vice presidents than any other type of organization. The reason is that bank customers want to be talking to someone important when they discuss their money. So if your goal in life is to be a vice president, your best chance would be to work for a bank.

Bank managers coordinate the activities of the financial institution's departments. They oversee programs to control and minimize the risks and losses that may arise from financial transactions. Loan officers review applications, check credit ratings, make decisions, and monitor payments. Managers of credit card operations establish criteria for granting credit. Reserve officers review financial statements and direct the purchase and sale of bonds and other securities to maintain the legally required ratio of assets to liabilities. Bank officers make decisions within a framework of existing laws and regulations and carry out policies set by the board of directors. They also advise individuals and businesses and participate in community projects.

Approximately 500,000 people hold positions as bank managers in the United States. Banks fill most of these positions by promoting skilled in-house personnel such as credit analysts or outstanding bank clerks or tellers who have demonstrated the potential for increased responsibilities. Bank management positions are generally filled by college graduates with majors in finance. Recently, however, other business majors such as marketing and management are becoming increasingly accepted.

The job outlook for bank managers and officers is expected to increase faster than the average for all occupations through the mid-1990s. Starting with a bachelor's degree, an individual can expect to earn in the range of $15,000 to $25,000, depending on his or her job experience and the region of the country. Typically, however, banking positions, except at top-management levels, pay relatively less than management jobs in other industries.

Securities Salespeople and Stockbrokers

Securities salespeople and stockbrokers buy and sell stocks and bonds for their clients. In their capacity as a salesperson and adviser, they discuss investment strategies and financial planning and learn the types of stocks and bonds that their clients would be interested in purchasing. Working within these guidelines, they read market reports and make recommendations. Many brokers also offer advice on the purchase of mutual funds, annuities, tax shelters, and other specialized investments.

At the present time, there are approximately 100,000 securities salespeople in the United States. A college degree is not absolutely required, but many securities salespeople have an undergraduate degree in business with a major in finance. Before working with clients, all securities salespeople must pass a series of examinations given by the Securities and Exchange Commission and by the state where they are employed. They also receive short courses and training from their employer.

New hires can expect to make $20,000 to $50,000 in their first year, depending on their commissions. As their list of clients increases and they become more experienced in the business, annual income can rise very high.

Career Opportunities (continued)

Actuaries

Actuaries normally work for the home office of an insurance company assembling and analyzing statistics to calculate the probabilities of death, sickness, injury, disability, property loss, and other hazards. To perform their duties effectively, actuaries keep informed about general economic and social trends, as well as legislative, health, and other developments that may affect insurance practices. Most actuaries specialize in either life and health insurance or property and liability insurance. In addition, a growing number are beginning to specialize in pension plans.

About 12,000 people are actuaries in the United States. The employment outlook for actuaries is expected to grow much faster than the average for all occupations through the mid-1990s. This position requires a bachelor's degree with considerable work in mathematics and statistics or a degree in actuarial science. Actuaries also must pass a series of difficult examinations.

New college graduates entering the field without having passed any actuarial exams can expect to earn in the range of $21,000 to $24,000. Those who have passed the first exam can expect to make about $3,000 more, and those who have passed the second exam can expect an additional $3,000. Top actuarial executives today earn in the range of $60,000 to $70,000 annually. Recent surveys indicate that this is the "hottest" job in the country, and salaries are soaring.

Insurance Salespeople

Insurance salespeople sell policies that provide individuals and businesses with financial protection against loss. They plan for the financial security and risk management of individuals, families, and businesses; advise about insurance protection for auto, home, business, or other property; prepare reports and maintain records; and help policyholders obtain settlement of their insurance claims. Most insurance salespeople specialize in a particular type of insurance: some sell life, property-liability, or health insurance; others sell auto insurance; still others offer comprehensive financial planning services.

Today there are approximately 400,000 insurance salespeople in the United States. Employment in insurance sales is expected to grow more slowly than the average for all occupations through the mid-1990s. Although many employers prefer college graduates, most will also hire people with only some college work, people with potential or proven sales ability, and people who have been successful in other types of work. For example, school teachers often are hired for insurance sales. Starting salaries for new insurance salespeople depend greatly on commissions but generally are around $16,000 annually. However, those who have five to ten years of experience and good sales skills can make considerably more — possibly even more than industry executives.

THE CHANGING LEGAL AND INTERNATIONAL ENVIRONMENT OF BUSINESS

Business operates in many different environments. The legal and international arenas are two of the most important, and they have one thing in common: constant change. Change is also occurring in international business. A decade ago, America was a big supplier of products and funds. Today, while the nation remains an enormous supplier, it is an even bigger buyer and borrower. Part VII examines the legal and international environments.

Chapter 21 examines business-government relations and laws affecting business. It discusses how government regulates business through legislation and how it collects funds and adjusts policy through taxation. Businesses, in turn, influence government policy through lobbying efforts and appeals to voters. A variety of laws affect business. This chapter describes laws pertaining to contracts, sales, negotiable instruments, property, patents, trademarks, copyrights, agency relationships, torts, and bankruptcy.

Chapter 22 focuses on international business. It describes how international trade influences American business and ways to measure international trade. It identifies the advantages and disadvantages managers weigh in considering whether to enter international markets, as well as special problems and opportunities. The chapter notes that trading internationally also requires paying attention to differences in language, customs, and culture. When firms decide to go international, they have a choice of arrangements; the basic options are described in the last part of the chapter.

When you have finished studying Part VII you should understand the basics of business-government relations. You should be acquainted with the major business laws and understand the reasons for government regulation of business. You also should know the challenges and benefits of doing international business, the ways that business people prepare themselves to enter the global marketplace, and the approaches they take in establishing an international operation. Upon completion of the book, you should have a broad understanding of modern business. This knowledge will be a foundation for entering the real world of business and for studying the specialized areas of business.

Source: Courtesy of Ford Motor Company.

C H A P T E R 21

Business-Government Relations

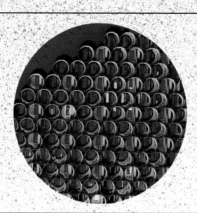

LEARNING OBJECTIVES

- Describe the major laws that regulate business and ensure competition.
- Identify the major types of federal, state, and local taxes.
- Present the major dimensions of contract and sales law.

- Discuss negotiable instruments and property law.
- Explain the responsibilities under agency and tort law.
- Relate the different ways of handling bankruptcy.

Your Business IQ

How much do you already know about business-government relations? Test your business IQ by labeling each statement *true* or *false*. Answers and explanations are at the end of the chapter.

1. According to federal law, companies planning to merge must notify the Federal Trade Commission (FTC) in advance.
2. Corporate income taxes contribute to about 35 percent of federal revenues, while individual income taxes contribute to about 10 percent.
3. Car dealers are often reluctant to sell to persons under 18 unless their parents participate in the contract, because young buyers are more likely to have an accident.
4. When you endorse a check made out to you, you can specify how the check may be used.
5. If a firm makes a product that is defective but can prove that it went out of its way to ensure that it was not defective, the courts will refuse to allow an injured party to pursue a lawsuit.

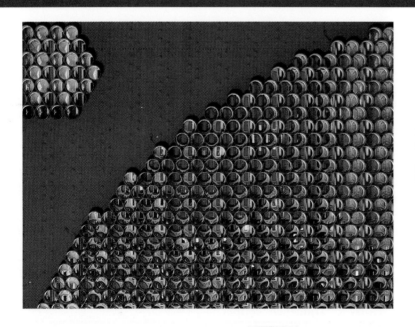

Government agencies are a major customer of many businesses. For example, Raytheon Company is making this radar for the Patriot air defense system.

Source: Courtesy of Raytheon Company.

Regulation is so much a part of some industries that some companies need a staff of experts to handle it. The pharmaceutical industry is a case in point. At Smith Kline & French Laboratories, project and product teams for new drugs rely on support from the company's regulatory operations department. Staff in this department sets policies for working with regulatory agencies around the world, develops strategies for obtaining approval of new drugs, ensures compliance with regulations, and monitors the safety of products on the market. The team shown here is preparing a submission for approval of a new drug.

Source: Courtesy of SmithKline Beckman Corporation.

Sherman Antitrust Act A federal law that prohibits all agreements created for the purpose of restraining trade in interstate commerce.

Looking Back and Ahead

In the United States, the consumption of foreign oil relative to that of domestic oil has recently been growing, and the efforts of the federal government to reverse this trend illustrate some of the ways that government actions influence business. The government has considered improving the relative economic position of domestic oil producers by taxing oil from overseas, which would force up its price, or by repealing a tax on domestic oil companies (called the windfall profits tax). The government has also considered giving companies increased rights to drill on federal property and subsidizing development of alternative energy sources. Another possibility is reducing regulation of the natural gas industry, which would probably lead to higher prices for natural gas, making oil more competitive. The government currently sets standards for the fuel efficiency of appliances, which could ultimately reduce demand for foreign oil. While the government is considering these actions, various business groups are trying to influence the government by lobbying for the changes they deem most advantageous.[1]

The relationship between business and government has been noted in connection with many of the topics discussed in preceding chapters. This chapter takes a closer look at the relationship. It begins by focusing on government regulation of business. Then it describes the government's power of taxation, in particular the kinds of taxes the government levies. The last half of the chapter is concerned with business law, first identifying the sources of law and then examining specific categories of law. These categories have to do with contracts, sales, negotiable instruments, property, agency relationships, torts, and bankruptcy.

Government Regulation

One of the most direct ways the government affects business is through regulations. Some legislation is designed to promote competition; other laws regulate particular industries.

Regulation to Promote Competition

Capitalism assumes that consumers benefit when businesses must compete for their money. To keep competition strong, Congress has passed a number of laws that prohibit businesses from restraining trade and engaging in unfair practices. Table 21.1 summarizes the major laws.

Sherman Antitrust Act One of the earliest and most famous of these laws is the **Sherman Antitrust Act** of 1890, which outlaws all agreements created for the purpose of restraining trade in interstate commerce. The act was initially used to break up giant monopolies of the late 1800s and early 1900s, which were preventing free competition. Probably the most famous case was that of the Standard Oil trust of John D. Rockefeller, Sr. At the time, Standard Oil held 90 percent of the nation's oil-refining capacity. The government used the Sherman Act to break up the trust.

Today, the Justice Department still uses this act to prevent what it believes is monopolistic power. For example, the government has recently used this act to prevent PepsiCo from taking over 7-Up, and to stymie Coca-Cola's efforts to acquire Dr Pepper.

Clayton Act To close loopholes in the Sherman Act, Congress amended it by passing the Clayton Act in 1914. The **Clayton Act** prohibits tying agreements, interlocking directorates, and certain anticompetitive stock acquisitions. In a tying agreement, sellers require customers to purchase unwanted merchandise in order to obtain what they want to buy. For example, a manufacturer of men's suits might require retailers to buy shirts and ties in order to get the suits, or a manufacturer of equipment might require that the buyer also purchase all of the materials and supplies needed to run the equipment. Recently, some computer manufacturers ran afoul of this law by requiring purchasers of their computer hardware to buy software and other related products. The government successfully argued in court that this constituted a violation of the Clayton Act.

An **interlocking directorate** is an arrangement in which a majority of the board of directors of two or more competing corporations with assets in excess of $1 million are the same people. Such an arrangement could enable the board members to establish company policies that would lessen competition between the companies. For example, they could raise prices at the same time. Today, many people serve on the boards of two or more corporations, but these directors must take care to avoid serving on the boards of competitors.

Federal Trade Commission Act In 1914, Congress passed the **Federal Trade Commission Act,** which prohibits unfair trade practices and established the Federal Trade Commission (FTC). The unfair trade practices mainly involve unfair competitive practices. The FTC's job is to help enforce the Clayton Act and to issue cease-and-desist orders when it finds a violation of antitrust laws. Over the years, the FTC has become known for "policing the business world."

Today, the commission surveys business practices, watches for false or misleading advertising, and investigates claims made by manufacturers.

Clayton Act A federal law that prohibits tying agreements, interlocking directorates, and certain anticompetitive stock acquisitions.

Interlocking directorate An arrangement in which a majority of the board of directors of two or more competing corporations with assets in excess of $1 million are the same people.

Federal Trade Commission Act A federal law that prohibits unfair trade practices and established the Federal Trade Commission (FTC).

Year	Federal Law	Consequences
1890	Sherman Antitrust Act	Outlaws all agreements created for the purpose of restraining trade in interstate commerce
1914	Clayton Act	Outlaws tying agreements, interlocking directorates, and certain anticompetitive stock acquisitions
1914	Federal Trade Commission Act	Outlaws unfair trade practices and established the Federal Trade Commission
1936	Robinson-Patman Act	Prohibits unfair pricing practices
1950	Celler-Kefauver Antimerger Act	Extended the prohibition of anticompetitive stock acquisitions of the Clayton Act to include mergers and major asset purchases that decrease competition in an industry
1974	Antitrust Procedures and Penalties Act	Increases fines and legal penalties for violation of the Sherman Act
1976	Antitrust Improvements Act	Requires companies planning to merge to notify the FTC in advance; allows injured parties to file lawsuits

T A B L E 21.1

Major Procompetition Legislation

Because of the recent public interest in the impact that a high blood cholesterol level may have on heart problems, food companies are trying to capitalize on this concern in their packaging and labeling. As Table 21.2 shows, products that are portrayed as being healthful and cholesterol-free may in fact contain saturated fat and palm and coconut oils, which are known to contribute to high levels of cholesterol. The agency may prosecute companies for making inaccurate or misleading claims. In other examples, the FTC has asked some aspirin manufacturers to support their claims regarding the potency of their product, has asked tire manufacturers to demonstrate the performance of their tires, and has required that some food manufacturers stop claiming their products provide special dietary benefits.

Robinson-Patman Act A federal law designed to eliminate unfair price competition.

Robinson-Patman Act Passed in 1936, the **Robinson-Patman Act** is designed to eliminate unfair price competition. The act prohibits a number of specific pricing practices. One is selling the same product at different prices unless the price differential is based on cost or the need to meet competition. For example, if a manufacturer receives an order from one wholesaler for 1,000 electrical components and a second order from a different wholesaler for 100 electrical components, the manufacturer may charge less per unit for the larger order, because manufacturing, packaging, and shipping big orders cost less per unit. The company may pass on the savings in the form of lower prices. However, if two wholesalers purchase the same number of units, the manufacturer may not charge one more than the other in an effort to drive one out of business or to provide the other with an unfair competitive advantage.

Other treatment must also be even-handed. The Robinson-Patman Act also forbids sellers from discriminating against customers in interstate commerce by selling basically identical goods but at different prices. Advertising allowances must also be given to all buyers on a proportionately equal basis. If a company that buys $100,000 of merchandise receives $1,000 toward its local advertising of the products, a firm that buys $50,000 of merchandise is entitled to $500 for local advertising.

T A B L E   21.2

Cholesterol Confusion

Common Food Labels	Potential Contribution to High Cholesterol Levels
"Cholesterol-free"	Many consumers believe this phrase, used on products ranging from cooking oils to prepared foods, means they are also free of saturated fat. Not so: they may contain palm or coconut oil.
"Health foods"	Not all "health foods" are good for the heart. About 10 percent of a bran muffin's calories come from saturated fat. Nature Valley Granola has 30 times more saturated fat than Sugar Smacks.
Nondairy creamer	Think dairy products are dangerous? Consider that powdered "coffee whitener," rich in coconut or palm oil, may contain twice as much saturated fat per tablespoon as half-and-half.
Two percent milk	Almost the same as skim? Not really: whole milk is only 3.3 percent fat to begin with. Some critics question the FDA law that allows 2 percent milk to be labeled "low fat." Skim milk has no fat.

The Robinson-Patman Act is regarded as fairly controversial because of the broad powers it gives to the FTC. For example, many economists believe that the act does more to discourage price competition than to eliminate monopolies. This is because the act does not focus enough attention on nonprice competition such as the domination of market channels, as is the case with giant goods manufacturers. In any event, the act has made business people acutely aware of the risks involved in unfair price competition.

Celler-Kefauver Antimerger Act To prohibit anticompetitive mergers, Congress passed the **Celler-Kefauver Antimerger Act** in 1950. This law broadened the scope of the Clayton Act, which had limited itself to forbidding companies to acquire the stock of competitive firms for the purpose of preventing competition. The Celler-Kefauver Act extended the prohibition to include mergers and major asset purchases that decrease competition in an industry. It also gave the FTC authority to approve mergers before they take place.

Celler-Kefauver Antimerger Act A federal law that prohibits mergers and major asset purchases that decrease competition in an industry.

More Recent Regulatory Acts The 1970s saw the passage of additional antitrust legislation. One was the **Antitrust Procedures and Penalties Act** of 1974, which increased the fines and penalties imposed for violation of the Sherman Act. Under the terms of this law, violation of the Sherman Act could result in a fine up to $100,000 for an individual and $10 million for a corporation. Such a violation was also made a felony and now carries a possible jail sentence of up to three years.

In 1976, Congress passed the **Antitrust Improvements Act,** which requires companies planning to merge to notify the FTC in advance and allows injured parties to file lawsuits. This act resulted in a host of suits designed to prevent mergers of firms in unrelated industries, for example, traditional manufacturing firms and high-tech companies, chemical firms and movie studios, and fast-food retailers and transportation companies.

Antitrust Procedures and Penalties Act A federal law that increased fines and penalties imposed for violation of the Sherman Antitrust Act.

Antitrust Improvements Act A federal law that requires companies planning to merge to notify the FTC in advance and allows injured parties to file lawsuits.

Regulation of Limited-Entry Industries

At certain times in history, the government has been concerned that too many businesses are unable or unwilling to look after the interests of workers and consumers. Congress has responded by passing laws encouraging companies to make safe products in safe workplaces and to provide accurate product information to consumers. In addition, the government has paid special attention to industries into which there has been limited entry because of size and resource commitments (for example, utilities and communications industries).

Electric and Gas Utilities Most electric and gas utilities could be called pure or natural monopolies. A pure monopoly is a business that provides services that are impractical to duplicate. For example, Consolidated Edison of New York serves the greater New York metropolitan area; Interstate Power Company supples power to parts of Iowa, Illinois, Wisconsin, and Minnesota; and Florida Power & Light serves the greater Miami area. It is thought cheaper for one large company to provide the energy than to have two power companies serving these areas, since they would unnecessarily duplicate costly power generation and distribution systems and the resulting higher costs would be passed on to the consumers.

However, the existence of pure monopolies eliminates the advantages of competition. For example, the utilities may lack an incentive to keep their rates low. Many people believe that a state or local government agency should monitor the firm and regulate how much it may charge — and this is exactly what happens throughout the country. Besides state and local public utility commissions, the federal government, through the Department of Energy, also oversees utility operations in areas such as preventing potentially catastrophic accidents like the one at the Three Mile Island nuclear power plant in Pennsylvania.

Communications Broadcasting is an example of limited entry into the communications industry, because the number of radio and television stations is physically limited. Radio and TV stations are therefore regulated by the Federal Communications Commission (FCC), which Congress originally created to license radio stations and set rates. Today, the FCC also licenses and regulates cable TV networks and ham radio operators.

Deregulation of Industry

Regulation in the United States has tended to occur in waves. For example, the initial procompetition laws were passed around the turn of the century, and many of the major consumer protection laws were passed during the 1930s and 1970s. During the 1980s, the government turned from regulation to deregulation of such businesses as telephone services, the airlines, and banking, as we have discussed in earlier chapters.

The debate over the merits of regulation versus deregulation will certainly continue. Some observers contend that many governmental rules and regulations continue to stifle business creativity and growth without providing substantive benefits to the general public. Others are concerned that deregulation has resulted in safety and financial risks and higher consumer prices. In some cases, the competition has become so intense, such as in the telephone industry, that rules are broken. For example, hoping to increase revenues or gain tactical advantage, some Bell salespeople were telling customers that optional services were required.[2] As a result, in the communications industry as well as in airlines and banking, the pendulum may swing back toward more regulation in the future.

Checkpoint

1. What are two major laws that ensure competition?
2. Why are utilities subject to greater regulation than most businesses?

Taxation

Besides making and enforcing regulations, government affects business in a fundamental way by collecting money in the form of taxes. Corporations pay taxes themselves, and they withhold taxes from the pay-

One business that has benefited from deregulation is USAir. Following passage of the Airline Deregulation Act of 1978, the company was able to expand from the Northeast to Texas, Florida, and eventually California. To reflect its national service, the company in 1979 changed its name from Allegheny Airlines to USAir. In 1987, USAir's parent company, USAir Group acquired California-based Pacific Southwest Airlines (PSA) and North Carolina-based Piedmont Aviation.

Source: © 1986 Mike Mitchell for U.S. Air Group, Incorporated. All rights reserved.

checks of employees and remit these monies to the government. In 1986, some major tax law changes began to go into effect, and because of the increasing concern over our huge federal debt, further changes are sure to be coming in the years ahead. Although the rates and impact will be changing,[3] the types of taxes discussed in the following sections will remain the same.

Federal Taxes

The federal government spends billions each year to pay its employees, operate the military, support social security and other programs, pay interest on its debts, and cover a variety of other expenses. While the government currently borrows 18 cents out of every dollar it spends, over half of its income comes from taxes. Figure 21.1 shows the sources and uses of federal funds.

Income Taxes The largest source of federal revenue is taxes on the income of individuals and corporations. As shown in Figure 21.2, top tax rates for each group have varied throughout this century. Top individual rates have varied from less than 10 percent in the early part of this century to more than 90 percent in the mid-1940s to mid-1950s. Top corporate rates have been less than top individual rates, ranging from under 10 percent to slightly over 50 percent.

Congress periodically adjusts tax rates and regulations, not only to alter the amount of revenues, but to set policy as well. For example, the government has a policy of encouraging home ownership, which it carries out by currently allowing individuals to deduct from their taxable income the interest they pay on their mortgage. In the past, the government has encouraged businesses to invest in equipment by allowing them to deduct from their taxes a percentage of the cost of new equipment. The government has also encouraged investment by allowing investors to pay a lower rate on gains from long-term investments than they pay on other income. Congress ended these last two incentives with its 1986 revision of the tax law, in order to lower tax rates without reducing total tax receipts.

FIGURE 21.1

The Federal Budget Dollar

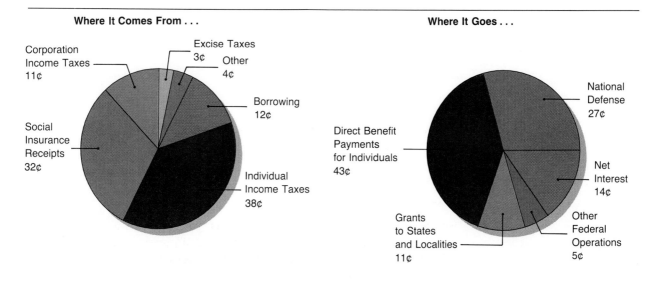

646

Progressive tax A tax that charges lower rates to taxpayers with lower incomes.

Excise tax A levy designed to limit the purchase of goods or make the users of certain services help pay for them.

Customs duties Taxes levied on imported goods.

As shown in Figure 21.1, the largest source of federal revenue is individual income taxes. These revenues come not only from employees, but also from sole proprietorships and partnerships, which pass their income to the owners for taxation at individual rates. In addition, certain small corporations may choose to be taxed as individuals, in which case, they are called S corporations (see Chapter 5). Other corporations pay corporate rates, which are scheduled to run up to 34 percent under present tax laws. Whether taxed at individual or corporate rates, all corporations file returns.

The federal income tax on individuals is sometimes referred to as a **progressive tax.** This means that people with low incomes pay tax at a lower rate than people with high incomes. The tax is progressive because it places a greater burden on those presumed to be in a better position to shoulder it. The 1986 tax revisions established two tax brackets, one at 15 percent and one at 28 percent, with a 5 percent surcharge for high-income taxpayers.

Excise Taxes The federal government also taxes certain purchases, using an excise tax. An **excise tax** is a levy designed to limit the purchase of goods or to make the users of certain services help pay for them. The excise tax on gasoline does both. It is designed to discourage excessive consumption and to pay for highway and road construction. In contrast, revenues from the excise tax on cigarettes are earmarked for general spending, not specifically for health research and medical care of smokers. Besides generating revenue, the tax provides an incentive to smoke less.

Customs Duties In the last century, the major source of federal revenue was **customs duties,** taxes levied on imported goods. The importer pays the government a percentage of the value of the goods. Besides generating revenue, duties give a price advantage to American producers.

FIGURE 21.2

Top Federal Income Tax Rates

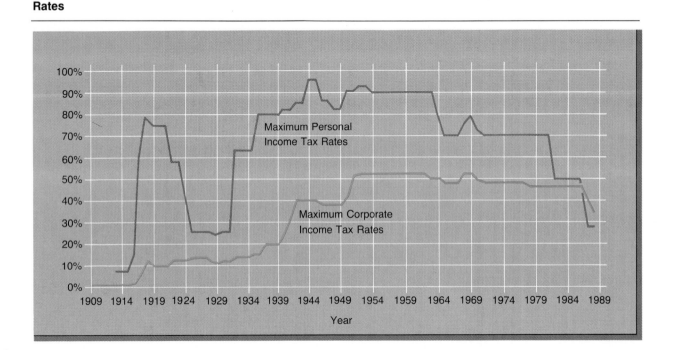

Currently, as evidenced by the huge U.S. trade deficit (imports are greater than exports), duties seem to have little impact on the desire of foreign companies to export their goods and on the desire of Americans to buy them.

State and Local Taxes

State and local governments also use taxes as a source of revenue. Some states and local governments have an income tax. However, the major source of revenue for most state governments is sales taxes, and the major source of revenue for local governments is property taxes.

Income Taxes Forty-one states currently assess an income tax. So do many local governments, especially large cities. Often, the state or local income tax is a fixed percentage of income, rather than a progressive tax. In calculating their income for federal income tax, taxpayers may deduct the state and local income taxes they paid for the year.

Sales Taxes Most states and some cities assess sales taxes. A **sales tax** is a levy on specified purchases. The taxing body decides what products the sales tax applies to. For example, in the state of Florida, the sales tax on retail goods is 6 percent. This means that a shirt that sells for $20 will cost the consumer $21.20. The retailer collects these taxes and forwards them to the appropriate state agency.

Some people object to sales taxes because they are a regressive tax. A **regressive tax** is one that hits low-income people harder than high-income people. Anyone who buys a $20 shirt in Florida must pay a $1.20 sales tax, but a rich person can more easily afford this tax. However, a sales tax is one of the easiest ways to raise money. With the federal government reducing the funds it sends to the states, many states will undoubtedly continue to assess and even increase sales taxes.

Often people are less aware of the effect of the sales tax on their pocketbook than they are of the impact of income taxes, because they pay sales tax a little at a time but see their total income tax when they file each spring. Also, the 1986 tax law ended the policy of being able to deduct sales taxes from taxable federal income, which will in effect increase the bite that sales taxes take out of gross income.

Property Taxes Local governments turn to property taxes for revenue. A **property tax** is a levy based on the assessed value of a piece of real estate. A tax assessor estimates the value of the property, and the tax is a proportion of that amount. If a house is assessed at $150,000 and the tax levy is $2.50 per $100, then the owner must pay $3,750 in property taxes ($150,000 ÷ $100 = 1,500; $1,500 × $2.50 = $3,750). The same approach is used in taxing office buildings, hotels, condominiums, and apartment buildings. Property taxes are deductible from income in the calculation of federal income tax.

A property tax is an example of a **proportional tax,** a tax in which the rate remains the same regardless of the base. If the house in the example above were to double in value over the next five years, the yearly tax bill would grow to $7,500.

Sales tax A levy on specified purchases.

Regressive tax A tax that hits low-income persons harder than high-income persons.

Property tax A levy based on the assessed value of a piece of real estate.

Proportional tax A tax in which the rate remains the same regardless of the base.

1. What are three federal taxes?
2. What are the major sources of revenue for state and local governments?

Business Law

Every day businesses and their employees undertake activities governed by laws. Most business people are not, and need not be, lawyers, but they do need a fundamental understanding of business law. As suggested in "Entrepreneurs Close-Up: Elizabeth J. Gulden," many business people also find it helpful to have an attorney nearby.

Sources of Law

In the United States, law arises from federal and state constitutions, federal and state statutes, administrative regulations, and court precedent. The U.S. Constitution is the highest law in the land; all other laws must be consistent with it. Each state has its own constitution, and the laws of the state are subject to its constitution.

Because legal considerations affect so many aspects of business, companies often hire experts in the law. This paralegal, on the staff of Ohio Bell, an Ameritech Company, is gathering data in the law library of the Cuyahoga County Courthouse. The legal department at Ohio Bell handles about 500 cases a year. Many of the cases are defenses against claims of personal injury or damage to property.

Source: Courtesy of Ohio Bell, an Ameritech Company.

The Congress of the United States and the state legislatures have the power to enact laws consistent with the Constitution. Together these laws form **statutory law.** These statutes may grant various administrative bodies the power to enact regulations, which retain the force of law, subject to legislative revision. Statutes and administrative regulations are sometimes called written law, because they are created as written documents.

Many businesses conduct their activities across state boundaries and therefore must keep up with the statutory law of various states. To simplify this, most states have adopted uniform codes governing a variety of activities. Of particular interest to business is the **Uniform Commercial Code (UCC),** which is a set of statutes that govern the legal dealings of business. The UCC has been adopted in its entirety by all states except Louisiana, which has adopted about half of it. The UCC covers a number of important areas of business law, including sales, commercial

Statutory law Law enacted by Congress and the state legislatures.

Uniform Commercial Code (UCC) A set of statutes that govern the legal dealings of business.

ENTREPRENEURS
CLOSE-UP

Elizabeth J. Gulden

Most lawyers work for corporations, partnerships, or the government, but Elizabeth J. Gulden runs her own business. However, she did not start out that way. Her initial job was as the first woman attorney with a 15-man firm. According to Gulden, her being a woman did not prevent the others from giving her excellent training, despite what she calls "minor silliness" (incidents such as being unable to lunch with her colleagues at an all-male club and being forbidden from wearing boots in the winter, according to the company's dress code for women).

After two-and-a-half years, a senior partner and an associate from the law office left to start a smaller firm, and Gulden joined them. She helped them purchase a building and establish the practice. She also helped decide which cases to accept and experienced the responsibility of bringing in business income and sharing it rather than counting on a salary.

Eventually Gulden's two partners moved on, leaving her with the remaining clients and the building. She first doubted her ability to carry on alone, but interviews with law firms led Gulden to conclude that she couldn't go back to working for someone else. So she rented out some of her building space to other lawyers and made a go of the

business. She specializes in trials of civil cases, unlike many lawyers who spend most of their time outside the courtroom on matters such as contracts and real estate closings.

One key to Gulden's success is her willingness to share strengths with colleagues. She participates in professional legal associations, through which she has developed a network of lawyers with whom she discusses cases. For extremely difficult cases, she sometimes hires a lawyer to assist her at the trial.

Gulden believes that being responsible for her business's earnings has made her especially sensitive to the importance of taking care of clients. She has heard former clients of other attorneys complain about a lack of information and interest from their attorneys, so Gulden emphasizes listening and concern.

Besides being an attorney and business owner, Gulden is a wife and mother. According to Gulden, running her own business allows her to limit her work load so that she can devote time to her children. Gulden believes that balancing the demands of being a lawyer in a very large firm with the demands of family life can lead to "excruciating emotional torment" that to her mind is "simply not worth it."

paper, bank deposits and collections, letters of credit, and investment securities.

Courts in the United States also rely on **common law,** the precedents established by prior court decisions, going back to English law. (However, reflecting that state's French heritage, Louisiana courts follow the Napoleonic Code instead.) Common law is sometimes called unwritten law, even though court decisions are recorded, to differentiate it from the documents of statutes and regulations. Today, statutes cover most areas of law, but judges rely on common law for guidance in interpreting statutes.

Contract Law

The branch of business law that governs most transactions is contract law. A **contract** is a legally binding promise. The promise stipulates that something shall or shall not happen. For example, a sporting goods manufacturer may promise to deliver 100 football helmets in exchange for $50 each, and a university may promise to deliver a check for $5,000 in exchange for 100 helmets. The same manufacturer might promise to pay a refuse collector for its services and also promise to refrain from hiring any other refuse collector that year, no matter how much refuse needs to be removed.

Forming a Contract To form a contract, at least one of the parties must make a promise. In many cases, good business practice is to put contracts in writing to make sure that both sides exactly understand the terms and conditions of the agreement. A clear understanding at the outset can prevent lawsuits later. If a lawsuit does arise, a written contract can make the conflict easier to resolve. Moreover, the law requires that contracts for the following transactions must be in writing:

> The sale of real estate
>
> The sale of goods valued at $500 or more
>
> Acts that will be performed one year or more after the contract is made
>
> The assumption of another person's financial obligation
>
> A promise made in contemplation of marriage

Most contracts are for such routine or immediate transactions that they are unwritten. The time and effort required to draw up formal written contracts does not justify the benefits to be gained. Often the contract is oral. For example, when a company calls up a regular supplier and orders ten boxes of computer paper to be delivered later that day, the company and the supplier have entered into an oral contract. A contract may even be formed by a person's actions. If you drive into a gas station, fill up your car, and hand the attendant $15, you have entered into a sales contract without saying a word. Your action of filling up the gas tank implied a promise to pay.

Types of Contracts Depending on how the contract is formed, it may be express or implied. An **express contract** is one in which the parties make oral or written promises. Contracts involving important dealings should always be express contracts. An **implied contract** is one created

---

Common law The precedents established by prior court decisions, going back to English law.

Contract A legally binding promise.

Express contract One in which the parties make oral or written promises.

Implied contract One created by the actions of one or more parties.

by the actions of one or more parties. For example, when people eat in a restaurant, the restaurant implies a promise that the food is fit for consumption. If a diner were to become sick from food poisoning, the restaurant would be responsible. Similarly, the diners imply that they will pay for the meal.

Conditions of an Enforceable Contract While any promise may form the basis of a contract, not all promises are enforceable in court. Several conditions must be present to make a contract legally enforceable. The contract must be based on a voluntary agreement between competent parties exchanging consideration for the performance of a lawful act.

A contract requires a voluntary agreement or meeting of the minds. The parties must agree on the specific terms. For example, if a seller says, "I will sell you this shirt for $20 right now," the buyer must realize that there is a time limit. The customer cannot return a week later and legally hold the seller to the $20 price. Nor can the buyer accept by saying, "I'll give you $18." Proposing a different price is making a counteroffer. If the seller accepts the counteroffer, then an agreement exists. The parties to a contract must also enter into the agreement voluntarily. If someone is threatened into signing a contract, the courts will not uphold it.

All parties to a legal agreement must be competent to contract. Convicts, persons under the influence of alcohol, and people suffering from severe mental illness are not regarded as legally competent. Neither are minors, which is why many stores or car dealers refuse to sell expensive merchandise to minors unless their parents also participate in the agreement. The minor may be able to set aside the contract, return the merchandise, and ask for a full refund.

For a contract to be binding, consideration must be present. Consideration is someting of value given in exchange for something else. For example, a business owner might give a real estate developer a $1,000 deposit on a parcel of land in return for the seller's promise to hold the land for ten days while the business owner lines up the necessary financing. The $1,000 is consideration given in exchange for the promise not to sell the lot during the ten-day period.

To be enforceable, a contract must have a lawful purpose. An agreement in which a company promises to pay a competitor's employee to steal trade secrets is not legally binding. If the employee took the money without providing any secrets, the company could not sue to recover the money. Similarly, financial contracts that specify payment of interest at rates higher than those permitted by law are unenforceable. The courts typically require the borrower to repay the loan but not the interest. This condition of enforceability means that changes in the law may result in changes in contracts.

If the law requires that a contract be in writing, this is a necessary condition of enforceability. For example, a buyer could not enforce an oral contract to sell real estate.

Breach of Contract If one of the parties fails to perform according to the terms of the agreement, this person has caused a breach of contract. When a party breaches an enforceable contract, the other party may sue to recover damages or to obtain specific performance.

Many problems can cause a breach of contract, including financial setbacks that make it too costly to continue with the agreement, and the decision to walk away from the agreement because it is not financially rewarding. For example, during the recession of the early 1980s, some owners of shopping centers found that the costs of operating the center exceeded revenues. The owners told their banks that they would discontinue running the center and would make no further payments on their outstanding loan. The banks stepped in, sold the shopping center, and, when the proceeds did not satisfy the mortgage on the property, sued the previous owners for the remainder of the debt. The owners, in essence, just walked away from their contracts with the banks.

In this case, the banks were the **plaintiffs**—the party that brought the legal action. The **defendant** is the party against whom a legal action is brought.

Statute of Limitations In cases of breach of contract, the plaintiff is restricted by the **statute of limitations.** This is the law that specifies the time period during which a wronged person may sue. After this statutory period, the defendant is protected from legal action.

Sales Law

All businesses enter into contracts to buy or sell. Therefore business people must be familiar with **sales law,** which involves the sale of goods for cash or credit. This law is exclusively concerned with transactions involving tangible property such as machinery, materials, supplies, or equipment.

Article 2 of the Uniform Commercial Code (UCC) covers sales contracts. For example, it spells out when sales contracts need to be in writing and provides for remedies should one or more parties fail to carry out the agreement. Article 2 also gives buyers the right to accept, reject, and inspect merchandise for sale. Finally, Article 2 addresses the use of warranties. A **warranty** is a guarantee.

Warranties may be express or implied. An **express warranty** is a guarantee offered orally or in writing. Figure 21.3 shows an example. By reading the warranty, the buyer is able to determine what guarantees

Plaintiff The party that brings a legal action.

Defendant The party against whom a legal action is brought.

Statute of limitations The law that specifies the time period during which a wronged person may sue.

Sales law The branch of law that involves the sale of goods for cash or credit.

Warranty A guarantee.

Express warranty A guarantee offered orally or in writing.

FIGURE   21.3

An Express Warranty

> **FULL THREE-YEAR WARRANTY**
>
> This Kodak instant camera is warranted by Kodak to function properly for three years from the date of purchase. Kodak makes no other express warranty for this camera. This warranty gives you specific legal rights, and you may also have other rights which vary from state to state
>
> Carefully read and follow the instructions in the manual to get good results and prevent damage to your camera.
>
> If this Kodak camera does not function properly within three years after purchase, Kodak will repair it without charge. If Kodak is unable to repair it, the option of replacement or refund of the purchase price will be available. These remedies are not available if the camera is damaged by misuse or other circumstances beyond Kodak's control, or if the improper functioning of the camera is caused by failure to follow the care and operating instructions in the manual.

the seller is making. An **implied warranty** is a guarantee that automatically accompanies the sale of a product. For example, products for sale are presumed to be safe for their intended use. General Motors does not need to provide an express warranty that its new cars are safe. This guarantee is implied by the fact that the firm has offered the autos for sale. Some companies such as G. D. Searle, a large pharmaceutical firm, have gone a step further. They now offer guarantees on all of their drug products. If customers find the drug ineffective or that it has any unpleasant side effects, they need only fill out a card, attach the sales receipt, and Searle will refund the money.[4]

Negotiable Instruments

In completing sales transactions, businesses use negotiable instruments. A **negotiable instrument** is a form of business paper that can be transferred from one person to another as a substitute for money. The most common example of a negotiable instrument is a check. Negotiable instruments facilitate the transfer of funds and make it easier to consummate business deals.

The value of negotiable instruments is in their negotiability, or transferability. To be negotiable, the instrument must meet certain criteria:

The instrument must be in writing and signed by the payer.

It must contain an unconditional promise to pay a specific amount of money. An instrument that says "pay John upon delivery of my car" would not be negotiable, because the promise is conditional and the amount is not specified.

The instrument must be payable on demand or at a specific future date. A check may be cashed on or after the date entered on it.

The instrument must be payable to bearer or order. Most checks say "Pay to the order of _____," meaning that only the person named may use it. If a check says only "Pay to _____," then anyone who has it (the bearer) may receive payment.

The payee, or recipient of the payment, must be indicated with reasonable certainty.

Properly filling out a standard check form creates a negotiable instrument.

To transfer the rights to a negotiable instrument, the payee endorses it. In the case of a check, the payee typically endorses it by signing it on the back. The endorsement is often designed to transfer to the bank the right to collect on it and deposit funds in the payee's account. The type of endorsement used determines the specific rights transferred. Figure 21.4 shows the basic types of endorsement.

As shown, a blank endorsement is simply the owner's signature at the top of the reverse side of a negotiable instrument. If you lose a check with a blank endorsement, anyone who finds it can cash it. That is why a restrictive endorsement, which specifies how the instrument may be used, is safer. A special endorsement specifies the person to whom the instrument is being transferred, and a qualified endorsement sets forth conditions on the transfer of the instrument. The most common wording on a qualified endorsement is "without recourse," which means that the endorser does not accept liability for payment of the instrument. For

Implied warranty A guarantee that automatically accompanies the sale of a product.

Negotiable instrument A form of business paper that can be transferred from one person to another as a substitute for money.

example, someone who accepts an instrument with the qualified endorsement of "without recourse" agrees not to pursue the endorser if the account has insufficient funds to cover the check.

Property Law

Property law The branch of law that involves the rights and duties associated with the ownership or use of real or personal property.

Real property Land and property attached to land.

Deed A document that establishes property ownership and is transferable to other parties.

Lease A document that allows the tenant to use the owner's property for a predetermined time period in exchange for consideration.

Personal property Any property that is not real property.

Another branch of law that concerns sales is property law, which addresses ownership as well as sales. More precisely, **property law** involves the rights and duties associated with the ownership or use of real or personal property.

Real property consists of land and property attached to land. The property must be permanently attached in the sense that it would be difficult to remove or that removing it would destroy it. Examples include a house, a factory, a warehouse, and a parking lot.

The instrument that conveys ownership of real property is typically a deed. A **deed** is a document that establishes property ownership and is transferable to other parties. The owner of real property may also grant use of the property by renting it. Small and medium-sized enterprises and businesses in major metropolitan areas often find it more economical to rent than to own property. The tenant signs a **lease,** a document that allows the tenant to use the owner's property for a predetermined time period in exchange for consideration (a rental fee).

Personal property is any property that is not real property. Furniture, videocassette recorders, typewriters, and pencils are all examples of personal property. So are stock and bond certificates. Personal property may be tangible or intangible. Tangible personal property consists of physical items such as equipment and inventory. Intangible personal property is property whose ownership is represented by a document or written instrument. For example, a person with a $500 check has a valuable property but the value is contained in what the check represents ($500 in cash) rather than what the check is (a mere piece of paper).

FIGURE 21.4

Basic Forms of Endorsement

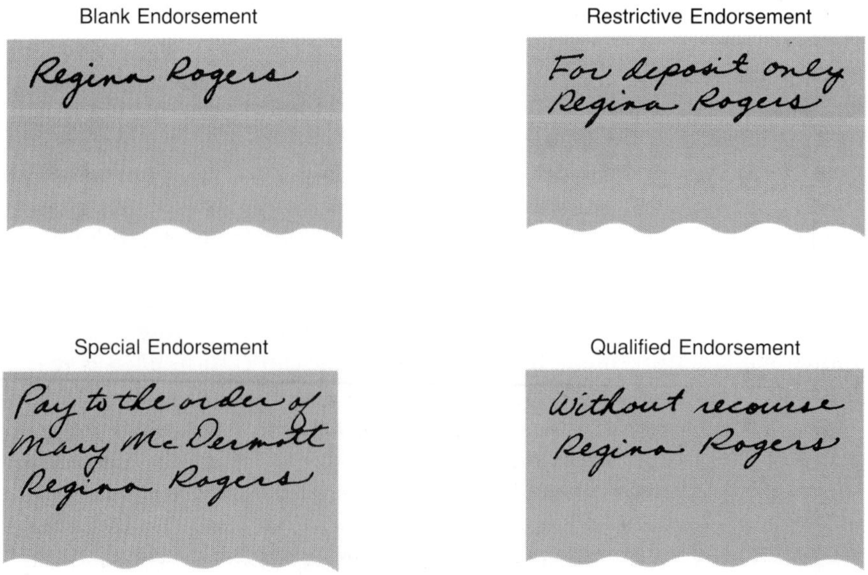

Mortgages, stock certificates, and trademarks are also examples of intangible personal property.

Understanding the difference between real and personal property is important because the laws and practices for transferring the two often differ. In addition, a business person buying or selling real estate, such as an office building, needs to know what items are real property and are therefore automatically included in the sale.

Patent, Trademark, and Copyright Law

Certain intangible property — patents, trademarks, and copyrights — provides its owner with protection from competition. To promote fair competition, a body of law protects owners' rights in these intangible assets.

Patents Developing a new product or manufacturing process often takes enormous amounts of time and money. Few businesses would bother with research if any competitor could immediately put the new idea to use. Thus an inventor with a new idea obtains a **patent,** a federal government grant of exclusive control over and use of a discovery or a new product or process. The U.S. Patent Office protects inventions for 17 years. The patent owner may manufacture the product exclusively or may sell other firms a license to use the patent.[5]

An applicant for a patent must demonstrate that the discovery is indeed new. Howard Head, famous for his invention of metal skis, later developed the now popular oversized tennis racket, the Prince. Initially, the government claimed he had not developed anything new — tennis rackets have been around for centuries. However, Head showed the patent office that the "sweet spot" (the part of the racket head used for returning a volley) on this racket was much larger than that on any conventional-sized racquet. The patent office then awarded him the legal right he sought. Within five years, the Prince oversized racket had become the best-selling tennis racket in the United States.

Trademark As you learned in Chapter 12, a **trademark** is a word or symbol used to distinguish a company's products. To protect the trademark from use or exploitation by others, the company must register it with the federal government and renew it every 20 years. In some cases, a trademark is a brand name such as Cadillac, Polaroid, or Excedrin. In other cases, it includes a logo such as McDonald's golden arches, Playboy's bunny, or Apple Computer's apple. Companies must protect their trademarks, because they will lose their exclusive right if the trademark becomes generic, describing a class of products rather than that of a particular company. For examples, see the discussion of trademarks in Chapter 12.

Copyrights The contents of creative works such as books and record albums varies because each new release is a unique endeavor requiring an investment of time and talent. A **copyright** is a legal protection of a particular work that allows its owner the exclusive right to reproduce, sell, and adapt the work. Copyrights protect literary and intellectual works such as books, magazines, plays, musicals, movies, videotapes, and computer software. The owner of the copyright registers this right by filing

This basket of fruit combined with the name *Welch's* is the trademark of Welch Foods Inc., A Cooperative. The company chose this trademark because it shows that the company's products are based on fruit, and it uses the company's widely recognized, longstanding brand name.

Source: Courtesy of Welch's.®

Patent A federal government grant of exclusive control over and use of a discovery or a new product or process for 17 years.

Trademark A word or symbol used to distinguish a company's products.

Copyright A legal protection of a particular work that allows its owner the exclusive right to reproduce, sell, and adapt the work.

with the U.S. Copyright Office. Copyrights obtained before 1977 last 75 years, while subsequent copyrights last for the lifetime of the creator plus 50 years. It is up to the owner of the copyright to protect this right, going to court if necessary.

One of the most common copyright infringements is unauthorized photocopying of materials. Ready access to photocopiers makes it easy and inexpensive to copy parts of or entire books and magazine articles. As a result of recent lawsuits, however, many companies and universities now restrict the use of photocopying in order to protect themselves from possible legal entanglements.

Some foreign countries (including Korea and China) have no copyright agreement with the United States. As a result, publishers in those countries often translate and sell American textbooks without paying the American authors or publishers a cent. Both authors of this text have experienced this problem firsthand. On a recent trip to Korea, Professor Luthans met numerous Korean professors who told him how much they and their students enjoyed using one of his textbooks, from which he had never received royalties. Professor Hodgetts was equally surprised when he recently received a copy of a book he had written that had been translated into Chinese for use at the University of Beijing. He had never received royalties from this book. Inside the front cover, the translator had autographed the book and asked whether he had written any other texts that could also be translated into Chinese!

Agency Law

Agency A legal relationship between an agent and a principal.

Agent A person authorized to act on behalf of another.

Principal A person represented by an agent.

Some dimensions of business law emphasize relationships between people rather than property rights. An important legal relationship is that of agency. An **agency** in business law is a legal relationship between an agent and a principal. An **agent** is a person authorized to act on behalf of another. A **principal** is a person represented by an agent. When an agent acts within the sphere of his or her agency responsibility, the principal is bound by those actions. Consequently, an agency relationship is one of trust. Any agent therefore owes the principal certain duties: care, obedience, accounting, and loyalty. This means that the agent must act carefully and follow instructions, must keep the principal informed about money and other matters, and must act in the best interests of the principal. The principal must compensate the agent and should be sure that the agent understands his or her duties.

Agents are important to business because they are a way to delegate authority. For example, a company may empower an attorney to enter into contracts for the firm. After hammering out an agreement, the attorney can commit the company to the contract. Businesses also authorize sales and purchasing agents to bind the company to sales contracts.

If agents exceed their authority, the enterprise can find itself embroiled in serious problems. If an agent commits an illegal or harmful act while representing the company, it may be held liable for the act. For example, even though it was unaware of the activity, the Japanese firm Toshiba found itself in trouble when an employee made unauthorized sales to the Soviet Union. Principals must also keep a careful eye on agents to make sure they are fulfilling their duties to the principal. "Social Responsibility Close-Up: Industrial Piracy" describes how some employees have violated their duty of loyalty.

Tort Law

As you can see from the discussion of agency, not every right and duty arises from a formal contract. In fact, the law recognizes that people inherently have certain rights, such as freedom from injury and the right to possess one's own property. An infringement of another person's inherent right that injures or damages that person is a **tort** (once a synonym for a wrong). For example, someone who punches or threatens another person is committing a tort. So is someone who steals or interferes with contractual relations.

Tort An infringement of a person's inherent right that injures or damages that person.

Sometimes one person injures or damages another unintentionally. For example, another student might walk off with your textbook, thinking it was his or her own. Carelessness that leads to an injury is called

---

SOCIAL RESPONSIBILITY   **CLOSE-UP**

Industrial Piracy

The contractor was adamant. "We can do the same quality job as General Electric and at a cheaper price," he told the prospective customer. To prove it, he produced blueprints of the turbine system that his company would build for the client. The materials contained a stamp that read "GE proprietary information." Armed with stolen GE blueprints, the contractor was in an excellent position to undercut GE by avoiding the costs of developing the system. This is unethical, if not illegal. In this case, the customer turned out to be a GE investigator, and the contractor found himself in big trouble. GE had won a battle in its war to close up leaks of trade secrets.

Unfortunately, companies seldom catch up with those who have stolen plans or other valuable information—at least until it is too late. Some companies are therefore losing millions of dollars of revenue every year because of industrial pirates.

IBM uses an aggressive legal staff to protect its intangible property. Since 1982, the firm has filed more than two dozen theft-of-information cases and has forced competitors to pay penalties or allow IBM to inspect their products for years. Pratt & Whitney, a large hi-tech firm, has sued employees caught selling company secrets. In one case, an employee was giving a competitor copies of Pratt & Whitney bids for military contracts. The man received a three-year prison term and a $10,000 fine. In another case, the court found a Ford Motor employee guilty of selling Ford technology to Romania. In still another instance, an employee of Intel Corporation and later the National Semiconductor Corporation was found guilty of selling secrets to Soviet-bloc countries.

Unfortunately, pirating employees are often able to avoid detection for years and, if caught, receive light sentences. For example, the employee who sold secrets to the Soviet-bloc countries received a sentence that will require him to spend no more than 16 months in jail. Because of the problems associated with finding and then prosecuting employees for industrial espionage, many firms are doing the next best thing: They are making it difficult for employees to have access to much information, and they are plugging some of the most obvious leaks with secrecy. For example, the Kellogg Company recently stopped all public tours at its Battle Creek, Michigan, plant when it learned that industrial spies had gathered valuable information during these visits.

negligence. Tort law covers both intentional tort and negligence. Therefore, the following examples fall within the bounds of tort law:

> The driver of a company truck loses control of the vehicle and strikes a pedestrian.
>
> A security officer arrests a suspected shoplifter after wrestling the alleged offender to the ground, but the person turns out to be innocent of the charge.
>
> A key financial officer absconds with $500,000 of the company's money.

An area of tort law that is becoming increasingly important to business is that of product liability, mentioned in Chapter 20 in the discussion of product liability insurance. Years ago, the courts established that a company was liable for the products it manufactured. In more recent years, this responsibility has been extended through the use of **strict product liability,** which holds that people or businesses are responsible for their acts, regardless of their intentions or degree of negligence. This means that even if a company tries very hard to make the best and safest product possible, if the product causes an injury, the company is still responsible. Consumers can now sue a manufacturer under this law if they can prove the following conditions: the product was defective; the defect caused the product to be unreasonably dangerous; and the defect was the probable cause of their injury. Companies can be found guilty of product liability even if they were not negligent or were unaware that the product was dangerous.[6]

Court cases illustrate the seriousness of product liability. In one of the most famous product liability cases to date, Ford Motor was charged with reckless homicide in the death of three young women who were burned to death in a Ford Pinto. The charge was that the company knew of the hazards of the car's design and did nothing about them. While the court found the company not guilty, the case helped show manufacturers how serious an area of concern product liability has become. Another example is the tragedy of the space shuttle *Challenger*. The families of some of the crew members have brought lawsuits against the designers and manufacturers of the shuttle's defective O-rings, which, along with mismanagement as discussed in Chapter 6, have been implicated in the explosion.

A recent survey indicated that many companies are shying away from introducing new products because they fear liability lawsuits. One legal expert noted that technology "is being frustrated to a certain extent by our tort system."[7]

Strict product liability
The principle that people or businesses are responsible for their acts, regardless of their intentions or degree of negligence.

Bankruptcy Law

Huge lawsuits, poor sales, and economic slumps are among the problems that have made some businesses unable to pay their debts and continue operating. **Bankruptcy law** specifies the legal steps for securing relief from debts. This law establishes procedures to protect an individual or business that cannot meet its financial obligations. The Bankruptcy Reform Act of 1978, as amended in 1984, spells out these procedures in three of the Act's chapters: liquidation (Chapter 7 of the Act), repayment (Chapter 13), and reorganization (Chapter 11).

Bankruptcy law The branch of law that specifies the legal steps for securing relief from debts.

Liquidation One approach to bankruptcy is **liquidation,** which is the sale of all assets to meet outstanding debts. Liquidation is often referred to as "straight" bankruptcy, because individuals or firms use it when they simply are unable to continue. A person who makes $30,000 a year and has debts of $600,000 will typically chose liquidation, because there is no way that person can hope to repay such a large debt. The best approach is to wipe the slate clean and start over again. When the court judges a person bankrupt, the person is relieved of all outstanding financial obligations.[8]

The decision to declare bankruptcy is often, but not always, voluntary. A voluntary bankruptcy is a legal proceeding brought by an individual or business that is unable to meet its financial obligations. An involuntary bankruptcy is a legal proceeding brought by creditors against an insolvent debtor. The creditors try to force the debtor to liquidate his or her assets and pay them their money. If the debtor has three or more creditors with total unsecured claims of $5,000 or more, the creditors may join together and file the petition. If the debtor has fewer than 12 creditors, one or more creditors with a claim of at least $5,000 may bring the involuntary bankruptcy action. If the debtor challenges these claims, the court will hear both sides and decide whether the bankruptcy proceeding may continue.

If the court rules that the individual or company is bankrupt, it appoints a trustee to preside over the debtor's property. The trustee administers the assets or operates the business during bankruptcy proceedings. If the assets are eventually sold, the Bankruptcy Act exempts certain property, including the following:[9]

Up to $7,500 in equity in a home and burial plot

Equity of up to $1,200 in a motor vehicle

Up to $200 each for household goods and furnishings, such as clothing, appliances, books, and so forth

Up to $500 of jewelry

Any other property up to a total of $400

Up to $750 in tools of the person's trade

In dividing up the assets, the court begins by allowing creditors with secured claims to repossess the collateral that backed up their claim. Any remaining funds then go to pay creditors who have unsecured claims, in this order:

1. The cost of the bankruptcy case
2. Business claims that arose after the bankruptcy proceedings began
3. Employee wages, salaries, and commissions up to a limit of $2,000 per person
4. Claims for contributions to employee benefit plans
5. Claims by creditors who have purchased products that have not been delivered, up to $900 per claimant
6. Federal and state taxes

Repayment Sometimes a person who is bankrupt can pay off the debts if given some time to do so. Repayment arrangements typically involve suspending interest on the debts and putting the bankrupt person on some type of repayment schedule. Individuals with a regular income, those with unsecured debts of less than $100,000, and those with secured debts of less than $350,000 can use this approach. Many creditors will go along with the plan because this is the only practical and realistic way of getting paid.

Reorganization Corporations often file for reorganization rather than liquidation. For example, in Texaco's court problems with Pennzoil over the attempted purchase of Getty Oil, the judgments against Texaco eventually forced them to file for Chapter 11 reorganization to set in motion the biggest case in bankruptcy-law history.[10] Under this form of bankruptcy, the creditors and the debtor prepare a plan under which the debtor will pay a portion of the debts and is discharged from the remainder. The company continues to operate as usual. If the court finds that the management is grossly incompetent, it will appoint a trustee to run the company. Large firms whose liquidation would cause a hardship for many people are often allowed to reorganize rather than to liquidate.

Checkpoint

1. What are two sources of law?
2. What are some legal obligations that are not spelled out in contracts?

Closing Comments

Business and the government influence one another in many ways—through laws, through taxes, through political influence, and through the exchange of goods and services. The government tries to protect businesses and consumers by ensuring fair trade and competition. Businesses must abide by laws governing contracts, negotiable instruments, property, patents, trademarks, copyrights, agency, torts, and bankruptcy. These laws are designed to ensure equity and honesty, not only for the general public, but for business itself.

Learning Objectives Revisited

1. **Describe the major laws that regulate business and ensure competition.**
   The Sherman Antitrust Act outlaws all agreements created for the purpose of restraining trade in interstate commerce. The Clayton Act outlaws tying agreements and interlocking directorates. The Federal Trade Commission Act established the Federal Trade Commission (FTC). The Robinson-Patman Act forbids types of unfair price competition. The Celler-Kefauver Act prohibits anticompetitive mergers. The Antitrust Procedures and Penalties Act increased penalties imposed for violating the Sherman Act. The Antitrust Improvements Act requires merging companies to notify the FTC in advance and allows injured parties to sue.

2. **Identify the major types of federal, state, and local taxes.**

   The major types of taxes levied at the federal level are individual and corporate income taxes, excise taxes, and customs duties. The major taxes assessed at the state and local levels are income taxes, sales taxes, and property taxes.

3. **Present the major dimensions of contract and sales law.**

   A contract is a legally binding promise. The promise may be expressed in words or implied by actions. For a contract to be enforceable, the parties must reach a voluntary agreement, they must all be competent to contract, consideration must be involved, and the contract's purpose must be lawful. In some cases, the agreement must be in writing. Sales law specifies when sales contracts must be in writing and what the buyer's rights are. It also addresses the use of warranties. An express warranty is a guarantee offered orally or in writing. An implied warranty is a guarantee such as the assurance of safety that automatically accompanies the sale of a product.

4. **Discuss negotiable instruments and property law.**

   A negotiable instrument is a form of business paper that people can transfer as a substitute for money. The payee transfers the instrument by endorsing it. Property law addresses the ownership and transfer of real and personal property. Real property consists of land and the things attached to it. Personal property is all other property. It includes intangible property such as patents, trademarks, and copyrights, which are governed by additional laws.

5. **Explain the responsibilities under agency and tort law.**

   Agency law governs the actions of agents — persons authorized to act on behalf of another (the principal) — and their principals. Agents owe the principal the duties of care, obedience, accounting, and loyalty. Principals should keep track of agents to make sure that they are fulfilling their responsibilities fully and behaving appropriately. A principal may be held liable for the unlawful acts of an agent. Tort law addresses breaches of duties held generally in the absence of a contract. This law addresses both intentional tort and negligence.

6. **Relate the different ways of handling bankruptcy.**

   One approach to bankruptcy is liquidation — selling all assets and paying debts with the proceeds. In voluntary bankruptcy, the debtor initiates this legal proceeding. An involuntary bankruptcy is a legal proceeding initiated by creditors. In some cases, the debtor will follow a repayment procedure, which involves repaying creditors on some type of schedule. Corporations also have the option of filing for reorganization rather than liquidation. Under reorganization, the debtor pays a portion of the debt and is discharged from the remainder.

Key Terms Reviewed

Review the following terms. For any that you do not know or are unsure of, look up the definitions and see how they were used in the chapter.

Sherman Antitrust Act
Clayton Act
interlocking directorate
Federal Trade Commission Act
Robinson-Patman Act
Celler-Kefauver Anti-merger Act
Antitrust Procedures and Penalties Act
Antitrust Improvements Act
progressive tax
excise tax
customs duties
sales tax
regressive tax
property tax
proportional tax
statutory law
Uniform Commercial Code (UCC)
common law
contract
express contract

implied contract
plaintiff
defendant
statute of limitations
sales law
warranty
express warranty
implied warranty
negotiable instrument
property law
real property
deed
lease
personal property
patent
trademark
copyright
agency
agent
principal
tort
strict product liability
bankruptcy law
liquidation

Review Questions

1. A large group of investors is planning to start a company that will make and sell snow blowers. So far, they have lined up $1.5 million in start-up financing. However, they are worried about how they will be able to compete with Toro. They are considering a scheme, proposed by one of the investors, in which they will ask some of Toro's board of directors to serve on the board of their company, in exchange for shares of stock. These directors would be interested in their company and would therefore give them tips on how to compete with Toro. What federal law addresses this arrangement? How does the law apply?
2. What is the role of the Federal Trade Commission?
3. Why are electric utilities regulated? Why are broadcasters regulated but not newspapers and magazines?

4. What is the major source of tax revenue for the federal government? For the state and local governments?

5. What general objectives does Congress try to meet by adjusting tax rates and regulations?

6. Identify one progressive tax and one regressive tax. What was your basis for selecting these taxes?

7. Who pays customs duties?

8. The Knapps have learned that their home has just been reassessed at $95,000. The tax rate for their suburb is $1.50 per $100 of assessed value. Last year they paid $8,000 in income taxes. How much do they owe in property taxes this year?

9. What are the major sources of law in the United States?

10. Which of the following are enforceable contracts? Explain your reasoning.
    a. Two adults arrive at an oral agreement to sell a parcel of real estate for $87,500.
    b. Two workers on their lunch break enter a restaurant and order hamburgers with grilled onions.
    c. When he turns 16, Phil buys a stereo on a deferred-payment plan. Five years later, Lucille tricks Phil into signing an agreement to sell his stereo to her for $5.

11. A cleaning company in Des Moines signs a contract in which it agrees to provide window-cleaning services for an office building in the city. Why might the cleaning company's lawyer need to be familiar with Iowa's statute of limitations?

12. To reduce the company's risk of liability, the managers of Grand Furniture Company have decided that in the future, Grand's furniture will carry no warranties, express or implied. Can the company do this? If so, how? If not, why not?

13. What criteria make business paper negotiable?

14. Which of the following are real property? Which are personal property?
    a. Trees growing in a lot
    b. Lumber in a lumberyard
    c. Lumber constructed into a house

15. What is the difference between a patent and a copyright?

16. Why do agents have special duties to the principal? What are those duties? Considering the risk that an agent may violate those duties, why do businesses use agents?

17. If you were a judge, would you impose stricter penalties for intentional torts or for negligence? Why?

18. If you burn yourself on your toaster, what do you have to demonstrate in order to win a lawsuit based on strict product liability? (Of course, any damages you could win would likely fall far short of the court costs.) Do these requirements seem fair to you? Why or why not?

Applied Exercises

1. At the library, find government statistics related to how the current federal budget dollar is being spent. Compare your data to those in Figure 21.1. How are they similar? How are they different? What conclusions can you draw from your comparison?
2. At the library, find government statistics related to state and local government sources of revenue. How does this compare to ten years ago? What conclusions can you draw from the comparison?
3. Visit a local tire dealer and discuss the type of warranty that the store offers with the purchase of one of their tires. Is this an express or implied warranty? Support your answer.
4. Visit a law office that handles bankruptcy cases. Explore with a lawyer the benefits and drawbacks of declaring personal bankruptcy. Write a short paper on what you have learned.

Your Business IQ: Answers

1. True. The Antitrust Improvements Act of 1976 requires that companies notify the FTC in advance.
2. False. These percentages are reversed. Individual income taxes contribute three to four times more than corporate income taxes.
3. False. Dealers are reluctant because minors, generally persons under 18, may be able to set aside the purchase contract, return the car, and ask for a full refund. Minors can do this because they are considered to lack competency to enter into a contract.
4. True. Such an endorsement is called a restrictive endorsement. The most common restrictive endorsement stipulates "for deposit only."
5. False. Under current laws providing for strict product liability, the company is responsible regardless of its efforts or intent to make a safe product.

Farmland Dairies Takes on New York City

Farmland Dairies, based in Wallington, New Jersey, processes and distributes the milk it buys from farmers. When Marc Goldman joined the family business in the 1970s, he was put in charge of new projects. He decided to cross the state line into New York.

The plan would take years to achieve, thanks to a mass of regulations. With federal price supports and state laws, the milk business is closely regulated by the federal and state governments. This is especially true in New York. A state law gave the commissioner of the Department of Agriculture and Markets the authority to forbid the dairy to sell milk if it would create "destructive competition in markets already adequately served." In New York City, five licensed dairies kept a close grip on the market by maintaining that they were adequately serving it. According to critics, however, this protectionism was costing New Yorkers at least $2 million a week in higher milk prices.

Farmland was already selling in Rockland and Orange Counties, just northwest of New York City. The company made an agreement to purchase a small dairy in Westchester County, northeast of the city. The sale was contingent on Farmland getting a local license to distribute milk. Getting the license took the work of two lawyers over two and a half years.

Finally, the company was ready to move south into New York City. With 9 million consumers there and in Long Island, it was the logical next step for selling a product that can't travel long distances.

Goldman fought his battle in the courts and with the public. He started by trying to get a license to distribute in Staten Island. When the commissioner didn't move on his license application, Goldman went to court. The day before his case was to come before the judge, the commissioner set a hearing date for his license. The hearings lasted for three months. Goldman visited dairy farmers to explain that the lack of competition reduced demand and therefore hurt them. He advertised to consumers, stirring up interest in increasing demand. He even hired a lobbyist in Albany to persuade the legislature to deregulate the milk industry. The application process dragged on, and Goldman went back to court to force a decision. Within days of his scheduled court date, the ruling came through. That was how Goldman finally won the right to sell milk in New York City.

Unfortunately for Goldman, Farmland's troubles were not over. The unpredictability of when the company could enter the New York market made it difficult to be prepared. Picketers in front of supermarkets protested that union jobs were being lost to an out-of-state processor. Goldman had to go to court to get injunctions to stop the pickets. Thugs beat up one of his drivers and have smashed windshields and radiators. Goldman has hired security guards for deliveries. And for all the trouble,

Farmland probably isn't even making much money in New York City. The average price of milk in New York City fell from $2.42 to $2.00 in six months.

Case Questions

1. How did the government make it more difficult for Farmland to enter the New York City market? Where did Farmland find help? (Were some sources of help also governmental?)
2. How did deregulation change the business environment for Farmland?
3. How would you suggest that Farmland meet the challenges of distributing milk in New York City? What will the role of government be in this strategy?

You Be the Adviser: The $100 Million Deal

Clara Bartlett is a special assistant to Sam Davis, the chief executive officer (CEO) of a large, prosperous firm. Sam often sends Clara on assignments that require her to represent the firm and conclude business agreements in the company's name. Clara is an attorney, and much of this work falls within her area of expertise.

Last month, Clara and Sam spent three days negotiating with a competitor who wants to retire and sell his business for $110 million. Sam has had his accountants go over the company's books, and this asking price is in the ballpark. However, Sam believes that they can purchase the company for $100 million.

After discussing the matter with Clara, Sam arranged a meeting with the competitor, Winston Green. He then told Clara, "I want you to represent me in this meeting. Have contracts drawn up promising to pay Green $100 million. Then negotiate him down to this price. You might consider starting out at about $90 million and letting him work you up the last $10 million. I'm going to have the people in the accounting department issue you a check for $1 million that I want you to use to seal the deal. Give it to Green as consideration, with the other $99 million due in 90 days. I will have the check made out to you."

At the meeting, Clara and Winston Green discussed many details of the deal. Winston was initially concerned about Sam's absence, but he seemed satisfied when Clara explained that she had the authority to strike a deal "if the price is right." The meeting lasted six hours, and when it was over, Winston had agreed to sell his company for $100 million. Clara would pay the first $1 million as soon as they signed the initial agreement. Another $24 million was due in cash in 30 days. The last $75 million was due in 90 days.

After Winston had signed the papers, Clara signed on the line designated for her company's signature. She then removed a check for $1 million from her briefcase, turned it over, endorsed it, and then gave it to Winston. He looked at both sides of the check, stood up, and extended his hand across the table. "Congratulations," he said, "you've just bought yourself a company."

Your Advice

1. From what you have learned in this case, do the two parties have a contract, or has Clara failed to do something? Explain.
2. Is the $1 million that Clara gave Winston Green adequate as consideration or should she have given him more? Explain.

International Business

LEARNING OBJECTIVES

- Describe the nature of international business.
- Present the major reasons for international business.
- Identify some government-imposed barriers to international trade.
- Relate some cultural differences that make international trade challenging.
- Explain some efforts to stimulate international business.
- Discuss some common approaches to entering international markets.

Your Business IQ

How much do you already know about international business? Test your business IQ by labeling each statement *true* or *false*. Answers and explanations are at the end of the chapter.

1. In recent years, thanks mostly to its production of high-tech goods, the United States has been exporting substantially more than it has been importing.
2. U.S. businesses often find that their advantage over foreign businesses comes from the large pool of skilled and innovative employees in the United States.
3. The government sometimes erects trade barriers to foreign businesses even when this leads to higher prices and limited choices.
4. The Common Market has been promoting free trade among member European countries since 1957.
5. For small companies, the most common way to enter global markets is to enter into a joint venture.

Coca-Cola is sold in more than 155 countries.

Source: Courtesy of The Coca-Cola Company.

Looking Back and Ahead

Once every four years, the two top soccer teams square off in the World Cup, a competition seen around the world. More than a billion fans watched the latest game on television, and another 11 billion saw the preceding playoffs. This giant audience attracted sponsors from around the world: Anheuser-Busch, Coca-Cola, Gillette, and R. J. Reynolds from the United States; Canon, Fuji, JVC, and Seiko from Japan; Cinzano, GM/Opel, and Philips from Europe; and Bata from Canada. Sponsors, who often spend as much as $10 million, get to put their corporate logos on the stadium walls and use their sponsorship in their advertising. The 1990 World Cup promises to be even larger; the approximately 16 billion viewers predicted should be an appealing target for advertisers.[1]

The environment of the World Cup sponsors is particularly complex. It includes the governmental and legal dimensions described in Chapter 21. But because these companies sell their products in many nations, they must understand and work with several governments and varying laws. The managers of international companies also must be aware of variations in demand and customs throughout the global marketplace.

This chapter begins its look at international business by describing the basics of international trade and its importance for the United States. The chapter then outlines the reasons for engaging in international business and selecting particular countries or regions. Next, the chapter discusses barriers facing international business and ways that countries encourage and promote trade. Finally, the chapter examines the ways companies enter international markets.

The Nature of International Business

Most businesses today are affected by the international arena. Some businesses directly engage in trade with suppliers and customers in other countries. When a company has operations in more than one country, has foreign sales, and/or has a nationality mix of managers and owners, it is commonly called a **multinational corporation (MNC)**. Although only one or two of the criteria have to exist for a company to be considered an MNC, most large corporations today — such as the auto companies, DuPont, United Technologies, IBM, and Eastman Kodak — meet all the characteristics and are truly MNCs. In fact, if a large company is not an MNC in today's global marketplace, it is probably headed for trouble.

Multinational corporation (MNC) A company having operations in more than one country, foreign sales, and/or a nationality mix of managers and owners.

Although a firm may not be an MNC because it sells only to domestic markets, it still may encounter competition from foreign-based companies. Other companies buy supplies, raw materials, or inventory from overseas businesses. Thus almost all businesses, small or large, are affected at least indirectly by international trade. For example, firms that have built a business on supplying parts to Detroit automakers have seen their sales slump when the automakers lost sales to imports. These businesses have had to cut back or find new customers.

Because the effects of international trade are so far-reaching, business people try to keep abreast of international business activity. They measure the extent of a country's international trade activity by looking at the balance of trade and the balance of payments.

The Balance of Trade

The **balance of trade** is the difference between the value of a nation's exports and the value of its imports. **Exports** are goods or services sold to other countries. **Imports** are goods or services brought into one's own country. As the definitions imply, one country's exports are another country's imports. Figure 22.1 shows trends in the U.S. balance of trade.

As Figure 22.1 shows, imports to the U.S. currently exceed exports. Because American companies and consumers have spent so much on imports in recent years, the United States has a **trade deficit.** This is a negative balance of trade, resulting from exports having a lower value than imports. The U.S. trade deficit has caused concern in recent years because it has reached record levels. The stock market crash in October 1987 was at least partly attributed to the pessimism surrounding the existing trade deficit. Even if the United States is able to cut its trade deficit in half, it is estimated that there will still be a $75 billion deficit by 1990.[2]

As Figure 22.2 shows, the U.S. share of the world export market went from 12 percent in 1980 to 11 percent in 1986. Although the United States is still exporting a significant amount of semiconductors (40 percent of the world market share), personal computers (68 percent), jet engines (90 percent), and services (health care, entertainment, and financial), and although certain companies such as Boeing (exports are 45 percent of sales) and MGM/UA Communications (exports 35 percent of sales) are very successful in world markets, the country may never make a significant comeback in mass-manufactured commodities such as textiles, shoes, consumer electronics, and machine tools.

Balance of trade The difference between the value of a nation's exports and the value of its imports.

Exports Goods or services sold to other countries.

Imports Goods or services brought into one's own country.

Trade deficit A negative balance of trade.

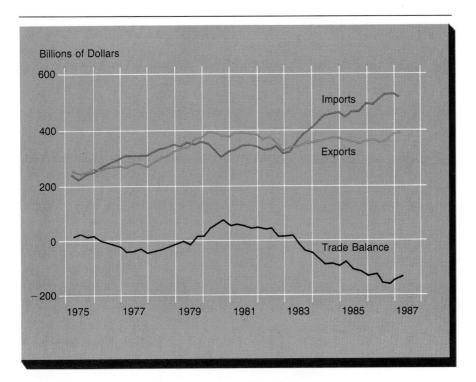

FIGURE 22.1

The U.S. Balance of Trade

Fortunately, there are recent encouraging signs that the U.S. trade balance may be getting better. Because of a weaker dollar (foreign countries buying American goods get them relatively cheaper and Americans buying from foreign countries pay relatively more) and the improved performance of the domestic manufacturing sector, the United States may become as competitive as ever in world markets.[3] For example, Lee Iacocca recently announced that for the first time in ten years, Chrysler would be selling cars in six Western European countries at lower prices than competitive European and Japanese models, and USX, the beleaguered steel company, recently sold 20,000 tons of hot-rolled bands of steel to an Osaka, Japan, tube company at a price 12 percent below what Japanese producers were offering. Such examples were unheard of during the early to mid-1980s. The head of USX noted that "we now have lower costs of producing steel for our customers in the United States than the Japanese industry has in providing steel to their customers in Japan."[4]

By getting the trade balance back into reasonable shape, American businesses can grow, and in the long run, the result can mean more income and jobs. In the short run, however, in their efforts to make themselves more competitive in world markets, many manufacturers have cut back jobs and rolled back wages.

The Balance of Payments

Balance of payments
The total cash flow out of a country minus the total inflow of cash.

A broader way to measure international trade is the **balance of payments,** which is the total cash flow out of a country minus the total inflow of cash. This measure thus incorporates not only purchases and sales, but also investments and government foreign aid. For almost four decades following World War II, the United States was the world's largest investor in other countries. Today, the country is still a big investor, but foreign investment in our debt (foreign investors as of 1987 owned 16 percent of the outstanding publicly held U.S. Treasury debt) makes the United States a net debtor. Our huge budget deficit led to high interest rates that in turn attracted foreign investors. America is now the largest debtor nation. By contrast, Japan is the world's largest creditor.

FIGURE 22.2

The World Export Market

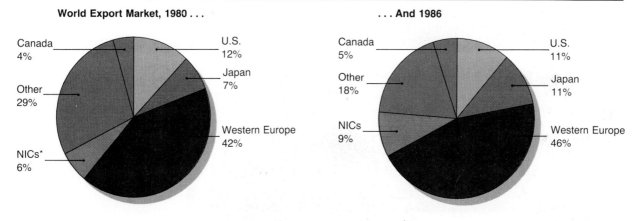

World Export Market, 1980 . . .

Canada 4%
Other 29%
NICs* 6%
U.S. 12%
Japan 7%
Western Europe 42%

. . . And 1986

Canada 5%
Other 18%
NICs 9%
U.S. 11%
Japan 11%
Western Europe 46%

ªNewly industrialized countries: South Korea, Brazil, Mexico, Hong Kong, Singapore, and Taiwan.

International Business and the American Economy

As these measures of exports, imports, and cash flows show, international business influences the American economy from two directions: American businesses participate in the economies of other countries, and foreign businesses participate in the U.S. economy. The interdependence between the United States and other countries of the world was borne out when the American stock market crash in October 1987 led to a chain reaction in stock market plunges around the globe.

U.S. products often meet with a warm reception overseas. This is particularly true for consumer goods and for products based on high technology. For example, the trademarks of Coke, Levi's, McDonald's, and Mickey Mouse (Disneylands are in Tokyo and soon to be in Paris) are known and appreciated worldwide. Lamson Corporation has predicted that expansion to foreign markets is the ticket to increased sales of its air pollution control equipment. The company's vice president, Harold La Tulip, claims that, technologically, Japanese competitors "can't touch us."[5] In general, U.S. manufacturers are especially competitive in markets where products are relatively complex and specialized.

At the same time, the United States is an important market for foreign companies. The size of the market alone draws foreign businesses to the United States. American consumers snap up Mercedes Benz automobiles, Sony electronic equipment, and Corona beer. Foreign companies also participate in the U.S. marketplace by investing in American companies and even buying them outright.[6] Today, Ball Park hot dogs and French's mustard are owned by a British conglomerate. In 1986 alone, foreign ownership in the United States jumped 25 percent to $1.3 trillion.[7] Table 22.1 shows some major purchases that have contributed to this climb. In addition, foreign businesses invest in the United States by purchasing government securities. Nevertheless, to put this in

Appropriately marketed American products often achieve wide popularity in other countries. In Japan, for example, the leading pain killer is Bufferin, a product of New York–based Bristol-Myers.

Source: © Burt Glinn. Magnum Photos, Inc.

The Mercedes-Benz dealership in Hollywood, California. Because these German automobiles have a reputation for superior quality, they continue to attract American buyers.

perspective, foreign investments in the United States account for only a small percentage of total investments.

International trade therefore opens opportunities for U.S. business owners and U.S. consumers. American business owners can try to make the whole world — the so-called global market — their marketplace and thus acquire more sources of funding. However, the influx of foreign competitors can also make maintaining their domestic market share a challenging job. Consumers can benefit from the greater choices and the sometimes lower prices available when more companies compete for their dollars. The records of the U.S. Patent Office illustrate both the enriched offerings and the challenging competition; in 1986, six of the top ten corporations receiving patents were foreign controlled.[8]

Checkpoint

1. What is the balance of trade?
2. Should the United States be concerned about having a negative balance of trade and being the world's largest debtor nation?

Reasons for International Business

Why do some companies expand into international markets, while others stay close to home? How do companies decide which countries to operate in? Some of the answers to these questions are found in the material you studied about production (Chapter 10) and marketing (Chapter 11). The managers of a company weigh its resources, opportunities, limitations, and strengths in an effort to determine what the company can do most effectively and profitably.

The Broader View: National Advantages

The types of products a nation's companies trade internationally depend in part on the things businesses in that nation tend to do well. These strengths stem from the nation's resources, such as raw materials, the

T A B L E   22.1

Major Foreign Investments in the United States

Country of Acquiring Company	Acquired American Company
Switzerland	Carnation
West Germany	Doubleday
Canada	Allied Stores (Brooks Brothers)
Great Britain	Smith & Wesson
Great Britain	Standard Oil
The Netherlands	Chesebrough-Ponds (Ragú, Vaseline, Q-Tips)
Japan	Dunes Hotel and Country Club

work ethic and educational levels of the people, and the degree of industrialization. Nations may have an absolute advantage or a comparative advantage. Business people looking for international opportunities might start by determining whether their company has such an advantage relative to businesses in other countries.

Absolute Advantage Some nations have a monopoly on certain products or can produce them for considerably less than anyone else. This advantage is an **absolute advantage**. For example, South Africa has most of the world's diamonds. Because of its monopoly in this natural resource, South Africa has an absolute advantage in the sale of diamonds. Most resources are distributed more widely, so absolute advantages are rare.

Comparative Advantage More often, a nation has a **comparative advantage**—it can sell certain products for relatively less than most other nations can. The reasons for this include cheap labor, abundant natural resources, a favorable climate, and an abundance of technical skill. For example, the United States has many skilled engineers and scientists who can develop products, such as computers and jet engines, that depend on sophisticated technology. Saudi Arabia has a generous supply of oil, so it sells oil to many countries. These advantages can shift over time. To learn how shifting advantages have influenced U.S. manufacturers, see "Small Business Close-Up: Made in America."

U.S. consumers can often get a better price by purchasing commodities imported from countries that have a comparative advantage. Table 22.2 provides some examples that show why some of the food on our table comes from other nations. Notice that even within the United States some states have a comparative advantage over others. For example, warm and sunny California is the major U.S. supplier of cantaloupe, while coastal Massachusetts supplies most of the nation's domestically harvested sea scallops.

Absolute advantage   A monopoly on certain products or the ability to produce them for considerably less than anyone else.

Comparative advantage The ability to sell certain products for relatively less than producers in most other nations can.

T A B L E   22.2 **Comparative Advantage for Selected Foods**

| Commodity | Major Source | | Price[a] | |
	Foreign	Domestic	Imported	Domestic
Eggplant	Mexico	Florida	$ .23	$ .27
Tomatoes	Mexico	Florida	.50	.58
Russet potatoes	Canada	Idaho	.12	.21
Red delicious apples	Chile	Washington	.48	.68
Cantaloupe	Mexico	California	.43	.58
Lemons	Spain	California	.31	.46
Choice steer	Australia	Nebraska	.47	.91
Choice and prime lamb	Australia	New Jersey	.26	1.50
Sea scallops	Japan	Massachusetts	4.75	5.40

[a]New York wholesale price per pound, in U.S. dollars.

The Narrower View: Sources of Advantage

Business people considering international trade might start by weighing whether their product has an absolute or comparative advantage over products supplied by companies in other countries. But at some point, a business's managers must consider the business's own advantages. Some sources of advantage include natural resources and climate, capital equipment and skilled personnel available, geographic location, and political climate.

SMALL BUSINESS **CLOSE-UP**

Made in America

Over the last ten years, the newly industrialized countries have surged ahead in labor-intensive manufacturing. In fact, many American producers are finding it cheaper to have their products made offshore and then imported than to make them at home. The biggest advantage of offshore manufacturing is the lower cost of labor. In some parts of the world, such as in Thailand, workers earn only a small percentage of the wages paid to comparable U.S. workers.

Recently, however, a countertrend has begun. Leading this trend are hard-nosed entrepreneurs who believe that their smaller businesses can keep costs down and earn a profit. At these companies, the benefits of manufacturing in small businesses at home may well outweigh the advantages of producing abroad.

Customers of complex products such as machinery want service and the ability to make modifications, not just the product itself. The higher the cost of the product, the more likely the customer will want direct contact with the firm. If the producer is 5,000 miles away, the local seller can hardly hope to meet the customer's demands for a quick response to a problem or an opportunity.

When machinery and equipment are manufactured locally, the management and production teams are located near one another. This gives them a chance to discuss problems that arise and work out solutions that can lead to higher quality. The offshore manufacturer is simply a producer of finished goods; the onshore manufacturer has a personal stake in the finished product. This can lead to better quality and service.

Onshore producers find that they can respond faster to new orders and to changes needed in the product line. They do not have to worry about coordinating their efforts with a manufacturer halfway across the world. This rapid response often makes the difference between getting repeat business and being left out in the cold on future orders.

In recent years, foreign labor costs (such as in Japan) have been going up, reducing the attractiveness of overseas production. Moreover, because domestic firms' costs have been higher all along, they have had to hustle to find ways of cutting costs and becoming more efficient. Many offshore producers are now seeing their profit margins dwindle, while onshore manufacturers are reaping the benefits of stable production costs, better technology, and more efficient and aggressive management practices.

Some small-business managers are predicting a trend back toward manufacturing in the United States. "Many of these offshore guys have failed to keep up with what is going on in the industry," notes one small-business person. "As a result, we're beginning to beat them to the punch more often than not."

Natural Resources Some countries have an abundance of certain natural resources. For example, the United States has about one-third of the entire world's known coal reserves. Mideast countries such as Saudi Arabia, Kuwait, and Iran are rich in oil, Bolivia has tin, and South Africa has diamonds. These natural resources can be exported in raw form or converted or refined into a finished component or product. Companies that sell or use these resources are likely to engage in international trade.

Climate and Terrain A favorable climate or terrain makes it possible to produce certain crops more efficiently than others. In the United States, for example, the Great Plains have a favorable climate and terrain for growing wheat. Farmers in Kansas, Nebraska, South Dakota, and North Dakota produce wheat for the United States and provide millions of tons of wheat for export. Farmers in other countries specialize in products suited to their climate and terrain; for example, farmers in Colombia and Brazil grow coffee beans, those in Cuba raise tobacco, Costa Rican farmers grow bananas, and Brazil is rich in rubber trees.

Countries whose climate gives them a comparative advantage for growing coffee beans include Colombia and Brazil. These coffee fields are in Colombia.

Source: Courtesy of The National Federation of Coffee Growers of Colombia.

Capital Equipment Manufacturers rely on capital resources such as high-tech plants, machinery, and equipment. The more capital equipment a company has, the greater its opportunity to meet domestic demand and have capacity left to produce exports. Businesses with idle capital equipment often turn to international selling as a means of using their productive capacity more fully.

Capital equipment also allows companies to diversify. Although Japanese companies have taken over the market for mass-produced silicon memory chips, America's Silicon Valley chip makers such as Cypreso Semiconductor have competed very well by offering diversity. This company makes 80 different types of chips in a facility that can accommodate several daily tool changes. Cypreso's president recently observed, "You can be very competitive with the Japanese if you understand what they're good at and don't bash into them head on."[9]

Human Resources Skilled workers are an important supplement to capital equipment. The United States, for example, has the high-tech equipment and traditionally has had skilled personnel who are able to produce and operate this complex equipment. However, there is some recent concern that the skill level of American workers is declining. For example, New York Telephone administered a test of fundamental skills to 22,880 job applicants and 84 percent failed.[10] So while the United States still has a ready supply of college-graduate professionals, entrepreneurs, and intrapreneurs (see Chapter 3), there may be a need for more skilled workers in order to remain competitive in the future.

The newly industrialized countries (NICs), which include South Korea, Singapore, Hong Kong, Taiwan, Mexico, and Brazil, have made their mark in world trade largely through their human resources. Employee wages in the NICs are considerably lower than their counterparts in Japan, Europe, and the United States. Not only are their human resources less costly, but they are becoming increasingly educated and skilled. Once dismissed as marginal producers of low-quality clothes and toys, the NICs have become producers of complex, high-quality goods because of their skilled workers. They now produce everything from VCRs and computers to cars and commuter planes.[11] For example, South Korea's Hyundai, which produces the subcompact Excel, is the hottest-selling new imported line of autos in U.S. history.

In the underdeveloped countries of Africa, the Middle East, and South America, businesses have been unable to take full advantage of high-tech markets. For example, even if they buy sophisticated computers, they are unable to use them to the fullest if they lack a well-trained, skilled work force that knows how to get the most out of these machines. Human resources help explain some of the productivity differences between businesses in the developed countries, the NICs, and the underdeveloped third-world nations.

Geographic Location A business's geographic location also influences its use of international trade. If demand exists in a nearby country, business people may sell there because the shorter distance keeps transportation costs down and makes foreign operations easier to control. For example, the West Coast has an advantage over the East Coast in trade with Asia. Access to roads, rail lines, and waterways also facilitates transportation.

Political Climate The political climate of a country can attract or discourage businesses. For example, many foreign countries are attracted to the stable political situation of the United States. Businesses tend to stay away from nations in turmoil. Of course, there are exceptions; the makers of security devices might look for trouble spots in which to sell their products!

Governments may also set policies specifically to encourage or discourage international trade. For example, the United States is interested in maintaining trade with the Philippines and Costa Rica because it wants to exert economic influence in order to discourage communism there. For parallel reasons, the Soviet Union buys millions of tons of sugar from Cuba at higher-than-market prices.

As government policy shifts, so do trade patterns. For example, 20 years ago, the United States and mainland China forbade trade with one another. Today, the governments allow it, and many American firms, from Coca-Cola to Sheraton Hotels to the Chase Manhattan Bank, are working hard to establish business links with China.

Checkpoint

1. How does absolute advantage differ from comparative advantage?
2. What are three sources of advantage business people consider in determining whether to engage in international trade?

Barriers to International Trade

Government policy can make it expensive or even illegal to engage in international trade. In addition, cultural differences can be a barrier to conducting business in the international arena.

Government Restrictions

Most governments erect some barriers to limit foreign businesses, since it is to the government's benefit when domestic businesses prosper and create more jobs and income for the citizenry. Most economists would also argue that trade restrictions lead to higher prices and limited choices, but these effects are more subtle.

The government also restricts foreign trade for security reasons. To avoid dependence on other countries for critical defense materials, the home government protects defense-related industries by limiting competition and foreign acquisitions. For example, the U.S. Defense Department recently prevented an attempt by Plessey Company, a major British electronics group, to acquire Harris Corporation, a Florida-based defense contractor. The Pentagon insisted on certain restrictions that would have left the British company without management control over the Harris divisions that produce sensitive defense-related goods.[12] Likewise, the government tries to protect innovations in defense technology by prohibiting sales of some high-technology items to certain countries, such as those allied with the Soviet Union.

Another reason the government erects trade barriers is to help the country reduce the trade deficit. Advocates of protectionist measures say that they would boost profits and reduce unemployment. Figure 22.3 shows that imports have captured a significant share of the U.S. market. To help this situation, the government imposes quotas, tariffs, and other regulations.

Quotas One of the most common government-imposed trade barriers is a **quota**. This is a restriction on the quantity or value of an item that

Quota A restriction on the quantity or value of an item that may be imported.

Honda overcomes some trade barriers by setting up factories in the countries where it wants to sell products. For example, this lawnmower manufacturing plant is located in North Carolina. By creating U.S. jobs, the Japanese company addresses the concern that buying from foreign businesses leads to domestic unemployment.

Source: Courtesy of American Honda Motor Company, Incorporated.

may be imported. For example, a quota could restrict the amount of Scottish wool imported into the United States in any calendar year to 5,000 tons. Another quota could restrict the amount of French wine imported into the United States to $10 million a year. In recent years Japanese automakers have used voluntary quotas on exporting autos to the United States to avoid having a quota imposed on them by the United States. Most quotas are expressed in terms of physical quantity, because goods are easier to measure and control on this basis.

Tariffs The government might also discourage imports by taxing them. A **tariff** is a duty or fee levied on imported goods. It discourages imports by making them more expensive in the hope that more consumers will switch to domestic brands. However, if a country's auto producers are less efficient than those of another, and the country competes by raising its tariff duties, the consumers in that country will pay more for their cars than they would otherwise have to.

Tariff A duty or fee levied on imported goods.

Regulation of Business Some governments regulate businesses more heavily than others. Sometimes these regulations discourage businesses from entering a market. In some nations, all international businesses must have local partners, meaning that a foreign company may not set up an operation without at least one national in the top management. In recent years, some countries, including Mexico, have attempted to ensure that the local partners hold a controlling interest. However, major firms like IBM have refused to do business on these grounds and have usually managed to get the foreign government to back down.

Government regulations limit what a company may do. For example, some countries require companies to file a plan indicating what they intend to produce, how many people they will hire, and how much they will pay the workers. The government reviews the plan to see whether the operations will fit into the government's economic master plan. If a company that wants to do business in the country does not fit into the master plan, it may not be allowed to set up operations unless it changes its plans. If the country decides to change its master plan, the firm again will find itself under pressure to go along with the changes.

FIGURE   22.3

Imports as a Percentage of the U.S. Market

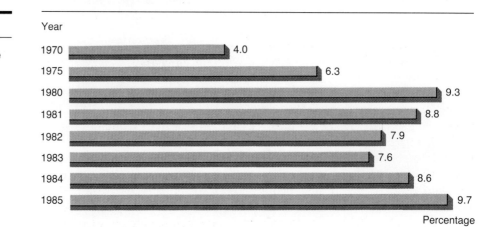

Year

1970	4.0
1975	6.3
1980	9.3
1981	8.8
1982	7.9
1983	7.6
1984	8.6
1985	9.7

Percentage

Currency Differences

Each nation issues its own currency, and the complications that result are another type of barrier to international trade. International business involves the extra task of converting money from the currency of one nation to that of another. For example, an American company that sends salespeople to London would exchange dollars for pounds for spending there. A company that operates stores in Japan would have to convert yen into dollars.

The arithmetic of dealing with the exchange rate is fairly simple, but planning for it is difficult in today's constantly changing world. For various reasons, the rate of exchange between the dollar and other currencies frequently changes. For example, if it currently does not take many U.S. dollars to buy a certain foreign currency, then Americans who travel in that country and American businesses who buy from that country can get a great deal more for their dollars than they can if later in the year it takes more dollars to buy the same amount of foreign currency. Obviously, American tourists and managers would have wanted to make purchases as early as possible that year, but predicting shifts in the exchange rate can be as tricky as forecasting the stock market.

In general, a strong dollar (worth more relative to foreign currencies) helps buyers of imports, because it keeps the price of imports down. A weak dollar (worth less relative to foreign currencies) helps exporters by making their products relatively less expensive in other countries. On paper, the earnings of an international business seem to change, too, with a strong dollar making overseas profits seem smaller than they would be with a weak dollar.[13]

Besides uncertainty over exchange rates, international businesses risk being unable to convert foreign earnings into the currency of their own country. Some countries try to keep funds in the country by refusing to allow companies to convert their currency, thus limiting the ways businesses can spend their earnings. Chapter 20 described how businesses can protect against this risk by purchasing inconvertibility insurance.

Cultural Differences

When people from different parts of the world come together, they often have trouble communicating. Even people with the best of intentions may baffle or even insult one another. Such problems arise because of cultural differences. **Culture** consists of the beliefs, attitudes, values, and behaviors that people learn in their society. When doing business abroad, incorrect assumptions about culture can be a major stumbling block. This is true not only for Americans doing business overseas, but also for foreign countries doing business in the United States.

Language and Communication Style While English is becoming the language of business, it is not the primary language of most people in the world. Reaching consumers worldwide requires the use of other languages, and foreign languages are also important in communicating with other business people. Most people appreciate the effort it takes to learn their language. When business people do not speak or read another country's language, they rely on translators. This can be very costly. At the rate of $20 to $25 a page to translate, some companies are spending

Culture The beliefs, attitudes, values, and behaviors that people learn in their society.

millions and not even realizing it. One company estimates that as its internationalization increases, the need for translation will jump from the present 50,000 to 200,000 pages by 1991.[14] But even when they use skilled translators, business people must be aware of differences in the way people of various cultures communicate.

Speaking styles, including the distances speakers maintain between themselves, are culturally based. For example, many Israeli business people speak English in an aggressive way, leading Americans who are unfamiliar with their speech habits to believe that their Israeli business counterparts are angry about something. However, this is simply the way many Israelis are accustomed to communicate. Arabic business people, in contrast, tend to speak softly and stand very close to their listener, which makes many Americans nervous. They may feel threatened by the closeness, which may seem pushy. Japanese business people, who value politeness above frankness, may seem to agree with all of an American visitor's ideas. However, the American might be dismayed later to discover that when saying yes, the Japanese business person merely meant, "I hear you," not "I agree with you."

Another language-related problem is the use of humor. Many Americans love to exaggerate, and some foreigners may take things literally. The American managers of a German subsidiary referred to the bald salesperson in their group as "Curly." They called their 6'10" engineer "Tiny," and the heavyset accountant "Slim." Most of the German managers were baffled by these names and simply wrote them off as the notions of those "crazy Americans."

Customs and Manners To make their foreign customers and colleagues comfortable and to avoid insult, managers need to be aware of customs and manners. For example, a U.S. custom is for people to wear black as a sign of mourning, but in China mourners wear white. In the United States, most businessmen go to work in a suit and tie, while in Israel almost no one does, and in Latin American countries, businessmen commonly wear a *guayavera* (an embroidered long overshirt).

These cultural differences in customs and manners need to be recognized by managers in the international business arena. Unfortunately, Americans have too often ignored cultural differences and have sometimes earned the title of "ugly Americans."

Concept of Time Most Americans have a high esteem for time and punctuality. In the United States, northern European countries, and England, for example, meetings are expected to start on time. However, in Latin countries, the pace is more leisurely; as a result, many American managers find themselves angrily cooling their heels for 15 to 30 minutes waiting for an appointment or meeting. In warm climates like Mexico, managers often take a long afternoon break but then go back to work after their evening meal, expecting their American counterparts to join them. American managers can save themselves a good deal of discomfort by learning these patterns in advance.

Culture in Perspective The way business people behave often varies from one country to another. But making business deals often depends on bonds of trust. To build these bonds, managers need to make the extra effort required to understand foreign cultures. Sometimes this involves finding out about a whole different way of looking at the world. For an example, see "International Close-Up: Building in Hong Kong." Making a product that meets a need is the heart of successful international business, but those efforts will be lost unless the company can overcome cultural barriers.

Checkpoint

1. What are some major ways governments erect barriers to international trade?
2. How do business practices vary among cultures?

Promoting International Trade

Despite the many barriers to international trade, which are mainly used to discourage imports, most countries have also made special efforts to promote trade. These efforts consist of creating free-trade zones, constructing trade agreements, and providing financial support.

Free-Trade Zones

A **free-trade zone (FTZ)** is a geographic area into which foreign goods can be imported without payment of duties. Applied to the United States, the importer moves the goods from the FTZ into the United States where a duty is then imposed. In other cases, the importer ships the products from the FTZ to other countries without ever paying a duty.

The primary benefit of FTZs is that they provide jobs for American workers and markets for U.S. goods. For example, the Brooklyn Navy Yard is now an FTZ at which over 150 firms do business. Many U.S. workers there repackage goods for shipment to foreign markets. Other firms use an FTZ as a temporary business site when they relocate from overseas back to the United States. This gives them a place from which to operate while their local facilities are being constructed. In still other cases, companies use an FTZ to delay customs duties on goods that are not yet ready for market. For example, a company in the New Orleans FTZ is aging its wine for future distribution.

Free-trade zone (FTZ) A geographic area into which foreign goods can be imported without payment of duties.

Agreements among Nations

Sometimes groups of nations agree to work together to promote trade among each other's businesses. One of the important existing trade agreements is the General Agreement on Tariffs and Trade. In addition, groups of nations form economic communities.

General Agreement on Tariffs and Trade (GATT) Over 90 nations have joined together in the **General Agreement on Tariffs and Trade (GATT),** an international agreement and organization designed to eliminate tariff barriers to worldwide trade. Since 1947, member nations of GATT have met periodically to negotiate tariff cuts and to remove other

General Agreement on Tariffs and Trade (GATT) An international agreement and organization designed to eliminate tariff barriers to worldwide trade.

trade barriers. A number of significant steps have been taken over the years. For example, the Kennedy Rounds (1962–1967) brought about an average tariff reduction of 40 percent on 60,000 separate items. The Tokyo Rounds (1973–1979) reduced tariffs by approximately 33 percent on 6,000 items. Recently, the United States has attempted to use GATT to solve trade disputes concerning Japanese quotas on American beef and citrus fruits.[15]

Common Market A group of European countries organized to eliminate trade barriers between all members.

Economic Communities Another way nations have attempted to remove trade barriers is by forming economic communities or unions. The best-known example is the European Economic Community (EEC), more commonly known as the Common Market. The **Common Market** is a group of European countries organized to eliminate trade barriers between all members. Specifically, there has been an attempt to eliminate tariffs and import quotas and to have free movement of capital and labor among Common Market members. Although there have been many roadblocks along the way, it is now generally predicted that by 1992 all intra-European trade barriers will end.[16] When this economic commu-

INTERNATIONAL

CLOSE-UP

Building in Hong Kong

Architects and builders around the world are subject to the principles of physics. These principles dictate how to make buildings strong enough for the stresses they must withstand. But in Hong Kong, builders are also expected to consult the principles of another discipline: *feng shui* (pronounced fung shway). This quasi-scientific surveying technique is more than 2,000 years old and is an important part of building in Hong Kong, Taiwan, Singapore, and other areas with large Chinese populations.

Before building in Hong Kong, most people have a *feng shui* master read the architectural plans to make sure that the new building won't destroy the harmonious movement of spirits. Managers of the Hong Kong and Shanghai Bank paid a fee of several thousand dollars for a *feng shui* master to review their plans for a new headquarters building. The master advised them to move a bank officer's door away from a nearby escalator to preserve the delicate balance derived from the Chinese philosophy of yin and yang. The managers complied.

Back in 1971, Singapore's Hyatt Regency was suffering from poor business. A *feng shui* master advised the hotel's management to remodel the hotel's fountain and facade to rid the hotel of unhappy spirits and lure back Chinese guests who were avoiding the hotel's bad *feng shui*. Today, the hotel reports a much better occupancy rate.

Following *feng shui* is not only good customer relations, it can be good employee relations. According to Michael Mathews, vice president of Hong Kong's Regent Hotel, "If we didn't go along with the local staff's beliefs, they might just decide to stay at home one day." The Regent has a panoramic picture window in response to a *feng shui* master's recommendation. The window is supposed to give the nine dragons who live nearby access to their favorite spot on Hong Kong Harbor. According to *feng shui*, dragons do not know how to use doors, but can pass through glass. Says the hotel's public relations chief, Lynn Grebstadt, "No one wants nine irritated dragons stranded in the lobby."

nity was founded in 1957 by the Treaty of Rome, it consisted of France, West Germany, the Netherlands, Belgium, Luxembourg, and Italy. Today, additional members are Ireland, England, Greece, Denmark, Portugal, and Spain, with Turkey as an associate member. Figure 22.4 shows the countries in the Common Market.

Financial Support for International Trade

Laws promoting free trade can encourage international business, but some companies need money to reach an international market. The U.S. government and the United Nations have created a number of financial institutions to help foster international trade:

The **Export-Import Bank (Exim Bank)** is a U.S. government lending agency that makes loans to importers and exporters that are unable to obtain adequate financing from private agencies.

The **International Monetary Fund (IMF)** is a UN organization that tries to stabilize exchange rates between world currencies.

Export-Import Bank (Exim Bank) A U.S. government lending agency that makes loans to importers and exporters unable to obtain private funding.

FIGURE 22.4

Common Market Countries

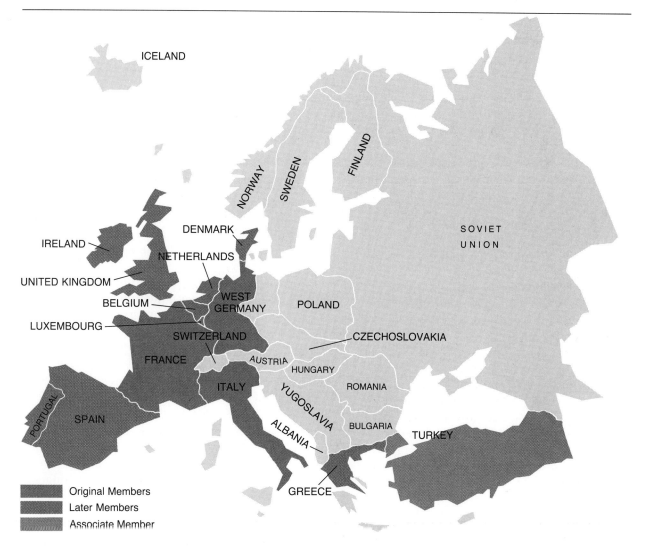

International Monetary Fund (IMF) A UN organization that tries to stabilize exchange rates between world currencies.

International Bank for Reconstruction and Development (World Bank) An agency that lends to underdeveloped countries to help them grow.

International Finance Corporation (IFC) An organization that invests in private enterprises in underdeveloped nations.

International Development Association (IDA) An organization that lends to underdeveloped countries.

The **International Bank for Reconstruction and Development (World Bank)** is an agency supported by about 150 member nations that lends to underdeveloped nations to help them stimulate their economy and grow.

The **International Finance Corporation (IFC),** an affiliate of the World Bank, invests in private enterprises in underdeveloped nations.

The **International Development Association (IDA),** an affiliate of the World Bank, makes loans to underdeveloped countries on more liberal terms than does the World Bank.

Checkpoint

1. What are two ways international trade is encouraged?
2. How does the federal government provide financing for international trade?

Going International

Many American firms have "gone international." The auto companies and aircraft companies export several billion dollars in goods each year. Smaller firms often use a much different approach from that employed by their larger counterparts. Small firms often start off by licensing or exporting their product, while larger firms are more likely to opt for a joint venture or to use a branch, subsidiary, or world company.

Licensing

License A legal agreement in which one firm gives another the right to manufacture and sell its product in return for paying a royalty.

When a company is small or simply does not want to underwrite the expense of entering a foreign market, it will sometimes seek a licensing agreement with an overseas firm. A **license** is a legal agreement in which one firm gives another the right to manufacture and sell its product in return for paying a royalty. This royalty is often a percentage of the income from the sale of the product.

Businesses with patents or trademarks that protect them against counterfeiters often use licensing because they have something special to bring to the licensing agreement, and both sides can profit from the deal. The licenser receives royalties and international marketing expertise. The licensee gains a successful product and the know-how required to manufacture it. The licenser often exercises strict quality control over the production of the goods, because its reputation is on the line. However, the specific selling practices are often up to the licensee, who typically knows more about how to sell the product in the foreign market.

Exporting

Businesses that want greater control over manufacturing can manufacture the product at home and then export it to foreign markets. The exporter's degree of involvement in the marketplace depends on its marketing strategy. In formulating such a strategy, exporters need to carefully examine basic demographics, growth potential, and political and economic climate.

Some firms sell their products to an export/import merchant, who assumes all of the selling risks. This merchant is similar to a wholesaler (discussed in Chapter 14), who takes goods off the manufacturer's hands and arranges for resale to retailers. In other cases, the company will use an export/import agent. In this case, the manufacturer retains title to the goods until the agent sells them to wholesalers or retailers in the foreign country. In still other cases, the exporter may set up its own sales offices or branches and take over distribution and sales of the product in the foreign country. This arrangement is more expensive than the other sales approaches, and therefore is usually limited to large firms.

Joint Ventures

In going international, smaller firms usually use the approach of licensing or exporting. Large firms may try a **joint venture** with a company in the targeted country. This is an arrangement in which two companies pool their resources to create, produce, and market a product. Many firms have used this arrangement because it helps them get a foothold in the international market without having to start from scratch. In the typical joint venture agreement, the American firm provides most of the funding and technical know-how for producing the product. The foreign firm takes responsibility for handling government red tape and fine tuning the sales pitch to the local market.

In some countries it is almost impossible to sell goods without having a local partner, hence the popularity of the joint venture. Garret, Mack Trucks, and KHD have used this approach to manufacture and sell gas turbine engines. International Harvester and Volvo have used it to

Joint venture An arrangement in which two companies pool their resources to create, produce, and market a product.

In some countries, Ford Motor Company establishes offices. In the Middle East, the company sells primarily by appointing dealers and exporting automobiles to them. Ford has dealers in Jordan, Kuwait, Saudi Arabia, Bahrain, Oman, Quatar, and the United Arab Emirates. The dealership shown here is Arabian Motors Group W.L.L. in Kuwait City.

Source: Courtesy of Ford Motor Company.

produce and sell tractor components. Recently, as a result of Gorbachev's policy of *glasnost* (the opening up of the Soviet Union to foreigners), U.S.-Soviet joint ventures are being signed. For example, a Connecticut engineering company will develop control systems for Russian oil refineries and petrochemical plants.[17] The venture benefits the Soviets by giving them needed technology, and benefits the Connecticut company by gaining them a foothold in the world's largest oil industry.

Branches and Subsidiaries

Branch organization An operation set up by a parent company in a foreign country for the purpose of accomplishing specific goals such as sales.

Subsidiary A company organized under the laws of a foreign country for the purpose of carrying out tasks, such as production and sales, assigned by the parent firm.

If a company's managers decide the company should handle the sales of its products abroad, they often establish a branch. A **branch organization** is an operation set up by a parent company in a foreign country for the purpose of accomplishing specific goals such as sales. The branch manager typically assumes the role of an overseas sales manager.

If the managers decide to go further and set up the company's own production facilities as well as marketing operations overseas, they typically will create a subsidiary. A **subsidiary** is a company organized under the laws of a foreign country for the purpose of carrying out tasks, such as production and sales, assigned by the parent firm. Some subsidiaries are highly dependent on the parent company for instructions and directions. As Chapter 6 pointed out, this would be an example of a centralized structure. Other subsidiaries operate autonomously because the home office management believes the on-site people are in the best position to make decisions. This would be a decentralized structure.

The Future of International Business

Multinational and global firms continue to be a growing presence in America. In addition, American firms continue to push into every corner of the globe to offer both goods and services. Some of the most recent expansion has involved international franchises, such as McDonald's and Kentucky Fried Chicken, and financial services, such as the offices

FIGURE 22.5

Share of Revenues Earned in Foreign Countries (Selected U.S. Multinational Corporations)

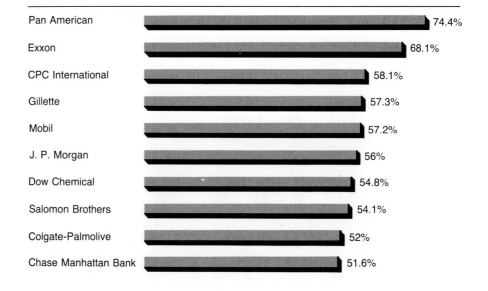

Pan American	74.4%
Exxon	68.1%
CPC International	58.1%
Gillette	57.3%
Mobil	57.2%
J. P. Morgan	56%
Dow Chemical	54.8%
Salomon Brothers	54.1%
Colgate-Palmolive	52%
Chase Manhattan Bank	51.6%

of large securities firms including First Boston, Merrill Lynch, Morgan Stanley, and Salomon Brothers in Europe and the Far East.[18] At the same time, large American banks such as Chase Manhattan and Citibank continue to maintain their financial relationships with nations around the world from China to Poland to Peru.

As Figure 22.5 shows, some U.S. firms rely on international operations for the bulk of their revenues. A major ethical challenge facing many multinational firms is how to conduct business in foreign lands. Does management follow their own home's rules and ethical standards, or those of the country in which they are doing business? Sometimes these standards are conflicting ones, but as has been stressed throughout this text, short-run ethical compromises may lead to long-run disasters. Businesses are learning that they must use the highest ethical standards not only as the right way to do business (even in another culture), but as the profitable way to do business in the long run.

In any event, we live in a global economy, and the future of business is surely an international one.

Checkpoint

1. What are three ways businesses can expand to overseas markets?
2. Why are small companies going international more likely to use licensing than foreign subsidiaries?

Closing Comments

International trade is a growing challenge for business. Many firms sell goods and services with appeal in the markets of several countries. This means that international trade offers both the additional opportunity of new markets and the additional challenge of new competition. Modern businesses need to think "international" rather than just in national terms. This includes having an expanded perspective of social responsibility to the people in every nation, not just to those on the home front. To the extent that companies can meet these important challenges, they stand a good chance not only of surviving, but also of being leaders in their respective industries.

Learning Objectives Revisited

1. **Describe the nature of international business.**
   International trade is the sale of exports (goods shipped to other countries) and purchase of imports (goods brought in from other countries). The balance of trade is total exports minus total imports. In the mid- to late 1980s, the United States has had a negative balance of trade, or a trade deficit. Therefore, although the United States is a major exporter of goods, an important part of international business affecting the United States is foreign businesses selling in domestic markets.

2. **Present the major reasons for international business.**

   Businesses sell in international markets when they have an absolute or comparative advantage. Sources of advantages include abundant natural resources, favorable climate and terrain, sufficient capital equipment, skilled personnel, accessible geographic location, and a stable political climate.

3. **Identify some government-imposed barriers to international trade.**

   Some of the principal barriers to international trade include quotas (import restrictions in terms of quantity or value) and tariffs (duties levied on imported goods). The government also restricts trade for security reasons and may impose regulations that make business operations more complex and costly. To keep money in the country, the government may limit conversion of funds.

4. **Relate some cultural differences that make international trade challenging.**

   Cultural differences create barriers when business people disregard them. Language and communication style are basic differences, but customs and manners may also vary. The concept of time differs between cultures, with punctuality being more important in some cultures than in others, and managers do not always work during the same hours.

5. **Explain some efforts to stimulate international business.**

   Some countries set up free-trade zones (FTZs) in the effort to promote trade. Countries have also cooperated through agreements such as the General Agreement on Tariffs and Trade (GATT) and communities such as the European Economic Community. The United Nations and U.S. government have established financial institutions that foster international trade, including the Export-Import Bank, the International Monetary Fund, and the International Bank for Reconstruction and Development (the World Bank).

6. **Discuss some common approaches to entering international markets.**

   The two most common approaches used by small businesses that want to go international are licensing and exporting. Firms that export use merchants or agents, or they set up their own sales office or branch. Large businesses that want more control use joint ventures, branch organizations, and subsidiaries.

Key Terms Reviewed

Review each of the following terms. For any that you do not know or are unsure of, look up the definitions and see how they were used in the chapter.

multinational corporation (MNC)	comparative advantage
balance of trade	quota
exports	tariff
imports	culture
trade deficit	free-trade zone (FTZ)
balance of payments	General Agreement on Tariffs and Trade (GATT)
absolute advantage	

Common Market

Export-Import Bank
(Exim Bank)

International Monetary
Fund (IMF)

International Bank for
Reconstruction and
Development
(World Bank)

International Finance
Corporation (IFC)

International Development
Association (IDA)

license

joint venture

branch organization

subsidiary

CHAPTER 22

International
Business

Review Questions

1. What is the difference between the balance of trade and the balance of payments?
2. What is the trade deficit? Why are some people concerned about the U.S. trade deficit?
3. What would give a country's businesses an absolute advantage? A comparative advantage? How would such advantages influence a decision to sell to foreign markets?
4. South Korean companies are beginning to produce durable goods such as automobiles and computers and ship many of them halfway around the world to sell in the United States. Why would these companies expand to such a distant market? What advantages do they have to offer U.S. customers? What advantages does the U.S. market offer the companies?
5. Imagine a country with few natural resources and land that is not particularly fertile. What advantages could such a country develop as a trading partner?
6. Why do governments restrict imports? Who benefits from such actions?
7. Managers of J&J Sweets are thinking of building a candy factory in Mexico. However, the Mexican government would require J&J to take on a Mexican partner in this venture. Why could this be disadvantageous to the company? What should the company's managers weigh in making this decision?
8. How do cultural differences make international business more difficult? How can U.S. managers cope with these differences?
9. How can businesses take advantage of free-trade zones?
10. Tina McCormick wants to expand her line of shoe stores into Latin America, but her bank has turned down her request for financing. Where else can Tina look for funding?
11. How do American businesses benefit from organizations that provide financing to underdeveloped nations?
12. Why do small firms usually enter international markets by licensing or exporting rather than by creating a subsidiary?

Applied Exercises

1. At the library, get the latest information on the U.S. trade deficit. What has happened to this deficit over the last five years? Can you discern any trend or pattern? Write a brief summary of your findings and present it to the class.

2. At the library, gather information on the most popular types of American exports and imports. How does comparative advantage help explain why America either exports and imports these goods?

3. Visit a company that is involved in international business. Ask one of the managers how culture affects the company's foreign operations. What are some of the biggest stumbling blocks culture creates for this company?

4. Do library research on one of the following countries: Norway, Kenya, or New Zealand. Based on your findings, what do you think this country's comparative advantage would be in world trade? Does the country have an absolute advantage? Support your answers in a two-page paper.

Your Business IQ: Answers

1. False. Overall, the United States in recent years has been importing substantially more than it has been exporting.

2. True. A large pool of skilled engineers and scientists gives the United States a relative advantage in businesses that rely on such talent. However, there is some evidence and concern that skills of lower-level American workers are declining.

3. True. Most economic experts agree that trade barriers can lead to higher prices and limited choices. However, the government may decide that certain advantages of trade barriers outweigh these disadvantages. For example, trade barriers may protect jobs in certain industries or may prevent the country from relying on foreign suppliers for critical defense materials.

4. True. This is the function of the Common Market, which was founded in 1957.

5. False. Smaller firms usually expand overseas by exporting or licensing. Joint ventures are more popular among large firms, such as the major automakers.

Chinese Opportunity for Foxboro   Case

In the late 1970s, China announced that it was opening the country to world trade. Not surprisingly, given the country's size and growth potential, the announcement was greeted enthusiastically around the world. Many companies reported that they planned to make long-term commitments with China, not saying that they also hoped for some quick profits. Then they encountered Chinese bureaucracy, and the hoopla has died down. Today, relatively few foreign businesses have established themselves profitably in China.

An exception is Foxboro Company in Foxboro, Massachusetts, which makes switchboards and control panels that help operate oil refineries, petrochemical plants, steel mills, cement factories, and other industries that convert natural resources into usable products. One of Foxboro's advantages is that it is supplying something China needs. The country is building basic industries such as the ones Foxboro supplies, and the government is seeking to modernize national industry, which Foxboro's modern technology can help it do.

Foxboro's management also has the advantage of patience. They spent four years traveling back and forth to negotiate a joint venture agreement establishing Shanghai-Foxboro Company Ltd. The company's board of directors, which consists of five Chinese officials and four Foxboro executives, handles long-range planning. Decisions are made by a two-thirds vote. Day-to-day operations are the joint responsibility of Ernest J. DeBellis, deputy general manager, and Yang Tong, the general manager, who also happens to be the factory's Communist Party secretary. This link to the Communist Party means that party decisions affecting the company are informed decisions.

Another reason Foxboro was able to enter the Chinese market is that it was willing to transfer advanced technology to its Shanghai operation. Companies entering joint ventures in other fields have tried to get by with outdated technology, but Shanghai-Foxboro's products are state of the art.

One of Shanghai-Foxboro's major challenges has involved currency. The joint venture agreement specified that the company would reinvest all profits earned during the first five years, limiting the company's use of that money. (The company has earned a profit since its second year in China, an unusually good track record for a joint venture in that country.) Furthermore, most of the earnings are in the form of *Renminbi*, or People's Money, the local currency, which cannot be used to buy imported parts and supplies. Until recently, the company had a difficult time converting *Renminbi* into currencies it could use to buy imports. In 1986, China set up a currency exchange center in Shanghai, which makes it possible to exchange *Renminbi*, but at a relatively expensive rate. Shanghai-Foxboro paid the higher price in order to have reserves of currency for future purchases.

Despite these difficulties, Foxboro's management is pleased with the company's prospects in China. Says DeBellis, "You have to believe China is going to industrialize, and our equipment is the key to much of that industrialization."

Case Questions

1. What comparative advantages does Foxboro bring to the Chinese market? Why does the Chinese market attract Foxboro's managers?
2. What barriers to international trade has Foxboro encountered in China? How has the company overcome or coped with them?
3. What risks is the company taking by sharing technology and decision-making responsibility with its Chinese partners? Do you think these risks are worthwhile?

You Be the Adviser:
Going International with Real Estate

Falworth Real Estate is a large landholder in Arizona and Florida. The firm owns a total of 1.2 million acres in these two states. Falworth both sells and develops land. The biggest revenues come from building speculative or customized homes, duplexes, and condos. However, the company also sells lots to those who want to build their own houses or hold the property as an investment.

Over the last five years the company has sold over 200,000 acres to smaller real estate developers and 400,000 acres to individual investors. The latter is the most profitable market niche and the one that the firm has targeted for the 1990s. The primary way in which Falworth sells this land is through agents working throughout the United States. For example, there is one agent who has the state of Illinois. He is authorized to sell Falworth land to Illinois residents and is given a percentage of the sales price. There are sales agents throughout all 50 states (some covering more than one state) and they have been selling a combined total of 1,250 acres a week.

Over the last year, James Falworth, the founder and president, has been thinking about opening up new sales territories in Europe and Asia. Foreign agents would be given exclusive sales territories and receive a commission on their sales. They could sell to anyone in their territory who is a native of that country. For example, an agent in France could sell an acre of land in Florida to a French couple but could not sell the land to an American family that was vacationing in France. Falworth would offer the same basic arrangement as that given to agents in the United States: each would be given a monthly draw of $1,000 that would be offset by sales commissions. There would also be an allowance for advertising, travel, and out-of-pocket expenses.

Mr. Falworth intends to make a final decision on this matter within the next two months. He and his staff have done considerable research and the major stumbling block appears to be the identification of overseas sales agents and the allocation of sales territories. But, as he reported in a preliminary report to the board of directors, "If we can sell 50,000 acres a year to Europeans and Asians, we can triple our annual profits. What we need to do now is to plan our strategy so that we have the same success overseas that we are having here in the states."

Your Advice

1. What cultural challenges will Falworth face if it decides to go into the European market? The Far East market?
2. What major pitfalls does the company face beside cultural problems if it decides to go international? Explain.
3. What would you specifically recommend the company do in preparing to go international?

Career Opportunities

The government is always part of the business environment, and international trade is growing. Therefore, many career opportunities are associated with the areas discussed in Part VII. Some of the most prominent include attorneys, legal assistants, FBI agents, and international managers.

Attorneys

Attorneys are extremely important to business. One of the most basic activities they perform is helping write and interpret legal documents. If they work exclusively for a particular business firm or specialize in a specific area such as patent law, they must stay abreast of their field in both legal and nonlegal matters. Their work involves contacting people for information, consulting with their clients to determine the details of specific problems, advising clients about the law, and recommending courses of action to resolve or avoid legal problems.

Approximately 500,000 people in the United States are now lawyers. Initial job requirements include graduating from a law school and passing a state bar exam. Most attorneys begin in a junior position with a law firm. Some work their way up the ladder to full-partner status, but many leave and start their own practices, work for the government, or join the corporate legal staff of a large business firm. Beginning lawyers can expect to make $30,000 to $40,000 the first year, depending on whether they enter private practice, where salaries are higher, or go to work for a company or the government. Successful attorneys can expect to make $100,000 or more annually.

Legal Assistants

Legal assistants work directly under the supervision of a lawyer. While the lawyer assumes responsibility for the assistant's work, the assistant is often allowed to perform all the functions of a lawyer other than accepting clients, setting legal fees, giving legal advice, or presenting a case in court. Legal assistants generally do background work for the lawyer such as investigating the facts of a case or doing legal research to identify the appropriate laws, judicial decisions, legal articles, and other materials that help the attorney determine whether the client has a good case and how to win it. Besides trial-related work, legal assistants may help draft documents such as contracts, mortgages, separation agreements, wills, and trust instruments. They also may help prepare tax returns and plan estates. Some legal assistants coordinate the activities of law office employees and keep the financial records for the office.

Legal assistants work in private practice, in business, and in the public sector, where they are employed at the federal, state, and local levels. At the community level, for example, they often serve on legal service staffs to help the poor, the aged, and other persons in need of legal aid. Some are trained on the job, but many attend formal programs in legal assistance, which are available from four-year colleges and universities, law schools, community and junior colleges, and private schools.

There are approximately 65,000 legal assistants in the United States. The number of job openings for legal assistants is expected to increase significantly through the mid-1990s. Earnings vary greatly. Most starting salaries are around $16,000. Top salaries for those with experience in the field are in the $30,000 to $40,000 range.

FBI Agents

FBI agents work under the direction of the U.S. Department of Justice. These agents investigate violations of federal law in connection with bank robberies, kidnappings, white-collar crimes, thefts of government property, organized crime, espionage, and sabotage. Because the FBI is a fact-gathering agency, its special agents function strictly as investigators, collecting information in cases in which the U.S. government is, or may be, an interested party.

At present, there are approximately 10,000 special agents. To be considered for such a position, applicants are usually required to have degrees in either law or accounting. Salaries are in the $25,000 to $35,000 range, depending on qualifications and experience. The employment outlook is that openings will increase about as fast as the average for all occupations.

International Managers

International managers handle the overseas operations of multinational corporations. Some international managers act as the chief executive officer for the company's foreign operations. While the specific demands of the job vary greatly from firm to firm, they resemble those of the head of the home office. The international manager examines overall strategies, helps formulate marketing plans, ensures that the financial plans are adequate to support operations, and reviews progress periodically. Most of these managers have had a great deal of international experience and are fluent in the language of their foreign operation. All of them have been in the business world for many years and have been in charge of major departments throughout the home organization.

About 100 international managers are overseas chief executives and approximately 500 more run international operations but have less authority. Salaries for these individuals vary widely, depending on the size of the overseas operation and the sales revenue of the firm. Most international managers earn $100,000 to $200,000 annually.

International managers other than the chief executive handle each of the functional areas (personnel, operations, marketing, and finance). These managers work in foreign branches and must have language skills of the host country. They have less experience than the chief executive but typically need a college degree. Starting salaries run about $20,000 to $25,000, depending on the company. In some assignments, the company pays extra for a higher cost of living or differences in quality of life.

Fundamentals of the Economy

This appendix discusses the economic foundation for American business. To grow and even to survive in America, businesses must recognize and operate successfully in the economic environment. The discussion begins by describing the overall nature of the economic environment. Going from broad to narrow, it then discusses the macro and micro dimensions of economics. The macro perspective of economics includes the gross national product, leading business indicators, and business cycles. Microeconomics is mainly concerned with the structure of markets.

The General Economic Environment

Economics The study of how societies use limited resources to fulfill their needs and wants for goods and services.

Economics is the study of how societies use limited resources to fulfill their needs and wants for goods and services. A simple example would be students needing textbooks for college classes. To produce college textbooks, publishing firms enter into contracts with knowledgeable authors (usually university professors). Under the terms of such a contract, the publishing firm agrees to pay the authors, who in turn research a subject, write about it, and submit a completed manuscript to the publisher. The publishing firm and the authors are fulfilling society's needs and wants for textbooks.

The process uses resources — labor, capital, and raw materials. Economists call these resources "scarce" because they are limited. This limited supply means that none of us can have as much of everything as we would like.

At the heart of economic activity are exchanges. In this example, a consumer is giving a supermarket money in the form of a check. In exchange, the supermarket is providing food and other goods.

Source: © John Blaustein 1987 for McKesson Corporation.

The exchange of goods and services takes place in the **economic environment,** which consists of buyers and sellers who are brought together through a series of markets. In the textbook example, the buyers are the students. The sellers consist of all the publishing firms that offer textbooks for a particular course (introduction to business, history of western civilization, principles of accounting, and so forth). The market in this case is your bookstore, where sellers and buyers meet.

Why Business Managers Need to Know Economics

The economic environment is very important for business. To a large degree, it dictates the types of decisions business people will make. Consequently, most successful business managers have a basic understanding of how the economic environment works and the changes taking place within it. They can read economic news and know how these developments are likely to affect their industry in general and their company in particular.[1] For example, book publishers know that as the birth rate slows, so will the number of future students. They also know that in good economic times, many young people bypass college, but in an economic recession, many cannot find jobs and so they go on to college. When enrollment increases, so does the demand for textbooks.

Understanding economic activity in the United States begins with a basic knowledge of the forces that drive the economic environment—supply and demand—and the pattern in which resources move through the economy.

The Role of Supply and Demand

The primary driving forces of economic activity in the free enterprise system are supply and demand. **Supply** indicates the amounts of a product that will be provided at varying prices. **Demand** indicates the amounts of a product that will be purchased at varying prices. Sellers will provide a great deal of a product at a high price, while buyers will purchase a great deal of a product at a low price. Business people are interested in supply and demand because, as the next example illustrates, these forces determine the price at which they can sell their products.

Figure A.1 provides a simple example of supply and demand. The figure shows various prices for a simple manufactured product; it also indicates how many units of the product the manufacturer would supply at each price and how many units a store would sell at each price. The supply and demand is also graphed. The graph makes it clear that the buyers (stores) will buy more at a low price, while the sellers (manufacturers) will sell more at a high price. At 40 cents per unit, manufacturers will ship 20,000 units of the product to stores, but the stores will be willing to buy only 1,000 units at this price. However, at 20 cents a unit, the stores will be willing to buy 20,000 units, but the manufacturer will ship only 1,000 units. At 25 cents per unit, the suppliers will ship 10,000 units, and the stores will pay for the same amount. So this is the price at which the parties will strike a deal—the price at which demand equals supply. This price is called the **equilibrium price.**

The relationship between supply and demand is vital to a basic understanding of economics. It is the way prices are determined in a competi-

Economic environment An environment in which buyers and sellers are brought together through an elaborate series of markets.

Supply The various amounts of a product that will be provided at varying prices.

Demand The various amounts of a product that will be purchased at varying prices.

Equilibrium price The price at which demand equals supply.

tive market. In other market structures, prices are set differently; this will be discussed later in the chapter.

Economic Activity: A Circular Flow

Money, goods, and services flow through the economy in a circular manner, as depicted in Figure A.2. Notice that there are three major transactors (government, businesses, and households) and two basic kinds of markets (resource markets and product markets). The participants in free enterprise markets exchange the resources that business and government need in order to operate: land, labor, capital, and entrepreneurial talent. For example, a business buys land, labor, and capital from resource markets and pays rents, wages, and interest for these resources. Households contribute land, labor, capital, and entrepreneurial talent to resource markets in exchange for income. In product markets, households spend money for consumer goods and services, and businesses provide these goods and services in exchange for sales revenue. The government provides services, such as the court system, to households and businesses. In turn, it receives taxes from them. It also uses the markets to purchase resources and products (e.g., guided missiles and the services of school teachers), paying for them with tax dollars.

An example will clarify these dimensions of the economy. Margaret Wilson, a student, works part-time at a local fast-food restaurant. Margaret is part of the labor provided by the resource market. In return for her labor, the restaurant pays her a wage. Margaret uses this income to pay her rent, buy food and clothing, and pay taxes. The business that employs Margaret takes the money it earns and pays its expenses. It buys soft drinks and food for resale, pays its personnel, and pays taxes. The government takes the tax money and uses it to buy goods and services for such uses as national defense, education, and health care. The government may also provide subsidies or make transfer payments, such

FIGURE A.1

Supply and Demand for a Product

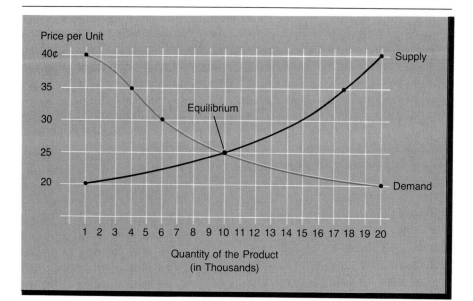

as to farmers or welfare recipients, for which it receives no products or services in return.

This example shows that business, government, and households are interdependent. Each of these three groups helps create and maintain economic activity in a process that continues over and over again, as shown in Figure A.2. From this pattern, business people learn that they must keep abreast of changes in households and government, as well as the activities of other businesses.

The Levels of Economic Analysis: Macro and Micro

The forces of supply and demand and the flow of goods and services provide a general overview of the economic environment for American business. But to gather enough information to make effective decisions, today's business managers try to fill in the details. They do so by learning more about economics, by studying its two major branches: macroeconomics and microeconomics.

Each of these branches examines the economy on a different level. **Macroeconomics** is the branch of economics that is concerned with the

Macroeconomics The branch of economics that is concerned with the overall economy.

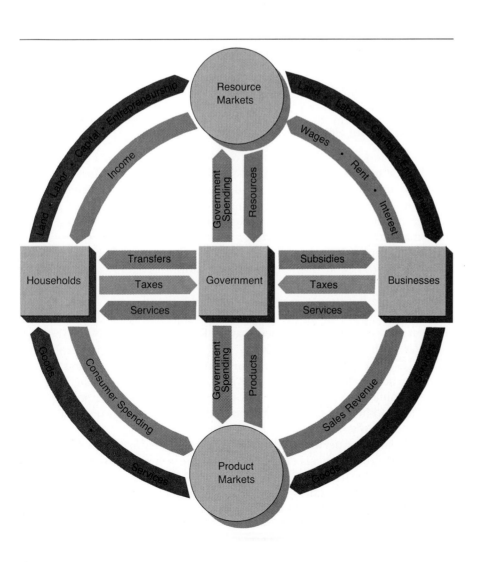

Microeconomics The branch of economics that is concerned with the individual firm or household.

overall economy. For example, when the local newspaper reports that inflation is down and the number of new housing starts is up, this tells business managers something about the economy in the aggregate, rather than about a particular firm or industry group. The other branch of economics, **microeconomics,** considers the individual firm, industry, or household. Microeconomics provides information about how prices are set in an industry, what influences consumer behavior, and how managers decide how much their business should produce. The rest of the chapter introduces you to these two levels of analysis.

Checkpoint

1. Why do business managers need to know economics?
2. How do supply and demand determine the price of a good or service?

Macroeconomics

Business firms are interested in macroeconomics because they want to know the state of the economy at large. Managers need some idea of where the economy is headed if they are to effectively plan for the future. There are many ways of focusing on and measuring macroeconomic activity. The two major measurements are gross national product (GNP) and leading indicators.

Gross National Product

Gross national product (GNP) The total market value of all goods and services produced in the economy in one year.

Most attention in macroeconomics focuses on **gross national product (GNP),** the total market value of all goods and services produced in the economy in one year. GNP is a good gauge of the health of the overall economy. When GNP is growing, managers assume that demand is strong. A flat or falling GNP may signal trouble and suggest that a business may have difficulty expanding.

In evaluating GNP, managers have to keep in mind the influence of price. To understand this, imagine a very simple economy in which the only goods produced are fish (to eat) and tents (to live in). Suppose that two years ago businesses caught five million fish and made one million tents, and they produced the same number this year. The GNP for both years is the same, right? Not necessarily. Remember that GNP is the *market value* of these goods and services. If the price of tents has risen from $70 to $75, the GNP will increase, implying that the economy has grown, when really the only change is in prices. We say that the growth is in "nominal" GNP—growth in name only. But if you're a manager and want to know whether the economy is really growing, not just prices, how can you tell?

Statisticians can perform calculations that correct for price changes. In statistical language, this is called holding price constant, and the resulting GNP figures are called "real" GNP, or GNP stated in "constant dollars." The real GNP reflects the actual quantity of goods and services produced. If real GNP goes up, more goods and services were produced this year than last year. Business usually views this as a good sign because it means more people were working and earning incomes, and more goods and services were produced and sold.

Trends in GNP During the Great Depression of the 1930s, the GNP dropped significantly. People were out of work, few could afford to buy much, and many were living hand-to-mouth. As the graph in Figure A.3 shows, between 1929 and 1933, the GNP dropped significantly. It was not until after World War II that the economy began its vigorous recovery. Today the GNP is higher than ever. However, taking into account both the dramatic drop in the stock market in 1987 and the huge federal and trade deficit, many economists feel that another recession may occur.

While nominal GNP has been growing steadily, note that during a recession real GNP often levels off or drops back. For example, real GNP dropped in 1980 and again in 1982 as the United States went through a significant recession. During that time, American auto production went from a high of over 12 million cars in 1977 to about 5 million cars in 1982. Of course, this production decline was not entirely the fault of the recession. Foreign competition and questionable management decisions also undoubtedly contributed.

Components of GNP GNP is the sum of four different types of spending: personal consumption expenditures *(C)*, private investment *(I)*, government purchases *(G)*, and net exports *(X_n)* of goods and services, or $GNP = C + I + G + X_n$. If the total of all four expenditures this year is greater than it was last year, GNP will rise. If the reverse is true, GNP will fall.

FIGURE A.3

U.S. Gross National Product for Selected Years

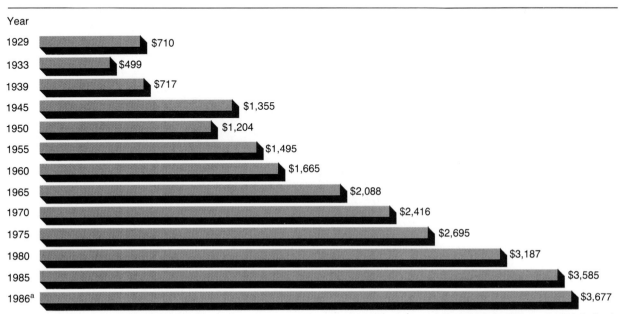

Year
1929 — $710
1933 — $499
1939 — $717
1945 — $1,355
1950 — $1,204
1955 — $1,495
1960 — $1,665
1965 — $2,088
1970 — $2,416
1975 — $2,695
1980 — $3,187
1985 — $3,585
1986[a] — $3,677

Real GNP (in Billions of 1982 Dollars)

[a]Estimated.

Personal Consumption Expenditures Personal consumption expenditures consist of all purchases made by individuals and families. As Table A.1 shows, about two-thirds of every dollar spent in the U.S. economy goes for personal consumption.

Durable goods Goods that do not wear out quickly.

Personal consumption comprises several subcategories. One is **durable goods,** which are goods that do not quickly wear out. Examples include washers, dryers, autos, television sets, and stereos. For years, American manufacturers dominated the market for durable goods. Since then the market has been dominated by Japanese and, more recently, Korean manufacturers.

Nondurable goods Goods that are used up or wear out quickly.

Another category of personal consumption is **nondurable goods.** These are goods that are used up or wear out quickly. Examples include toothpaste, soap, food, and gasoline.

Other personal consumption expenditures include services, such as medical care, education, domestic help, and legal and accounting assistance. Purchases of services by Americans have been dramatically increasing in recent years and have become a dominant component of American consumer spending.

Private investment Total expenditures for capital goods during a year.

Private Investment The **private investment** area of GNP is total expenditures for capital goods during a year. **Capital goods** include machinery, equipment, tools, and facilities. In other words, as Chapter 1 pointed out, these capital goods represent the technological dimension of business. Another major part of private investment is changes in business inventories, which take such forms as raw materials, work in process, and finished goods. Notice that this definition excludes what we often think of as investing: buying stock, for example, or putting money into a certificate of deposit.

Capital goods Machinery, equipment, tools, and facilities.

Government Purchases of Goods and Services The government spends billions of dollars every year. The pie chart in Figure A.4 shows that at the federal level, a large percentage of the money is spent on running the military and for health and human services. At the state and local level, governments spend billions on education, police and fire protection, and road and building maintenance. At the present, government purchases account for approximately one-fifth of GNP.

T A B L E   A.1

Breakdown of U.S. GNP

Type of Spending	Amount (in billions of 1982 dollars)	Percentage of Total
Goods and services purchased by individuals	$2,450.5	66%
Private investment	654.0	18
Government purchases of goods and services	754.5	20
Net exports of goods and services	−145.8	−4
Total	$3,713.3	100.0%

Net Exports of Goods and Services The fourth component of GNP is net exports of goods and services. The United States imports and exports goods and services. Rather than treating them separately, in calculating GNP the difference between the two is taken. Thus, net exports refers to the amount by which foreign spending on American goods and services exceeds American spending on foreign goods and services.[2] For example, if foreigners buy $100 billion worth of U.S. exports and Americans buy $50 billion worth of foreign imports in a year, then net exports will be a positive $50 billion.

Unfortunately, in recent years the United States has been importing more than it has been exporting, so this figure is negative, as Table A.1 shows. In 1987 there was $171 billion trade deficit (imports were greater

	Fiscal 1985 (in Millions)	Percentage
Executive Office	$111	.01%
President	$11,277	1.4
Agriculture	$49,596	6.0
Defense	$262,898	31.6
Health and Human Services	$315,553	38.0
Treasury	$165,043	19.8
Labor	$23,893	2.9
Justice	$3,518	.4

F I G U R E   A.4

U.S. Government Spending[a]

[a]For fiscal year 1985.

Hyundai Excel automobiles, such as this one, are among the popular goods imported from South Korea. In recent years, the total value of imports sold in the United States has exceeded the value of U.S. goods sold in other countries. South Korean companies including Hyundai have been among the most successful at increasing their share of the U.S. market.

Nothing succeeds like cars that make sense.
Hyundai.

A new home under construction. The number of new homes on which construction has started is one of the leading business indicators, that is, it is linked to future changes in the economy at large. One possible reason is that sales of homes lead to increased sales of other goods and services, such as large appliances, mortgage lending, and lawn-care products and services. Thus, when the number of housing starts rises, business people view the trend as a sign of future economic growth.

Source: © 1986 Steve Weber: CLICK/Chicago.

Composite of leading indicators A set of measurements that provides clues about which way the economy is moving.

than exports by $171 billion).[3] A whopping $59 billion of that negative balance was in trade with Japan. If such a large deficit persists for an extended period, this trade imbalance is an unhealthy sign for the American economy. The stock market crash in October 1987 was the result of a number of factors, but many experts cited the trade deficit as a — if not *the* — major precipitating cause.

Largely because of the trade deficit, the United States became a debtor nation in 1985 for the first time since 1914. In fact, we are now by far the world's largest debtor nation. This means that foreigners now own more in U.S. investments than Americans own in foreign investments. This has been a rapid plunge, because in 1982 we were the largest creditor nation. In 1986 foreign investment in the United States shot up 26 percent, which dwarfed our 13 percent increase in investments overseas. The debt at the end of fiscal 1987 was $268.4 billion and the annual interest paid to foreigners was $23.5 billion.[4] The way that we can reduce the debt is by running surpluses in merchandise trade accounts. Most economists do not see this happening in the foreseeable future and estimate that the U.S. foreign debt could hit $1 trillion by the early 1990s.[5] Chapter 22 discusses international trade in greater detail.

Leading Business Indicators

Business is particularly interested in changes in GNP because these reflect changes in the economy at large, at the macro level. However, rather than wait for changes to occur, business people like to anticipate or forecast what is going to happen and prepare for it.[6] For example, if the economy is likely to grow, business managers want to be ready to expand appropriately. If a downturn is likely, they want to cut back operations and prepare to weather the economic storm.

For this reason, managers pay close attention to the **composite of leading indicators,** which is a set of measurements that provide clues about which way the economy is moving. Table A.2 shows the 12 indicators that the U.S. Department of Commerce tracks. The Commerce Department combines these indicators into one composite index.

T A B L E   A.2

Leading Business Indicators

1. The average work week of production workers in manufacturing
2. The layoff rate in manufacturing
3. The value of manufacturers' new orders for consumer goods and materials in constant dollars
4. New business foundations
5. Standard & Poor's index of 500 common-stock prices
6. Contracts and orders for plant and equipment in constant dollars
7. The number of new private housing starts
8. Net changes in inventories on hand and new orders
9. The percentage of companies reporting slower deliveries
10. Changes in prices of key raw materials such as foods, feeds, and fibers
11. Changes in liquid (easily sellable) wealth held by private investors
12. The money supply in constant dollars

A brief review of some of these variables shows why they are good indicators of what is going to happen in the economy. For example, if the average work week of production workers (#1) is up, layoffs are down (#2), new orders for plant and equipment are up (#3), and inventories are up (#8), business is beginning to pick up and the economy is likely to spurt ahead. If just the opposite is happening, the economy is beginning to slow down. In either case, the length of the lead may be weeks or months. Many business managers keep close track on these leading indicators for clues about how to adjust their strategies appropriately. Yet despite the availability of these predictors, the stock market crash in 1987 caught most business people and economic experts by surprise. In some cases, they failed to believe what the indicators were saying, and in some ways the indicators did not pick up on what was happening.

Business Cycles

The GNP and the leading indicators provide information about whether the economic environment is growing, shrinking, or stagnant. This behavior of the economy is part of another area of macroeconomics, **business cycles.** These cycles are fluctuations in business activity that progress through four major phases.

The Phases of the Business Cycle The **peak** phase of the business cycle is the period when national output reaches its highest level. This peak or period of prosperity is followed by **recession,** an economic period during which the economy begins to slow and move downward. Recessions are typically characterized by sales declines, employee layoffs, and a general business retrenchment. If economic conditions do not stabilize, the result can be a **depression,** an economic period characterized by prolonged recession and massive unemployment, low wages, and large numbers of people living in poverty. When the cycle bottoms out it reaches a "trough." As the economy begins to turn around, it enters a **recovery,** an economic period during which demand for goods and services is on the rise. During this period, production increases, employees are called back to work, and wages start to rise.

Trends in the Business Cycle The last 50 years provide a good picture of business cycles in action. This history is shown in Figure A.5. The Great Depression came to an end with the start of World War II. At the end of the war, some people predicted that the economy would enter a recession. However, except for a dip in 1949, the economy stabilized and experienced positive growth through the 1950s.

The 1960s started slowly, but a tax credit for purchases of new machinery (capital goods) and an $11 billion tax cut for individual taxpayers helped spur the economy on. However, the latter part of the decade saw a rise in **inflation,** which is a general increase in the level of prices. Under inflation, purchasing power is eroded; it costs more and more to buy less and less. Inflation has had a particularly strong impact on expenditures in such areas as energy, medical care, and transportation.

The 1970s saw the emergence of a new economic phenomenon: stagflation. **Stagflation** is stagnant economic growth coupled with inflation. Before the 1970s, economists believed that inflation occurred only after

Business cycles Fluctuations in business activity.

Peak The phase of the business cycle when national output reaches its highest level.

Recession An economic period during which the economy begins to slow and move downward.

Depression An economic period characterized by prolonged recession, massive unemployment, low wages, and large numbers of people living in poverty.

Recovery An economic period during which demand for goods and services is on the rise.

Inflation A general increase in the level of prices.

Stagflation Stagnant economic growth coupled with inflation.

the economy was at full employment. Now, they realize that it could occur in an economy where economic growth was still quite low and there was a good deal of unemployment. The Arab oil embargo worsened the situation, and by the end of the 1970s, the United States was bogged down in the worst economic decline since the Great Depression.

The 1980s began on a sour note. For the first couple of years, unemployment remained high, while inflation and interest rates for loans (which had reached 20 percent and more) slowly came down. By the middle of the decade, the group of Arab oil exporters known as OPEC had all but collapsed, leading to a decrease in oil prices, and inflation was under control. On the other hand, economic growth remained fairly slow, and the government was running massive deficits. Overall, however, the economic climate for business, except for the escalating trade deficit, was better than it had been the decade before.

Causes of Business Cycles

What causes business cycles? Wars, tax policies, and good and bad economic times are obvious contributors. Often two or more of them are influential at the same time. Also, not every sector of the economy or every part of the country faces the same business cycle at the same time. If a downturn starts with, say, a slowdown in the demand for manufactured goods, then industrial areas of the country such as the Northeast and large urban areas will feel the effect quickly, but rural areas will not. Conversely, if the price of farm products begins to decline, farmers and small rural communities will feel the negative effects almost immediately, while city dwellers will not. If these problems persist, however, there will be a ripple effect. Eventually the entire country will begin to feel the economic crunch. The far-reaching changes can stem from any of the factors that cause business cycles.

In a purely capitalistic system, competitive market forces would be allowed to regulate the business cycles through supply and demand alone. However, in the American free enterprise system, the government attempts to influence the economy through fiscal and monetary policies. **Fiscal policy** is the use of government spending and tax collection to

Fiscal policy The use of government spending and tax collection to attain full employment and a noninflationary high level of GNP.

F I G U R E   A.5

The Business Cycle in Action

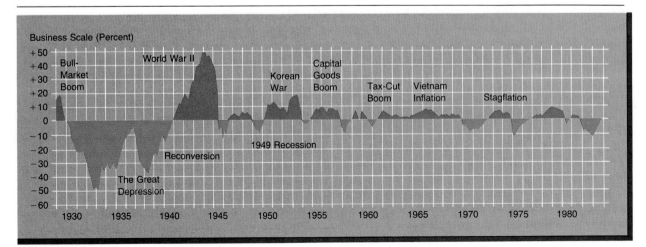

attain full employment and a noninflationary high level of GNP. **Monetary policy** is government regulation of the money supply to attain full employment and a noninflationary high level of GNP. These policies, which change spending or the money supply, can have a big impact on business cycles.

Changes in Total Spending The major immediate cause of business cycles is changes in total spending. For example, if the federal government decided to spend no more than it collected in taxes (a balanced budget), deficit spending would end. As a result, the government would spend dramatically less. The government might, for example, cut expenses for military weapons and supplies, research and development, and computers. The resulting decline in the demand for these products may hurt the sales of many industries: defense contractors and aerospace, high-tech, and computer firms to name but a few.

By the same token, by balancing the budget, the cost of the debt would be reduced and there might be a positive long-range impact on trade with other countries. Traditionally, most economists have called for deficit spending to spur employment and economic growth, but, especially after the stock market crash in 1987, a growing number of economists and politicians are calling for a reduction in the national debt, which means less government spending and/or increased taxes.

Changes in the Money Supply Another influence on business cycles is changes in the money supply. These changes result from federal government activities described in Chapter 17. An increase in the amount of money in circulation makes it easier to obtain; a decrease makes it more difficult to obtain. When money is easy to obtain, interest rates for loans are low. Businesses and people borrow more and spend more, and the economy expands. When money becomes more difficult to obtain, interest rates for loans will rise. Businesses and people cut back on their borrowing; they have less to spend, and the economy slows down.

By monitoring and manipulating the amount of money in circulation, the government can help move the economy forward or slow it down. During a recession, the government wants to turn things around, so it will tend to increase the supply of money. This is called an "easy-money policy." When the economy is moving ahead too quickly, resulting in inflation, the government will slow it down by reducing the amount of money in circulation. This approach is a "tight-money policy."

Changes in Business Investments A third cause of business cycles is changes in business investments. Businesses invest in many things, including factory buildings, machinery, equipment, warehouses, and inventory. As companies spend money in these areas, their expenditures help increase GNP and move the economy forward. But if the demand for goods and services declines, managers will begin reducing inventory and will avoid expanding facilities or replacing or upgrading equipment. Instead, they will wait for the economy to turn around.

Although managers may make investments based on expectations, changes in business investment often directly follow trends in the economy. As managers notice that the economy is starting to turn down, they will begin trimming purchases. As they see the economy starting to turn

Monetary policy
Government regulation of the money supply to attain full employment and a noninflationary high level of GNP.

up, they will begin increasing inventory and expanding facilities and equipment and upgrading their technology.

Population Changes Another influence on business cycles is changes in the population. The population of the United States continues to increase every year. More people mean an increased demand for goods and services. Over the last half-decade, the U.S. population has grown a little over 1 percent a year.

However, the population in each geographic region does not change in the same proportion. For example, southern and western states, the so-called Sun Belt, accounted for 90 percent of the population growth in the last half-decade. During the 1980s, Florida's population has increased dramatically, as has that of Texas and California. The Northeast, meanwhile, has seen a relative decline in the population. These variations mean that business people must examine population increases from both a national and a regional standpoint.

Both the number of people and their age breakdown affect the demand for particular goods and services. For example, if there are relatively more young people, the demand for educational services and supplies will increase; if there are relatively more older people, the demand for health services and supplies will increase. Thus, as the age breakdown changes over the long run, some industries will pick up business, and others will lose it.

Expectations Besides changes in demand and spending patterns, business cycles are also greatly responsive to expectations such as pessimism and optimism. If people believe that prices are going to rise rapidly next year, they are likely to buy this year. If people believe the economy will continue its prosperity for another couple of years, they will be more likely to take a loan and buy a home or car or go on a dream vacation.

The behavior that results from these expectations can influence the economy. A strong economy can be thrown into a recession if consumers suddenly stop spending because they believe the economy is going downhill. Actually, it would be their own lack of spending that caused the economic decline, but it is often difficult to get people to recognize this fact. The good news is that expectations are unlikely to start a change in the business cycle, and they can facilitate or speed up an economic turnaround. The bad news is that expectations can worsen an economic downturn.

Checkpoint

1. What are two ways business people evaluate the macroeconomic environment?
2. If you were planning to expand your taxicab business, which measurements would you be most interested in?

Microeconomics

Besides the general economic environment, business managers want to know about their particular industry and their particular company. What price should they charge? How much should they produce? How will consumers respond to a price increase? For these answers, managers turn to microeconomics, the branch of economics that helps explain how businesses make decisions.

The Economic Basis of Business Decisions

When economists analyze business decisions, they assume that managers are rational—that when managers make decisions, they weigh the costs and benefits and choose the option with the greatest net benefits. To use a simple example, if you can spend 50 cents for one apple or the same amount for two apples of comparable quality, you will choose two apples. (If you aren't hungry enough to eat two apples, you can save the second one or exchange it for something else.) Likewise, if you were the owner of a business and could choose between earning $1 million and $2 million this year, chances are you'd opt for $2 million, other things being equal. This would be the rational thing to do.

In a free enterprise economy, the benefit that businesses seek to maximize is profit. Remember from Chapter 1 that profit is the company's total revenue minus its expenses. Therefore, to obtain the maximum profit, which is the rational approach, managers must keep production costs as low as possible and revenues as high as possible.

Long-Term versus Short-Term Profits If the objective of business is to maximize profits, there may be a conflict with being socially responsible, as Chapter 2 pointed out. The resolution of this conflict may be found in the difference between long-term and short-term profits. Companies that want to remain profitable over the long term need good relationships with customers and the community. For example, a hair-styling business may decide that it can save a lot of money by hiring untrained stylists fresh out of high school and using substandard or even dangerous supplies, but after a few customers had their hair styled there, word would get around and the shop would be out of business.

When effective business people seek to maximize profits, they consider the lifetime of the company. They try to make products and provide services that people will value enough to buy again, and they try to develop a good reputation in the community. This approach makes some decisions complicated—a more expensive manufacturing process, higher wages, or fewer sales may seem to hurt the company in the short run but may be beneficial in the long run. In addition, a focus on long-term profitability may seem expensive at the outset, but it increases earnings and growth over the company's existence.

Measuring Profits Chapter 15 discusses in detail the accounting statements used for measuring a company's profits, but for purposes of the present discussion it can simply be said that to measure profits, managers have to calculate the company's total revenue and total expenses. To find total revenue, they multiply the price of their product by the quantity sold. To calculate total costs, they multiply the cost of producing one unit of their product by the number of units produced and add the costs that are there no matter how many units are produced (for example, lights, heat, and rent). In general, the amount the company will want to produce is the quantity at which the difference between revenues and costs is greatest.

One way a company could increase profits would be to sell the same quantity at a higher price. But remember that in a competitive economic environment, demand falls with an increase in price. If the quantity sold decreases sharply, the company can actually earn less profit by charging a higher price. Therefore, business people try to determine how sensitive consumers are to the price of their product. For example, since some consumers are relatively insensitive to the prices of luxuries such as designer clothing, sellers of designer clothes can charge high prices. In general, sensitivity to price is influenced by the type of competition the supplier faces.

Competition and Market Structure

To learn about the kind of competitive environment they face, managers try to understand the type of market structure in which their business is operating. The market structure influences how buyers and competitors make decisions. In particular, knowing this helps managers determine price and develop other competitive strategies.

The market structures in which businesses in a free enterprise economic system operate fall into four major categories: pure monopoly, oligopoly, monopolistic competition, and pure competition.

Pure monopoly A market in which there is only one seller or producer and there are no substitutes for the product or service.

Pure Monopoly A **pure monopoly** is a market in which there is only one seller or producer and there are no substitutes for the product or service. The most common examples are public utilities, which are established and regulated by the government. These utilities, such as the local power company, have the exclusive right to sell their output to area residents and businesses.

Pure monopolies are discouraged legally and philosophically in a free enterprise economy and thus rarely occur in the private sector. Nevertheless, some companies such as Polaroid come close. When Polaroid first produced the "instant picture" camera, it had a monopoly because, as Kodak learned the hard way, no one else was able to duplicate this product. The company was able to maintain its monopoly because it applied for, and was granted, a **patent,** a federal government grant of exclusive control over and use of a discovery or a new product or process for 17 years. Although seldom associated with monopolies, patents can temporarily create a monopoly-like situation for a company.[7]

Patent A federal government grant of exclusive control over and use of a discovery or a new product or process for 17 years.

Another possible way for a firm to resemble a monopoly is to own the raw materials for a particular product. For example, the DeBeers Company of South Africa owns most of the world's diamond mines and, through agreements, controls other sources it does not own. The International Nickel Company of Canada controls most of the world's known nickel reserves. In essence, these companies have monopolies. They are practically the only seller, and their products have no close substitutes.

Still another possible way for a private firm to create a monopoly-like situation is to obtain the exclusive rights to sell a particular good or service. The local garbage collection service, for example, provides all of the refuse collection for a given area. Because of the investment needed to provide this service, it is cheaper for one company to do this than many small ones. This is why a city or town will create a monopoly position for the refuse firm by granting it an exclusive contract.

The way a monopoly sets prices depends on whether it is regulated or not. A regulated monopoly such as a utility can charge only what the regulating agency will allow. The firm requests periodic price increases to allow it to keep up with inflation and plant maintenance and expansion, but the regulators determine the final price. In an unregulated monopoly, the business sets the price that provides the greatest profit. This does *not* mean charging the highest price, because at this price, there will be very few customers. Although there are no substitutes, the customer may choose to go without. Nor does it mean charging an extremely low price, because at this level, the profit may be very small.

Oligopoly An **oligopoly** is a market structure in which a small percentage or number of firms dominate the industry. For example, of, say, 40 companies in an industry, three or four of them may account for 70 or 80 percent of the sales. In the automobile business, General Motors, Ford, Chrysler, and a handful of foreign competitors dominate the industry. The tire industry is dominated by Goodyear, Goodrich, Firestone, and General Tire. The giants in the long-distance telephone industry are American Telephone & Telegraph (AT&T), which until recently had a monopoly on the telephone business, and some relatively new arrivals such as Sprint and MCI.

In an oligopoly, the strategy of each firm affects the others. If one lowers its price, the others must follow or will lose customers. If one raises its price and the others do not follow, the first must lower its price or lose customers. An illustrative case is the airline industry. Before deregulation in 1978, many major airlines competed for passengers. The same was true several years after deregulation. Eventually, however, only a few companies survived the fierce price competition. By 1987, at the top 15 airports, half the airline passenger business was controlled by either one carrier, or two carriers shared at least 70 percent.[8] For example, in St. Louis, TWA handled 82 percent of the passengers and at Denver, United and Continental together handled 88 percent. Because only a few survive in the end, firms in an oligopoly typically try to avoid competing on the basis of price and turn to nonprice competition instead.

Nonprice Competition Competition in an oligopoly usually consists of **nonprice competition**—trying to win over customers with advertising and personal selling rather than price. This form of promotion (covered in Chapter 13) is used to differentiate a standardized product or service. For example, everyone wants good telephone service, and it is irrelevant who provides it. In the mid-1980s, AT&T used an effective advertising program to convince customers that it had always provided outstanding service and would continue to do so with the new, and untried, competitors entering the markets. The price for AT&T's service may be somewhat higher than that of the competition, but because customers think the firm provides excellent service, they may choose to remain loyal. If

Oligopoly A market in which a small percentage of the firms dominate the industry.

Nonprice competition The effort to win over customers with advertising and personal selling rather than price.

this happens, AT&T has managed to differentiate itself from the competition, even though all firms in the oligopolistic market structure are selling a standardized service.

Barriers to Entry Another important characteristic of an oligopoly is that entry into the industry is difficult. It costs a lot of money to enter an oligopolistic industry because the firms already there have made huge capital outlays for large plants or other facilities, up-to-date expensive equipment, research and development laboratories staffed by specialists creating new products, and patents to protect their current products and processes. Taken as whole, these assets constitute what are called "barriers to entry." Any firm that cannot overcome these barriers is effectively blocked from entering the oligopolistic market.

Monopolistic competition A market structure in which there are many firms, each producing only a small share of the total output demanded.

Monopolistic Competition In contrast to the few firms dominating an oligopoly, in **monopolistic competition** there are many firms, each producing only a small share of the total output demanded. Firms readily enter such a market because there are relatively few barriers to entry. Under monopolistic competition, each firm attempts to differentiate its products and services from those of the competition. Similar to oligopolistic firms, nonprice competition is important because the large number of competitors makes it difficult to raise prices. Customers have access to too many other sources of the product at a better price. To compete, businesses in this market structure try to develop a reputation among their clientele and to improve product quality.

Service stations are a good example. While one gallon of gasoline is much like another, the services that accompany the gas may vary. At some service stations, when the customer drives in, employees check under the car's hood, wash the windows, and ensure that the tire pressure is correct. Many customers will pay the extra money for the gas because they think that the accompanying services are worth it.

Another example of monopolistic competition is the market for college graduates with degrees in computer science. Many students graduate with such a degree, but each student is unique. Some employees are willing to pay a little more to obtain the services of a graduate with a particularly desirable background, such as relevant work experience or a minor in business.

Pure competition A market structure in which there are many independent sellers, each offering products at the current market price.

Pure Competition Under a **pure competition** market structure, there are many independent sellers, each offering products at the current market price. Just as there are no absolutely pure monopolies in modern America, there are also no really pure competitive markets. Although the U.S. government to a degree does influence price and the amount produced, agricultural products come the closest. These products are standardized; consumers cannot distinguish one farmer's or company's offerings from those of another. Also, no supplier is large enough to influence the price. Each is selling only a small percentage of the total output being demanded. For example, a farmer selling corn or wheat will sell at the going price per bushel. Buyers cannot distinguish between Farmer Anderson's corn or wheat and Farmer Brown's corn or wheat, so the farmer simply brings the crops to market and sells them at the going price. The same is true in dealing with vegetables or cattle.

In pure competition, supply and demand are critical to the price of goods and services. Additional factors such as advertising and personal selling, used to influence the transaction in other market structures, are unimportant to those operating in pure competition.

To summarize, Table A.3 compares and contrasts the four market structures. Managers find that understanding the type of structure in which they are operating is an important part of making effective business decisions involving, say, pricing and advertising, and of making a profit.

Checkpoint

1. What are the four basic market structures found in the micro analysis of the American economy?
2. How do business people decide how much to produce?

When many firms compete for a share of the market, businesses look for ways to differentiate their products. If customers find better price or quality elsewhere, they can easily change companies. Automobile dealers operate in such an economic environment, called monopolistic competition. The auto manufacturers, on the other hand, operate in an oligopolistic market.

Source: © 1987 Don Smetzer: CLICK/Chicago.

T A B L E   A.3   **Characteristics of the Four Basic Market Structures**

	Market Structure			
Characteristics	**Pure Monopoly**	**Oligopoly**	**Monopolistic Competition**	**Pure Competition**
Number of firms in the market	One	A small number	Many	Many
Control over price	A great deal	Depends on what the others do	Some	None
Type of product	Unique	Unique or differentiated	Differentiated	Standardized
Ease of entry into the industry	Not possible	Very difficult	Relatively easy	Very easy
Use of nonprice competition	Some; mostly public relations, advertising	Quite a lot; advertising, quality, and service	Quite a lot; advertising, quality and service	None
Examples	Local utilities, garbage service	Steel, autos, household appliances, banks	Retail stores, household items, clothing, restaurants, beauty salons	Agriculture

Business Statistics and Research

For many people, both inside and outside the business world, the mere mention of the words *statistics* and *research* is enough to inspire fear. However, you have already been using statistics and research results in your study of business. For example, if you have studied economics or read Appendix A, when you looked at the pattern of business cycles and the growth in gross national product, you were evaluating statistics. Marketing and accounting also rely on statistical methods: conducting and interpreting marketing research involves statistics and research, as do the techniques for analyzing financial statements. In fact, research results are used in every chapter of this text. As you can see from these examples, business statistics and research are a practical source of information for managers and not necessarily difficult to comprehend.

This appendix shows how business researchers gather, analyze, and present data. After first presenting the nature and sources of statistical information, the discussion turns to the various ways to analyze data. These techniques include frequency distributions, averages, index numbers, and correlations. The next part is devoted to presenting information through the use of tables and graphs. The final section provides guidelines for using statistical research information to make more effective decisions.

The Nature and Meaning of Business Statistics

When the Coca-Cola Company introduced "new" Coke a few years ago, it announced that research showed that consumers prefer a cola that tastes sweeter and less tangy. Coca-Cola's managers were in for a rude awakening. Within weeks, sales figures showed that Pepsi-Cola was making serious inroads into Coke's market. Further investigation revealed that while many people liked the new taste, they didn't want an old favorite to be tampered with. From this information, Coca-Cola's managers realized that withdrawing "old" Coke had been a serious mistake. They brought back the original product and labeled it "Classic" Coke. Although Classic Coke outsells the newer version, data indicate that the overall market share for Coke has increased.

In making this series of decisions, Coca-Cola's managers used **business statistics** — the systematic collection, presentation, and interpretation of data related to business problems. To collect information, they used marketing research into consumer preferences and motivations, as well as sales figures for its own and its competitors' product. They interpreted the data when they assigned meaning to numbers such as the percentage of consumers preferring a particular flavor or buying a particular brand.

This activity has a variety of applications to all kinds of businesses. Store managers evaluate sales records to determine which products are selling. Marketers conduct research to evaluate who wants and needs a particular kind of product. Economists and finance managers use statistics to measure and predict trends in the economy. Statistics also play a

Most companies provide some sources of secondary data, if only a few subscriptions to business periodicals. Some companies provide extensive support, such as the libraries of Smith Kline & French Laboratories, a major pharmaceutical company. Shown here is the company's research library in the United Kingdom, which contains over 4,000 books, subscribes to 350 journals, and maintains more than 15,000 bound volumes. Smith Kline & French's libraries also offer access to computerized information searches.

Source: Courtesy of SmithKline Beckman Corporation.

Business statistics The systematic collection, presentation, and interpretation of data related to business problems.

role in quality control, evaluating costs, and testing the results of business decisions.

Checkpoint

1. What are business statistics?
2. What are three ways in which business people use statistical information?

Data Collection

The activities of business statistics and research begin with data collection. Managers want to collect data that will provide accurate information at a reasonable cost. To make informed choices, they must be able to weigh the relative merits of the various techniques used for data collection. Chapter 11 presents the various types of data relevant to marketing decisions; these are relevant here as well.

Collecting Secondary Data

Secondary data
Information that already is available from sources outside the firm.

When they can, business researchers start by collecting **secondary data** — information that already is available from sources outside the firm. The government is a major source of secondary data. For example, census data describe agriculture, retail and wholesale trade, the service industry, housing, manufacturing, and the population. The federal government also produces important economic documents such as the *Federal Reserve Bulletin, Survey of Current Business,* and *Monthly Labor Review,* as well as the *Statistical Abstracts of the United States.* At the state level, documents and pamphlets describe regional economic conditions and general population statistics. At the local level, statistics related to employment, production, and sales activities are typically available at city hall or the Chamber of Commerce. State and municipal colleges and universities also generate data of local interest.

Besides government publications, researchers can tap a number of private sources of information. One of the most popular sources are trade associations that collect data concerning the industry. Some national companies sell information to subscribers who pay a fee to receive data periodically. For those interested in sales information, the A. C. Nielsen Company gathers product sales data every 60 days for items stocked in drugstores and food stores. For those interested in financial information, Moody's, Dun & Bradstreet, and Standard & Poor's provide a wealth of information to their subscribers. Still other common sources of information are business magazines and newspapers such as *Business Week* and *The Wall Street Journal.*

Collecting Primary Data

Primary data Original information gathered in order to investigate a particular problem or to determine the status of a particular operation.

Secondary data are relatively inexpensive to collect, but managers often need information that more specifically addresses a particular issue. For this, they turn to **primary data** — original information gathered in order to investigate a specific problem or to determine the status of a particular operation. For example, if a manager wanted to find out why assembly line A has twice as many hours of down time as assembly line B, the manager could collect primary data on the problem. Such data might include interviewing people on the line, reviewing equipment maintenance on the two assembly lines, and talking to supervisors in both areas. Based on these data, the manager would draw conclusions and take action. Most primary data come from company records, observation, and surveys.

Company Records The most common form of primary data are internal records. A business's records often provide valuable insights into specific problems and operations. For example, if a brewing company added a new light beer to its line, and began selling the product through all of its current outlets, it would want to find out how well it was doing. The initial sales records might show that the firm's biggest sales region is the western part of the United States.

Information such as this may suggest possible relationships to investigate further. For example, the brewing company might find that people on the West Coast are more willing to try new products. By generating a hypothesis such as this, the manager can narrow the scope of future primary research, thereby cutting research costs. Company records put a great deal of important data right at the manager's fingertips.

Observation To gain insights into the reasons underlying numerical patterns, managers find it helpful to observe what is happening directly. For example, consider a company that is having trouble reducing defects in the products its workers are assembling. The production engineers say that technically 99 out of 100 units should be up to standards, so something besides the machinery must be causing the problem. One way of determining what is wrong is to visit the production floor and observe what is going on. The observer may find that the workers are unable to inspect the finished product because they are short-handed, or the workers may be making honest mistakes because they need additional training. Whatever the reason, direct observation may well reveal the problem and help managers resolve it. However, as you learned in Chapter 7's discussion of human behavior in the workplace, if the workers know that management is observing them, they may alter their behavior, rendering the observational data inaccurate.

Surveys A common way to gather primary data is through a survey. Surveys are especially useful in obtaining data about opinions or subjective evaluations. There are three basic types of surveys: telephone and mail surveys and personal interviews.

A telephone survey provides rapid feedback and can be a fairly inexpensive method of collecting data. Companies that often conduct telephone surveys use WATS lines, telephone lines that are leased at a relatively low cost. New technology, such as automatic dialing machines, also can make the survey easier to conduct.

Telephone interviewers typically follow written instructions, first identifying themselves and relating the purpose of the call, and then asking the questions. This procedure usually takes less than two or three minutes, making it an efficient method of data collection. However, it is often difficult to gather much information from the respondent, because few people are willing to stay on the line more than a few minutes. In addition, the research excludes people without telephones, those who are away from their phones, and — if the caller is using a telephone book to generate phone numbers — those with unlisted numbers.

The least expensive survey method is the mail questionnaire. Little labor is involved; the major costs are for paper, postage, and designing and printing the questionnaire. The biggest problem is that the response rate is often low. People receive so much promotional mail that they may not even bother to open the survey. Usually, less than 10 percent of those polled in any national survey ever respond; some marketing research firms feel that a return of 1 to 2 percent is good.

To get in-depth information, the most effective type of survey is the personal interview. The interviewer can ask follow-up questions, offer an explanation when the respondent seems puzzled by a question, and even take note of the respondent's facial expressions. However, personal interviews are also the most expensive and time-consuming of the survey methods. This approach requires well-trained, well-paid interviewers and often involves travel expenses. For these reasons, personal interviews are often used as a supplement to other techniques, rather than as the primary method of collecting data.

Sampling

Seldom if ever can a company survey every customer and potential customer. Even if the company has a massive research budget, it seldom has the time required. Instead, researchers try to measure a representative subgroup of the total. The portion of the group that is being investigated is called a **sample.** If the managers of a utility want to know whether people in the community feel the company is socially responsible, they can interview a sample of community residents. If a battery maker wants to find out whether its batteries work for at least four years as advertised, the company can survey a sample of those who bought the battery four years ago.

The intent of sampling is to obtain results that are representative of the whole population. To achieve this, researchers use random sampling. A **random sample** is one in which each member of the population has an equal chance of being chosen. An important part of planning primary research or evaluating secondary research is making sure that the sample is random.

Sample   A portion of a population that is being investigated.

Random sample   A sample in which each member of the population being investigated has an equal chance of being chosen.

Checkpoint

1. What are the differences between primary and secondary data?
2. Why do researchers try to use secondary data before designing their own studies?

Analysis of Data

Regardless of how the data are collected, they are seldom in a form that allows a manager to draw accurate conclusions. To make the data a useful source of information, the researcher almost always needs to analyze them. This can be done in a number of ways. Some of the most common techniques used in data analysis are frequency distributions, averages, index numbers, and correlations.

Frequency Distributions

Often, the data a researcher collects consists of many individual measurements, such as the number of cassette tapes consumers buy or say they would buy at a particular price, the lifetimes of hundreds of products tested in a laboratory, or the salaries companies in a particular area pay their skilled employees. Table B.1 shows data giving the ages of a sample of apartment renters in an imaginary city. The raw data are not arranged or categorized in any way.

How can researchers draw conclusions from such a list, especially if they have collected hundreds or thousands of numbers or values? They might start by creating an **array,** which is a list of the values in ascending or descending order. This relatively simple task gives the researcher a sense of the range of values encompassed by the results. For example, the designers of bicycles or automobile interiors want to know the range of heights of bike riders or drivers, so that they can design their products to accommodate most or all of the range.

In most cases, however, the researcher wants to know more about the pattern of the numbers within the extremes. Consequently, the researcher constructs a **frequency distribution,** or an arrangement of data that shows the number of times each value (or range of values) occurs.

Array A list of values in ascending or descending order.

Frequency distribution An arrangement of data that shows the number of times each value or range of values occurs.

27	70	23	61	77
19	62	67	43	21
68	24	62	20	19
40	20	75	22	20
65	45	71	63	65
22	36	72	23	66
22	27	26	41	71
30	20	67	24	23
21	22	52	37	46
68	66	21	76	21

TABLE B.1

Raw Data: Ages of a Sample of Apartment Renters

If the data contain more than about a dozen different values, the researcher typically groups the data into categories, each with a range of the same size. Table B.2 shows possible categories for the data in Table B.1; note that each group covers an age range of ten years. The researcher may keep a tally to count the number of occurrences in each age range. The totals for each category are the frequency distribution.

The frequency distribution suggests patterns in the data. It may indicate that many of the values fall into a few categories, perhaps near the top, bottom, or middle of the distribution. This may help the researcher come up with hypotheses to explain consumer or product behavior, or it may help a marketer select a significant target market. For example, the data in Table B.2 suggest that a marketer selling products designed for apartment dwellers may want to target either young adults or the elderly.

Averages

Average A measure of central tendency.

If you have ever computed your grade point average or the batting averages of your favorite baseball players, you are already familiar with another technique for statistical analysis, the average. An **average** is a measure of central tendency; that is, it describes the values that are in the middle of a group of data. While an array of your grades would tell you your best and worst grades, your grade point average gives you an idea of the grades you typically earn, not your peak or bottom grades.

Business people use averages to make comparisons. A production manager might decide whether workers are producing at least the average quantity for the company or the industry. Marketers might be interested in the average price of a particular product. Human resource managers look at average wages for particular jobs. Figure B.1 shows a comparison of electricity rates in Chicago with the average electricity rates charged in the rest of the United States. Because most companies want to have above-average profits and below-average costs, a reasonable hypothesis is that companies looking for a place to open a new plant might try to avoid the higher electricity costs of Chicago. Local government officials and managers looking for a place to locate a business would want to investigate this finding further.

T A B L E   B.2

Frequency Distribution of Ages

Age Group	Tally	Number of Observations
Under 20	| |	2
20–29	卌 卌 卌 卌	20
30–39	| | |	3
40–49	卌	5
50–59	|	1
60–69	卌 卌 | |	12
70–79	卌 | |	7
		Total 50

Depending on the way the data are distributed, the researcher calculates averages by using the mean, median, or mode. Sometimes the researcher uses all three as a check.

Mean A popular way to calculate an average is to find the mean. A **mean** is an arithmetic average, determined by adding all of the values and then dividing this total by the number of values in the sample. For example, a human resource manager who wants to know the starting salaries for mechanical engineers in the area might call ten local businesses and obtain the figures in Table B.3. To find the average of these salaries, the manager then adds the values and divides the total by ten. The average starting salary is $24,529.

Mean An arithmetic average; the sum of the values divided by the number of values.

Starting Salary
$ 22,190
23,500
25,000
24,200
26,100
22,100
23,650
28,400
24,900
25,250 ÷ 10 = $24,529
$245,290

T A B L E   B.3

Calculating the Mean

F I G U R E   B.1

**The Average as a Basis
for Comparison:
Electricity Rates**

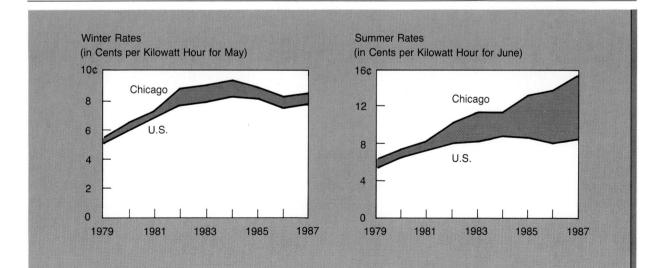

Winter Rates
(in Cents per Kilowatt Hour for May)

Summer Rates
(in Cents per Kilowatt Hour for June)

Median The middle value
in an array.

Mode The value that
occurs most frequently in a
sample.

Index number A
statistical tool for
measuring changes in a
group of related items over
a specific period of time.

Median If a set of data contains several extreme values, they can skew the mean (bias the direction one way or the other). In that case, the researcher may want to compute the **median,** the middle value in an array. The median has as many values less than it as greater than it. If the array contains an odd number of values, the median is easy to compute. The researcher merely identifies which value falls in the middle. For example, in an array of five numbers, the median is the third number. In an array of 15 numbers, it is the eighth number. In an array of 101 numbers, it is the 51st number. If the array contains an even number of values, the median is the mean of the two numbers in the middle. For example, in an array of six numbers, the median is the average of the third and fourth numbers, and in an array of 30 numbers, it is the average of the 15th and 16th numbers.

The median is useful for managers who want to price their goods in the middle of the pack. Additionally, the median may sometimes be a better gauge of central tendency than the mean because it cannot be affected by one or two large numbers in the array.

Mode Decision makers who are interested in the most popular or widely used practices want to know the **mode** — the value that occurs most frequently in a sample. If a company wants to follow the leader and charge what most others do, it will choose the mode. For many kinds of data, the mode usually occurs near the middle of an array.

The mode is also useful for examining beginning salaries. A new college graduate may learn that the mean starting salary for accountants is $27,500 at a particular Big Eight accounting firm. However, this number is misleading because it does not provide any information regarding who is being hired for more than $27,500 or who is being hired for less. If students graduating from Ivy League schools with master's degrees are starting at twice this figure, others are earning much less. Probably the most relevant question for the new graduate is "How much are most people getting?" The answer is the mode, not the mean.

Index Numbers

While averages describe information at one particular time, business researchers are also interested in changes over time. For this, they use **index numbers,** which are a statistical tool for measuring changes in a group of related items over a specific period of time. Government and business statisticians use index numbers to examine the rise and fall of wholesale prices, consumer prices, the general cost of living, stock prices, and other economic-oriented data.

To calculate an index number, divide the value for the current year by the value of the base year. Sometimes the base year is given; if not, you can select a base year. Table B.4 illustrates this process for an index of the price of four commonly purchased consumer goods: gasoline, eggs, bread, and milk. The price for these goods rose from $477.36 in the base year to $1,175.20 in the current year. Dividing $1,175.20 by $477.35 gives an index for the current year of 246.2 percent. (Usually, business researchers state indexes without the percent sign.) Thus, this index says the prices of these consumer goods more than doubled during the period under analysis. An index number of 110.0 indicates that the price of the good has gone up 10 percent from the base year. An index number of 90.0 indicates that the price has dropped by 10 percent from the base year.

Managers use index numbers in various ways. For example, the manager calculating a cost-of-living allowance uses a price index to calculate how much of a pay raise will be needed to offset an increase in the cost of living. If the price index increases by 8 points, the human resource manager may be advised to increase wages by 8 percent. Managers may use the price index when interpreting their revenues and profits to determine whether increases or decreases are due to prices or performance.

Correlation Analysis

An important part of business research is looking for relationships between variables. To accomplish this, researchers use a technique called correlation analysis. A **correlation** is the degree to which two or more variables are related. It indicates the degree to which the variables move together or are found most often in the presence or absence of one another. For example, a researcher in the personnel department may want to know if scores on a job satisfaction questionnaire correlate with absenteeism and turnover. When two variables increase or decrease in tandem, the correlation is positive. When they move in opposite directions, the correlation is negative. Although some relationships are obvious (for example, age of employees and turnover), if numerical analysis is needed, mathematical calculations using correlation formulas are used. Computer statistical packages now commonly make correlational calculations.

Correlation The degree to which two or more variables are related.

Correlation versus Causation Business researchers using correlation analysis must take care to avoid the trap of confusing correlation with causation, or a cause-and-effect relationship. Because two things happen at the same time or in the absence of one another does not mean that one thing actually causes the other to happen or not happen. For example, in the Hawthorne studies discussed in Chapter 8, the researchers found

Amount of Consumer Good	Base Year		Current Year	
	Price per Unit	Total	Price per Unit	Total
520 gallons of unleaded gas	$0.35	$182.00	$1.00	$ 520.00
52 dozen eggs	0.60	31.20	1.00	52.00
104 loaves of bread	0.34	35.36	1.02	106.08
208 gallons of milk	1.10	228.80	2.39	497.12
		$477.36		$1,175.20

Index Number for Current year $= \dfrac{\$1,175.20}{\$477.36} = 2.462$, or 246.2 percent

T A B L E   B.4

Calculating a Price Index of Four Consumer Goods

that increased illumination was correlated with higher output. Did the increase in the light level *cause* the output to increase? Only after the researchers tried decreasing illumination, and output rose again, was the hypothesis that light caused output discounted.

Unfortunately, while researchers often have an easier time finding correlations, managers frequently would be more interested in knowing causations, because this information gives them more ability to control an outcome. For example, investors are always on the lookout for information that will help predict the future of the stock market. One observer has suggested a correlation between rising and falling dress hemlines and rising and falling stock prices (see Figure B.2). With enough correlational evidence, predictions can improve, but to say that based on correlational evidence one variable caused the other is not justified. Thus, the evidence on the relationship between hemlines and stock prices may help predict stock prices, but it does not say that rising hemlines will cause stock prices to go up. If it did, the government would have ordered that miniskirts be required attire after the stock market crash in 1987!

Applications of Correlation Analysis This difference between correlation and causation indicates the possible applications of correlation analysis. It allows business researchers to predict outcomes and act accordingly. For example, in a light-hearted manner, someone once calculated a high positive correlation between storks' nests in the steeples of Munich, Germany, and the birth rate of that city. Does this indicate that storks *cause*

F I G U R E   B.2

The Hemline Indicator, 1897–1986

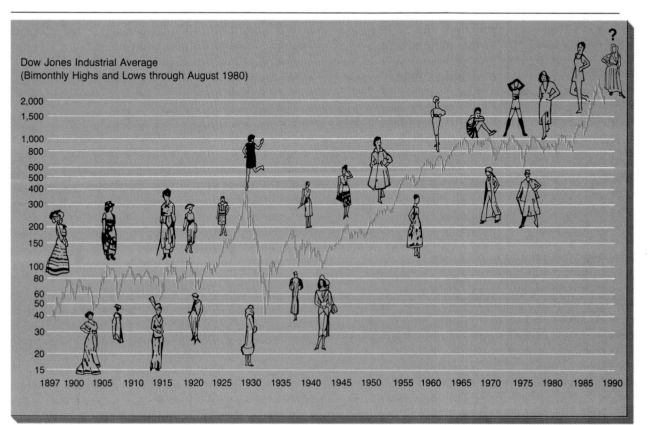

births in this city? No, but the high correlation could be used for *predicting* the number of births. If you were in charge of planning the staffing and supply needs for the newborn section of Munich Hospital, you might want to go out and count storks' nests. However, if you were in charge of a Munich birth control agency, you would be foolish to go around knocking down storks' nests. In other words, correlation helps to predict, not to control, outcomes.

Applied to business decisions, correlation analysis is useful in areas such as forecasting economic changes. For example, many of the large banks have designed economic forecasting models based on correlation analysis that help them predict what is going to happen in the economy in general and certain sectors in particular. A well-designed forecasting model can answer questions such as the following:

> What level of business sales can be predicted with a 5 percent inflation rate?
>
> If national unemployment rises by 1 percent, what predictions can be made for firms in the local area?
>
> If the economy is turning around, how might regional construction firms be affected?

Based on the answers, bank managers can predict which lending strategies will be wisest.

Checkpoint

1. What are three types of statistical analysis?
2. A real estate agent wants to know what a typical first-time home buyer is like. Which analytical techniques might be most helpful in determining this?

Data Presentation

No matter how well the business researcher has collected and analyzed the data, the information is useless to managers unless it is presented in an understandable and usable fashion. The researcher can make statistical presentations clear by being sensitive to the audience's needs and following a logical approach. In addition, well-constructed tables and graphs help make the data more meaningful.

Summary Tables

To display complex information, researchers often use a **summary table** —a table that lists data in various categories along with totals or percentages. Financial statements, described in Chapter 15, are a type of summary table. Table B.5, which reports U.S. employment by occupation, provides another example. Note the information not only provides the relative percentages for each occupation, but also breaks the data down by sex. The reader of this table can compare the relative size of categories and how they compare by sex. The summary table makes the information collected easier to read and comprehend.

Summary table A table that lists data in various categories along with totals or percentages.

Graphs

The summary table in Table B.5 provides a lot of information but doesn't highlight any particular relationships or trends. To present statistical information that focuses on relationships or trends, researchers use graphs. Translating the numbers into a visual relationship makes the information easier to recognize and understand. The most commonly used types of graphs are bar charts, pie charts, and line charts.

Bar Charts To illustrate changes in one or a few categories over time or to show the relative size of various groups, researchers often use **bar charts.** These are graphs of a series of values using bars that vary in length according to the size of each value. Figure B.3 is a bar chart showing the aging of America. It shows that the percentage of older Americans is rapidly growing. This information could be presented in a summary table, but the data are easier to understand and compare in the form of a bar chart. This trend is of interest to managers who work for nursing homes, hospitals, insurance companies, textile manufacturers, pharmaceutical firms, and other companies whose business is affected by the size of older age groups.

Bar chart A graph of a series of values using bars that vary in length according to the size of each value.

T A B L E   B.5

U.S. Employment by Occupation

Occupation Category	Total	Men	Women
Managerial and professional	24.2%	24.3%	23.9%
Technical, sales, and administrative support	30.8	19.6	44.9
Service occupations	13.4	9.4	18.3
Precision production, craft, and repair	12.1	19.9	2.4
Operators, fabricators, and laborers	15.8	21.1	9.1
Farming, forestry, and fishing	3.8	5.6	1.4
	100.1%[a]	99.9%[a]	100.0%

[a]Due to rounding, does not total 100.

F I G U R E   B.3

Bar Charts: Age Distribution of Americans by Percentage

By 2020, almost one-third of the U.S. population is expected to be at least age 55.

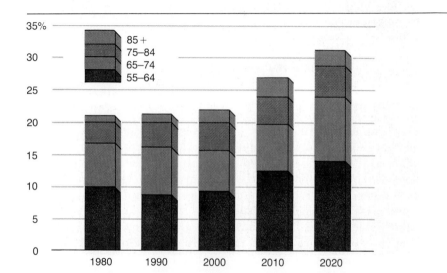

Pie Charts To show the relative size of the parts of a whole, researchers use **pie charts.** These are circles divided into sectors that are proportional in angle and area to the relative size of each category of data. Figure B.4 provides an example. This pie chart shows the levels of charitable giving reported by a survey sample. Charitable organizations might want to learn more about those who give at least 6 percent of their incomes, so that they can target these people for fund raising. Or they might want to try reaching as many people as possible, on the basis that each is unlikely to give a lot.

This form of presentation is a useful way to show how an organization spends its money. Governmental agencies use pie charts to illustrate where tax dollars go. Businesses often use pie charts to show the major categories on the income statement.

Line Charts To show changes in one or more categories over time, researchers often use a **line chart.** This chart graphs information over a period of time by using a line to represent the values of each category of information. Figure B.5 shows such a line chart that shows the median earnings of men and women over 23 years. By simply looking across the chart from left to right, you can see how fast these earnings are growing and their relationship to one another. When information is presented over an extended period of time, a line chart is often superior to any other form of graph.

Pie chart A graph in the form of a circle divided into sectors that are proportional in angle and area to the relative size of each category of data.

Line chart A graph of information over a period of time that uses a line to represent the values of each category of information.

Today, computers help business people prepare charts. The man in this photo is using a CompuServe graphics program to make a bar chart in five colors.

Source: Courtesy of H&R Block, Inc.

**Pie Chart: Levels of
Charitable Giving**

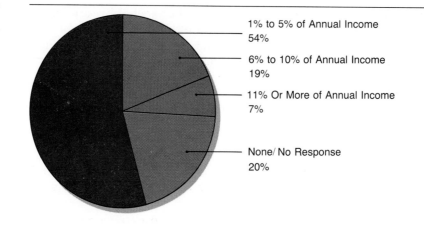

1% to 5% of Annual Income
54%

6% to 10% of Annual Income
19%

11% Or More of Annual Income
7%

None/ No Response
20%

**Line Chart: Median
Earnings for Men and
Women Working Full
Time**

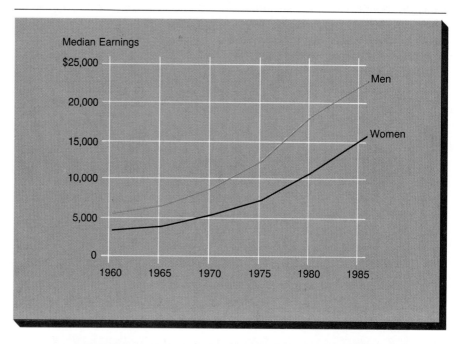

Checkpoint

1. What are three ways to present statistical information?
2. How might a researcher present the relative market shares of a company and its competitors?

Interpretation of Statistics

Once researchers have gathered, analyzed, and presented statistical information, they are faced with the challenge of interpretation. What do the data mean? What actions do they suggest? During this process of interpreting data, business statistics and research becomes either a valuable tool for decision making or a source of misinformation.

If the business researcher has carefully determined the types of information that are necessary and has designed data collection procedures around these needs, interpretation of the information can be clear-cut. However, mistakes can still occur. Someone might make a mistake when adding columns of numbers. More subtle problems arise in areas of judgment, such as in choosing the type of average to compute or in deciding whether a correlation suggests a predictive relationship.

Unfortunately, "how to lie with statistics" has become an established art form. The following adage should be followed by all those using statistics: "Do not put your faith in what statistics say until you have carefully considered what they do not say."

Users must be on the lookout for the biases of those collecting, analyzing, and presenting business statistics. If the researcher who conducts the study manipulates or presents the data to favor a particular point of view, the results can be misleading. For example, a business researcher who feels that the firm should tighten its credit requirements can present the information in a way that favors this view. The researcher calculating the statistics may find that the percentage of uncollectible accounts has doubled since the firm introduced an easier credit policy. Saying that these accounts have gone up 100 percent implies that credit policies should be made tougher. But the firm may have tripled its sales by easing up its credit policies, so that uncollectible accounts have actually declined as a percentage of overall accounts receivable. Thus what the researcher fails to report is sometimes more important than what is reported.

To avoid such problems, users of business statistics must be prepared to ask questions and to challenge the conclusions of statistical data. In particular, managers using business statistics should ask how calculations were made and what assumptions were made. The answers to these questions can enable managers to identify potential biases and take them into account.

Checkpoint

1. In what ways can decision makers be misled by statistics?
2. How can decision makers detect bias in statistical reports?

NOTES

Chapter 1

1. Joan O'C. Hamilton, "Birth of a Blockbuster: How Genentech Delivered the Goods," *Business Week*, November 30, 1987, pp. 138–142.

2. Johnnie L. Roberts, "US West, Demanding Further Deregulation, Sparks Much Criticism," *The Wall Street Journal*, September 4, 1987, p. 10.

3. Stephen Koepp, "Rolling Back Regulation," *Time*, July 6, 1987, pp. 50–52.

4. "Air Travel Complaints on Increase," *Lincoln Journal*, July 15, 1987, p. 24.

5. Calvin A. Kent, "Entrepreneurship Suffers Textbook Case of Neglect," *The Wall Street Journal*, September 4, 1987, p. 10.

6. Gifford Pinchot III, *Intrapreneuring* (New York: Harper & Row, 1985).

7. Tom Peters and Nancy Austin, *A Passion for Excellence* (New York: Random House, 1985), p. 131.

8. Ibid.

9. "IBM Announces Reorganization to Decentralize," *Lincoln Journal*, January 29, 1988, p. 18.

10. "Computers at College," *The Wall Street Journal*, May 13, 1987, p. 33.

11. "Russia Gropes for a Way to Enter the High-Tech Age," *Business Week*, November 11, 1985, p. 102.

12. "Cities Paying Industry to Provide Public Services," *New York Times*, May 28, 1985, p. 9.

13. David Winder, "Governments Cut Themselves Out of Business Worldwide," *Christian Science Monitor*, May 26, 1987, p. 1.

14. "Capitalism in China," *Business Week*, January 14, 1985, pp. 53–59; Barry Kramer, "The Chinese Economy Appears to Be Firmly on the Reform Path," *The Wall Street Journal*, May 14, 1987, pp. 1, 12.

15. Alan Riding, "Brazil Acts to Tame State Ownership," *New York Times*, November 25, 1985, p. 30.

16. Winder, "Governments Cut Themselves Out of Business Worldwide," p. 1.

17. "Some of Europe Tops U.S. in Hourly Pay," *Omaha World-Herald*, October 23, 1987, p. 21.

18. *World Almanac* (New York: Newspaper Enterprise Association, 1986), p. 105.

19. George Russell, "Rebuilding to Survive," *Time*, February 16, 1987, p. 45.

20. Sylvia Nasar, "America's Competitive Revival," *Fortune*, January 4, 1988, pp. 44–52.

21. Lindley H. Clark, Jr., "Manufacturers Grow Much More Efficient, But Employment Lags," *The Wall Street Journal*, December 24, 1986, p. 1.

22. J. Peterson, "Much-Heralded American Service Economy Has Arrived," *Lincoln Journal*, September 24, 1987, p. 28.

23. "Fighting Back: It Can Work," *Business Week*, August 26, 1985, pp. 62–68.

24. Cynthia Hutton, "America's Most Admired Corporations," *Fortune*, January 6, 1986, p. 20.

25. Richard A. Morans and Norman Deets, "Professional Retraining: Meeting the Technological Challenge," *Training and Development Journal*, May 1985, p. 99.

26. "HRM Update," *Personnel Administrator*, September 1984, p. 16.

27. "Review and Outlook," *The Wall Street Journal*, June 30, 1987, p. 26.

28. Ron Scherer, "Steel Makes a Comeback," *Christian Science Monitor*, August 13, 1987, pp. 14–15.

29. Nasar, "America's Competitive Revival," p. 44.

30. "Duty Privileges End for 4 Asian Nations," *Omaha World-Herald*, January 30, 1988, p. 1.

Chapter 2

1. Daniel B. Moskowitz, "Why ATVs Could Land in a Heap of Trouble," *Business Week*, November 30, 1987, p. 38.

2. "Labor Letter," *The Wall Street Journal*, January 19, 1988, p. 1.

3. "The Forgotten Americans," *Business Week*, September 2, 1985, p. 50.

4. "Gap Cut in '87," *Omaha World-Herald*, February 2, 1988, p. 12.

5. "Labor Letter," *The Wall Street Journal*, January 12, 1988, p. 1; "Attitudes in Black and White," *Time*, February 2, 1987, p. 21.

6. *The Wall Street Journal*, November 18, 1986, p. 1.

7. "Labor Letter," *The Wall Street Journal*, May 5, 1987, p. 1.

8. "Women Entrepreneurs Lead in Rate of Growth," *Omaha World-Herald*, January 5, 1988, p. 6.

9. *The Wall Street Journal*, December 30, 1986, p. 1.

10. Eric Morgenthaler, "A Florida Utility Wins Naturalists' Praise for Guarding Wildlife," *The Wall Street Journal*, May 7, 1987, p. 1.

11. Matt Moffett, "Mexican Consumers Have a Stout Friend in Arturo Lomeli," *The Wall Street Journal*, January 18, 1988, p. 1.

12. "Having It All, Then Throwing It All Away," *Time*, May 25, 1987, p. 22.

13. Ibid.

14. "Ethical Behavior," *The Wall Street Journal*, January 18, 1988, p. 13.

15. "Where Business Goes to Stock Up on Ethics," *Business Week*, October 14, 1985, p. 63.

16. "Labor Letter," *The Wall Street Journal*, December 29, 1987, p. 1.

Chapter 3

1. "Orville Redenbacher Still Popping at 80," *Chicago Tribune*, July 22, 1987, Sec. 8, p. 4.

2. Gifford Pinchot III, *Intrapreneuring* (New York: Harper & Row, 1985).

3. *The Foresight Intrapreneur*, January-February 1987, p. 76.

4. Wilson Harrell, "Entrepreneurial Terror," *Inc.*, February 1987, p. 76.

5. William Echikson, "In Italy, an Industrial Renaissance Thrives," *Christian Science Monitor*, April 7, 1987, pp. 1, 14.

6. Tom Peters and Nancy Austin, *A Passion for Excellence* (New York: Random House, 1985), p. xxii.

7. Sanford L. Jacobs, "Big-Firm Alumni Apt to Be Growth-Oriented Entrepreneurs," *The Wall Street Journal*, March 31, 1985, p. 27.

8. Linda Watkins, "Minority Entrepreneurs Venturing into Broader Range of Businesses," *The Wall Street Journal*, March 31, 1987, p. 31.

9. "100 Ideas for New Businesses," *Venture*, November 1985, pp. 40–80; "100 Ideas for New Businesses," *Venture*, December 1986, p. 29.

10. "A Lack of Creativity?" *The Wall Street Journal*, January 15, 1988, p. 19.

11. Cynthia Hutton, "America's Most Admired Corporations," *Fortune*, January 6, 1986, p. 19.

12. "How to Make a Breakthrough," *The Economist*, January 24, 1987, p. 66.

13. Jacquelyn Wonder and Priscilla Donovan, *Whole-Brain Thinking* (New York: William Morrow, 1984), pp. 102–104.

14. Clare Ansberry, "Eastman Kodak Co. Had Arduous Struggle to Regain Lost Edge," *The Wall Street Journal*, April 2, 1987, p. 1.

15. Other techniques include morphological analysis (a system of breaking an idea or problem into its components for study), visualization, lists, lateral thinking, and divergent thinking. See Ron Zemke, "The Creativity Jargon Jungle," *Training*, May 1986, pp. 32–33, for details of each.

16. "Retiring Westinghouse Chief Executive Talks of Issues Facing Firms and Managers," *The Wall Street Journal*, December 30, 1987, p. 15.

17. Julia Kagan, "Survey: Work in the 1980s and 1990s," *Working Woman*, May 1985, p. 24.

18. Charles N. Weaver and Michael D. Matthews, "What White Males Want from Their Jobs: Ten Years Later," *Personnel*, September 1987, p. 62.

19. "How to Make a Breakthrough," p. 66.

20. Thomas J. Peters and Robert H. Waterman, Jr., *In Search of Excellence* (New York: Harper & Row, 1982).

21. Thomas J. Peters, *Thriving on Chaos: Handbook for a Management Revolution* (New York: Knopf, 1987).

22. Karl Albrecht and Ron Zemke, *Service America* (Homewood, Ill.: Dow Jones–Irwin, 1985), p. 49.

23. "Workstyle," *Inc.*, January 1986, p. 50.

24. Albrecht and Zemke, *Service America*, pp. 149, 152.

25. For a critical analysis of the Peters and Waterman work, see Michael A. Hitt and R. Duane Ireland, "Peters and Waterman Revisited: The Unended Quest for Excellence," *Academy of Management Executives*, May 1987, pp. 91–98.

26. Tom Richman, "The Hottest Entrepreneur in America," *Inc.*, February 1987, p. 51.

27. "Women Entrepreneurs Lead in Rate of Growth," *Omaha World-Herald*, January 5, 1988, p. 6.

28. Ibid.

29. Leslie Wayne, "Buyouts Altering Face of Corporate America," *New York Times*, November 23, 1985, p. 1.

30. "Private Lives," *Inc.*, December 1985, pp. 66–69, 91.

31. "American Dream Realized," *Lincoln Journal-Star*, February 15, 1987, p. C1.

Chapter 4

1. "Women Entrepreneurs Lead in Rate of Growth," *Omaha World-Herald*, January 5, 1988, p. 6.

2. Richard M. Hodgetts and Donald F. Kuratko, *Effective Small Business Management*, 2nd ed. (Orlando, Fla.: Academic Press, 1986), p. 5.

3. "Pul-eeze! Will Somebody Help Me?" *Time*, February 2, 1987, p. 50.

4. These examples are from Susan Benway, "Presto! The Convenience Industry: Making Life a Little Simpler," *Business Week*, April 27, 1987, pp. 86–94.

5. "Are Money and Status Losing Their Allure?" *The Wall Street Journal*, January 12, 1988, p. 31.

6. "Business Failures," *The Wall Street Journal*, March 3, 1987, p. 37.

7. "Paper Shuffle Hits Small Firms Hardest," *The Wall Street Journal*, July 27, 1987, p. 17.

8. Roger Lowenstein, "Many Successful Athletes Suffer Setbacks in Business," *The Wall Street Journal*, January 27, 1987, p. 29.

9. Steven P. Galante, "Group Tries Broadening Firms' Horizons," *The Wall Street Journal*, January 31, 1988, p. 31.

10. Steven P. Galante, "Small Manufacturers Shifting to 'Just-in-Time' Techniques," *The Wall Street Journal*, December 21, 1987, p. 21.

11. Samuel Rowe, "Getting in on the Franchising Act," *Black Enterprise*, September 1987, p. 71. The quote is by Stan Wilson of the International Franchise Association.

12. Janice Castro, "Franchising Fever," *Time*, August 31, 1987, p. 36.

13. George Kurian, *What's What in American Business* (Chicago: Probus, 1986), p. 75.

14. Sabin Russell, "A Formula That Works," *Venture*, September 1985, pp. 36–39.

15. Ibid.

16. "Labor Letter," *The Wall Street Journal*, February 24, 1987, p. 1.

17. "Truth in Franchising," *The Wall Street Journal*, September 21, 1987, p. 25.

18. "Franchises Seen as a Middle Ground," *The Wall Street Journal*, January 15, 1988, p. 19.

19. Castro, "Franchising Fever," p. 36.

20. "Chinese Eating Chicken with Col. 'Elderly Head'," *Omaha World-Herald*, November 14, 1987, p. 4.

21. Castro, "Franchising Fever," p. 36.

Chapter 5

1. Del Marth, "Building Up, Spreading Out," *Nation's Business*, January 1987, pp. 58–59.

2. Tom Richman, "The Hottest Entrepreneur in America," *Inc.*, February 1987, p. 51.

3. Susan Benway, "Presto! The Convenience Industry: Making Life a Little Simpler," *Business Week*, April 27, 1987, pp. 86–94.

4. Correspondence from Small Business Administration (1985).

5. John F. Persinos, "The Advice Squad," *Inc.*, January 1986, pp. 80–84.

6. Julie Amparano, "A Lawyer Flourishes by Suing Corporations for Their Shareholders," *The Wall Street Journal*, April 28, 1987, p. 1.

7. "Labor Letter," *The Wall Street Journal*, March 24, 1987, p. 1.

8. Janice Castro, "Tougher Than the Rest," *Time*, February 8, 1988, pp. 48–49.

9. "Rebuilding to Survive," *Time*, February 16, 1987, p. 45.

Chapter 6

1. Aimée L. Stern, "GF Tries the Old Restructure Ploy," *Business Month*, November 1987, pp. 37–39.

2. This classification was originally given by Robert L. Katz, "Skills of an Effective Administrator," *Harvard Busi-*

ness Review, January-February 1955, pp. 33–42. See also Robert L. Katz, "Retrospective Commentary," Harvard Business Review, September-October 1974, pp. 101–102.

3. Richard L. Daft, Management (Hinsdale, Ill.: Dryden, 1988), p. 17.

4. For example, see Tom Peters, Thriving on Chaos: Handbook for a Management Revolution (New York: Knopf, 1987); Fred Luthans, Richard M. Hodgetts, and Stuart A. Rosenkrantz, Real Managers (Cambridge, Mass.: Ballinger, 1988).

5. "Bristol-Myers Bucks the Odds in Search of a Blockbuster Drug," Business Week, October 29, 1984, pp. 136–140.

6. Michael Brody, "NASA's Challenge: Ending Isolation at the Top," Fortune, May 12, 1986, pp. 26–28, 32.

7. Tom Peters and Nancy Austin, A Passion for Excellence (New York: Random House, 1985), p. 313.

8. Ibid.

9. Thomas McCarroll, "Can This Elephant Dance?" Time, February 8, 1988, p. 52.

10. "The Old Foreman Is On the Way Out, and the New One Will Be More Important," Business Week, April 25, 1983, p. 14.

11. Christopher J. Chipello, "Matter of Honor: Japanese Top Managers Quick to Resign When Trouble Hits Firm," The Wall Street Journal, July 10, 1987, p. 19.

12. John Naisbitt and Patricia Aburdene, Reinventing the Corporation (New York: Warner Books, 1985), p. 33.

13. Peters and Austin, A Passion for Excellence, p. 54.

14. Ibid., p. 319.

15. Don Hellriegel and John W. Slocum, Jr., Management, 4th ed. (Reading, Mass.: Addison-Wesley, 1986), p. 333.

16. "IBM Announces Reorganization to Decentralize," Lincoln Journal, January 29, 1988, p. 18.

17. Hellriegel and Slocum, Management, pp. 334–335.

18. George Russell, "Rebuilding to Survive," Time, February 16, 1987, p. 45.

19. Fred Luthans, Stuart A. Rosenkrantz, and Harry W. Hennessey, "What Do Successful Managers Really Do?" Journal of Applied Behavioral Science, August 1985, pp. 255–270.

20. "The Un-Manager," Inc., August 1982, p. 36.

21. "Labor Letter," The Wall Street Journal, May 12, 1987, p. 1.

22. M. N. Vamos, "Rescuing Flops—or How to Buy Cat Litter and Sell Sawdust," Business Week, December 3, 1984, p. 128.

23. Andrew D. Szilagyi, Jr., and Marc J. Wallace, Organizational Behavior and Performance (Glenview, Ill.: Scott, Foresman, 1983), p. 349.

24. Peters and Austin, A Passion for Excellence, p. 11.

25. Ralph H. Kilmann, "Corporate Culture," Psychology Today, April 1985, p. 63.

26. Much of the material in this section can be found in Terrence D. Deal and Allan A. Kennedy, Corporate Cultures: The Rites and Rituals of Corporate Life (Reading, Mass.: Addison-Wesley, 1982).

27. Larry Reibstein, "Federal Express Faces Challenges to Its Grip on Overnight Delivery," The Wall Street Journal, January 8, 1988, p. 1.

28. See Deal and Kennedy, Corporate Cultures, Ch. 6.

Chapter 7

1. Bob Wiedrich, "Every Worker's King at White Castle," Chicago Tribune, November 30, 1987, Sec. 4, pp. 1, 6; Bob Wiedrich, "From 28 Cents an Hour to Chicago Manager," Chicago Tribune, November 30, 1987, Sec. 4, p. 6.

2. Edwin T. Layton, Jr., The Revolt of the Engineers: Social Responsibility and the American Engineering Profession (Baltimore, Md.: The Johns Hopkins University Press, 1986), pp. 134–153.

3. Today, the term Hawthorne effect refers to a change in the behavior of research subjects caused by the fact that they are being studied and given special attention.

4. Arthur Sharplin, Strategic Management (New York: McGraw-Hill, 1985), p. 468.

5. "MIT Report Says Poor Management Hurting Productivity," Lincoln Journal, February 16, 1988, pp. 1, 9.

6. Ernesto J. Poza and M. Lynn Markus, "Success Story: The Team Approach to Work Restructuring," Organizational Dynamics, Winter 1980, pp. 3–25.

7. "Labor Letter," The Wall Street Journal, December 22, 1987, p. 1.

8. "Labor Letter," The Wall Street Journal, January 12, 1988, p. 1.

9. Ibid.

10. Paul J. Champagne, "Explaining Job Enrichment," Supervisory Management, November 1979, pp. 24–34.

11. John Naisbitt and Patricia Aburdene, Reinventing the Corporation (New York: Warner, 1985), pp. 38–39.

12. Ibid., p. 93.

13. Donald F. Petersen, "Flexitime in the United States: The Lessons of Experience," Personnel, January-February 1980, pp. 21–31.

14. Naisbitt and Aburdene, Re-inventing the Corporation, p. 93.

15. "Labor Letter," The Wall Street Journal, June 2, 1987, p. 1.

16. Sam E. White, Terence R. Mitchell, and Cecil H. Bell, Jr., "Goal-Setting, Evaluation Apprehension, and Social Cues as Determinants of Job Performance and Job Satisfaction in a Simulated Organization," Journal of Applied Psychology, December 1977, pp. 665–673.

17. Gary P. Latham and Gary A. Yukl, "A Review of Research on the Application of Goal-Setting in Organizations," Academy of Management Journal, December 1975, pp. 824–845.

18. John M. Ivancevich, "Effects of Goal Setting on Performance and Job Satisfaction," Journal of Applied Psychology, October 1976, pp. 605–612.

19. Jay S. Kim and W. Clay Hamner, "Effect of Performance Feedback and Goal Setting on Productivity and Satisfaction in an Organizational Setting," Journal of Applied Psychology, February 1976, pp. 45–57.

20. Based on Don Hellriegel, John W. Slocum, and Richard W. Woodman, Organizational Behavior, 4th ed. (St. Paul, Minn.: West, 1986), p. 516.

21. Jerry E. Bishop, "Prognosis for the 'Type A' Personality Improves in a New Heart Disease Study," The Wall Street Journal, January 14, 1988, p. 29.

22. Naisbitt and Aburdene, Reinventing the Corporation, p. 198.

23. Ibid., p. 197.

24. "Labor Letter," The Wall Street Journal, May 19, 1987, p. 1.

25. Douglas McGregor, The Human Side of Enterprise (New York: McGraw-Hill, 1960), pp. 33–34.

26. Ibid., pp. 47–48.

27. William G. Ouchi, Theory Z (New York: Avon, 1981).

28. Fred E. Fiedler, A Theory of Leadership Effectiveness (New York: McGraw-Hill, 1967).

29. Steve Swartz, "How Eccentric Chief Built Up Hutton, Hastened Its Demise," *The Wall Street Journal,* February 17, 1988, p. 1.

30. "At Ease; Fall Out for Executive Meetings," *The Wall Street Journal,* January 15, 1988, p. 19. The study was conducted by the Center for Creative Leadership.

Chapter 8

1. "L. L. Bean's Employees Live the Great Outdoors," *Chicago Tribune,* October 18, 1987, Sec. 7, p. 10D.

2. "Human Resources Managers Aren't Corporate Nobodies Anymore," *Business Week,* December 2, 1985, pp. 58–59.

3. Robert Levering, Milton Moskowitz, and Michael Katz, *The 100 Best Companies to Work for in America* (New York: Addison-Wesley, 1985), p. 30.

4. Personnel Policies Forum Survey (Washington, D.C.: Bureau of National Affairs, 1979).

5. Larry Reibstein, "More Firms Use Personality Tests for Entry-Level, Blue-Collar Jobs," *The Wall Street Journal,* January 16, 1986, p. 31.

6. "Labor Letter," *The Wall Street Journal,* December 29, 1987, p. 1.

7. Edward L. Levin and Stephen M. Rudolf, *Reference Checking for Personnel Selection: The State of the Art* (New York: American Society for Personnel Administration, 1977), p. 70.

8. "Poll: Fear of AIDS Strong in Workplace," *Omaha World-Herald,* February 8, 1988, p. 14.

9. R. Richard Ritti and G. Ray Funkhouser, *The Ropes to Skip and the Ropes to Know,* 2nd ed. (Columbus, Ohio: Grid, 1982).

10. Paula Popvich and John P. Wanous, "The Realistic Job Preview as a Persuasive Communication," *Academy of Management Review,* July 1982, pp. 570–578.

11. Michael A. Hitt, R. Dennis Middlemist, and Robert L. Mathis, *Management,* 2nd ed. (St. Paul, Minn.: West, 1986), p. 472.

12. "In Chicago: Seminars Everywhere," *Time,* October 12, 1987, p. 12.

13. Herbert G. Heneman III, "Self-Assessment: A Critical Analysis," *Personnel Psychology,* Summer 1980, pp. 279–300; Herbert H. Meyer, "Self-Appraisal of Job Performance," *Personnel Psychology,* Summer 1980, pp. 291–295; and George C. Thorton, "Psychometric Properties of Self-Appraisals in Job Performance," *Personnel Psychology,* Summer 1980, pp. 263–271.

14. Jacob M. Schlesinger, "GM's New Compensation Plan Reflects General Trend Tying Pay to Performance," *The Wall Street Journal,* January 26, 1988, p. 33.

15. Cindy Skrzycki, "Pay for Performance Is Changing U.S. Workplace," *Omaha World-Herald,* May 28, 1987, p. 43.

16. U.S. Department of Labor, Bureau of Labor Statistics, *Employer Benefits in Medium and Large Firms, 1983,* Bulletin 2213, August 1984, p. 2.

17. John Naisbitt and Patricia Aburdene, *Reinventing the Corporation* (New York: Warner, 1985), pp. 168, 220.

18. "Labor Letter," *The Wall Street Journal,* January 26, 1988, p. 1.

19. Naisbitt and Aburdene, *Re-inventing the Corporation,* p. 99.

20. See Dennis W. Organ and Thomas Bateman, *Organizational Behavior,* 3rd ed. (Plano, Tex.: Business Publications, 1986), Chap. 14.

21. Kenneth B. McRae, "Career-Management Planning: A Boon to Managers and Employees," *Personnel,* May 1985, p. 56.

22. "Labor Letter," *The Wall Street Journal,* January 19, 1988, p. 1.

23. Kerry E. Knobeisdorff, "Fast Growth for Outplacement," *Christian Science Monitor,* July 14, 1987, p. 23.

24. "Finnish Men Claim Sex Harassment," *Lincoln Journal,* October 7, 1987, p. 26.

25. Terry L. Leap and Edmund R. Gray, "Corporate Responsibility in Cases of Sexual Harassment," *Business Horizons,* October 1980, pp. 58–65; Kathryn A. Thurston, "Sexual Harassment: An Organizational Perspective," *Personnel Administrator,* December 1980, pp. 59–64; and George K. Kronenberger and David L. Bourke, "Effective Training and the Elimination of Sexual Harassment," *Personnel Journal,* November 1981, pp. 879–883.

26. Donald J. Petersen, "Paving the Way for Hiring the Handicapped," *Personnel,* March-April 1981, p. 50.

27. "Labor Letter," *The Wall Street Journal,* May 19, 1987, p. 1.

28. Sara M. Freedman and Robert T. Keller, "The Handicapped in the Workforce," *Academy of Management Review,* July 1981, p. 453.

29. John Hoerr et al., "Privacy," *Business Week,* March 28, 1988, pp. 61–68.

30. "Respecting Employee Privacy," *Business Week,* January 11, 1982, p. 130.

31. John Hoerr, "It's Getting Harder to Pass Out Pink Slips," *Business Week,* March 28, 1988, p. 68.

32. Naisbitt and Aburdene, *Re-inventing the Corporation,* p. 104.

Chapter 9

1. U.S. Department of Labor, Bureau of Labor Statistics, *Employment and Earnings,* January 1987, p. 219. The statistics on union membership include employee associations that act as unions.

2. Thomas A. Kochan, "How American Workers View Labor Unions," *Monthly Labor Review,* April 1979, pp. 29–30.

3. "Organized Labor Maintained 36% Wage Gap," *Omaha World-Herald,* January 23, 1988, p. 41.

4. Cathy Frost, "Unions Court People in Service-Type Work to Stem Fall in Ranks," *The Wall Street Journal,* September 19, 1986, p. 12.

5. "Labor Letter," *The Wall Street Journal,* February 16, 1988, p. 1.

6. Daniel D. Cook, "Divorce Union Style," *Industry Week,* June 25, 1979, p. 38.

7. John Holusha, "Innovative Pact Wins Approval of Auto Union," *New York Times,* July 27, 1985, p. 6.

8. R. S. Greenberger, "Work-Rule Changes Quietly Spread as Firms Try to Raise Productivity," *The Wall Street Journal,* January 23, 1983, p. 35.

9. "Labor Letter," *The Wall Street Journal,* April 14, 1987, p. 1.

10. "BW/Harris Poll: Confidence in Unions Is Crumbling," *Business Week,* July 8, 1985, p. 76.

11. "Pul-eeze! Will Somebody Help Me?" *Time,* February 2, 1987, p. 50.

12. "Labor Letter," *The Wall Street Journal,* February 3, 1987, p. 1.

13. "Labor Letter," *The Wall Street Journal,* February 11, 1986, p. 1.

14. Alex Kotlowitz, "Unions May Be Poised to End Long Decline, Recover Some Clout," *The Wall Street Journal,* August 28, 1987, pp. 1, 8.

Chapter 10

1. See Sylvia Nasar, "America's Competitive Revival," *Fortune*, January 4, 1988, pp. 44–52; Alan Murray, "Aided by Weak Dollar, Factory Output Leads Economy Once Again," *The Wall Street Journal*, January 26, 1988, p. 1.

2. "Manufacturers Grow Much More Efficient but Employment Lags," *The Wall Street Journal*, December 4, 1986, p. 1.

3. This example is discussed in James L. Heskett, *Managing in the Service Economy* (Boston: Harvard Business School Press, 1986), pp. 21–22.

4. Don Hellriegel and John W. Slocum, *Management*, 4th ed. (Reading, Mass.: Addison-Wesley, 1986), p. 677.

5. Vincent G. Reuters, "Value Engineering/Value Analysis: Valuable Management Techniques," *Industrial Management*, November-December 1983, p. 2.

6. Ellen Posner, "Architecture: Computers Do It Faster," *The Wall Street Journal*, February 25, 1986, p. 28.

7. Gordon Bock, "Limping along in Robot Land," *Time*, July 13, 1987, p. 46.

8. Ibid.

9. Bela Gold, "CAM Sets New Rules for Production," *Harvard Business Review*, November-December 1982, p. 90.

10. Barbara Bradley, "The Flexible Factory Reshapes American Industry," *Christian Science Monitor*, June 1, 1987.

11. Richard Brandt and Otis Port, "How Automation Could Save the Day," *Business Week*, March 3, 1986, p. 74.

12. Donald K. Clifford, Jr., and Richard E. Cavanagh, *The Winning Performance* (New York: Bantam Books, 1985), p. 230.

13. Tom Peters and Nancy Austin, *A Passion for Excellence* (New York: Random House, 1985), p. 88.

14. Steven P. Galante, "Small Manufacturers Shifting to 'Just-in-Time' Techniques," *The Wall Street Journal*, December 1987, p. 21.

15. Hellriegel and Slocum, *Management*, p. 676.

16. Andrew Collier, "U.S. Auto Parts Companies Feel Pressure to Cut Costs and Compete," *Christian Science Monitor*, June 2, 1987, p. 21.

17. D. Halberstam, "Yes We Can," *Parade Magazine*, July 8, 1984, p. 5.

18. Jeremy Main, "Toward Service without a Snarl," *Fortune*, March 23, 1981, p. 66.

19. Clifford and Cavanagh, *The Winning Performance*, p. 229.

20. Peters and Austin, *A Passion for Excellence*, p. 99.

21. Ibid., p. 57.

22. Otis Port, "The Push for Quality," *Business Week*, June 8, 1987, p. 134.

23. "Higher Quality Helps Boost U.S. Products," *The Wall Street Journal*, January 11, 1988, p. 1.

24. Paul A. Eisenstein, "Turnaround Makes Ford No. 1 in Profits," *Christian Science Monitor*, May 8, 1987, p. 23.

25. The quote comes from George F. Will and is found in Karl Albrecht and Ron Zemke, *Service America* (Homewood, Ill.: Dow Jones–Irwin, 1985), p. 1. This book champions the role of the service industry in American business.

26. "Where the Customer Is Still King," *Time*, February 2, 1987, pp. 56–57. The examples of Nordstrom, Mini Maid, and Amica are adapted from this source. For details on other top service companies, see Bro Uttal, "Companies That Serve You Best," *Fortune*, December 7, 1987, pp. 98–116.

Chapter 11

1. Tom Peters and Nancy Austin, *A Passion for Excellence* (New York: Random House, 1985), p. 38.

2. Stephen J. Fansweet, "Dick Woolworth Builds a Better Mousetrap—and Falls Flat on His Face," *The Wall Street Journal*, September 24, 1970, p. 1.

3. Monci Jo Williams, "McDonald's Refuses to Plateau," *Fortune*, November 12, 1984, p. 36.

4. Eileen White, "Future Flights: Jetliners May Offer More Exotic, But Costly, Features," *The Wall Street Journal*, January 23, 1987, p. 19.

5. *The Wall Street Journal*, May 26, 1987, p. 29.

6. Martha Brannigan, "Pseudo Polls: More Surveys Draw Criticism for Motives and Methods," *The Wall Street Journal*, January 29, 1987, p. 27.

7. John Holusha, "A Noted Voice on Car Buying," *New York Times*, January 21, 1986, p. 29.

8. Ellen Graham, "As Kids Gain Power of Purse, Marketing Takes Aim at Them," *The Wall Street Journal*, January 19, 1988, p. 1.

9. "Shifting Population," *The Wall Street Journal*, February 9, 1988, p. 33.

10. *The Wall Street Journal*, February 9, 1988, p. 33.

11. "My, What Ugly Mugs," *Time*, October 2, 1987, p. 116.

12. Wendy L. Wall, "NutraSweet's Fat Substitute, Seen Beating P&G to Market, Promises Diet Revolution," *The Wall Street Journal*, January 28, 1988, p. 25.

13. John P. Tarpey, Lois Therrien, Kimberly Carpenter, and Zachary Schiller, "The Pasta Pot Is Boiling—But No One Can Serve Up a National Brand," *Business Week*, September 9, 1985, pp. 54–55.

Chapter 12

1. Albert R. Karr, "Growers Press Bid to Produce Better Tomato," *The Wall Street Journal*, June 4, 1987, p. 27.

2. "Business Bulletin," *The Wall Street Journal*, February 11, 1988, p. 1.

3. "Will the Same Machine Also Make Juice?" *The Wall Street Journal*, February 8, 1988, p. 25.

4. Philip R. McDonald and Joseph O. Eastback, Jr., "Top Management Involvement with New Products," *Business Horizons*, December 1971, p. 24.

5. Michael E. Porter, *Competitive Advantage* (New York: Free Press, 1985), Chap. 8.

6. "Kodak Slips Its Disc," *Time*, February 15, 1988, p. 85.

7. John Bussey and Douglas R. Sease, "Manufacturers Strive to Slice Time Needed to Develop Products," *The Wall Street Journal*, February 23, 1988, p. 1.

8. "Judge Backs Firm Raising Stink Over Liz's Perfume," *Omaha World-Herald*, November 20, 1987, p. 3.

9. Amy Dunkin, "Want to Wake Up a Tired Old Product? Repackage It," *Business Week*, July 15, 1985, pp. 130, 134.

10. Fred Langan, "New Plastic Could Help Roadside Litter Do a Better Vanishing Act," *Christian Science Monitor*, May 5, 1987, p. 22.

11. "Just How Much Juice Is in a Fruit Drink?" *The Wall Street Journal*, February 9, 1988, p. 33.

12. Lynn Asinof, "Business Bulletin," *The Wall Street Journal*, March 5, 1987, p. 1.

13. Michael E. Porter, *Competitive Strategy* (New York: Free Press, 1980), p. 43.

Chapter 13

1. "Howling Success for a Hired Gun," *Sales and Marketing Management*, July 1987, pp. 23, 25.

2. Belinda Hulin-Salkin, "Newspapers: Stretching to Deliver Readers' Needs," *Advertising Age*, July 20, 1987, pp. S1–S8.

3. Ronald Alsop, "More Companies Squeeze Ads into Bargain 15-Second Spots," *The Wall Street Journal*, January 19, 1987, p. 27.

4. Joanne Lipman, "Need a Commercial Bread? Viewers Take Ads Home to Play on VCRs," *The Wall Street Journal*, June 5, 1987, p. 21.

5. Ronald Alsop, "Consumer Products Become Movie Stars," *The Wall Street Journal*, February 29, 1988, p. 21.

6. For more on advertising effectiveness, see "Study of Magazine Ads Yields Some Eye-Opening Findings," *The Wall Street Journal*, December 5, 1985, p. 33.

7. Robert L. Simison, "Why Are Auto Sales Strictly for the Birds? Just Ask Any Pigeon," *The Wall Street Journal*, December 15, 1982, p. 1.

8. Matt Moffett and Laurie McGinley, "NASA, Once a Master of Publicity, Fumbles in Handling Shuttle Crisis," *The Wall Street Journal*, February 14, 1986, p. 23.

9. For example, see Anastasia Toufexis, "Have Your Cake—and Eat It Too," *Time*, February 8, 1988, p. 72.

10. Tom Ineck, "New Pictionary Draws Consumers," *Sunday Lincoln Journal-Star*, February 7, 1988, p. 1C.

11. Naomi S. Travers, "Get the Champagne; Today Is Sure to Be Something's Birthday," *The Wall Street Journal*, July 23, 1987, pp. 1, 20.

12. Jacob M. Schlesinger, "GM, with Hoopla, Seeks to Trade in Its Current Image," *The Wall Street Journal*, January 4, 1988, p. 6.

Chapter 14

1. Ronald Alsop, "Izod Alligator Makes Its Move to Get Off Endangered List," *The Wall Street Journal*, May 21, 1987, p. 25.

2. Lynn Asinof, "Business Bulletin," *The Wall Street Journal*, March 5, 1987, p. 1.

3. "Fuller Brush to Open Two Stores," *Chicago Tribune*, July 26, 1987, Sec. 7, p. 9C.

4. "Eye-Stopping Design in the Supermarket," *The Wall Street Journal*, January 21, 1988, p. 21.

5. Barry Stavro, "Minding The Store," *Forbes*, April 7, 1986, pp. 31–32.

6. "Shaping a Sears Financial Empire," *New York Times*, February 12, 1984, pp. 1, 6–7.

7. Barry Stavro, "Mass Appeal," *Forbes*, May 5, 1986, pp. 128, 130.

8. "A Grocer's Touch of Theater," *New York Times*, May 3, 1986, pp. 21, 23.

9. "Eye-Stopping Design in the Supermarket," p. 21.

10. Denise Frenner, "From Piano to Sushi Bars, Grocers Jazz Up Service," *Advertising Age*, May 4, 1987, pp. S1–S2.

11. Lori Kesler, "St. Louis' Dierbergs Serves More Than Usual Fare," *Advertising Age*, May 4, 1987, pp. S4, S6.

12. Claire Wilson, "Europe's Hypermarkets Making Waves Here," *Advertising Age*, May 4, 1987, pp. S18–S19.

13. Antonio Fins, "Sunglass Huts: Thriving in Nooks and Crannies," *Business Week*, July 27, 1987, p. 77.

14. Steven P. Galante, "Bookshop 'Superstore' Reflects the Latest Word in Retailing," *The Wall Street Journal*, February 23, 1987, p. 21.

15. "Financial Services Join Trend in Catalog Sales," *The Wall Street Journal*, January 19, 1988, p. 33.

16. Mark Gill, "The Rise and Rise of HSN," *Esquire*, April 1987, p. 70; "Home Shopping Networks: 'We're No Fad,' " *Sales and Marketing Management*, July 1987, p. 92.

17. "Where the Customer Is Still King," *Time*, February 2, 1987, p. 57.

Chapter 15

1. Russell Mitchell, "Jack Welch: How Good a Manager?" *Business Week*, December 14, 1987, pp. 92–103.

2. Lee Berton and Daniel Akst, "CPAs May Soon Have to Report Fraud Earlier," *The Wall Street Journal*, January 2, 1988, p. 21.

3. Lee Berton, "Accounting Group Will Fight Efforts by FTC to Lift Ban on Contingent Fees," *The Wall Street Journal*, July 28, 1987, p. 10.

4. Daniel Akst and Lee Berton, "Accountants Who Specialize in Detecting Fraud Find Themselves in Great Demand," *The Wall Street Journal*, February 26, 1988, p. 17.

5. "Business Bulletin," *The Wall Street Journal*, February 11, 1988, p. 1.

6. "It's Fancy, It's Fun, It's an Annual Report," *The Wall Street Journal*, January 22, 1988, p. 21.

Chapter 16

1. Bob Davis, "As Government Keeps More Tabs on People, False Accusations Rise," *The Wall Street Journal*, August 20, 1987, pp. 1, 16.

2. John Naisbitt and Patricia Aburdene, *Re-inventing the Corporation* (New York: Warner Books, 1985), p. 19.

3. Fred V. Guterl, "Computers Think for Business," *Dun's Business Month*, October 1986, p. 32.

4. For more on artificial intelligence, see David E. Whiteside, "Artificial Intelligence Finally Hits the Desktop," *Business Week*, June 9, 1986, pp. 68, 70; "The Next Computers," *Newsweek*, April 6, 1987, p. 60.

5. "The Compact Disk Turns into an Informational Tool," *Business Week*, July 7, 1986, p. 71.

6. "Computer Graphics Speed Data Search," *The Wall Street Journal*, August 31, 1987, p. 19.

7. John M. Leighty, "NASA Unveils Supercomputer," *Lincoln Journal*, March 9, 1987, p. 12.

8. "Scientists Set Computing Speed Record," *Lincoln Star*, March 14, 1988, p. 3.

9. Robert Koester and Fred Luthans, "The Impact of the Computer on the Choice Activity of Decision Makers: A Replication with Actual Users of Computerized MIS," *Academy of Management Journal*, June 1979, pp. 416–422.

10. "White-Collar Jobs Continue to Vanish," *Chicago Tribune*, July 12, 1987, Sec. 8, p. 1.

11. "Computers Monitor Work Habits of Millions," *Lincoln Journal*, September 21, 1987, p. 17.

12. Gene Kelly, "Desktop Publishing Invades the Office," *Lincoln Journal-Star*, June 14, 1987, p. 13D.

13. Julie Amparano, "A Wide Variety of Information Services Will Soon Be Available on Phone Lines," *The Wall Street Journal*, March 11, 1988, p. 19.

Chapter 17

1. Campbell R. McConnell, *Economics* (New York: McGraw-Hill, 1987), pp. 339–340.

2. Earl C. Gottschalk, "Money Funds Bear Scrutiny, Analysts Assert," *The Wall Street Journal,* March 10, 1988, p. 23.

3. "Hitching a Ride on Tuition Bills," *Time,* October 5, 1987, p. 57.

4. Jeff Bailey, "Sears Is Discovering Discover Credit Card Isn't Hitting Pay Dirt," *The Wall Street Journal,* February 10, 1988, p. 1.

5. "A Heaping Helping Hand," *Time,* February 15, 1988, p. 85.

6. Robert E. Taylor, "Data on Banks to Be Available to Customers," *The Wall Street Journal,* March 3, 1988, p. 17.

7. "Bank Profits Least Since the Depression," *Omaha World-Herald,* March 3, 1988, p. 19.

8. Charles McCoy, "Financial Fraud: Theories behind Nationwide Surge in Bank Swindles," *The Wall Street Journal,* October 10, 1987, p. 15.

9. Steve Jordan, "Author: Endless Service Is the Means to Success," *Omaha World-Herald,* November 18, 1987, p. 58. Quotes author Nancy Austin, who co-authored the book *A Passion for Excellence* with Tom Peters.

10. "Tom Peters Tells U.S. Businesses: Serve and Take Care of Customers," *Lincoln Journal,* March 16, 1987, p. 15.

11. Sarah Bartlett, "Borrower vs. Banker: The Newest Lawsuit in Town," *Business Week,* July 14, 1986, p. 59.

12. Jim Jurlock and Todd Mason, "A Ten-Gallon Feud over the Hunts' Bank Loans," *Business Week,* July 7, 1986, pp. 33, 36.

Chapter 18

1. Christopher Farrell and Jeffrey M. Laderman, "Wringing More Profits from Idle Corporate Cash," *Business Week,* May 12, 1986, pp. 85–86.

2. Jeff Bailey, "Sears Is Discovering Discover Credit Card Isn't Hitting Pay Dirt," *The Wall Street Journal,* February 10, 1988, p. 1.

3. "Growth Capital Can Still Be Found," *The Wall Street Journal,* January 31, 1988, p. 31.

4. Frank McCoy, "Venture Capital Is Changing Course," *Business Week,* August 31, 1987, p. 71.

5. David Elsner, "The Oak Forest Whiz Whom Forbes Missed," *Chicago Tribune,* September 13, 1987, Sec. 7, p. 1.

6. "The New Dealmakers," *Newsweek,* May 26, 1986, pp. 47–50.

7. Anthony Bianco and Chris Farrell, "Power on Wall Street," *Business Week,* July 7, 1986, pp. 56–62.

Chapter 19

1. Dean Foust. "Why Federal Express Has Overnight Anxiety," *Business Week,* November 9, 1987, pp. 62, 66.

2. Gene Koretz, "College May Cost More, But Look at the Payoff," *Business Week,* May 25, 1987, p. 24.

3. Stephen Koepp, "Riding the Wild Bull," *Time,* July 27, 1987, p. 50.

4. Ibid.

5. "Big Board Membership Sells for Record $1 Million," *The Wall Street Journal,* April 24, 1987, p. 13.

6. "Turmoil Spurs Gallows Humor among Brokers," *Omaha World-Herald,* October 23, 1987, p. 21.

7. "System Failure," *Time,* February 8, 1988, p. 52.

8. "Crash of 1929 Wasn't That Bad," *Lincoln Sunday Journal-Star,* October 25, 1987, p. 3C.

9. Dennis Farney, "Main Street's View of the Crash Is Far from Wall Street's," *The Wall Street Journal,* December 30, 1987, pp. 1, 4.

10. Anthony Bianco, "Charles Schwab vs. Les Quick: Discount Brokering's Main Event," *Business Week,* May 12, 1986, pp. 80–83.

11. For a good example, see Jonathan B. Levine, "Don't Sell the Feschback Brothers Quick," *Business Week,* June 20, 1986, pp. 117–118.

12. Jeffrey M. Laderman, "Protecting Stock Profits If the Bear Attacks," *Business Week,* March 31, 1986, p. 62.

13. See, for example, Anthony Bianco, "Mutual Funds: Foreign Stock and Big Risks Pay Off," *Business Week,* August 4, 1986, pp. 64–65.

14. John Dorfman, "Stocks Brokers Buy Often Don't Do Well," *The Wall Street Journal,* April 24, 1987, p. 13.

15. John Dorfman, "Do Brokers' Stock Picks Perform Well?" *The Wall Street Journal,* February 5, 1988, p. 19.

16. Anise Wallace, "Seven Mistakes Investors Make Over and Over," *New York Times,* November 18, 1984, Sec. 12, pp. 18, 20.

Chapter 20

1. Ronald W. Vinson, "Insuring a Growing Country," *Nation's Business,* September 1987, pp. 89, 92, 96.

2. Christopher Farrell, et al., "The Crisis Is Over—But Insurance Will Never Be the Same," *Business Week,* May 25, 1987, pp. 122–123.

3. "A Question of Liability," *Time,* April 4, 1988, p. 61.

4. Farrell, "The Crisis Is Over," p. 122.

5. Karen Slater, "Return on Universal Life Insurance Can Be a Lot Less Than Expected," *The Wall Street Journal,* February 11, 1986, p. 35.

6. "Labor Letter," *The Wall Street Journal,* February 3, 1987, p. 1.

Chapter 21

1. John M. Barry, "Congress Pushes Homegrown Energy Again," *Business Month,* November 1987, pp. 70–71.

2. Laurie Hays and Mary LuCarnevale, "Regional Phone Firms Bend Rules and Invade Each Other's Territory," *The Wall Street Journal,* March 9, 1988, pp. 1, 18.

3. Karen Slater, "For Rich, Aftermath of Tax Overhaul Might Be a Bigger Bill from the State," *The Wall Street Journal,* February 29, 1988, p. 21.

4. "Easing Pains in the Wallet," *Time,* September 28, 1987, p. 54.

5. Nancy J. Perry, "The Surprising New Power of Patents," *Fortune,* June 23, 1986, pp. 57–63.

6. Kenneth W. Clarkson, et al., *West's Business Law: Alternative UCC Comprehensive Edition* (St. Paul, Minn.: West, 1981), p. 253.

7. "Business Bulletin," *The Wall Street Journal,* December 24, 1987, p. 1.

8. Addie M. Rimmer, "Bankrupt Find Starting Over Isn't So Easy," *The Wall Street Journal,* November 11, 1985, p. 27.

9. Clarkson, *West's Business Law,* p. 387.

10. "Texaco Files Petition for Chapter 11 as Talks with Pennzoil Collapse," *The Wall Street Journal,* April 13, 1987, p. 1.

Chapter 22

1. Brenton Welling, "The Selling of the Biggest Game on Earth," *Business Week,* June 9, 1986, pp. 102–103.

2. Bruce Nussbaum, "The New Economy: Say Hello to the Lean Years," *Business Week,* November 16, 1987, p. 163.

3. Barbara Rudolph, "Big Wheels Turning," *Time,* March 14, 1988, pp. 48–50.

4. Stephen Koepp, "Taking on the World," *Time,* October 19, 1987, p. 46.

5. Douglas R. Sease, "U.S. Exporters Begin to Post Sizable Gains in a Variety of Lines," *The Wall Street Journal,* August 31, 1987, pp. 1, 10.

6. Robert Johnson, "More U.S. Companies Are Selling Operations to Foreign Concerns," *The Wall Street Journal,* February 24, 1988, p. 1.

7. Stephen Koepp, "For Sale: America," *Time,* September 14, 1987, pp. 52–62.

8. Lynn Asinof, "Business Bulletin," *The Wall Street Journal,* September 24, 1987, p. 1.

9. Koepp, "Taking on the World," p. 47.

10. Ibid.

11. Glen Garelik, "Low Costs, High Growth," *Time,* October 19, 1987, p. 52.

12. Stephen D. Moore, "Pentagon Rebuffed Plessey Plan to Buy Harris Corp. of U.S. Earlier This Year," *The Wall Street Journal,* September 23, 1987, p. 27.

13. For more on the impact of exchange rates on international trade, see Leslie Helm, et al., "Will Japan Really Change?" *Business Week,* May 12, 1986, pp. 47–58; and Sease, "U.S. Exporters Begin to Post Sizable Gains."

14. "Business Bulletin," *The Wall Street Journal,* July 23, 1987, p. 1.

15. "Japan Blocks U.S. Try to Settle Trade Dispute through GATT," *Lincoln Journal,* April 8, 1988, p. 23.

16. Philip Revzin, "Despite Difficulties, Moves to Strengthen Common Market Gain," *The Wall Street Journal,* February 23, 1988, p. 1.

17. "Glasnost Makes a Deal," *Time,* November 23, 1987, p. 57.

18. James Sterngold, "Redrawing the Financial Map," *New York Times,* April 1, 1986, pp. 29, 33.

Appendix A

1. See Karen Pennar, "Jitters: Unsettling Economic Signs Have Americans on Edge," *Business Week,* May 11, 1987, pp. 40–41.

2. Campbell R. McConnell, *Economics* (New York: McGraw-Hill, 1987), p. 151.

3. "Trade Deficit Dips in Year-End Quarter," *Lincoln Journal,* February 24, 1988, p. 29.

4. "Cost of Paying the Foreign Piper," *The Wall Street Journal,* January 18, 1988, p. 1.

5. "U.S. Is World's Largest Debtor Nation," *Lincoln Journal,* June 23, 1987, p. 14.

6. Todd May, Jr., "The Economy Will Tough It Out," *Fortune,* June 22, 1987, pp. 47, 50.

7. Reginald Rhein, Jr., "Patent Pirates May Soon Be Walking the Plank," *Business Week,* June 15, 1987, pp. 62–63.

8. Scott Kilman, "An Unexpected Result of Airline Decontrol Is Return to Monopolies," *The Wall Street Journal,* July 20, 1987, p. 1.

Sources

Chapter 1

p. 11 Entrepreneurs Close-Up: Adapted from Joshua Hyatt, "Coming Distractions," *Inc.*, October 1987, p. 11.

p. 13 Figure 1.1: *Statistical Abstracts of the United States*, 1987, p. 827.

p. 14 Figure 1.2: *Reader's Digest 1987 Almanac and Yearbook*, pp. 480–483.

p. 20 Small Business Close-Up: "Small Is Beautiful Now in Manufacturing," *Business Week*, October 22, 1984, pp. 152–156; "Small Is Beautiful," *Business Week*, May 27, 1985, pp. 88–90; and Richard M. Hodgetts and Donald F. Kuratko, *Effective Small Business Management*, 2nd ed., (Orlando, FL.: Academic Press, 1986), Chapter 2.

p. 21 Table 1.1: Adapted from "Who Makes Technology Work: A Special Report," *The Wall Street Journal*, June 12, 1987, Section 4, pp. 5D, 8D, 9D.

p. 30 Case: Adapted from Paulette Thomas, "In Denver, Tensions Flare as Two Airlines Trade Barbs and Smiles," *The Wall Street Journal*, June 23, 1987, pp. 1, 17.

Chapter 2

p. 37 Social Responsibility Close-Up: "Is a Stampede Starting in South Africa?" *Business Week*, August 26, 1985, pp. 35, 38; John Nielsen, "Time to Quit South Africa?" *Fortune*, September 30, 1985, pp. 18–23; Karen Elliott House, "Don't Push South Africa to the Wall," *The Wall Street Journal*, October 30, 1985, p. 28; "GM Vows to Aid Workers Charged under Apartheid," *Omaha World-Herald*, February 24, 1986, p. 4; Barbara Rudolph, "Cutting Ties to a Troubled Land," *Time*, June 29, 1987, pp. 44–45.

p. 40 Table 2.2: *Economic Report of the President*, 1987, p. 288.

p. 41 Figure 2.2: U.S. Department of Labor, 1987.

p. 45 Social Responsibility Close-Up: Adapted from Dexter Hutchins, "The Drive to Kick Smoking at Work," *Fortune*, September 15, 1986, pp. 42–43.

p. 54 Case: Tim Smart, "Costly Cleanups at the Gas Pump," *Business Week*, April 20, 1987, pp. 28–29.

p. 56 Career Opportunities: Adapted from Walecia Konrad and Joan Tedeschi, "The 25 Hottest Careers in 1987," *Working Woman*, July 1987, pp. 57–62; 90–91.

Chapter 3

p. 66 Entrepreneurs Close-Up: Adapted from Brenton R. Schlender, "Microsoft's Gates Uses Products and Pressure to Gain Power in PCs," *The Wall Street Journal*, September 25, 1987, pp. 1, 6.

p. 69 Technology Close-Up: "One-Arm Bandits That Will Take Plastic," *Business Week*, August 12, 1985, p. 59; "Maintaining a Dialogue with Your Tires," *Business Week*, September 30, 1985, p. 87; and Tom Post, "The Year's Best Entrepreneurial Ideas," *Venture*, December 1986, pp. 30–31.

p. 82 Case: Adapted from Tom Richman, "Calibrake, Inc.," *Inc.*, December 1985, pp. 72, 77.

Chapter 4

p. 90 Small Business Close-Up: Adapted from " 'Iowa Nuts' Venture May Amount to More Than a Hill of Beans," *Chicago Tribune*, July 5, 1987, Sec. 7, p. 8.

p. 98 Figure 4.2: U.S. Department of Commerce, International Trade Administration, "Franchising in the Economy," *Statistical Abstracts of the United States*, 1987.

p. 99 Entrepreneurs Close-Up: Adapted from Pamela Sherrod, "Franchising: Land of Opportunity," *Chicago Tribune*, November 23, 1987, Sec. 4, pp. 1, 4, 5.

p. 103 Figure 4.3: U.S. Department of Commerce, International Trade Administration, "Franchising in the Economy," *Statistical Abstracts of the United States*, 1987; *U.S. Industrial Outlook*, 1987, pp. 57–62.

p. 109 Case: Adapted from Steven P. Galante, "Auto-Related Franchises Join the Ranks of Home Services," *The Wall Street Journal*, May 18, 1987, p. 21.

Chapter 5

p. 115 Figure 5.1: *Statistical Abstracts of the United States*, 1987, p. 503.

p. 125 Table 5.2: Adapted from *Fortune*, April 25, 1988, p. D11.

p. 139 Case: Adapted from Robert Mulder, "Sole Proprietor," *Inc.*, November 1986, pp. 96, 99.

Chapter 6

p. 153 Competitiveness Close-Up: Adapted from George H. Labovitz, "Keeping Your Internal Customers Satisfied." *The Wall Street Journal*, July 6, 1987, p. 12.

p. 162 Small Business Close-Up: Adapted from Bruce G. Posner, "Smart Money," *Inc.*, January 1986, pp. 58–68.

p. 179 Case: Adapted from William M. Bulkeley, "Two Computer Firms with Clashing Styles Fight for Market Niche," *The Wall Street Journal*, July 6, 1987, pp. 1, 16.

Chapter 7

p. 198 Social Responsibility Close-Up: Adapted from Bill Saporito, "Cutting Costs without Cutting People," *Fortune*, May 25, 1987, pp. 26–32.

p. 201 Case: Adapted from Paul B. Brown, "Stop the Treadmill, I Want to Get Off," *Inc.*, May 1987, pp. 92–98.

Chapter 8

p. 217 Social Responsibility Close-Up: Irene Pave, "Move Me, Move My Spouse: Relocating the Corporate Couple," *Business Week*, December 16, 1985, pp. 57, 60; William R. Greer, "Assisting Spouses in Transfers," *New York Times*, February 4, 1986, p. 33.

p. 219 Technology Close-Up: Adapted from John Knowlton, " 'Smile for the Camera': Job Seekers Make More Use of Video Resumes," *The Wall Street Journal*, June 22, 1987, p. 25.

p. 226 International Close-Up: Adapted from Richard M. Hodgetts, Ronald G. Greenwood, and David S. Cohen, "A Comparison of Human Resources Development between American Multinational and Private National Taiwan Firms" (Paper presented at the Pan-Pacific Business Conference, November 1986) and "Labor Letter," *The Wall Street Journal*, December 22, 1987, p. 1.

p. 229 Figure 8.3: Adapted from Peggy Simpson, "If the Wage System Doesn't Work, Fix It," *Working Woman*, October 1985, p. 118.

p. 240 Case: Adapted from Martha Brannigan, "Women Who Fought Sex Bias on Job Prove to Be a Varied Group," *The Wall Street Journal*, June 8, 1987, pp. 1, 8.

Chapter 9

p. 245 Figure 9.1: U.S. Bureau of Census and Bureau of Labor Statistics; "Unions Continued to Lose Members in 1987," *Omaha World-Herald*, January 23, 1988, p. 41.

p. 261 Social Responsibility Close-Up: Jonathan Tasini and Patrick Houston, "Letting Workers Help Handle Workers' Gripes," *Business Week*, September 15, 1986, pp. 82, 86.

p. 264 Small Business Close-Up: Adapted from Sabin Russell, "Living with Unions," *Venture*, February 1986, pp. 33–36.

p. 272 Case: Adapted from "Talking Union," *Forbes*, April 6, 1987, pp. 35–36.

Chapter 10

p. 281 Technology Close-Up: Adapted from Brian Dumaine, "Still A-OK: The Promise of Factories in Space," *Fortune*, March 3, 1986, pp. 49–50.

p. 292 International Close-Up: Leslie Helm and Maralyn Edid, "Life on the Line: Two Auto Workers Who Are Worlds Apart," *Business Week*, September 30, 1985, pp. 76–78; "Special Report: Japan's Troubled Future," *Fortune*, March 30, 1987, pp. 21–24.

p. 295 Figure 10.7: Richard Brandt and Otis Port, "How Automation Could Save the Day," *Business Week*, March 3, 1986, p. 73.

p. 300 Social Responsibility Close-Up: Some of the information in this example can be found in Laurie McGinley, "Group Faults Audi Shift Lock for 5000 Series," *The Wall Street Journal*, July 30, 1987, p. 6.

p. 308 Case: Tom Nicholson, Richard Manning, William J. Cook, and Connie Leslie, "GM's 'Saturn' Satellite," *Newsweek*, January 21, 1985, pp. 56–57; William J. Hampton, "Will Saturn Ever Leave the Launchpad?" *Business Week*, March 16, 1987, p. 107; Dale D. Buss, "GM Slows Big Drive for Saturn to Produce Small Car in Five Years," *The Wall Street Journal*, October 30, 1986, pp. 1, 27.

Chapter 11

p. 319 Social Responsibility Close-Up: Adapted from Jonathan Dajel, "Complaint Department: Airlines Find New Ways to Enrage Fliers," *The Wall Street Journal*, June 1, 1987, p. 19; "Airline Consumer Bill OK'd," *Lincoln Journal*, October 30, 1987.

p. 329 Table 11.1: John Holusha, "A Noted Voice on Car Buying," *New York Times*, January 21, 1986, p. 29.

p. 336 Small Business Close-Up: Adapted from Steve Kichen and Matthew Schifrin, "Niche List," *Forbes*, November 3, 1986, pp. 160–164.

p. 344 Case: Mark Clayton, "Small Towns Think Japan," *Christian Science Monitor*, May 11, 1987, pp. 1, 16; Michael Tackett, "Indiana Cultural Bridge Lures Japanese Plant," *Chicago Tribune*, June 21, 1987, Sec. 1, p. 3.

Chapter 12

p. 355 Social Responsibility Close-Up: Amy Dunkin et al., "The Spirited Battle for Those Who Want to Drink Light," *Business Week*, June 16, 1986, pp. 84–86.

p. 364 Small Business Close-Up: John P. Tarpey, "Home Exercise Gear: Another Industry Gets Fat on Fitness," *Business Week*, January 20, 1985, p. 118; Jonathan B. Levin, "Precor: Pulling Ahead by Stressing Design," *Business Week*, January 20, 1985, p. 119; Jonathan Levin, "Soloflex Puts More Muscle in Its Hard Sell," *Business Week*, January 20, 1985, p. 122; Jo Ellen Davis, "So Long, Bench Press: Thanks for the Pep Talk," *Business Week*, January 26, 1987, pp. 72, 74.

p. 373 Case: Richard Zoglin, "MTV Faces a Mid-Life Crisis," *Time*, June 29, 1987, p. 67.

Chapter 13

p. 381 Table 13.1: Adapted from *Advertising Age*, September 24, 1987, pp. 1, 162. Table 13.2: Adapted from *Advertising Age*, September 24, 1987, p. 165.

p. 384 Figure 13.2: *1987 Information Please Almanac* (Boston: Houghton-Mifflin, 1987), p. 66; *Statistical Abstracts of the United States*, 1987.

p. 387 Competitiveness Close-Up: Adapted from Debbie Seaman, "Chemical Blasts Off in Battle of the Banks," *Adweek*, July 20, 1987, p. 22.

p. 388 Figure 13.3: *Advertising Age*, January 20, 1986, p. 1.

p. 394 Technology Close-Up: Jack Falvey, "Car Phones Become the Sales Force's Fifth Wheel," *The Wall Street Journal*, July 27, 1987, p. 14.

p. 405 Case: Adapted from Beth Austin, "Quaker Wins Legal Bout in Cereal Wars," *Advertising Age*, July 20, 1987, Sec. 1, p. 1; Steve Weiner, "Food Fight!" *Forbes*, July 27, 1987, pp. 86, 89.

Chapter 14

p. 414 Business Ethics Close-Up: Adapted from John Schwartz, "Now, One-Stop Medicine?" *Newsweek*, May 25, 1987, pp. 32–33.

p. 425 International Close-Up: Adapted from John S. DeMott, "The Store That Runs on a Wrench," *Time*, July 27, 1987, p. 54.

p. 433 Figure 14.10: U.S. Interstate Commerce Commission, *Freight Commodity Statistics*, annual, *Statistical Abstracts of the United States*, 1987.

Chapter 15

p. 448 Social Responsibility Close-Up: Paula Dwyer and Lawrence J. Tell, "Wedtech: Where Fingers Are Pointing Now," *Business Week*, October 5, 1987, pp. 34–35 and "Wedtech Defendants Enter Scandal Trial," *Omaha World-Herald*, March 12, 1988, p. 6.

p. 467 Business Communication Close-Up: Jonathon B. Levine, "Déjà Vu at BankAmerica," *Business Week*, May 25, 1987, p. 59.

Chapter 16

p. 480 Small Business Close-Up: Anne R. Field, "The Next Boom in Computers: Services," *Business Week*, July 7, 1986, pp. 72–73; Randall Smith, "Lost Dreams: Computer Retailing Is Littered with Those Who Failed," *The Wall Street Journal*, May 22, 1986, p. 33; Christine Winter, "'Rent' Becomes a Password in Computer World," *Chicago Tribune*, August 31, 1987, Sec. 4, pp. 1, 5.

p. 481 Figure 16.1: Adapted from J. Daniel Couger and Fred R. McFadden, *First Course in Data Processing*, 2nd ed. (New York: Wiley, 1984), p. 401.

p. 487 Figure 16.2: Adapted from *Newsweek*, November 18, 1985, p. 71.

p. 494 International Close-Up: David E. Sanger, "Snags Imperil Japan's Dream of World's Fastest Computer," *New York Times*, November 28, 1986, pp. 1, 31; "Scientists Set Computing Speed Record," *The Lincoln Star*, March 14, 1988, p. 3.

p. 502 Figure 16.4: Adapted from Joel Dreyfuss, "Networking: Japan's Latest Computer Craze," *Fortune*, July 17, 1986, p. 95.

p. 507 Case: Susan M. Gelfond and Jo Ellen David, "Now, the 'Paperless' Expense Account," *Business Week*, September 2, 1987, p. 106.

Chapter 17

p. 517 International Close-Up: Blanca Riemer et al., "The Lords of Money," *Business Week*, April 28, 1986, pp. 72, 74–75 and Barbara Rudolph, "Big Wheels Turning," *Time*, March 14, 1988, p. 48.

p. 522 Figure 17.2: *American Banker*, March 19, 1987, p. 11.

p. 535 Social Responsibility Close-Up: Blanca Riemer et al., "Liberty, Justice, and Bank Accounts for All," *Business Week*, July 1, 1985, pp. 68–69 and *Ethics in American Business*, a report by Touche Ross & Co., January 1988, p. 8.

p. 541 Case: Martin Mayer, "The Watchful Eye of Charlie Rice," *Business Month*, September 1987, pp. 34–37, 40.

Chapter 18

p. 549 Small Business Close-Up: Adapted from Merrill Goozner, "Age-Old Tradition Bankrolls Koreans," *Chicago Tribune*, July 19, 1987, Sec. 7, pp. 1, 2.

p. 567 Case: Ruth Simon, "The Price of Quick Riches," *Forbes*, September 21, 1987, pp. 112, 117.

Chapter 19

p. 573 Figure 19.1: Stephen Koepp, "Riding the Wild Bull," *Time*, July 27, 1987, pp. 50–52.

p. 577 Table 19.2: Adapted from George Curian, *What's What in American Business* (Chicago: Probus Publishing, 1986), p. 163.

p. 581 Computer Technology Close-Up: Denise M. Topolnicki, "Investing by Computer," *Money*, December 1984, pp. 171–178; "Software for Seasoned Investors," *Changing Times*, November 1986, pp. 91–95; and "System Failure," *Time*, February 8, 1988, p. 52.

p. 590 Business Communication Close-Up: Adapted from Carol Jouzaitis, "Broker Speaks Language of the Deaf," *Chicago Tribune*, August 10, 1987, Sec. 4, p. 3.

p. 602 Case: Adapted from Timothy K. Smith, "By End of This Year, Poultry Will Surpass Beef in the U.S. Diet," *The Wall Street Journal*, September 17, 1987, pp. 1, 14; Timothy K. Smith, "The Cyclical Nature of Chicken Firms Is Problem for Investors," *The Wall Street Journal*, September 17, 1987, p. 14.

Chapter 20

p. 615 Table 20.2: *Fortune*, June 8, 1987, p. 208.

p. 617 Computer Technology Close-Up: Adapted from David J. Solomon, "Hotlines and Hefty Rewards: Retailers Step Up Efforts to Curb Employee Theft," *The Wall Street Journal*, September 17, 1987, p. 33.

p. 619 International Close-Up: Adapted from Peggy Berkowitz, "In Canada Different Legal and Popular Views Prevail," *The Wall Street Journal*, April 4, 1986, p. 23.

p. 623 Figure 20.3: Department of Health and Human Services, 1986; *U.S. Industrial Outlook*, 1987, pp. 54–1, 54–5.

p. 631 Case: Adapted from Burr Leonard, "Life after Death," *Forbes*, May 4, 1987, pp. 132–133.

Chapter 21

p. 642 Table 21.2: Adapted from *Newsweek*, October 19, 1987, p. 97.

p. 645 Figure 21.1: Adapted from "Reagan Presents 'Give-and-Take' Budget," *Lincoln Journal*, February 18, 1988, p. 1.

p. 646 Figure 21.2: U.S. Treasury Department.

p. 649 Entrepreneurs Close-Up: Adapted from Elizabeth J. Gulden, "Flying Solo as a Woman," *The Compleat Lawyer* (American Bar Association), Summer 1987, pp. 25–26.

p. 657 Social Responsibility Close-Up: Gregory L. Miles, "Information Thieves Are Now Corporate Enemy No. 1," *Business Week*, May 5, 1986, pp. 120–125.

p. 665 Case: Adapted from John Grossmann, "Milk Fight," *Inc.*, September 1987, pp. 37, 40–44.

Chapter 22

p. 671 Figure 22.1: Adapted from *Economic Review*, July/August 1987, p. 26.

p. 672 Figure 22.2: Adapted from Stephen Koepp, "Taking on the World," *Time*, October 19, 1987, pp. 46–47.

p. 674 Table 22.1: Adapted from Stephen Koepp, "For Sale: America," *Time*, September 14, 1987, pp. 52–62.

p. 675 Table 22.2: *New York Times*, August 3, 1986, p. F9. Data from U.S. Department of Commerce and U.S. Department of Agriculture.

p. 676 Small Business Close-Up: Some of the material in this story is from Joel Kotkin, "The Case for Manufacturing in America," *Inc.*, March 1985, pp. 49–54; and Jeremy Main, "Detroit's Cars Really Are Getting Better," *Fortune*, February 2, 1987, pp. 90–98.

p. 680 Figure 22.3: *Statistical Abstracts of the United States*, U.S. Department of Commerce, 1987.

p. 684 International Close-Up: Howard G. Chua-Eoan, "How to Keep the Dragons Happy," *Time*, June 22, 1987, p. 44.

p. 688 Figure 22.5: Adapted from *Forbes*, July 28, 1986, pp. 207–208.

p. 693 Case: Adapted from Joseph A. Reaves, "U.S. Firm Keeps China Door Open," *Chicago Tribune*, May 16, 1987, sec. 3, pp. 1, 8.

Appendix A

p. A5 Figure A.3: Adapted from *Economic Report of the President*, 1987, pp. 244–246.

p. A6 Table A.1: Adapted from *Economic Indicators*, August 1987, p. 2. Figures are for fiscal 1986.

p. A7 Figure A.4: Adapted from *The World Almanac and Book of Facts* (New York: Pharos Books, 1987), p. 115.

Appendix B

p. B7 Figure B.1: Adapted from *Chicago Tribune*, August 9, 1987, Sec. 7, p. 1. Data from the U.S. Department of Commerce.

p. B10 Figure B.2: Smith Barney Harris Upham, Incorporated.

p. B12 Table B.5: *Employment and Earnings*, U.S. Department of Labor, August 1987, p. 29. Figure B.3: *Statistical Abstracts of the United States* (Washington, D.C.: U.S. Department of Commerce, 1987), p. 14; *The Wall Street Journal*, January 22, 1988, p. 21.

p. B14 Figure B.4: Adapted from *The Wall Street Journal*, August 7, 1987, p. 21. Figure B.5: Department of Commerce, Bureau of the Census, 1987 for the data through 1980; 1987 data was reported by the U.S. Labor Department on February 1, 1988.

GLOSSARY

Absolute advantage A monopoly on certain products or the ability to produce them for considerably less than anyone else.

Accounting The process of measuring, interpreting, evaluating, and communicating financial information for the purpose of effective decision making and control.

Accounting equation The relationship stating that assets equal liabilities plus owners' equity.

Acid-test ratio The ratio of highly liquid assets to current liabilities.

Acquisition The purchase of one company by another, in which the purchasing company takes over the acquired company's operations and property.

Activity format Classifies cash inflows and outflows in terms of operating, investing, and financing activities.

Actuaries Experts in collecting statistics about losses and using this information to make predictions.

Advertising A nonpersonal form of promotion in which a firm attempts to persuade someone to a particular point of view.

Affirmative-action programs Programs designed to seek out minorities, women, the handicapped, and others with problems finding work and to hire, train, develop, and promote them.

Agency A legal relationship between an agent and a principal.

Agency shop A company at which the employees do not have to join the union but nevertheless have to pay union dues.

Agent A person authorized to act on behalf of another.

Agent intermediaries Wholesalers that do not take title to the goods they distribute.

Alien corporation A business incorporated in one country but operating in another.

American Federation of Labor (AFL) The most important craft union federation in the United States.

American Stock Exchange (AMEX) The second-largest exchange in the United States.

Analytic manufacturing process A process that reduces a raw material to its component parts for the purpose of obtaining one or more products.

Antitrust Improvements Act A federal law that requires companies planning to merge to notify the FTC in advance and allows injured parties to file lawsuits.

Antitrust Procedures and Penalties Act A federal law that increased fines and penalties imposed for violation of the Sherman Antitrust Act.

Apprentice training Training a new employee by assigning a more experienced employee to teach procedures, rules, and techniques, over a relatively long period.

Arbitration A resolution method in which a neutral third party listens to both sides and then directs each side in what to do.

Array A list of values in ascending or descending order.

Assets Everything of value owned by an enterprise.

Authority The right to command.

Authorization card A request that the union represent the workers.

Average A measure of central tendency.

Aviation insurance Coverage of losses involving airliners and their passengers.

Bait and switch Advertising a product at a very low price and then telling customers the product is either out of stock or of low quality and recommending a higher-priced alternative.

Balance of payments The total cash flow out of a country minus the total inflow of cash.

Balance of trade The difference between the value of a nation's exports and the value of its imports.

Balance sheet A financial statement showing the position of a firm as of a particular date.

Bank money market accounts Short-term, special deposit accounts that offer competitive interest rates.

Bankruptcy law The branch of law that specifies the legal steps for securing relief from debts.

Bar chart A graph of a series of values using bars that vary in length according to the size of each value.

Bear An investor who believes that stock prices are going to fall.

Benefit segmentation Dividing up a market on the basis of the benefits that people seek.

Binding arbitration Arbitration in which both parties agree to follow the arbitrator's decision.

Blue-chip stocks Stocks of large, high-quality companies with a proven track record.

Blue-collar jobs Jobs in manufacturing or ones that call for employees to work with their hands.

Board of directors The top governing body of a corporation.

Bonds Long-term debts with a term of 20 to 30 years that are sold to raise funds.

Boycott An organized effort to convince people to refrain from buying goods or services from a targeted business.

Brainstorming A creative technique for groups in which participants generate as many ideas as possible for solving a problem without considering at first the merits of each idea.

Branch organization An operation set up by a parent company in a foreign country for the purpose of accomplishing specific goals such as sales.

Brand A name, term, symbol, or combination of these used to identify a firm's products and differentiate them from competing products.

Breakeven point The level of production at which total revenues from selling the products equal total expenses incurred in making them.

Broker An agent intermediary that brings buyers and sellers together.

Budget A financial plan that specifies revenues and expenses for a given time period.

Bull An investor who believes that stock prices are going to rise.

Bumping An arrangement permitting employees laid off from one department to go to another department in the company and re-place, or bump, someone there who has less seniority.

Burnout Mental and/or physical exhaustion caused by excess stress.

Business An organized, profit-seeking approach to providing people with the goods and services they want.

Business cycles Fluctuations in business activity.

Business ethics Standards that govern business behavior.

Business interruption insurance Coverage of losses from temporary business closings.

Business statistics The systematic collection, presentation, and interpretation of data related to business problems.

Buying Deciding the type and amount of goods to be purchased.

Byte A character of data.

Call option An option to buy a specific security.

Call provision A bond provision that allows the firm to repurchase the bonds before maturity.

Capital The money and technology used for operating the enterprise.

Capital goods Machinery, equipment, tools, and facilities.

Career pathing The process of identifying a sequence of job assignments through which a person can move from one position to another laterally or up the hierarchy.

Carrying costs The expenses associated with keeping inventory on hand.

Cash discount A discount given for paying a bill within a predetermined time period.

Cash value The amount of money in a life insurance policy that the insured can borrow or obtain by canceling the policy.

Celler-Kefauver Antimerger Act A federal law that prohibits mergers and major asset purchases that decrease competition in an industry.

Centralization Upper management levels make most of the important decisions.

Central processing unit (CPU) The component that controls what the computer does.

Certificates of deposit (CDs) Fixed-term accounts that pay a predetermined rate of interest.

Certified management accountant (CMA) A private accountant who has met certain education and professional requirements and has passed a series of exams.

Certified public accountant (CPA) A public accountant who has met state certification requirements of education and job experience and has passed a comprehensive examination.

Channel of distribution The path a product follows from production to final sale.

Checkoff Deducting union dues directly from each member's paycheck.

Class-action suit A lawsuit in which a group of buyers join together to sue the seller.

Clayton Act A federal law that prohibits tying agreements, interlocking directorates, and certain anticompetitive stock acquisitions.

Collective bargaining The process in which management and the employees, represented by the union of their choice, negotiate over wages, hours, and conditions of employment.

Commercial bank A financial institution that accepts deposits and provides a wide array of financial services.

Commercial finance company Lending institution that provides short-term, collateralized loans to businesses.

Commercial paper An unsecured promissory note.

Common carrier A transportation company that performs services within a particular line of business for the general public.

Common law The precedents established by prior court decisions, going back to English law.

Common Market A group of European countries organized to eliminate trade barriers between all members.

Common stock An ownership share in a corporation.

Communism An economic system where the government owns all property and makes all decisions regarding production of goods and services.

Comparable worth The idea that jobs requiring equal amounts of skill and responsibility are of equal value to the employer and therefore should receive equal pay.

Comparative advantage The ability to sell certain products for relatively less than producers in most other nations can.

Composite of leading indicators A set of measurements that provides clues about which way the economy is moving.

Computer-integrated manufacturing (CIM) A manufacturing system that automates all of the factory functions and links them with company headquarters.

Computer network A system that allows for multiple users and multiple activities.

Computer program A series of coded instructions that tells the computer what to do.

Concentrated marketing Focusing marketing efforts on a single market segment.

Congress of Industrial Organizations (CIO) The most important industrial union federation in the United States.

Conscious motives The reasons for buying that people are willing to express.

Consumer behavior The way consumers go about making their purchase decisions.

Consumer finance company A financial institution that makes short-term loans to individuals.

Consumer good or service A good or service destined to be used by a consumer.

Consumerism A movement designed to provide buyers with the information and bargaining power necessary for obtaining high-quality, safe products and services.

Consumer-oriented marketing Based on the belief that a company must find out what the customer wants before providing a good or service.

Consumer pretest A test of advertising effectiveness that asks people to examine ads and rank them on their ability to capture and retain interest.

Contingency leadership The leadership technique of using the style that will be most effective in a specific situation.

Continuous production A production sequence in which the flow of materials is steady and constant.

Contract A legally binding promise.

Contract carrier A transportation company that performs services called for by an individual contract.

Contrarianism An investment strategy based on the belief that the market will move in the direction opposite to that predicted by the general public.

Controlling Comparing actual results against expected performance.

Convenience store A limited-line store that specializes in fast service.

Conversion privilege A provision permitting conversion of bonds into a stated number of shares of common stock.

Cooperative advertising Advertising for a product in which the manufacturer and merchant share the costs.

Coordination A systematic, unified group effort in the pursuit of common objectives.

Copyright A legal protection of a particular work that allows its owner the exclusive right to reproduce, sell, and adapt the work.

Core hours Those times when everyone must be on the job under a flexible work schedule.

Corporate officers Individuals legally empowered to represent the corporation and to bind it to contracts.

Corporation A body established by law and existing distinct from the individuals who invest in and control it.

Correlation The degree to which two or more variables are related.

Cost of goods sold The costs involved in producing or acquiring a product to sell.

Couponing A sales promotion technique that offers buyers a specified discount if they redeem a coupon.

Creative process Generating new or unique ideas, involving four steps: preparation, incubation, illumination, and verification.

Creative selling Determining the buyer's needs and matching them with the products for sale.

Credit card An instrument used for obtaining a short-term loan for a cash purchase.

Credit union A savings cooperative that lends money to its members.

Critical path The sequence of activities that identifies the longest possible time a project will take.

Cross training An expanded version of job rotation, in which the employee learns different skills or perspectives.

Culture The beliefs, attitudes, values, and behaviors that people learn in their society.

Currency Coins and paper money.

Current assets Assets that the company will use or convert into cash within the year.

Current liabilities Financial obligations that will fall due within the year.

Current ratio The ratio of current assets to current liabilities.

Customer departmentalization The structure of a level of an organization on the basis of customer needs.

Customs duties Taxes levied on imported goods.

Data base An organization of data for rapid search and retrieval.

Debenture An unsecured bond.

Debt-asset ratio The ratio of the firm's total debt to its total assets.

Debt-equity ratio The ratio of total debt to total equity.

Decentralization Delegation of many important decisions to lower management levels.

Decertification The process of dropping a union as the bargaining agent for the workers.

Deductible The amount that a policyholder must pay before the insurance company pays any part of a claim.

Deed A document that establishes property ownership and is transferable to other parties.

Defendant The party against whom a legal action is brought.

Delegation The distribution of work and authority to subordinates.

Demand The amount of a good purchased at a particular price.

Demand deposits Checking accounts.

Demographic segmentation Dividing up a market on the basis of socioeconomic characteristics.

Departmentalization The structure of a given level of an organization on the basis of some common characteristics.

Department store A large store that offers a wide variety of merchandise grouped into departments.

Depreciation A deduction from the value of a fixed asset to account for its gradual wearing out.

Depression An economic period characterized by prolonged recession, massive unemployment, low wages, and large numbers of people living in poverty.

Derivative plan The plan for a series of actions that convert the strategic plan into an operational plan.

Desktop publishing A computer system that allows companies to publish newsletters, charts, brochures, and other printed material in-house.

Development The process of helping people gain the skills and experiences they need to become or remain successful in their jobs.

Differentiated marketing Selling a range of related products to specific market segments.

Direct channel A distribution channel that bypasses all intermediaries.

Directing Getting human resources to work effectively and efficiently.

Directors' and officers' liability insurance Coverage of the costs of lawsuits against board members and senior corporate executives arising out of their actions.

Discount An amount subtracted from the list price; the amount by which a bond's price is less than its face value.

Discount rate The interest rate that the Fed charges member banks for loans.

Discount store A retail store that offers lower prices and fewer customer services than other retailers.

Discretionary order An order that gives the stockbroker the right to execute it immediately or wait for a better price.

Distributive bargaining Bargaining in which a gain to one side is a loss to the other.

Divestiture The selling off of a business holding.

Domestic corporation A business operating in the state where it is incorporated.

Door-to-door retailer A salesperson who sells products house to house.

Dormant partner A partner who is not known as a partner to the general public and plays no active role in the company.

Double-entry bookkeeping The use of two entries for every transaction.

Downward processing A materials flow in which different parts of the same product are produced on different floors.

Durable goods Goods that do not wear out quickly.

Earnings per share The ratio of net income to common stock shares outstanding.

Ecology The interrelationship of living things and their environment.

Economic environment An environment in which buyers and sellers are brought together through an elaborate series of markets.

Economic order quantity (EOQ) model An inventory-ordering model that balances order and carrying costs and reduces the likelihood of running out of inventory.

Economics The study of how societies use limited resources to fulfill their needs and wants for goods and services.

Electronic funds transfer system A computerized system for depositing and withdrawing funds electronically.

Electronic mail A system for sending and receiving messages through computers.

Employee stock ownership plans (ESOPs) Financial arrangements that allow employees to buy the company that employs them.

Employer associations Employer-sponsored lobbying and public relations organizations primarily designed to promote promanagement legislation.

Employment at will The principle that the employer can retain or dismiss personnel as it wishes.

Endowment life insurance Life insurance that combines a death benefit with a great deal of savings.

Entrepreneur The creator and/or organizer of a venture.

Entrepreneurship The process of organizing, operating, and assuming the risks associated with a business venture.

Equal Employment Opportunity Commission (EEOC) The commission charged with overseeing enforcement of the Civil Rights Act of 1964 by investigating complaints and taking appropriate action.

Equilibrium price The price at which demand equals supply.

Equity-asset ratio The ratio of owners' equity to total assets.

Equity financing The sale of ownership in a firm.

Exception principle Management should concern itself only with significant deviations or exceptions.

Excise tax A levy designed to limit the purchase of goods or make the users of certain services help pay for them.

Exclusive distribution A channel strategy in which only one intermediary distributes a product in a given area.

Export-Import Bank (Exim Bank) A U.S. government lending agency that makes loans to importers and exporters unable to obtain private funding.

Exports Goods or services sold to other countries.

Express contract One in which the parties make oral or written promises.

Express warranty A guarantee offered orally or in writing.

Expropriation and inconvertibility insurance Political risk insurance that covers nationalization of property and conversion of currency.

Fabrication Combining materials or parts in order to form or assemble them into a finished product.

Factor A financial institution that purchases accounts receivable.

Family brand A brand used with all of the products a firm sells.

Fast freight The rapid conveyance of perishable goods by train.

Federal Deposit Insurance Corporation (FDIC) A federal agency that insures bank deposits up to $100,000 in case of bank failure.

Federal Reserve System (Fed) A network of regional banks that regulate banking in America.

Federal Savings and Loan Insurance Corporation (FSLIC) A federal agency that insures deposits up to $100,000 at savings and loan associations.

Federal Trade Commission Act A federal law that prohibits unfair trade practices and established the Federal Trade Commission (FTC).

Fidelity bond Coverage of losses caused by employee embezzlement or theft.

FIFO An inventory valuation system under which the first goods produced or acquired are considered the first ones sold (**F**irst **I**n, **F**irst **O**ut).

Financial manager The person responsible for developing, implementing, and controlling the financial plan.

Fiscal policy The use of government spending and tax collection to attain full employment and a non-inflationary high level of GNP.

Fiscal year The 12 months that constitute an organization's annual operation.

Fixed assets Assets that the company intends to keep for more than one year and use in the operation of the business.

Fixed-price technique A pricing technique in which the marketer sells at the announced price.

Flat structure Structure with few levels and long spans of control.

Flex benefits approach An employee benefit arrangement that allows each worker to tailor his or her own benefit package.

Flexible manufacturing system (FMS) A manufacturing system in which computer-controlled machining centers produce complicated parts at high speed.

Flexible pricing Selling a product at a price that is negotiable.

Flexible work schedule A schedule that allows workers to set their own work hours within limitations established by the organization.

Flextime Another name for a flexible work schedule.

Foreign corporation A business that has been incorporated in another state.

Formal organization structure The explicitly established lines of authority and responsibility designed by management.

Franchise A system of distribution in which a producer or supplier arranges for a dealer to handle a product or service under mutually agreed-upon conditions.

Franchisee The dealer in a franchise system.

Franchisor The supplier in a franchise system.

Freedom of choice Businesses are free to hire people, invest money, purchase machinery and equipment, and choose the markets where they wish to operate.

Free enterprise system An economic system under which businesses are free to decide what to supply and are rewarded based on how well they meet customer needs.

Free-trade zone (FTZ) A geographic area into which foreign goods can be imported without payment of duties.

Freight forwarder A common carrier that leases or contracts space from other carriers and resells it to small-volume shippers.

Frequency distribution An arrangement of data that shows the number of times each value or range of values occurs.

Functional departmentalization The structure of the level of an organization on the basis of major activities.

Fundamental analysis The process of comparing a company's current financial position and prospects for the future with those of other firms.

Gantt chart A tool for production scheduling and control that keeps track of projected and actual work progress over time.

General Agreement on Tariffs and Trade (GATT) An international agreement and organization designed to eliminate tariff barriers to worldwide trade.

General partner A partner who is active in the operation of a business and has unlimited liability.

Generic product A product with no brand and simple packaging.

Geographic departmentalization The structure of the level of an organization along territorial lines.

Geographic segmentation Dividing up a market on the basis of where people live.

Goal setting The process of establishing specific objectives for an individual to pursue.

Grading Sorting goods into classes based on quality.

Grievance A complaint brought by an employee who feels that he or she has been treated improperly.

Gross national product (GNP) The total market value of all goods and services produced in the economy in one year.

Gross profit margin ratio The ratio of gross margin to net sales.

Group incentive plan Compensation to units, departments, and sometimes the entire organization for meeting or exceeding a goal.

Halo effect The tendency to allow an overall positive evaluation of a person to influence the specific characteristics being rated.

Hardware The machinery and physical components of a computer.

Hawthorne studies Pioneering research studies on worker behavior and motivation.

Horizontal flow A materials flow in which all production takes place on the same floor.

Human relations A management approach that brings employees and the organization together to achieve the objectives of both.

Human resource management The process of planning personnel needs; staffing the organization; and training, developing, appraising, and maintaining an organization's personnel.

Human resource planning The process of forecasting personnel needs and developing the necessary strategies for meeting those needs.

Hygiene factors Job characteristics that do not motivate people but that cause dissatisfaction when absent, including money, working conditions, and job security.

Hypermarket A giant store selling a combination of groceries and general merchandise at low prices.

Illumination Stage of the creative process during which the answer to the problem or issue becomes apparent.

Implied contract One created by the actions of one or more parties.

Implied warranty A guarantee that automatically accompanies the sale of a product.

Imports Goods or services brought into one's own country.

Impulse items Goods that consumers buy on the spur of the moment.

Income statement A financial statement that summarizes the firm's operations for a given period of time, usually one year.

Incubation Stage of the creative process that involves sitting back and letting the subconscious mind work on the problem.

Indenture agreement A document that sets forth the terms of a bond issue.

Index number A statistical tool for measuring changes in a group of related items over a specific period of time.

Individual brand A brand used exclusively for one of the products a firm sells.

Individual incentive payment plan Compensation that rewards a specific worker for high performance.

Industrial good or service A good or service used to produce still other goods or services.

Inflation A general increase in the level of prices.

Informal organization structure The structure created by the personnel on the basis of friendship and common interests.

Inland marine insurance Coverage of damage to or loss of goods shipped by rail, truck, airplane, or inland barge.

Input Any resource needed to produce a desired good or service.

Input unit A component that converts data into a form that the computer can understand.

Inside directors Directors who are employees of the firm.

Institutional advertising Advertising designed to create goodwill and build a desired company image.

Institutional investors Organizations that buy securities with their own funds or with funds held in trust for others.

Insurance A financial arrangement under which the cost of unexpected losses is distributed among those who are insured.

Insurance benefit programs Benefits designed to provide various forms of coverage against accident, illness, or death.

Intangible assets Assets such as patents or goodwill that do not have physical presence.

Integrated circuit A network of dozens of tiny transistors etched onto a silicon wafer.

Integrative bargaining Bargaining in which both sides work together to solve a mutual problem.

Intensive distribution A channel strategy of saturating in which the producer sells its product through every available outlet.

Interlocking directorate An arrangement in which a majority of the board of directors of two or more competing corporations with assets in excess of $1 million are the same people.

Intermittent production A production sequence in which the flow of materials is noncontinuous.

International Bank for Reconstruction and Development (World Bank) An agency that lends to underdeveloped countries to help them grow.

International Development Association (IDA) An organization that lends to underdeveloped countries.

International Finance Corporation (IFC) An organization that invests in private enterprises in underdeveloped nations.

International Monetary Fund (IMF) A UN organization that tries to stabilize exchange rates between world currencies.

In-transit privileges Permission to stop a train shipment along the way in order to perform a function and then continue the shipment.

Intrapreneur Manager or staff expert who creates and controls new, usually risky projects within an existing business.

Intrapreneuring Managers and staff experts creating and controlling new, usually risky projects within an existing business.

Inventory management Efficiently balancing inventory with sales orders.

Inventory turnover The number of times that inventory is replaced during the year, expressed as the ratio of cost of goods sold to average inventory.

Investment bank A financial intermediary that purchases and resells bonds and stocks.

Job enrichment A technique for motivating employees by adding motivator factors to their jobs.

Job rotation Development of broad experience by moving an employee from one job to another.

Job sharing Employing two or more part-time workers to fulfill the requirements of a single full-time position.

Joint venture A type of joint ownership that, when viewed as a partnership, is usually temporary and is created for the purpose of carrying out a single business project; an arrangement in which two companies pool their resources to create, produce, and market a product.

Just-in-time (JIT) inventory A system of receiving inventory just before it is needed in the production process.

Kidnap, ransom, and extortion insurance Political risk insurance that covers costs associated with these criminal acts.

Knights of Labor The most important federation of unions for skilled and unskilled workers in the years following the Civil War.

Label The part of a package that presents information about its contents.

Labor The people who produce the goods and services that the business provides.

Laissez-faire The doctrine of government noninterference in the affairs of business.

Land The geographic territory and natural resources used in producing goods and services.

Leadership The process of influencing people to direct their efforts toward the achievement of particular objectives.

Lease A document that allows the tenant to use the owner's property for a predetermined time period in exchange for consideration.

Leniency error A rating error in which a manager rates most employees above average or excellent.

Leverage The use of borrowed funds to increase the return on equity.

Liabilities Creditors' claims on an enterprise's assets.

License A legal agreement in which one firm gives another the right to manufacture and sell its product in return for paying a royalty.

LIFO An inventory valuation system under which the last goods produced or acquired are considered the first ones sold (**L**ast **I**n, **F**irst **O**ut).

Limited partner A partner whose liability is limited to his or her investment in the business.

Limited-pay life insurance Whole life insurance that limits the number of years the insured must pay premiums.

Limit order An order that specifies the highest price at which the broker may buy stock or the lowest price at which the broker may sell stock.

Line-and-staff organization structure Specialists help those directly responsible for attaining organization objectives.

Line chart A graph of information over a period of time that uses a line to represent the values of each category of information.

Line of credit A stated cash reserve available whenever the business wants to draw on it.

Line organization structure Organization flows directly from the top of the organization to the bottom.

Liquidation The sale of all assets to meet outstanding debts.

Liquidity The ease with which an asset can be converted into cash.

List price The price announced for a good.

Local ad A television ad carried only in the immediate area.

Local union The basic unit of the union structure, representing members in a limited area.

Lockout A company's refusal to allow workers to enter a facility.

Long-term liabilities Debts that will be due one or more years in the future.

Long-term loan A loan that has a term of at least one year.

Loss leader A product that is priced below cost to attract people into a store.

M1 A measure of the money supply equal to currency and demand deposits.

Macroeconomics The branch of economics that is concerned with the overall economy.

Mail-order house A retailer that sells goods through a mail-order catalog.

Mainframe computer A large computer system with considerable storage capacity and fast processing capability.

Maintenance-of-membership provision A requirement that those who join the union must remain members.

Management The process of setting objectives and coordinating employees' efforts to attain them.

Management by objectives (MBO) The system in which managers and subordinates jointly set objectives to use as the basis for operating the business and evaluating performance.

Management by walking around (MBWA) The management practice of visiting the workplace to find out what is going on.

Management information system (MIS) A method for collecting, analyzing, and disseminating timely information to support decision making.

Margin trading Buying stock without putting up the full value of the transaction.

Marine insurance Coverage of losses to boats, ships, trucks, railcars and engines, and planes.

Market A group of customers who have the money and desire to purchase goods and services.

Marketing Identifying the goods and services the customer wants and providing them at the right price and place.

Marketing mix The combination of a firm's strategies for product, price, place, and promotion.

Marketing research Investigating marketing problems and identifying market opportunities.

Market order An order to purchase or sell a stock at the best possible price at the present time.

Market segmentation Dividing markets into groups that have similar characteristics.

Master production schedule A plan that coordinates all the raw materials, parts, equipment, manufacturing processes, and assembly operations necessary to produce goods.

Materials handling Overseeing the movement of goods within the company's facilities.

Matrix organization structure Combines elements of a line organization with elements of a project organization.

Mean An arithmetic average; the sum of the values divided by the number of values.

Median The middle value in an array.

Mediation A resolution method in which a neutral third party with no formal authority helps both sides reach a settlement.

Medicare A federal program providing hospital and medical insurance to the elderly.

Mentor An experienced employee who coaches an identified person with advice and assistance and helps the person achieve career goals.

Merchant wholesalers Intermediaries that take title to the goods they distribute.

Merger The joining together of two companies to form a new company.

Microcomputer A small desktop computer that relies on a microprocessor.

Microeconomics The branch of economics that is concerned with the individual firm or household.

Microprocessor An integrated circuit on one chip that is the equivalent of the central processing unit in a larger computer.

Minicomputer A medium-sized computer in terms of physical dimensions and storage capacity.

Minority enterprise small business investment company (MESBIC) An SBIC that provides capital and equity financing to small businesses whose owners are economically or socially disadvantaged.

Missionary selling A type of personal selling in which one salesperson supports the sales efforts of others.

Mixed economy Combines characteristics of free enterprise, communist, and/or socialist economies.

Mode The value that occurs most frequently in a sample.

Modem A device that enables computers to communicate with one another over telephone lines.

Modification The process of changing raw materials into a product.

Monetary policy Government regulation of the money supply to attain full employment and a noninflationary high level of GNP.

Money Anything a society generally accepts in payment for goods and services.

Money market mutual funds Shares in mutual funds that make short-term investments in securities of the federal government and major corporations.

Monopolistic competition A market structure in which there are many firms, each producing only a small share of the total output demanded.

Motivation The process through which needs or wants lead to drives aimed at goals or incentives.

Motivator factors Job characteristics that make people feel exceptionally good about their jobs, including challenge, recognition, and responsibility.

Multinational corporation (MNC) A company having operations in more than one country, foreign sales, and/or a nationality mix of managers and owners.

Mutual fund An investment company that pools the contributions of investors; the fund is carefully managed by buying and selling securities to meet the investment objectives.

Mutual insurance company A type of cooperative in which the policyholders become shareholders of the insurance company.

Mutual savings bank State-chartered bank that offers many of the same services as S&Ls.

National banks Commercial banks chartered by the federal government.

National brand A brand owned by a manufacturer.

National Credit Union Administration A federal agency that insures deposits up to $100,000 at federal- or state-chartered credit unions.

National union The parent organization for local unions, which focuses on long-range considerations that affect all of the locals.

Near money Certain highly liquid assets that do not function as a medium of exchange.

Negotiable instrument A form of business paper that can be transferred from one person to another as a substitute for money.

Negotiable order of withdrawal (NOW) account A checking account that pays interest.

Net profit margin ratio The ratio of net income to net sales.

Network ad A television ad directed at a major audience around the country.

New York Stock Exchange (NYSE) The largest and best-known exchange in the United States.

No-fault insurance Coverage providing compensation regardless of who was at fault in an accident.

Nominal partner A partner who lends his or her name to the partnership but plays no role in the operation.

Nondurable goods Goods that are used up or wear out quickly.

Nonprice competition The effort to win over customers with advertising and personal selling rather than price.

Ocean marine insurance Coverage of losses that occur to ships or their cargo on the high seas or in port.

Odd lot Any number of stock shares less than 100.

Odd pricing Setting a price just below a round number for psychological reasons.

Old-Age, Survivors, Disability, and Health Insurance (OASDHI) A federal insurance program that provides retirement, medical, disability, and death benefits.

Oligopoly A market in which a small percentage of the firms dominate the industry.

On-the-job training Informal instruction conducted at the job site.

Open-market operations The buying and selling of government securities by the Fed.

Open order An order that instructs the broker to leave it on the books until it is executed or the investor cancels it.

Open shop A company at which the workers do not have to join a union or pay union dues.

Operational objectives Short-range objectives that help management control its internal resources and implement the strategic plan.

Operational plan A short-range plan.

Options Contracts that permit an investor to either purchase or sell a particular security at a predetermined price and within a certain time period.

Order costs The expenses associated with ordering inventory.

Order processing Taking sales orders, checking them, and then seeing that the product is shipped to the customer.

Order taking Processing orders from customers who have decided they want to buy.

Organizational culture An organization's norms, beliefs, attitudes, and values.

Organizing Efficiently bringing together human and material resources to attain objectives.

Outplacement Human resource management efforts to help reduce the consequences of job loss.

Output The finished good or service that results from the production process.

Outside directors Directors who come from outside the company.

Over-the-counter (OTC) market A marketplace for unlisted securities that trade outside of the organized securities exchanges.

Owner or executive insurance Life insurance that reimburses an organization upon the death of a key employee.

Owner's equity The owner's claim on the assets of an enterprise.

Partnership An association of two or more persons to carry on as co-owners of a business for profit.

Passbook savings accounts Non-checkable interest-bearing accounts.

Patent A federal government grant of exclusive control over and use of a discovery or a new product or process for 17 years.

Paternalistic approach Taking care of employees similar to the way that parents take care of children.

Peak The phase of the business cycle when national output reaches its highest level.

Peer rating A performance appraisal in which the workers all rate each other.

Pension fund A pool of money set aside and invested to take care of retirement obligations.

People-meter An electronic instrument attached to a TV that records the channel to which the set is tuned.

Perpetual inventory A system for keeping track of inventory by subtracting what the company uses up or sells and adding what the company purchases.

Personal investors Individuals who trade securities for their own account.

Personal property Any property that is not real property.

Personnel managers Managers responsible for staffing the organization and training, developing, appraising, and maintaining its employees.

Physical distribution The activities necessary to move goods from the producer to the final user.

Physical inventory The process of counting the amount of inventory on hand.

Picket An assembly of workers stationed outside the premises for the purpose of calling attention to their grievances.

Pie chart A graph in the form of a circle divided into sectors that are proportional in angle and area to the relative size of each category of data.

Piggyback service The shipment of a fully loaded truck trailer on a specially designed railroad flatcar.

Place The location where a good or service is available for purchase.

Plaintiff The party that brings a legal action.

Planning Setting objectives and formulating the steps to attain them.

Point-of-purchase (POP) displays In-store displays of a product that draw attention to it.

Point-of-sale terminal A computer terminal that allows retail customers to use a debit card to transfer funds from their bank account to that of the merchant.

Pollution Contamination of the air, water, land, or environment in which life exists.

Portfolio analysis A method for developing a product strategy based on the attractiveness of a market and the product's share of that market.

Preferred stock Stock that provides preferential treatment in the payment of dividends and the distribution of assets.

Premium (for bonds) the price paid for a bond over and above its face value; (in insurance) a fee to cover the costs of an insurance policy.

Premiums Goods offered to potential customers as an incentive to purchase a product.

Preparation Stage of the creative process that involves gathering information on the problem or issue under analysis.

Price The cost of the product to the purchaser.

Price level The price being charged in the industry.

Primary data Original information gathered in order to investigate a particular problem or to determine the status of a particular operation.

Primary-demand advertising Advertising designed to increase the total demand for a good or service, rather than for a particular brand.

Primary needs Physiological needs, such as food, water, sex, sleep, clothing, and shelter.

Principal A person represented by an agent.

Private brand A brand owned by a retailer.

Private carrier A transportation company owned by the company whose goods it transports.

Private investment Total expenditures for capital goods during a year.

Private warehouse A storage facility owned or leased by the company whose goods it stores.

Process layout A production layout that groups machines and equipment on the basis of function.

Product Any good or service that the firm offers to the customer.

Product departmentalization The structure of a level of an organization on the basis of product lines.

Product design The process of deciding the specific physical dimensions of the good or service to be produced.

Production The process of transforming inputs such as raw materials and labor into outputs, or finished products.

Production-oriented marketing Based on the belief that a good product or service will sell itself.

Production planning The process whereby managers determine the most profitable way to produce the goods and services the company will sell.

Productivity The amount of output divided by the input.

Product layout A production layout in which all machines are set up along a product-flow line, and the units to be manufactured move down this line.

Profit The difference between revenues and expenses.

Program evaluation and review technique (PERT) A planning and control tool useful on complex projects requiring coordination.

Progressive tax A tax that charges lower rates to taxpayers with lower incomes.

Project organization structure A structure formed for the purpose of attaining a particular objective and then disbanded.

Promotion The process of stimulating demand for a company's goods and services.

Property law The branch of law that involves the rights and duties associated with the ownership or use of real or personal property.

Property tax A levy based on the assessed value of a piece of real estate.

Proportional tax A tax in which the rate remains the same regardless of the base.

Prospecting Researching potential buyers and choosing those who are the most likely customers.

Protestant work ethic A belief that people should work hard and save their money.

Proxy A written authorization that allows a specified person to cast a stockholder's vote.

Psychographic segmentation Dividing up a market on the basis of the customer's life-style, values, or personality.

Publicity Product- or company-related information that the firm does not pay the media to carry and that the firm does not control.

Public relations All activities directed toward creating and maintaining a favorable public image.

Public warehouse A public storage facility whose owner is not the company storing goods there.

Purchasing The process of buying inventory and other assets.

Pure competition A market structure in which there are many independent sellers, each offering products at the current market price.

Pure monopoly A market in which there is only one seller or producer and there are no substitutes for the product or service.

Pure risk The threat of a loss without the possibility of a gain.

Put option An option to sell a specific security.

Quality control The process of ensuring that goods and services are produced or provided within predetermined specifications.

Quality-control circle A group of workers who meet regularly to discuss the way they do their jobs and to recommend changes.

Quality of work life (QWL) Efforts to improve the job environment and to make work life more enjoyable and meaningful.

Quantity discount A discount given to buyers who place larger-than-average orders.

Quota A restriction on the quantity or value of an item that may be imported.

Random sample A sample in which each member of the population being investigated has an equal chance of being chosen.

Random walk theory An investment strategy holding that stock prices are independent of past stock prices.

Readership report A test of advertising effectiveness that asks people to look at ads that have appeared in publications and identify those that they recognize and those that they have read.

Realistic job previews Orientations that attempt to tell the full story about the job instead of creating false expectations.

Real property Land and property attached to land.

Recession An economic period during which the economy begins to slow and move downward.

Recovery An economic period during which demand for goods and services is on the rise.

Redemption premium A bonus the company pays to bondholders for early redemption of bonds.

Regional stock exchanges Exchanges that trade the stocks of firms that serve regional markets.

Regressive tax A tax that hits low-income persons harder than high-income persons.

Regular checking An account that pays no interest but allows the depositor to write checks on the funds.

Reliable Tests that give consistent and accurate results.

Reserve requirement The percentage of all deposits that a bank must keep on hand at the bank or on deposit with the Fed.

Resolution methods Approaches used to overcome union-management disagreements.

Retailer An intermediary that sells goods and services to the final consumer.

Retained earnings Profits that have been reinvested in the company.

Return on owners' investment The ratio of net income to total owners' equity.

Right to private property The right to own, use, buy, sell, or give away property.

Right to rewards The owner's right to all of the profits, after taxes, that accrue from business activity.

Right-to-work laws State laws that prohibit union shops and other such union security arrangements.

Risk management The reduction of loss caused by uncontrollable events.

Robinson-Patman Act A federal law designed to eliminate unfair price competition.

Robot A machine capable of doing a variety of tasks based on computer-programmed manipulations of materials and tools.

Round lot One hundred shares of stock.

Sales finance company A financial institution that purchases installment sales contracts.

Sales law The branch of law that involves the sale of goods for cash or credit.

Sales promotion Promotional activities other than advertising and personal selling that stimulate consumer purchasing and dealer effectiveness.

Sales tax A levy on specified purchases.

Sample A portion of a population that is being investigated.

Sampling The process of inspecting some of the goods and using the results to judge the overall quality of all the goods.

Savings and loan association (S&L) Financial institution that emphasizes savings accounts and home mortgage loans.

Scientific management An approach started around 1900 that used engineering techniques such as time-and-motion analysis to increase plant efficiency, by establishing the one best method for each task.

S corporation A corporation that has fewer than 35 stockholders and is taxed as a partnership but maintains the rights and liabilities of a corporation.

Scrambled merchandising Diversifying the store's selection of products in order to increase sales volume.

Seasonal discount A discount given during particular times of the year.

Secondary data Information that already is available from sources outside the firm.

Secondary needs Psychological needs such as friendship, recognition, power, and achievement.

Secret partner A partner who is not known as a partner to the general public but who plays an active role in running the business.

Secured loan A loan that is backed up with collateral.

Securities Evidence of ownership (stocks) or debt (bonds).

Securities exchange A marketplace where securities such as stocks and bonds are bought and sold.

Selective advertising Advertising designed to increase the demand for a particular brand of product.

Selective distribution A channel strategy in which only a few intermediaries distribute a product.

Self-rating A performance appraisal in which the employees evaluate themselves.

Selling Identifying buyers, developing a promotion campaign to attract their business, and concluding the sale.

Selling short Selling borrowed stock in the hope of later buying it on the open market at a lower price.

Semistructured interview An interview that consists of prepared questions to direct the interview but allows the interviewee to develop ideas that seem important.

Severity error A rating error in which a manager rates all of the subordinates lower than they deserve.

Sexual harassment Any unwelcome sexual advance.

Sherman Antitrust Act A federal law that prohibits all agreements that are created for the purpose of restraining trade in interstate commerce.

Short-term financing Raising funds to meet obligations that will come due within the next 12 months.

Silent partner A partner known to be an owner in the business but who plays no active role in running the operation.

Small business Independently owned and operated business that is not dominant in its field of operation and meets certain standards of size in terms of employees or annual receipts.

Small Business Administration (SBA) The principal government agency concerned with the economic welfare of small U.S. firms.

Small business investment company (SBIC) A company licensed by the SBA for the purpose of providing venture capital to small businesses.

Socialism An economic system under which the government controls primary industries, but most other businesses remain in private hands.

Social responsibility The obligation of business to the society in which it operates.

Social security A legally required benefit that provides disability payments, old-age benefits, and survivors' benefits.

Sole proprietorship A business owned by one individual.

Software The series of instructions, or programming, that tells the computer what to do.

Span of control The number of subordinates directly reporting to a supervisor.

Speculation The assumption of large risks in the hope of large returns.

Speculative risk The threat of a loss coupled with the chance of a gain.

Spot ad A television ad broadcast over one or more stations at various times.

Spreadsheets Data arranged in tables of rows and columns.

Stagflation Stagnant economic growth coupled with inflation.

Standardizing Establishing specifications or categories for products.

Standard of living The measure of how well off people of a country are economically.

State banks Commercial banks chartered by an individual state.

Statement of cash flows Provides information regarding a firm's cash receipts and cash payments.

Static layout A production layout in which the product stays in one place and the workers come to the product.

Statute of limitations The law that specifies the time period during which a wronged person may sue.

Statutory law Law enacted by Congress and the state legislatures.

Steel-collar jobs Jobs performed by robots and computers.

Steward An on-site union representative whose job is to protect the rights of members.

Stockbroker An individual who has demonstrated knowledge by passing a series of exams on buying and selling securities and who, for a fee, performs this function for clients.

Stock exchange An organization whose members provide a trading place for buying and selling securities for clients.

Stockholders Individuals who have purchased shares of stock in a corporation.

Stock insurance company A corporation that sells insurance for profit.

Storing Warehousing goods.

Straight piecework A compensation plan in which employees are paid in direct relation to their output.

Strategic objectives Long-range objectives that help an organization compare itself with the competition.

Strategic plan A long-range plan.

Stress The body's response to an action or situation that places demands on a person.

Strict product liability The principle that people or businesses are responsible for their acts, regardless of their intentions or degree of negligence.

Strike A collective refusal to work until a dispute is resolved.

Strikebreaker A nonunion worker hired to do the job of a striking union employee.

Structured interview An interview that follows a prepared format that consists of a series of direct questions.

Subordinate rating A performance appraisal in which the workers evaluate their superior.

Subsidiary A company organized under the laws of a foreign country for the purpose of carrying out tasks, such as production and sales, assigned by the parent firm.

Summary table A table that lists data in various categories along with totals or percentages.

Supermarket A large store that sells a wide variety of food products as well as some nonfood offerings.

Supervisory appraisal A performance appraisal in which the immediate supervisor evaluates the performance of a subordinate.

Supply The amount of a good provided at a particular price.

Suppressed motives The reasons for buying that people are unwilling to express.

Surety bond Coverage against the risk that someone will fail to perform on a contract.

Synthetic manufacturing process A process that converts a number of raw materials or parts into a finished product.

Tall structure Structure with many levels and short spans of control.

Target market A group of customers who are likely to buy a company's goods or services.

Tariff A duty or fee levied on imported goods.

Technical analysis The process of using the pattern of a stock's price over time to predict the stock's future price movement.

Technology The application of knowledge to production, physical equipment, and machinery.

Telecommunicating Using a modem to send information between two computers or between a terminal and a processing unit.

Terminal A keyboard combined with a screen or printer and wired to a processing unit in another location.

Term life insurance Coverage for a death benefit during a stated number of years.

Theory X The assumption that people are basically lazy and have to be coerced or threatened before they will work.

Theory Y The assumption that people are creative and responsible and will work hard under the proper conditions.

Theory Z The assumption that the key to productivity is to create a climate or culture of openness and trust that leads to increased employee involvement.

Time deposits Savings accounts that require the depositor to give notice before withdrawing funds or to pay a penalty for withdrawing the funds before a specified date.

Tort An infringement of a person's inherent right that injures or damages that person.

Trade credit The purchase of merchandise on an open account.

Trade deficit A negative balance of trade.

Trade discount A discount given to merchants in the distribution channel.

Trademark A brand the owner has the legal and exclusive right to use; a word or symbol used to distinguish a company's products.

Training The process of teaching employees the procedures and techniques to efficiently do their jobs.

Transformation process Those activities that change inputs into the desired outputs.

Transporting Moving goods from where they were manufactured or purchased to where they are needed.

Traveler's check A check that is sold with a preset value and is redeemable if lost.

Type A personality A personality characterized by a drive to get more and more done in less and less time.

Unconscious motives The reasons for buying that people are unaware of.

Undifferentiated marketing Selling a single product to all customers.

Unemployment The involuntary idleness of people who are actively seeking work.

Unemployment insurance A state program that provides benefits to workers who have been laid off.

Uniform Commercial Code (UCC) A set of statutes that govern the legal dealings of business.

Union An organization of workers who have joined forces to achieve common goals, such as higher wages and improved working conditions.

Union shop A company at which all employees, as a condition of employment, must join the union after a predetermined time period.

Unity of command Every person should have only one boss.

Universal life insurance Life insurance that combines term insurance with a tax-deferred savings plan.

Unlimited liability Total responsibility for all debts of a company.

Unsecured loan A loan that requires no collateral.

User-friendly program A computer program that is easy to understand and master.

Valid Tests that measure what they are intended to measure.

Value-added network (VAN) A system providing electronic links between an organization and outside personnel.

Value analysis The evaluation of current products to determine how they can be improved.

Value engineering The evaluation of new products and the application of research and development to design the highest-quality, lowest-priced output.

Vending machine A mechanical retail outlet that stores products and dispenses them directly to customers.

Venture A new business or a new or different approach or product/service in an existing business.

Venture capital firm Financial intermediaries that specialize in funding ventures with special promise.

Venture capitalist An investor who specializes in small firms that offer potential for rapid growth and high returns.

Verification Stage of the creative process that involves testing the solution, and, if necessary, modifying it.

Vertical marketing system (VMS) A planned distribution system in which all levels are brought under unified control.

Warehousing Storing goods until they are ready to be shipped.

Warranty A guarantee.

Whistle blowers Employees who alert management or public bodies to illegal or unethical practices.

White-collar jobs Jobs that involve clerical, office, or managerial work.

Whole life insurance A combination of a death benefit and tax-deferred savings.

Wholesaler An intermediary that normally purchases goods and sells them to buyers for the purpose of resale.

Word processing A system to store, retrieve, edit, and print text.

Workers' compensation A legally required benefit that provides compensation to those who suffer job-related injuries or illnesses.

Workers' compensation insurance A state program that provides benefits to workers who suffer job-related injury or illness.

Yield The percentage return from stock dividends, or the dividend divided by the selling price per share.

Name Index

Subject Index